I0890718

Building Consumer-Brand Relationship in Luxury Brand Management

Paula Rodrigues
Lusíada University of Porto, Portugal

Ana Pinto Borges
Instituto Superior de Administração e Gestão, Portugal

IGI Global
PUBLISHER of TIMELY KNOWLEDGE

A volume in the Advances in Marketing, Customer Relationship Management, and E-Services (AMCRMES) Book Series

Published in the United States of America by
IGI Global
Business Science Reference (an imprint of IGI Global)
701 E. Chocolate Avenue
Hershey PA, USA 17033
Tel: 717-533-8845
Fax: 717-533-8661
E-mail: cust@igi-global.com
Web site: http://www.igi-global.com

Copyright © 2021 by IGI Global. All rights reserved. No part of this publication may be reproduced, stored or distributed in any form or by any means, electronic or mechanical, including photocopying, without written permission from the publisher. Product or company names used in this set are for identification purposes only. Inclusion of the names of the products or companies does not indicate a claim of ownership by IGI Global of the trademark or registered trademark.

Library of Congress Cataloging-in-Publication Data

Names: Rodrigues, Paula Cristina Lopes, 1970- editor. | Borges, Ana Pinto, 1980- editor.
Title: Building consumer-brand relationship in luxury brand management / Paula Rodrigues and Ana Pinto Borges, editors.
Description: Hershey : Business Science Reference, 2020. | Includes bibliographical references and index. | Summary: "This book focuses on the conception and marketing of luxury as an experience and explores more integrative and comprehensive approaches to modeling and understanding the consumer-brand relationship with luxury brands and their sustainability in a global and multicultural world"-- Provided by publisher.
Identifiers: LCCN 2020000238 (print) | LCCN 2020000239 (ebook) | ISBN 9781799843696 (hardcover) | ISBN 9781799852445 (paperback) | ISBN 9781799843702 (ebook)
Subjects: LCSH: Luxuries--Marketing. | Brand name products--Management. | Customer relations.
Classification: LCC HD9999.L852 B85 2020 (print) | LCC HD9999.L852 (ebook) | DDC 658.8/27--dc23
LC record available at https://lccn.loc.gov/2020000238
LC ebook record available at https://lccn.loc.gov/2020000239

This book is published in the IGI Global book series Advances in Marketing, Customer Relationship Management, and E-Services (AMCRMES) (ISSN: 2327-5502; eISSN: 2327-5529)

British Cataloguing in Publication Data
A Cataloguing in Publication record for this book is available from the British Library.

All work contributed to this book is new, previously-unpublished material. The views expressed in this book are those of the authors, but not necessarily of the publisher.

For electronic access to this publication, please contact: eresources@igi-global.com.

Advances in Marketing, Customer Relationship Management, and E-Services (AMCRMES) Book Series

Eldon Y. Li
National Chengchi University, Taiwan & California Polytechnic State University, USA

ISSN:2327-5502
EISSN:2327-5529

Mission

Business processes, services, and communications are important factors in the management of good customer relationship, which is the foundation of any well organized business. Technology continues to play a vital role in the organization and automation of business processes for marketing, sales, and customer service. These features aid in the attraction of new clients and maintaining existing relationships.

The Advances in Marketing, Customer Relationship Management, and E-Services (AMCRMES) Book Series

addresses success factors for customer relationship management, marketing, and electronic services and its performance outcomes. This collection of reference source covers aspects of consumer behavior and marketing business strategies aiming towards researchers, scholars, and practitioners in the fields of marketing management.

Coverage

- B2B marketing
- Mobile CRM
- Text Mining and Marketing
- Ethical Considerations in E-Marketing
- Cases on Electronic Services
- CRM strategies
- CRM in financial services
- Social Networking and Marketing
- E-Service Innovation
- Legal Considerations in E-Marketing

IGI Global is currently accepting manuscripts for publication within this series. To submit a proposal for a volume in this series, please contact our Acquisition Editors at Acquisitions@igi-global.com or visit: http://www.igi-global.com/publish/.

The Advances in Marketing, Customer Relationship Management, and E-Services (AMCRMES) Book Series (ISSN 2327-5502) is published by IGI Global, 701 E. Chocolate Avenue, Hershey, PA 17033-1240, USA, www.igi-global.com. This series is composed of titles available for purchase individually; each title is edited to be contextually exclusive from any other title within the series. For pricing and ordering information please visit http://www.igi-global.com/book-series/advances-marketing-customer-relationship-management/37150. Postmaster: Send all address changes to above address. Copyright © 2021 IGI Global. All rights, including translation in other languages reserved by the publisher. No part of this series may be reproduced or used in any form or by any means – graphics, electronic, or mechanical, including photocopying, recording, taping, or information and retrieval systems – without written permission from the publisher, except for non commercial, educational use, including classroom teaching purposes. The views expressed in this series are those of the authors, but not necessarily of IGI Global.

Titles in this Series

For a list of additional titles in this series, please visit:
http://www.igi-global.com/book-series/advances-marketing-customer-relationship-management/37150

Innovations in Digital Branding and Content Marketing
Subhankar Das (Duy Tan University, Vietnam) and Subhra Rani Mondal (Duy Tan University, Vietnam)
Business Science Reference • © 2021 • 311pp • H/C (ISBN: 9781799844204) • US $195.00

Handbook of Research on Applied AI for International Business and Marketing Applications
Bryan Christiansen (Global Training Group, Ltd, UK) and Tihana Škrinjarić (University of Zagreb, Croatia)
Business Science Reference • © 2021 • 702pp • H/C (ISBN: 9781799850779) • US $295.00

Handbook of Research on Technology Applications for Effective Customer Engagement
Norazah Mohd Suki (Universiti Utara Malaysia, Malaysia)
Business Science Reference • © 2021 • 391pp • H/C (ISBN: 9781799847724) • US $295.00

New Techniques for Brand Management in the Healthcare Sector
Ana Pinto Borges (ISAG - European Business School and Research Group of ISAG (NIDISAG), Portugal) and Paula Rodrigues (Lusíada University of Porto, Portugal)
Business Science Reference • © 2021 • 300pp • H/C (ISBN: 9781799830344) • US $225.00

Leveraging Consumer Behavior and Psychology in the Digital Economy
Norazah Mohd Suki (Universiti Malaysia Sabah, Malaysia) and Norbayah Mohd Suki (Universiti Utara Malaysia, Malaysia)
Business Science Reference • © 2020 • 299pp • H/C (ISBN: 9781799830429) • US $195.00

Analyzing the Strategic Role of Neuromarketing and Consumer Neuroscience
Dincer Atli (Uskudar University, Turkey)
Business Science Reference • © 2020 • 304pp • H/C (ISBN: 9781799831266) • US $225.00

Managing Customer Experiences in an Omnichannel World
Taşkın Dirsehan (Marmara University, Turkey)
Business Science Reference • © 2020 • 300pp • H/C (ISBN: 9781799850069) • US $195.00

Millennial Consumer Trends and Their Impact on the Global Economy
Abhijit Pandit (Amity University, India) and Jayjit Chakraborty (University of Calcutta, India)
Business Science Reference • © 2020 • 300pp • H/C (ISBN: 9781799844297) • US $215.00

IGI Global
PUBLISHER of TIMELY KNOWLEDGE

701 East Chocolate Avenue, Hershey, PA 17033, USA
Tel: 717-533-8845 x100 • Fax: 717-533-8661
E-Mail: cust@igi-global.com • www.igi-global.com

Editorial Advisory Board

Aaron C. Ahuvia, *University of Michigan, Dearborn, USA*
Luciana de Araujo Gil, *Faculty of Business, University Diego Portales (UDP), Santiago, Chile*
Michael Chattalas, *Monmouth University, USA*
Sandra Maria Correia Loureiro, *BRU, ISCTE, Lisbon University Institute, Portugal*
Marc Fetscherin, *Rollins College, USA*
Mónica Gómez-Suárez, *Universidad Autónoma de Madrid, Spain*
Sang-Lin Han, *School of Business, Hanyang University, South Korea*
Khalid Hussain, *COMSATS University Islamabad, Pakistan*
Alicia Izquierdo-Yusta, *University of Burgos, Spain*
Muhammad Junaid, *COMSATS University Islamabad, Pakistan*
Daniela Langaro, *BRU, ISCTE, Lisbon University Institute, Portugal*
Arnaldo Fernandes de Matos Coelho, *Faculdade de Economia, Universidade de Coimbra, Portugal*
Sebastian Molinillo, *University of Malaga, Spain*
Pablo Antonio Muñoz-Gallego, *Universidad de Salamanca, Spain*
Clarinda Rodrigues, *Linnaeus University, Sweden*
Carlos M. Rodriguez, *College of Business, Center for the Study of Innovation Management (CSIM), Delaware State University, USA*
Jaime Romero, *Universidad Autónoma de Madrid, Spain*
Marika Taishoff, *International University of Monaco, Monaco*

Table of Contents

Detailed Table of Contents

Understanding the concept of luxury and knowing what luxury means is still necessary and pertinent research because the definition of what luxury is has not proved to be consensual, and those that exist leave out the understanding of how fragmented meanings of today's society appear and influence consumers' perceptions of luxury. While the terms of new and old luxury have gained popularity in the literature, there remains little empirical research comparing consumers' perceptions of new and old luxury brands. Therefore, it can be said that previous research on luxury contributes to improvements under the point of view centred on the product of the meaning of luxury while the current era of popularization and democratization of luxury causes confusion and, what luxury means today, remains unclear. This research intends, through an extensive literature review, to clarify the main differences between the concepts of new and old luxury brands.

With luxury consumption still growing fast despite various challenges such as increasing competition, rise in rental luxuries, and in counterfeits, luxury brands are challenged with an additional and complex development: consumers' interest towards inconspicuous luxury products. Being one of the major characteristics of luxury goods, conspicuousness is losing its value among some luxury shoppers necessitating a new definition for luxury and a new value proposition for luxury brands. This chapter initially provides a review on luxury and on the different motivations that determine luxury consumption. Next, socio-economic changes that trigger the shift from conspicuous to inconspicuous luxury consumption is examined briefly. And finally, a discussion on why inconspicuous consumption is valued by consumers is followed by a theoretical framework on the motivations for inconspicuous luxury brand usage. The chapter then concludes with theoretical and managerial implications.

The extant research highlights that the strength of consumer-brand relationships is very much shaped by consumers' experiences with brands. Given the inherent characteristics of luxury brands, it is no surprise that luxury consumers expect much more intense experiences, and thus the delivery of a superior brand experience is a necessity in the luxury market. Therefore, both marketing scholars and brand managers in the luxury market need to acknowledge the power of brand experiences as a way to strengthen consumer-brand relationships. However, despite the need for a deeper understanding of brand experience in the context of luxury brands, still much remains unknown regarding the factors that can be used to enhance brand experience. Building on this gap in the literature, this chapter investigates the relational outcomes of brand experience and subsequently discusses the various drivers that luxury brands can use to enhance luxury brand experience and thus develop stronger consumer-brand relationships.

Luxury restaurants are expected to offer outstanding culinary talent and expertise; be authentic, creative and consistent; and provide exciting quality food. Currently, culinary art discourses include a social dimension in which social networking sites are used to share gastronomic experiences and check recommendations. User-generated reviews are thus an intersection of participatory culture and 'foodie' discoures. This study's main objective was to examine this phenomenon by analysing web reviews to identify the expressive dimensions that describe guests' experiences. Mixed-method content analysis was selected for this research, using qualitative text interpretation to supplement quantitative word counts and factor analyses. Content analysis of reviews of the top three Michelin-starred restaurants (i.e., two stars) in Portugal identified concepts used to assess haute cuisine experiences from the client's perspective. The results include a concept map encompassing the following dimensions: 'food', 'restaurant', 'experience', 'menu', 'wine', 'special (dinner)', 'view', 'beautiful (food)', 'friendly (staff)', 'chef', 'visit' and 'dessert'.

The primary purpose of the present research is to develop a methodology which can accurately analyse online public reviews on Google using Netnography studies combined with text mining analyses. By analysing the current techniques applied to a lifestyle hotel brand in nine properties in different countries and carefully studying how negative reviews are expressed online by costumers, this study aims to create a pattern of lifestyle customer complaints. This research seeks to demonstrate patterns of consumer behaviour that are not fully satisfied with the hotel service and how it can negatively affect the brand. This study identifies the areas that five stars lifestyle hoteliers and hotel managers need to pay attention to improve services, considering online reviews on online platforms, such as social networks and other tourism sites. Today, online reviews and customer experiences have a significant impact on the choice of a hotel.

Luxury management can be considered the management of paradoxes between intangibility and functionality, rationality and emotion, modern technology with traditional craftsmanship, showing that luxury comes from creation, timelessness, emotion, excellence, heritage, and authenticity. This chapter results from two methods, a qualitative analysis, which presents an analysis grid with the most varied characteristics; these are divided into six groups: identification, content, product page, utility, entertainment and complementary relationship, speed and other presences visible on three websites of luxury furniture brands. The other method is the quantitative one, which was a questionnaire with the understanding the perceived quality of the website using the WebQual scale, as well as understanding the purchase intention and the importance of the internet in the purchase decision process.

Today, there are different digital communication opportunities that companies use to communicate with their customers. These are especially web sites and social networks. International brands are adapting to all changes in this communication environment while determining their communication strategies and then they communicate with their target audiences. Brands communicate with their target audiences and potential or unfamiliar audiences through communication opportunities without borders. This is also seen in the luxury brand market and consumers. In this study, luxury brand, luxury brand consumption, and finally website and social media applications used in international luxury brand communication are explained. In addition, comparative content analysis of corporate web sites and social media environments of Ferrari and Porsche companies, in which they are producing and marketing luxury products, were conducted and evaluations were made in the context of international luxury brand communication.

As one of the essential elements of culture, the role of religiosity in consumer behavior has long been established and number of consumer research on Muslim individuals has been increasing rapidly in recent years. With the rapid increase of the Muslim population and the developing welfare level of the Islamic countries, it is observed that Islamic luxury consumption has also become widespread too. In this chapter, it is aimed to determine the conceptual framework of Islamic luxury consumption together with current trends. Three halal concepts which are considered as include more explicit examples of Islamic luxury are chosen and analyzed: halal fashion, halal cosmetics, and halal tourism. Throughout the text and in the conclusion part, it is aimed to create insights for marketers who interested in Islamic luxury.

SMM (social media marketing) aims to produce content that users share in their various social media applications in order to increase brand exposure and broaden customer reach. There are numerous marketing techniques to apply in social media in order to involve the customer, some of which have costs and others do not. Digitization was a real challenge for any hotel company, requiring cautious and well-planned action to be successful. In this sense, the nature of social networks demands the adoption of a constructivist perspective, that is, a perspective that involves affirmations of knowledge based on individual and collective experiences. Presently, being present in social networks presents itself as a high value advantage, allowing to expose the brand, product, or idea, at a low cost, to a high audience. This

Foreword

Over the last two decades, the topic of Consumer Brand Relationships as gained interest and has become an important stream of research in the marketing literature. The topic of relationships between consumers and brands has always been at the center of marketing strategies, initiatives and is a major driver of successful marketing.

A simple search on Google scholar reveals that there are over 9,000 hits for the search term "consumer brand relationships" (as of 30. September 2020). Next to the thousands of research papers written, there are a few special issues in academic journals like the one in the *Journal of Brand Management* (Fetscherin and Heinrich, 2014) as well as in the *Journal of Product and Brand Management* (Fetscherin et al., 2016; Fetscherin et al., 2019). Next to that, there were also a few edited books such as the one by MacInnis, Park and Priester (2009), Fournier, Breazeale, Fetscherin (2012), Fournier, Breazeale, Avery (2015) and Fetscherin and Heilmann (2015). The most recent edited book by Paula Rodrigues and Ana Pinto Borges is a great addition to the existing body of literature. While the first edited books looked at various aspects of brand relationships, this book does this within the context of luxury goods. Brand relationships within luxury goods is important as the intrinsic value of luxury goods is related to value rather than costs. Luxury brand management shifted from materialism, conspicuous and hedonic consumption to one that embraces enrichment and experiences for consumers. While luxury goods were accessible a few centuries ago to a few, this changed in the last decade. With liberalization and economic growth, a growing middle class and technology advances making luxury goods more exposed and accessible than ever before. While the concept of luxury and luxury goods is different across cultures and times, they share the common denominator of not being essential but goods, which are highly desired and associated with affluent or wealthy people.

Gladly, the editors have collected an impressive edition with authors from different international backgrounds to these research pursuits, offering their global perspectives to brand relationships in the luxury industry. Both, practitioners and researchers will benefit from these contributions and gain valuable insights and a richer understanding and appreciation of the different facets of this topic. In sum, the book with over 300 pages, provides with the 12 chapters a neat summary of latest research of relationships consumers have with luxury goods. The chapters offer a stimulating treatment of the topic and offers to any branding scholar or practitioner a valuable addition.

Marc Fetscherin
Rollins College, USA

REFERENCES

Fetscherin, M., Cayolla, R. R., Guzmán, F., & Veloutsou, C. (2016). Editorial. *Journal of Product and Brand Management*, *25*(6), 505–506. doi:10.1108/JPBM-07-2016-1268

Fetscherin, M., Guzman, F., Veloutsou, C., & Cayolla, R. R. (2019). Latest research on brand relationships: Introduction to the special issue. *Journal of Product and Brand Management*, *28*(2), 133–139. doi:10.1108/JPBM-12-2018-2167

Fetscherin, M., & Heilmann, T. (2015). Brand relationships rule. In *Consumer Brand Relationships* (pp. 1–12). Palgrave Macmillan. doi:10.1057/9781137427120_1

Fetscherin, M., & Heinrich, D. (2014). Consumer brand relationships: A research landscape. *Journal of Brand Management*, *21*(5), 366–371. doi:10.1057/bm.2014.22

Fournier, S., Breazeale, M., & Avery, J. (Eds.). (2015). *Strong brands, strong relationships*. Routledge. doi:10.4324/9781315767079

Fournier, S., Breazeale, M., & Fetscherin, M. (Eds.). (2012). *Consumer-brand relationships: theory and practice*. Routledge. doi:10.4324/9780203128794

MacInnis, D. J., Park, C. W., & Priester, J. W. (2009). *Handbook of brand relationships*. M.E. Sharpe.

Foreword

The personal luxury segment, which has tripled its size over the past 20 years, is now facing an enormous challenge like never before due to the Covid 19 outbreak. After falling by an estimated 25 percent in the first quarter of 2020, the slowdown would even accelerate in the second quarter and could lead to an estimated total contraction of between 20 percent to 35 percent for the full 2020 year[1]. Worth pointing out the fact that Chinese consumers are still set to strengthen their status as crucial drivers of the industry, accounting for nearly 50 percent of the market by 2025. Moreover, luxury purchases made online have increased throughout the crisis and could represent up to 30 percent of the market by 2025.

Nonetheless, it will take time for the market to recover. According to Bain & Company, a recovery to 2019 levels will not occur until 2022 or 2023. Market growth will resume gradually from then on, reaching an estimated €320-330 billion by 2025. If hence one can expect a recovery for the luxury market, the industry will be profoundly transformed. Indeed, according to Federica Levato, Bain & Company partner, "*the speed of future market growth will depend on luxury players' strategic responses to the current crisis and their ability to transform the industry on behalf of the customer*"[2]

All in all, everything seems nowadays to lie in the consumers' hands. The paradox is that, luxury, once the ordinary of extraordinary people, has become the extraordinary of ordinary people too (Kapferer and Valette-Florence, 2018). Thus, the luxury market is changing with global shifts across national borders. One major question for the managers of highly successful luxury brands is defining how well and how far they can generalize the notion that luxury brands' desirability rests on maintaining some form of rarity and exclusivity. Continued growth and rarity seem two opposed notions. Moreover, despite the ubiquitous visibility of luxury brands and luxury malls in capital cities of the world, the question "*what is really luxury*?" is still debated among academics. Not only are there as many definitions as researchers but also these definitions changed through time.

Nonetheless, the essence of luxury may still be elusive, yet its existence is clear for all consumers. When it comes to the market, luxury is not a "*concept*" but a reality incarnated by brands and their glamorous stores concentrated on high streets where the luxury malls in Seoul, Taipei or Shanghai tell what brands are the "*luxury brands*". This shapes the new consumers' vision of what luxury is. This is why brands are at the core of luxury today. The ubiquitous existence of the same luxury brands, luxury products, luxury malls and communications across countries creates a quite homogeneous consumer experience and, hence, a global vision of what is luxury.

All in all, recent research (Kapferer and Valette-Florence, 2018) has put forward the relevance of the hypothesis of the universality of the rarity principle, also known as the '*dream equation*'. Their overall contribution refers to three main conceptual frameworks. First, it mostly rests on Brock's commodity theory on the psychological effects of scarcity. Secondly, it also rests on cultural differences between the western culture and the Asian one, for instance as far as the need for uniqueness is concerned. Thirdly, it makes reference to bandwagon effect versus snob effect theory. Bandwagon effects, when one's choice follows the choice of the many, should be prevalent in countries where conformity is rewarded, such as China, or in new markets, where the consumers have not enough confidence in their own choice. Snob effects may appear in luxury mature markets where new riches need to differentiate themselves and adopt newer and lesser known brands with less penetration. The overall effect of increased market penetration on luxury desirability remains negative, while the impact of awareness remains always positive

Readers will have understood, the world of luxury has changed and it is becoming essential to find new forms of investigation. This book, edited by Paula Rodrigues and Ana Pinto Borges, hence represents an outstanding contribution in that respect. With over 300 pages, it provides trough 12 chapters a global overview of latest research of relationships consumers have with luxury goods. The selected papers of this book have touched upon, yet are but not limited to, the few issues outlined above. Fascinating chapters deal with up to date luxury research and explore different aspects of luxury branding such as, just to name quite a few, old and new luxury, luxury counterfeiting, inconspicuous luxury consumption, and luxury brand experience or virtual luxury communication. All in all, we strongly recommend reading these papers as all of them do provide real new insights into the luxury business and hence will serve as a fertile platform for further interest, discussion and research.

Pierre Valette-Florence
Grenoble IAE, France

REFERENCES

Kapferer, J.-N., & Valette-Florence, P. (2018). The impact of brand penetration and awareness on luxury brand desirability: A cross country analysis of the relevance of the rarity principle. *Journal of Business Research*, *83*, 38–50. doi:10.1016/j.jbusres.2017.09.025

ENDNOTES

1 https://www.bain.com/about/media-center/press-releases/2020/spring-luxury-report/ (retrieved, September 28th, 2020)

2 https://www.consultancy.eu/news/4171/bain-personal-luxury-goods-market-will-need-years-to-recover (retrieved, September 28th, 2020)

Foreword

Consumer-brand relationship is a field of research embedded in relationship marketing that has attracted diverse researchers and witnessed important developments. Among the most representative publications, we can point out the Fournier's seminal anthropomorphic model brand relationship quality in the *Journal of Consumer Research.* Following this approach, Jennifer Aaker develop brand personality as a set of human characteristics which are associated with a brand and publish the findings in The Journal of Marketing Research. Muniz, McAlexander and other colleagues (publishing in *Journal of Marketing and Journal of Consumer Research*) devoted their research around the concept of brand community, meaning a specialized, non-geographically bound community aggregating those who are admirers of a brand.

The attachment theory coming from the studies of parent-child relationships developed by Bowlby and colleagues. The core aspects of such theory have been transferred to the marketing by diverse authors (e.g., Schouten, McAlexande, Yuksel, Thomson, Park) who suggest that emotional attachment is created between human and animals, places, destinations, objects, or brands. Thomson, MacInnis, and Park, for instance, identified a higher-order emotional attachment construct – published in Journal of Consumer Psychology- consisting of three factors: affection, passion, and connection. This way, attachments reflect an emotional bond similar to love, what according to the triangular theory of love of Sternberg several concepts emerge as crucial, that is, passion, intimacy and commitment. Yet, more facets are in the game when talking about the relational love that it is possible to stablish between consumers and certain brands. Brand love published in 2012 in Journal of Marketing uncovered such facets by the hands of Batra, Ahuvia and Bagozzi.

Park, Eisingerich, and Park published in Journal of Consumer Psychology a very promising model designated as Attachment–aversion (AA). This model uses two key properties, the degree of brand-self distance and brand prominence. The first regards the perceived distance between the self and the brand and the second is the perceived memory accessibility of a brand to an individual. Attachment–aversion represents two essential and opposite ends components of the relationship spectrum at a moment in time.

Recently, another prototype emerged in Journal of Marketing called brand coolness. After more than eight years working on the subject, the team constituted by Warren, Batra, Loureiro and Bagozzi published the 10 characteristics that cool brands have perceived to be extraordinary, aesthetically appealing, energetic, high status, rebellious, original, authentic, subcultural, iconic, and popular. To give a glimpse, generating strategies and tactics to raise a brand's scores on the characteristic components of brand coolness requires considerable creativity. Creating a perception of extraordinary quality likely requires performance/functional specs that are "next-generation" or that deliver unsurpassed customer experience/service rather than incremental improvements. Aesthetic appeal routes suggest the need for eye-popping design. Both the energetic and originality subcomponents require continuous innovation, dynamism, and momentum. Authenticity may require reminding consumers of the history and deeply held values of a brand and its founders, while avoiding the use of strategies associated with mass marketed brands. High status comes from associations with glamour and sophistication. Iconic perceptions might be raised by using and publicizing distinctive packaging, advertising style, or telling a brand myth that resonates with consumers.

Within this context, this book provides a valuable contribute to the field by focusing on the luxury sector. Luxury is hard to be defined and constantly change. Luxury implies different things to different groups of people across time and cultures. Yet, academics and managers tend to agree that luxury brands bear symbolic meanings that are employed by consumers to meet their social goals. Luxury is traditionally associated to premium brand characteristics, uniqueness, and exclusivity. Symbolic properties are requisite aspects of a luxury brand what lead us to the conspicuous consumption, focusing on ostentatious signalling of one's wealth and social strata. However, luxury market has evolved from traditional conspicuous consumption model to an experiential consumer self-orientation model and thus, become even more complex to understand. These aspects are discussed in a chapter dedicated to new luxury versus old luxury.

The book *Building Consumer-Brand Relationship in Luxury Brand Management* conducts us in a journey into this market. The collection of chapters illustrates different perspectives from hospitality, tourism to furniture or automotive industry.

Several relevant issues are discussed. This is the case of luxury counterfeiting and how brands lead with this market and create anti-counterfeiting strategies. Another issue is the Islamic luxury and its trends. The online environment was not forgotten in chapters devoted to tourism and hospitality, where were employed methodologies such as netnography and text-mining.

In this vein, the challenge of writing chapters and all the work of reviewing and editing this book has been largely overcome, resulting in an interesting piece of work for academics, PhD students, and practitioners.

Sandra Maria Correia Loureiro
BRU, ISCTE, Lisbon University Institute, Portugal

Sandra Maria Correia Loureiro*'s research interests include consumer-brand relationship and its implications with VR, AR and AI. Her papers have been published in a variety of peer reviewed journals that include Journal of Marketing, Journal of Retailing, Journal of Service Management, or Journal of Business Research. Her work has also been presented at respected international conferences such as EMAC, ANZMAC, and KAMS-GMC. Sandra serves as a reviewer for several international journals and conferences and has participated in several research projects funded by the EU and FCT (Foundation for Science and Technology). She recently won several awards, such as: the 2012 Best Paper Premier Award presented by the Global Marketing Conference (comprised of EMAC, ANZMAC, KSMS, and the Japanese Association of Marketing), Highly Commended paper Award 2014 - 7th EuroMed Conference and EuroMed Research Business Institute (EMRBI), Highly Commended paper Award 2016 - 9th EuroMed Conference and EuroMed Research Business Institute (EMRBI), Best Paper Award 2016- ICCMI 2016. In 2017 and 2018 she also won high commended papers award from editor Emerald. Best paper award at the Fashion Management Conference 2019.*

Preface

In the last years a large number of papers have been published on the topic of researching of luxury branding and consumer-brand relationships. Luxury brands and consumer-brand relationships are both closely related (Amatulli & Guido, 2011; Bahari-Ammari, Coulibaly & Mimoun, 2020; Batat, 2019; Bian & Forsythe, 2012; Chandon, Laurent & Valette-Florance, 2016; Cristini, Kauppinen-Räisäinen, Barthod-Prothade & Woodside, 2017; Kapferer & Valette-Florance, 2018; Ko, Costello & Taylor, 2019).

Since the consumer-brand relationship is a key aspect for brand management at the corporate level, it becomes much more important when it comes to luxury brands (Eastman, Shin & Ruhland, 2020). Its importance, at the business level, is related to the fact that the creation of a long-term relationship implies large investments of financial and human resources, whose objectives is to return to the level of certain consumer behaviors (Fournier, 1998). Understanding the factors that lead to the creation of a strong emotional connection with luxury brands is a relevant theme in brand management (Cristini et al., 2017; Nobre & Simões, 2019; Rodrigues & Rodrigues, 2019; Rodrigues, Brandão & Rodrigues, 2018).

In this context, luxury is no longer a privilege of the high net worth individuals but becomes accessible to all (Chandon, Laurent & Valette-Florance, 2016). This has become possible because the essence of luxury has changed: from something based upon materialism, conspicuous and hedonic consumption to one that embraces enrichment and experiences for the consumers (Dion & Borraz, 2017; Ko, Costello & Taylor, 2019). This evolution creates challenges for luxury brands and for the managers of luxury brands (Batat, 2019; Cristini et al., 2017).

The meaning of luxury is changing. Structural changes in the types of relationship between brands and consumers affect the concept of luxury for consumers. With the growth in the middle classes, luxury has become accessible and democratised (Batat, 2019; Chandon, Laurent & Valette-Florance, 2016; Kapferer & Michaut-Denizeau, 2020).

On the other hand, the concept of luxury is incredibly fluid and changes dramatically across time and culture (Abalkhal, 2020; Aksoy & Abdulfatai, 2019; Cristini et al., 2017; Kapferer & Valette-Florance, 2018; Kapferer & Michaut-Denizeau, 2020).

The consumer, nowadays, differentiates him or herself not only through the goods and services they buy but also by the experiences they enjoy (Atwal & Williams, 2009, Batat, 2019). These include the experience of time, space, authenticity, community individuality and well-being (Beverland, 2006; Loureiro, Plaza & Taghion, 2020). The luxury and the consumer relationship with luxury becomes the desire to enrich their daily lives by experiencing new things and to undertake activities which deliver a sense of improvement, enjoyment and refreshment, something that is called experience economy (Brandão, Pinto & Rodrigues, 2019; Eastman, Shin & Ruhland, 2020).

The mega-rich often own or influence very potent cultural objects and favour certain social causes, they drive both expectation and behaviour on the part of the more ordinary citizen and then, the mega-rich are bound closely together as a niche of consumers isolated from the mainstream (Cristini et al., 2017; Dion & Borraz, 2017; Katanakis & Balabanis, 2012). This segment of market highlights the rising prestige communities which are based on status and economic class and, in contrast to lifestyle communities, are not promoted for their facilities but rather for their exclusivity, both in physical design and in social composition (Batat, 2019; Goor, Odabayeva, Keinan & Crener, 2020; Kapferer & Michaut-Denizeau, 2020; Katanakis & Balabanis, 2012).

Female and male consumers do not favour the same luxury values and owing to gender differences in the influence of luxury value drivers (Roux, Tafani & Vigneron, 2017; Semaan, Lindsay, Williams & Ashill, 2019). Then, each gender possesses a specific relationship to luxury brands in accordance with its position in the social structure and related beliefs and roles that implicate different consumer-brand relationships (Alserhan, Bataineh, Halkias & Komodromos, 2014; Batat, 2019; Eastman, Shin & Ruhland, 2020).

Changes in science, innovation and technology allow us to personalize luxury experiences and consumer behaviour. The Internet revolution creates many new questions for the luxury industry, while also opening many new research avenues to marketing academics (Arrigo, 2018; Baker, Ashill, Amer & Diah, 2018; Brandão, Pinto & Rodrigues, 2019; Fazeli, Shukla & Perks, 2020; Jain & Schultz, 2019; Kim, 2019). Additionally, it addresses the urgent need for more integrative and comprehensive approaches to modelling and understanding the consumer-brand relationship with luxury brands and their sustainability in a global and multicultural world (Boidvet & Ashill, 2018; Eastman, Shin & Ruhland, 2020; Rajanasingsawad, Ryding & Barnes, 2020).

The consumer-brand relationship is a multidisciplinary, multidimensional and multiconceptual construct, that is, with a variety of concepts, constructs and underlying theories that derive from different fields, such as marketing, psychology, sociology, anthropology or neuroscience (Belard & Temessek Behil, 2011; Fetscherin & Heinrich, 2015; Fournier, 1998).

One can classify the different concepts of relationship with the brand in relationships based on functional connection, emotional connection or a combination or the two, that is, functional with emotional connection. Functional connections are found only when functional needs are at stake. Emotional connection results if only the emotional need of consumers are met. You can also group them into relationships (weak vs. strong) and consumer feelings towards brands (negative vs. positive), considering only the emotional dimensions of consumer-brand relationship (Chaudhuri, 2006; Fournier & Alvarez, 2013).

A review of recent research in consumer-brand relationship is structured in terms of the three foundational elements entity: first, the bond between consumer and brand, second, the brand as relationship partner, and third, the consumer as relationship partner (Fetscherin & Heinrich, 2015; Fournier, 1998). The construction of this relationship is also subject to all challenges and constraints of the luxury brand market. The purpose of this book is to understand the relationship of the consumer with the luxury brands with all the new challenges that are in the market today (Eastman, Shin & Ruhland, 2020).

The importance of understanding how managers can create and manage a strong emotional relationship with consumers of luxury brands must bear in mind that the luxury market: (1) is a very attractive, global but volatile market, in the need of presence in omnichannels; (2) it has consumers with different characteristics and (3) it is a market with the appearance of new brands.

The main objective of the book is to contribute to the dissemination of knowledge, both to academics and professionals, in the area of branding and consumer relationship in the luxury market.

Empirical and theoretical works will be presented in order to reach several audiences and diversity of subjects. It is expected to have a high impact because it is focused on the aspects of the consumer's emotional relationship with luxury brands. Thus, it is necessary to define strategies that necessarily pass through analysis and planning on how a luxury brand in a new context is perceived in the market. The value of the book is to be pioneer in the field and become a reference. Among book*'s* targeted audience are marketing academics, PhD students, and practitioners (e.g., marketing researches and consulting professionals) and other interested groups and individuals.

The book is structured in the following manner: it is divided into four section with twelve chapters. Section one has four chapters that address the relationship between luxury brands and the consumer-brand relationship. Section two has three chapters that focus on aspects of consumer relationships with luxury brands from the point of view of experiences. Section three has two chapters on the importance of the Internet, Social Media, and Websites in building, developing, and maintaining consumer relationship with luxury brands. And, finally, section four has three more chapters that address different but very pertinent themes in the luxury brand management.

Chapter 1 presents a new framework that proposes antecedents reflecting both external and internal point of references as well as luxury accessibility levels that impact the consumer behaviour toward luxury brands, having obtain three propositions to summarize the framework.

Chapter 2 presents a literature review with the purpose to examine consumers' behaviour and perceptions of luxury brands.

Chapter 3 tries to understanding the concept of luxury through an extensive literature review, to clarify the main differences between the concepts of new and old luxury brands.

Chapter 4 explains the consumers' interest towards inconspicuous luxury products. Provides a review on luxury and on the different motivations that determine luxury consumption. Socio-economic changes that trigger the shift from conspicuous to inconspicuous luxury consumption is examined briefly. And, a discussion on why inconspicuous consumption is valued by consumers is followed by a theoretical framework on the motivations for inconspicuous luxury brand usage.

Chapter 5 highlights that the strength of consumer-brand relationships is very much shaped by consumers' experiences with luxury brands. This chapter investigates the relational outcomes of brand experience and discusses the various drivers that can be used to enhance luxury brand experience and developed stronger consumer-brand relationships.

Chapter 6 has the main objective to analyse Web reviews to identify the expressive dimensions that describe guests' experiences in luxury restaurants, using content analysis of reviews of Michelin-starred restaurants.

Chapter 7 used Netnography technique applied to a five stars lifestyle hotel brands in different countries for studying the negative reviews expressed online by consumers and create a pattern of lifestyle consumers' complaints, in luxury hotels.

Chapter 8 identifies six groups of characteristics of luxury in furniture brands on three websites - identification, content, product page, utility, entertainment, and complementary relationship – to understanding the perceived quality of the website and the internet in the purchase decision process.

Chapter 9 compares two website and social media for two luxury automobile sector to evaluate the strategies of marketing and communication in the context of international luxury brand.

Chapter 10 examines the element of culture, the role of religiosity in consumer luxury behaviour using three halal concepts as an example – halal fashion, halal cosmetics and halal tourism.

Chapter 11 studies the social media marketing in luxury hotels. Aims to systematize some relational marketing best practices – communication - that are identified in the luxury hotel segment in Europe.

Chapter 12 publishes a research on the characteristics of those who are more likely to purchase counterfeits, and investigates the social and emotional motives that underlie counterfeit users. Makes a reviews of the literature, particularly in marketing, in order to provide some insight to brand managers, policymakers and law enforcement agencies who are attempting to curb counterfeit consumption.

REFERENCES

Abalkhail, T. S. (2020). The impact of religiosity on luxury brand consumption: the case of Saudi consumers. *Journal of Islamic Marketing*. Ahead-of-print. doi:10.1108/JIMA-11-2016-0091

Aksoy, H., & Abdulfatai, O. (2019). Exploring the impact of religiousness and culture on luxury fashion goods purchasing intention: A behavioural study on Nigerian Muslim consumers. *Journal of Islamic Marketing*, *10*(3), 768–789. doi:10.1108/JIMA-01-2018-0022

Alserhan, B. A., Bataineh, M. K., Halkias, D., & Komodromos, M. (2014). Measuring luxury brand consumption and female consumers' religiosity in the UAE. *Journal of Developmental Entrepreneurship*, *19*(2), 1–16. doi:10.1142/S1084946714500095

Amatulli, C., & Guido, G. (2012). Externalised vs. internalised consumption of luxury goods: Propositions and implications for luxury retail marketing. *International Review of Retail, Distribution and Consumer Research*, *22*(2), 189–207. doi:10.1080/09593969.2011.652647

Arrigo, E. (2018). Social media marketing in luxury brands: A systematic literature review and implications for management research. *Management Research Review*, *41*(6), 657–679. doi:10.1108/MRR-04-2017-0134

Atwal, G., & Williams, A. (2009). Luxury brand marketing – the experience is everything! *Journal of Brand Management*, *16*(5-6), 338–346. doi:10.1057/bm.2008.48

Bahri-Ammari, N., Coulibaly, D., & Mimoun, M. S. B. (2020). The bandwagon luxury consumption in Tunisian case: The roles of independent and interdependent self-concept. *Journal of Retailing and Consumer Services*, *52*, 101903. doi:10.1016/j.jretconser.2019.101903

Baker, J., Ashill, N., Amer, N., & Diab, E. (2018). The internet dilemma: An exploratory study of luxury firms' usage of internet-based technologies. *Journal of Retailing and Consumer Services*, *41*, 37–47. doi:10.1016/j.jretconser.2017.11.007

Batat, W. (2019). *The new luxury experience*. Springer International Publishing. doi:10.1007/978-3-030-01671-5

Belaid, S., & Temessek Behi, A. (2011). The role of attachment in building consumer-brand relationships: An empirical investigation in the utilitarian consumption context. *Journal of Product and Brand Management*, *20*(1), 37–47. doi:10.1108/10610421111108003

Beverland, M. (2006). The 'real thing': Branding authenticity in the luxury wine trade. *Journal of Business Research*, *59*(2), 251–258. doi:10.1016/j.jbusres.2005.04.007

Bian, Q., & Forsythe, S. (2012). Purchase intention for luxury brands: A cross cultural comparison. *Journal of Business Research*, *65*(10), 1443–1451. doi:10.1016/j.jbusres.2011.10.010

Boisvert, J., & Ashill, N. J. (2018). The impact of branding strategies on horizontal and downward line extension of luxury brands: A cross-national study. *International Marketing Review*, *35*(6), 1033–1052. doi:10.1108/IMR-10-2017-0208

Brandão, A., Pinho, E., & Rodrigues, P. (2019). Antecedents and consequences of luxury brand engagement in social media. *Spanish Journal of Marketing-ESIC*, *23*(2), 163–183. doi:10.1108/SJME-11-2018-0052

Chandon, J. L., Laurent, G., & Valette-Florence, P. (2016). Pursuing the concept of luxury: Introduction to the JBR Special Issue on "Luxury Marketing from Tradition to Innovation". *Journal of Business Research*, *69*(1), 299–303. doi:10.1016/j.jbusres.2015.08.001

Chaudhuri, A. (2006). *Emotion and reason in consumer behavior*. Routledge. doi:10.4324/9780080461762

Cristini, H., Kauppinen-Räisänen, H., Barthod-Prothade, M., & Woodside, A. (2017). Toward a general theory of luxury: Advancing from workbench definitions and theoretical transformations. *Journal of Business Research*, *70*, 101–107. doi:10.1016/j.jbusres.2016.07.001

Dion, D., & Borraz, S. (2017). Managing status: How luxury brands shape class subjectivities in the service encounter. *Journal of Marketing*, *81*(5), 67–85. doi:10.1509/jm.15.0291

Eastman, J. K., Shin, H., & Ruhland, K. (2020). The picture of luxury: A comprehensive examination of college student consumers' relationship with luxury brands. *Psychology and Marketing*, *37*(1), 56–73. doi:10.1002/mar.21280

Fazeli, Z., Shukla, P., & Perks, K. (2020). Digital buying behavior: The role of regulatory fit and self-construal in online luxury goods purchase intentions. *Psychology and Marketing*, *37*(1), 15–26. doi:10.1002/mar.21276

Fetscherin, M., & Heinrich, D. (2015). Consumer brand relationships research: A bibliometric citation meta-analysis. *Journal of Business Research*, *68*(2), 380–390. doi:10.1016/j.jbusres.2014.06.010

Fournier, S. (1998). Consumers and their brands: Developing relationship theory in consumer research. *The Journal of Consumer Research*, *24*(4), 343–353. doi:10.1086/209515

Fournier, S., & Alvarez, C. (2013). Relating badly to brands. *Journal of Consumer Psychology*, *23*(2), 253–264. doi:10.1016/j.jcps.2013.01.004

Goor, D., Odabayeva, N., Keinan, A., & Crener, S. (2020). The impostor syndrome from luxury consumption. *The Journal of Consumer Research*, *46*(6), 1031–1051. doi:10.1093/jcr/ucz044

Jain, V., & Schultz, D. E. (2019). How digital platforms influence luxury purchase behavior in India? *Journal of Marketing Communications*, *25*(1), 41–64. doi:10.1080/13527266.2016.1197295

Kapferer, J.-N., & Michaut-Denizeau, A. (2020). Are millennials really more sensitive to sustainable luxury? A cross-generational international comparison of sustainability consciousness when buying luxury. *Journal of Brand Management*, *27*(1), 35–47. doi:10.105741262-019-00165-7

Kapferer, J. N., & Valette-Florence, P. (2018). The impact of brand penetration and awareness on luxury brand desirability: A cross country analysis of the relevance of the rarity principle. *Journal of Business Research*, *83*, 38–50. doi:10.1016/j.jbusres.2017.09.025

Kastanakis, M. N., & Balabanis, G. (2012). Between the mass and the class: Antecedents of the "bandwagon" luxury consumption behavior. *Journal of Business Research*, *65*(10), 1399–1407. doi:10.1016/j.jbusres.2011.10.005

Kim, J. H. (2019). Imperative challenge for luxury brands: Generation Y consumers' perceptions of luxury fashion brands' e-commerce sites. *International Journal of Retail & Distribution Management*, *47*(2), 220–244. doi:10.1108/IJRDM-06-2017-0128

Ko, E., Costello, J. P., & Taylor, C. R. (2019). What is a luxury brand? A new definition and review of the literature. *Journal of Business Research*, *99*, 405–413. doi:10.1016/j.jbusres.2017.08.023

Loureiro, S. M. C., de Plaza, M. A. P., & Taghian, M. (2020). The effect of benign and malicious envies on desire to buy luxury fashion items. *Journal of Retailing and Consumer Services*, *52*, 101688. doi:10.1016/j.jretconser.2018.10.005

Nobre, H., & Simões, C. (2019). NewLux Brand Relationship Scale: Capturing the scope of mass-consumed luxury brand relationships. *Journal of Business Research*, *102*, 328–338. doi:10.1016/j.jbusres.2019.01.047

Rodrigues, C., & Rodrigues, P. (2019). Brand Love Matters to Millenials: The relevance of mystery, sensuality and intimacy to neo-luxury brands. *Journal of Product and Brand Management*, *28*(7), 830–848. doi:10.1108/JPBM-04-2018-1842

Rodrigues, P., Brandão, A., & Rodrigues, C. (2018). The importance of self in brand love in consumer luxury brand relationships. *Journal of Customer Behaviour*, *18*(3), 189–210. doi:10.1362/147539218X15434304746036

Rojanasingsawad, M., Ryding, D., & Barnes, L. (2020). Consumer decision-making styles for grey luxury goods: a study on Thailand. *International Journal of Sales, Retailing & Marketing*, *9*(1).

Roux, E., Tafani, E., & Vigneron, F. (2017). Values associated with luxury brand consumption and the role of gender. *Journal of Business Research*, *71*, 102–113. doi:10.1016/j.jbusres.2016.10.012

Semaan, R. W., Lindsay, V., Williams, P., & Ashill, N. (2019). The influence of gender roles in the drivers of luxury consumption for women: Insights from the gulf region. *Journal of Retailing and Consumer Services*, *51*(November), 165–175. doi:10.1016/j.jretconser.2019.06.006

Acknowledgment

All the chapters were double-blind review. The editors would like to acknowledge the help of all the people involved in this project and, more specifically, to the authors and reviewers that took part in the review process. Without their support, this book would not have become a reality.

First, the editors would like to thank each one of the authors for their contributions. Our sincere gratitude goes to the chapter's authors who contributed their time and expertise to this book.

Second, the editors wish to acknowledge the valuable contributions of the reviewers regarding the improvement of quality, coherence, and content presentation of chapters. Most of the authors also served as referees; we highly appreciate their double task.

Finally, a special acknowledgement to Isabel Cristina Pereira Barbosa, a student of a Master scholarship in Management, of COMEGI (*(Research Centre in Organizations, Markets and Industrial Management)* and Universidade Lusíada – Norte.

Paula Rodrigues
Lusiada University of Porto, Portugal

Ana Pinto Borges
Instituto Superior de Administração e Gestão, Portugal

Chapter 1
Understanding the Luxury Brand Consumer:
A Proposed Conceptual Framework

Natalie A. Mitchell
University of North Florida, USA

Christine Kowalczyk
East Carolina University, USA

ABSTRACT

The definition of luxury brands has been long debated among marketing scholars; however, understanding how consumers perceive luxury is important too. This research presents a new framework that includes antecedents reflecting external and internal points of reference, luxury accessibility levels that ultimately impact consumer behavior toward luxury brands. It is understood that consumers have different lived experiences and may also have access to different goods in the marketplace. Hence, the proposed framework contributes to the luxury marketing literature by highlighting these important antecedents which induce various perceptions of luxury. Three propositions are presented to summarize the framework, which also supports future research aims.

INTRODUCTION

Increasingly, the luxury goods market continues to grow (Kim, 2019; Interbrand, 2013; Christodoulides et al., 2009). Luxury brand managers are challenged to understand the changes of the luxury industry and consumer needs and wants (Fionda & Moore, 2009). Since the 1990's, the luxury market has experienced an annual growth rate of 10-15 percent and has exceeded the growth rates in other consumer goods categories (Matthiesen & Phau, 2005). Its rapid global success has propelled the luxury market to be one of the fastest-growing industries in the world (Fionda & Moore, 2009). Continued spikes in luxury consumption in the marketplace influences consumer culture and consumers' experience throughout their lives (Fazeli, Shukla, & Perks, 2020). For example, consumers are bombarded by 3,000 adver-

DOI: 10.4018/978-1-7998-4369-6.ch001

Copyright © 2021, IGI Global. Copying or distributing in print or electronic forms without written permission of IGI Global is prohibited.

tised messages or brand contact points daily, some of which may also include luxury brands (Henke & Fontenot, 2011). Regardless of costs or status, each brand contact, whether casual or direct, serves as a brand introduction or reminder to possibly consider luxury brands.

During one's socialization process, consumers are exposed to various points of reference that reflect their upbringings at home. Points of reference may represent family, social class, race, gender and family, among other demographic factors. Accessibility to goods also varies based on the aforementioned points of reference. Privileged consumers raised in trendy global cities, such as New York, with families who may actively engage in luxury consumption, undoubtedly will have access to luxury goods. This may be based on their family's income and luxury awareness, in addition to the accessibility to luxury retailers in Manhattan, and the overall consumer culture in the Northeast region. Further, identity formation occurs during childhood and continues through adulthood (Moschis, 1987). Consumers develop identities based on both gender and racial status. Hence, racial and gender identities will also influence their position in the marketplace, their perceptions of brands, in addition to their access to such brands. During the formative years, points of references leave lasting impressions on consumers' values, beliefs, and purchase intentions.

Many brands, including luxury, are shifting to a more consumer-focused business model. Consumers' changing preferences and access to luxury and media consumption suggest that more theorizing is needed to understand the ultimate luxury market. Luxury marketers are challenged to better understand luxury consumers in order to better target consumers and increase marketplace presence. To do so, marketers need more in-depth knowledge about consumer behavior within the luxury market. The aim of this research is to further develop a conceptualization of luxury consumers, which includes antecedents that serve as their points of reference in the luxury marketplace. Specifically, the conceptual framework highlights the role of advertising on luxury consumer perception. It is important for marketers to holistically consider the consumer, including their life experiences, rather than just the motivational drivers of luxury consumption. Focusing on the consumer perspective is important because consumers have individual needs (Wiedmann et al., 2007; Kapferer & Bastien, 2012). Further, researchers have suggested more examination is needed to understand the concept of luxury from the consumer perspective (Berthon et al., 2009; Chandon, Laurent, & Vallette-Florence, 2016). To date, one research team developed a luxury consumer buying behavior model theorizing luxury consumption in India (Jain et al., 2015). While it included external stimuli that influence consumers and consumer behavior, a more nuanced framework is needed to address other key points of reference not previously identified.

A myriad of factors likely influence consumer perception of luxury. Such factors reflect varying degrees of consumer socialization and luxury accessibility. Not all consumers share the same body of knowledge, attraction, and accessibility to luxury brands. It is understood that luxury may be desired by most consumers, but that may not always be true. Luxury consumption in some cases can be associated with materialism, which is the preoccupation of consumption for hedonic pleasures only and not for utility (Belk, 2001). While materialism is criticized for eroding consumer morality, some consumers may strongly oppose luxury brands and not desire them at all. Therefore, more insight about luxury consumers provides a deeper understanding.

The proposed conceptual framework departs from previous typologies and frameworks that strictly focused on defining luxury based on macro-level conditions. Instead, this framework suggests a closer exploration of the micro-level, personal factors central to understanding luxury consumers. For example, consumers' personal interpretation of advertised messages and how they potentially find meaning of luxury goods. Further, this research also underscores the value of consumer perspectives of luxury, since the consumer is the final decision-maker for purchase or non-purchase behavior. Consumer personal values and cultural values should be more involved in the conceptualization of luxury. To address this, the framework proposes external and internal points of references, in addition to varying luxury accessibility levels, as influencers of consumer behavior. In turn, the conceptual framework aims to address the following research questions:

RQ1: What points of reference are driving consumer interest in luxury brands?
RQ2: How is a consumer's access to luxury brands driven by his/her points of reference?
RQ3: What consumer behaviors result from a consumer's access to luxury brands?

This chapter includes a literature review of luxury brands, the proliferation of mass prestige luxury marketing, and luxury consumer points of reference. Also, two conceptual luxury models are critiqued. Then, a proposed conceptual framework, highlighting the points of references for luxury consumers, is introduced, along with research propositions, marketing implications, and future research opportunities.

BACKGROUND

Overview of the Luxury Brand Market

Luxury brands tend to attract consumers based on the brand's strong brand heritage, appealing aesthetics, and quality. Due to various meanings and interests describing luxury brands, researchers have long debated the best luxury definition to describe them (Ko et al., 2019; Berthon et al., 2009; Beverland, 2004). To date, the literature is devoid of a specific definition of luxury (Sung et al., 2014). The subjective nature of luxury perception adds to this challenge. For example, consumer perception of a personal vehicle in one country may be considered a luxury to consumers in developing countries. Expensive products do not always reflect luxury. Often, luxury brands are defined by its characteristics (Kim, 2019). For purposes of this research, luxury brands are defined as "images in the minds of consumers that comprise associations above a high level of price, quality aesthetics, rarity, extraordinariness and a high degree of non-functional associations" (Heine, 2012, p. 60). This definition is suitable to describe luxury brands because it considers consumer perceptions and how they identify luxury. It is important to better understand how consumers identify luxury because it varies by consumer. Moreover, it has been found that consumers can associate luxury brands with quality, emotions, and rarity (Pileiene, 2012). It is noted that luxury brands also offer consumers functional, symbolic, and experiential values (Berthon et al., 2009).

The luxury goods market has experienced significant growth because of changes in consumer lifestyles and income (Interbrand, 2013). The scope of luxury consumers is getting broader as luxury brands extend their reach and marketing efforts. The increased frequency of luxury depictions in media is also a contributing factor (Christodoulides et al., 2009; Phau & Teah, 2009). The global luxury market is expected to reach $40 trillion by 2020 (Jain & Schultz, 2019). It is estimated the demand for luxury products will continue to grow at the rate of 4 to 5 percent annually (Jain, 2018). The rapid growth of the luxury market demonstrates the strong economic implications associated with luxury goods and consumer culture. Much of this growth is a result of the growth of the internet and more accessible and affordable luxury products (Kim, 2019; Jain & Schultz, 2019).

Luxury Growth Known as Masstige

Consumption of goods has been categorized into four levels: necessary, basic, affluence and luxury (Smith, 1776); whereas, luxury has been categorized as products which are rare or exclusive. Alleres (1990) suggested that luxury brands can be marketed based on three categories: inaccessible luxury, intermediate luxury, and accessible luxury. The inaccessible luxury brands are considered to be of exceptional quality, rare, high price and extremely selective in its target market. Intermediate luxury still has high quality but targets a larger market who wants to distinguish one's self from others. The accessible luxury is mass produced and marketed to consumers. It is a competitive market that is strongly influenced by advertising.

In the 1990s, consumer confidence was at an all-time high with rising stock prices, growth in disposable personal income, and a global redistribution of wealth, which led to an increase in demand for luxury brands. Nueno and Quelch (1998) suggested "the mass marketing of luxury" with increased accessibility and wider circulation of luxury products to meet consumer needs and wants. This led to distinctions between "supra-luxury" and "mass luxe" (Jordan Keane & McMillan, 2004).

As the economy plummeted in the 2000's, luxury brands utilized mass marketing techniques with a growing aspirational consumer segment known as "masstige" (mass and prestige) (De Barnier et al., 2012). As the term masstige grew, the idea of luxury versus necessity products may vary from society to society (Christodoulides et al., 2009). While one product may be considered basic in one culture, the same product may be considered a luxury item in a developing country. For luxury brands, the degree of luxury can be distributed along a continuum depending on the product and brand name (Kapferer, 1997; Vigneron & Johnson, 2004). Silverstein and Fiske (2003) referred to "new luxury" products as those that are available to middle class U.S. market consumers who are willing to pay a premium price. This "new luxury" consumer is known to have an emotional attachment to luxury goods with the development of a relationship with the product, including more than just the high-end functional aspect of the product. This aspirational segment categorizes luxury brands based on three categories: accessible super-premium, old luxury brand extensions, and masstige (Silverstein & Fiske, 2003). The accessible super-premium luxury items are priced near the top of the product category, but are affordable to the middle-market of consumers. Examples include Starbucks beverages, Cuban cigars, and spa treatments. Old luxury brand extensions include once inaccessible luxury brands like BMW and Louis Vuitton. These companies have extended their product lines to offer more accessible, lower-priced versions of their luxury product. The masstige brands fall between the mass-market and high-end products and command a premium price, but are priced below super-premium goods. Coach handbags and luxury designs sold at Target are examples of the masstige category.

Granot et al., (2013) proposed a new luxury paradigm known as "populence" (i.e., popular opulence), that is defined as a category of new luxury goods and services consumed by a larger aspirational segment. As the middle class grows in global economies like China, there is an increase in the desire for luxury goods (Lannes & Han 2010). Populence is theoretically depicted through a four-stage approach of the luxury concept. Stage I is conspicuous consumption where products are displayed in social settings and consumed only by the very rich. Stage II also focuses on consumers who are interested in prestige and social status of luxury products, but do not focus on financial superiority of products. Stage III is populence, the new mass luxury market, which is accessible, intimate, ubiquitous, and includes consumption experiences. Based on the populence paradigm, Granot et al., (2013) suggests luxury is not just for the affluent. The authors anticipate the future for luxury (Stage IV) will likely result in a clearer distinction between products and experiences. The populence paradigm proposes a shift from the producer to the consumer and the demand side over the supply side (Granot et al., 2013).

The evolution of the masstige market has provided challenges for luxury brands but also has provided opportunities for growth. The luxury brand consumer of today is not the same as generations prior. Thus, just defining how consumers perceive luxury is not enough.

Luxury Framework Critiques

As stated throughout the chapter, the concept of luxury is unclear, broad, and varies on a spectrum of different concepts (Berthon et al., 2009; Beverland, 2004; Jain, 2018). In turn, truly defining luxury and what it entails, is debated amongst scholars and proves to be challenging to determine the true essence of its concept. The subjective nature of luxury is one of the reasons conceptualizing it is challenging (Kapferer, 1998). Luxury items, like material items, provide value above tangible and functional needs. The novelty of luxury brands is grounded in its concept, brand meaning, and personality (Sung et al., 2014). Hence, the concept of luxury extends past just simply price and exuded status. While several scholars have debated the definition and meaning of luxury, two have proposed frameworks to explain the varying consumer perceptions of luxury in the marketplace. Hennigs et al. (2013) presented a conceptual framework to test antecedents of consumer luxury perceptions and its relationship with luxury brand strength. In more recent years, a framework of motivations of luxury buying behavior was developed and tested by Jain et al. (2015). Both frameworks are discussed next.

Luxury Brand Perceptions Model

Similar to our goal, Hennigs et al., (2013) explored the different concepts of consumer luxury perception and how it impacts the aspects of luxury brand strength. Their presented framework focused on antecedents of luxury brand perceptions and the relationship to cognitive, affective, and connotative components of luxury brand strength as seen in Figure 1. It is widely understood that conspicuous consumption is a driver of luxury consumption. However, more personal factors influence consumer interest in luxury goods (Wong & Ahuvia, 1998; Wiedmann et al., (2009). Consumers generally rate luxury brands based on financial, functional, and social considerations, which all serve as antecedents in the proposed Hennigs et al., (2013) model. For example, consumers consider high price products to deliver greater value, which is a financial expectation (Wiedmann et al., 2007). The functional dimension focuses on the sole benefit and use of luxury goods depicting quality; while the social dimension represents the perceived value that consumers gain when viewed by reference groups while consuming luxury goods.

Considering luxury brand strength is vital for brand management, managers are compelled to determine it and distinguish the brand from other competitors to ensure superior quality. As such, understanding the relationship between consumer luxury perception and brand strength supports the strong identity and enhanced emotional and symbolic associations tied to luxury brands (Megehee & Spake, 2012). The model includes three outcomes of luxury brand perception representing the strength of consumer attitudes toward the brand as cognitive, affective, and behavioral responses (Eagly & Chaiken, 1993; Chaudhuri, 2006). Using survey research, the research team found luxury brand perceptions were greatly influenced by functional, financial, and social evaluations of luxury brands. In addition, luxury brand perception also showed to significantly affect luxury brand strength as well. This conceptual framework is of merit and examines luxury consumer perceptions. However, more detailed antecedents about the personal

Figure 1.

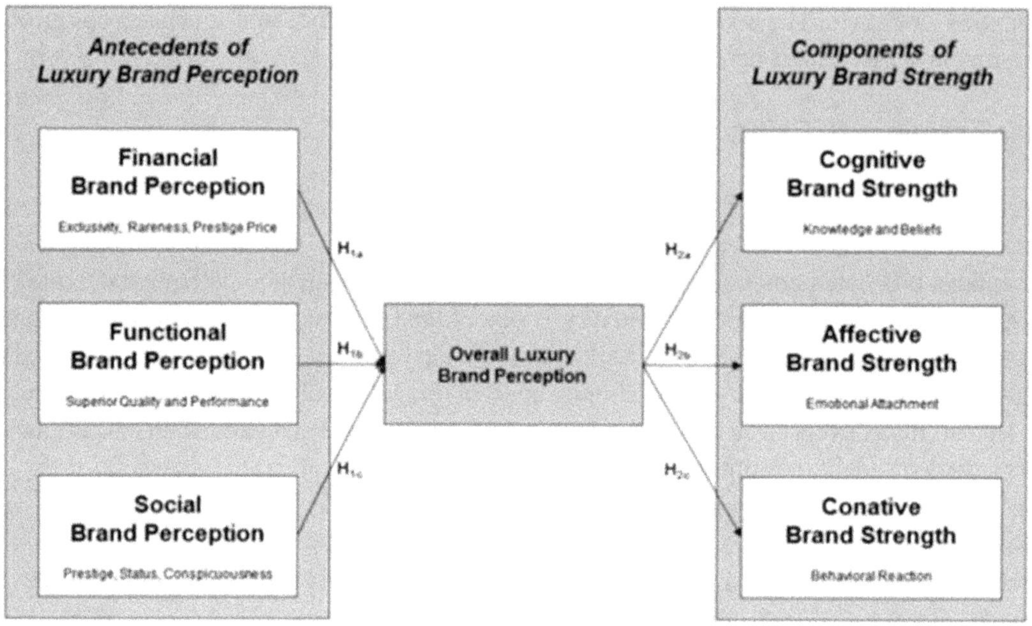

factors that influence consumer luxury perception is not considered, such as demographic information and personal values. Secondly, while Hennig et al., (2013) measured luxury brand strength, it is equally important to explore potential consumer behavior, which is undetermined in the current model.

Motivations for Luxury Buying Behavior Model

Aiming to better understand consumer luxury buying intentions, researchers Jain et al., (2015) developed a conceptual framework. The major contribution of the framework highlights consumer perspectives of luxury buying behavior in one country and among gender. Although, the framework was centered on Indian consumers, it is likely applicable for any consumer segment. Using the Keegan et al. (1992) S-O-R (stimuli-organism-response) model, Jain et al. 2015 adapted it to theorize a new consumer buying behavior model as seen in Figure 2. Stimuli is represented by regional culture, which varies by nation at the macro level, and even differs further at the regional or micro levels. India's keen interest in luxury reflects the regional population tested in the study. It is akin to an expressed interest in luxury consumption in western cultures like America, but with a more heightened interest in metro cities such as Los Angeles, Miami, or New York. This is true as the model includes two influencers -- challenges (macroeconomic forces, infrastructure, demand) and opportunities (rising income, awareness, influence of media). Awareness and exposure of luxury goods, coupled with rising incomes, contributes to luxury consumption interest.

Consumers are referenced as organisms in the model that transfer through several psychological processes and includes internal and external motivational factors, luxury associations, and perceptions.

Figure 2.

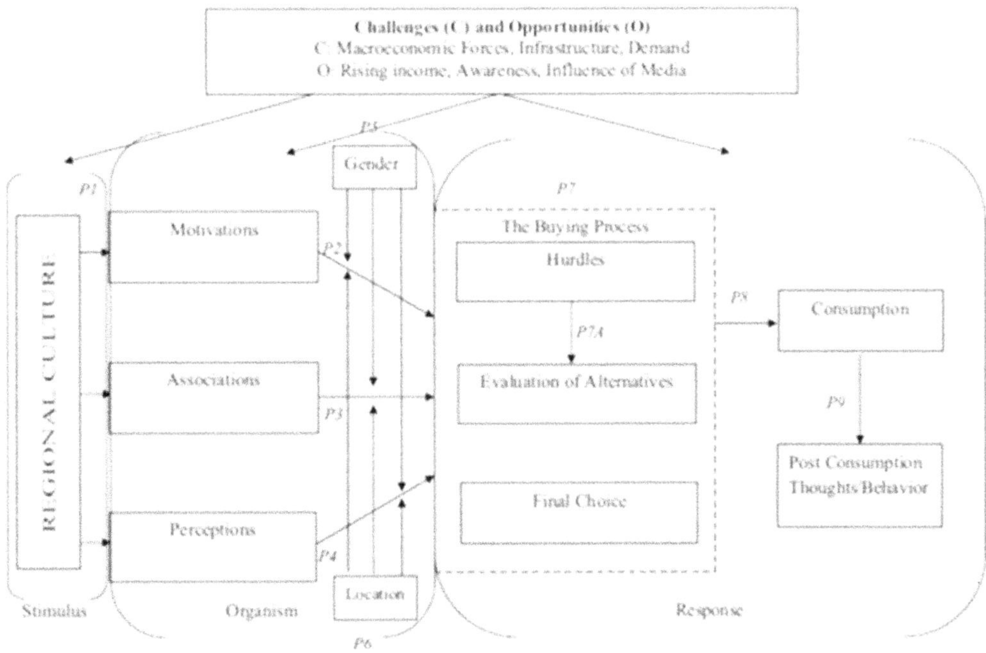

These three processes are considered antecedents for luxury consumption, while gender and geographical location function as moderators to influence the relationship strength between the antecedents and the buying process. The next phase in the model involves the buying process, which is considered a response to both the stimuli and organisms presented earlier. In a lock-step process, perceived hurdles to luxury buying in turn, influences the evaluations of alternatives and ultimately the final purchase decision. Hurdles could be time, price, or accessibility, which yields different luxury product alternatives for consumers who are selecting. All these aforementioned factors ultimately influence consumption effects, the actual purchase and post-purchase behaviors. In sum, the research proposed the model after conducting focus groups with luxury consumers and practitioners represents the study findings. The practitioner focus groups were added to verify and validate the findings regarding consumer perceptions on the macro-level influencers in the buying model. The overall model presents an updated framework that is also of merit. However, the model does not explain factors that contribute to one's perception and definition of luxury. Further, accessibility, in addition to awareness, which were excluded from the model, are key for consumer consideration of luxury goods, which are likely driven by advertised messages. Consumers must have access to luxury brands before entering the buying process (response) to evaluate or consider product alternatives. A more nuanced theorization about luxury consumers' socialization process and points of reference should be considered.

LUXURY PERCEPTIONS OF INFLUENCES FRAMEWORK

While most of the luxury brand literature helps to better understand the definition of luxury, the literature fails to fully define the luxury brand consumer. The definition of luxury can be defined by the consumer and the situation (Chattalas & Paurav, 2015). Most luxury research focuses on how the consumer defines luxury based on functionality as well as personal and social orientation (Kapferer, 1997; Phau & Prendergast, 2000; Mason, 1999; Dubois & Laurent, 1994; Tsai 2005; Wiedmann et al., 2007, 2009). While luxury brand marketers try to develop meaning behind their luxury brands, consumer perceptions vary from individual to individual and a focus is needed on these personal experiences, not the luxury brand (Roper et al., 2013). Few studies have clearly defined the consumer who aspires luxury products, as well as who purchases such products. To further define the consumer who is interested in luxury brand products, services and even experiences, it is proposed that the consumer's point of references be considered, externally, internally and demographically, in addition to accessibility to luxury brands which may ultimately determine purchase behavior. The next section discusses each point of reference and is also included in Table 1.

Thus, the proposed conceptual framework consists of three points of reference leading to potential purchase behaviors. These points of reference include: *internal influences* (personal values, cultural values, demographics, and family), *external influences* (price, product category, mass media, and celebrity culture), *accessibility* (inaccessible, intermediate, accessible, and mass accessible), and potential consumer behavior (buy luxury, won't buy luxury, buy counterfeit luxury). Each component is discussed below.

External Points of References

Price

When a consumer considers a luxury brand, price, the product category and advertising and celebrities, serve as a point of reference. Price can be the actual or perceived cost of the luxury brand. Luxury products are defined based on their price and because they are costly (Ng, 1987). Wiedmann et al. (2009) recognized the financial dimension of luxury perceptions to address the direct monetary aspects, which can include the core benefit and the basic functions of the luxury product. While emphasis has been placed on the experiential and symbolic values of luxury brands, the growth of accessible luxury brands known as masstige or luxury to the masses has placed an important emphasis on price of luxury brands. According to Kapferer and Laurent (2014), price is a stronger predictor of consumers' perceptions of luxury, and consumers have a "common hierarchy of luxury products" based on perceived prices. However, perceptions of price for luxury products does increase with the consumer's immersion in luxury, income, ownership of costly goods and they age (Kapferer & Laurent, 2014).

Product Category

Price can categorize luxury brands as luxury items; however, the term "luxury brand" has been found to be "ambiguous and ubiquitous," according to a recent study (Jain et al., 2015). Jain et al., (2015) found that the term serves as a substitute for various forms of quality and may depend on whether it is a product, service, or consumer experience. Through downward vertical product extensions, the product category can allow products to become more accessible to consumers. Accessories with the luxury brand logo,

External Points of Reference	**Definition**	**Supporting Literature**
Price	How much an item cost.	Kapferer &Laurent, 2014; Wiedman et al, 2009
Product Category	Types of products sold	Jain et al, 2015; Yang & Mattila, 2014; Atwal & Williams, 2009; Roy & Rabbanee, 2015
Mass and Social Media	Sources of information via mas media outlets (i.e. television) or social media sites	Hung et al, 2011; Jain et al, 2015; Mandel et al, 2006; Tanner, et al, 2007
Internal Points of Reference	**Definition**	**Supporting Literature**
Value Expression	Individualistic approach based on new needs and desires for experiences.	Atwal & Williams, 2007; Nia &Zaichowsky, 2000
Conspicuous Consumption	Consumers purchase expensive items to display wealth and income.	Mason, 1981; Vigneron & Johnson, 2004; Yann, 2010
Personal Aspiration	Goals to achieve things in life.	Yann, 2010
Culture	Group of people who share similar and distinct physical characteristics.	Dubois & Duquesne, 1993; Gardyn, 2002
Demographics	**Definition**	**Supporting Literature**
Gender	Male or female	Gardyn, 2002; Meyers-Levy; 1989; Meyers-Levy & Maheswaran, 1991; Meyers-Levy & Sternthal, 1991
Age	How old is the consumer	Silverstein and Fiske, 2003; Kapferer & Laurent, 2014; Park et al 2008; Dubois & Duquesne, 1993
Socioeconomic Class	Economic and sociological factors to measure of a person's work experience and economic and social position in relation to others, based on income, education, and occupation.	Alleres, 1990; Dubois & Duquesne, 1993; Granot et al, 2013

including sunglasses and key chains, may allow consumers to purchase part of the luxury brand product line; however, are more accessible in price to handbags or shoes (Kapferer & Laurent, 2014). In addition, businesses now offer a wide variety of new-luxury products, ranging from automobiles, fashion, home furnishings, toys and even food and beverage (Silverstein & Fiske, 2003). It has been found that luxury services, in particular, the luxury hospitality market, may be evaluated differently by the affluent than other luxury product categories and can target the less affluent without hurting attitudes and perceptions (Yang & Mattila, 2014). Further, Atwal and Williams (2009) stated that the experiences are central to consumption of luxury brands, and experiential marketing offers the best opportunity for the luxury market to capitalize luxury consumers. Thus, a new level of consumption - luxury experiences - should be considered when evaluating luxury brands. Highlighting unique personal experiences with luxury brand consumption may attract consumers (Roy & Rabbanee, 2015).

Mass Media

Advertising, as well as the celebrity culture represented in marketing communications, we believe, influences consumer perception. Hung et al. (2011) argued that consumption of luxury products will rise when the environment promotes these types of images to consumers and cited the example of the rapid growth in Taiwan. Jain et al. (2015) found that in India, social media sites, like Facebook, were influential on participants' consumption of luxury brands. Moreover, the accessible luxury brands are advertised as luxury and are perceived to be luxury by consumers (Kapferer & Laurent, 2014). This representation in marketing and advertising messages encourages consumers to aspire to want more through convincing messages and alluring imagery. This is true as the implicit meaning of luxury brands is promoted through narrative transportation in advertising (Kim, Lloyd, & Cervellon, 2015), which refers to experience through heightened engagement (Green & Brock, 2000). Specifically, transportation is described "as a convergent process, where all mental systems and capacities become focused on events occurring in the narrative" (Green & Brock, 200, p. 701). Integrated storylines absorbed and consumed by the consumer in advertising in a relatable manner reflects narratives. The advertised depictions of success were found to influence consumer desire for luxury brands (Mandel et al., 2006). By comparing one's self to advertised images of those who are wealthier or more successful, consumers increase their luxury brand preferences. To that end, it is also assumed that marketing communications (e.g. traditional advertising, social media, reality television programming, etc.) promotes luxury goods, and may evoke interest in luxury (Richins, 1995; Belk, 2001). Consumers' judgement of functional and symbolic appeals in luxury brand advertising is determined by their personalities as fixed (impermeable) or malleable (Kwon, Seo, Ko, 2016). Social media now provides two-way communication for brands, celebrities, and users to create content promoting luxury brand consumption to millions of consumers. Hence, some consumers may be drawn to such consumption because of the frequent images posted by social media contacts, which reflects consumption mimicry (Tanner et al., 2007).

Internal Points of References

Personal Values

Personality is a set of unique individual qualities that produce distinct behaviors, cognitions, and emotions across similar situations. When considering one's own personality type as it relates to luxury products, the two most common qualities are personal value perceptions and conspicuous consumption. Personal value perceptions are a growing area of research as it relates to the motives of luxury consumption (Tsai, 2005). Wong and Ahuvia (1998) found that the consumption of luxury products is based on the self-concept. Based on this self-concept, consumers may aspire to be associated with certain prestige groups reflecting their ownership of luxury brands (Christodoulides, Michaelidou & Li, 2009). Personal aspiration is defined as an individual's achievement of goals in life. It is suggested that consumers who are status-seekers are also luxury brand purchasers (Eastman et al., 1999). Moreover, individuals who possess conspicuous consumption behaviors are motivated by the ability to pay high prices to not only impress others, but to display their wealth to others. This behavior is also supported by social-adjustive attitude, suggesting consumers enjoy luxury brand for self-presentation purposes among peers (Katz 1960, Smith, Bruner, and White, 1956). Godey et al. (2013) found in their cross-cultural study that two extremes exist for defining luxury, with conspicuous on one side and emotional on the other. Truong et al. (2010) found that extrinsic motivations of status seekers were stronger for luxury brand preferences than intrinsic motivations, but there were not conceptual grounds for these behaviors. However, aspiration can be perceived as being a part of the group or being unique from the group too (Roy & Rabbanee, 2015). Further, consumers' appeal to luxury goods may involve more than one set of emotions. Silverstein and Fiske (2003) suggest four "emotional pools" (Taking Care of Me, Questing, Connecting and Individual Style) to better understand the unique personal nature of the new luxury brand consumer. Recent research has found that luxury consumption can produce impostor syndrome in consumers, making them feel inauthentic in their luxury (Goor et al., 2020).

Cultural Values

Cultural values can also provide a role in shaping the minds of the luxury brand consumer, in particular their motivations for purchasing (Christodoulides et al., 2009). Wong and Ahuvia (1998) examined the cultural differences between Southeast Asian and Western societies and how this impacts luxury consumption in these cultures. It has been found that Eastern Asian cultures use more holistic reasoning when evaluating products, whereas, Western cultures are more analytical in nature (Christodoulides, Michaelidou, & Li, 2009). In addition, risk acceptance and control of one's source of opportunities for the self are culturally related values for evaluation (Dubois & Duquesne, 1993). Since most research has been conducted in Western cultures, Hung et al. (2011) attempted to expand the knowledge of luxury brands to Eastern Asian culture with an examination of Chinese luxury brand consumers and concluded that social influence has a significant relationship with purchase intentions. Most research studies have only focused on one cultural consumer or just Western cultures. Few studies have attempted to analyze the cross-cultural perceptions of luxury and luxury products. Godey et al. (2013) used an undergraduate student sample across five different countries (Germany, France, Italy, Japan, China and the United States), however, it was not identified if the students were or were not current luxury consumers. However, a complex picture was obtained as it related to the stage of luxury consumption by country. Understanding the luxury consumer in greater depth within the Western culture, like the United States, is equally important as well. But the current literature is devoid of examining luxury consumption among specific ethnic/racial groups. Such ethnic/racial groups represent a growing consumer base in the United States that is gradually surpassing the majority market and signals opportunities for more tailored marketing (Selig Center for Economic Growth, 2014). According to the 2014 Multicultural Economy Report conducted by the Selig Center for Economic Growth, the buying power for the Hispanic market is $1.3 trillion, which is greater than the economy of all but 15 global countries (2014). Similarly, high, the African American buying power rose to $1.1 trillion, $770 billion for the Asian American market, and the Native American buying power rose to $100 billion, representing a 149 percent increase since 2000

(2014). Research has proposed that differences may exist at the intra-country level based on individual levels before one examines the country-level effects (Stathopouloua & Balabanis, 2019). Thus, the inclusion of cultural/racial groups in understanding luxury consumers is important as the aforementioned groups have large buying power and their perceptions impact consumer behavior in the marketplace. More importantly, consumers' sense of self is based on their cultural group member, which is supported by social identity theory (Tajfel & Turner, 1979).

Family

Consumer socialization is the process that children learn and develop as consumers, including skills, knowledge and attitudes (Ward, 1974). Families are believed to have the greatest influence on the consumer socialization of children (Moschis, 1987). Research has found that this parental influence carries into young adulthood, in particular mothers and daughters share similarities in marketplace beliefs and behaviors (Moore and Lutz, 1988) and brand preferences (Mandrik et al., 2005), suggesting that mothers' attitudes can have a long-term impact on their children's behaviors. Moreover, the preference-pester-purchase (PPP) planning framework has proposed that children are influencers on their parents' purchase decisions which can assist marketers who target children (Sharma & Dasgupta, 2009). A few studies have started to examine children's understanding of luxury and luxury brands (Dhillon, Rapindar, & Roberts, 2020; Shaikh, 2019). It is important that researchers understand the role and influence of family members on their children as consumers to potentially predict subsequent behaviors including luxury consumption.

Demographics

Gender

Consumer behavior is shaped partially by social cultural theory, meaning consumer perspectives on life reflects their social and cultural contact based on race, gender, and nationality (Sanderson, 2010). Women differ from men in their response about luxury brands. For example, women have more positive attitudes towards luxury brands in the clothing, perfume, and watch product category than men; and are a highly sought-after consumer segment (Stokburger-Sauer & Teichmann, 2011). Further, luxury brands offer women more uniqueness, prestige, social value among peers, than non-traditional brands (Stokburger-Sauer & Teichmann, 2011). A study of Gulf Arab women highlighted the complexity female towards luxury consumption (Semaan et al., 2019). Only one study has attempted to address gender as a potential moderator to luxury brand purchase behavior (Jain et al., 2015). This study found that men are more aware of brands, style and price and were quick to make decisions for purchases, while women were more focused on the aesthetics, design, and style of the products, but were slower in their shopping. Research also indicates genders may differ on how they process information, with women being more comprehensive processors and males being more selective (Roux et al., 2017; Meyers-Levy & Loken, 2015); however, these studies did not focus on luxury products.

Age

Age can be an important factor for luxury brand consumers. While most of the research has been conducted with student samples, many students may not be active consumers of luxury products. As a consumer ages, the consumer will earn more, and their luxury perceptions may increase (Kapferer & Laurent, 2014). In addition, it is believed that consumer luxury purchasing power will grow as they age (Park et al., 2008). Since luxury products are expensive, income is an important factor to consider. At one time, luxury products were only considered to be enjoyed by those of "privileged economic status" and who must be able to find value (Dubois & Duquesne, 1993).

Socioeconomic Status

Finally, the socioeconomic status (SES) should be evaluated for luxury brand consumers. Socioeconomic status, also known as an individual's social class, is measured as a combination of education, income and occupation. Alleres (1990) proposed that one's socioeconomic status should be considered as it relates to luxury brands. According to Alleres, those individuals in the middle class would be able to attain accessible luxury products, whereas, intermediate luxury levels are accessible by the "professional" class, and the inaccessible luxury items are only attainable by the "elite." Alleres' (1990) study failed to address the lowest level of SES, who may only aspire luxury products, but do not have the income to obtain them. Granot et al. (2013) argued accessibility and consumption to luxury products is not restricted by social class, but it is driven by aspiration and emotional connections. Roy and Rabbanee (2015) suggest that luxury brand images should be developed based on the status of its potential owners, which can then potentially attract those who aspire to be part of that status level.

Thus, it is important to understand the types of luxury consumers. Luxury research should not be driven to define the luxury brand, but to define the consumer who buys the brands. Consumer's points of references are the driving factor that we posit influences consumer perceptions of luxury, which has not been fully addressed in the literature.

Based on the literature review, a new framework is presented in Figure 3. The framework is centered on antecedents that influence consumer luxury perception. It includes two spheres, points of reference and accessibility levels, in addition to, potential behavioral outcomes. At the core of this framework is the consumer because greater understandings of their perceptions of luxury brands is warranted. Antecedents that contribute to consumer perceptions begin with the innermost sphere, which consists of points of reference. Referring back to the socialization process, these reference points -- personal values, cultural values, family, and demographics -- represent both personal and controlled influences that internally impacts consumers. Consumers' personal values, cultural identity, family, and demographics (e.g. income, age, gender) dictates the types of brands consumers are exposed to during their formative years (Kapferer & Laurent 2014; Alleres 1990; Jain et al., 2015). Consumers are more susceptible to normative influences that will likely influence consumption decisions (Zhan & He, 2012). For example, elite consumers who were reared in higher income households, who enjoy conspicuous consumption, may believe owning a BMW vehicle is expected among consumers with similar status and cultural values. This is true based upon the aforementioned antecedents that influence their perceptions of luxury. Normative influences, such as owning a BMW, reflect consumption habits that are common within specific social classes, racial groups, and gender.

Aside from internal influences, consumers are also influenced by external factors that shape their perceptions of luxury goods. External influences, which are uncontrolled, are integrated in the framework and include price, product category, mass media, and celebrity culture. Largely, the mass media plays a strong force in promoting desired lifestyles luxury goods, which goods consumers ought to buy (Mandel et al., 2006; Belk, 2001; Richins, 1995). Innovative social media platforms, such as Instagram and Facebook, enable such imagery to proliferate. It yields strong brand messaging of luxury brands and lifestyles which are highly influential among consumers, especially those that are vulnerable.

Figure 3.

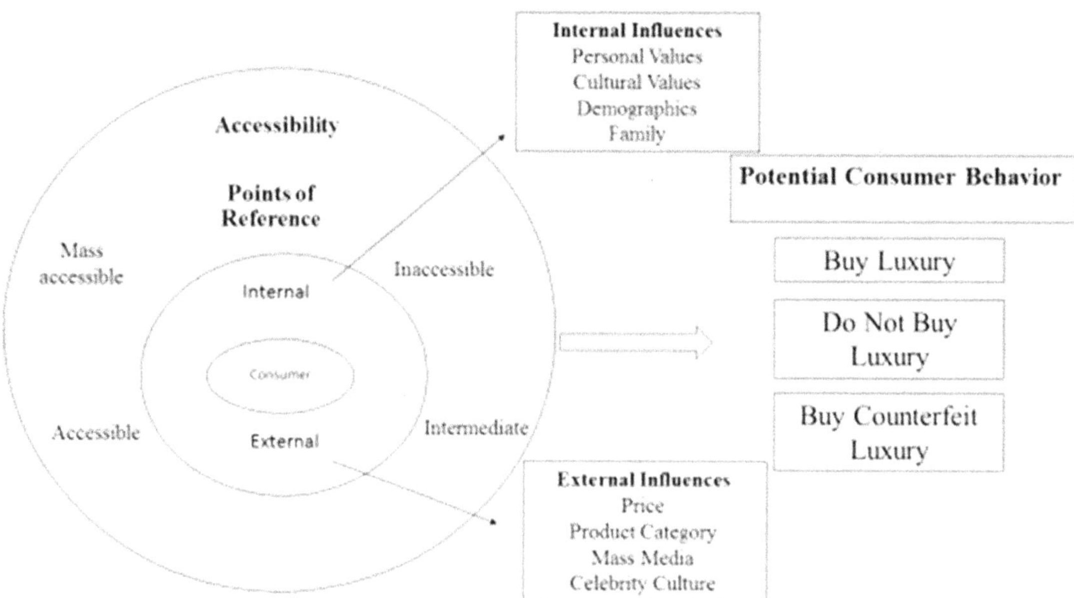

A major contribution of this framework includes the luxury accessibility sphere. This sphere represents an adaptation of Alleres (1990)'s hierarchy of luxury levels. While that model was centered on three levels (accessible, intermediate, and inaccessible) to exclusively describe luxury brands, we believe updating it with a consumer focus is useful. We posit that consumer luxury accessibility is dependent upon the aforementioned antecedents. Not all consumers have access to luxury goods; geography, social class, and media, strongly influence one's accessibility (Jain et al., 2015).

For example, consumers in Wyoming may have limited exposure to luxury goods, such as Hermes Birkin or Christian Louboutin. Owning a Ford F-350, several hundred acres of land, and livestock, may be highly valued and considered luxury goods within that region, but not so much for the affluent society of New York consumers. Conversely, poor Flint, Michigan consumers may consider a clean and healthy water supply, which is a basic necessity, as a luxury, while college students may not perceive their Apple Macbooks luxury, because it is highly accessible, although it is expensive. Vast variations of consumer perceptions of luxury brands underscore the benefits of expanding the Allere's (1990) framework with a consumer perspective. It enables scholars to better understand the variation of luxury based on consumer perspectives reflecting the point of reference influences identified in Figure 2. Secondly, the Alleres (1990) model is dated and does not consider innovative luxury marketing tactics. Masstige, which is a common marketing strategy used by luxury brand managers, targets an emerging consumer segment by promoting luxury brands at lower prices to the mass market. Mass accessibility is an added antecedent to encompass a new access point for consumers who may be non-traditional luxury consumers.

The final component of the framework entails potential consumer behavior. The Jain et al. (2015) luxury buying behavior model only considered product selection as a behavior outcome. But there are obvious cases where consumers may have access to luxury, been exposed through points of reference, and may elect to not buy luxury goods. Therefore, the proposed framework includes three potential behaviors: buy luxury good, do not buy luxury good, and buy a counterfeit luxury good. These potential behavioral outcomes are supported by consumer culture theory, as consumers' decisions to purchase or not purchase luxury goods reflects their social and cultural perspectives, which is displayed in the aforementioned antecedents (Arnould & Thompson, 2005). The final two consumption behaviors are important to consider because antecedents may not lead to a luxury purchase. Further, some consumers may elect to purchase counterfeit luxury goods instead of real luxury goods for a variety of reasons including, price, strained resources, or limited access. Considering the presented luxury perception influences framework, we offer research propositions next.

CONCEPTUAL FRAMEWORK PROPOSITIONS

Based on the proposed framework, the following propositions are presented:

- Proposition 1: Consumer interest in luxury brands is influenced by their points of reference.
- Proposition 2: Consumer points of reference is influenced by their access to luxury brands.
- Proposition 3: Consumer access to luxury brands influences potential consumer behavior.

Proposition 1 correlates with the innermost sphere encompassing points of reference mentioned earlier. Both internal and external influences are believed to influence consumer perceptions of luxury goods. Then in the outer sphere, consumer points of references are suggested to influence consumer access to luxury brands, which represents Proposition 2. It is understood one's access to luxury goods is representative of internal (e.g. demographics, personal values) and external (e.g. mass media) factors that they are exposed to in their daily lives. As Propositions 1 and 2 are linearly connected, based on the spheres -- points of reference and accessibility levels -- ultimately, those propositions influence and determine potential luxury consumer behavior as indicated in Proposition 3.

CONCLUSION AND FUTURE RESEARCH

The goal of this chapter was to present a conceptual framework highlighting the potentially important antecedents of luxury consumer perception and its influence on consumer behavior. As the luxury product market grows globally and expands with new accessible luxury brand lines, luxury brand marketers are shifting to a more consumer-focused business model, as they are challenged to reach their current and future customers. Consumers' changing preferences, access to luxury and media consumption, as well as varied demographics, suggests more theorizing was needed to understand the ultimate luxury market. Thus, the proposed conceptual framework was developed.

In developing the new conceptual framework, it was important to explore the frameworks previously introduced by Hennig et al. (2013) and Jain et al. (2015), with a similar focus on consumer luxury perceptions. Following the steps of developing a conceptual framework, the authors' goal involved drawing connections between relevant constructs (MacInnis, 2011). In turn, the authors identified key similarities and differences to reveal novel gaps in the literature where questions were understudied. The process of comparing and contrasting the two models enabled the integration of models presented by Jain et al. (2015), Hennig et al. (2013), and Alleres (1990) into the new Luxury Perceptions of Influences framework, which showcases different thinking of existing relationships, while highlighting differences to further expand the models (Yadav, 2014).

This research makes two conceptual contributions to luxury marketing literature. First, it provides a more nuanced conceptual framework suggesting the personal influences that impacts luxury consumer perception that is supported by theory. Recognizing the personal backgrounds of consumers that are founded in their socialization process enables scholars to consider the whole consumer. Further, as depicted in the proposed framework, the complexity and fluidity of the luxury consumer experience is illustrated. No one consumer is the same. Consumers have different needs, unique experiences, and various bodies of knowledge, attitudes and preferences that all influence their perceptions, which in turn impacts decisions in the marketplace. Given the greater level of detail found in the proposed framework, this research enhances the marketing literature by expanding the Jain et al. (2013) buying behavior framework, which makes a meaningful addition.

The second contribution of the current research is the integration of Alleres' (1990) luxury accessibility levels framework. As stated throughout the literature and in this paper, the concept of luxury has primarily been defined according to luxury brands. Little research focusing on the concept of luxury from the consumer perspective exists. Hence, applying the Alleres' (1990) framework to the proposed conceptual framework of luxury consumer perception adds value. It was a valuable addition as it supported the framework. Based on the consumer socialization process, consumers have different levels of access to luxury goods. Adding the Alleres' (1990) framework addresses the variance of consumers' accessibility to luxury. Moreover, the proposed framework also expanded the Alleres (1990) accessibility luxury levels by adding mass accessibility as an entry point to luxury to the current three levels (accessible, intermediate, and inaccessible). Considering the rise in masstige marketing, an update was needed to incorporate another access point which consumers may have that is based on the points of reference antecedents in the proposed framework (De Barnier et al., 2012). Hence, the three propositions presented illustrate the linear connection depicted in the proposed conceptual framework: Consumer interest in luxury brands is influenced by their points of reference, while consumer points of reference is influenced by their access to luxury brands; and ultimately, consumer access to luxury brands influence potential consumer behavior.

Based on the current research, the proposed luxury perception influences framework provides profound insights for marketers. More theorizing was warranted to better understand the detailed complexities of the luxury consumer. The antecedents presented in the framework suggest factors marketers should consider when targeting luxury consumers. These factors have potential to impact the entire luxury marketing process. For example, the framework components may influence the selection of retail channels, advertising decisions, pricing strategies, product positioning, and consumer targeting. With the aid of this framework, marketers can make informed marketing strategy decisions.

A follow-up study guided by the research propositions is suggested for future exploration. Using in-depth interviews would unveil more specific and vivid insights about consumer points of reference that influence consumer perceptions, accessibility, and purchase intentions of luxury. Including a more diverse research sample representing various racial and social classes would enhance the current literature as it is currently devoid. This suggestion is feasible considering the growth of diverse and minority consumers in the United States. Further, future research should include empirically testing the antecedents in the proposed luxury perception influences framework. Examining the multi-variables through consumers' external and internal points of reference, as well as demographic information, will provide a more holistic approach to understanding who is and may be the luxury consumer. Two potential studies are recommended. First, an investigation using surveys to measure the causal relationship between the antecedents and potential consumer behavior is suggested. Such research would demonstrate the validity of the proposed framework. From a global perspective, the proposed framework could also be tested in cross-cultural studies to focus on the heterogeneous nature of current and potential luxury consumers. Including both eastern and western consumers will be beneficial to closing the knowledge gap. Also, student samples are not enough to understand the luxury consumers, since most students are not current luxury purchasers. Giving attention to these knowledge gaps will help further understanding of the luxury market and its consumers.

REFERENCES

Alleres, D. (1990). *Luxe—Strategies Marketing*. Economica.

Arnould, E. J., & Thompson, C. J. (2005). Consumer culture theory (CCT): Twenty years of research. *The Journal of Consumer Research, 31*(4), 868–882. doi:10.1086/426626

Atwal, G., & Williams, A. (2009). Luxury brand marketing – The experience is everything! *Journal of Brand Management, 16*(5-6), 338–346. doi:10.1057/bm.2008.48

Bastien, V., & Kapferer, J. N. (2012). *Luxe oblige*. Editions Eyrolles.

Belk, R. W. (2001). Materialism and you. *Journal of Research for Consumers, 1*(1), 291–297.

Berthon, P., Pitt, L., Parent, M., & Berthon, J. P. (2009). Aesthetics and ephemerality: Observing and preserving the luxury brand. *California Management Review, 52*(1), 45–66. doi:10.1525/cmr.2009.52.1.45

Beverland, M. (2004). Uncovering "theories-in-use": Building luxury wine brands. *European Journal of Marketing, 38*(3/4), 446–466. doi:10.1108/03090560410518648

Chandon, J. L., Laurent, G., & Valette-Florence, P. (2016). Pursuing the concept of luxury: Introduction to the JBR Special Issue on "Luxury Marketing from Tradition to Innovation". *Journal of Business Research, 69*(1), 299–303. doi:10.1016/j.jbusres.2015.08.001

Chattalas, M., & Paurav, S. (2015). Impact of value perceptions on luxury purchase intentions: A developed market comparison. *Luxury Research Journal, 1*(1), 40–57. doi:10.1504/LRJ.2015.069806

Chaudhuri, A. (2006). *Emotion and reason in consumer behavior*. Routledge. doi:10.4324/9780080461762

Christodoulides, G., Michaelidou, N., & Li, C. H. (2009). Measuring perceived brand luxury: An evaluation of the BLI scale. *Journal of Brand Management, 16*(5/6), 395–405. doi:10.1057/bm.2008.49

De Barnier, V., Falcy, S., & Valette-Florence, P. (2012). Do consumers perceive three levels of luxury; A comparison of accessible, intermediate and inaccessible luxury brands. *Journal of Brand Management, 19*(7), 623–636. doi:10.1057/bm.2012.11

Dhillon, S., Rapindar, Y., & Roberts, J. (2020). *An exploration of children's understanding of luxury: A visual approach. Luxury: History, Culture*. Consumption.

Dubois, B., & Duquesne, P. (1993). The market for luxury goods: Income versus culture. *European Journal of Marketing, 27*(1), 35–45. doi:10.1108/03090569310024530

Eagly, A. H., & Chaiken, S. (1993). *The psychology of attitudes*. Harcourt Brace Jovanovich College Publishers.

Eastman, J. K., Goldsmith, R. E., & Flynn, L. R. (1999). Status consumption in consumer behavior: Scale development and validation. *Journal of Marketing Theory and Practice, 7*(3), 41–51. doi:10.1080/10696679.1999.11501839

Eng, T., & Bogaert, J. (2010). Psychological and cultural insights into consumption of luxury Western brands in India. *Journal of Customer Behaviour, 9*(1), 55–75. doi:10.1362/147539210X497620

Fazeli, Z., Shukla, P., & Perks, K. (2020). Digital buying behavior: The role of regulatory fit and self-construal in online luxury goods purchase intentions. *Psychology and Marketing, 37*(1), 15–26. doi:10.1002/mar.21276

Fionda, A. M., & Moore, C. M. (2009). The anatomy of the luxury fashion brand. *Journal of Brand Management, 16*(5), 347–363. doi:10.1057/bm.2008.45

Gardyn, R. (2002). Oh, the good life. *Advertising Age, 24*(10), 31–35.

Godey, B., Pederzoli, D., Aiell, G., Donvito, R., Wiedmann, K. P., & Hennigs, N. (2013). A cross-cultural exploratory content analysis of the perception of luxury from six countries. *Journal of Product and Brand Management, 22*(3), 229–237. doi:10.1108/JPBM-02-2013-0254

Goor, D., Odabayeva, N., Keinan, A. & Crener, S. (2020). The impostor syndrome from luxury consumption. *Journal of Consumer Research, 46*(6), 031–1051.

Granot, E., Russell, L. M., & Brashear-Alejandro, T. G. (2013). Populence: Exploring luxury for the masses. *Journal of Marketing Theory and Practice, 21*(1), 31–44. doi:10.2753/MTP1069-6679210102

Green, M. C., & Brock, T. C. (2000). The role of transportation in the persuasiveness of public narratives. *Journal of Personality and Social Psychology, 79*(5), 701–721. doi:10.1037/0022-3514.79.5.701

Henke, L. L., & Fontenot, G. (2011). Why advertising does not cause smoking initiation. *Journal of Business & Economics Research, 3*(5), 65–70. doi:10.19030/jber.v3i5.2778

Hennigs, N., Wiedmann, K. P., Behrens, S., & Klarmann, C. (2013). Unleashing the power of luxury: Antecedents of luxury brand perceptions and effect on luxury brand strength. *Journal of Brand Management, 20*(8), 705–715. doi:10.1057/bm.2013.11

Hung, K. P., Chen, A. H., Peng, N., Hackely, C., Tiwsakul, R. A., & Chou, C. I. (2011). Antecedents of luxury brand purchase intentions. *Journal of Product and Brand Management, 20*(6), 457–467. doi:10.1108/10610421111166603

Interbrand. (2013). *2013 ranking of the top 100 brands*. https://www.interbrand.com/en/best-global-brands/2013/Best-Global-Brands-2013-Brand-View.aspx

Jain, V. (2018). Luxury: Not for consumption but developing extended digital self. *Journal of Human Values, 24*(1), 25–38. doi:10.1177/0971685817733570

Jain, V., Roy, S., & Ranchhod, A. (2015). Conceptualizing luxury buying behavior: The Indian perspective. *Journal of Product and Brand Management, 24*(3), 211–228. doi:10.1108/JPBM-07-2014-0655

Jain, V., & Schultz, D. E. (2019). How digital platforms influence luxury purchase behavior in India? *Journal of Marketing Communications, 25*(1), 41–64. doi:10.1080/13527266.2016.1197295

Jordan Keane, M., & McMillan, Z. (2004). Above and beyond (brand papers). *Brand Strategy, 187*, 30.

Kapferer, J. N. (1997). Managing luxury brands. *Journal of Brand Management, 4*(4), 251–259. doi:10.1057/bm.1997.4

Kapferer, J. N. (1998). Why are we seduced by luxury brands? *Journal of Brand Management, 6*(1), 44–49. doi:10.1057/bm.1998.43

Kapferer, J. N., & Laurent, G. (2014). Where do consumers think luxury begins? A study of perceived minimum price for 21 luxury goods in 7 countries. *Journal of Business Research, 69*(1), 332–340. doi:10.1016/j.jbusres.2015.08.005

Katz, D. (1960). The functional approach to the study of attitudes. *Public Opinion Quarterly, 24*(2), 163–204. doi:10.1086/266945

Kim, J. (2019). Luxury fashion goods ownership and collecting behavior in an omni-channel retail environment. *Research Journal of Textile and Apparel, 23*(3), 212–231. doi:10.1108/RJTA-01-2019-0001

Kim, J. E., Lloyd, S., & Cervellon, M. C. (2016). Narrative-transportation storylines in luxury brand advertising: Motivating consumer engagement. *Journal of Business Research, 69*(1), 304–313. doi:10.1016/j.jbusres.2015.08.002

Kim, J. H. (2019). Imperative challenge for luxury brands: Generation Y consumers' perceptions of luxury fashion brands' e-commerce sites. *International Journal of Retail & Distribution Management, 47*(2), 220–244. doi:10.1108/IJRDM-06-2017-0128

Ko, E., Costello, J. P., & Taylor, C. R. (2019). What is a luxury brand? A new definition and review of the literature. *Journal of Business Research, 99*, 405–413. doi:10.1016/j.jbusres.2017.08.023

Kwon, J., Seo, Y., & Ko, D. (2016). Effective luxury-brand advertising: The es–if matching (entity–symbolic versus incremental–functional) model. *Journal of Advertising*, *45*(4), 459–471. doi:10.1080/00913367.2016.1226995

Lannes, B., & Han, W. (2010). Selling luxury to the Chinese masses. *The Wall Street Journal Asia.*

Liu, F., Li, J., Mizerski, D., & Soh, H. (2012). Self-congruity, brand attitude, and brand loyalty: A study on luxury brands. *European Journal of Marketing*, *46*(7/8), 922–937. doi:10.1108/03090561211230098

MacInnis, D. J. (2011). A framework for conceptual contributions in marketing. *Journal of Marketing*, *75*(4), 136–154. doi:10.1509/jmkg.75.4.136

Mandel, N., Petrova, P., & Cialdini, R. (2006). Images of success and the preference of luxury brands. *Journal of Consumer Psychology*, *16*(1), 57–69. doi:10.120715327663jcp1601_8

Mandrik, C., Fern, E., & Bao, Y. (2005). Intergenerational influence: Roles of conformity to peers and communication effectiveness. *Psychology and Marketing*, *22*(10), 813–832. doi:10.1002/mar.20087

Mason, R. (1981). *Conspicuous consumption: A study of exceptional consumer behaviour*. Gower Publishing Company.

Matthiesen, I., & Phau, I. (2005). The 'HUGO BOSS' connection: Achieving global brand consistency across countries. *Journal of Brand Management*, *12*(5), 325–338. doi:10.1057/palgrave.bm.2540229

Megehee, C. M., & Spake, D. F. (2012). Consumer enactments of archetypes using luxury brands. *Journal of Business Research*, *65*(10), 1434–1442. doi:10.1016/j.jbusres.2011.10.009

Meyers-Levy, J. (1989). Gender differences in information processing: A selectivity interpretation. In Cognitive and Affective Responses to Advertising. Lexington Press.

Meyers-Levy, J., & Loken, B. (2015). Revisiting gender differences: What we know and what lies ahead. *Journal of Consumer Psychology*, *25*(1), 129–149. doi:10.1016/j.jcps.2014.06.003

Moore, E., & Lutz, R. (1988). Intergenerational influences in the formation of consumer attitudes and beliefs about the marketplace: Mothers and daughters. *Advances in Consumer Research. Association for Consumer Research (U. S.)*, *15*, 461–467.

Moschis, G. (1987). *Consumer socialization: A life cycle perspective*. Lexington Press.

Ng, Y.-K. (1987). Diamonds are a government's best friend: Burden free taxes on goods valued for their values. *The American Economic Review*, *77*, 186–191.

Nia, A., & Zaichkowsky, J. L. (2000). Do counterfeits devalue the ownership of luxury brands? *Journal of Product and Brand Management*, *9*(7), 485–497. doi:10.1108/10610420010351402

Nueno, J. L., & Quelch, J. A. (1998). The mass marketing of luxury. *Business Horizons*, *41*(6), 61–68. doi:10.1016/S0007-6813(98)90023-4

Park, H. J., Rabolt, N. J., & Jeon, K. S. (2008). Purchasing global luxury brands among young Korean consumers. *Journal of Fashion Marketing and Management*, *12*(2), 244–259. doi:10.1108/13612020810874917

Phau, I., & Prendergast, G. (2000). Consuming luxury brands: The relevance of the 'rarity principle'. *Journal of Brand Management*, *8*(2), 122–138. doi:10.1057/palgrave.bm.2540013

Phau, I., & Teah, M. (2009). Devil wears (counterfeit) Prada: A study of antecedents and outcomes of attitudes towards counterfeits of luxury brands. *Journal of Consumer Marketing*, *26*(1), 15–27. doi:10.1108/07363760910927019

Richins, M. L. (1995). Social comparison, advertising, and consumer discontent. *The American Behavioral Scientist*, *3*(4), 593–607. doi:10.1177/0002764295038004009

Roper, S., Caruana, R., Medway, D., & Murphy, P. (2013). Constructing luxury brands: Exploring the role of consumer discourse. *European Journal of Marketing*, *47*(3/4), 375–400. doi:10.1108/03090561311297382

Roux, E., Tafani, E., & Vigneron, F. (2017). Values associated with luxury brand consumption and the role of gender. *Journal of Business Research*, *71*, 102–113. doi:10.1016/j.jbusres.2016.10.012

Roy, R., & Rabbanee, F. K. (2015). Antecedents and consequences of self-congruity. *European Journal of Marketing*, *49*(3/4), 444–466. doi:10.1108/EJM-12-2013-0739

Sanderson, C. (2009). *Social psychology*. John Wiley & Sons, Ltd.

Selig Center for Economic Growth. (2014). *Multicultural Economy Report*. https://news.uga.edu/releases/article/multicultural-economy-report-2014/

Semaan, R. W., Lindsay, V., Williams, P., & Ashill, N. (2019). The influence of gender roles in the drivers of luxury consumption for women: Insights from the gulf region. *Journal of Retailing and Consumer Services*, *51*(November), 165–175. doi:10.1016/j.jretconser.2019.06.006

Shaikh, S. (2019). The malleable self-concept-relationships between young adolescents' self-concept and bandwagon luxury consumption. *Journal of Marketing Development and Competitiveness*, *13*(5), 33–44.

Sharma, R. W., & Dasgupta, P. (2009). Marketing to children: A planning framework. *Young Consumers*, *10*(3), 180–187. doi:10.1108/17473610910985991

Silverstein, M., & Fiske, N. (2003). Luxury for the masses. *Harvard Business Review*, *81*(4), 48–57.

Smith, A. (1776). *An Inquiry into the Nature and Causes of the Wealth of Nations*. Strahan & T. Cadell.

Smith, M. B., Bruner, J. S., & White, R. W. (1956). *Opinions and personality*. Wiley.

Srivastava, R. K., Bhanot, S., & Srinivasan, R. (2016). Segmenting markets along multiple dimensions of luxury values: The Case of India. *Journal of Promotion Management*, *22*(1), 175–193. doi:10.1080/10496491.2015.1088925

Stathopoulou, A., & Balabanis, G. (2019). The effect of cultural value orientation on consumers' perceptions of luxury value and proclivity for luxury consumption. *Journal of Business Research*, *102*, 298–312. doi:10.1016/j.jbusres.2019.02.053

Stokburger-Sauer, N., & Teichmann, K. (2011). Influences of culture, gender, and age: why is luxury appealing? Exploring consumer's brand response with a special focus on gender. Chicago, IL: American Marketing Association.

Sung, Y., Choi, S. M., Ahn, H., & Song, Y. A. (2015). Dimensions of luxury brand personality: Scale development and validation. *Psychology and Marketing*, *32*(1), 121–132. doi:10.1002/mar.20767

Tajfel, H., & Turner, J. C. (1979). An integrative theory of intergroup conflict. *The Social Psychology of Intergroup Relations*, *33*(47), 74.

Tanner, R. J., Ferraro, R., Chartrand, T. L., Bettman, J. R., & Van Baaren, R. (2008). Of chameleons and consumption: The impact of mimicry on choice and preferences. *The Journal of Consumer Research*, *34*(6), 754–766. doi:10.1086/522322

Truong, Y., McColl, R., & Kitchen, P. J. (2009). Uncovering the relationships between aspirations and luxury brand preference. *Journal of Product and Brand Management*, *19*(5), 346–355. doi:10.1108/10610421011068586

Tsai, S. P. (2005). Impact of personal orientation on luxury-brand purchase value: An international investigation. *International Journal of Market Research*, *47*(4), 429–454. doi:10.1177/147078530504700403

Vigneron, F., & Johnson, L. W. (2004). Measuring perceptions of brand luxury. *Brand Management*, *11*(6), 484–506. doi:10.1057/palgrave.bm.2540194

Ward, S. (1974). Consumer socialization. *The Journal of Consumer Research*, *1*(2), 1–14. doi:10.1086/208584

Wiedmann, K. P., Hennigs, N., & Siebels, A. (2007). Measuring consumers' luxury value perception: A cross-cultural framework. *Academy of Marketing Science Review*, *7*(7), 333–361.

Wiedmann, K. P., Hennings, N., & Siebels, A. (2009). Value based segmentation of luxury consumption behaviour. *Psychology and Marketing*, *26*(7), 625–651. doi:10.1002/mar.20292

Wong, N. Y., & Ahuvia, A. C. (1998). Personal taste and family face: Luxury consumption in Confucian and Western societies. *Psychology and Marketing*, *15*(5), 423–432. doi:10.1002/(SICI)1520-6793(199808)15:5<423::AID-MAR2>3.0.CO;2-9

Yadav, M. S. (2014). Enhancing theory development in marketing. *AMS Review*, *4*(1-2), 1–4. doi:10.100713162-014-0059-z

Yang, W., & Mattila, A. S. (2004). Do affluent customers care when luxury brands go mass? The role of product type and status seeking on luxury brand attitude. *International Journal of Contemporary Hospitality Management*, *26*(4), 526–543. doi:10.1108/IJCHM-03-2013-0124

Yann, T. (2010). Personal aspirations and the consumption of luxury goods. *International Journal of Market Research*, *52*(5), 653–671.

KEY TERMS AND DEFINITIONS

Accessibility: Refers to a consumer's entrance point into the luxury product category, introducing four levels – inaccessible, intermediate, accessible, and mass accessible. Accessibility to luxury goods can vary based on the consumer's points of reference.

Luxury Consumer Behavior Framework: The antecedents which reflect both external and internal points of reference as well as luxury accessibility levels that ultimately impact consumer behavior toward luxury brands.

Luxury Brand: Images created in the minds of consumers which is associated with price, quality, aesthetics, rarity, extraordinariness and symbolism.

Luxury Consumer Perception: Customer's awareness and impressions of luxury products and brands.

Luxury Influences: The antecedents that influence consumer behavior toward luxury products and brands.

Luxury Marketing: The process of understanding the luxury consumer and products and building relationships with them, based on a strong brand heritage, appealing aesthetics, and quality.

Points of Reference: During one's socialization process, consumers are exposed to various points of reference that reflect their upbringings at home. Points of reference may represent family, social class, race, gender and family, among other demographic factors.

Chapter 2
Consumer Behaviors and Perceptions Towards Luxury Brands

Pınar Yürük-Kayapınar
https://orcid.org/0000-0002-7460-6465
Trakya University, Turkey

Senem Ergan
Çanakkale Onsekiz Mart University, Turkey

ABSTRACT

The main objective of this chapter is to examine consumers' behavior and perceptions of luxury products and brands. For this purpose, literature review was made by considering the issues related to luxury consumers. The behavior of consumers who purchase luxury products differs from that of other consumers. Because these consumers are especially different from the purpose of buying luxury products. The luxury product for them is more about satisfying their psychological needs than satisfying their physical needs. Therefore, the characteristics of these consumers, their purchasing styles, their segments in the market, their perceptions and values towards the product also differ. When buying luxury products, consumers are most influenced by reference groups and they affect them the most. Therefore, they turn to counterfeit products in order to feel only belonging to the luxury world and to be like reference groups.

INTRODUCTION

While luxury brands and/or products were reached, purchased and used only by a certain small group of society in previous periods, today, due to consumers have become aware of, income status differentiation, changing preferences and access to the desired product at any time and place, and increase in access possibilities, almost all consumers have become products. This situation has led to an increase in the variety and market of luxury brands and/or products, an important market situation and a change in the behavior and perceptions of consumers.

DOI: 10.4018/978-1-7998-4369-6.ch002

Copyright © 2021, IGI Global. Copying or distributing in print or electronic forms without written permission of IGI Global is prohibited.

Along with this change in consumer behavior and perceptions, developments in information and communication technologies and globalization have changed the behaviors of companies and as a result of these changes, the awareness of consumers on luxury products has increased. Because these products, which are difficult to reach before, have become the products that consumers can easily reach anytime and anywhere thanks to digital media.

The curiosity of consumers to have this luxury product is to achieve their own psychological satisfaction, that is, to achieve social success. These products will give an image, power, reputation and social status to the consumers in the society and create a sense of belonging to a special segment in the society. Therefore, luxury products are a symbol for them, they are symbolic, and the functionality of these products is not important. In addition, thanks to this digitalization, consumers have the opportunity to share this satisfaction with reference groups immediately, and they can also immediately learn about the luxury product consumption of the reference groups. Therefore, the expectations, motivations and segments within the market of the luxury product consumers are also different. Because of this difference, companies and marketers develop different strategies for consumers who consume luxury products.

The motivations and perceptions of luxury consumers are so strong that they are also trying different alternatives, such as purchasing counterfeit products, for the purposes of just being or belonging to others. Even though consumers know that these products are damaging to themselves and the national economies and are not ethically appropriate, they still only buy them for psychological satisfaction.

This section, which draws attention to the importance of consumer behavior and perceptions of luxury products, is designed as follows. Firstly, the basic characteristics of the consumers who buy luxury products, namely luxury consumers, why they buy these products and how they are divided into segments in the market unlike other consumers are examined. In addition, the meanings and definitions that consumers place on luxury products are researched. Afterwards, it is mentioned about the perception of luxury products in consumers, what are the values of consumers in the luxury world and the effects of consumption on luxury products. The reference groups that are especially important for luxury products were investigated. It is stated how consumers are affected by the reference groups when they buy or decide to buy luxury products and how they affect them. Finally, the behavior of consumers towards counterfeit products, an alternative to the desire of consumers to belong to the luxury world, is examined.

LITERATURE REVIEW

Characteristics and Segments of Luxury Consumers

When purchasing products or services, firstly consumers want to satisfy the basic needs of physiological and safety, such as Maslow's hierarchy of needs. They do not make a special effort in satisfying these needs and the aim is to satisfy their basic needs rather than their psychology. But there are some consumers whose main purpose is to establish a special symbolic identity in order to achieve psychological satisfaction and to show it to other consumers in society. Therefore, they have the intention of purchasing luxury products. In order to fully understand the behaviors of these consumers, behaviors towards luxury products/brands draw attention. As Mostofa & Arnaout (2020) stated that if consumers' attitudes and intentions towards luxury brands are positive, they want to buy and consume that brand.

Consumers aiming to meet a physical need when buying a product, while buying a luxury brand or product, aim to feel pleasure, happiness and satisfaction, and most importantly, to feel part of a certain segment of society. Using a luxury product for consumers is an important force that forms an image of their social classes and status in society. Therefore, consumers want to benefit from the image and identity features of luxury products (Phau & Teah, 2009) and try to create a social identity (Atwal & Williams, 2009).

In other words, luxury products are not consumed as tangible by consumers. The main benefit and functionality of the product is taken to the second plan and the spiritual image of the product is consumed. These products become a reflector of that social class or lifestyle for the consumers. By using these luxury products, consumers determine their social classes and status, create a special role and a special identity in the society, and provide themselves with the feeling of belonging to a particular segment of society. Therefore, consuming luxury products is completely symbolic for most consumers, functionality is not important. Heine (2012: 79) expressed the symbolic features of luxury products as follows. *"In fact, there is no other product category with a similar relevance of symbolic benefits, which often even exceeds its functional benefits."*

As a result of the researches, there are 4 basic dimensions that consumers find necessary for a brand to belong to the luxury world and according to the these dimensions, when consumers position the concept of luxury, their meanings are given in Table 1. As can be seen from Table 1, the value that consumers attach to luxury for the purposes of belonging to the luxury world is expressed in terms of product and perception. In the product, consumers focus on brand and manifestation, and on perception, they focus on creating social and personal perception. The brand of the product is an indicator of strength for consumers, and with a luxury brand, consumers think they have earned prestige, reputation and fame. Manifestations of product means high quality and high priced products for consumers. The second definition is based on consumer perceptions. The fact that consumers have a luxury product creates a social perception and consumers perceive that they belong to the elite layer of society. Their personal perceptions focus on the pleasure and enjoyment of having a luxury product. These definitions are the dimensions of the features that consumers want from that luxury brand (Chevalier & Mazzalovo, 2012).

Table 1. Positioning of the Luxury Definition Given by Consumers

<table>
<tr><th colspan="4">Nature of Luxury</th></tr>
<tr><th colspan="4">Mechanisms</th></tr>
<tr><td colspan="2">of production</td><td colspan="2">of perception</td></tr>
<tr><td>Brand</td><td>Power
Reputation</td><td>Social</td><td>Elitism</td></tr>
<tr><td>Manifestations</td><td>Quality
High Price</td><td>Personal</td><td>Hedonism</td></tr>
</table>

Source: Chevalier & Mazzalovo, 2012.

- First, ***elitism*** is an indicator of social success for consumers. It creates a sense of belonging to a group and is the basic dimension for luxury products. Roux, Tafani & Vigneron (2017) stated in their research that whether or not elitism varies according to gender, that men attach more importance to elitism and that elitism has a stronger and more positive effect for them than women.
- The second basic dimension is that luxury products are ***a quality and high price*** indicator for consumers.

- The third dimension is ***hedonism,*** which has a weak relationship. It expresses the emotional elements of luxury products for consumers.
- Another dimension is ***the power of the brand.*** It is the dimension of the brand's reputation and uniqueness derived from past decisions and actions.

These are the common characteristics of consumers and these features include the motives and expectations of consumers from a luxury product. But when buying luxury products, consumers are evaluated under different segments. Because, while the classes of the so-called luxury products or brands differ, so do the classes of consumers who buy them.

According to the Truong & McColl (2011), intrinsic and extrinsic purchasing objectives of consumers for luxury products express their motivation and expectations. Intrinsic motivation is the consumer's self-realization goals. Extrinsic, the main motivation factor for luxury products. It is the importance the consumer attaches to the perceptions of others. It is the thought of what others think or feel.

Therefore, consumers are divided into segments according to the way they have the money and the status of buying luxury products with this money. In the study of Chevalier & Mazzalovo (2012), these consumers are divided into classes according to the distinction made by Don Ziccardi and and this distinction is about how consumers earn their money.

- **Millennium Money:** This segment includes celebrities, sports men or women and those engaged in the internet business, which grew at the beginning of this century.
- **Old Money:** This class includes those who earn a living through inheritance, who manage their work, and who have a professional life.
- **New Money:** These consumers are those who earn their money by working themselves, usually not young people, who come to work with their money, not by their money, and who knows how to make money.
- **Middle Money:** This is the segment of consumers, the most important source of income salaries, who generally make reasonable expenditures and belong to the upper middle class.

Another segment of consumers' towards luxury products is included in the study of Som & Blanckaert (2015). This segmentation that obtained as a result of the literature review reveals the consumer typologies which is defined for the luxury industry. As shown in Figure 1, these segments are consumer types which is expressed that at first ***"haves/rich"*** and ***"have nots/poor"*** and at second ***"status seekers/public"*** and ***"nonstatus seekers/private".***

The consumer types in Figure 1 above relate to whether consumers are rich or poor in a society and whether they seek status. Therefore, it does not determine the behaviors of the consumers towards luxury products but helps to determine them. According to the consumer types in Figure 1, the consumer segments for luxury products are handled in 4 different ways (Som & Blanckaert, 2015). First segment is ***luxury hedonists.*** The luxury hedonists are not in seeker of status. This segment usually made up of successful and more optimistic young consumers. They like to follow trends, spend for themselves, travel. The purpose of buying luxury brands or products is to express themselves to the world. They usually want to purchase such as Marc Jacobs, D&G, Michael Kors. Second segment is ***the aspirational consumers.*** Compared to the previous consumer group, this segment is composed of more mature, usually male consumers. They like to spend on themselves, but they don't follow the media too much to get information about luxury products. They learn more about these products through word of mouth

Figure 1. Different Types of Consumers
Source: Som & Blanckaert (2015).

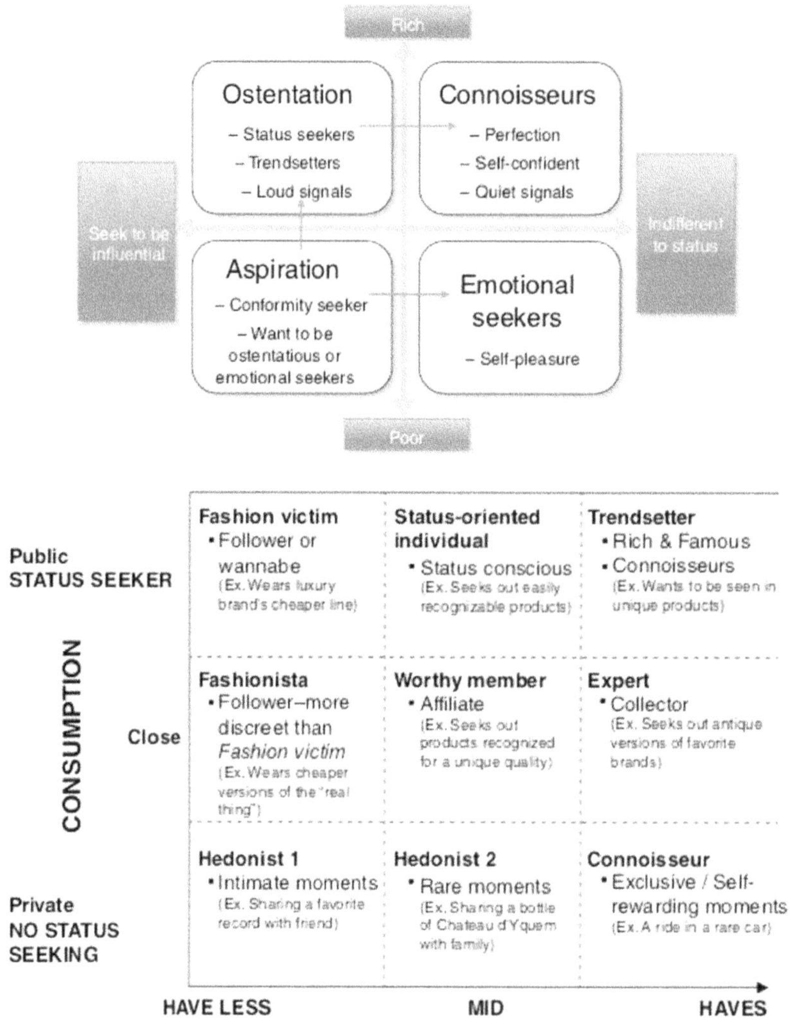

marketing. The traditional ones are consumers. Third segment is ***the luxury experts, the connoisseurs.*** This consumer group consists of the richest and most educated consumers. The concepts that precisely define this segment are high creativity, discerning and openness. They are always open to new products and brands, they pay attention to the products, they want to be of superior quality, they do not buy luxury products as status symbol. The most important products for them are natural products. They focus to purchase such as Hermes, Chanel and Bentley. And last segment is ***the ostentatious, status-oriented individuals.*** They cannot buy all luxury products because they are financially limited, it is important for them to travel abroad. Male and female consumers in this segment are very sensitive about logo and brands. They want to show their brands and logos. They spend a lot of time grooming themselves. They tend to prefer brands such as Armani, Gucci, Prada, BMW.

Segments determined for luxury products are examined by considering different product categories. One of these studies is the study of Wang & Somogyi (2020), which examines the motivations of consumers in luxury seafood consumption in China. In this study, consumers are divided into two main segments. The first is *dual value seeker* and the second is *food value seeker*. The characteristics of the consumers in both segments are as follows: Consumers in the dual value seeker segment pay more attention to food and symbolic values than food value seeker while consuming luxury seafood and they tend to consume more of these products. The demographic characteristics of dual value seeker in general are as follows: These consumers are in the high or middle income group, have a high level of occupation and educational level, and are generally married.

Gong (2001) stated that consumers who buy luxury products should be grouped into 4 main groups. These groups have been made according to the benefits that consumers target when purchasing luxury products. Consumers:

- Who value the beauty, the perfection, its fascination and unique of the products,
- Who cares about creativity and the feelings that the product creates in themselves,
- Who want the product to be magical and beautiful but who want their preferred products to be classic and never go out of fashion.
- Who expect the product to be most special to them, want to have few people who can buy the product and prefer to be a member of a privileged small group.

CONSUMERS' PERCEPTIONS AND VALUES IN THE LUXURY WORLD

As Vigneron & Johnson (2004: 489) argue, "*The consumption of luxury brands may be important to individuals in search of social representation and position. This means that social status associated with a brand is an important factor in conspicuous consumption*". Understanding the nature of value for luxury goods requires consideration of what constitutes a luxury brand. Luxury goods exist at one end of a continuum with ordinary goods, so where the ordinary ends and luxury starts is a matter of degree as judged by consumers (Tynan et al., 2010). Kapferer & Bastien (2009: 316) state that for luxury brands "*being unique is what counts, not any comparison with a competitor*".

According to Heine (2012), luxury products can be classified in 5 ways for consumers, as shown in Figure 2. These classes constitute consumers' perceptions of luxury products.

Regional Relativity focuses on whether a product is luxurious according to the availability of resources in the region. Because some products are very common in some regions. For those consumers in the region, those products are not luxurious. But if there are no products in that particular area, then for consumers in that area, they are luxury products (Heine, 2012). For example, skiing is not a luxury purchase for people who live very close to the ski resort in winter, it is considered a luxury consumption for those in warmer areas.

Temporal Relativity: It is based on the change of resources over time. The increase in productivity has led to a decrease in the prices of the products, so for some consumers these products have become easier to buy (Matsuyama, 2002). In the past, while unreachable products are considered as luxury, they have become more accessible with technological changes and developments. For this reason, the products that were considered luxury in time became the products that were easily found and purchased by all consumers.

Figure 2. Types of relativity
Source: Heine, 2012.

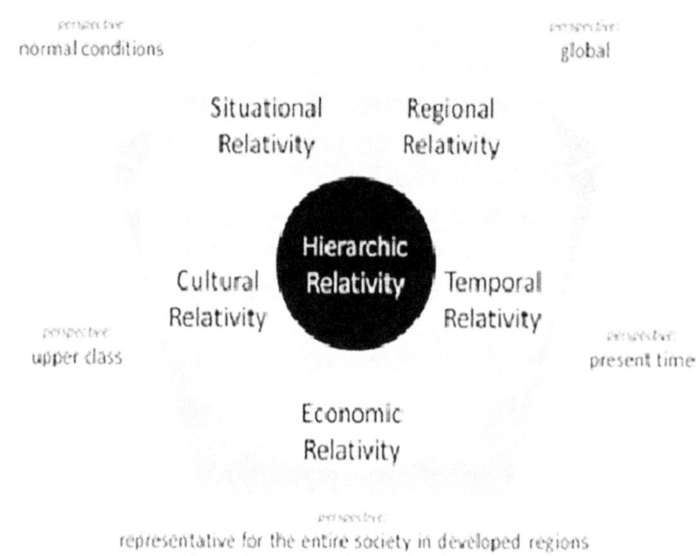

Economic Relativity is based on the different economic situation of consumers and countries. An ordinary product for most consumers can be considered luxury for low income consumers in underdeveloped economies (Heine, 2012). Since these societies and consumers' cultures also change according to their economic situation, it also varies whether or not the products are luxury products (Christodoulides et al. 2009).

Cultural Relativity: Culturally, luxury means a necessary and extraordinary product. A product which is consumed as luxury according to a culture is an unwanted product according to some cultures (Kemp, 1998). Mortelmans (2005: 497, 504) stated that "*Every social group can be said to have its own lux- ury. Every social group has in fact a different kind of luxury. Luxury may be present in all times and in all cultures, its appearance differs all the time.*"

Situational Relativity: It is the state of consumers deciding whether a product is luxury according to the changing situation over time. Before buying a product, consumers may think it is a luxury product. But after purchasing and using the product, the product may lose its luxury meaning to that consumer. Therefore, this concept includes the perception of luxury according to the status of the consumer.

CONSUMPTION EFFECTS OF LUXURY CONSUMERS

Initially, economists believed that consumers' consumption decisions made independently of other actors in the market. In contrast, according to Veblen (1899) as people's income increases and spreads to society, their buying reasons change. People are not only buying to satisfy their needs but also they are buying to draw others' attention and earn their respect. Duesenberry (1949) claims the level of consumption of a person depends not only on the level of spending but also on comparing with others. People are affected, through "demonstration effects", from consumption patterns of their reference groups and try to copy those patterns. Leibenstein (1950) theorizes three different consumption effects; bandwagon effect, snob effect and veblen effect (Kastanakis & Balabanis, 2012).

Bandwagon Effect: According to Leibenstein (1950), the bandwagon effect is an increase in the demand for a product because others consume the same product. This behavior occurs as a result of being affected by peer pressure (Agraval, Gupta & Vora, 2020). In the context of consuming luxury products, this effect expresses the desire to be associated with people in the upper class (Mainolfi 2019). According to the bandwagon effect, consumers buy a popular luxury brand to get approval from the group they belong to or identify themselves with that group. The other words bandwagon effect can be seen as a tendency to adapt to social norms (Tsai et al., 2013). A person who acts with bandwagon effect buys in order to be part of a group, in order to conform with the people they wish to be in a relationship with, in order to be in vogue or stylish, or in order to be part of the group (Leibenstein, 1950). Therefore, the bandwagon effect can also be named as herd psychology.

In order to explain Bandwagon luxury consumption, psychological and socio-logical factors should also be examined. The study on this subject supports this. Because consumers who have an independent self-concept want to belong to a certain group and look like them when purchasing luxury products. Consumers who have an independent self and an interdependent self tend to explain the status, success and prestige created by having luxury goods to the group they feel belong to (Bahri-Ammari, Coulibaly & Mimoun, 2020).

The bandwagon effect creates a positive effect on being increased demand for a good. Bandwagon effects have two consumption behaviours. Bandwagon effects arise from the actions of others and depend on the actions of others. Therefore, they are consumption behaviours related to social origin. They are also directed to similar audiences and further strengthen the consumption behaviour of other bandwagons. Therefore, it is a consumption behaviour with social value (Kastanakis & Balabanis, 2012). Bandwagon consumption happens when consumers buy luxury products because of their popularity (Kastanakis & Balabanis, 2014). In the study of Stepień (2018), it has been determined that consumers under the bandwagon effect want to have a higher social class and are not prone to luxury consumption.

Researches (O'Guinn and Shrum 1997; Dittmar 1994) show that consumers use television to get information about the affluent lifestyle, and then try to imitate the stereotype of being wealthy by consuming similar products of prestige products they learn from television. O'Guinn and Shrum (1997) examined consumers' watch to television to create social reality. They examined the relationship between the prevalence of products and activities associated with a rich lifestyle and television exposure. As a result, they found a positive relationship between them (Vigneron & Johnson, 1999).

Bandwagon consumers buy brands that have growing awareness because they buy reference groups that they see as their role models. However, brands that have growing awareness disturbs the original consumers who buy with the motivation to differentiate from others. Thus, bandwagon consumers who are affected by the reference groups also stop buying those brands. Because the reference groups don't show a commitment to that brand. For this reason, luxury brands should pay attention to this when investing in their reputation (Heine, 2012).

Snob Effect: According to Snyder & Fromkin (1977), people want to distinguish from others. When people think that they are too similar to others, they may feel their identities are threatened. This situation can require them to behave in a way that makes them feel different. Unique value refers to the perceived exclusivity of a product. Some consumers who seeking uniqueness avoid buying the products that buying by the general mass of people (Sun, D'Alessandro & Johnson, 2016). The bandwagon can not explain this situation. Therefore, a new term has created; snob effect. Unlike the bandwagon effect, the snob effect occurs when an individual wants to consume a product that is not consumed by the people around him (Agraval, Gupta & Vora, 2020). Therefore, a consumer under the snob effects is looking for high-quality and high-priced products that some consumers cannot reach and buy (Kapferer & Valette-Florence, 2018).

Leibenstein (1950) defines the snob effect as the decrease in the demand of a product due to the consumption of that product by others or the increasing consumption of that product by others. The snob effect reflects one person's sense of separation from the group and being special (Tsai et al., 2013).

The snob effect can occur in two situations. On the first situation; when a new product is launched, snob consumer will adopt that product which a limited number of consumers who will use it first, and on the second situation; status sensitive consumers refuse to buy a particular product when they see it consumed by the large mass of people (Vigneron & Johnson, 1999).

According to a lot of research, when a product which the consumers perceive limited in number produced, the consumers pay more attention and that product's value increases (Vigneron & Johnson, 1999; Pantzalis, 1995; Lynn, 1991; Verhallen, 1982).

Many studies show that luxury products are scary. Because the prices of luxury products are high. They are also sold in limited locations. Therefore, it is the right approach to buy luxury products to differentiate and become unique from others. The studies of some authors, such as Bian & Forsythe 2012; Stokburger-Sauer & Teichmann 2013, show that consumers' unique needs supply with luxury products. Therefore, the perceived uniqueness value should be in a positive relationship with consumers' purchases (Sun, D'Alessandro & Johnson, 2016).

In addition to this result Solomon (1994), limited number of products sale have a high value. On the other hand, products that can be purchased from anywhere are less desirable. The products that find difficult have prestige and the snob consumers search for prestige brands offering uniqueness (Vigneron & Johnson, 1999).

The bandwagon effect helps consumers to create an image that is associated with high lifestyles or to be fashionable. On the other hand the snob effect defines a person's desire to distinguish himself/herself from common people, so the purchase and consumption of popular and widely accessible goods is rejected (Patsiaouras & Fitchett, 2012).

Veblen Effect: Several authors, such as Erickson & Johansson 1995; Lichtenstein, Bloch, & Black 1988; Tellis & Gaeth 1990, referred that the price of the products may have a positive effect on perceived quality. These studies have shown that consumers frequently use price when evaluating different brands according to quality. In practice, a higher price means higher quality. In addition, studies that perceived price as an indicator of quality, suggest that price is a positive indicator for prestige. According to these results, consumers use price as an indicator of prestige. Veblenian consumers attach great importance to price since their main goal is to impress others. Because, according to them, price is an important indicator of prestige (Vigneron & Johnson, 1999). Therefore, veblen effect is used by consumers as a status symbol (Loureiro, de Plaza & Taghine, 2002). Therefore, veblen products are luxury products that make consumers more proud in a society. The price increase applied to these products also increases the demand for these products (Agraval, Gupta & Vora, 2020).

Veblen effect is the increase in product demand owing to the price increase (Yang & Mattila, 2016). Veblen effect assumes increased demand for a product with the price increase. Consumers prefer to buy more expensive products to prove their wealth levels (Yang & Mattila, 2016).

Veblen effect is closely related to conspicuous consumption (Pepall & Reiff, 2016). Veblen considers separating oneself from others as the basis of conspicuous consumption. Therefore, conspicuous consumption represents the socially-directed characteristics of luxury consumption (Sun, D'Alessandro & Johnson, 2016).

Eventually, the snob effect is the purchase of a luxury product in a situation that very few people have it, while the Veblen effect is the purchase of a luxury product when the price increases (Kastanakis & Balabanis, 2012). Usually luxury brands use the effect of Veblen and snob. Because of the higher the price, the better Veblen consumers can show their wealth. Also, the snob consumers can show their status as the general mass of people can't buy the luxury products. In this way, luxury brands encourage consumers to buy more quickly (Heine, 2012).

THE EFFECTS OF THE REFERENCE GROUP ON THE LUXURY CONSUMERS

Vigneron & Johnson (1999), stated that using luxury brands or products is the result of social influences. Reference groups affect consumers' product and brand evaluations, especially in their buying behavior of luxury goods (Amaldoss & Jain, 2008; Childers & Rao, 1992). This is done in order to receive support, acceptance and approval from the reference groups (Vel et al. 2011). Due to the fear of social rejection, consumers need more belonging to reference groups (Khalifa & Shukla, 2017). Because consumers think that reference group members are experts on luxury brands or products. They even give up buying counterfeit products because they fear that reference groups will detect counterfeit products immediately. Therefore, luxury brands are influenced by reference groups in their purchasing behavior (Ngo et al., 2020). To order to show their prestige and achievement to their targeted social groups, socially oriented consumers are motivated to own luxury brands (Tsai, 2005). Consumers prefer to imitate the buying actions of the group members they want to belong to 'Reference Group'. Lascu and Zinkhan (1999) also explained that reference group influences are more likely to be stronger for luxury items, products or brands which have social visibility. As with the Bandwagon Effect, some consumers only buy the same products as reference groups buy luxury products and follow the reference group members (Guido et al., 2020; Amatulli & Guido, 2012).

According to Bearden & Etzel (1982), the basis of the reasons why consumers are affected by reference groups is based on 3 factors. ***Informational influence*** is based on the desire to make informed decisions. Faced with uncertainty, an individual will seek information. ***Utilitarian reference group influence*** is reflected in attempts to comply with the wishes of others to achieve rewards or avoid punishments. A third type of influence, ***value-expressive***, is characterized by the need for psychological association with a person or group and is reflected in the acceptance of positions expressed by others. This association can take two forms. One form is an attempt to resemble or be like the reference group. The second type of value-expressive influence flows from an attachment or liking for the group. The individual is responsive to the reference group out of a feeling for it, not because of a desire to be associated with it. The way consumers are influenced by reference groups is value-expressive influence. In the study conducted on women, on these three main reference group factors, although there are differences in different women segments, women are affected by all three factors (Fernanades & Panda, 2018).

In the case of reference groups, social influences should also be taken into account. Because social influences reveal how an individual is affected by others in their shopping or expectations. Therefore, social influences are an important variable that affects the consumer purchasing process (Zhang, Chen & Zaccour, 2020). So, especially reference group and social influences are two of the most important issues particularly consumer purchase decision for the luxury products or brands. Even consumers can buy counterfeit of luxury products, both in order to feel belonging to a certain social class in the society and to gain a social status, despite the fear of being understood. If the counterfeit product is visually identical to the original and has the desired symbolic value, consumers intend to purchase or purchase luxury products. Eventually, it is important to investigate how customers feel and act on this issue.

Reference groups affect consumers' brand decisions in two ways. The first is the exclusive of a product, and the second is the decisions that others see and define. This distinction relates to where the product is consumed. It is a combination of the concepts of public or private consumption and luxury or necessity. Therefore, there are 4 basic combinations (Bearden & Etzel, 1982; Childers & Rao, 1992).

- **Publicly consumed luxury:** It is a luxury product that is consumed publicly. Whether he or she has a luxury product and which brand is purchased will be seen and influenced by others. In this combination, because the consumption of the product is seen by others and the product is luxurious, the brand of the product must be very strong. These are products such as golf clubs, snow skis.
- **Privately consumed luxury:** These are luxury products that are consumed in a non-public manner and cannot be used very widely. The consumer chooses the product individually and this decision is an important and voluntary decision for the consumer. Consuming this luxury product will have a family effect. The effect of the product is strong because it is luxury for themselves. But others will not see this product, so the brand may be weak. These are products such as TV games, compactor, icemaker.
- **Publicly consumed necessity:** They are consumed publicly and are used more widely than other luxury products and differ according to brand type. In this combination the product is a requirement for consumers so the effect should be weak but the brand should be strong as the product will be observed by others. These are products such as automobile, wristwatch.
- **Privately consumed necessity:** They are purchased by almost all consumers because of the characteristics of the product rather than the effects of the product. In this combination, the product and brand are not socially visible. Therefore, the effect of the product and the brand are weak. The consumer needs and buys for himself or herself. These are products such as refrigerator, mattress.

In the study of Fernandes & Panda (2019) on the combination of publicly and privately, it was found that reference groups had more impact on publicly luxury purchases rather than privately necessity. In publicly consumed luxury product purchases, it was emphasized that consumers were more affected by reference groups (Dong &Koo, 2018).

In the study of Mainolfi (2019), it was examined that reference groups positively affect the choice of luxury brands and products, as Chinese consumers care about what their reference group members use and buy. Similar results were obtained in the study of Wang & Foosiri (2018) conducted on Chinese consumers. Consumers are influenced by reference groups when making decisions about luxury products and brands. In the study of Eastman, Shin & Ruhland (2020) on students, they found that reference groups played a bigger and stronger role than the family in purchasing luxury brands for students. They also found that luxury brand purchasing situations may vary depending on whether they are included in the reference groups. As Kostritsa et al. (2020) stated that the brand is an important tool for social integration. Therefore, when any brand is used by the reference group, the consumer establishes a stronger bond with the brand. Rojanasingsawad, Ryding & Barnes (2020) stated that Thai consumers are very exposed to the information they receive from social reference groups during their decision making process. In addition, it was revealed that these consumers were very worried about social acceptance and adaptation to the reference group and consumed luxury products for this. In the study of Jain & Schultz (2019), which examined the purchases of Indian consumers in digital media, it was revealed that these consumers were largely digitally attached to reference groups in their luxury purchasing behavior and brand choices. Contrary to these studies, in study on luxury perfumes of Wijanarko & Fachrodji (2020) shows that reference groups do not have a direct effect on purchasing, but they recommend it to members of the reference group. The emergence of this result revealed that everyone has different tastes about perfume. In the study of Fernandes & Panda (2018), it was examined that women were affected by reference groups more than men. In addition, in the examination made according to women's ages, young women were found to be more sensitive to reference group effects than older women. As a result, it has been emphasized that reference groups are of vital importance on women consumer behavior.

COUNTERFEIT PRODUCTS AND CONSUMERS

Luxury products, which are an indicator of wealth and a symbol of belonging, are the products that only a certain rich segment constitutes a small group within the society and that a certain segment wants to have but cannot have due to their income. The most preferred and most important of these ways is to buy and use counterfeit products.

Counterfeits is the reproduction of a trademark that is the same or very similar to the original products. This reproduction covers all the processes required for a product such as packaging and labeling (Phau & Teah, 2009). Counterfeiting is defined by McCarthy as: *"the act of producing or selling a product containing an intentional and calculated reproduction of a genuine trademark. A counterfeit mark is identical to or substantially indistinguishable from a genuine mark."* (Yoo & Lee, 2012: 1507). According to the Bian & Moutinho (2009: 368), "*counterfeits are those products bearing a trademark that is identical to, or indistinguishable from, a trademark registered to another party, thus infringing the rights of the holder of the trademark.*" As a result of the research, Phau & Teah (2009) has revealed consumers who purchase two types of counterfeit products. According to Grossman & Shapiro (1988), these two types are deceptive counterfeiting and nondeceptive counterfeiting. First, consumers who buy without knowing that they are counterfeit products because they are very similar to the original products. So you are a victim of them. The second is consumers who knowingly and willingly buy counterfeit products. They know that these products are illegal, but they still buy. Consumers have many reasons for this. Some consumers tend to buy counterfeits because they are looking for novelty and variety. Consumers in this seeking buy cheaper products more often (Yoo & Lee, 2012). Because consumers think that by purchasing cheaper products, they will save money and gain economic benefits and these products are indistinguishable because the counterfeit products look exactly the same as the real luxury product (Harun et al., 2020). Other reason is higher social status. Consumers consider the symbolic value of these products rather than their functionality and therefore buy them (Gentry et al. 2001). They intend to buy counterfeit products in order not to be exposed to social pressure and to establish positive relationships with the society(Harun et al., 2020). The third is price advantage of counterfeits. Counterfeit products are cheaper than luxury products (Prendergast, Hign Chuen & Phau, 2002). Together with these reasons, the factors that affect the attitudes and behaviors of consumers towards counterfeits of luxury products are social factors and personality factors (Phau & Teah, 2009). Social factors affecting consumers are collectivism and reference groups that influence the consumer from the outside. Personality factors are social status, novelty seeking, a sense of accomplishment, social recognition.

Although counterfeit products are not legal and ethical, they continue to be produced and purchased by consumers according to all these attitudes and behaviors of consumers. With today's technological advances, it is even more difficult to determine whether the counterfeit products are the same or very similar in shape and appearance with their originals. The rapid expansion and development of mass media and information technologies enables products to move around the world faster. Thanks to this digital environment, consumers can easily be aware of the latest fashion trends in fashion leading countries and can easily access these products. Furthermore, thanks to this digital environment, consumers have the opportunity to reach more reference groups and share their experiences with these reference groups in an unlimited way.

In the study of Wee, Tan & Cheok (1995), it was revealed that there was a high level of meaningful relationship between consumers' intention to purchase counterfeit wallet and their personal appearance. In another study, Tom et al. (1998) found that consumers with low incomes and educational level were more inclined to buy counterfeit products. According to the study of Gentry et al. (2001), consumers were identified as the main reasons for the purchase of counterfeit products, representing a brand and providing innovation. Ang et al. (2001) revealed that consumers' counterfeit buying behaviors were largely due to the low price of counterfeit products. Penz & Stöttinger (2005) reached the same conclusion as this study. They have been found that consumers intend to purchase counterfeit products because they are low priced.

Mwihaki (2019) found that price consciousness has a significant impact on consumers' purchasing intentions for counterfeit products. In the study of Bupalan et al. (2019), which measures the intentions of consumers to purchase counterfeit products, it is determined that the brand image and attitude are important factors affecting the purchase intent for counterfeit products. In another study of Bajwa & Singh (2019), where the effects of demographic factors on the purchase of counterfeit products in cosmetic brands were examined, it was found that education, marital status, family size and self income had a significant effect on the behavior of buying counterfeit products. In addition, single women were found to buy more counterfeit cosmetics than married women. In the study of Pratt & Zeng (2020), which measures whether the behavior of purchasing counterfeit goods in Hong Kong varies depending on age and gender, it was found that the behavior of buying counterfeit goods does not change according to gender and age. Priporas et al. (2020) examined the buying behavior of upper middle class consumers in China for counterfeit goods. According to the results obtained, it was revealed that the upper middle class consumers (i.e. high-income level, great sense of security, and advanced level of education and societal status) have largely negative opinions about consuming counterfeit products. In the study of Karahan & Sahin (2020), which examines the behavior of Turkish consumers towards counterfeit products, it has been determined that perceived risk and experience factors have a significant effect on consumers' attitudes towards buying counterfeit goods. However, social status, ethical awareness and low price factors were found to have no significant effect.

FUTURE RESEARCH DIRECTIONS

This study theoretically examines how consumers behave and perceive luxury products in general. The topics included in the study can be a guideline on which topics should be focused more on understanding luxury consumers. This study deals with consumer behavior towards luxury products in general. Empirical research on this subject will provide a more detailed discussion of the topic. Empirical research on the ethnicity and social status of consumers can be done on this subject. In addition, it can be examined which consumers are particularly affected by reference groups when buying luxury products and which counterfeit products they buy. It is hoped that the study will serve as a resource for future studies and contribute to the literature in addition to the previous ones.

CONCLUSION

As explained above, consumers do not make a purchase only to meet their functional needs. they can buy a product because of belong to a group, of feeling like a part of the group, of showing or proving their assets and wealth, of being respected by society, being different from the majority, and of showing that they are in a position above the majority. Consumers can provide motivation to buy a product with emotional or psychological reasons.

Four types of consumers are mentioned in the consumption of luxury products. These are the luxury hedonists, the aspirational consumers, the luxury experts, the connoisseurs and the ostentatious, status-oriented individuals. The luxury hedonists are not in seeker of status. This group that generally consisting of successful and more optimistic young likes to follow trends, spends for themselves, travel. They buy luxury products to introduce themselves to the world. The aspirational consumers are more mature consumers than hedonist consumers and are usually male consumers. They are traditional, like to spend for themselves, and use word-of-mouth marketing to learn about luxury products. The luxury experts, the connoisseurs, which are made up of the richest and most educated consumers are always open to new products and brands, they want to be of superior quality, they do not buy luxury products as a status symbol. The ostentatious, status-oriented individuals are very sensitive about logo and brands. So they want to show their brands and logos. Because they are financially limited, it is important for them to travel abroad.

There are some factors that affect the consumption of luxury products. Some consumption effects such as bandwagon effect, snob effect, veblen effect are effective in the purchase of luxury products. Bandwagon effect occurs when consumers purchase luxury products in order to be included in the reference groups they take as role models or to look like a member of them. Snob effect is the opposite to bandwagon effect. As the demand for a product increases, the consumer moves away from that product in snob effect. The snob consumer does not buy the product that the majority buys. Veblen effect is the consumer's purchase of a product to impress others. The consumer aims to provide prestige and reputation with the product purchased. Therefore price is an important indicator of the veblen effect.

One of the motivations that affect consumers in the consumption of luxury products is the reference groups. Because many consumers want to belong to a reference group. These consumers prefer to imitate the purchase of members of the Reference Group they wish to belong to. In this way, they want to get the support, approval and acceptance of the reference group. The reasons why consumers are affected by reference groups are based on three factors. These are informational influence, utilitarian reference group influence and value-expressive. Informational influence is about the desire to make informed decisions. A person who faces uncertainty will ask for information. Utilitarian reference group influence is to comply with others' wishes to win prizes or to avoid punishment and final influence that value-expressive is characterized by the need for psychological relationships with one person or group. That influence is reflected in the acceptance of positions expressed by others.

As seen in this study, consumption of luxury products is realized from social, emotional and psychological needs rather than functional purposes. The current position of the consumer or the position of the consumer's want in society is seen as an important factor in luxury product consumption. In addition, it is stated that consumption effects are related to individual characteristics of the person. Some consumers buy to belong to a group, while others want to get away from the majority with the product they buy. Luxury brands need to take these into consideration and develop strategies that will affect the consumer's buying behavior.

REFERENCES

Agrawal, A. K., Gupta, A. A., & Vora, M. K. (2020). Pricing and lot-sizing policies for products with demand under Veblen effect. *Operations Management Research,* 1-9.

Amaldoss, W., & Jain, S. (2008). Trading up: A strategic analysis of reference group effects. *Marketing Science*, *27*(5), 932–942. doi:10.1287/mksc.1070.0350

Amatulli, C., & Guido, G. (2012). Externalised vs. internalised consumption of luxury goods: Propositions and implications for luxury retail marketing. *International Review of Retail, Distribution and Consumer Research*, *22*(2), 189–207. doi:10.1080/09593969.2011.652647

Ang, S. H., Cheng, P. S., Lim, E. A., & Tambyah, S. K. (2001). Spot the difference: Consumer responses towards counterfeits. *Journal of Consumer Marketing*, *18*(3), 219–235. doi:10.1108/07363760110392967

Atwal, G., & Williams, A. (2009). Luxury brand marketing – the experience is everything! *Journal of Brand Management*, *16*(5-6), 338–346. doi:10.1057/bm.2008.48

Bahri-Ammari, N., Coulibaly, D., & Mimoun, M. S. B. (2020). The bandwagon luxury consumption in Tunisian case: The roles of independent and interdependent self concept. *Journal of Retailing and Consumer Services*, *52*, 101903. doi:10.1016/j.jretconser.2019.101903

Bajwa, S., & Singh, S. (2019). Demographic characteristics and consumer purchase behaviour towards counterfeit cosmetic brands. *PIMT Journal of Research*, *12*(1), 83–93.

Bearden, W. O., & Etzel, M. J. (1982). Reference group influence on product and brand purchase decisions. *The Journal of Consumer Research*, *9*(2), 183–194. doi:10.1086/208911

Bian, Q., & Forsythe, S. (2012). Purchase intention for luxury brands: A cross cultural comparison. *Journal of Business Research*, *65*(10), 1443–1451. doi:10.1016/j.jbusres.2011.10.010

Bian, X., & Moutinho, L. (2009). An investigation of determinants of counterfeit purchase consideration. *Journal of Business Research*, *62*(3), 368–378. doi:10.1016/j.jbusres.2008.05.012

Bupalan, K., Rahim, S. A., Ahmi, A., & Rahman, N. A. A. (2019). Consumers' repurchase intention towards counterfeit products. *Int. J Sup. Chain. Mgt*, *8*(3), 973–981.

Chevalier, M., & Mazzalovo, G. (2013). *Luxury Brand Management: A World of Privilege.* Wiley.

Childers, T. L., & Rao, A. R. (1992). The influence of familial and peer-based reference groups on consumer decisions. *The Journal of Consumer Research, 19*(2), 198–211. doi:10.1086/209296

Christodoulides, G., Michaelidou, N., & Li, C. H. (2009). Measuring perceived brand luxury: An evaluation of the BLI scale. *Journal of Brand Management, 16*(5-6), 395–405. doi:10.1057/bm.2008.49

Dittmar, H. (1994). Material possessions as stereotypes: Material images of different socio-economic groups. *Journal of Economic Psychology, 15*(4), 561–585. doi:10.1016/0167-4870(94)90011-6

Dong, H. B., & Koo, J. (2018). Conspicuous and inconspicuous luxury consumption: a content analysis of BMW advertisements. reinvention. *An International Journal of Undergraduate Research, 11*(2).

Duesenberry, J. S. (1949). *Income, Saving and The Theory of Consumer Behavior.* Harvard University Press.

Eastman, J. K., Shin, H., & Ruhland, K. (2020). The picture of luxury: A comprehensive examination of college student consumers' relationship with luxury brands. *Psychology and Marketing, 37*(1), 56–73. doi:10.1002/mar.21280

Erickson, G. M., & Johansson, J. K. (1985). The role of price in multi-attribute product evaluations. *The Journal of Consumer Research, 12*(2), 195–199. doi:10.1086/208508

Fernandes, S., & Panda, R. (2019). Influence of social reference groups on consumer buying behavior: A review. *Journal of Management Research, 19*(2), 131–142.

Fernandes, S. F., & Panda, R. (2018). Social reference group influence on women buying behaviour: A review. *Journal of Commerce and Management Thought, 9*(2), 273–291. doi:10.5958/0976-478X.2018.00019.8

Gentry, J. W., Putrevu, S., II, & Commuri, S. (2001). How now Ralph Lauren? The separation of brand and product in a counterfeit culture. *ACR North American Advances, 28*, 258-265.

Gong, Y. (2001). *Anomaly of consumption: Asian's extravagance in luxury goods.* Academic Press.

Grossman, G. M., & Shapiro, C. (1988). Foreign counterfeiting of status goods. *The Quarterly Journal of Economics, 103*(1), 79–100. doi:10.2307/1882643

Guido, G., Amatulli, C., Peluso, A. M., De Matteis, C., Piper, L., & Pino, G. (2020). Measuring internalized versus externalized luxury consumption motivations and consumers' segmentation. *Italian. Journal of Marketing*, 1–23.

Harun, A., Mahmud, M., Othman, B., Ali, R., & Ismael, D. (2020). Understanding experienced consumers towards repeat purchase of counterfeit products: The mediating effect of attitude. *Management Science Letters, 10*(1), 13–28. doi:10.5267/j.msl.2019.8.019

Heine, K. (2012). The concept of luxury brands. *Luxury Brand Management, 1.*

Jain, V., & Schultz, D. E. (2019). How digital platforms influence luxury purchase behavior in India? *Journal of Marketing Communications, 25*(1), 41–64. doi:10.1080/13527266.2016.1197295

Kapferer, J. N., & Bastien, V. (2009). The specificity of luxury management: Turning marketing upside down. *Journal of Brand Management, 16*(5-6), 311–322. doi:10.1057/bm.2008.51

Kapferer, J. N., & Valette-Florence, P. (2018). The impact of brand penetration and awareness on luxury brand desirability: A cross country analysis of the relevance of the rarity principle. *Journal of Business Research, 83*, 38–50. doi:10.1016/j.jbusres.2017.09.025

Karahan, M. O., & Şahin, F. (2020). Tüketicilerin taklit ürün satın alma tutumlarını ve niyetlerini etkileyen faktörlerin belirlenmesi: Nicel bir araştırma. *Gümüşhane Üniversitesi Sosyal Bilimler Enstitüsü Elektronik Dergisi, 11*(1), 154–170.

Kastanakis, M. N., & Balabanis, G. (2012). Between the mass and the class: Antecedents of the "bandwagon" luxury consumption behavior. *Journal of Business Research, 65*(10), 1399–1407. doi:10.1016/j.jbusres.2011.10.005

Kastanakis, M. N., & Balabanis, G. (2014). Explaining variation in conspicuous luxury consumption: An individual differences' perspective. *Journal of Business Research, 67*(10), 2147–2154. doi:10.1016/j.jbusres.2014.04.024

Kemp, S. (1998). Perceiving luxury and necessity. *Journal of Economic Psychology, 19*(5), 591–606. doi:10.1016/S0167-4870(98)00026-9

Khalifa, D., & Shukla, P. (2017). Me, my brand and I: Consumer responses to luxury brand rejection. *Journal of Business Research, 81*, 156–162. doi:10.1016/j.jbusres.2017.05.032

Kostritsa, M., Liebl, H., Beinhauer, R., & Turčínková, J. (2020). Consumer Brand Love for Luxury Brands in India. *Acta Universitatis Agriculturae et Silviculturae Mendelianae Brunensis, 68*(1), 189–197. doi:10.11118/actaun202068010189

Lascu, D. N., & Zinkhan, G. (1999). Consumer conformity: Review and applications for marketing theory and practice. *Journal of Marketing Theory and Practice, 7*(3), 1–12. doi:10.1080/10696679.1999.11501836

Leibenstein, H. (1950). Bandwagon, snob, and Veblen effects in the theory of consumers' demand. *The Quarterly Journal of Economics, 64*(2), 183–207. doi:10.2307/1882692

Lichtenstein, D. R., Bloch, P. H., & Black, W. C. (1988). Correlates of price acceptability. *The Journal of Consumer Research, 15*(2), 243–252. doi:10.1086/209161

Loureiro, S. M. C., de Plaza, M. A. P., & Taghian, M. (2020). The effect of benign and malicious envies on desire to buy luxury fashion items. *Journal of Retailing and Consumer Services, 52*, 101688. doi:10.1016/j.jretconser.2018.10.005

Lynn, M. (1991). Scarcity effects on value: A quantitative review of the commodity theory literature. *Psychology and Marketing, 8*(1), 45–57. doi:10.1002/mar.4220080105

Mainolfi, G. (2019). Exploring materialistic bandwagon behaviour in online fashion consumption: A survey of Chinese luxury consumers. *Journal of Business Research*. doi:10.1016/j.jbusres.2019.11.038

Matsuyama, K. (2002). The rise of mass consumption societies. *Journal of Political Economy*, *110*(5), 1035–1070. doi:10.1086/341873

Mortelmans, D. (2005). Sign values in processes of distinction: The concept of luxury. *Semiotica*, *2005*(157), 497–520. doi:10.1515emi.2005.2005.157.1-4.497

Mostafa, M. M., & Arnaout, J. P. (2020). What drives Kuwaiti consumers to purchase luxury brands? *International Review of Retail, Distribution and Consumer Research*, *30*(1), 86–102. doi:10.1080/09593969.2019.1626259

Mwihaki, B. W. (2020). Effects of personality factors on consumer attitude toward the acquisitions of counterfeit products. *African Multidisciplinary Journal of Research*, *4*(2), 1–23.

Ngo, L. V., Northey, G., Tran, Q., & Septianto, F. (2020). The Devil might wear Prada, but Narcissus wears counterfeit Gucci! How social adjustive functions influence counterfeit luxury purchases. *Journal of Retailing and Consumer Services*, *52*, 52. doi:10.1016/j.jretconser.2018.09.003

O'Guinn, T. C., & Shrum, L. J. (1997). The role of television in the construction of consumer reality. *The Journal of Consumer Research*, *23*(4), 278–294. doi:10.1086/209483

Pantzalis, I. (1995). *Exclusivity Strategies in Pricing and Brand Extension* (Unpublished Doctoral Dissertation). University of Arizona.

Patsiaouras, G., & Fitchett, J. A. (2012). The evolution of conspicuous consumption. *Journal of Historical Research in Marketing*, *4*(1), 154–176. doi:10.1108/17557501211195109

Penz, E., & Stöttinger, B. (2008). Original brands and counterfeit brands—Do they have anything in common? *Journal of Consumer Behaviour: An International Research Review*, *7*(2), 146–163. doi:10.1002/cb.243

Pepall, L., & Reiff, J. (2016). The "Veblen" effect, targeted advertising and consumer welfare. *Economics Letters*, *145*, 218–220. doi:10.1016/j.econlet.2016.06.024

Phau, I., & Teah, M. (2009). Devil wears (counterfeit) prada: A study of antecedents and outcomes of attitudes towards counterfeits of luxury brands. *Journal of Consumer Marketing*, *26*(1), 15–27. doi:10.1108/07363760910927019

Pratt, S., & Zeng, C. Y. (2020). The economic value and determinants of tourists' counterfeit purchases: The case of Hong Kong. *Tourism Economics*, *26*(1), 155–178. doi:10.1177/1354816619834482

Prendergast, G., Hing Chuen, L., & Phau, I. (2002). Understanding consumer demand for non-deceptive pirated brands. *Marketing Intelligence & Planning*, *20*(7), 405–416. doi:10.1108/02634500210450846

Priporas, C. V., Chen, Y., Zhao, S., & Tan, H. (2020). An exploratory study of the upper middle-class consumer attitudes towards counterfeiting in China. *Journal of Retailing and Consumer Services*, *53*, 101959. doi:10.1016/j.jretconser.2019.101959

Rojanasingsawad, M., Ryding, D., & Barnes, L. (2020). Consumer decision-making styles for grey luxury goods: a study on Thailand. *International Journal of Sales, Retailing & Marketing, 9*(1).

Roux, E., Tafani, E., & Vigneron, F. (2017). Values associated with luxury brand consumption and the role of gender. *Journal of Business Research*, *71*, 102–113. doi:10.1016/j.jbusres.2016.10.012

Snyder, C. R., & Fromkin, H. L. (1977). Abnormality as a positive characteristic: The development and validation of a scale measuring need for uniqueness. *Journal of Abnormal Psychology*, *86*(5), 518–527. doi:10.1037/0021-843X.86.5.518

Solomon, M. R. (1994). *Consumer Behavior* (2nd ed.). Allyn and Bacon.

Som, A., & Blanckaert, C. (2015). *The Road To Luxury, The Evoluation, Markets, and Strategies of Luxury Brand Management*. Wiley. doi:10.1002/9781118814321

Stępień, B. (2018). Snobbish bandwagoners: Ambiguity of luxury goods' perception. *Journal of Management and Business Administration. Central Europe*, *26*(1), 79–99.

Stokburger-Sauer, N. E., & Teichmann, K. (2013). Is luxury just a female thing? The role of gender in luxury brand consumption? *Journal of Business Research*, *66*(7), 889–896. doi:10.1016/j.jbusres.2011.12.007

Sun, G., D'Alessandro, S., & Johnson, L. W. (2016). Exploring luxury value perceptions in China direct and indirect effects. *International Journal of Market Research*, *58*(5), 711–731. doi:10.2501/IJMR-2016-021

Tom, G., Garibaldi, B., Zeng, Y., & Pilcher, J. (1998). Consumer demand for counterfeit goods. *Psychology and Marketing*, *15*(5), 405–421. doi:10.1002/(SICI)1520-6793(199808)15:5<405::AID-MAR1>3.0.CO;2-B

Truong, Y., & McColl, R. (2011). Intrinsic motivations, self-esteem, and luxury goods consumption. *Journal of Retailing and Consumer Services*, *18*(6), 555–561. doi:10.1016/j.jretconser.2011.08.004

Tsai, S. P. (2005). Impact of personal orientation on luxury-brand purchase value: An international investigation. *International Journal of Market Research*, *47*(4), 427–452. doi:10.1177/147078530504700403

Tsai, W. S., Yang, Q., & Liu, Y. (2013). Young Chinese consumers' snob and bandwagon luxury consumption preferences. *Journal of International Consumer Marketing*, *25*(5), 290–304. doi:10.1080/08961530.2013.827081

Tynan, C., McKechnie, S., & Chhuon, C. (2010). Co-creating value for luxury brands. *Journal of Business Research*, *63*(11), 1156–1163. doi:10.1016/j.jbusres.2009.10.012

Veblen, T. (1899). *The Theory of The Leisure Class*. Macmillan.

Vel, K. P., Captain, A., Al-Abbas, R., & Al Hashemi, B. (2011). Luxury buying in the United Arab Emirates. *Journal of Business and Behavioural Sciences*, *23*(3), 145–160.

Verhallen, T. M. (1982). Scarcity and consumer choice behavior. *Journal of Economic Psychology*, *2*(2), 299–321. doi:10.1016/0167-4870(82)90034-4

Vigneron, F., & Johnson, L. W. (1999). A Review and a Conceptual Framework of Prestige Seeking Consumer Behavior. Academy of Marketing Science Review, (3/1), 2-8.

Vigneron, F., & Johnson, L. W. (2004). Measuring perceptions of brand luxury. *Journal of Brand Management*, *11*(6), 484–506. doi:10.1057/palgrave.bm.2540194

Wang, J., & Foosiri, P. (2018). Factors related to consumer behavior on luxury goods purchasing in China. *UTCC International Journal of Business & Economics*, *10*(1), 19–36.

Wang, O., & Somogyi, S. (2020). Motives for luxury seafood consumption in first-tier cities in China. *Food Quality and Preference*, *79*, 103780. doi:10.1016/j.foodqual.2019.103780

Wee, C. H., Ta, S. J., & Cheok, K. H. (1995). Non-price determinants of intention to purchase counterfeit goods: An exploratory study. *International Marketing Review*, *12*(6), 19–46. doi:10.1108/02651339510102949

Wijanarko, B., & Fachrodji, A. (2020). The analysis towards the ınfluence of motivation, brand ımage, price, and groups reference on purchasing decisions of original perfume products (Study Case of Meruya Campus Undergraduate Students, Mercu Buana University). *International Journal of Innovative Science and Research Technology*, *5*(1), 932–941.

Yang, W., & Mattila, A. (2016). Why do we buy luxury experiences? Measuring value perceptions of luxury hospitality services. *International Journal of Contemporary Hospitality Management*, *28*(9), 1848–1867. doi:10.1108/IJCHM-11-2014-0579

Yoo, B., & Lee, S. H. (2012). Asymmetrical effects of past experiences with genuine fashion luxury brands and their counterfeits on purchase intention of each. *Journal of Business Research*, *65*(10), 1507–1515. doi:10.1016/j.jbusres.2011.10.018

Zhang, Q., Chen, J., & Zaccour, G. (2020). Market targeting and information sharing with social influences in a luxury supply chain. *Transportation Research Part E, Logistics and Transportation Review*, *133*, 133. doi:10.1016/j.tre.2019.101822

ADDITIONAL READING

Atwal, G., & Williams, A. (2017). Luxury brand marketing–the experience is everything! In *Advances in luxury brand management* (pp. 43–57). Palgrave Macmillan. doi:10.1007/978-3-319-51127-6_3

Brun, A., & Castelli, C. (2013). The nature of luxury: A consumer perspective. *International Journal of Retail & Distribution Management*, *41*(11/12), 823–847. doi:10.1108/IJRDM-01-2013-0006

Chevalier, M., & Mazzalovo, G. (2013). *Luxury Brand Management: A World of Privilege*. Wiley.

Clifford, H. (Ed.). (1999). *Consumers and luxury: consumer culture in Europe 1650-1850*. Manchester University Press.

Dubois, B., Czellar, S., & Laurent, G. (2005). Consumer segments based on attitudes toward luxury: Empirical evidence from twenty countries. *Marketing Letters*, *16*(2), 115–128. doi:10.100711002-005-2172-0

Heine, K. (2012). The concept of luxury brands. *Luxury brand management*, 1, 2193-1208.

Husic, M., & Cicic, M. (2009). Luxury consumption factors. *Journal of Fashion Marketing and Management*, *13*(2), 231–245. doi:10.1108/13612020910957734

Phau, I., & Teah, M. (2009). Devil wears (counterfeit) prada: A study of antecedents and outcomes of attitudes towards counterfeits of luxury brands. *Journal of Consumer Marketing*, *26*(1), 15–27. doi:10.1108/07363760910927019

Vigneron, F., & Johnson, L. W. (1999). A Review and a Conceptual Framework of Prestige Seeking Consumer Behavior. Academy of Marketing Science Review, (3/1), 2-8.

Yeoman, I. (2011). The changing behaviours of luxury consumption. *Journal of Revenue and Pricing Management*, *10*(1), 47–50. doi:10.1057/rpm.2010.43

KEY TERMS AND DEFINITIONS

Bandwagon Effects: The bandwagon effect is an increase in the demand for a product because others consume the same product.

Counterfeit: They are produced in a manner similar to luxury products, which are very similar or identical to their originals bearing their characteristics.

Elitism: It is the most basic feature of the luxury products that consumers buy in order to gain social success and to belong to a group.

Hedonism: It is emotional factor such as pleasure, enjoyment for consumers to buy luxury products.

Luxury Consumer: They are consumers who buy luxury products.

Reference Group: Particularly when buying luxury products, they are the consumer groups that consumers are affected by them and want to be like them.

Snob Effects: The snob effect is the decreasing in the demand for a product due to the consumption of that product by others or the increasing consumption of that product by others.

Veblen Effects: Veblen effect is the increase in product demand owing to the price increase.

Chapter 3
New Luxury vs. Old Luxury:
What Is the Definition of Luxury Brand?

Paula Rodrigues
https://orcid.org/0000-0003-2967-2583
Lusíada University of Porto, Portugal

Ana Pinto Borges
https://orcid.org/0000-0002-4942-079X
Instituto Superior de Administração e Gestão, Portugal

ABSTRACT

Understanding the concept of luxury and knowing what luxury means is still necessary and pertinent research because the definition of what luxury is has not proved to be consensual, and those that exist leave out the understanding of how fragmented meanings of today's society appear and influence consumers' perceptions of luxury. While the terms of new and old luxury have gained popularity in the literature, there remains little empirical research comparing consumers' perceptions of new and old luxury brands. Therefore, it can be said that previous research on luxury contributes to improvements under the point of view centred on the product of the meaning of luxury while the current era of popularization and democratization of luxury causes confusion and, what luxury means today, remains unclear. This research intends, through an extensive literature review, to clarify the main differences between the concepts of new and old luxury brands.

INTRODUCTION

Over the past two decades, in particular, luxury and luxury brands have undergone profound changes (Kapferer, 2017; Kapferer & Laurent, 2016). What was once an extremely limited offer for a target group considered as an elite, has become a mass product for a high-end sector (Ko, Costello & Taylor, 2019). And, as such, the question arises whether something more generalized and accessible, can continue to be called "luxury" in the classic sense of the term.

DOI: 10.4018/978-1-7998-4369-6.ch003

Copyright © 2021, IGI Global. Copying or distributing in print or electronic forms without written permission of IGI Global is prohibited.

Pure luxury probably no longer exists in relation to what today are the big luxury brands globally (Nobre & Simões, 2019). The new communication technologies have contributed to the globalization and democratization of many luxury goods and, thus, it can be established that they are no longer pure elitist goods.

In addition, there is a new generation of consumers emergent on the market – generation Y or Millennials – a consumer generation with high levels of education and characterized by a tech-savvy lifestyle (Kapferer & Michaut-Denizeau, 2020). In this way, a more hedonic behaviour is expected, in a more egocentric society, where individuals mainly seek fun, pleasure, experiences and sensual desires (Kapferer & Valette-Florence, 2019). It is a generation always looking for new trends and who define themselves not quite for what they have but more for what they experience (Kapferer & Valette-Florence, 2019; Kapferer & Michaut-Denizeau, 2020).

On the other hand, brands like Prada and Louis Vuitton are currently seen as mass-luxury items, as opposed to old luxury brands as Roll Royce cars, Patek Philippe watches or Hermés fashion brand (Silverstein & Fiske, 2003; Heine & Phan, 2011).All of this indicates that in addition to the traditional luxury brands, new luxury brands are beginning to appear, no longer supported by a long tradition and no longer exclusive from European countries (Deloitte, 2017). The 100 largest luxury companies in the world generated $217 billion in sales, in 2016, according to the 5th edition of Deloitte's (2017) *Global Powers of Luxury Goods*. According to the same study, the Top 5 worldwide continues to be led by the brands LVMH, Estée Lauder, Richemont, Luxottica and Kering. China, France, Germany, Italy, Spain, Switzerland, the UK and the USA together account for 83 of the top 100 luxury goods companies worldwide and 90% of the sales. And the most interesting thing is that Spain and France have the highest growth rate according to Deloitte (2017). However, consumers in emerging markets continue to help the sector's growth (Kapferer & Valette-Florance, 2019). China, Russia and United Arab Emirates are categorized as emerging luxury markets by Deloitte (2017) and the percentage of consumers increased their spending by 70% when compared to the 53% of more mature markets such as the USA, Europe and Japan. The Deloitte (2017) report also concludes that the sales of luxury goods continue to accelerate despite their high volatility, and that there are two major trends for this market: the shift from physical products to digital experiences, and, despite globalization's influence in the luxury market, it will move from standardization (mass-prestige) to personalization (co-creation) (Merz et al., 2018).

Thus, in this context, and in the sense of helping luxury brand managers, it makes sense to understand the extent to which consumers perceive brands as being new luxury or old luxury brands.

The objective of this chapter is to verify through the literature review and according to the consumer's perspective, what are the main characteristics of the new luxury and old luxury brands, and thereby help the luxury brand managers to position their brands in the global market.

BACKGROUND

What is Luxury and Luxury Brands?

The luxury concept is difficult to define because it represents a social context (Nueno & Quelch, 1998) that follows a cultural evolution. Thus, it is consensual to consider that it is an alterable and extremely subjective concept (Phau & Prendergast, 2000; Amatulli & Guido, 2011, Nobre & Simões, 2019).

Many definitions of luxury have been suggested, both by academics and managers. The explanation for this reality results from the fact that these definitions reflect more the individual conceptions about what luxury is than the definition of the concept itself (Bian & Forsythe, 2012; Chattalas & Shuka, 2015; Cristini, Kauppinen-Räisänen, Barthod-Prothade, & Wooside, 2017; Ko, Costello & Taylor, 2019; Shukla & Purani, 2012; Tsai, 2005; Wiedmann, Hennigs & Siebles, 2009; Kapferer 2014, 2017; Kapferer & Michaut, 2016; Kapferer & Valette-Florence, 2019).

Although the word "luxury" is used in everyday life to refer to a certain lifestyle, the definition underlying the construct is specific to the consumer and to the situation or context. Cornell (2002) states that luxury is a difficult term to define, due to the strong involvement of individual cognition and the recognition of status by the others.

Brun and Castelli (2013: 828-829) consider that "luxury has been transformed over time reveals how is multifaceted nature makes it difficult to establish a clear definition of luxury" and "avoid these ambiguities, some authors have chosen to focus on the primary characteristics of luxury brands and products in the current market rather than to determinate how to define luxury".

Luxury in the historical/traditional sense, in marketing terms, refers to "class-oriented exclusivity goods and services that only a small segment of population can afford or is willing to purchase" (Granot, Russel & Brashear-Alejandro, 2013: 32). Historically, luxury is "always associated with wealth, exclusivity and power" (Brun & Castelli, 2013: 826).

Luxury goods are defined as drivers of pleasure and comfort and are also difficult to obtain (Chattalas & Shukla, 2015). By providing exceptional value and total excellence, luxury products enable consumers to satisfy both socio-psychological and functional needs (Shukla, 2012; Wiedmann, Hennigs & Siebels, 2009; Hennigs, Wiedmann, Klarmann, 2012). Kapferer (2017) suggests an experiential approach to understanding the concept of luxury, according to which luxury items provide extra pleasure when using all the senses at once. Wiedmann, Hennigs and Siebels (2009) propose that the individual need for luxury singularity has a fundamental role in luxury products consumption.

There is still no accepted definition of what constitutes a luxury brand (Ko, Costelo & Taylor, 2019). Although some academics argue that there are certain codes for luxury, with consistency across disciplines and ages (Larraufie & Kourdoughli, 2014), there are a number of challenges in composing a definition of luxury brands, including the fact that luxury is a relative concept (Mortelmans, 2005) and the perception of what constitutes luxury has changed over time (Cristini et al., 2017). Furthermore, it has been argued that the definition and measure of luxury is highly subjective, although some authors believe that luxury may not be inherently a subjective construct (Godey et al., 2012; Ko, Costello & Taylor, 2019).

Therefore, in order to understand what luxury is, it is crucial to understand the components or facets of a luxury product. Dubois, Czellar and Laurent (2005) developed a work in which they describe the multifaceted nature of a luxury product. For the authors, a luxury product must contain six facets: excellent quality, a high price, scarcity and uniqueness, aesthetics and poly-sensuality, ancestral heritage and personal history and, finally, be superfluous. Also for Veblen (1994), one of the components of luxury is rarity.

De Barnier, Falcy and Valette-Florence (2012) identified seven common elements that characterize luxury: (1) exceptional quality; (2) hedonism (beauty and pleasure); (3) (high) price; (4) rarity (which is not a scarcity); (5) selective distribution and personalized services; (6) exclusive character (prestige and privilege); and (7) creativity (art and avant-garde). These seven criteria are all necessary to differentiate luxury goods from other types of goods, such as premium goods or fashion goods (Kapferer & Bastien, 2012).

The consumption of luxury products is often associated with conspicuous consumption or consumption of status (O'Cass & Frost, 2002). The desire to gain social status and social prestige can be fulfilled through the conspicuous consumption of luxury products (Giovannini, Xu, & Thomas, 2015). Chaudhuri, Mazermdar and Ghoshal (2011) found that conspicuous consumption behaviours are influenced by consumer characteristics, including individualism, social visibility, individuality desire, self-esteem and materialism.

It is also known that one of the functions of luxury is social signalling (Wiedmann, Henning & Siebels, 2009; Sun, Wang, Chen, Li & Chen, 2017). This function encourages conspicuous consumption that is seen as the essence of luxury (Veblen, 1994). Conspicuous consumption shows status as an indicator of a great need for recognition, which can be filled through the bandwagon effect (Kastakanis & Babalanis, 2012), in such a way that, individuals buy well-known brands and products that seem to represent the taste of a group of consumers who wish to imitate, or the snob effect (Amaldoss & Jain, 2005), in such a way that they intend to express status when buying niche brands.

From a sociological and social-psychological perspective, based on the company's management theory, consumers use brands as symbols to create a favourable social image (Eagly & Chaiken, 1993). In this context, conspicuous consumption has traditionally been seen as the main source of purchase for luxury brands (O'Cass & Frost, 2002; Vigneron & Johnson, 2004). Conspicuous consumption is explained by the need for singularity, a theory that focuses on consumers trying to differentiate themselves from each other through material goods (Knight & Kim, 2007; Tian, Bearden & Hunter, 2001).

Academic literature broadly defines luxury brands based on consumer perceptions and/or certain dimensions of management, such as marketing activities and product attributes (Wiedmann, Hennigs & Siebels, 2009; Truong, Simmons, McColl & Kitchen, 2008; Vickers & Renand, 2003).

What constitutes a luxury brand must follow an integrative approach to what luxury is and consider the multifaceted desires that an individual wants to achieve with luxury consumption (Hennigs et al., 2013).

Luxury brands are known for being shaped by their cultural and historical heritage (Kapferer & Bastien, 2012). In view of the subjective nature of luxury and its definition, the perception of luxury brands is not consistent across market segments and geographic locations (Phau & Prendergast, 2000), as this depends heavily on each consumer's perception of indulgence.

Luxury brand consumption is largely determined by the social attitudes function (self-expression and self-presentation attitudes), as consumers express their individuality (need for uniqueness) and exhibit their social position (self-monitoring) through luxury brands (Wilcox, Kim & Sen, 2009).

In addition to the reasons that socially determine luxury consumption (Wilcox, Kim & Sen, 2009), a more personal orientation about luxury brands, also influences the decision process of luxury consumption (Wong & Ahuvia, 1998; Wiedmann, Henning, & Siebels, 2009). Following this perspective, consumers evaluate luxury brands based on financial, functional and emotional considerations (Wiedmann, Hennigs & Siebels, 2009).

Vigneron and Johnson (2004) consider the perceived quality, uniqueness, conspicuous consumption, the perceived extended-self and the perceived hedonism as a whole set of perceptions that increase the likelihood of consumers preferring luxury brands. However, they distinguish between luxury brands' perceptions that are not personally oriented (perceived quality, perceived uniqueness, perceived conspicuous consumption) from those that are personally oriented (perceived extended-self and perceived hedonism).

Considering the concept of customer perceived value (Sweeney & Soutar, 2001; Smith & Colgate, 2007) and the perception of the value of luxury (Wiedmann, Hennigs & Siebels, 2009), the key elements of luxury value proposed by Wiedmann, Hennigs and Siebels (2009) constitute the luxury brands perception.

The key elements, according to the authors, that make consumers evaluate luxury brands based on **four latent dimensions** of luxury value, are the following: financial, functional, individual and social dimension (Table 1).

Table 1. Elements of Luxury Value

Elements	Latent Dimension
Financial	Refers to direct monetary aspects.
Functional	Refers to the main benefit and basic utility of a luxury product.
Individual	Focuses on the consumer's personal orientation towards luxury consumption
Social	Value of the perception of luxury related to the perceived individual utility acquired when consuming products or services recognized by the social group.

Source: Authors elaboration

The perception of luxury brands is not consistent across market segments because luxury is a subjective concept (Phau & Prendergast, 2000) that depends on the perception of each consumer about the value of indulgence. Phau and Prendergast (2000) focus on the dimension of luxury exclusivity, arguing that luxury brands compete in the ability to evoke selectivity, which, in turn, is strongly associated with perceived quality.

Thus, in order to explain consumer behavior in relation to luxury brands, several aspects must be considered, namely, separating social orientation from pride and conspicuity (Mason, 1996) from personal orientation, hedonic or materialistic motives (Dubois & Laurent, 1996; Tsai, 2005) of quality and uniqueness functional value associations (Wiedmann, Hennigs & Siebels, 2009; Tsai, 2005), among others.

By providing exceptional value and total excellence, luxury brands allow consumers to satisfy both socio-psychological and functional needs (Shukla, 2012; Wiedmann, Hennigs & Siebels, 2009; Hennigs, Wiedmann & Klarmann, 2012). In luxury brands it is therefore important to understand the consumer's thoughts, perceptions, attitudes, feelings and the factors that influence them.

Luxury brands have a set of characteristics that differentiate them from other brands, being divided into two large blocks according to their functional characteristics and the characteristics of symbolic value in the consumer's mind (Dubois, Czellar, & Laurent, 2005): premium price; excellent quality; aesthetics and poly-sensuality; unique character and scarcity; ancestral heritage and personal history and superfluity.

Another way to understand the consumers' interest in luxury brands is to identify the reasons why they prefer luxury brands (Wilcox, Kim & Sen, 2009). Luxury brands attract consumers for extrinsic or interpersonal and intrinsic or personal reasons (Truong, 2010; Truong & McColl, 2011).

Within **extrinsic or interpersonal reasons,** three can be highlighted:

(1) **Veblen effect or conspicuous consumption:** where individuals like to show their wealth and status, they spend money to acquire and maintain their position in society, so luxury brands become a means of expressing a social position. Luxury brands are symbols of success and social status.

(2) **Snob effect or elite club**: where consumers tend to buy luxury brands to satisfy their psychological needs. This need results from the social comparison in which the individual wants to differentiate himself and express his unique character;
(3) **Bandwagon effect or search for affirmation:** refers to the consumer's desire to identify with social status groups or differentiate themselves from others that are not appreciated. Here, the consumption of luxury brands allows consumers to present their public self.

Within the **intrinsic reasons**, two stand out:

(1) **Hedonic Effect**: The hedonic effect or pleasure, above all, translates into an emotional value, which is an important component in luxury brands, therefore, hedonic consumption makes individuals buy luxury brands for pure pleasure (Tsai, 2005). Hedonism is associated with self-pleasure, when enjoying life and luxury takes on a central role in the individual lives.
(2) **Perfectionism Effect**. The perfectionism effect means that buying luxury brands that have a superior quality translates to a perfectionist, who focuses on details and exceptional manual work (Wiedmann, Hennigs & Siebels, 2009).

Luxury brands are usually defined as having external attributes that position these products away from other products (Vigneron & Johnson, 2004; Kapferer, 2008). The product attributes are sufficiently differentiating to maintain luxury by itself (Berthon et al., 2009) and, because luxury brand products are more than a set of physical attributes, not all rare and expensive, well designed high quality products can also be seen as luxury goods.

A luxury brand can be defined as "*a branded product that is carefully crafted, unique and conspicuous*" (Hung et al., 2011: 458).

Despite the aspects related to the products, the experiential and symbolic dimensions also play an important role in defining luxury brands. The mix of **functional**, **experiential** and **symbolic dimensions** differentiates luxury items from the others (Vickers & Renand, 2003). The **functional dimension** is based on the attributes of the products and their ability to satisfy the utilitarian performance needs of consumers or to solve the consumers' problems (Olson, 1999).

The **experiential dimension** develops the personal and hedonic nature of luxury brands (Berthon et al., 2009). It is generally recognized by consumers who want products that provide sensory pleasure (Holbrook & Hirschman, 1982).

Symbolic aspects are an integral part of brands. The **symbolic dimension** captures the fundamental value and desire of luxury brands (Dubois, Laurent & Czellar, 2001), but to achieve this status, the social context assumes considerable importance in the creation of symbolic meanings because the signs need to be recognized by others (Berthon et al., 2009). In addition to signaling to others, the meanings of the luxury brand can be used as symbolic resources for the construction and maintenance of their identity, thus symbolizing the consumer's own self (Elliott & Wattanasuwan, 1998).

In this way, luxury goods have often been linked to symbolic meanings that signal the status of those who own them (Han, Nunes & Drèze, 2010; Eastman, Goldsmith & Flynn, 1999). These symbolic meanings are traditionally seen as derived from exclusivity that is often related to service experiences (Tynan, McKenchie, & Chuon, 2010). Current luxury brand consumers also appreciate sustainability, revealing that they consider this value to be complementary to others (Kapferer & Laurent, 2016).

Although a substantial body of knowledge about luxury management has emerged in recent decades, it remains a very important area of research (Okonkwo, 2009). However, the theoretical and empirical results remain difficult to reconcile since the body of literature on the topic remains generic. The fundamental concepts of luxury remain with conceptual gaps and, as such, need further investigation (Barnier, Falcy, & Valette-Florance, 2012; Tynan, McKechnie, & Chhuon, 2010).

From what has been said, it is possible to perceive certain patterns in which some authors agree on what luxury is (Larraufie & Kourdoughli, 2014), namely, that the definition of what a luxury brand is remains a great challenge, considering luxury is a relative concept (Ko, Costello & Taylor, 2019; Mortelmans, 2005) and because the perception of what constitutes luxury changes over time (Cristini et al., 2017; Rodrigues & Rodrigues, 2019).

In addition, it has been stated that the definition and measurement of luxury has been highly subjective despite the fact that luxury is not an inherent subjective construct (Godey et al., 2012).

Thus, it is clear that it is desirable to define what a luxury brand is and, above all, define what is a new and an old luxury brand. Or, as defended by Ko, Costello and Taylor (2019: 406) to "measure the degree to which a given brand is a luxury brand".

The main goal of this chapter is to analyse the existence of differences between the consumers' perception of old and new luxury brands and if those concepts, "old luxury" and "new luxury", could be useful for luxury brand managers.

Old Luxury

Academic literature, in general, defines luxury brands based on the consumer's perception or from the point of view of business management, determining a set of dimensions or characteristics that this type of brands must contain. Most of these definitions consider a more or less wide range of multiple attributes, dimensions or characteristics. However, some of these dimensions appear in a generalized way in almost all definitions, namely, high quality, rarity, high price and a high level of design or aesthetics. But where there is truly consensus is that whether a brand is considered luxury or not, that depends on the consumer (Ko, Costello & Taylor, 2019).

Ko, Costello and Taylor (2019) made an extensive review of the academic literature on the definition of a luxury brand. After identifying a set of key dimensions, the authors concluded that the definition of a luxury brand must contain five elements perceived by the consumer: (1) the brand must have a high level of quality, (2) offer authentic value through desired benefits (whether functional or emotional), (3) have a prestigious image created by the market through qualities such as, "'handmade,, handcrafted or quality of service provided, (4) to be worth the premium price it requires and (5) to be able to inspire a strong connection or resonance with the consumer.

Luxury products generally refer to non-essential but highly desired goods and services, as they have associated characteristics of great quality in terms of design, materials and production. Traditionally, a premium image, high prices, superior quality, unique character/scarcity, superfluous and aesthetic is what characterizes luxury goods and brands, which are produced as a means of social distinction (Han, Nunes & Drèze, 2010).

Luxury brands are different from other types of brands because they follow a logic based on sociological characteristics that are fundamentally different from other brands on the market (Dion & Borraz, 2017). It is not the object or the brand itself that defines luxury but the social relationships that are developed around them (Dion & Arnould, 2011). As a rule, luxury is based on a social stratification and is considered a privilege of an elite, who use luxury as a sign of distinction or affirmation of their status (Kastanakis & Babalanis, 2012; Ordabayeva & Chandon, 2011).

The brand's prestige refers to the status or esteem associated with the brand (Stokburger-Sauer, Ratneshwar & Sen, 2012). The symbolic meanings imbued in a brand (Steenkamp, Batra & Alden, 2003), high prices and scarcity, represent the sources of creation of the brand's most prestigious appeal (Bearden & Etzel, 1982).

With regard to the prestige of the brand, Kirmani, Sood and Bridges (1999) argue that consumers choose not only the brand for its quality but also for its status and conspicuous consumption. When consumers believe that the brand has high reputation, self-improvement will be established (Kressmann et al., 2006).

Luxury means value and belonging and symbolizes a search for status (Kastanaki & Balabanis, 2012; Kauppinen-Raisanen et al., 2014), which implies that luxury serves a lot of personal interests - the desire to have, own and use luxury through the brands. According to Young, Hwang, McDonald and Oates (2010), luxury exists for the benefit of consumers in their private space but also for their public prominence. The current desire for luxury is not only related to the inherent characteristics of the products themselves, but also to the brands and images that are transmitted through the prominence of the brand (Kastanakis & Balabanis, 2012; Han, Nunes & Drèze, 2010). As such, it can be argued that luxury is no longer linked to what the product is but to what the brand represents (Thomas, 2007; Han, Nunes & Drèze, 2010).

According to Yeoman and Mcmahon-Beattre (2005), the concept of luxury is traditionally associated with affluence and consumption exclusively available to an elite. Typically, luxury brands are strongly associated with the exclusivity and rarity of products - attributes that increase the desire and preference for them (Verhallen, 1982; Lynn, 1991). Also traditionally, underlying the concept of luxury goods is the principle of rarity (Veblen, 1994).

The inherent excellence is one of the main meanings linked to luxury. Excellence means something better than the ordinary, excellence is a dimension of quality that contains superiority, greatness, splendor, magnificence and even, potentially, perfection (Kauppinen-Raisanen et al., 2014).

Luxury brands have characteristics such as premium quality, heritage of craftsmanship, recognized style, premium price, unique character and global reputation (Nueno & Quelch, 1998). Consumers buy luxury brands mainly for symbolic reasons that reflect their individual and social goals (Wilcox, Kim & Sen, 2009).

Until a few decades ago, luxury was still an expression of excellence, something that was exclusive and unique and seen by everyone as something creative and made by hand or handcrafted with exquisite materials (Thomas, 2007). Craftsmanship or skill and expertise is synonymous with time and the need for specialized work to produce an object with value, a symbol of tradition that is passed on from generation to generation, the fruit of manual know-how (Amatulli & Guido, 2011).

For Blevis et al. (2007), the traditional notion of luxury can be understood as something that is concerned with expensive and exclusive products, of high status, fashion and high comfort. Phau and Prendergast (2000) focus on the dimension of luxury exclusivity, arguing that luxury brands compete in the ability to evoke selectivity, which in turn, is strongly associated with perceived quality.

On the other hand, historically, luxury was only used by the rich and powerful. However, if today's society has become a mass consumer society, making the desire for luxury in terms of luxury brands, luxury has moved into something that can be excellent and creative but is no longer exclusive to a minority (Kapferer, 2017). With the transformation of luxury into something like a sensation, the appetite for self-serving manages to trivialize the concept, as well as dropping some of its inherent meanings (Kapferer, 2017; Silverstein & Fiske, 2003).

The first identity of luxury as being excellent, creative and exclusive has changed towards the notion of affordable luxury (Yeoman, 2011) or, at least, evoking this illusion. This is called the new luxury (Kapferer & Laurent, 2016), and it appears to be based on an ultra-utilitarian model, whose sustainability, ethical responsibility and long-term approach can be changed.

The use in marketing of the term "luxury" refers specifically to a high-price offer in almost all categories of products or services (Dubois, Laurent, & Czellar, 2005). The management of luxury brands currently lives in a conflict between meeting the rising demand for luxury in the global market and the effort to protect unique and exclusive luxury products (Tynan, McKenchie, & Chhuon, 2010).

Luxury brands are for a luxury consumer market, synonymous with high prices and limited supply (Granot & Brashear, 2008; Granot, Russell & Brashear-Alejandro, 2013; Turunen & Laaksonen, 2011). This is now commonly described as the old luxury, especially when contrasted in discussions comparing it the new luxury (Granot & Brashear, 2008; Gil et al., 2012).

As has already been said, the concept of luxury is highly subjective, depending on situational contingencies and on the consumer's experience and individual needs (Wiedmann, Hennigs & Siebels, 2009; Kapferer & Bastien, 2012). What constitutes a luxury brand must follow an integrative approach to what luxury is and consider the multifaceted desires that an individual wants to achieve with the consumption of luxury products / brands (Hennigs et al., 2013). The concept of luxury remains "incredibly fluid and changes dramatically across time and culture" (Yeoman & McMahon-Beattie, 2005: 320). As a result, new forms of luxury have emerged on the market.

The motivation to buy luxury products or brands is traditionally linked to the desire to "impress others" because the purchase and possession of luxury brands can, to some extent, help to create a favorable social image by developing prominence goals (Tsai, 2005). The consumption of luxury products is associated with conspicuous consumption or status (O'Cass & Frost, 2002). The desire to obtain social status and social prestige can be fulfilled through the consumption of luxury products (Giovannini, Xu & Thomas, 2015). Chaudhuri, Mazumdar and Ghosal (2011) consider that conspicuous consumption behavior is influenced by the characteristics of consumers, which include individualism, social visibility, exclusivity desire, self-esteem and materialism.

Thus, in this research work and considering the review carried out by old luxury brands, it is understood that these are brands that have characteristics such as premium quality, heritage of craftsmanship, recognized style, premium price, unique character, exclusivity and a global reputation, strongly linked to the status, value and images they convey from those who own them.

New Luxury

The term used by Silverstein and Fiske (2003) more than a decade ago, the new luxury, refers to the democratization of luxury, where both symbolic meanings and the form of luxury consumption have changed significantly (Gil et al., 2012). An important issue related to the definition and measurement of luxury derives from the subjectivity of its character (De Barnier, Falcy & Valette-Florence, 2012). Hagtveded and Patrick (2009) adopted the centrality of the hedonic dimension and, more specifically, the emotional orientation linked to the consumption of luxury brands. These authors understand a luxury brand as a premium product, providing pleasure as a central benefit and connecting with consumers on an emotional level.

However, just as there is no consensus for the definition of what luxury is, there is no consensus for a definition of new luxury. The basis of this new luxury has a distinctly different economic identity than that of the old luxury or the so-called traditional luxury (Blevis et al., 2007). It has been argued that luxury products are now available to a large number of consumers, at least in some ways (Thomas, 2007; Corbellini & Saviolo, 2009).

Thanks to the democratic and liberal system, luxury became accessible to more and more people, with the birth of the consumer society and through the development of the industrial revolution that shaped and transformed tastes and preferences (McKendrick, 1984).

The traditional meaning of luxury associations with excellence, creativity and exclusivity (Okonkwo, 2009; Jackson & Shaw, 2009) is less and less prevalent in the approach to luxury today sought by brands, that is, luxury can appear without one of these three conditions and continue to be perceived as luxury. However, lately, luxury continues to require that all conditions reach high level standards.

One explanation for this phenomenon, also called the "democratization of luxury", was that the technological development allows luxury products to be more available and that the Internet, in particular, has made it possible to purchase luxury products from different sources (Okonkwo, 2009). With the emergence of the new luxury, luxury consumption is no longer limited to only a selected few, limited only to goods that are rare and exclusive and are charged at very high prices.

The new luxury can be defined as "products and services that possess higher levels of quality, taste and aspiration that other goods in the category but are not so expensive as to be out of reach" (Silverstein, Fiske & Butman, 2003:1).

The new luxury implies that luxury is not so exclusive or so old and is also not so expensive or inaccessible (Silverstein & Fiske, 2005). The democratization of luxury results in mass luxury, much more linked to brands, which occurs when these brands extend cheaper offers and connect to new product groups (Cristini et al., 2017). Also for Silverstein and Fiske (2005), luxury continues to evolve into a process of transforming "having" into "being" essentially related to being, sharing and feeling, instead of being based on the very current desire to have, to possess and use (Cristini et al., 2017).

In the mainstream of consumer society, the media influence tastes and values and potentially reinforce the aura of short-term consumption. This transformation also implies that the media moderate and shape the appetite for mass-produced luxury brands (Cristini et al., 2017).

In the age of experience, luxury ends up on the Internet, increasing the appetite for luxury with new technologies (Atwal & Williams, 2009). However, this presents some difficulties, namely, while feeling the impression of luxury online in the first place is possible, the abundance of information befits all that is known and accessible, which in turn can create impatience. Unique and customized luxury is difficult to respond to an instantaneous desire, which is contrary to mass production and the offer of new luxury brands (Cristini et al., 2017; Kapferer, 2017).

Another significant characteristic of luxury is related to the fact that luxury is intrinsically associated with creativity (Lipovetsky, 2003; Michaud, 2003), therefore it is synonymous with something unique and a customized creation. Luxury may remain excellent, creative and exclusive, but what was previously related to art is now related to the ability to do business and generate profit (Thomas, 2007). This means that the influence of creativity has changed, not creativity itself, but the way in which artists see luxury is what has changed, it has gone from creativity to profitability (Cristini et al., 2017).

Atwal and Williams (2009) add that creativity has changed and that today in the era of self-interest, luxury serves individual needs and can be referred to as individual luxury, while creativity seen in its traditional form, continues to be expressed and presented by having, owning and using luxury brands.

This supports the view that luxury has become something that has moved from public to private space, favoring conspicuity (Cristini et al., 2017).

For Blevis et al. (2007), the notion of the new luxury can be characterized by products and services that offer the same function as traditional luxury, but whose target is the mass or semi-mass market. For these authors, luxury and new luxury must be seen in relative terms, meaning that if you can buy something that others cannot buy, that is luxury if you can buy something that you previously could not, but that has now become accessible at a lower cost, bringing something more expensive in something that can be purchased, this is called new luxury.

The term *masstige* (mass + prestige) appears with reference to luxury products for a pasta market (De Barnier, Falcy & Valette-Florence, 2012). Researchers studying luxury often find themselves faced with the difficulty that exists between three concepts: upmarket products, expensive products and luxury products. According to Alleres (1991), luxury consists of three domains: inaccessible luxury, intermediate luxury and affordable luxury, constituted by the way brands are on the market.

There are several forms of new luxury (Granot, Russell & Brashear-Alejandro, 2013; Silverstein & Fiske, 2003; Truong, McColl & Kitchen, 2009) that include:

(1) affordable super-premium products - products with prices close to the top in their categories, but for middle market consumers who can buy them because they are relatively low-ticket items (ex: Café Starbucks, Nespresso);
(2) extensions of old luxury brands - when old luxury brands (ex: Louis Vuitton, Chanel, Dior) extend product lines for more affordable offers, low end versions of their high end versions;
(3) *masstige* (mass + prestige) - are premium goods that have a premium price, but remain well below high-priced products in the category and far from traditional super-premium or Old Luxury goods (ex: Ralf Lauren, Calvin Klein) and;
(4) *populence* (represents popular opulence) - includes mass production and distribution of premium products.

Also for Hagtveded and Patrick (2009), brands with value satisfy the consumers and luxury brands delight them.

While luxury continues to transform the tangible into the intangible, it will appear as a controversial phenomenon, due to its inherent meanings and considering that the new conditions make it a paradox (Cristini et al., 2017). Luxury is typically associated with rarity but broadening the concept of scarcity and Commodity Theory, Lynn (1991) demonstrated that scarcity increases the desire for ownership only when consumers think that products will be more expensive. Recent research has re-investigated the Veblen effect, according to which, the demand for luxury increases when prices increase (Kapferer & Laurent, 2016).

In this research, the concept of new luxury brands is understood as affordable luxury goods that have high levels of quality, good taste and that represent status for those who use them.

It can be stated that the old luxury brands and the new luxury brands have some differences that can be developed by the luxury brand managers, according to their brand positioning (Table 2).

Table 2. Comparison of Old and New Luxury Components

Components	Old Luxury	New Luxury
Excellent quality	Ö	Ö
High price	Ö	
Scarcity/rarity	Ö	
Singularity	Ö	Ö
Aesthetics	Ö	Ö
Ancestral Heritage	Ö	
Personal History	Ö	
Conspicuous	Ö	Ö
Functionality	Ö	Ö
Experience	Ö	Ö
Symbolism	Ö	Ö
Status	Ö	Ö
Sustainability		Ö

Source: Own elaboration

SOLUTIONS AND RECOMMENDATIONS

The world of luxury brands attracts a lot of attention, both at the academic level and at the business level, because it is considered the greatest symbol of the consumer society that dominates today (Kapferer & Michaut, 2015; Kapferer & Vallete-Florence, 2019). In most academic research, luxury is associated with a set of characteristics, such as high quality, know-how, slow time, preservation of manual tradition, transmission of generation to generation of timeless products - all of which are associations made according to the notion of sustainability (Ko, Costello & Taylor, 2019; Hennigs, Wiedmann, Behrens & Klarmann, 2013; Kapferer & Laurent, 2016; Bian & Forsythe, 2012).

However, the luxury market is changing. Currently, many brands claim to be luxury brands, because luxury is sold on the world market (Kapferer, 2017). To expand the definition of this type of luxury, new terms have been created, such as, new luxury, affordable luxury, popular luxury, premium brands and causal luxury, with the aim of taking advantage of the "luxury" label from brands that know they are not luxury brands (Kapferer, 2017). Academics have endeavored to solve this problem by proposing a new definition of luxury but without reaching a consensus, because luxury is inherently a subjective notion, although the criteria are generally well known and accepted (De Barnier, Falcy, & Valette -Florence, 2012).

To attract new consumers, existing brands have adopted an abundant rarity strategy (Kapferer, 2012) expanding their product portfolio, typically through a vertical extension, from top to bottom, with cheaper and more profitable items (ex: accessories, watches, glasses, bags, perfumes, etc.). To expand their sales, protecting the brand value, several luxury brands have created secondary lines to offer goods at more affordable prices, leading to the emergence of the so-called mass prestige; simultaneously, new and more accessible brands have developed and appeared in the markets (Kapferer & Laurent, 2016).

However, some continue to defend, at the academic level, that luxury is associated with something truly exceptional, in terms of rarity, the quality of the rare components used in its execution, the qualification of something that is handmade, taking all this up to high prices that characterize luxury brands (Kapferer, 1998; Vigneron & Johnson, 2004; Dubois, Czellar & Laurent, 2005; Wiedmann, Henning, & Siebels, 2009; De Barnier, Falcy & Valette-Florence, 2012). On the demand side, modern luxury has developed based on consumers who are beyond the happy few. Many consist of a vast number of new and occasional customers, who do not need to be wealthy to buy goods that they consider to be luxury goods/brands (Dubois & Laurent, 1996; Kapferer & Laurent, 2016).

FUTURE RESEARCH DIRECTIONS

From what has been said, it becomes very relevant to consider an alternative approach where the need to empirically explore how consumers are recognized and themselves identify luxury today, after decades of growth in the sector, and what they perceive as new or old luxury brands.

The debate around the notion of luxury consumption suggests a new definition of luxury based on its nature and empowered with symbolism and subjectivity related to the consumer's context.

CONCLUSION

From the literature review, arises the need to make a comparison between the existing components of the new and old luxury brands, in order to understand to what extent they are perceived as different. Thus, the components that effectively distinguish the two concepts are linked to aspects of price, scarcity/rarity, heritage & history and concerns for sustainability. In the new luxury, the components of price scarcity/rarity, heritage & history have a smaller weight compared to the old luxury brands. On the other hand, with regard to sustainability, it appears that it has a greater weight in new luxury brands compared to the old.

However, the nature of mass consumption and new luxury derives from the "intersection of exclusivity and mass consumption" (Kastanakis & Balabanis, 2012, p.1399). This new paradigm of luxury brand consumption requires new approaches to brand management (Nobre & Simões, 2019; Rodrigues & Rodrigues, 2019; Kapferer & Michaut-Denizeau, 2020).

REFERENCES

Alleres, D. (1991). Spécificités et stratégies marketing des différents univers du luxe. *Revue Française du Marketing*, *132*(33), 71–95.

Amaldoss, W., & Jain, S. (2005). Conspicuous Consumption and Sophisticated Thinking. *Management Science*, *51*(10), 1449–1466. doi:10.1287/mnsc.1050.0399

Amatulli, C., & Guido, G. (2011). Determinants of purchasing intentions of fashion luxury goods in the Italian market: A laddering approach. *Journal of Fashion Marketing and Management*, *15*(1), 123–136. doi:10.1108/13612021111112386

Atwal, G., & Williams, A. (2009). Luxury brand marketing— The experience is everything! *Journal of Brand Management, 16*(5-6), 338–346. doi:10.1057/bm.2008.48

Bearden, W. O., & Etzel, M. J. (1982). Reference group influence on product and brand purchase decisions. *The Journal of Consumer Research, 9*(2), 183–194. doi:10.1086/208911

Berthon, P., Pitt, L., Parent, M., & Berthon, J. P. (2009). Aesthetics and ephemerality: Observing and preserving the luxury brand. *California Management Review, 52*(1), 45–66. doi:10.1525/cmr.2009.52.1.45

Bian, Q., & Forsythe, S. (2012). Purchase intention for luxury brands: A cross cultural comparison. *Journal of Business Research, 65*(10), 1443–1451. doi:10.1016/j.jbusres.2011.10.010

Blevis, E., Makice, K., Odom, W., Roedl, D., Beck, C., & Blevis, S. A. (2007). Luxury; New Luxury, Quality; Equality. Sustainable Interaction Design Research Group, School of Informatics, Indiana University at Bloomington. doi:10.1145/1314161.1314188

Brun, A., & Castelli, C. (2013). The nature of luxury: A consumer perspective. *International Journal of Retail & Distribution Management, 41*(11/12), 823–847. doi:10.1108/IJRDM-01-2013-0006

Chattalas, M., & Shukla, P. (2015). Impact of value perceptions on luxury purchase intentions: A developed market comparison. *Luxury Research Journal, 1*(1), 40–57. doi:10.1504/LRJ.2015.069806

Chaudhuri, H. R., Mazumdar, S., & Ghoshal, A. (2011). Conspicuous consumption orientation: Conceptualisation, scale development and validation. *Journal of Consumer Behaviour. An International Research Review, 10*(4), 216–224.

Corbellini, E., & Saviolo, S. (2009). *Managing fashion and luxury companies*. Etas.

Cornell, A. (2002). Cult of luxury: The new opiate of the masses. *Australian Financial Review, 27*(April), 47.

Cristini, H., Kauppinen-Räisänen, H., Barthod-Prothade, M., & Woodside, A. (2017). Toward a general theory of luxury: Advancing from workbench definitions and theoretical transformations. *Journal of Business Research, 70*, 101–107. doi:10.1016/j.jbusres.2016.07.001

De Barnier, V., Falcy, S., & Valette-Florence, P. (2012). Do consumers perceive three levels of luxury? A comparison of accessible, intermediate and inaccessible luxury brands. *Journal of Brand Management, 19*(7), 623–636. doi:10.1057/bm.2012.11

Deloitte. (2017). *Global powers of luxury goods 2017: The new luxury consumer*. Retrieved July 30, 2019, from https://www2.deloitte.com/content/dam/ Deloitte/global/Documents/consumer-industrial-products/gx-cip-globalpowers-luxury-2017.pdf

Dion, D., & Arnould, E. J. (2011). Retail Luxury Strategy: Assembling Charisma through Art and Magic. *Journal of Retailing, 87*(4), 502–520. doi:10.1016/j.jretai.2011.09.001

Dion, D., & Borraz, S. (2017). Managing Status: How luxury brands shape class subjectivities in the service encounter. *Journal of Marketing, 81*(5), 67–85. doi:10.1509/jm.15.0291

Dubois, B., Czellar, S., & Laurent, G. (2005). Consumer Segments Based on Attitudes Toward Luxury: Empirical Evidence from Twenty Countries. *Marketing Letters*, *16*(2), 115–128. doi:10.100711002-005-2172-0

Dubois, B., & Laurent, G. (1996). Le luxe par-delà les frontières: Une etude exploratoire dans douze pays. *Décisions Marketing*, *9*, 35–43. doi:10.7193/DM.009.35.42

Dubois, B., Laurent, G., & Czellar, S. (2001). *Consumer rapport to luxury: Analyzing complex and ambivalent attitudes.* Working Paper 736, HEC School of Management, Jouy-en-Josas.

Eagly, A. H., & Chaiken, S. (1993). *The psychology of attitudes.* Harcourt Brace Jovanovich.

Eastman, J. K., Goldsmith, R. E., & Flynn, L. R. (1999). Status Consumption in Consumer Behaviour: Scale Development and Validation. *Journal of Marketing Theory and Practice*, *7*(3), 41–52. doi:10.1080/10696679.1999.11501839

Elliott, R., & Wattanasuwan, K. (1998). Brand as symbolic resources for the construction of identity. *International Journal of Advertising*, *17*(2), 131–144. doi:10.1080/02650487.1998.11104712

Gil, L. A., Kwon, K. N., Good, L. K., & Johnson, L. W. (2012). Impact of self on attitudes toward luxury brands among teens. *Journal of Business Research*, *65*(10), 1425–1433. doi:10.1016/j.jbusres.2011.10.008

Giovannini, S., Xu, Y., & Thomas, J. (2015). Luxury fashion consumption and Generation Y consumers: Self, brand consciousness, and consumption motivations. *Journal of Fashion Marketing and Management*, *19*(1), 22–40. doi:10.1108/JFMM-08-2013-0096

Godey, B., Pederzoli, D., Aiello, G., Donvito, R., Chan, P., Oh, H., Singh, R., Skorobogatykh, I. I., Tsuchiya, J., & Weitz, B. (2012). Brand and country-of-origin effect on consumers' decision to purchase luxury products. *Journal of Business Research*, *65*(10), 1461–1470. doi:10.1016/j.jbusres.2011.10.012

Granot, E., & Brashear, T. (2008). *From luxury to populence: Inconspicuous consumption as described by female consumers.* Paper presented at the Advances in Consumer Research Volume 35, Duluth, MN.

Granot, E., Russell, L. T. M., & Brashear-Alejandro, T. G. (2013). Populence: Exploring luxury for the masses. *Journal of Marketing Theory and Practice*, *21*(1), 31–44. doi:10.2753/MTP1069-6679210102

Hagtveded, H., & Patrick, V. (2009). The broad embrace of luxury: Hedonic potential as a driver of brand extendibility. *Journal of Consumer Psychology*, *19*(4), 608–619. doi:10.1016/j.jcps.2009.05.007

Han, Y. J., Nunes, J. C., & Dreze, X. (2010). Signaling Status with Luxury Goods: The Role of Brand Prominence. *Journal of Marketing*, *74*(July), 15–30. doi:10.1509/jmkg.74.4.015

Heine, K., & Phan, M. (2011). Trading-up mass-market goods to luxury products. *Australasian Marketing Journal*, *19*(2), 108–114. doi:10.1016/j.ausmj.2011.03.001

Hennigs, N., Wiedmann, K.-P., Behrens, S., & Klarman, C. (2013). Antecedents of luxury brand perception and effects of luxury brand strength. *Journal of Brand Management*, *20*(8), 705–715. doi:10.1057/bm.2013.11

Hennigs, N., Wiedmann, K.-P., & Klarmann, C. (2012). Luxury brands in the digital age: Exclusivity versus ubiquity. *Marketing Review St. Gallen*, *29*(1), 30–35. doi:10.100711621-012-0108-7

Holbrook, M. B., & Hirschman, E. C. (1982). The Experiential aspects of consumption: Consumer fantasies, feelings and fun. *The Journal of Consumer Research*, *9*(2), 132–140. doi:10.1086/208906

Hung, K. P., Huiling Chen, A., Peng, N., Hackley, C., Amy Tiwsakul, R., & Chou, C. L. (2011). Antecedents of luxury brand purchase intention. *Journal of Product and Brand Management*, *20*(6), 457–467. doi:10.1108/10610421111166603

Jackson, T., & Shaw, D. (2009). *Mastering Fashion Marketing*. Palgrave Macmillan. doi:10.1007/978-1-137-09271-7

Kapferer, J.-N. (1998). Why are we seduced by luxury brands? *Journal of Brand Management*, *6*(1), 44–49. doi:10.1057/bm.1998.43

Kapferer, J.-N. (2010). All that glitters is not green: The challenge of sustainable luxury'. *European Business Review*, (November–December), 40–45.

Kapferer, J.-N. (2012). Abundant rarity: The key to luxury growth. *Business Horizons*, *55*(5), 453–462. doi:10.1016/j.bushor.2012.04.002

Kapferer, J. N. (2017). Managing luxury brands. In J. N. Kapferer, J. Kernstock, T. Brexendorf, & S. Powell (Eds.), *Advances in Luxury Brand Management*. Palgrave Macmillan. doi:10.1007/978-3-319-51127-6_11

Kapferer, J.-N., & Bastien, V. (2012). *The Luxury Strategy: Break the Rules of Marketing to Build Luxury Brands*. Kogan Page.

Kapferer, J. N., & Laurent, G. (2016). Where do consumers think luxury begins? A study of perceived minimum price for 21 luxury goods in 7 countries. *Journal of Business Research*, *69*(1), 332–340. doi:10.1016/j.jbusres.2015.08.005

Kapferer, J.-N., & Michaut, A. (2015). Luxury and sustainability: A common future? The match depends on how consumers define luxury. *Luxury Research Journal*, *1*(1), 3–17. doi:10.1504/LRJ.2015.069828

Kapferer, J.-N., & Michaut, A. (2016). Pursuing the Concept of Luxury A cross-country comparison and segmentation of luxury buyers' perception of luxury. *Journal of International Marketing Strategy*, *4*(1), 6–23.

Kapferer, J.-N., & Michaut-Denizeau, A. (2020). Are millennials really more sensitive to sustainable luxury? A cross-generational international comparison of sustainability consciousness when buying luxury. *Journal of Brand Management*, *27*(1), 35–47. doi:10.105741262-019-00165-7

Kapferer, J.-N., & Valette-Florance, P. (2019). How self-success drives luxury demand: An integrated model of luxury growth and country comparisons. *Journal of Business Research*, *102*(September), 273–288. doi:10.1016/j.jbusres.2019.02.002

Kastanakis, M. N., & Balabanis, G. (2012). Between the Mass and the Class: Antecedents of the 'Bandwagon' Luxury Consumption Behavior. *Journal of Business Research*, *65*(10), 1399–1407. doi:10.1016/j.jbusres.2011.10.005

Kauppinen-Räisänen, H., Gummerus, J., von Koskull, C., Finne, A., Helkkula, A., Kowalkowski, C., & Rindell, A. (2014). Am I worth it? Gifting myself with luxury. *Journal of Fashion Marketing and Management, 18*(2), 112–132. doi:10.1108/JFMM-04-2013-0062

Kirmani, A., Sood, S., & Bridges, S. (1999). The Ownership Effect in Consumer Responses to Brand Line Stretches. *Journal of Marketing, 63*(January), 88–101. doi:10.1177/002224299906300107

Knight, D. K., & Kim, E. Y. (2007). Japanese consumers' need for uniqueness: Effects on brand perceptions and purchase intention. *Journal of Fashion Marketing and Management, 11*(2), 270–280. doi:10.1108/13612020710751428

Ko, E., Costello, J. P., & Taylor, C. R. (2019). What is a luxury brand? A new definition and review of the literature. *Journal of Business Research, 99*, 405–413. doi:10.1016/j.jbusres.2017.08.023

Kressman, F., Sirgy, M. J., Herrman, A., Huber, F., Huber, S., & Lee, D.-J. (2006). Direct and indirect effects of self-image congruence on brand loyalty. *Journal of Business Research, 59*(6), 955–964. doi:10.1016/j.jbusres.2006.06.001

Larraufie, A.-F. M., & Kourdoughli, A. (2014). The e-semiotics of luxury. *Journal of Global Fashion Marketing, 5*(3), 197–208. doi:10.1080/20932685.2014.906120

Lipovetsky, G. (2003). *De l'Age du sacré au temps des marques* [From the age of the sacred to the age of the brands]. Gallimard.

Lynn, M. (1991). Scarcity effects on value: A quantitative review of the commodity theory literature. *Psychology and Marketing, 8*(1), 43–57. doi:10.1002/mar.4220080105

Mason, R. (1996). Measuring the demand for status goods: An evaluation of means-end chains and laddering. In F. Hansen (Ed.), *European Advances for Consumer Research* (pp. 78–82).

McKendrick, N. (1984). *The birth of a consumer society: Commercialization of eighteenth century England*. Harper Collins Publishers Ltd.

Michaud, Y. (2003). *Essai sur le triomphe de l'esthétique* [Essay on the triumph of the aesthetic]. Stock.

Mortelmans, D. (2005). Sign values in processes of distinction: The concept of luxury. *Semiotica, 157*(1/4), 497–520. doi:10.1515emi.2005.2005.157.1-4.497

Nobre, H., & Simões, C. (2019). NewLux Brand Relationship Scale: Capturing the scope of mass-consumed luxury brand relationships. *Journal of Business Research, 102*, 328–338. doi:10.1016/j.jbusres.2019.01.047

Nueno, J. L., & Quelch, J. (1998). The mass marketing of luxury. *Business Horizons, 41*(6), 61–68. doi:10.1016/S0007-6813(98)90023-4

O'Cass, A., & Frost, H. (2002). Status brands: Examining the effects of non-product related brand associations on status and conspicuous consumption. *Journal of Product and Brand Management, 11*(2), 67–88. doi:10.1108/10610420210423455

Okonkwo, U. (2009). The luxury brand strategy challenge. *Journal of Brand Management, 16*(5), 287–289. doi:10.1057/bm.2008.53

Olson, E. (1999). Bottled Water: Pure Drink or Pure Hype? Natural Resources Defense Council (NRDC).

Ordabayeva, N., & Chandon, P. (2011). Getting Ahead of the Joneses: When Equality Increases Conspicuous Consumption Among Bottom-Tier Consumers. *The Journal of Consumer Research, 38*(1), 27–41. doi:10.1086/658165

Phau, I., & Prendergast, G. (2000). Consuming luxury brands: The relevance of the "rarity principle. *Journal of Brand Management, 8*(2), 122–138. doi:10.1057/palgrave.bm.2540013

Rodrigues, C., & Rodrigues, P. (2019). Brand Love Matters to Millenials: The relevance of mystery, sensuality and intimacy to neo-luxury brands. *Journal of Product and Brand Management, 28*(7), 830–848. doi:10.1108/JPBM-04-2018-1842

Shukla, P. (2012). The influence of value perceptions on luxury purchase intentions in developed and emerging markets. *International Marketing Review, 29*(6), 574–596. doi:10.1108/02651331211277955

Shukla, P., & Purani, K. (2012). Comparing the importance of luxury value perceptions in cross-national contexts. *Journal of Business Research, 65*(10), 1417–1424. doi:10.1016/j.jbusres.2011.10.007

Silverstein, M., & Fiske, N. (2005). *Trading up: Why consumers want new luxury goods, and how companies create them* (rev. ed.). Portfolio.

Silverstein, M. J., & Fiske, N. (2003). Luxury for themasses. *Harvard Business Review, 81*, 48–57.

Smith, J. B., & Colgate, M. (2007). Customer value creation: A practical framework. *Journal of Marketing Theory and Practice, 15*(1), 7–23. doi:10.2753/MTP1069-6679150101

Steenkamp, J. B., Batra, R., & Alden, D. (2003). How perceived brand globalness creates brand value. *Journal of International Business Studies, 34*(1), 53–65. doi:10.1057/palgrave.jibs.8400002

Stokburger-Sauer, N., Ratneshwar, S., & Sen, S. (2012). Drivers of consumer–brand identification. *International Journal of Research in Marketing, 29*(4), 406–418. doi:10.1016/j.ijresmar.2012.06.001

Sun, G., Wang, W., Cheng, Z., Li, J., & Chen, J. (2017). The intermediate linkage between materialism and luxury consumption: Evidence from the emerging market of China. *Social Indicators Research, 132*(1), 475–487. doi:10.100711205-016-1273-x

Sweeney, J. C., & Soutar, G. N. (2001). Consumer perceived value: The development of a multiple item scale. *Journal of Retailing, 77*(2), 203–220. doi:10.1016/S0022-4359(01)00041-0

Thomas, D. (2007). *Deluxe: How Luxury Lost Its Luster*. The Penguin Press.

Tian, K. T., Bearden, W. O., & Hunter, G. L. (2001). Consumers' need for uniqueness: Scale development and validation. *The Journal of Consumer Research, 28*(1), 50–66. doi:10.1086/321947

Truong, Y. (2010). Personal aspirations and the consumption of luxury goods. *International Journal of Market Research, 52*(5), 653–671. doi:10.2501/S1470785310201521

Truong, Y., & McColl, R. (2011). Intrinsic motivations, self-esteem, and luxury goods consumption. *Journal of Retailing and Consumer Services, 18*(6), 555–561. doi:10.1016/j.jretconser.2011.08.004

Truong, Y., McColl, R., & Kitchen, P. J. (2009). New luxury brand positioning and the emergence of masstige brands. *Journal of Brand Management, 16*(5/6), 375–382. doi:10.1057/bm.2009.1

Truong, Y., Simmons, G., McColl, R., & Kitchen, P. J. (2008). Status and conspicuousness – are they related? Strategic marketing implications for luxury brands. *Journal of Strategic Marketing, 16*(3), 189–203. doi:10.1080/09652540802117124

Tsai, S.-P. (2005). Impact of personal orientation on luxury-brand purchase value. *International Journal of Market Research, 47*(4), 429–454. doi:10.1177/147078530504700403

Turunen, L. L. M., & Laaksonen, P. (2011). Diffusing the boundaries between luxury and counterfeits. *Journal of Product and Brand Management, 20*(6), 468–474. doi:10.1108/10610421111166612

Tynan, C., McKechnie, S., & Chhuon, C. (2010). Co-creating value for luxury brands. *Journal of Business Research, 63*(11), 1156–1163. doi:10.1016/j.jbusres.2009.10.012

Veblen, T. (1994). *The collected works of Thorstein Veblen*. Routledge/Thoemms Press.

Verhallen, T. M. (1982). Scarcity and consumer choice behavior. *Journal of Economic Psychology, 2*(4), 299–321. doi:10.1016/0167-4870(82)90034-4

Vickers, J. S., & Renand, F. (2003). The marketing of luxury brands: An exploratory study – three conceptual dimensions. *The Marketing Review, 3*(4), 459–479. doi:10.1362/146934703771910071

Vigneron, F., & Johnson, L. (2004). Measuring perceptions of brand luxury. *Journal of Brand Management, 11*(6), 484–506. doi:10.1057/palgrave.bm.2540194

Wiedmann, K.-P., Hennigs, N., & Siebels, A. (2009). Value-based segmentation of luxury consumption behavior. *Psychology and Marketing, 26*(7), 625–651. doi:10.1002/mar.20292

Wilcox, K., Kim, H. M., & Sen, S. (2009). Why do consumers buy counterfeit luxury brands? *JMR, Journal of Marketing Research, 46*(2), 247–259. doi:10.1509/jmkr.46.2.247

Wong, N. Y., & Ahuvia, A. C. (1998). Personal Taste and Family Face: Luxury Consumption in Confucian and Western Societies. *Psychology and Marketing, 15*(August), 423–441. doi:10.1002/(SICI)1520-6793(199808)15:5<423::AID-MAR2>3.0.CO;2-9

Yeoman, I. (2011). The changing behaviours of luxury consumption. *Journal of Revenue and Pricing Management, 10*(1), 47–50. doi:10.1057/rpm.2010.43

Yeoman, I., & McMahon-Beattie, U. (2005). Luxury Markets and Premium Pricing. *Journal of Revenue and Pricing Management, 4*(4), 319–328. doi:10.1057/palgrave.rpm.5170155

Young, W., Hwang, K., McDonald, S., & Oates, C. J. (2010). Sustainable consumption: Green consumer behavior when purchasing products. *Sustainable Development, 18*(1), 20–31.

KEY TERMS AND DEFINITIONS

New Luxury Brands: Affordable luxury goods that have high levels of quality, good taste and that represent status for those who use them.

Old Luxury Brands: Brands that have characteristics such as premium quality, heritage of craftsmanship, recognized style, premium price, unique character, exclusives and a global reputation, strongly linked to the status, value and images that convey who owns them.

Chapter 4
Inconspicuous Luxury Consumption:
Another Form of New Luxury?

Aslı Tolunay Kuşçu
https://orcid.org/0000-0003-3856-8518
Yeditepe University, Turkey

ABSTRACT

With luxury consumption still growing fast despite various challenges such as increasing competition, rise in rental luxuries, and in counterfeits, luxury brands are challenged with an additional and complex development: consumers' interest towards inconspicuous luxury products. Being one of the major characteristics of luxury goods, conspicuousness is losing its value among some luxury shoppers necessitating a new definition for luxury and a new value proposition for luxury brands. This chapter initially provides a review on luxury and on the different motivations that determine luxury consumption. Next, socio-economic changes that trigger the shift from conspicuous to inconspicuous luxury consumption is examined briefly. And finally, a discussion on why inconspicuous consumption is valued by consumers is followed by a theoretical framework on the motivations for inconspicuous luxury brand usage. The chapter then concludes with theoretical and managerial implications.

INTRODUCTION

Even though many major economies are going through tough times and consumer spending is significantly affected worldwide (Bhattarai, 2019), luxury consumption is still steadily growing (Bain & Company, 2019). The wealthy upper segment buys luxury conspicuous goods to be disassociated from the middle class, whilst middle class consumers buy the same products to be associated with the wealthy upper class, creating a luxury market that grew to 1.2 trillion Euros worldwide in 2018 by an increase of 5% and is further expected to grow by 3-5% each year (Bain & Company, 2019). As can be seen by the numbers, the future seems to be promising for most luxury brands; yet they are still challenged by several factors. Apart from the economic challenges and increasing competition, there are other emerging issues such

DOI: 10.4018/978-1-7998-4369-6.ch004

Copyright © 2021, IGI Global. Copying or distributing in print or electronic forms without written permission of IGI Global is prohibited.

as rise in counterfeits (Bian, Wang, Smith, & Yannopoulou, 2016) and in liquid consumption in the form of rental luxuries (Eckhardt & Bardhi, 2019) as well as changing consumer demands and increase in individualisation, that are threatening the sector and call for different strategies to keep up with the changing market. These lead luxury brands to use democratization strategy (Silverstein & Fiske, 2003), to add experiential and customized luxury to their portfolios (Atwal & Williams, 2009; Chatikavanij, 2019) or to develop omni-channel strategies similar to mass-market brands. Particularly, with the rise of democratization, a new form of luxury emerged, which is referred as "new luxury" that targets masses through affordability and reachability (Silverstein & Fiske, 2003). Nonetheless, luxury brands employing this strategy face dilution challenges, as luxury for long has been associated with visibly status signaling goods, in other words with conspicuousness, which a mass consumer cannot effort (Veblen, 1899). According to Phau and Predergast (2000) "luxury brands evoke exclusivity, have a well-known identity, enjoy high brand awareness and perceived quality" (p.123). Therefore, luxury consumption is linked with characteristics such as prestige (Vigneron & Johnson, 1999), rarity (Phau & Predergast, 2000) and with being of high price and quality (Kapferer, 1997), but mostly with being high in conspicuousness to fuel awareness and associations (Berthon, Pitt, Parent, & Berthon, 2009; Truong, Simmons, McColl, & Kitchen, 2008). As a result, being available to a larger group rather than to the privileged elite and therefore not signaling wealth and exclusivity as it used to be, blur the boundaries of luxury (Kapferer & Laurent, 2016). According to Dubois and Laurent (1995) "other's luxury" may not only trigger negative feelings; but use of counterfeits and democratized luxury by the masses also signals unwanted identification to some regular luxury consumers. In that sense, a rising number of consumers, who are referred as "the insiders" by Eckhard, Belk, and Wilson (2015), choose to enjoy luxury in a certain unrecognizable way and purposely stay away from conspicuous products. These consumers apparently still choose high quality luxury products to create and signify their selves but follow a more private and "less is more" approach (Berger & Ward, 2010; Eckhardt et al., 2015; Shao, Grace, & Ross, 2019a).

Generating a new way of competitive advantage over other luxury brands, inconspicuous consumption, which is defined as the use of products with subtle signs, that are only appreciated by a small group of individuals rather than the mass (Berger & Ward, 2010) is thus rising as a trend not only in the developed as well as in the developing countries (Shukla, 2012) challenging the traditional view of conspicuousness as a value being strongly associated with luxury (Makkar & Yap, 2018a; Mylan, 2019; Wiedmann, Hennigs, & Siebels, 2009). Although some established luxury brands such as Louis Vuitton or Bottega Veneta targeting "the insiders" are producing product lines without any logo or visible signs yet providing the same up-to-date fashion and handmade quality that is only recognizable by the ones who are in the "know", others are faced with a strategic crossroads on whether to embrace this new paradigm and to rebrand accordingly or to keep on investing in the conspicuousness, whilst being left with little academic research and practical knowledge on this emerging phenomenon (Eckhardt et al., 2015).

Against this background, inconspicuous luxury consumption deserves more academic and practical attention. Initially, as a growing consumer segment that deviates from the majority due to social and personal reasons, understanding inconspicuous luxury consumers may provide competitive advantage to luxury brands in correlating with the changing market with respect to how these new cohort of consumers perceive luxury, what values they associate with and what they expect from luxury brands. Although as stated in Ko, Costello, & Taylor (2019) that understanding individual differences between luxury consumers is important, a general understanding of inconspicuous luxury consumers will aid luxury brands to decide on their upcoming competitive strategy and positioning. Further, from a theoretical standpoint, inconspicuous luxury consumption operates against the rules and beyond the boundaries of luxury consumption and challenges the prior definitions provided for luxury consumption emphasizing the use of luxury as a sign of wealth and superiority. Acknowledging inconspicuousness as part of luxury consumption may require a broadening of the luxury concept to include invisibility over visibility, snob effect over bandwagon influence on luxury and to examine possible relationships between values associated with inconspicuous luxury and consumers' affectual and behavioral responses to luxury.

With this aim, this chapter focuses on the underlying reasons of inconspicuous luxury consumption and aims to elaborate the definitional and perceptual changes of luxury. Following a review on previous definitions of luxury and on the different motivations that determine luxury consumption, a theoretical framework on the motivations for inconspicuous luxury brand use is suggested. The chapter then concludes with theoretical and managerial implications.

BACKGROUND

Characteristics Associated with Traditional Luxury

Luxury is among the major perceived distinctive aspects of any product or service within its category shaping consumer choice and behaviour (Dubois & Duquesne, 1993; Kapferer, 1997). Luxury as a concept is highly abstract, changes from one individual to the other (Vigneron & Johnson, 1999) and is further prone to changes due to culture and time (Vickers & Renand, 2003; Yeoman, 2011). Therefore, within literature the definition of luxury is inconsistent, and the conceptual boundaries of luxury are also subjective (Godey et al., 2012) and not well defined (Miller & Mills, 2012). Although there have been various different definitions of luxury identified in the literature (Ko et al., 2019) and yet no consensus arrived among scholars (Vickers & Renand, 2003), as the term comes from the Latin word "luxus" which stands for "excess and extravagance", luxury is mostly associated within consumers' minds with being self-indulgent and even in some cases as a "sin" (Berthon et al., 2009). Among the initial definitions, Kapferer (1997) refers to luxury as "art applied to functional items" (p.253). According to him, luxury offers pleasure and is "enlightening", which are the most typical aspects of luxury over non-luxury. Most of the definitions provided in literature follow his way of thinking and talk about the aesthetics of luxury products along with the quality over the others in the market, which is not only expected as well as is perceived by the consumers in most of the cases (Ko et al., 2019).

Perception of luxury is subjective, personally and culturally defined, creating several diverse multi-dimensional motivations and attached benefits/values for luxury consumers (Kemp, 1998; Tsai, Yang & Liu, 2013; Vickers & Renand, 2003). Therefore, as expected, Hudders, Pandelaere, and Vyncke (2013) find three distinct segments of luxury consumers, each ascribing a different meaning to luxury. One group is just oriented towards the aesthetics and functional utility, whilst another values the expressiveness of luxury, with the third group of consumers putting emphasis on both. However, there are some common themes associated with luxury consumption and discussed in literature which consistently articulates that consumers' motives for luxury brand purchase are completely different than mass brands (Ko et al., 2019). For instance, Vigneron and Johnson (2004) identify two personal (hedonic and extended self) and three non-personal (conspicuousness, uniqueness and quality) benefits that are perceived by the luxury consumers that further justify premium pricing for luxury products. In this vein of research, although some scholars believe that luxury items do not possess any utilitarian value (Hagtvedt & Patrick, 2008), not only functional benefits such as quality (Berthon et al., 2009) but also experiential and emotional ones such as pleasure, prestige and status (Vigneron & Johnson, 1999) have been associated with luxury by many (Vickers & Renald, 2003). According to Berthon et al. (2009), luxury consumption entails values that relate to the material (objective), the individual (subjective) and the collective environment (social). Hence, luxury products are believed to offer not only superior functional utility because of the high-quality, unique handiwork and raw materials used in their manufacture; but they are also social representations of the identity for self-expression and are regarded by many as symbols for superiority within the society. Conspicuousness, in other words displaying highly visible and easily identifiable symbols related with the brand, used by the individuals to expose their wealth, success and prestige to the society (Shukla, 2008; Trigg, 2001) and obtain social status (Grace & Griffin, 2009; Veblen, 1899) is thus a key factor associated with luxury brands (Dubois et al., 2001; Shukla, 2008; Vigneron & Johnson, 2004). Thereafter, as stated in Truong et al. (2008) "conspicuous consumption is more oriented toward the evident display of expensive possessions" (p. 190) and is strictly related with why consumers choose luxury over mass brands (Wiedmann et al., 2009). Within this perspective social encounters and interactions with others interdependently provide meaning to the self, society and possessions. Hence, products or brands consumers possess are major contributors to and reflections of their identities and have important implications to their self-concepts (Escalas & Bettman 2003). People see themselves through the eyes of others and form self-concepts via the reactions of others based on these meanings. Consumers by using specific brands in "symbolic, iconic, or indexical ways" (Schembri, Merrilees, & Kristiansen, 2010, p.634) not only gain self-enhancement (Grubb & Grathwahl 1967), but also approval, acceptance, a superior prestigious image (Keller, 2009) and status within the social environment, which significantly affect a person's social behavior (Jackson & Smith 1999). As discussed by Elliott and Wattanasuwan (1998) and by Firat and Venkatesh (1995), the individual in the postmodern society is struggling to construct and maintain a self-concept through a rapidly changing, highly fragmented environment. The age of postmodernism is in fact the age of symbols, where the consumers are no longer loyal to brands but to images and symbols, especially the ones that they produce while they consume and are not just after to satisfy some need but after to construct themselves (Firat & Venkatesh 1995). Hence, brands that are used, are treated as extensions of the self (Belk, 1988) and as stated by Dittmar (1992, p. 2) "by buying goods, we magically acquire a different persona."

Heine (2012), states that "luxury brands are regarded as images in the minds of consumers that comprise associations about a high level of price, quality, aesthetics, rarity, extraordinariness and a high degree of non-functional associations" (p.62). Here, the image associated with the brand and message transferred through the use of it matters more rather than the functional characteristics and features (Han, Nunes, & Drèze, 2010). As asserted by Dubois and Duquesne (1993), "motivated by a desire to impress others, with the ability to pay particularly high prices, this form of consumption is primarily concerned with the ostentatious display of wealth" (p. 43). Within this perspective, owning and publicly displaying a Chanel bag with a visible logo or an iconic Chanel bag that everybody can easily recognize offer apart from the functional benefits (e.g. being able to carry items in the bag and durability of the product), a hedonic fulfillment through the reflection of prestige, uniqueness and direct and indirect associations related with the brand (e.g. being able to afford a Chanel bag). Those associations are shaped and built within the social environment and being worth for a luxury product, through the visible and identifiable symbols of the brand, further in return symbolizes the social status of the person even to the most irrelevant people (Kastanakis & Balabanis, 2012). They altogether justify a higher price, which is another main feature of luxury identified within literature (Ko et al., 2019).

Accordingly, not all consumers are believed to have access to luxury, which in return enhances the value attached to it, specifically in a way that a deeper connection is created within the ones who can afford and enjoy it (Ko et al., 2019). Luxury is therefore also associated with being rare, authentic and exclusive (Beverland, 2006; Cornell, 2002; Phau & Prendergast, 2000; Vickers & Renand, 2003), yet displaying higher brand awareness (Phau & Prendergast, 2000). Wiedmann et al. (2009) further extend these contentions and differentiate between four values, namely social, functional, individual and financial, which are further divided into sub-values such as conspicuousness, prestige, usability, quality, uniqueness, self-identity, hedonic, materialistic and price. As socioeconomic and technological conditions change though, the meaning and understanding of luxury is shaped towards an overall image transfer conveyed most significantly through the experiential benefits offered by the brands, yet the overall value proposition offered to the luxury consumer remains mainly intact (Cristini, Kauppinen-Räisänen, Barthod-Prothade, & Woodside, 2016). In a recent article, Seo and Buchanan-Oliver (2019) identify five distinctive ways of luxury consumption. According to the authors, luxury is used by the consumers as an investment and a tool that assist them to run away from the reality, to be socially connected and identified as an affluent individual and to portray their social status and construct themselves. As a result, Ko et al. (2019) define a luxury brand as "a branded product or service that consumers perceive to: (1) be high quality; (2) offer authentic value via desired benefits, whether functional or emotional; (3) have a prestigious image within the market built on qualities such as artisanship, craftsmanship, or service quality; (4) be worthy of commanding a premium price; and (5) be capable of inspiring a deep connection, or resonance, with the consumer" (p. 2.)

FROM CONSPICIOUS TO INCONSPICIOUS LUXURY

Shifts in Luxury Consumption

Luxury brands, as mentioned above, in general are regarded as branded goods with high quality and prestigious image, displaying both tangible and intangible benefits to their premium paying consumers (Wiedmann et al., 2009) with the intangible and symbolic benefits outweighing tangible ones (Cristini et al., 2016; Nia & Zaichkowsky, 2000; Nueno & Quelch, 1998; Vickers & Renand, 2003). Nonetheless, with the emergence of strategies such as democratization, a new experiential as well as personally and symbolically relevant yet more affordable luxury emerged, which is referred as "new luxury" (Silverstein & Fiske, 2003; Truong et al., 2009). New luxury is defined as "products and services that possess higher levels of quality, taste, and aspiration than other goods in the category but are not so expensive as to be out of reach" (Silverstein & Fiske, 2003, p.1). Many luxury and mass brands thus employ democratization or premiumization strategy to expand to bigger markets by offering products or services that appeal to the luxury-savvy and mostly younger mass, who previously did not afford luxury (e.g. Rolex watches with affordable prices; luxury brand collaborations with H&M; more affordable chocolates by Godiva). Hence, this perspective acknowledges all aspects of luxury (apart from higher prices and low availability) previously identified by various scholars, specifically the ones that are symbolic and provide social advancement through conspicuousness. With the emergence of this new form, a bandwagon effect defined as "the extent to which the demand for a commodity is increased due to the fact that others are also consuming the same commodity" (Leibenstein, 1950, p.189) occurred such that additional product categories started to be linked with luxury, enabling the middle-class experience a prosperous and luxurious lifestyle in a way that the society was not used to before. In contrast to the conventional understanding of the "old luxury", the "new luxury" is not distant from the mass; on the contrary, it is widely inclusive and accessible, which for some "real luxury buyers" dilutes the meaning of luxury as a signal for prestige and uniqueness (Ferraro, Kirmani & Matherly, 2013; Roper,Caruana, Medway, & Murphy, 2013).

Further, counterfeit consumption, which is buying products that resemble luxury goods but lack the quality, performance and craftsmanship, is gaining impetus as can be seen by the world trade and EU import numbers in 2016 (3.3% worldwide and 6.8% of the EU trade from third world countries) compared to the numbers in 2013 (2.5% and 5% respectively) (OECD/EUIPO, 2019). Underlying reasons and motives for consumers' interest in counterfeit products are again rooted in consumers' demand for luxury (Hoe, Hogg, & Hart, 2003; Wilcox, Kim, & Sen, 2009). Studies find that consumers, who want to enjoy specifically social and symbolic benefits of luxury, but are not interested in the tangible ones and not willing to or cannot pay the price premium, turn to counterfeits instead (Bian & Veloutsou, 2007; Bian, Wang, Smith, & Yannopoulou, 2016; Sharma & Chan, 2017). With the rise in counterfeit products, which are in some cases higher in circulation than the genuine product (e.g. Louis Vuitton bags or Alexander Mcqueen sneakers), counterfeit products have become a major problem for luxury brands affecting their reputation and consumers' commitment to luxury (Wilke & Zaichkowsky, 1999).

Another important development is the rise of liquid consumption, where specifically luxury products can be either barrowed or let again due to their power of their symbolism. Represented by online companies such as "Renttherunway", "Bagtropolis" or "Bagromance", with this new form of "ownership", that revolves around visible signs of luxury, social meanings and hedonic benefits constructed around luxury are cracking. Motivated by the social-adjustive and value-expressive function of the luxury (Wilcox et al., 2009), this type of fluid ownership leads to the emergence of a confusion in the meaning of luxury within a particular segment's minds (Kapferer, 2010) and calls for a different form of luxury to satisfy those consumers, who whilst still being involved in luxurious superior quality consumption do not want to be associated with the mass and are therefore increasingly interested in the consumption of inconspicuous luxury (Eckhardt et al., 2015; Han et al., 2010; Wu, Luo, Schroeder, & Borgerson, 2017).

Inconspicuous Luxury

Contrary to conspicuous consumption, which is pushed as a normative way of consumption and is used to show affluence and to gain higher status within society through the purchase and use of visibly lavish items (Kastanakis and Balabanis, 2012), according to Shove and Warde (2002), inconspicuous consumption is "a realm ignored by consumer culture that are enthralled by the significance of immediate visual clues to social meaning" (p. 247). Although, Thomsen, Holmqvisk, von Wallpach, Hemetsberger, and Belk (2020) add that it is the opposite to product-focused traditional luxury that involves consumption of unconventional luxury products with no social clue, Berger and Ward (2010) state that inconspicuous consumption is "the use of subtle signals that are only observable to people with the requisite knowledge to decode their meaning" (p. 559), while those signs remain unrecognized by the mainstream (Eckhardt et al., 2015). In other words, what differentiates inconspicuously luxurious products from the conspicuous ones in the eyes of a certain consumer group is some hidden yet sophisticated and appealing characteristics such as the leather of a Loewe or Mansur Gavriel bag or the back flopping of a Jacquemus hat, rather than the usual, highly visible and easily identifiable ones such as monograms on Louis Vuitton bags, large metallic buckles on Gucci belts or high platforms of Balenciaga sneakers. Figure 1 provides visual examples of inconspicuous versus conspicuous luxury products.

Figure 1. Examples of inconspicuous vs conspicuous luxury products

Motivated by the snob effect defined by Leibenstein (1950, p. 189) as "the extent to which the demand for a consumer's good is decreased owing to the fact that others are also consuming the same commodity", inconspicuous consumers are therefore interested in qualities such as heritage, rarity, authenticity, functionality, quality and exclusivity offered by luxury products and services (Makkar & Yap, 2018b). Yet, they don't gain status through the realization of luxury by others, as they already possess a status within the society without the brand prominence (Han et al.,2010). Charles, Hurst, and Roussanov (2007) find supporting evidence that individuals with higher income incline towards inconspicuous consumption, whilst low-income individuals are discovered to purchase luxury more extravagantly. In fact, Berger and Ward (2010) and Carbajal, Hall and Li (2016) discuss that perceived inconspicuousness value increases when the luxury product's price rises. Nevertheless, Wu et al. (2017) warn from generalizations with respect to the inconspicuous luxury shoppers and suggest that even though they may prefer inconspicuous luxury, the main motivation may vary. Eckhardt et al. (2015) refer to those well-luxury-informed individuals, who can easily recognize a Gucci or Burberry bag even though it's made of black nylon rather than their usual checked or colored canvas material, as "the insiders" because they are part of a group bonded together with an unspoken and unseen link and are most likely more in the know of luxury than the average mass consumer. As mentioned by Han et al. (2010) "wealthy consumers low in need for status want to associate with their own kind and pay a premium for quiet goods only they can recognize" (p. 15), which in fact may run counter to the conspicuousness and extended-self benefits associated with luxury. As a result, inconspicuous luxury consumers are believed to be more interested in other benefits of luxury. In other words, "the relationship between brands and conspicuousness is weakening" (Eckhardt et al., 2015, p. 808).

Motivations for Inconspicuous Luxury Consumption

Existing yet scant qualitative research on inconspicuous luxury consumption and consumers has identified some motivations and mechanisms. Specifically, the relationship between inconspicuous luxury usage and identity deserves attention for two reasons. First, this link has been extensively discussed in previous conspicuous luxury literature with the contention that conspicuousness is mainly motivated with identity construction and representation (Gurzki & Woisetschläger, 2016). Second, although inconspicuous luxury consumption may seem to contradict what is known about luxury consumption, there is still a link in a socially constructed symbolic way.

Inconspicuous Luxury and Identity

Most of luxury consumption is believed to be directed towards the aim of impression management, in other words self-presentation (Goffman, 1959) or identity management, which "refers to the process by which individuals attempt to control the impressions others form of them" (Leary & Kowalski, 1990, p. 34) and self-construction, which refers to the identity development and presentation based on one's current and ideal self-perception and desired and undesired images (Baumeister & Hutton, 1987; Leary & Kowalski, 1990). Leary and Kowalski (1990) define impression management as a process with two components and distinguish between impression motivation and impression construction, with the former being motivated by the desired goals and the difference between the current and desired image and the latter being a development of strategy based on the evaluation of the current and anticipated states of the self, identity and image. Self-presentation is a very recent terminology that has entered the social psychology research arena within the last three decades and many scholars use it interchangeably with impression management, whereas others point out differences between them (Leary & Kowalski, 1990). Nevertheless, in both cases it is regarded as a goal-directed activity (Schlenker, 2012). Individuals are believed to manage their impressions with the motivation that they will gain a more favorable and rewarding identity within their social environment, develop friendships and get financial and/or psychological benefits in return. Against this background, some scholars believe that impression management activities are conscious manipulations designed to impress an audience (Leary & Kowalski, 1990; Schlenker, Britt, & Pennington, 1996). Nonetheless, Schlenker (2012) suggests that it is beyond conscious evaluations and is in fact autonomous and involuntary. This means that individuals do not always plan the activities beforehand but lean towards gains automatically and naturally. Therefore, within this perspective individuals monitor their socially-reflected image regularly and manage their reflections within their social environment through their acts and/or consumption behaviors. Hence, self-presentation activities are usually designed in a way to create and signal a "better or polished self", to maximize the return, as well as to overcome doubts about oneself (Schlenker, 2012). Self-presentation is therefore different from self-expression (Schlenker, 2012). Within self-expression individuals are reflecting themselves as they are in their authentic way. Whereas, self-presentation is inauthentic, depending on the environment and being based on the reactions of others. Further, Tice, Butler, Muraven and Stillwell (1995) suggest that individuals modify some parts of their impression management activities based on the characteristics of the ones they interact with, such as gender, social tie or social status. Hence, identity management is a social phenomenon as the identity is. The main motivation behind self-presentation is therefore self-enhancement (Leary & Baumeister, 2000) and both social comparison theory (Festinger, 1954) or social identity theory (Tajfel, 1981) suggest that people strive to attain a desirable place within the society and want to improve their current state and climb the social ladder. Hence, individuals make choices and choose brands that would make them construct a more "successful" and "suitable" perceived identity in their social settings and obey the ones that do not.

In the context of inconspicuous luxury, though some scholars such as Ting, Goh, and Isa (2018) find no value expressiveness in inconspicuous consumption, the social status is no longer defined by the visibility and acknowledgement of the luxury by the mass (Eckhardt et al., 2015), rather according to Wu et al. (2017) consumers by using discreet signs of luxury are reflecting a privately imagined and owned self-image or social identity. As a matter of fact, both extrinsically and intrinsically motivated consumers choose subtle signs on luxury (Shao et al., 2019a), whilst extrinsically motivated in other words socially motivated ones show more inclination towards both subtle and visible signs of luxury (Shao, Grace, & Ross, 2019b), supporting Hudders et al. (2013) in their finding of a group of inner-oriented luxury.

In addition, as outlined by Wu et al. (2017), specifically young consumers are also motivated by inconspicuousness as they fancy an imaginary lifestyle of a certain group and want to live up to that identity. By acquiring inconspicuous luxuries, that are owned only by the elite, they enhance themselves. This further generates a feeling of self-reward or self-gratification (Hume & Mills, 2013) but also satisfies their need to be unique. Either case, they either enhance or defend their own image and identity that is referred as emotional self-defense, emotional social-defense and emotional self-enhancement by Makkar and Yap (2018a). Emotional defense (self or social) occurs when the individual does not want to show off but still would like to stay true to his/her own identity, whereas self-enhancement through inconspicuousness is gained by knowing that it appeals only to a small audience (Makkar & Yap, 2018b). As a result, although some inconspicuous luxury consumers are excluding themselves from the young, luxury-enthusiastic masstige or democratized luxury consumers (Feltovich, Harbaugh, & To, 2002; Han et al., 2010, Berger & Ward, 2010), they are still motivated to "signal the self to desirable others" (Makkar & Yap, 2018a, p. 134) and to communicate and enhance their self-image; but this time through differentiation (Hume & Mills, 2013; Wu et al., 2017). Berger and Health (2008) state that individuals may want to differentiate themselves from others due to high resemblance that may cause misidentification. As the number of people purchasing luxury is increasing, this "elite" group gets irritated and would like to differentiate themselves as much as possible, whilst still enjoying the superior functional benefits provided by the luxuries and be associated with a certain group that can understand the hidden value (Han, Nunes, & Drèze, 2010; Zhang, 2019). For the more mature and classical consumers it may be reflected in the form of purchasing Victoria Beckham clothes, Patek Philippe watches or Bottega Veneta bags, where for the younger and fashion-oriented audiences the interest may be directed towards Off-White products such as the ones depicted in Figure 2. Nevertheless, this effect is specifically evident in the ones that are intrinsically motivated and value uniqueness in their choices (Shao et al., 2019b).

Additional Motivations of Inconspicuous Luxury

Berger and Ward (2010) assert that through avoiding obvious luxury signals and preferring unrecognizable subtle signs, consumers are hiding behind luxuries and staying unrecognized by the group they want to dissociate themselves from while still reflecting their social identities, that only a small group with "domain-specific social capital" can recognize. In other words, motivated by emotional defense (Makkar

Figure 2. Luxury brands positioned on inconspicuousness

Victoria Beckham Dress Off-White Backpack Bottega Veneta Bag Patek Philippe Watch

& Yap, 2018b), only the ones that are knowledgeable about this luxury brand would know that they have it. On top of differentiation and group membership, this approach further helps wealthy consumers to feel self-gratified and pleased with themselves (Hume & Mills, 2013). Being able to experience the superior benefits of luxury products and services without showing off to the public therefore provides self-indulgence. Hence, this perspective entails that inconspicuousness to some extent replaces the role previously served by conspicuousness. Put differently, contrary to the past, where visible signs were signaling luxury benefits to the society, now invisible signals provide the same result. Yet, this time it is within a certain small group of individuals privileged with money and social capital.

While some are motivated with the aforementioned individual and social benefits, some value inconspicuousness as it does not trigger any negative feelings such as anger or envy within the jealous mass (Wu et al., 2017). In fact, an investigation on inconspicuous consumption reveals that this was case in China during the Cultural Revolution in the 60's, experienced not only in terms of fashion but also in the fields of arts and entertainment (Zhang, 2019). Similarly, Abalkhail (2020) shows that Saudi Arabians are also choosing less subtle luxuries due to the outburst that can be caused by others because of the religion. Eventually, some luxury consumers hide behind high fashion luxury products that resemble mass products in the "luxury-uneducated" eye but diverge distinctively from the mass and from each other in the "insider" point of view. With this strategy they avoid all negativity that may arise in the public.

Overall Motivational Drivers of Inconspicuous Luxury Consumption

As outlined in the above discussion, the motivational drivers of inconspicuous consumption are depicted below in Figure 3. In general, it can be suggested that consumers are either personally or socially motivated for inconspicuous luxury consumption and are therefore looking for ways (1) to enhance themselves, (2) to socially reflect their identity and differentiate themselves from the others, (3) to personally feel better, (4) avoid envy and (5) to experience functional and aesthetic luxury (Berger & Ward, 2010; Makkar & Yap, 2018a; Makkar & Yap, 2018b; Wu et al., 2017). Self-enhancement, self-gratification and functional gratification are related with the individual, whereas self-presentation, differentiation and willingness to remain unrecognized and avoid negative reactions are socially constructed.

Figure 3. Motivational Drivers of Inconspicuous Luxury Consumption

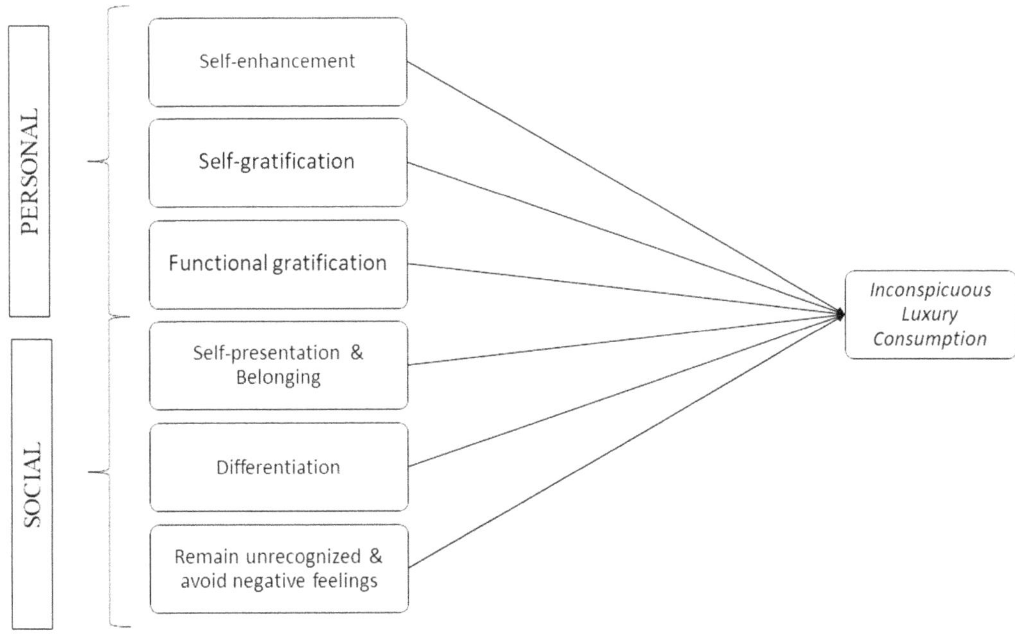

RECOMMENDATIONS FOR LUXURY BRANDS

From a practical perspective, understanding changes within consumer culture and making necessary adjustments are inevitable to survive in the competitive luxury industry. One segment that has emerged recently and stayed mainly invisible is formed by inconspicuous luxury consumers. Even though luxury branding is still growing and the number of consumers who want to show off with luxury is believed to be still expanding, recent research finds that the main motivation for luxury consumption is not status seeking (Kastanakis & Balabanis, 2014). As discussed in Eckhardt and Bardhi (2019), the rules of social status development and transfer are changing, creating new ways for consumers to signal wealth and status. Obviously, this understanding requires a dramatic shift with respect to luxury brand management and the way brand managers develop strategies for luxury brands. For years, brands specifically luxury brands have been purchased for what they symbolise, and the visibility of those symbols meant a lot to the consumers. Iconic logos (e.g. Louis Vuitton or Chanel), iconic patterns (e.g. Goyard) or iconic designs (e.g. Rolex Submariner or Daytona) have been all built around this understanding as is the whole counterfeit industry. Nevertheless, luxury brands need to know that there is a growing trend and demand towards inconspicuousness, that oddly enough similar to conspicuous luxury is mostly built on individuals' evaluations based on self-image and social identity.

As outlined in this chapter, inconspicuous luxury consumption contrary to common expectations is highly intertwined with the self-image and social identity of the consumer. Yet, concentrating on the symbolic benefits does not mean that brands should not focus on functional and hedonic ones. Against the common belief that luxury value resides in the overall meaning of the brand rather than in the product, luxury products will always be sought after by the consumers for their superior quality and performance as well as the joy associated with luxury consumption. Only ensuring all will justify price premium.

For instance, Tesla with just a "T" displayed in front of the car is a great example conjoining all these benefits and fulfilling all personal and social expectations of the inconspicuous consumers. However, the previous discussion also highlights that inconspicuous luxury consumers have several other motivations and may therefore be inhomogeneous. Some consumers even prefer inconspicuous luxury items to be invisible and to avoid negative reactions. As a result, whilst some consumers are strongly involved and emotionally invested in inconspicuous consumption due to intrinsic motivations, some may still be motivated for self-enhancement or self-protection. One probable distinction within inconspicuous luxury consumers for instance might be between younger consumers and older ones in the motivations outlined, which requires strategies and most of the communication to be designed accordingly and makes it not easy for luxury brands to create a single strategy in their route towards embracing inconspicuousness. Nevertheless, this group is willing to pay more without acquiring the visible characteristics, that are previously strongly associated with and demanded from luxuries.

Apart from advantages in targeting unmet needs and previously ignored segments, there are additional significant benefits of inconspicuous luxury. Recent research suggests that conspicuous brand usage damages the brand image perceived by the consumers who are not strongly attached to the brand in the first place (Ferraro et al., 2013). This finding shows that visible brand signals do not add new admirers. On the contrary, it creates a negative perception and dilutes the brand's image. Further, compared to traditional luxury goods, that are easily recognized by many through the logo or other elements that can be easily replicated, risk of counterfeiting inconspicuous luxury items is extra low, as what makes them unique and worthy of interest for the luxury consumers cannot be achieved in an economic way by the counterfeits. From the brand management perspective, this raises great opportunities for luxury brands which are positioned on quality and distinctiveness of their offerings rather than on the logo and other visible signs.

The topics discussed in this chapter and examples provided are designed in a way to provide an understanding on this emerging group of consumers. Nevertheless, as fruitful as it might look for luxury brands, obviously there will not be an instant shift from conspicuousness to inconspicuousness neither in terms of consumer demands nor in terms of brands' strategies. As a result, sympathizing with and targeting inconspicuous luxury consumers coupled with the finances to afford luxury, initially necessitates a thorough analysis and understanding of this segment and the probable sub-segments, followed by the redesigning of products through concealing/hiding or reducing the size and the number of logo on the product and other brand signs (e.g. Lacoste resized their crocodile), which requires companies either to add a line to the overall brand portfolio specifically designed in this way or to totally reposition the brand accordingly. Additionally, specific tailoring of all brand-related activities and choices such as managing the distribution network and designing communication is a must to stay out-of-sight of the mass but to be recognizable only by the ones in-the-know. Most luxury brand are already very selective in their communication and distribution. Yet, their value resides in the level of consumers' awareness. However, inconspicuous luxury brands are not looking forward to increasing awareness in the general public. As a result, they need to be more immersive and only be there where their target audiences are, which can only be achieved successfully when the inconspicuous luxury consumer persona has been studied in detail.

FUTURE RESEARCH DIRECTIONS

Although recent research on luxury consumption implicitly discovers that luxury products do not always have to be conspicuous (Gurzki & Woisetschläger, 2016) and awareness on inconspicuousness' value rises (Wu et al., 2017), there is still insufficient research on the topic (Hume & Mills, 2013; Gurzki & Woisetschläger, 2016). As a result, there are several fruitful research areas waiting to be discovered by luxury brand researchers.

Initially, as this chapter is exploratory and conceptual only, research should concentrate on qualitative in-depth identification of the drivers of inconspicuous luxury consumption, which can be based on previous theories employed by luxury branding literature (for a summary of these theories please see Ko et al. 2019, p. 5), and needs to be elaborated further through empirical investigations as the next step. Wiedmann and Hannies (2013) state that definitions of luxury are more grounded when they are based on consumers' perceptions. This necessitates a deeper analysis on what luxury consumers perceive as inconspicuous, who inconspicuous luxury consumers are and what motivates them to purchase silently luxurious products. As luxury as a concept is highly abstract, subjective (Vigneron & Johnson, 1999) and culturally defined (Ko et al., 2019; Vickers & Renand, 2003; Yeoman, 2011), this understanding requires cross-cultural and cross-segmented analyses. There can be distinct segments represented in inconspicuous consumers as demonstrated by Hudders et al. (2013) for general luxury consumption. An additional avenue of research that is linked to these concepts is the social understanding of inconspicuous consumption. For instance, within the traditional luxury context, Desmichel, Ordabayeva, and Kocher (2020) show that ephemeral luxuries in comparison to iconic luxuries signal more social status in the society. Similar to conspicuous consumption use of inconspicuous luxury also entails a meaning transfer between the user and the society. Therefore, as it is the case in general luxury research that needs to be focusing on both personal and social meaning (Seo & Buchanan-Oliver, 2019), inconspicuous luxury should also reflect both perspectives. In line with that, Rucker (2020) suggests luxury researchers to analyze inconspicuous consumption both from the actor and the observer's perspective. Yet, much of the research so far only concentrated on subtle self-presentation rather than on the self-construction and on the signaling of an upper social status, that can also be achieved invisibly. As mentioned in Gurzki and Woisetschläger (2016) social and symbolic gains of inconspicuous consumption should not be neglected. Another line of research that needs emphasis is the analysis of the personality traits' influence on motivations and attitudes of consumers to inconspicuous luxuries, just as it is shown by Greenberg et al. (2019) using Big Five personality traits in the context of prominent and extravagant brands. Further, similar to research investigating gender roles in luxury consumption (e.g. Hume & Mills, 2013; Stokburger-Sauer & Teichmann, 2013), gender-based differences may be evident not only in the motivations but also in the consumption of inconspicuous luxury.

CONCLUSION

As the importance of luxury consumption for many consumers as a signal of status, quality, functionality and superiority is unquestionable, both academics and practitioners concentrated on luxury brands and tried to identify the underlying reasons of consumers' demand for luxury goods. In vein of research, there have been various perceived benefits and underlying motivations linked with luxury, nonetheless according to many scholars, conspicuousness, in other worlds publicly displaying highly visible and easily identifiable symbols related with expensive goods, is one of main reasons why consumers choose luxury over mass brands. However, due to the recent changes in consumer culture and in the worldwide socio-economic environment, inconspicuous luxury consumption is gaining popularity not only in the developing but also specifically in BRIC countries (Brazil, Russia, India and China) (Postrel, 2008) resulting in the emergence of a new segment, that is called inconspicuous luxury consumers. Contrary to conspicuous consumption, inconspicuous consumption involves purchase and usage of unconventional luxury products with no visible clues that are only meaningful to the ones that are knowledgeable, rather than to the mass. This view contradicts with most definitions of luxury emphasizing luxury products' highly visible symbols used by many to expose their wealth, success and prestige to the society and obtain social status. As a result, as the number of inconspicuous luxury consumers ignored by consumer culture escalates, the strongly established link between conspicuousness and luxury to fuel awareness and associations is fading and understanding why some luxury consumers choose to spend their money in invisible luxury increases in importance to create a competitive advantage in a highly competitive and turbulent environment.

Accordingly, this chapter through a literature review tries to analyse inconspicuous consumers, that whilst preferring to be differentiated from the ones using luxury products extravagantly to live a dream or reflect a certain lifestyle and status, would still like to be recognized by the like-minded individuals and want to live up to their standards as well as to their utilitarian and individual expectations. With this purpose, the chapter, while relying on the extensive luxury literature, discusses several aspects in relation with inconspicuous luxury consumption and provides an exploratory investigation on the motivations that lead to the emergence of inconspicuous luxury demand. In this regard, the current chapter identifies self-enhancement, self-gratification and functional gratification as individual motivated and self-presentation, differentiation and willingness to remain unrecognized and avoid negative reactions as socially motivated drivers of inconspicuous luxury consumption.

In total, the theoretical and practical contributions of this chapter are manifold. Initially, the chapter provides an understanding on recently emerged trends in luxury consumption and their influence on luxury brands in general. Secondly, this chapter argues that inconspicuous consumption is rising as a competitive advantage for luxury brands to differentiate themselves and to increase their sales if they can detect this opportunity and investigate the underlying consumer motivations for inconspicuous luxury consumption. The chapter, contrary to the common believes that inconspicuous consumption lacks the social benefits of luxury, specifically highlights the role of self-concept and social identity in inconspicuous consumption and advises brands to carefully analyze their target audiences with respect to in-group/out-group identification and changes in the consumer culture. From a theoretical perspective, the topics discussed in the chapter do not only highlight possible motivational drivers of inconspicuous luxury consumption but makes it also evident that a new definition of luxury is needed.

REFERENCES

Abalkhail, T. S. (2020). The impact of religiosity on luxury brand consumption: the case of Saudi consumers. *Journal of Islamic Marketing*. Ahead-of-print. doi:10.1108/JIMA-11-2016-0091

Atwal, G., & Williams, A. (2009). Luxury brand marketing— The experience is everything! *Journal of Brand Management*, *16*(5-6), 338–346. doi:10.1057/bm.2008.48

Bain & Company. (2019). *Luxury goods worldwide market study - – Spring 2019 Update Report.* Retrieved from https://www.bain.com/insights/luxury-report/

Bardhi, F., & Eckhardt, G. M. (2017). Liquid consumption. *The Journal of Consumer Research, 44*(3), 582–597. doi:10.1093/jcr/ucx050

Baumeister, R. F., & Hutton, D. G. (1987). Self-presentation theory: Self-construction and audience pleasing. In B. Mullen & G. R. Goethals (Eds.), *Theories of Group Behavior* (pp. 71–87). Springer. doi:10.1007/978-1-4612-4634-3_4

Belk, R. W. (1988). Possessions and the extended self. *The Journal of Consumer Research, 15*(2), 139–168. doi:10.1086/209154

Berger, J., & Heath, C. (2008). Who drives divergence? Identity signaling, outgroup dissimilarity, and the abandonment of cultural tastes. *Journal of Personality and Social Psychology, 95*(3), 593–607. doi:10.1037/0022-3514.95.3.593

Berger, J., & Ward, M. (2010). Subtle signals of inconspicuous consumption. *The Journal of Consumer Research, 37*(4), 555–569. doi:10.1086/655445

Berthon, P., Pitt, L., Parent, M., & Berthon, J. P. (2009). Aesthetics and ephemerality: Observing and preserving the luxury brand. *California Management Review, 52*(1), 45–66. doi:10.1525/cmr.2009.52.1.45

Beverland, M. (2006). The 'real thing': Branding authenticity in the luxury wine trade. *Journal of Business Research, 59*(2), 251–258. doi:10.1016/j.jbusres.2005.04.007

Bhattarai, A. (2019, April 16). Consumers around the world are spending less on almost everything. Even booze. *The Washington Post.* Retrieved from https://www.washingtonpost.com/business/2019/04/16/consumers-around-world-are-spending-less-almost-everything-even-booze/

Bian, X., & Veloutsou, C. (2007). Consumers' attitudes regarding non-deceptive counterfeit brands in the UK and China. *Journal of Brand Management, 12*(3), 211–222. doi:10.1057/palgrave.bm.2550046

Bian, X., Wang, K. Y., Smith, A., & Yannopoulou, N. (2016). New insights into unethical counterfeit consumption. *Journal of Business Research, 69*(10), 4249–4258. doi:10.1016/j.jbusres.2016.02.038

Carbajal, J. C., Hall, J., & Li, H. (2015). Inconspicuous conspicuous consumption. Peruvian Economic Association, (38), 1-20.

Charles, K., Hurst, E., & Roussanov, N. (2007). *Conspicuous consumption and race.* Working Paper 13392, National Bureau of Economic Research, Cambridge, MA.

Chatikavanij, K. (2019, February 12). The luxury brands taking personalisation to a new level. *The Style.* Retrieved from https://www.lifestyleasia.com/bk/style/fashion/the-luxury-brands-taking-personalisation-to-a-new-level/

Cornell, A. (2002). Cult of luxury: The new opiate of the masses. *Australian Financial Review*, 47.

Cristini, H., Kauppinen-Räisänen, H., Barthod-Prothade, M., & Woodside, A. (2017). Toward a general theory of luxury: Advancing from workbench definitions and theoretical transformations. *Journal of Business Research, 70*, 101–107. doi:10.1016/j.jbusres.2016.07.001

Desmichel, P., Ordabayeva, N., & Kocher, B. (2020). What if diamonds did not last forever? Signaling status achievement through ephemeral versus iconic luxury goods. *Organizational Behavior and Human Decision Processes, 158*, 49–65. doi:10.1016/j.obhdp.2020.01.002

Dittmar, H. (1992). Perceived material wealth and first impressions. *British Journal of Social Psychology, 31*(4), 379–391. doi:10.1111/j.2044-8309.1992.tb00980.x

Dubois, B., & Duquesne, P. (1993). The market for luxury goods: Income versus culture. *European Journal of Marketing, 27*(1), 35–44. doi:10.1108/03090569310024530

Dubois, B., & Laurent, G. (1995). Luxury Possessions and Practices, an Empirical Scale. In F. Hansen (Ed.), *European Advances in Consumer Research* (Vol. 2, pp. 69–77). Association for Consumer Research.

Dubois, B., Laurent, G., & Czellar, S. (2001). *Consumer rapport to luxury: Analyzing complex and ambivalent attitudes.* Working Paper 736, HEC School of Management, Jouy-en-Josas.

Eckhardt, G. M., & Bardhi, F. (2019). New dynamics of social status and distinction. *Marketing Theory, 20*(1), 85–102. doi:10.1177/1470593119856650

Eckhardt, G. M., Belk, R. W., & Wilson, J. A. (2015). The rise of inconspicuous consumption. *Journal of Marketing Management, 31*(7-8), 807–826. doi:10.1080/0267257X.2014.989890

Elliott, R., & Wattanasuwan, K. (1998). Brands as symbolic resources for the construction of identity. *International Journal of Advertising, 17*(2), 131–144. doi:10.1080/02650487.1998.11104712

Escalas, J. E., & Bettman, J. R. (2003). You are what they eat: The influence of reference groups on consumers' connections to brands. *Journal of Consumer Psychology, 13*(3), 339–348. doi:10.1207/S15327663JCP1303_14

Feltovich, N., Harbaugh, R., & To, T. (2002). Too cool for school? Signalling and Countersignalling. *The RAND Journal of Economics, 33*(4), 630–349. doi:10.2307/3087478

Ferraro, R., Kirmani, A., & Matherly, T. (2013). Look at me! Look at me! Conspicuous brand usage, self-brand connection, and dilution. *JMR, Journal of Marketing Research, 50*(4), 477–488. doi:10.1509/jmr.11.0342

Festinger, L. (1954). A theory of social comparison processes. *Human Relations, 7*(2), 117–140. doi:10.1177/001872675400700202

Firat, A. F., & Venkatesh, A. (1995). Liberatory postmodernism and the reenchantment of consumption. *The Journal of Consumer Research, 22*(3), 239–267. doi:10.1086/209448

Godey, B., Pederzoli, D., Aiello, G., Donvito, R., Chan, P., Oh, H., Singh, R., Skorobogatykh, I. I., Tsuchiya, J., & Weitz, B. (2012). Brand a.nd country-of-origin effect on consumers' decision to purchase luxury products. *Journal of Business Research, 65*(10), 1461–1470. doi:10.1016/j.jbusres.2011.10.012

Goffman, E. (1959). *The presentation of self in everyday life*. Doubleday Anchor.

Greenberg, D., Ehrensperger, E., Schulte-Mecklenbeck, M., Hoyer, W. D., Zhang, Z. J., & Krohmer, H. (2020). The role of brand prominence and extravagance of product design in luxury brand building: What drives consumers' preferences for loud versus quiet luxury? *Journal of Brand Management*, *27*(2), 195–210. doi:10.105741262-019-00175-5

Grubb, E. L., & Grathwohl, H. L. (1967). Consumer self-concept, symbolism and market behavior: A theoretical approach. *Journal of Marketing*, *31*(4), 22–27. doi:10.1177/002224296703100405

Gurzki, H., & Woisetschläger, D. M. (2017). Mapping the luxury research landscape: A bibliometric citation analysis. *Journal of Business Research*, *77*, 147–166. doi:10.1016/j.jbusres.2016.11.009

Hagtvedt, H., & Patrick, V. M. (2008). Art infusion: The influence of visual art on the perception and evaluation of consumer products. *JMR, Journal of Marketing Research*, *45*(3), 379–389. doi:10.1509/jmkr.45.3.379

Han, Y. J., Nunes, J. C., & Drèze, X. (2010). Signaling status with luxury goods: The role of brand prominence. *Journal of Marketing*, *74*(4), 15–30. doi:10.1509/jmkg.74.4.015

Heine, K. (2012). *The Concept of Luxury*. Retrieved from https://upmarkit.com/sites/default/files/content/20130403_Heine_The_Concept_of_Luxury_Brands.pdf

Hoe, L., Hogg, G., & Hart, S. (2003). Faking it: Counterfeiting and consumer contradictions. *European Advances in Consumer Behaviour*, *6*, 60–67.

Hudders, L., Pandelaere, M., & Vyncke, P. (2013). Consumer meaning making: The meaning of luxury brands in a democratised luxury world. *International Journal of Market Research*, *55*(3), 391–412. doi:10.2501/IJMR-2013-036

Hume, M., & Mills, M. (2013). Uncovering Victoria's Secret: Exploring women's luxury perceptions of intimate apparel and purchasing behaviour. *Journal of Fashion Marketing and Management*, *17*(4), 460–485. doi:10.1108/JFMM-03-2013-0020

Kapferer, J. N. (1997). Managing luxury brands. *Journal of Brand Management*, *4*(4), 251–259. doi:10.1057/bm.1997.4

Kapferer, J. N. (2010). Luxury after the crisis: Pro logo or no logo. *European Business Review*, (September-October), 42–46.

Kapferer, J. N., & Laurent, G. (2016). Where do consumers think luxury begins? A study of perceived minimum price for 21 luxury goods in 7 countries. *Journal of Business Research*, *69*(1), 332–340. doi:10.1016/j.jbusres.2015.08.005

Kastanakis, M. N., & Balabanis, G. (2012). Between the mass and the class: Antecedents of the "bandwagon" luxury consumption behavior. *Journal of Business Research*, *65*(10), 1399–1407. doi:10.1016/j.jbusres.2011.10.005

Kastanakis, M. N., & Balabanis, G. (2014). Explaining variation in conspicuous luxury consumption: An individual differences' perspective. *Journal of Business Research*, *67*(10), 2147–2154. doi:10.1016/j.jbusres.2014.04.024

Keller, K. L. (2009). Building strong brands in a modern marketing communications environment. *Journal of Marketing Communications*, *15*(2-3), 139–155. doi:10.1080/13527260902757530

Kemp, S. (1998). Perceiving luxury and necessity. *Journal of Economic Psychology*, *19*(5), 591–606. doi:10.1016/S0167-4870(98)00026-9

Ko, E., Costello, J. P., & Taylor, C. R. (2019). What is a luxury brand? A new definition and review of the literature. *Journal of Business Research*, *99*, 405–413. doi:10.1016/j.jbusres.2017.08.023

Leary, M. R., & Kowalski, R. M. (1990). Impression management: A literature review and two-component model. *Psychological Bulletin*, *107*(1), 34–47. doi:10.1037/0033-2909.107.1.34

Leibenstein, H. (1950). Bandwagon, snob, and Veblen effects in the theory of consumers' demand. *The Quarterly Journal of Economics*, *64*(2), 183–207. doi:10.2307/1882692

Makkar, M., & Yap, S. F. (2018a). Emotional experiences behind the pursuit of inconspicuous luxury. *Journal of Retailing and Consumer Services*, *44*, 222–234. doi:10.1016/j.jretconser.2018.07.001

Makkar, M., & Yap, S. F. (2018b). The anatomy of the inconspicuous luxury fashion experience. *Journal of Fashion Marketing and Management*, *22*(1), 129–156. doi:10.1108/JFMM-08-2017-0083

Miller, K. W., & Mills, M. K. (2012). Contributing clarity by examining brand luxury in the fashion market. *Journal of Business Research*, *65*(10), 1471–1479. doi:10.1016/j.jbusres.2011.10.013

Mylan, J. (2019). Sustainable innovation, consumption and everyday life. In F. Boons & A. McMeekin (Eds.), *Handbook of Sustainable Innovation* (pp. 252–266). Edward Elgar Publishing. doi:10.4337/9781788112574.00023

Nia, A., & Lynne Zaichkowsky, J. (2000). Do counterfeits devalue the ownership of luxury brands? *Journal of Product and Brand Management*, *9*(7), 485–497. doi:10.1108/10610420010351402

Nueno, J. L., & Quelch, J. A. (1998). The mass marketing of luxury. *Business Horizons*, *41*(6), 61–61. doi:10.1016/S0007-6813(98)90023-4

OECD/EUIPO. (2019, March 18). *Trends in Trade in Counterfeit and Pirated Goods*. . doi:10.1787/g2g9f533-en

Phau, I., & Prendergast, G. (2000). Consuming luxury brands: The relevance of the 'rarity principle'. *Journal of Brand Management*, *8*(2), 122–138. doi:10.1057/palgrave.bm.2540013

Postrel, V. (2006, July/August). Inconspicuous consumption: A new theory of the leisure class. *The Atlantic*. Retrieved from https://www.theatlantic.com/magazine/archive/2008/07/inconspicuous-consumption/306845/

Roper, S., Caruana, R., Medway, D., & Murphy, P. (2013). Constructing luxury brands: Exploring the role of consumer discourse. *European Journal of Marketing*, *47*(3/4), 375–400. doi:10.1108/03090561311297382

Rucker, D. D. (2020). Social rank: Implications for consumers as actors and observers. *Current Opinion in Psychology*, *33*, 57–61. doi:10.1016/j.copsyc.2019.07.024

Schembri, S., Merrilees, B., & Kristiansen, S. (2010). Brand consumption and narrative of the self. *Psychology and Marketing*, *27*(6), 623–637. doi:10.1002/mar.20348

Schlenker, B. R. (2012). Self-presentation. In M. R. Leary & J. P. Tangney (Eds.), *Handbook of self and identity* (pp. 542–570). The Guilford Press.

Schlenker, B. R., Britt, T. W., & Pennington, J. (1996). Impression regulation and management: Highlights of a theory of self-identification. In R. M. Sorrentino & E. T. Higgins (Eds.), Handbook of motivation and cognition. Handbook of motivation and cognition, Vol. 3. The interpersonal context (pp. 118-147). New York, NY: The Guilford Press.

Seo, Y., & Buchanan-Oliver, M. (2019). Constructing a typology of luxury brand consumption practices. *Journal of Business Research*, *99*, 414–421. doi:10.1016/j.jbusres.2017.09.019

Shao, W., Grace, D., & Ross, M. (2019). Consumer motivation and luxury consumption: Testing moderating effects. *Journal of Retailing and Consumer Services*, *46*, 33–44. doi:10.1016/j.jretconser.2018.10.003

Shao, W., Grace, D., & Ross, M. (2019a). Investigating brand visibility in luxury consumption. *Journal of Retailing and Consumer Services*, *49*, 357–370. doi:10.1016/j.jretconser.2019.04.017

Sharma, P., & Chan, R. Y. (2017). Exploring the role of attitudinal functions in counterfeit purchase behavior via an extended conceptual framework. *Psychology and Marketing*, *34*(3), 294–308. doi:10.1002/mar.20989

Shove, E., & Warde, A. (2002). Inconspicuous consumption: the sociology of consumption, lifestyles and the environment. *Sociological Theory and the Environment: Classical Foundations. Contemporary Insights*, *230*, 51.

Shukla, P. (2012). The influence of value perceptions on luxury purchase intentions in developed and emerging markets. *International Marketing Review*, *29*(6), 574–596. doi:10.1108/02651331211277955

Silverstein, M. J., & Fiske, N. (2003). Luxury for the masses. *Harvard Business Review*, *81*(4), 48–57.

Stokburger-Sauer, N. E., & Teichmann, K. (2013). Is luxury just a female thing? The role of gender in luxury brand consumption. *Journal of Business Research*, *66*(7), 889–896. doi:10.1016/j.jbusres.2011.12.007

Tajfel, H. (1981). *Human groups and social categories: Studies in social psychology*. Cambridge University Press.

Thomsen, T. U., Holmqvist, J., von Wallpach, S., Hemetsberger, A., & Belk, R. W. (2020). *Conceptualizing unconventional luxury. Journal of Business Research*. Ahead-of-print., doi:10.1016/j.jbusres.2020.01.058

Tice, D. M., Butler, J. L., Muraven, M. B., & Stillwell, A. M. (1995). When modesty prevails: Differential favorability of self-presentation to friends and strangers. *Journal of Personality and Social Psychology*, *69*(6), 1120–1138. doi:10.1037/0022-3514.69.6.1120

Ting, M. S., Goh, Y. N., & Isa, S. M. (2018). Inconspicuous consumption of luxury fashion goods among Malaysian adults: An investigation. *Global Business and Management Research*, *10*(1), 313–330.

Trigg, A. B. (2001). Veblen, Bourdieu, and conspicuous consumption. *Journal of Economic Issues*, *35*(1), 99–115. doi:10.1080/00213624.2001.11506342

Truong, Y., Simmons, G., McColl, R., & Kitchen, P. J. (2008). Status and conspicuousness–are they related? Strategic marketing implications for luxury brands. *Journal of Strategic Marketing, 16*(3), 189–203. doi:10.1080/09652540802117124

Tsai, W. S., Yang, Q., & Liu, Y. (2013). Young Chinese consumers' snob and bandwagon luxury consumption preferences. *Journal of International Consumer Marketing, 25*(5), 290–304. doi:10.1080/08961530.2013.827081

Veblen, T. (1899). *The Theory of the Leisure Class*. Penguin.

Vickers, J. S., & Renand, F. (2003). The marketing of luxury goods: An exploratory study–three conceptual dimensions. *The Marketing Review, 3*(4), 459–478. doi:10.1362/146934703771910071

Vigneron, F., & Johnson, L. W. (1999). A review and a conceptual framework of prestige-seeking consumer behavior. *Academy of Marketing Science Review, 1*(1), 1–15.

Vigneron, F., & Johnson, L. W. (2004). Measuring perceptions of brand luxury. *Journal of Brand Management, 11*(6), 484–506. doi:10.1057/palgrave.bm.2540194

Wiedmann, K. P., Hennigs, N., & Siebels, A. (2009). Value-based segmentation of luxury consumption behavior. *Psychology and Marketing, 26*(7), 625–651. doi:10.1002/mar.20292

Wilcox, K., Kim, H. M., & Sen, S. (2009). Why do consumers buy counterfeit luxury brands? *JMR, Journal of Marketing Research, 46*(2), 247–259. doi:10.1509/jmkr.46.2.247

Wilke, R., & Zaichkowsky, J. L. (1999). Brand imitation and its effects on innovation, competition, and brand equity. *Business Horizons, 42*(6), 9–9. doi:10.1016/S0007-6813(99)80033-0

Yeoman, I. (2011). The changing behaviours of luxury consumption. *Journal of Revenue and Pricing Management, 10*(1), 47–50. doi:10.1057/rpm.2010.43

Zhang, W. (2019). Politicizing fashion: Inconspicuous consumption and anti-intellectualism during the Cultural Revolution in China. *Journal of Consumer Culture*. Advance online publication. doi:10.1177/1469540519889989

ADDITIONAL READING

Bagwell, L. S., & Bernheim, B. D. (1996). Veblen effects in a theory of conspicuous consumption. *The American Economic Review*, 349–373.

Belk, R. W. (1988). Possessions and the extended self. *The Journal of Consumer Research, 15*(2), 139–168. doi:10.1086/209154

Braun, O. L., & Wicklund, R. A. (1989). Psychological antecedents of conspicuous consumption. *Journal of Economic Psychology, 10*(2), 161–187. doi:10.1016/0167-4870(89)90018-4

Danzinger, P. N. (2018, Dec 18). 4 Mega-trends ahead for the luxury market in 2019: expect turmoil and slowing sales. *Forbes*. Retrieved from https://www.forbes.com/sites/pamdanziger/2018/12/18/whats-ahead-for-the-luxury-market-in-2019-expect-turmoil-and-slowing-sales/#20320d646578

Kapferer, J. N. (2014). The artification of luxury: From artisans to artists. *Business Horizons*, *57*(3), 371–380. doi:10.1016/j.bushor.2013.12.007

Kapferer, J. N. (2015). *Kapferer on luxury: How luxury brands can grow yet remain rare*. Kogan Page Publishers.

Kapferer, J. N., Kernstock, J., Brexendorf, T. O., & Powell, S. M. (2017). *Advances in luxury brand management*. Springer. doi:10.1007/978-3-319-51127-6

O'cass, A., & McEwen, H. (2004). Exploring consumer status and conspicuous consumption. *Journal of Consumer Behaviour: An International Research Review*, *4*(1), 25–39. doi:10.1002/cb.155

Wilson, J., Eckhardt, G., & Belk, R. (2015). Luxury branding below the radar. *Harvard Business Review*, 26–27.

KEY TERMS AND DEFINITIONS

Brand Prominence: How visible is a brand's logo or trademark signaling what the brand constitutes to an average consumer.

Counterfeit: A product that has been manufactured in an unethical and unauthorized way to look exact or similar to the genuine branded product. Those products in general rely on brand prominence to create an association with the real product.

Democratization: Extending the luxury brand's portfolio by adding more affordable products, so that it is more easily accessible by the mass.

Inconspicuousness: Not having an easily recognizable characteristics such as a logo, pattern or texture or any other sign that signals a specific brand to the average user.

Luxury Consumer: Someone who is knowledgeable in luxury brands and what they offer and buys luxury on a frequent basis rather than occasionally.

Motivation: Desire that forces the individual to do something to get fulfilled. Motivation plays therefore a significant role in shaping behavior. Motivation can be driven internally by the individual (intrinsic) or by externally by the outside world (extrinsic) through rewards.

Self-Concept: Who a person believes s/he is. It is the sum of the perceptions and beliefs of the individual about himself/herself as a human being.

Social Identity: Part of the self-concept that is built within the society through the social interactions and roles of the individual within his/her social environment. Individuals can have multiple social identities in connection with multiple roles they have in life.

Symbolism: Using socially approved and well-known symbols and abstract signals to communicate and portray something to others.

Chapter 5
Enhancing Consumer-Brand Relationships Through Luxury Brand Experiences

Esra Arıkan
Istanbul Bilgi University, Turkey

ABSTRACT

The extant research highlights that the strength of consumer-brand relationships is very much shaped by consumers' experiences with brands. Given the inherent characteristics of luxury brands, it is no surprise that luxury consumers expect much more intense experiences, and thus the delivery of a superior brand experience is a necessity in the luxury market. Therefore, both marketing scholars and brand managers in the luxury market need to acknowledge the power of brand experiences as a way to strengthen consumer-brand relationships. However, despite the need for a deeper understanding of brand experience in the context of luxury brands, still much remains unknown regarding the factors that can be used to enhance brand experience. Building on this gap in the literature, this chapter investigates the relational outcomes of brand experience and subsequently discusses the various drivers that luxury brands can use to enhance luxury brand experience and thus develop stronger consumer-brand relationships.

INTRODUCTION

Building strong and long-term relationships with consumers is essential for the success of brands (Fournier, 1998); thus, research on consumer-brand relationships has flourished since the beginning of the 2000s. The importance of consumer-brand relationships is also widely acknowledged in the context of luxury brands (e.g., Eastman, Shin, & Ruhland, 2020; Rodrigues, Brandao, & Rodrigues, 2018). However, even if the luxury market is expected to grow further over the years, industry experts warn that today's luxury consumers are less loyal and more likely to shop around (Shimul, Phau, & Lwin, 2019). The intensifying competition accompanied by the proliferation of luxury brands in the market and consequent opportunities for consumers to switch necessitate both marketing scholars and brand managers to identify the factors that can enhance the development and maintenance of consumer-brand

DOI: 10.4018/978-1-7998-4369-6.ch005

Copyright © 2021, IGI Global. Copying or distributing in print or electronic forms without written permission of IGI Global is prohibited.

relationships (Shukla, Banerjee, & Singh, 2016). Within this respect, brand experience can play a highly critical role. The extant research highlights that the strength of consumer-brand relationships is very much shaped by consumers' experience with the brand (e.g., Prentice, Wang, & Loureiro, 2019). The importance of brand experience as a way to build strong relationships is also recognized in terms of managerial practice (e.g., Andreini, Pedeliento, Zarantonello, & Solerio, 2018).

A review of the literature reveals that many studies conducted in this stream of research (e.g., Dolbec & Chebat, 2013; van der Westhuizen, 2018) use the theoretical perspective provided by Brakus, Schmitt, and Zarantonello (2009) in their discussions. This perspective is built on the experiential value of consumption (Holbrook & Hirschman, 1982) and experiential marketing (Schmitt, 1999). Brakus et al. (2009, p. 53) define brand experience as "subjective, internal consumer responses (sensations, feelings, and cognitions) and behavioral responses evoked by brand-related stimuli that are part of a brand's design and identity, packaging, communications, and environments." The effect of brand experience on consumer-brand relationships is studied across different product categories and markets (e.g., Japutra & Molinillo, 2019; Ramaseshan& Stein, 2014). However, such brand-related stimuli are particularly crucial for providing superior experiences in the luxury market (de Kerviler & Rodriguez, 2019). This can be explained by the unique characteristics of luxury brands. Luxury brands are often defined in terms of their strong heritage, distinctive style, superior quality, exclusive and prestigious outlets, and high transaction value (Fionda & Moore, 2009; de Kerviler & Rodriguez, 2019). Given these characteristics, it is no surprise that consumers of luxury brands expect intense experiences; thus, the delivery of a superior brand experience is not merely an option but a necessity in this market (Chandon, Laurent, & Valette-Florence, 2017). As luxury consumption involves the search for enrichment through indulgent and recreational experiences (de Kerviler &Rodriguez, 2019), both marketing scholars and brand managers in the luxury market need to acknowledge the power of brand experiences as a way to strengthen consumer-brand relationships. Despite this need for a deeper understanding of brand experience in the context of luxury brands (Seo & Buchanan-Oliver, 2019), still much remains unknown regarding the factors that can be used to enhance brand experience and the mechanisms through which brand experience allows consumers to develop stronger relationships with luxury brands (de Kerviler & Rodriguez, 2019). Building on this gap in the literature, this chapter aims to investigate the relational outcomes of brand experience and subsequently discuss the different drivers that luxury brand managers can use to enhance luxury brand experience and thus develop stronger consumer-brand relationships.

BRAND EXPERIENCE AND ITS DIMENSIONS

In the last decades, both the marketing theory and practice have started emphasizing the strategically important role that the experiential characteristics of brands can play in terms of creating more valuable experiences with consumers (e.g., Andreini et al., 2018; Dwivedi, Nayeem, & Murshed, 2018). The starting point referenced in most of these studies is the study by Brakus et al. (2009). Building on Schmitt's (1999) conceptual work, Brakus et al. (2009) conceptualize brand experience as consumer sensations, feelings, cognitions, and behavioral responses evoked by brand-related stimuli and name its four dimensions as sensory, affective, intellectual, and behavioral. The sensory dimension relates to consumers' five senses and captures the degree to which the consumers find the brand attractive in a sensory way (Brakus et al., 2009; Iglesias, Markovic, & Rialp, 2019). From this standpoint, all the tactile, visual, auditory, olfactory, and gustatory stimulations generated by brands during their purchase, consumption, or use can have a positive effect on consumers' sensory experience (Hultén, 2011). Thus, the sensory dimension of brand experience has been the focus of many studies and it has been found that such sensory stimulations (e.g., music, smell, colors, or designs associated with the product or in-store) can significantly enhance the brand experience (e.g., Hepola, Karjaluoto, & Hintikka, 2017; Iglesias et al., 2019). Of the other dimensions, while the affective dimension is generally concerned with the consumers' emotions and feelings that are evoked by brands and captures the degree to which consumers perceive brands as emotional, the intellectual dimension is related to the analytical and imaginative thinking that brands induce and captures the degree to which brands encourage consumers to think by stimulating their curiosity and problem-solving capabilities (Brakus et al., 2009; Iglesias et al., 2019). Finally, the behavioral dimension compromises the consumer behaviors or intentions that are caused by brands and captures the degree to which consumers engage in physical behavior and bodily experiences while using the brand (Brakus et al., 2009; Iglesias et al., 2019).

As shown in Table 1, these four dimensions are commonly adopted within this field of research. Even if the earlier studies mostly study the importance of brand experience across a variety of product categories (e.g., Iglesias, Singh, & Batista-Foguet, 2011; Ramaseshan& Stein, 2014), some studies examine its importance specifically in the context of luxury products. For example, Wiedman, Labenz, Haase, and Hennigs (2018) investigate the relationships among multisensory marketing, brand experience, customer perceived value, and brand strength in the context of luxury hotels. Measuring brand experience through the four dimensions proposed by Brakus et al. (2009), the researchers show that brand experience has a significant effect on all types of customer perceived value, which in turn increases brand strength. In a similar context, Islam, Hollebeek, Rahman, Khan, and Rasool (2019) also use these dimensions and find that customer engagement has a positive effect on the brand experience of luxury hotel guests. These studies show that brand experiences can indeed play a very significant role in the luxury markets. Thus, these dimensions need to be given particular emphasis to be able to create favorable brand experiences.

Despite the popularity of these four dimensions in the literature, some studies also acknowledge the importance of another dimension (e.g., Bapat, 2017; Huang, Lee, Kim, & Evans, 2015). These studies state that the SENSE, FEEL, THINK, ACT, and RELATE modules of experiential marketing, as proposed by Schmitt (1999), correspond with the sensory, affective, cognitive, behavioral, and social (relational) dimensions respectively and thus, the social dimension should also be considered. The social dimension refers to the relationship one has with others and his/her ideal-self (Gentile, Spiller, & Noci, 2007) and it can undoubtedly be vital in terms of enhancing the experience with luxury brands given their inherent characteristics. Thus, it is not a surprise that some studies highlight the social dimension as a critical factor. For example, Ramirez and Merunka (2019) examine the effect of brand experience on brand attachment in a context that also covers luxury brands and highlight the importance of using the social dimension along with others. In another study, de Kerviler and Rodriguez (2019) investigate the effect of luxury brand experiences based on four dimensions, which are sensory, affective, intellectual, and social. The researchers argue that the social dimension is especially important for luxury brands as consumers usually buy luxury brands to gain social approval.

BRAND EXPERIENCE AND CONSUMER-BRAND RELATIONSHIPS

Consumer-brand relationships have gained tremendous popularity among scholars and managers, especially after Fournier's (1998) seminal work that provides the theoretical foundation for this stream of

Table 1. Dimensions of brand experience: Representative research

		Dimensions of Brand Experience				
Authors	**Context**	**Sensory**	**Affective**	**Behavioral**	**Intellectual**	**Social**
Iglesias et al., 2011	Car, laptop and sneaker	✓	✓	✓	✓	
Dolbec & Chebat, 2013	Mid-tier fashion brand	✓	✓	✓	✓	
Nysveen, Pedersen,& Skard, 2013	Telecommunication	✓	✓	✓	✓	✓
Francisco-Maffezzolli, Semprebon, & Prado, 2014	Perfume and bath soap	✓	✓	✓	✓	
Ramaseshan& Stein, 2014	Consumer products, electronics and fast-food	✓	✓	✓	✓	
Ding & Tseng, 2015	Burger King, Cold Stone, Creamery, Mc Donald's, and Starbucks	✓	✓	✓	✓	✓
Huang et al., 2015	Apparel	✓	✓		✓	✓
Klein, Falk, Esch, & Gloukhovtsevi, 2016	Luxury car pop-up stores	✓	✓			
Bapat, 2017	Financial services	✓	✓	✓	✓	✓
Hepola et al., 2017	Tableware	✓				
Huang, 2017	Mobile phone	✓		✓	✓	
Kang, Manthiou, Sumarjan, & Tang, 2017	Lodging: Name-brand hotels	✓	✓	✓	✓	
Dwivedi et al., 2018	Automobiles	✓	✓	✓	✓	
Ong, Poon, & Zhang, 2018	Casual dining restaurants	✓	✓	✓	✓	
van der Westhuizen, 2018	Multiple categories	✓	✓	✓	✓	
Wiedmann et al., 2018	Luxury hotels	✓	✓	✓	✓	
Das, Agarwal, Malhotra, & Varshneya, 2019	Apparel	✓	✓	✓	✓	
de Kerviler & Rodrigues, 2019	Personal intimate luxury and non- luxury	✓	✓		✓	✓
Ferreira, Rodrigues, & Rodrigues, 2019	Fashion brand retail store	✓	✓	✓	✓	
Islam et al., 2019	Luxury hotels	✓	✓	✓	✓	
Japutra& Molinillo, 2019	Multiple categories	✓	✓	✓	✓	
Prentice et al., 2019	Airline	✓	✓	✓	✓	
Ramirez & Merunka, 2019	Multiple categories, including casual dining and luxury hotel	✓	✓	✓	✓	✓

research. As consumer-brand relationships are considered as a powerful mechanism that drives brand loyalty, these relationships offer several benefits to brands such as increased market share and profits (Khamitov, Wang, & Thomson, 2019). Building strong relationships with their consumers is especially important for luxury brands as these are products that are not purchased daily and creating long-term relationships is very critical for future purchases (Eastman et al., 2020). Thus, there exist many studies that investigate consumer-brand relationships in the context of luxury brands. These studies highlight various brand relationship variables, such as brand commitment (e.g., Pham, Valette-Florence, & Vigneron, 2018), brand attachment (e.g., Peng& Chen, 2019), and brand love (e.g., Rodrigues et al., 2018) and discuss the importance of building strong consumer-luxury brand relationships through these variables.

As brand relationships emerge from the experiences that consumers establish with brands over time (Nobre& Simoes, 2019), the nature of brand experiences plays a determining role in the strength of consumer-brand relationships. A systematic review of the literature reveals that favorable brand experiences are mostly studied concerning their positive effect on brand loyalty. When consumers assess their brand experiences as unique and highly differentiated, these experiences are stored in consumer memory as such; thus, consumers are more likely to repeat their purchases and become loyal (Brakus et al., 2009). There exist many studies supporting the view that favorable brand experiences help brands create both purchase and attitudinal loyalty (e.g., Khan& Fatma, 2017; Ramaseshan& Stein, 2014; van der Westhuizen, 2018). However, some of these studies deserve particular emphasis as they argue that it is essential to investigate the effect of each brand experience dimension separately, as each may have a different impact on brand loyalty. For example, in their study, Ong et al. (2018) examine the effects that the dimensions of brand experience have on different brand loyalty components and claim that practitioners should focus on enhancing different dimensions of brand experience based on their loyalty-related goal.

In line with brand loyalty, the effect of favorable brand experiences on brand commitment is also examined in the literature. In some studies, brand commitment is investigated as a direct outcome of favorable brand experiences (e.g., Ramaseshan& Stein, 2014). However, in other studies, its critical role as a mediator between brand experience and brand loyalty is emphasized (e.g., Iglesias et al., 2011). Acknowledging the effect that brand experience has on brand commitment, some recent studies also examine the effect of the different dimensions of brand experience on brand commitment. For example, in their latest research, Iglesias et al. (2019) support that favorable sensory brand experiences increase brand equity through their positive effect on brand commitment. Pointing out that the literature on brand commitment usually focuses on the non-luxury domain, Shukla et al. (2016) argue that it is vital to understand the relationship between brand experience and brand commitment in the luxury domain. The researchers claim that favorable experience with luxury brands has a positive effect on especially on affective commitment that is considered as the foundation on which relationships are built (Fullerton, 2005).

Since brand experiences can strategically be vital for enhancing consumer-brand relationships, the effect of brand experiences on other brand relationship variables is also studied considerably. Brand trust and brand attachment are the two crucial relationship variables that deserve special attention, especially in the context of luxury brands. Thus, it is essential to understand the effect of brand experience on these variables. Since the process by which consumers attribute trust to a brand is mainly determined by their experience with that brand (Delgado-Ballester & Munuera-Alemán, 2001), brand experience may play a significant effect on brand trust. In his study on mobile phone brands, Huang (2017) shows that brand trust is very much affected by sensory experiences and acts as a mediator on the relationships between brand experience and brand loyalty. Sahin, Kitapci, Altındag, and Gok (2017) also conduct a similar study in the context of automobile brands and find that favorable brand experiences promote the development of brand trust, which in turn positively affects behavioral intentions. Besides brand trust, the relationship between brand experience and brand attachment also attracts attention in academia. For example, Dolbec and Chebat (2013) conduct a study that investigates how retailers may use the in-store brand experience to their benefit and find that brand experience has a positive impact on brand attachment. This result is further supported by Nierobisch, Toporowski, Dannewald, and Jahn (2017), who reveal that flagship store-fueled brand experience positively influences brand attachment. Very recently, Arya, Sethi, and Paul (2019) also argue that as favorable brand experiences help the consumer form stronger bonds with brands both at the individual and social levels, such experiences have a positive impact on brand attachment.

In the literature, there also exist studies that simultaneously investigate the effect of two or more relationship variables. For example, in their study, Ramaseshan and Stein (2014) examine the link between brand experience and three brand relationship variables, namely brand commitment, brand trust, and brand attachment. The researchers find that brand experience has a direct positive effect on brand attachment and brand commitment, but not on brand trust. They presume this to be related to the choice of product categories used in the study; as for brand trust to rise, high involvement and familiarity with that brand are required. However, in some more recent studies, the significant effect of brand experience on brand trust is supported along with the effect of brand experience on brand attachment. For example, in their study on conducted in the lodging industry, Kang et al. (2017) find not only that that brand experience significantly affects brand attachment and brand trust, but also that brand trust is affected by brand attachment. Ramirez and Merunka (2019) also conduct a similar study that examines the effects of brand experience on brand attachment and brand trust. In line with the previous findings, they conclude that brand experience has a positive effect on brand attachment and brand trust partially mediates this relationship. Even if these are the variables that are mostly studied within this field of research, there exist a few but recent studies that acknowledge the importance of other relationship-based variables, such as brand love (e.g., Ferreira et al., 2019), brand passion (e.g., Das et al., 2019), self-brand-connection (e.g., van der Westhuizen, 2018) and brand-relationship quality (e.g., Pulh, Mencarelli, & Chaney, 2019).

All these studies provide strong evidence that brand experiences should be carefully considered both by scholars and managers, given that they play a very critical role in terms of enhancing consumer-brand relationships. Even if the importance of creating favorable brand experiences in the context of luxury products has been partially discussed in some studies that investigate the role of brand experience on various relationship-based variables along with other product types (de Oliveira Santini, Ladeira, Sampaio, & Pinto, 2018), the number of studies that specifically focus on the luxury market has been limited, at least until recently. However, with the recognition that experiences constitute a significant part of the luxury market, an experiential perspective has gained ground in the luxury research and researchers have started examining how these experiences can enhance the relationships consumers have with luxury brands (Holmqvist, Ruiz, & Penaloza, 2019). For example, in their study on Millennials, de Kerviler and Rodriguez (2019) especially examine the effect of luxury brand experiences on consumer-brand relationships and show that luxury brand experiences can enhance relationship quality and consumer-brand identification through self-expansion. Initially proposed by Aron and Aron (1986), the theory of self-expansion mainly focuses on how people think, feel, and act in their close relationships with people and how they are driven by the desire to expand their selves by incorporating others into their conception. As consumers can form such relationships with brands, this theory is also highly referenced in the context of consumer-brand relationships (Reimann &Aron, 2009). Building on this theory, de Kerviler and Rodriguez (2019) claim that through favorable experiences, luxury brands provoke a high degree of arousal among consumers, which triggers self-expansion, and consumers feel a stronger desire to maintain their relationships with these brands which provide them a valuable opportunity for self-growth. Given that other studies also draw on the self-expansion theory to provide insights into the relationships consumer have with luxury brands (e.g., Castano & Perez, 2014; Stöttinger &Penz, 2015), both marketing scholars and brand managers need to acknowledge the effects that favorable brand experiences can have on consumer-brand relationships through self-expansion.

DRIVERS OF LUXURY BRAND EXPERIENCE

Even if the conceptualization provided by Brakus et al. (2009) claims that brand design and identity, packaging, retail environment, communication, and events can all be used to enhance the experience consumers have with brands, the studies that focus on identifying the potential drivers of brand experience have been quite rare in the marketing literature (Coelho, Bairrada, &Coelho, 2020). Nevertheless, the intensifying competition within the business environment and the opportunities created by the technological changes have urged both marketing scholars and brand managers to take a more active stance. Accordingly, identifying the potential factors that can enhance brand experience and thus, strengthen consumer-brand relationships has recently become a priority in terms of academic research and firm strategy. Based on a thorough literature review, this chapter proposes the conceptual model shown in Figure 1. This model studies the potential drivers for enhancing the luxury brand experience under two broad categories: retail environment and online communication. The model also highlights the significance of some personal and cultural factors that are important for assessing the effect of luxury brand experience on consumer-brand relationships.

Figure 1. Conceptual Model

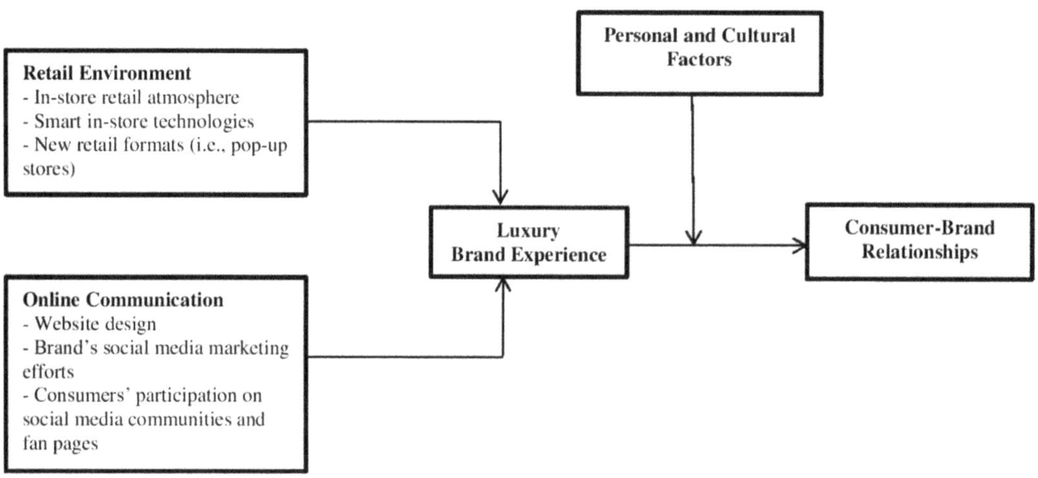

Retail Environment

One factor that is quite influential in terms of shaping the brand experience is the in-store retail atmosphere itself. As Bitner (1990) argues in her landmark article, the elements of the physical environment, including the atmosphere, can have a significant impact on the experiences of consumers. As luxury brands aim to attract consumers by offering them a hedonic, multisensory appeal, the retail atmosphere is considered as an essential part of the positioning strategy of luxury brands (Pantano, Passavanti, Priporas, & Verteramo, 2018). Given that, luxury brand managers need to support their positioning strategies with an attractive retail atmosphere that enhances the brand experience and helps the brand develop stronger relationships with its consumers. Despite its importance, the number of studies that examine the effect of the in-store retail atmosphere, specifically in the context of luxury brands, has been somewhat limited. Still, it is imperative to note the findings of these studies as they can provide valuable insights for enhancing the luxury brand experience. For example, in their study conducted in a luxury goods store, Grewal, Baker, Levy, and Voss (2003) first test the effect of in-store cues on wait expectations and store atmosphere evaluations and then test the effects of these two on store patronage intentions. Their findings reveal especially the positive effect that classical music has on store atmosphere evaluations and, thus on store patronage intentions. In another study, Klein et al. (2016) find that store atmosphere, together with hedonic shopping value, has a positive effect on brand experience in luxury retail. Recently, Zhang and Zhao (2019) also conduct a study that investigates the different dimensions of luxury value and argue that the store atmosphere itself is crucial for the experiential dimension of luxury value. All these studies highlight the significant role that in-store store retail atmosphere can play in terms of enhancing the brand experience and thus develop stronger consumer-brand relationships.

In line with the exclusive, high-status image luxury brands aim to build, the in-store retail atmosphere of luxury brands also usually expresses high levels of art, status, and creativity and acts as etiquette that identifies the consumers who are socially legitimate to shop from these stores (Dion& Borraz, 2017). Thus, it is not surprising that some luxury brands use highly creative designs in their retail environments. Sometimes these environments are so artistically appealing that some consumers even perceive the luxury brand stores as art institutions (Joy, Wang, Chan, Sherry, &Cui, 2014) or as places that assembly charisma through art and magic (Dion &Arnould, 2011). In the literature, there exist studies that especially emphasize the importance of the use of visual arts and the undertaking of arts-based initiatives by luxury brands as both have the potential to enhance the brand experience and strengthen consumer-brand relationships (e.g., Koronaki, Kyrousi, & Panigyrakis, 2018; Lee, Chen, & Wang, 2015).

P1: In-store retail atmosphere enhances the luxury brand experience and thus strengthens the consumer-brand relationships.

While the in-store retail atmosphere of luxury brands can play a very significant role in terms of enhancing the brand experience, new technologies can also be important for brand managers as luxury brands are in need of finding attractive ways of providing brand experiences to both existing and new target groups (Klein et al., 2016). These technologies can be highly influential in the sense that they not only improve shopping processes but also provide a superior experience by engaging and entertaining consumers (Dacko, 2017; Pantano et al., 2018). Within this context, aside from the digital technologies that include social media and online channels and the mobile technologies that include the mobile apps, the smart in-store technologies that include ibeacons, interactive storefronts, and displays can provide a superior experience to consumers and improve the retail management strategies of luxury brands (Pantano et al., 2018). Even if the effective use of smart technologies has been quite limited in the luxury market, these unconventional yet innovative systems have been incorporated successfully into daily practices in other retail markets (Papagiannidis, Pantano, See-To, Dennis, & Bourlakis, 2017). For example, in-store screen networks that are called digital signages are widely used in retail spaces with the belief that they are useful tools for enhancing the shopping experience and they positively affect consumers' in-store behavior (Dennis, Brakus, Gupta, & Alamanos, 2014).

The effect of other smart systems such as self-service technologies, interactive displays, touch screens, and informative touchpoints on retail experience has also been studied and supportive evidence for the significant role that these systems can play in terms of enhancing perceived shopping value, engagement and retail experience for consumers has been provided (e.g., Adapa, Fazal-e-Hasan, Makam, Azeem, & Mortimer,2020; Roy, Balaji, Quazi, & Quaddus, 2018). As a result of the rising popularity of these systems, there have been some recent attempts to incorporate these innovative systems into the luxury market and this has created interest among consumers as well as scholars (e.g., Chung, Ko, Joung, & Kim, 2018; Jung, Yu, Seo, & Ko, 2019). For example, examining the use of e-service agents, namely Chatbot agents, by luxury fashion retail brands, Chung et al. (2018) state that these agents offer superior and more engaging service encounters by providing "convenient, personal and unique customer assistance" (p.1) and thus support the use of these agents as a new and entertaining way of serving consumers. The researchers also cite the use of the Chatbot agents by Louis Vuitton as a successful example that perfectly fits with the luxury retail brand value of offering superior service. They claim that these agents can play a very critical role in terms of developing consumer-brand relationships.

P2: The use of smart in-store technologies enhances the luxury brand experience and thus strengthens the consumer-brand relationships.

Recognizing the demand among luxury consumers for memorable experiences, some luxury brands also introduce pop-up brand stores as a new retail format for creating a superior brand experience in luxury retail (Lunardo &Mouangue, 2019; Taube & Warnaby, 2017). Pop-up stores are "retail environments that carry a single brand, are controlled by the brand's manufacturer, and are operated with the intention of reinforcing the brand experience rather than selling products at a profit" (Klein et al., 2016, p. 5761-5762). These stores can act as a very influential marketing tool for luxury brand managers since the hedonic shopping value and store atmosphere associated with these stores not only enhance the brand experience but also stimulate positive word-of-mouth (Klein et al., 2016). Moreover, since these stores are perceived to be less luxurious than traditional luxury stores due to their design, consumers feel more comfortable, experience less embarrassment in these stores and accordingly, exhibit more favorable store evaluations in this new and appealing retail format (Lunardo& Mouangue, 2019). Feeling comfortable in the retail environment is an essential factor that contributes significantly to brand experience; thus, luxury brand managers should seriously consider using such new retail formats.

P3: The use of new retail formats (i.e., pop-up stores) enhances the luxury brand experience and thus strengthens the consumer-brand relationships.

Online Communication

Another critical issue for luxury brand managers is related to managing online communication with and among consumers. The luxury market has been relatively slow in terms of embracing the Internet compared to other consumer markets since the exclusive aura of the luxury brands in a way seems to conflict with the highly open and borderless nature of the Internet (Baker, Ashill, Amer, & Diab, 2018; Shen, Vel, & Khalifa, 2016). However, as Millennials are recognized as a significant target for luxury goods, luxury brand managers have started employing the Internet as a vital strategic tool to reach this technologically savvy group of consumers who highly use the Internet in their daily lives for shopping (Rodrigues & Rodrigues, 2019). Within this respect, the websites of luxury brands need to be carefully designed since websites can play a very critical role in terms of attracting new consumers and developing their relationships with the current consumers by offering an enhanced online experience. Thus, not only luxury brand managers but also marketing scholars have recently started giving much more emphasis to the design of the luxury websites. For example, in their study, Shen et al. (2016) examine how website design can positively contribute to the sense of luxury experienced and hence improve brand equity. Their results reveal that aesthetic appeal is very critical in terms of enhancing the brand experience; thus, the luxury brand managers should design creative and impressive websites that will stimulate consumers to convey a sense of luxury, which will contribute to positive evaluations of overall brand equity. In another study, Baker et al. (2018) also refer to the dilemma faced by luxury brands in terms of preserving their exclusive image within the Internet mass medium. The researchers state that as luxury brands can use their websites to gather data from the consumers, this wealth of information can be used for enhancing the brand experience and building stronger consumer-brand relationships. Other studies also acknowledge the significant role that websites can play within this respect (e.g., Kim, Choi, & Lee, 2015; Kim & Kim, 2018). Thus, it is highly suggested that luxury brand managers approach websites as a valuable touchpoint that can enrich the brand experience (Heine & Berghaus, 2014).

P4: Website design enhances the luxury brand experience and thus strengthens the consumer-brand relationships.

Another challenge that awaits luxury brands is the increasing popularity of social media among consumers in general. Even if today many brands actively use social media platforms as a new and more interactive way of interacting with consumers, luxury brands at first acted rather cautiously in their attempts to connect with their consumers via popular social media platforms (Kim &Ko, 2012). For many years, the compatibility between the exclusive aura of luxury brands and social media has been questioned (Liu, Shin, & Burns, 2019) and these platforms have not been preferred much by luxury brands. However, recently both scholars and brand managers have turned their attention to how luxury brands may embrace social media marketing activities to enhance the luxury brand experience and develop stronger consumer-brand relationships (e.g., Godey et al., 2016; Leban, Seo, & Voyer, 2019). In these studies, the researchers specifically examine the effect of social media activities on luxury brand consumers. For example, Godey et al. (2016) show that social media marketing activities can strategically be vital for luxury brands as they positively affect brand equity and consequently, some key consumer responses such as brand preference, price premium, and loyalty. The researchers highlight that social media marketing efforts incorporate five different dimensions, which are entertainment, interaction, trendiness, customization, and word-of-mouth. They argue that luxury brand managers should seek to promote each of these dimensions while designing their social media sites in order to enrich the brand experience and strengthen consumer-brand relationships. In a similar context, Liu et al. (2019) also investigate the impact of social media marketing on consumer engagement in the luxury market. The researchers claim that luxury brand managers should focus on the entertainment, interaction, and trendiness dimensions of social media marketing activities in order to formulate more effective strategies since these are the dimensions that significantly increase consumer engagement with the brand-related social media content. Moreover, Mandler, Johnen, and Grave (2019) specifically investigate the effect of non-personal (quality, heritage, conspicuousness, uniqueness) and personal (hedonism, extended self) brand luxury dimensions on consumers' affective responses to luxury brand posts on social media. As the results reveal that the non-personal luxury dimensions trigger relatively more positive affect compared to the personal luxury dimensions, brand managers should design their social media content accordingly in order to enhance the luxury brand experience and thus strengthen consumer-brand relationships.

P5: Brand's marketing efforts on social media enhance the luxury brand experience and thus strengthen the consumer-brand relationships.

Lately, marketing scholars and luxury brand managers also explore the consumer-driven social media communities and fan pages devoted to specific luxury brands as a way of better understanding the brand experience and thus, strengthening the consumer-brand relationships. For example, in their recent study, Kim and Lee (2019) examine the luxury brand communities by utilizing the concept of integration and interactivity and reveal that perceived interactivity plays a highly critical role in terms of enhancing relationship outcomes such as brand attitude, purchase intention, and brand loyalty. Based on this finding, the researchers argue that it is essential for luxury brand managers to encourage greater interactivity on social media since interactivity has a favorable, long-term effect on consumer-brand relationships. In another study, Kefi and Maar (2018) emphasize the importance of luxury brand fan pages and show that both the hedonic and informative content of these pages should be carefully designed as the content can significantly affect the experience of the followers and thereby, the relationship they have with luxury brands.

Furthermore, Khan and Rahman (2015) highlight the vital role that stories can play and cite storytelling as a driver for brand experience. For many years, the literature has mainly focused on how firm-originated stories influence consumer brand experience (e.g., Lundqvist, Liljander, Gummerus, & van Riel, 2013). However, with the increasing popularity of social media, more consumers have started sharing their consumption stories on social media platforms and shaping the brand experience of not only their own but also others. Thus, the power of symbolically rich stories as a means of co-constructing brand culture has received the attention of marketing scholars (Schembri & Latimer, 2016). Recently, the literature on luxury branding has also started acknowledging the power of brand stories as a means of enhancing brand experience. For example, Hughes, Bendoni, and Pehlivan (2016) introduce the concept of storygiving and argue that storygiving is especially crucial in the context of luxury brands since these stories feed the experiential and symbolic dimensions which represent the essence of luxury brands. Thus, the researchers promote storygiving as a powerful co-creation tool and suggest that luxury brand managers create motivations and incentives for storygiving.

P6: Consumers' active participation on social media communities and fan pages (including storygiving) enhances the luxury brand experience and thus strengthens the consumer-brand relationships.

Personal and Cultural Factors

Some personal and cultural factors that are important for assessing luxury brand experience and consumer-brand relationships should also be acknowledged within this context. For example, Millennials should be given particular emphasis as they are not only more interested in luxury products compared to other generations, but also more motivated to spend money for status (Shin, Eastman, & Mothersbaugh, 2017). However, Millennials constitute a significant challenge for luxury brand managers as Millennials are less likely to be emotionally attached to brands; thus, it is harder for them to form strong relationships (de Kerviler & Rodriguez, 2019). Since Millennials value experiences more than the possessions they own (Oyedele& Simpson, 2018), luxury brand managers should ensure that they offer enhanced brand experiences to Millennial consumers. Within this context, scholars and practitioners should also consider some personal factors, such as the need for uniqueness and self-monitoring (e.g., Shao, Grace, & Ross, 2019), novelty seeking (e.g., de Kerviler & Rodriguez, 2019), and personal values (e.g., Zhang& Zhao, 2019) since all of these may have an impact on the relationship between brand experience and consumer-brand relationships. Scholars and practitioners should also recognize the significance of cultural factors as this will be very important in terms of creating the right brand experience, especially the online experience (Choi, Seo, Wagner, & Yoon, 2018; Shobeiri, Mazaheri, & Laroche, 2018).

P7: Personal and cultural factors moderate the impact of luxury brand experience on consumer-brand relationships.

THEORETICAL AND MANAGERIAL IMPLICATIONS

This chapter serves to extend the literature on brand experience in the context of luxury brands by providing some valuable insights. Even if there exist studies that draw attention to the importance of brand experience for the marketing literature (e.g., Andreini et al., 2018; Brakus et al., 2009; de Oliveira Santini et al., 2018), there exist only a few studies that examine its effect specifically in the context of luxury brands (e.g., de Kerviler & Rodrigues, 2019; Wiedmann et al., 2018). Realizing this gap in the literature, this chapter states the vital role that luxury brand experience can play in terms of strengthening consumer-brand relationships, which is considered as a highly valuable asset for luxury brands in today's extremely competitive business environment. The chapter discusses that enhanced brand experience can positively contribute to relationship-based variables such as brand loyalty, brand commitment, brand trust, and brand attachment and argues that investigating the ways of enhancing the brand experience should be a priority for marketing scholars and luxury brand managers. Within this context, the chapter also highlights the need for integrating the self-expansion theory into the related discussion. This theory is essential to understand how enhanced brand experiences contribute to stronger consumer-brand relationships, supporting de Kerviler and Rodriguez (2019). More importantly, this chapter contributes to the literature by suggesting an integrative framework on the potential drivers of brand experience in the context of luxury brands which might be useful to guide future research as the potential drivers of brand experience are rarely investigated in the related literature (Coelho et al., 2020).

In addition to these theoretical implications, this chapter also offers some managerial implications and suggestions for luxury brand managers. This chapter argues that enhancing the luxury brand experience is of utmost strategic importance for luxury brands as a way of building stronger relationships with consumers and discusses some of the factors that can be quite influential in terms of shaping the brand experience. Thus, luxury brand managers should acknowledge the importance of these factors and incorporate these factors into their strategic brand management decisions. Within this context, luxury brand managers should give particular emphasis to the in-store retail atmosphere as an attractive atmosphere can enhance brand experience and help the brand develop stronger relationships with its consumers. As luxury brands are in need of finding new and attractive ways of providing brand experiences to both existing and new target groups (Klein et al., 2016), luxury brand managers should also consider the use of smart in-store technologies and new retail formats (i.e., pop-up stores) that can enhance the brand experience. Moreover, luxury brand managers should encourage the use of visual arts and the undertaking of arts-based initiatives, as both have the potential to enhance the luxury brand experience and strengthen consumer-brand relationships (Koronaki et al., 2018; Lee et al., 2015).

Given that the use of the Internet and social media platforms have become popular among luxury consumers, it is also important that luxury brand managers employ the Internet as an essential strategic tool to reach their target consumers. Within this context, luxury brand managers should carefully design their website and develop social media marketing activities so that with enriched brand experience, they can form stronger relationships with their consumers. Luxury brand managers should also encourage their consumers to take active participation on social media communities and fan pages and to co-construct the brand culture through storygiving, as the sharing of consumption experiences and stories can indeed enhance the brand experience and strengthen the consumer-brand relationships (Hughes et al., 2016).

DIRECTIONS FOR FUTURE RESEARCH

Even if the critical role that brand experience can play in the luxury market in terms of developing stronger consumer-brand relationships has been partly acknowledged by both marketing scholars and luxury brand managers, there are still underexplored yet promising areas for future research. First of all, future studies must expand the knowledge on brand experience by adopting a multi-perspective approach that examines the various psychological, relational, social and cultural factors that can be influential within this context; thus "a renaissance of brand experience" is highly needed (Andreini et al., 2018, p. 123). Future research should also give more emphasis to identifying the potential drivers of luxury brand experience and empirically test the effects of these factors. Also, the multi-dimensional nature of the brand experience should further be investigated by considering both the effect of each potential driver on the different dimensions of brand experience and the effect of each dimension on various relationship-based variables. Even if the theoretical perspective provided by Brakus et al. (2009) is widely used, the significant role that the social dimension proposed by Schmitt (1999) also warrants attention and thus need to be further examined in future studies since the relationship one has with others and his/her ideal-self can be very important in terms enhancing the luxury brand experience. Furthermore, most of the studies on brand experience, especially the ones that investigate its effects on consumer-brand relationships, use the relationship theory (Fournier, 1998) to support their discussions (e.g., Prentice et al., 2019; Ramaseshan& Stein, 2014). However, other theoretical perspectives such as the self-expansion theory (e.g., de Kerviler & Rodriguez, 2019) and construal level theory of psychological distance (e.g., Park, Im, & Kim, 2018) can also be used within this line of research. The inclusion and further discussion of these theories can provide some interesting insights and guidance to both marketing scholars and luxury brand managers. Finally, future research that provides cross-cultural comparative analyses is highly encouraged.

CONCLUSION

This chapter discusses the critical role that luxury brand experience can play in terms of strengthening consumer-brand relationships in the luxury market and highlights some of the potential drivers that can be used by luxury brand managers to enhance the brand experience of luxury consumers. Given that today's luxury consumers are less loyal and more likely to shop around (Shimul et al., 2019), the importance of brand experience has increased significantly. Within that respect, the role that the retail environment and online communication can play has become more critical than ever. By enriching the in-store retail atmosphere, promoting the use of smart in-store technologies and new retail formats, improving website design, increasing social media marketing efforts, and encouraging consumers' active participation on social media platforms, it is possible to enhance brand experiences. Thus, both marketing scholars and luxury brand managers should truly acknowledge and emphasize the power of enhanced brand experiences as a way to develop stronger relationships with luxury consumers.

REFERENCES

Adapa, S., Fazal-e-Hasan, S. M., Makam, S. B., Azeem, M. M., & Mortimer, G. (2020). Examining the antecedents and consequences of perceived shopping value through smart retail technology. *Journal of Retailing and Consumer Services*, *52*, 101901. doi:10.1016/j.jretconser.2019.101901

Andreini, D., Pedeliento, G., Zarantonello, L., & Solerio, C. (2018). A renaissance of brand experience: Advancing the concept through a multi-perspective analysis. *Journal of Business Research*, *91*, 123–133. doi:10.1016/j.jbusres.2018.05.046

Aron, A., & Aron, E. N. (1986). *Love and the expansion of self: Understanding attraction and satisfaction*. Hemisphere Publishing Corp/Harper & Row Publishers.

Arya, V., Sethi, D., & Paul, J. (2019). Does digital footprint act as a digital asset? Enhancing brand experience through remarketing. *International Journal of Information Management*, *49*, 142–156. doi:10.1016/j.ijinfomgt.2019.03.013

Baker, J., Ashill, N., Amer, N., & Diab, E. (2018). The internet dilemma: An exploratory study of luxury firms' usage of internet-based technologies. *Journal of Retailing and Consumer Services*, *41*, 37–47. doi:10.1016/j.jretconser.2017.11.007

Bapat, D. (2017). Impact of brand familiarity on brands experience dimensions for financial services brands. *International Journal of Bank Marketing*, *35*(4), 637–648. doi:10.1108/IJBM-05-2016-0066

Bitner, M. J. (1990). Evaluating service encounters: The effects of physical surroundings and employee responses. *Journal of Marketing*, *54*(2), 69–82. doi:10.1177/002224299005400206

Brakus, J. J., Schmitt, B. H., & Zarantonello, L. (2009). Brand experience: What is it? How is it measured? Does it affect loyalty? *Journal of Marketing*, *73*(3), 52–68. doi:10.1509/jmkg.73.3.052

Castano, R., & Perez, M. E. (2014). A matter of love: Consumers' relationships with original brands and their counterfeits. *Journal of Consumer Marketing*, *31*(6/7), 475–482. doi:10.1108/JCM-05-2014-0970

Chandon, J. L., Laurent, G., & Valette-Florence, P. (2017). In search of new planets in the luxury galaxy. *Journal of Business Research*, *77*(August), 140–146. doi:10.1016/j.jbusres.2017.04.006

Choi, Y. K., Seo, Y., Wagner, U., & Yoon, S. (2018). (in press). Matching luxury brand appeals with attitude functions on social media across cultures. *Journal of Business Research*. Advance online publication. doi:10.1016/j.jbusres.2018.10.003

Chung, M., Ko, E., Joung, H., & Kim, S. J. (2018). (in press). Chatbot e-service and customer satisfaction regarding luxury brands. *Journal of Business Research*.

Coelho, F. J., Bairrada, C. M., & de Matos Coelho, A. F. (2020). Functional brand qualities and perceived value: The mediating role of brand experience and brand personality. *Psychology and Marketing*, *37*(1), 41–55. doi:10.1002/mar.21279

Dacko, S. G. (2017). Enabling smart retail settings via mobile augmented reality shopping apps. *Technological Forecasting and Social Change*, *124*, 243–256. doi:10.1016/j.techfore.2016.09.032

Das, G., Agarwal, J., Malhotra, N. K., & Varshneya, G. (2019). Does brand experience translate into brand commitment?: A mediated-moderation model of brand passion and perceived brand ethicality. *Journal of Business Research*, *95*, 479–490. doi:10.1016/j.jbusres.2018.05.026

de Kerviler, G., & Rodriguez, C. M. (2019). Luxury brand experiences and relationship quality for Millennials: The role of self-expansion. *Journal of Business Research*, *102*, 250–262. doi:10.1016/j.jbusres.2019.01.046

de Oliveira Santini, F., Ladeira, W. J., Sampaio, C. H., & Pinto, D. C. (2018). The brand experience extended model: A meta-analysis. *Journal of Brand Management*, *25*(6), 519–535. doi:10.105741262-018-0104-6

Delgado-Ballester, E., & Munuera-Alemán, J. L. (2001). Brand trust in the context of consumer loyalty. *European Journal of Marketing*, *35*(11/12), 1238–1258. doi:10.1108/EUM0000000006475

Dennis, C., Brakus, J. J., Gupta, S., & Alamanos, E. (2014). The effect of digital signage on shoppers' behavior: The role of the evoked experience. *Journal of Business Research*, *67*(11), 2250–2257. doi:10.1016/j.jbusres.2014.06.013

Ding, C. G., & Tseng, T. H. (2015). On the relationships among brand experience, hedonic emotions, and brand equity. *European Journal of Marketing*, *49*(7/8), 994–1015. doi:10.1108/EJM-04-2013-0200

Dion, D., & Arnould, E. (2011). Retail luxury strategy: Assembling charisma through art and magic. *Journal of Retailing*, *87*(4), 502–520. doi:10.1016/j.jretai.2011.09.001

Dion, D., & Borraz, S. (2017). Managing status: How luxury brands shape class subjectivities in the service encounter. *Journal of Marketing*, *81*(5), 67–85. doi:10.1509/jm.15.0291

Dolbec, P. Y., & Chebat, J. C. (2013). The impact of a flagship vs. a brand store on brand attitude, brand attachment and brand equity. *Journal of Retailing*, *89*(4), 460–466. doi:10.1016/j.jretai.2013.06.003

Dwivedi, A., Nayeem, T., & Murshed, F. (2018). Brand experience and consumers' willingness-to-pay (WTP) a price premium: Mediating role of brand credibility and perceived uniqueness. *Journal of Retailing and Consumer Services*, *44*, 100–107. doi:10.1016/j.jretconser.2018.06.009

Eastman, J. K., Shin, H., & Ruhland, K. (2020). The picture of luxury: A comprehensive examination of college student consumers' relationship with luxury brands. *Psychology and Marketing*, *37*(1), 56–73. doi:10.1002/mar.21280

Ferreira, P., Rodrigues, P., & Rodrigues, P. (2019). Brand love as mediator of the brand experience-satisfaction-loyalty relationship in a retail fashion brand. *Management & Marketing. Challenges for the Knowledge Society*, *14*(3), 278–291. doi:10.2478/mmcks-2019-0020

Fionda, A. M., & Moore, C. M. (2009). The anatomy of the luxury fashion brand. *Journal of Brand Management, 16*(5-6), 347–363. doi:10.1057/bm.2008.45

Fournier, S. (1998). Consumers and their brands: Developing relationship theory in consumer research. *The Journal of Consumer Research, 24*(4), 343–353. doi:10.1086/209515

Francisco-Maffezzolli, E. C., Semprebon, E., & Prado, P. H. M. (2014). Construing loyalty through brand experience: The mediating role of brand relationship quality. *Journal of Brand Management, 21*(5), 446–458. doi:10.1057/bm.2014.16

Fullerton, G. (2005). How commitment both enables and undermines marketing relationships. *European Journal of Marketing, 39*(11/12), 1372–1388. doi:10.1108/03090560510623307

Gentile, C., Spiller, N., & Noci, G. (2007). How to sustain the customer experience: An overview of experience components that co-create value with the customer. *European Management Journal, 25*(5), 395–410. doi:10.1016/j.emj.2007.08.005

Godey, B., Manthiou, A., Pederzoli, D., Rokka, J., Aiello, G., Donvito, R., & Singh, R. (2016). Social media marketing efforts of luxury brands: Influence on brand equity and consumer behavior. *Journal of Business Research, 69*(12), 5833–5841. doi:10.1016/j.jbusres.2016.04.181

Grewal, D., Baker, J., Levy, M., & Voss, G. B. (2003). The effects of wait expectations and store atmosphere evaluations on patronage intentions in service-intensive retail stores. *Journal of Retailing, 79*(4), 259–268. doi:10.1016/j.jretai.2003.09.006

Heine, K., & Berghaus, B. (2014). Luxury goes digital: How to tackle the digital luxury brand-consumer touchpoints. *Journal of Global Fashion Marketing, 5*(3), 223–234. doi:10.1080/20932685.2014.907606

Hepola, J., Karjaluoto, H., & Hintikka, A. (2017). The effect of sensory brand experience and involvement on brand equity directly and indirectly through consumer brand engagement. *Journal of Product and Brand Management, 26*(3), 282–293. doi:10.1108/JPBM-10-2016-1348

Holbrook, M. B., & Hirschman, E. C. (1982). The experiential aspects of consumption: Consumer fantasies, feelings, and fun. *The Journal of Consumer Research, 9*(2), 132–140. doi:10.1086/208906

Holmqvist, J., Ruiz, C. D., & Penaloza, L. (2019). Moments of luxury: Hedonic escapism as a luxury experience. *Journal of Business Research, 116*, 503–513. doi:10.1016/j.jbusres.2019.10.015

Huang, C. C. (2017). The impacts of brand experiences on brand loyalty: Mediators of brand love and trust. *Management Decision, 55*(5), 915–934. doi:10.1108/MD-10-2015-0465

Huang, R., Lee, S. H., Kim, H., & Evans, L. (2015). The impact of brand experiences on brand resonance in multi-channel fashion retailing. *Journal of Research in Interactive Marketing, 9*(2), 129–147. doi:10.1108/JRIM-06-2014-0042

Hughes, M. U., Bendoni, W. K., & Pehlivan, E. (2016). Storygiving as a co-creation tool for luxury brands in the age of the internet: A love story by Tiffany and thousands of lovers. *Journal of Product and Brand Management, 25*(4), 357–364. doi:10.1108/JPBM-09-2015-0970

Hultén, B. (2011). Sensory marketing: The multi-sensory brand-experience concept. *European Business Review*, *23*(3), 256–273. doi:10.1108/09555341111130245

Iglesias, O., Markovic, S., & Rialp, J. (2019). How does sensory brand experience influence brand equity? Considering the roles of customer satisfaction, customer affective commitment, and employee empathy. *Journal of Business Research*, *96*, 343–354. doi:10.1016/j.jbusres.2018.05.043

Iglesias, O., Singh, J. J., & Batista-Foguet, J. M. (2011). The role of brand experience and affective commitment in determining brand loyalty. *Journal of Brand Management*, *18*(8), 570–582. doi:10.1057/bm.2010.58

Islam, J. U., Hollebeek, L. D., Rahman, Z., Khan, I., & Rasool, A. (2019). Customer engagement in the service context: An empirical investigation of the construct, its antecedents and consequences. *Journal of Retailing and Consumer Services*, *50*, 277–285. doi:10.1016/j.jretconser.2019.05.018

Japutra, A., & Molinillo, S. (2019). Responsible and active brand personality: On the relationships with brand experience and key relationship constructs. *Journal of Business Research*, *99*, 464–471. doi:10.1016/j.jbusres.2017.08.027

Joy, A., Wang, J. J., Chan, T. S., Sherry, J. F. Jr, & Cui, G. (2014). M (Art) worlds: Consumer perceptions of how luxury brand stores become art institutions. *Journal of Retailing*, *90*(3), 347–364. doi:10.1016/j.jretai.2014.01.002

Jung, J., Yu, J., Seo, Y., & Ko, E. (2019). (in press). Consumer experiences of virtual reality: Insights from VR luxury brand fashion shows. *Journal of Business Research*. Advance online publication. doi:10.1016/j.jbusres.2019.10.038

Kang, J., Manthiou, A., Sumarjan, N., & Tang, L. (2017). An investigation of brand experience on brand attachment, knowledge, and trust in the lodging industry. *Journal of Hospitality Marketing & Management*, *26*(1), 1–22. doi:10.1080/19368623.2016.1172534

Kefi, H., & Maar, D. (2018). (in press). The power of lurking: Assessing the online experience of luxury brand fan page followers. *Journal of Business Research*. Advance online publication. doi:10.1016/j.jbusres.2018.08.012

Khamitov, M., Wang, X. S., & Thomson, M. (2019). How well do consumer-brand relationships drive customer brand loyalty? Generalizations from a meta-analysis of brand relationship elasticities. *The Journal of Consumer Research*, *46*(3), 435–459. doi:10.1093/jcr/ucz006

Khan, I., & Fatma, M. (2017). Antecedents and outcomes of brand experience: An empirical study. *Journal of Brand Management*, *24*(5), 439–452. doi:10.105741262-017-0040-x

Khan, I., & Rahman, Z. (2015). Brand experience anatomy in retailing: An interpretive structural modeling approach. *Journal of Retailing and Consumer Services*, *24*, 60–69. doi:10.1016/j.jretconser.2015.02.003

Kim, A. J., & Ko, E. (2012). Do social media marketing activities enhance customer equity? An empirical study of luxury fashion brand. *Journal of Business Research*, *65*(10), 1480–1486. doi:10.1016/j.jbusres.2011.10.014

Kim, H., Choi, Y. J., & Lee, Y. (2015). Web atmospheric qualities in luxury fashion brand web sites. *Journal of Fashion Marketing and Management, 19*(4), 384–401. doi:10.1108/JFMM-09-2013-0103

Kim, J., & Lee, K. H. (2019). Influence of integration on interactivity in social media luxury brand communities. *Journal of Business Research, 99*, 422–429. doi:10.1016/j.jbusres.2017.10.001

Kim, J. H., & Kim, M. (2018). Conceptualization and assessment of e-service quality for luxury brands. *Service Industries Journal*, •••, 1–35. doi:10.1080/02642069.2018.1461842

Klein, J. F., Falk, T., Esch, F. R., & Gloukhovtsev, A. (2016). Linking pop-up brand stores to brand experience and word of mouth: The case of luxury retail. *Journal of Business Research, 69*(12), 5761–5767. doi:10.1016/j.jbusres.2016.04.172

Koronaki, E., Kyrousi, A. G., & Panigyrakis, G. G. (2018). The emotional value of arts-based initiatives: Strengthening the luxury brand-consumer relationship. *Journal of Business Research, 85*, 406–413. doi:10.1016/j.jbusres.2017.10.018

Leban, M., Seo, Y., & Voyer, B. G. (2019). Transformational effects of social media lurking practices on luxury consumption. *Journal of Business Research, 116*, 514–521. doi:10.1016/j.jbusres.2019.09.010

Lee, H. C., Chen, W. W., & Wang, C. W. (2015). The role of visual art in enhancing perceived prestige of luxury brands. *Marketing Letters, 26*(4), 593–606. doi:10.100711002-014-9292-3

Liu, X., Shin, H., & Burns, A. C. (2019). (in press). Examining the impact of luxury brand's social media marketing on customer engagement: Using big data analytics and natural language processing. *Journal of Business Research*. Advance online publication. doi:10.1016/j.jbusres.2019.04.042

Lunardo, R., & Mouangue, E. (2019). Getting over discomfort in luxury brand stores: How pop-up stores affect perceptions of luxury, embarrassment, and store evaluations. *Journal of Retailing and Consumer Services, 49*, 77–85. doi:10.1016/j.jretconser.2019.03.005

Lundqvist, A., Liljander, V., Gummerus, J., & van Riel, A. (2013). The impact of storytelling on the consumer brand experience: The case of a firm-originated story. *Journal of Brand Management, 20*(4), 283–297. doi:10.1057/bm.2012.15

Mandler, T., Johnen, M., & Grave, J. F. (2019). (in press). Can't help falling in love? How brand luxury generates positive consumer affect in social media. *Journal of Business Research*. Advance online publication. doi:10.1016/j.jbusres.2019.10.010

Nierobisch, T., Toporowski, W., Dannewald, T., & Jahn, S. (2017). Flagship stores for FMCG national brands: Do they improve brand cognitions and create favorable consumer reactions? *Journal of Retailing and Consumer Services, 34*, 117–137. doi:10.1016/j.jretconser.2016.09.014

Nobre, H., & Simoes, C. (2019). NewLux Brand Relationship Scale: Capturing the scope of mass-consumed luxury brand relationships. *Journal of Business Research, 102*, 328–338. doi:10.1016/j.jbusres.2019.01.047

Nysveen, H., Pedersen, P. E., & Skard, S. (2013). Brand experiences in service organizations: Exploring the individual effects of brand experience dimensions. *Journal of Brand Management, 20*(5), 404–423. doi:10.1057/bm.2012.31

Ong, C. H., Lee, H. W., & Ramayah, T. (2018). Impact of brand experience on loyalty. *Journal of Hospitality Marketing & Management, 27*(7), 755–774. doi:10.1080/19368623.2018.1445055

Oyedele, A., & Simpson, P. (2018). Emerging adulthood, sharing utilities and intention to use sharing services. *Journal of Services Marketing, 32*(2), 161–174. doi:10.1108/JSM-09-2016-0344

Pantano, E., Passavanti, R., Priporas, C. V., & Verteramo, S. (2018). To what extent luxury retailing can be smart? *Journal of Retailing and Consumer Services, 43*, 94–100. doi:10.1016/j.jretconser.2018.03.012

Papagiannidis, S., Pantano, E., See-To, E. W., Dennis, C., & Bourlakis, M. (2017). To immerse or not? Experimenting with two virtual retail environments. *Information Technology & People, 30*(1), 163–188. doi:10.1108/ITP-03-2015-0069

Park, M., Im, H., & Kim, H. Y. (2018). (in press). "You are too friendly!" The negative effects of social media marketing on value perceptions of luxury fashion brands. *Journal of Business Research.*

Peng, N., & Chen, A. (2019). Examining consumers' luxury hotel stay repurchase intentions-incorporating a luxury hotel brand attachment variable into a luxury consumption value model. *International Journal of Contemporary Hospitality Management, 31*(3), 1348–1366. doi:10.1108/IJCHM-04-2018-0332

Pham, M., Valette-Florence, P., & Vigneron, F. (2018). Luxury brand desirability and fashion equity: The joint moderating effect on consumers' commitment toward luxury brands. *Psychology and Marketing, 35*(12), 902–912. doi:10.1002/mar.21143

Prentice, C., Wang, X., & Loureiro, S. M. C. (2019). The influence of brand experience and service quality on customer engagement. *Journal of Retailing and Consumer Services, 50*, 50–59. doi:10.1016/j.jretconser.2019.04.020

Pulh, M., Mencarelli, R., & Chaney, D. (2019). The consequences of the heritage experience in brand museums on the consumer-brand relationship. *European Journal of Marketing, 53*(10), 2193–2212. doi:10.1108/EJM-03-2017-0233

Ramaseshan, B., & Stein, A. (2014). Connecting the dots between brand experience and brand loyalty: The mediating role of brand personality and brand relationships. *Journal of Brand Management, 21*(7-8), 664–683. doi:10.1057/bm.2014.23

Ramirez, R., & Merunka, D. (2019). Brand experience effects on brand attachment: The role of brand trust, age, and income. *European Business Review, 31*(5), 610–645. doi:10.1108/EBR-02-2017-0039

Reimann, M., & Aron, A. (2009). Self-expansion motivation and inclusion of brands in self. In D. J. MacInnis, C. Whan Park, & J. W. Priester (Eds.), *Handbook of brand relationships* (pp. 87–103). Routledge.

Rodrigues, C., & Rodrigues, P. (2019). Brand love matters to Millennials: The relevance of mystery, sensuality and intimacy to neo-luxury brands. *Journal of Product and Brand Management, 28*(7), 830–848. doi:10.1108/JPBM-04-2018-1842

Rodrigues, P., Brandao, A., & Rodrigues, C. (2018). The importance of self in brand love in consumer luxury brand relationships. *Journal of Customer Behaviour, 18*(3), 189–210. doi:10.1362/147539218X15434304746036

Roy, S. K., Balaji, M. S., Quazi, A., & Quaddus, M. (2018). Predictors of customer acceptance of and resistance to smart technologies in the retail sector. *Journal of Retailing and Consumer Services*, *42*, 147–160. doi:10.1016/j.jretconser.2018.02.005

Sahin, A., Kitapci, H., Altindag, E., & Gok, S. (2017). Investigating the impacts of brand experience and service quality. *International Journal of Market Research*, *59*(6), 707–724. doi:10.2501/IJMR-2017-051

Schembri, S., & Latimer, L. (2016). Online brand communities: Constructing and co-constructing brand culture. *Journal of Marketing Management*, *32*(7-8), 628–651. doi:10.1080/0267257X.2015.1117518

Schmitt, B. (1999). Experiential marketing. *Journal of Marketing Management*, *15*(1/3), 53–67. doi:10.1362/026725799784870496

Seo, Y., & Buchanan-Oliver, M. (2019). Constructing a typology of luxury brand consumption practices. *Journal of Business Research*, *99*, 414–421. doi:10.1016/j.jbusres.2017.09.019

Shao, W., Grace, D., & Ross, M. (2019). Consumer motivation and luxury consumption: Testing moderating effects. *Journal of Retailing and Consumer Services*, *46*, 33–44. doi:10.1016/j.jretconser.2018.10.003

Shen, K. N., Vel, P., & Khalifa, M. (2016). Website design: Place for luxury brands in cyberspace? *Behaviour & Information Technology*, *35*(12), 1115–1129. doi:10.1080/0144929X.2016.1188987

Shimul, A. S., Phau, I., & Lwin, M. (2019). Conceptualising luxury brand attachment: Scale development and validation. *Journal of Brand Management*, *26*(6), 675–690. doi:10.105741262-019-00158-6

Shin, H., Eastman, J. K., & Mothersbaugh, D. (2017). The effect of a limited-edition offer following brand dilution on consumer attitudes toward a luxury brand. *Journal of Retailing and Consumer Services*, *38*, 59–70. doi:10.1016/j.jretconser.2017.05.009

Shobeiri, S., Mazaheri, E., & Laroche, M. (2018). Creating the right customer experience online: The influence of culture. *Journal of Marketing Communications*, *24*(3), 270–290. doi:10.1080/13527266.2015.1054859

Shukla, P., Banerjee, M., & Singh, J. (2016). Customer commitment to luxury brands: Antecedents and consequences. *Journal of Business Research*, *69*(1), 323–331. doi:10.1016/j.jbusres.2015.08.004

Stöttinger, B., & Penz, E. (2015). Concurrent ownership of brands and counterfeits: Conceptualization and temporal transformation from a consumer perspective. *Psychology and Marketing*, *32*(4), 373–391. doi:10.1002/mar.20786

Taube, J., & Warnaby, G. (2017). How brand interaction in pop-up shops influences consumers' perceptions of luxury fashion retailers. *Journal of Fashion Marketing and Management*, *21*(3), 385–399. doi:10.1108/JFMM-08-2016-0074

van der Westhuizen, L. M. (2018). Brand loyalty: Exploring self-brand connection and brand experience. *Journal of Product and Brand Management*, *27*(2), 172–184. doi:10.1108/JPBM-07-2016-1281

Wiedmann, K. P., Labenz, F., Haase, J., & Hennigs, N. (2018). The power of experiential marketing: Exploring the causal relationships among multisensory marketing, brand experience, customer perceived value and brand strength. *Journal of Brand Management*, *25*(2), 101–118. doi:10.105741262-017-0061-5

Zhang, L., & Zhao, H. (2019). Personal value vs. luxury value: What are Chinese luxury consumers shopping for when buying luxury fashion goods? *Journal of Retailing and Consumer Services*, *51*, 62–71. doi:10.1016/j.jretconser.2019.05.027

ADDITIONAL READING

Arrigo, E. (2018). Social media marketing in luxury brands: A systematic literature review and implications for management research. *Management Research Review*, *41*(6), 657–679. doi:10.1108/MRR-04-2017-0134

Batat, W. (2019). *The new luxury experience*. Springer International Publishing. doi:10.1007/978-3-030-01671-5

Fetscherin, M., & Heinrich, D. (2015). Consumer brand relationships research: A bibliometric citation meta-analysis. *Journal of Business Research*, *68*(2), 380–390. doi:10.1016/j.jbusres.2014.06.010

Kapferer, J. N., & Bastien, V. (2012). *The luxury strategy: Break the rules of marketing to build luxury brands*. Kogan Page Publishers.

Pini, F. M., & Pelleschi, V. (2017). Creating a seamless experience for luxury consumers integrating online and offline communication. In *New luxury management* (pp. 217–237). Palgrave Macmillan. doi:10.1007/978-3-319-41727-1_12

Reimann, M., Castaño, R., Zaichkowsky, J., & Bechara, A. (2012). How we relate to brands: Psychological and neurophysiological insights into consumer-brand relationships. *Journal of Consumer Psychology*, *22*(1), 128–142. doi:10.1016/j.jcps.2011.11.003

Roy, S. K., Balaji, M. S., Sadeque, S., Nguyen, B., & Melewar, T. C. (2017). Constituents and consequences of smart customer experience in retailing. *Technological Forecasting and Social Change*, *124*, 257–270. doi:10.1016/j.techfore.2016.09.022

Woodside, A. G., Sood, S., & Miller, K. (2008). When consumers and brands talk: Storytelling theory and research in psychology and marketing. *Psychology and Marketing*, *25*(2), 97–145. doi:10.1002/mar.20203

KEY TERMS AND DEFINITIONS

Brand Experience: Subjective consumer responses shown in response to brand-related stimuli.

Experiential Marketing: A marketing strategy that aims to create memorable, real-life experiences between brands and consumers.

Multisensory Marketing: A marketing strategy that aims to improve brand perceptions and experience by focusing on the human senses and their interactions.

Pop-Up Store: A new retail format that carries a single brand and that is operated to reinforce the brand experience.

Smart Retailing: A group of smart technologies that are used for providing consumers with an enhanced shopping experience that is faster and smarter.

Social Media Marketing: The process of promoting a product or service through the use of social media platforms.

Storygiving: The practice of creation and sharing of brand stories among consumers.

Chapter 6
Excellent Cuisine Worth a Detour:
Dimensions of Luxury Dining Experiences

Fernando Oliveira-Brochado
ISCTE, Lisbon University Institute, Portugal

ABSTRACT

Luxury restaurants are expected to offer outstanding culinary talent and expertise; be authentic, creative and consistent; and provide exciting quality food. Currently, culinary art discourses include a social dimension in which social networking sites are used to share gastronomic experiences and check recommendations. User-generated reviews are thus an intersection of participatory culture and 'foodie' discoures. This study's main objective was to examine this phenomenon by analysing web reviews to identify the expressive dimensions that describe guests' experiences. Mixed-method content analysis was selected for this research, using qualitative text interpretation to supplement quantitative word counts and factor analyses. Content analysis of reviews of the top three Michelin-starred restaurants (i.e., two stars) in Portugal identified concepts used to assess haute cuisine experiences from the client's perspective. The results include a concept map encompassing the following dimensions: 'food', 'restaurant', 'experience', 'menu', 'wine', 'special (dinner)', 'view', 'beautiful (food)', 'friendly (staff)', 'chef', 'visit' and 'dessert'.

INTRODUCTION

Restaurants provide experiences, and, because they operate in highly competitive business environments, a distinctive dining experience is often a critical factor for increasingly demanding customers (Johnson, Surlemont, Nicod and Revaz, 2005). High quality restaurants need to have outstanding culinary talent and expertise (Johnson et al., 2005); be authentic, creative and consistent; and offer exciting quality food to create a unique identity recognisable to customers and differentiated from the competition (Gehrels & Kristanto, 2007). According to Pizam (2010, p. 343), what drives guests' 'willingness to pay high prices for hospitality "products" is the quality of the experience'.

DOI: 10.4018/978-1-7998-4369-6.ch006

Copyright © 2021, IGI Global. Copying or distributing in print or electronic forms without written permission of IGI Global is prohibited.

The Michelin Guide is a gastronomy guide (Gehrels & Kristanto, 2007; Johnson et al., 2005; Surlemont & Johnson, 2005) that has mainly categorised the highest quality segment of restaurants since 1933. *The Michelin Guide* uses a star system ranging from one to three stars according to the quality of the food. This system's 'mystique' culture and clandestine nature are both its key features and essential elements, contributing to preserving creativity and individuality within the restaurant sector and avoiding standardisation (Johnson et al., 2005; Surlemont & Johnson, 2005). No guidelines or written criteria have been published regarding the quality required for the various levels in the Michelin star rating system (Johnson et al., 2005; Surlemont & Johnson, 2005). A selective, rigorously trained team of inspectors anonymously make unannounced visits and rate restaurants (Johnson et al., 2005).

The team's emphasis on consistent quality and – to some extent – tradition has attracted some criticism but has also contributed to making *The Michelin Guide* a reliable source of information (Johnson et al., 2005; Surlemont & Johnson, 2005) and an advertising channel for luxury restaurants (Hlee, Lee, Yang & Koo, 2019). It is widely accepted as the definitive reference book for gourmands and followers of haute cuisine in Europe, and its influence within the industry and with the dining-out public is unquestionable. Given this system's undisputed reputation, being awarded a Michelin star is viewed as duly deserved recognition of culinary achievement and excellence (Surlemont & Johnson, 2005). Thus, the Michelin Guide potentially has great influence on restaurant choices and a major impact on restaurants' seat occupancy, turnover and profitability (Surlemont & Johnson, 2005).

The luxury segment of the restaurant industry has grown rapidly over the last two decades (Han & Hyun, 2017). This segment of the restaurant industry is a niche market that attracts tourists and consumers with high levels of expenditure who demand high quality products (Johnson et al., 2005; Palmer, Cooper & Burns, 2010; Tommaso, Petruzzelli & Vito, 2017). Previous studies have analysed luxury restaurants from different perspectives. These have included the Michelin star system's characteristics and effects (e.g. Bóka & Kovács, 2015; Johnson et al., 2005; Surlemont & Johnson, 2005), marketing mechanisms (e.g. Gehrels & Kristanto, 2007; Miranda, Rubio & Chamorro, 2015), innovation processes in developing new food creations (e.g. Ottenbacher & Harrington, 2007). Other research has focused on culinary team composition (Tommaso et al., 2017) and social and cultural processes underpinning the formation of chefs' identities (e.g. Palmer et al., 2010).

In addition, studies have examined consumer behaviours in luxury restaurants, diners' consumption patterns and factors contributing to guests' loyalty (e.g. Peng & Chen, 2015) and online complaints (e.g. Vásquez & Chik, 2015). Researchers have also studied the type of information (e.g. utilitarian and hedonic) shared online by guests (Hlee et al., 2019) and consumers' willingness to pay premium prices (Kiatkawsin & Han, 2019). A trend observed in the luxury restaurant segment is an increase in information shared by consumers in Web reviews about their experiences, which has contributed to enhancing foodie discourse (Rousseau, 2012; Vásquez & Chik, 2015). Engaging in culinary discourses, therefore, includes a social dimension in which social networking sites are used to share gastronomic experiences.

These sites provide 'affinity spaces' (Gee, 2005) for people who want to reach an audience likely to have similar interests. Online restaurant review sites also provide the means for individuals to display their culinary capital as they demonstrate expertise in matters such as authenticity, taste and quality and discuss the perceived value of their dining experiences with those who share parallel interests (Vásquez & Chik, 2015). Naccarato and Lebesco (2012:) conceptualise culinary capital as engagement in 'food related practices that reflect a certain set of values that are privileged over others'.

A further trend towards democratisation can be observed in the circulation of information about food, especially for restaurant reviews. Food bloggers have made use of the full potential of participatory forms of digital media, writing their own reviews and changing various conventions associated with restaurant reviewing (Rousseau, 2012). User-generated restaurant reviews can also be considered a manifestation of this cultural shift from a few-to-many food writers, turning restaurant reviewing into a widespread phenomenon. This has meant a shift from an exclusive cultural activity restricted to an elite to a cultural practice that has now fully entered the vernacular realm and that can be done by anyone. User-generated restaurant reviews thus represent an interesting intersection of participatory culture and foodie discourse (Vásquez & Chik, 2015).

In addition, an increasing tendency over the last two decades has been noted towards democratisation in certain culinary practices. More individuals representing a wider range of social classes have gained information about – as well as access to – a broader spectrum of dining options than ever before. In recent decades, dining in higher-end restaurants has become less exclusive and more affordable than it ever was before – whether done regularly, intermittently or exceptionally (Lane, 2014).

Online food discourses about luxury restaurants also show this trend towards democratisation. Online review sites allow a greater diversity of voices, perspectives and opinions about high-end dining compared with elite forms of restaurant reviewing. However, review sites can simultaneously reproduce existing social hierarchies, as only individuals in possession of sufficient economic capital can afford to dine at – and, consequently, post reviews on – high-end restaurants.

The present study is based on the argument that Web reviews of luxury dining experiences offer a valuable source of information regarding the determinants of luxury restaurants that are worth a special visit. The main objective was thus to identify the factors contributing to overall satisfaction with haute cuisine in the post-experience phase, based on online user-generated content. The central research question was defined as follows: What are the main narratives shared by tourists online about luxury dining experiences and the dimensions of these tourists' service experiences with luxury restaurants?

This paper is structured as follows. The next section discusses the relevant literature on service quality in restaurants and content analysis of Web reviews in service quality studies. The third section describes the methodology, including the research context, data collection and data analysis procedure. The fourth section presents the results of quantitative (i.e. concept map) and qualitative (i.e. narrative) analyses of the Web reviews. The final section contains conclusions, limitations and avenues for future research.

LITERATURE REVIEW

This section discusses three main topics relevant to the present research. These are (1) service quality measurement in a restaurant setting, (2) the role of user-generated content in service quality studies and (3) content analysis of Web reviews.

Service Quality Management in a Restaurant Setting

As is the case of most service-oriented businesses, customers' experience of quality is recognised as vital to restaurants (Kaminakis, Karantinou, Koritos & Gounaris, 2019).

Research on perceived quality in restaurant settings has identified and studied the different attributes of restaurant quality that affect customer satisfaction and/or future behavioural intentions (Bojanic & Rosen, 1994; Bujisic et al., 2014; Chow et al., 2007; Gupta et al., 2007; Ha & Jang, 2010, 2012; Iglesias & Guillén, 2004; Kivela et al., 2000).

The three most commonly agreed-upon attributes of restaurant quality are food, service and environment (Ryu & Han, 2010). Studies have shown that all three are vital components that directly influence guests' perception of the quality of restaurants and, therefore, customers' overall satisfaction with restaurant experiences and their post-dining behavioural intentions (Loureiro & Kastenholz, 2011; Loureiro, Miranda & Breazeale, 2014).

Over time, researchers have added other components that create clients' overall impression of services rendered, such as physical setting, hygiene, value for money (, convenience, price and value (Kim, Ng & Kim, 2009). Some of the most widely accepted restaurant quality attributes have been included in well-established theoretical frameworks (Bujisic, Hutchinson & Parsa, 2014), such as SERVQUAL (Parasuraman et al., 1988) and DINESERV (Kim et al., 2009; Stevens, Knutson & Patton, 1995).

Service quality in the restaurant industry is nevertheless difficult to evaluate because assessments are made not only based on service outcomes but also on service delivery processes. To understand all characteristics of restaurant service quality, an appropriate measurement instrument is required (Markovic, Raspor & Šegaric, 2010). Stevens et al. (1995) developed the DINESERV scale to measure perceived service quality in restaurants (Liu & Jang, 2009). This instrument is considered to be a reliable, relatively simple tool for determining how consumers view a restaurant's quality (Kim et al., 2009). DINESERV consists of a 29-item questionnaire that measures the five areas of service quality specific to restaurant contexts, which are evaluated on a seven-point scale, as follows:

(1) Tangibles – a restaurant's physical design, appearance of staff and cleanliness
(2) Reliability – the food's freshness and temperature, accurate billing and reception of ordered food
(3) Responsiveness – staff assistance with the menu or wine list or appropriate and prompt response to customers' needs and requests
(4) Assurance – trustworthiness of the staff's recommendations, confidence that the food is free from contamination and ability to express any concerns without fear
(5) Empathy – personalised attention to customers by anticipating special dietary requirements or by being sympathetic about customers' problems

The goal of the DINESERV scale is to give restaurant operators and owners a tool to get a reading on how customers view their restaurant's quality, to identify problematic areas and to take the necessary actions so that gaps can be filled or services adjusted to meet customers' needs and wants (Hansen, 2014; Kim et al., 2009). DINESERV also provides restaurateurs with a quantified measure of what customers expect in restaurants, which is important because unfulfilled expectations create dissatisfied customers, who may leave in silence or spread negative word-of-mouth (WOM). Satisfied and returning customers who patronise restaurants regularly represent a fixed source of income and tell others about their positive experiences (Barber, Goodman & Goh, 2011).

DINESERV has been validated (Kim et al., 2009), and it covers a wide variety of restaurant types (e.g. sit down and fast food). In addition, this scale is a performance-based measure that assesses perceived service outcomes. More recently, Hanks, Linea and Kim (2017) used the dimensions of DINESERV to study the impact of restaurant type and human and built density on perceptions of interpersonal service quality. Namin (2017) concluded that service quality, food quality and price-value ratio have an impact on guests' satisfaction specifically with fast food restaurants. Reliability proved to be the most important dimension and tangibles the least important. Overall quality in a restaurant setting encompasses both tangible components, such as physical facilities and food, and intangible elements, such as employee services and experiences (Han & Hyun, 2017). Kuo, Chen and Cheng's (2018) research revealed that DINESERV dimensions' influence on customer satisfaction varies for first-time and returning customers. Front-line service staff's responsiveness also affects ðrst-time customers' satisfaction, while dining atmosphere is the most important determinant of repeat visits.

Guests of Michelin-starred restaurants rarely criticise service while dining, but they complain – after dining experiences – on review sites. Most diners consider high prices justified by the excellent quality of meals, but reviewers frequently discuss and often question this aspect. Online review sites may generally be dismissed as not having a significant influence in terms of tastemaking. However, websites with user-generated reviews of Michelin-starred restaurants provide an audience for individuals who wish to claim culinary capital and share their gastronomic experiences with others (Naccarato & Lebesco, 2012; Rousseau, 2012).

By exercising their right to evaluate Michelin-starred restaurants publicly, online reviewers, even if not perceived as tastemakers, are clearly still arbiters of taste. By participating in the larger discussion about Michelin standards, they stand alongside culinary elites and professional food reviewers. Vásquez and Chik (2015) suggest that narratives shared online by luxury restaurants' customers have allowed consumers to gain access to a greater diversity of voices speaking about high-end dining than ever before. The present study was based on the argument that, in a luxury setting, different approaches need to be applied to assess the perceived quality of services in order to avoid disturbing customers. In this research context, online reviews offer a valuable source of information.

Role of Customer-Generated Web Content in Service Quality Studies

WOM is often the most important means by which consumers can learn about products or services' attributes (Pan, MacLaurin & Crotts, 2007). This refers to informal communication between consumers regarding the characteristics, ownership and usage of services or products (Westbrook, 1987).

Internet technologies and, in particular, Web 2.0 have revolutionised the distribution and influence of WOM (Goldenberg, Libai & Muller, 2001; Stokes & Lomax, 2002) and expanded or changed the nature of WOM communication, which has evolved to include digitised forms. According to Au, Buhalis and Law (2014, p. 255), Web 2.0 is 'also known as the "interactive [W]eb", [as] it refers to the second generation of [W]eb-based communities and hosted services available on the worldwide [W]eb that allows people to generate content, collaborate, and share information online'. Customers can now easily broadcast opinions and leave feedback online for everyone to see (Au et al., 2014; Zhang, Ye, Song & Liu, 2015), and these online public channels are being used increasingly to post comments, experiences and advice regarding products or services (Ekiz, Khoo-Lattimore & Memarzadeh, 2012). Content generated by Web 2.0 users – also called user-generated content (Au et al., 2014) – and, more specifically, online customer reviews and ratings has been termed 'electronic WOM' (eWOM) (Zhang & Cole, 2016; Zhang et al., 2015).

Consumer decision-making processes are strongly influenced by WOM from other consumers (Goldenberg et al., 2001). As WOM is mainly based on personal experiences, other consumers find this third-party perspective more convincing, credible, trustworthy and unbiased than marketing information from commercial sources or through mass media (Au et al., 2014). Thus, customers tend to rely on online feedback, particularly when making their choices in service industries such as the hospitality and tourism industry, which is traditionally more dependent on perceived image and reputation (Au et al., 2014; Ekiz et al., 2012; Loureiro & Kastenholz, 2011; Vasquez, 2011).

In this industry, freely accessible eWOM provides a budget- and time-efficient and, ultimately, cost-effective channel for collecting consumer feedback. Industry-wide trends can, in this way, be identified through costumers' voices (Jeong & Jeon, 2008), as can the demands and expectations of the market (Carson, 2008; Litvin, Goldsmith & Pan, 2008; Pan et al., 2007; Wenger, 2008; Zhang & Mao, 2012; Zhang & Cole, 2016). In addition, eWOM is a valuable source of information for organisations' management about what affects brand perceptions and customer relations (Lu & Stepchenkova, 2012). This can help companies identify their brand image, understand the attributes generating customer purchase decisions and recognise the qualities needed to enhance customer loyalty (Drennan et al., 2015; Zhang & Mao, 2012).

Zhang and Cole (2016, p. 16) argue that knowledge acquired from eWOM should guide 'businesses' future practices of service promotion and delivery'. Thus, online platforms have 'great potential to become the leading marketing tools and branding enhancers in the near future' (Zhang & Mao, 2012, p. 118).

Traditional methods of doing marketing research on consumer experiences and perceived service quality, such as surveys and guest comment cards, have limitations, namely, poor response rates and information that cannot be explored further by researchers. In contrast, online eWOM in user-generated content is a particularly appropriate source of accessible, reliable, credible and readily available information for both consumers and researchers (Lu & Stepchenkova, 2012). Its use as a source of data on consumer experiences has thus grown in several areas of tourism research (Lu & Stepchenkova, 2012; Zhang & Cole, 2016).

Besides conveying individuals' actual experiences and providing direct information on user-perceived quality (Zhang & Cole, 2016), online tourist-generated content, in particular, is considered to be a valuable data source by tourism researchers. Hookway (2008) states, 'it provides immediately available information that is also "uncontaminated" by researchers during data creation and collection.' Zhang and Cole (2016, p. 16) report that 'eWOM has thus been recognised as a natural setting for the study of travellers' lived experiences'.

Researchers have previously analysed Web travel reviews to identify service attributes that are determinants of customer satisfaction and to improve service design (Zhang & Cole, 2016) and management accordingly. For instance, Zhang and Mao (2012) studied customers' Web reviews of major United States (US) hotel brands, and Lu and Stepchenkova (2012) analysed ecotourists' experiences. Au et al. (2014), in turn, examined online complaints about hotels, while Zhang et al. (2015) examined tourists' cruise satisfaction and Zhang and Cole (2016) analysed travel reviews about lodging services written by individuals with mobility challenges.

In the luxury market, Ekiz et al. (2012) investigated online complaints about luxury hotels, and Brochado, Troilo, Rodrigues and Oliveira-Brochado (2019) focused on the dimensions of clients' overall experience of luxury wine hotels. Brochado and Brochado (2019) further conducted content analysis of Web reviews of luxury camping, while Brochado, Oliveira, Rita and Oliveira-Brochado's (2018) research targeted luxury shopping malls. However, a survey of the existing literature did not reveal any studies about service quality in haute cuisine settings based on Web-generated content.

Qualitative and Quantitative Approaches to Customer-Generated Content

Content analysis has gained increasing popularity as an effective method for interpreting the fast-growing body of Web communications (Banyai, 2012; Romano, Donovan, Chen & Nunamaker, 2003). This method allows researchers to gather general information regarding the subject under study. Both qualitative and quantitative analyses can be used to analyse text data.

Quantitative content analysis involves techniques used to analyse the characteristics of messages, examine human interactions, investigate word usage by means of computers (Banyai & Glover, 2012) and, according to Neuendorf (2002, p. 1), 'so much more'. In word occurrence frequency analysis, keywords with top occurrence frequencies are associated into clusters by their cooccurrence, as well as being subjected to factor analysis and frequency counts (Stepchenkova & Morrison, 2006). This word-count and measurement approach extracts concepts of interest from textual data in a relatively unobtrusive and objective way. Quantitative methods are useful when analysing large amounts of textual data, which can be quickly processed by computer software and used to make general conclusions (Banyai & Glover, 2012; Zhang & Cole, 2016).

Qualitative content analysis involves techniques used to observe, deconstruct and interpret texts based on existing theories. Researchers can then interpret the data by coding and grouping quotations, words or images into categories or themes that feature the major issues that studies need to address (Banyai & Glover, 2012; Zhang & Cole, 2016). Individualised details and subjective feelings are further interpreted by researchers through the more subjective technique of thematic analysis, which primarily relies on researchers' judgment (Krippendorff, 2004). This approach also addresses the data's interpretive nature and its contextual variations (Banyai & Havitz, 2013; Zhang & Cole, 2016). However, these techniques are criticised for requiring too much effort, consuming large amounts of time in large-scale data analyses and introducing more subjective bias into data interpretation (Banyai & Glover, 2012; Stepchenkova & Morrison, 2008).

In summary, content analysis can be empirical or subjective while involving the counting of words or phrases, measuring observable text characteristics (Smith, 2010) or making sense of what is written (Banyai & Glover, 2012). Krippendorff (2004) argues that both types of content analysis are indispensable in research. A mixed-method content analysis approach combines structured quantitative methods with unstructured qualitative methods to capture different and broader components in texts (Baloglu & Mangaloglu, 2001; Banyai & Havitz, 2013; Choi, Chan & Wu, 1999). Quantitative methods can be used to find out general information or make systematic comparisons between different samples. Alternatively, qualitative methods can be used to extract latent meanings from data, thereby highlighting subjective reality and meanings. The value of applying both qualitative and quantitative methods lies in using different data collection procedures to gather both latent and manifest meaning in data (Banyai & Glover, 2012).

Given the complexity of content analysis and the enormous quantity of text-embedded eWOM available, a combination of quantitative and qualitative content analyses was selected as an effective research method in the present study. In service research, many keywords in service settings portray different service attributes that are dependent on the context, which makes identifying service attributes from textual data too complex through quantitative content analysis alone (Zhang & Cole, 2016). Thus, after quantitative factor analysis summarises significant service attributes, the meaningful cooccurrence of keywords needs to be confirmed further by qualitative in-text interpretation of the most frequent keywords that comprise each service attribute.

This kind of research also requires an interpretation of both generic service attributes and concrete service details as summarised by the identified attributes. Generic attributes facilitate a structured understanding of customer service needs and further statistical analysis to clarify the relationships between attribute performance and customer satisfaction. Concrete details on each service attribute, in turn, can provide businesses with practical guidance by identifying specific services to be emphasised (Zhang

& Cole, 2016). Therefore, after a quantitative analysis of the Web textual data was carried out in order to extract generic attributes, the present study applied a qualitative approach to interpret the specific service details for each service attribute. The content analysis followed the procedure suggested by other researchers who have focused on various luxury sectors (Brochado et al., 2018; Brochado & Brochado, 2019; Brochado et al., 2019).

METHODOLOGY

Research Context: Portugal – Two-Star Michelin Restaurants

The study targeted the most highly awarded (i.e. two-stars) Michelin-starred restaurants in Portugal in 2016. The selected restaurants are located in three Portuguese cities: Belcanto in Lisbon, Vila Joya in Albufeira and Ocean in Almancil.

Research Method

Data source. The data were collected from user-generated reviews shared on TripAdvisor's website. All guests of these selected restaurants are encouraged to write comments and rate their experiences after their visits. Reviewers create a title, write a review and assign a rating between 1 and 5.

These comments represent a large part of TripAdvisor's content and keep the system running. The website's credibility is higher than that of other online communities because users are strongly advised to create a complete profile as either a host or client. Thus, only verified members with a complete profile have a good chance of being accepted by readers as a guest reviewer. All these aspects make the TripAdvisor website a rich source of research data.

Data collection. Visitors' reviews of their experiences in two-star Michelin restaurants were gathered from TripAdvisor. As in previous studies of the luxury market (Brochado et al, 2018; Brochado & Brochado, 2019; Brochado et al., 2019), the data collected included the review title, review and rating. Reviewers' country of origin was also identified whenever possible in the present study. Each review was coded as a case in an Excel document. In all, the 600 reviews collected included only the most recent

Table 1. Consumers' Ratings (N = 600)

Rating	1	2	1 + 2	3		4	5	4 + 5	Total
Belcanto	1	4	2.5%	9	4.5%	22	164	93.0%	200
Ocean	5	3	4.0%	11	5.5%	18	163	90.5%	200
Vila Joya	2	3	2.5%	7	3.5%	19	169	94.0%	200
Total	8	10	3.0%	27	4.5%	59	496	92.5%	600

Source: Author

ones written in English for each city – with a total of 61,539 words. Around 92.5% of guests gave the three restaurants a 4 or 5 out of 5.

The majority of the guest reviewers are from European countries (69.7%), primarily from the UK (33%) and Portugal (14.3%). Guests from the US and Canada represent 11.7% of the sample.

Data analysis. Leximancer 4.5 software was used to analyse reviews of the three restaurants selected. Leximancer is a relatively new tool for transforming lexical cooccurrence information from natural language into semantic patterns. The software's procedure is consistent with a naturalistic and grounded theory approach, and this tool helps avoid researcher bias since the categories emerge from the cooccurrence of terms, unlike externally imposed classifications (e.g. Brochado & Brochado, 2019).

Table 2. Geographical Distribution of Reviewers

Countries	N	%
Europe	418	69.7%
UK	198	33.0%
Portugal	86	14.3%
France	19	3.2%
Spain	18	3.0%
Germany	14	2.3%
Denmark	13	2.2%
Netherland	10	1.7%
Other	60	10.0%
US & Canada	70	11.7%
Asia	10	1.7%
Australia & New Zealand	9	1.5%
Latin America	8	1.3%
Africa	2	0.3%
Missing	83	13.8%

Note. N = 600. UK = United Kingdom.
Source: Author

Leximancer seeks to assist researchers by analysing texts 'from words to meaning to insight'. This type of analysis has been applied most recently in hospitality and tourism research (Brochado et al., 2018; Brochado & Brochado, 2019; Brochado et al., 2019). The software performs two stages of cooccurrence information extraction – semantic and relational – using a machine learning algorithm to facilitate the determination of main topics within texts. This programme also highlights how topics relate to each other and indicates which source files or individual authors and/or speakers' communications contain particular topics (Brochado & Brochado, 2019).

In addition, Leximancer generates concept maps and statistical output to help analysts efficiently gain insights into, and an understanding of, natural language (e.g. reviews, interviews and focus group discussions). The software accomplishes this through the process of (1) conducting semantic information retrieval of key themes and concepts, (2) viewing bodies of data in a graphical format (i.e. concept maps) and (3) navigating through the concepts while mining the text for deeper contextual associations).

Results

The concept map generated for the present study revealed 12 themes and 36 concepts (i.e. theme size = 30%). The themes are as follows: 'food', 'restaurant', 'experience', 'menu', 'wine', 'special (dinner)', 'view', 'beautiful (food)', 'friendly (staff)', 'chef', 'visit' and 'dessert'.

The theme of food includes the concepts 'food', 'service', 'excellent (food)' and 'amazing (food)'. A typical review reads, '[t]he food itself was amazing and the service was . . . [of a] very [high]. . . professional standard'. Another guest wrote more simply, '[t]he food is amazing.' A further customer said the restaurant offers 'great food and service'. An additional review states, '[this is] one of the best restaurants I have eaten in[;] [with such] great original food, excellent wine and great service, [it] could be pushing for 3 stars.'

The theme of restaurant encompasses the concepts 'restaurant', 'Michelin', 'best (restaurant)', 'place' and 'world'. A guest shared, '[this is the] best restaurant in the world. [It already has] 2 . . . Michelin [stars] . . . and I truly hope it gets the 3rd one next year.' A second guest stated, '[this restaurant has] a well[-]deserved reputation [and a] well-deserved ranking . . . [among the] 50 best restaurants of the world!'

The theme of experience comprises the concepts 'experience', 'dinner', 'meal' and 'worth (a visit)'. One guest shared, '[w]e were very satisfied and [it was] well worth the drive from our resort which is about an hour away. [This restaurant is w]ell worth a visit, if you want [a] top-quality dining (or lunch) experience.'

The theme of menu combines the concepts 'menu', 'courses', 'tasting (menu)', 'surprises', 'flavours' and 'delicious (food)'. For instance, a guest said:

We opted for the tasting menu at 105 per head and left after a relaxing four-hour lunch with full bellies and smiles on our faces after a fantastic culinary experience which offered much more than the four[-]course menu suggested. We were treated to surprise after surprise by the chefs, each one more delicious than the last.

Another guest wrote, 'I got the tasting menu and every course was an amazing surprise, not only for the presentation, but also for the flavours and the way ingredients were utilised.' A further client reported, '[t]he lunch tasting menu, with added surprises, lived up [to] the Michelin 2-star ranking, [as there was a] meticulous creative presentation of textures, tastes, flavors, ingredients and combinations which we wouldn't ever contemplate in our home kitchen.'

The theme of wine covers the concepts 'wine', 'dish' and 'perfect(ion)'. A guest shared, '[t]he wine selections were perfect and really complimented the flavours of each dish.' Another review reads, '[w]e also ordered the wine menu which adds a little extra to each dish as the wine complimented the food perfectly.' An additional customer wrote, '[t]he [s]ommelier was also excellent and explained in detail the wine pairing which included all Portuguese wines.'

The special (dinner) theme comprises the concepts 'special (occasion)', 'time', 'expensive (restaurant)' and 'kitchen'. A guest reported, '[we had a] special dinner tonight. . . . [It's been] a long time . . . [since] the kitchen of a chef . . . [has delight]ed us as much.' A final review reads, '[this restaurant is] great for a special occasion.'

Another theme is the view, which included the concepts 'view' and 'Portugal'. A reviewer wrote:

Figure 1. Concept Map of Two-star Michelin Restaurants
Source: Author

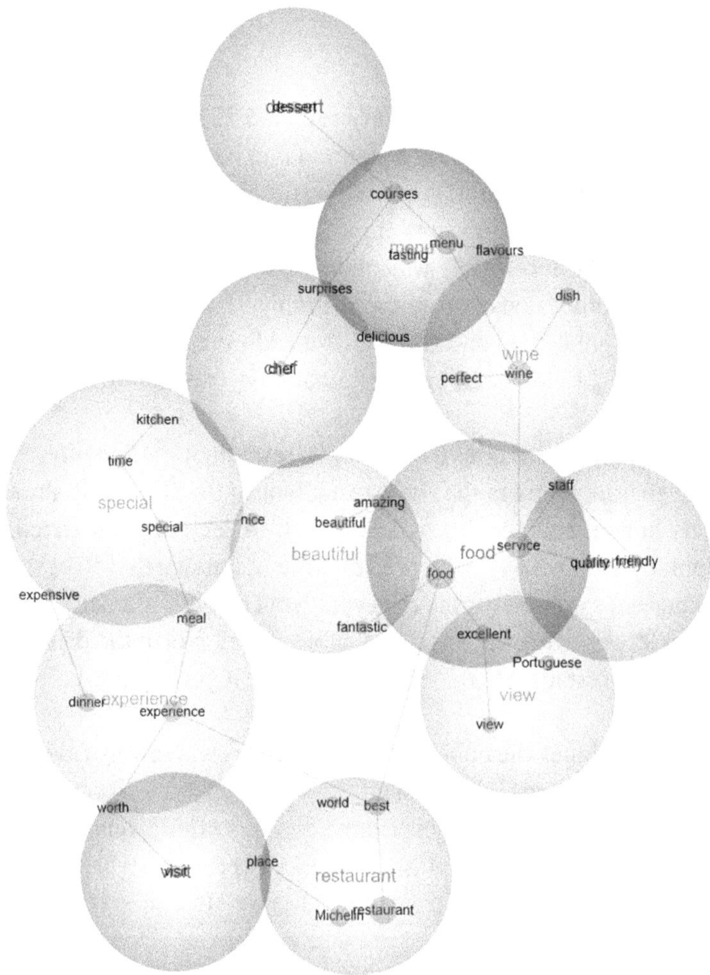

I am writing this review only to document my wonderful memory . . . for future reference. A ladies['] luncheon on a beautiful day in sunny PORTUGAL [sic] started with an outdoor view overlooking the grounds of this lovely resort.

Another guest stated, '[i]t is located in a beautiful setting on PORTUGAL's [sic] south coast; sitting at the tables on the terrace affords a delightful view over the sea.'

The theme of beautiful (food) encompasses the concepts 'beautiful (food)', 'fantastic (food)' and 'amazing (food)'. A review shared by a guest states, 'it was absolutely outstanding. [E]verything was perfect, beautiful and [almost] too nice to eat. [It was] fantastic . . . [and] beautifully presented food.'

The theme of friendly (staff) encompassed the concepts 'friendly (service)', 'quality (food)' and 'staff'. A guest wrote about 'the staff who are well trained and extremely friendly'. Another recalled '[v]ery friendly service and good quality food'. An additional review reads, '[the restaurant offers p] rofessional service, [which is] friendly and uncomplicated, without the snobbery that we sometimes see in restaurants of this level.'

The theme of chef includes only the concept 'chef'. The reviews often mention the name of the chef. One guest highlighted that 'the chef was there to greet me'. Another client shared, 'WOW [sic]! We ate at the chef's table and wow!' A further guest said, '[the restaurant has a g]reat chef.'

Another theme – and concept – is that of visit. A reviewer wrote, 'BELCANTO's [sic] Michelin stars are well deserved! BELCANTO [sic] is a must for foodies visiting LISBON [sic].' Another guest said, '[the meal was e]xcellent from start to finish. We booked lunch at VILA JOYA [sic] on our latest visit to the ALGARVE [sic], and it was everything, and more, that we thought it would be.'

The final theme of dessert also has one concept with the same name. A guest shared, '[the] dessert was over the top.' Another reviewer wrote, 'the [most] famous [dessert is the] tangerina. [I]f you love mousse, sorbet and everything delightfully tangerine – this is your dessert [of] choice.' A further customer said, 'we also appreciated the complimentary dessert to celebrate our anniversary. [T]hanks for a wonderful night.' Still another reported, 'the mandarin dessert will live on in my taste buds for a long time.'

CONCLUSION

This study sought to answer a predefined research question: What are the main narratives shared by tourists online about luxury dining experiences and the dimensions of these tourists' service experiences with luxury restaurants?

Fine dining is a luxury product (Jin et al., 2016). Consumers of fine dining – also known as luxury dining – pay premium prices for unique experiences that include a variety of food and beverages, luxury atmosphere and personalised service (Jin et al., 2015). The Michelin star system is the most respected ranking system of fine dining restaurants. Thus, the present research examined guests' narratives about and main dimensions of luxury dining experiences in two-star Michelin-rated restaurants.

The existing literature in this field reports that content analysis of online reviews provides valuable results for both empirical studies of and managers in this sector of the hospitality and tourism industry (Brochado & Brochado, 2019). This approach has also proved useful in research on luxury services as a way to avoid disturbing customers during their dining experience, as compared with alternative data collection methods (e.g. surveys).

The current results confirm the value of online reviews in haute cuisine as a means of sharing culinary capital with an audience with similar interests (Naccarato & Lebesco, 2012; Vásquez & Chik, 2015). Content analyses of these Web reviews produced a broad overview of the main dimensions of an exceptional haute cuisine experience based on user-generated content. The main dimensions identified are food, restaurant, experience, menu, wine, special (dinner), view, beautiful (food), friendly (staff), chef, visit and dessert. These results underline that luxury dining experiences need to be evaluated using a multi-attribute approach (Chen, Raab & Chen, 2017).

Guests emphasised primarily the themes of restaurant and visit. For most clients, Michelin-starred restaurants are worth a visit. Guests appear to feel that the restaurants' Michelin star status is the main reason for a visit and part of the assessment of their experiences. This result is in accordance with previous research (Vásquez & Chik, 2015) that has stressed the importance of prestige linked with dining in this category of restaurants.

Moreover, the themes of experience and special (dinner) highlight the role of a visit to high-end restaurants as an exceptional occasion. Previous research (Vásquez & Chik, 2015) has highlighted the diversity of motivations when visiting Michelin-starred restaurants. Some individuals use a Michelin star experience to celebrate a special occasion, while wealthier customers are especially loyal to this luxury segment of the restaurant industry.

With regard to human resources, guests value not only the staff but also the chef. The chef is the team leader, and his or her team is responsible for the innovation process and knowledge transfer (Tommaso et al., 2017). Chefs of upscale restaurants are considered celebrities (Chen et al., 2017). Customers, therefore, evaluate chef-related services (e.g. creativity) when assessing upscale restaurants. Clients greatly value not only having staff assistance with the menu and wine list but also engaging with the creators of the menu.

Overall, in fine dining restaurants, the staff are expected to be highly educated about food and beverages and well trained to address all consumer needs (Hanks et al., 2017). High quality staff has been previously confirmed to be an importance component in enhancing overall satisfaction with luxury restaurants (Han & Hyun, 2017).

The theme of food is also a central topic. Related words are dessert, menu, wine and beautiful (food). Guests value the ingredients, the menu and its components (e.g. desserts), wine-food pairings and the aesthetics of dishes (i.e. beautiful food). According to the literature on food quality, food can be evaluated based on a set of attributes that include not only taste but also presentation (Chen et al., 2017). Leong, Yeh, Fan and Huan (2020) report that aesthetics is the most influential factor for customers' emotions about haute cuisine.

The theme of view highlights the role of the ambience in luxury restaurant visits. The physical surroundings are made up of sounds, lighting, scents and colours that influence consumers' perceptions and behaviours (Chen et al., 2017).

From a theoretical point of view, the present study is expected to add to the literature on food tourism by providing a better understanding of the dimensions of dining experiences in the high-end segment of the restaurant industry, namely, two-star Michelin-rated restaurants. The results offer a comprehensive description of luxury dining experiences. Overall, dining experiences combine food and beverage themes, tangible and tangible aspects and emotional outcomes.

From a managerial point of view, the present findings confirm the validity of new methodological approaches to dealing with Web review content and demonstrate the usefulness of these data for the restaurants under analysis. WOM has previously been found to be an important consumer behaviour outcome and a significant marketing tool for Michelin-starred restaurants (Gehrels & Kristanto, 2007). As the Michelin star system is widely recognised as a reputed authority on high-end restaurants, customers' negative ratings can damage not only chefs and restaurants' image but also the Michelin star system's reputation. Therefore, while restaurants need to pay attention to Web reviews to ensure outstanding quality and recover from service failures, *The Michelin Guide*'s management also must take these reviews seriously.

This study's results offer Michelin-starred chefs and restaurant managers and owners a fuller picture of the overall experiences shared by customers. The chef's signature dish, menu, meal, wine, dessert, food service, presentation of dishes, relationship with the staff and positive emotions describe two-star Michelin restaurant experiences from the customers' perspective. Fine dining restaurants should develop food designs and flavour combinations that appeal to all of the clients' senses. Creativity, innovation and surprise are necessary elements that make guests feel special. Restaurant managers should also concentrate on hiring employees who are well trained and who have a positive work attitude, as well as offering the training required for staff members to meet customers' needs. As chefs are an important component of these experiences, their visits to tables can contribute to making their restaurants unique.

Despite having useful theoretical and managerial implications, this study has some limitations. Online reviewing is a global phenomenon, but this study focused only on two-star restaurants located in a single country. This study could thus be extended to consider restaurants on different Michelin star levels around the world.

REFERENCES

Au, N., Buhalis, D., & Law, R. (2014). Online complaining behavior in mainland China hotels: The perception of Chinese and non-Chinese customers. *International Journal of Hospitality & Tourism Administration*, *15*(3), 248–274. doi:10.1080/15256480.2014.925722

Baloglu, S., & Mangaloglu, M. (2001). Tourism destination images of Turkey, Egypt, Greece, and Italy as perceived by US-based tour operators and travel agents. *Tourism Management*, *22*(1), 1–9. doi:10.1016/S0261-5177(00)00030-3

Banyai, M. (2012). Travel blogs: A reflection of positioning strategies? *Journal of Hospitality Marketing & Management*, *21*(4), 421–439. doi:10.1080/19368623.2012.624297

Banyai, M., & Glover, T. D. (2012). Evaluating research methods on travel blogs. *Journal of Travel Research*, *51*(3), 267–277. doi:10.1177/0047287511410323

Banyai, M., & Havitz, M. E. (2013). Analyzing travel blogs using a realist evaluation approach. *Journal of Hospitality Marketing & Management*, *22*(2), 229–241. doi:10.1080/19368623.2012.680239

Barber, N., Goodman, R. J., & Goh, B. K. (2011). Restaurant consumers repeat patronage: A service quality concern. *International Journal of Hospitality Management*, *30*(2), 329–336. doi:10.1016/j.ijhm.2010.08.008

Bóka, Z., & Kovács, I. S. (2015). Hungarian cuisine with respect to restaurant awards and consumers' opinions. *Journal of International Food & Agribusiness Marketing*, *27*(1), 33–49. doi:10.1080/08974438.2013.807417

Brochado, A., & Brochado, F. (2019). What makes a glamping experience great? *Journal of Hospitality and Tourism Technology*, *10*(1), 15–27. doi:10.1108/JHTT-06-2017-0039

Brochado, A., Oliveira, C., Rita, P., & Oliveira-Brochado, F. (2018). Shopping centres beyond purchasing of luxury goods: A tourism perspective. *Annals of Leisure Research*, *22*(4), 484–505. doi:10.1080/11745398.2018.1522594

Brochado, A., Troilo, M., Rodrigues, H., & Oliveira-Brochado, F. (2019). Dimensions of wine hotel experiences shared online. *International Journal of Wine Business Research*, *32*(1), 59–77. doi:10.1108/IJWBR-12-2018-0072

Bujisic, M., Hutchinson, J., & Parsa, H. G. (2014). The Effects of Restaurant Quality Attributes on Customer Behavioral Intentions. *International Journal of Contemporary Hospitality Management*, *26*(8), 1270–1291. doi:10.1108/IJCHM-04-2013-0162

Carson, D. (2008). The 'blogosphere' as a market research tool for tourism destinations: A case study of Australia's Northern Territory. *Journal of Vacation Marketing*, *14*(2), 111–119. doi:10.1177/1356766707087518

Chen, Y. S., Raab, C., & Chen, C.-C. (2017). The influence of celebrity chefs on restaurant customers' behavior. *Journal of Hospitality Marketing & Management*, *26*(5), 489–510. doi:10.1080/19368623.2017.1269305

Choi, W., Chan, A., & Wu, J. (1999). A qualitative and quantitative assessment of Hong Kong's image as a tourist destination. *Tourism Management*, *20*(3), 361–365. doi:10.1016/S0261-5177(98)00116-2

Drennan, J., Bianchi, C., Cacho-Elizondo, S., Loureiro, S., Guibert, N., & Proud, B. (2015). Examining the role of wine brand love on brand loyalty: A multi-country comparison. *International Journal of Hospitality Management*, *49*, 47–55. doi:10.1016/j.ijhm.2015.04.012

Ekiz, E., Khoo-Lattimore, C., & Memarzadeh, F. (2012). Air the anger: Investigating online complaints on luxury hotels. *Journal of Hospitality and Tourism Technology*, *3*(2), 96–106. doi:10.1108/17579881211248817

Gee, J. P. (2005). Social semiotic spaces and affinity spaces. In D. Barton & K. Tusting (Eds.), *Beyond communities of practice* (pp. 214–232). Cambridge University Press. doi:10.1017/CBO9780511610554.012

Gehrels, S. A., & Kristanto, S. (2007). Marketing of Dutch culinary restaurants: An exploration from the entrepreneur's perspective. *Journal of Culinary Science & Technology*, *5*(2/3), 23–37.

Goldenberg, J., Libai, B., & Muller, E. (2001). Talk of the network: A complex systems look at the underlying process of word-of-mouth. *Marketing Letters*, *12*(3), 211–223. doi:10.1023/A:1011122126881

Han, H., & Hyun, S. S. (2017). Impact of hotel-restaurant image and quality of physical-environment, service, and food on satisfaction and intention. *International Journal of Hospitality Management*, *63*, 82–92. doi:10.1016/j.ijhm.2017.03.006

Hanks, L., Linea, N., & Kim, W. G. (2017). The impact of the social servicescape, density, and restaurant type on perceptions of interpersonal service quality. *International Journal of Hospitality Management*, *61*, 35–44. doi:10.1016/j.ijhm.2016.10.009

Hansen, K. V. (2014). Development of SERVQUAL and DINESERV for measuring meal experiences in eating establishments. *Scandinavian Journal of Hospitality and Tourism*, *14*(2), 116–134. doi:10.1080/15022250.2014.886094

Hlee, S., Lee, J., Yang, S.-B., & Koo, C. (2019). The moderating effect of restaurant type on hedonic versus utilitarian review evaluations. *International Journal of Hospitality Management*, *77*, 195–206. doi:10.1016/j.ijhm.2018.06.030

Hookway, N. (2008). "Entering the Blogosphere" Some Strategies for Using Blogs in Social Research. *Qualitative Research*, *8*(1), 91–113. doi:10.1177/1468794107085298

Jeong, M., & Jeon, M. M. (2008). Customer reviews of hotel experiences through consumer-generated media (CGM). *Journal of Hospitality & Leisure Marketing*, *17*(1/2), 121–138. doi:10.1080/10507050801978265

Jin, N., Goh, B., Huffman, L., & Yuan, J. J. (2015). Predictors and outcomes of perceived image of restaurant innovativeness in fine-dining restaurants. *Journal of Hospitality Marketing & Management*, *24*(5), 457–485. doi:10.1080/19368623.2014.915781

Jin, N., Line, N. D., & Merkebu, J. (2016). Examining the Impact of Consumer Innovativeness and and Innovative Restaurant Image in Upscale Restaurants. *Cornell Hospitality Quarterly*, *57*(3), 268–281. doi:10.1177/1938965515619229

Johns, N., & Pine, R. (2002). Customer behavior in the food service industry: A review. *International Journal of Hospitality Management*, *21*(2), 119–134. doi:10.1016/S0278-4319(02)00008-7

Johnson, C., Surlemont, B., Nicod, P., & Revaz, F. (2005). Behind the stars – A concise typology of Michelin restaurants in Europe. *The Cornell Hotel and Restaurant Administration Quarterly*, *46*(2), 170–187. doi:10.1177/0010880405275115

Kaminakis, K., Karantinou, K., Koritos, C., & Gounaris, S. (2019). Hospitality servicescape effects on customer-employee interactions: A multilevel study. *Tourism Management*, *72*, 130–144. doi:10.1016/j.tourman.2018.11.013

Kiatkawsin, K., & Han, H. (2019). What drives customers' willingness to pay price premiums for luxury gastronomic experiences at Michelin-starred restaurants? *International Journal of Hospitality Management*, *82*, 209–219. doi:10.1016/j.ijhm.2019.04.024

Kim, W. G., Ng, C. Y. N., & Kim, Y.-S. (2009). Influence of institutional DINESERV on consumer satisfaction, return intentions, and word-of-mouth. *International Journal of Hospitality Management*, *28*(1), 10–17. doi:10.1016/j.ijhm.2008.03.005

Krippendorff, K. (2004). *Content analysis: An introduction to its methodology*. Sage.

Kuo, T., Chen, C. T., & Cheng, W. J. (2018). Service quality evaluation: Moderating influences of first-time and revisiting customers. *Total Quality Management & Business Excellence*, *29*(4), 429–440. doi:10.1080/14783363.2016.1209405

Lane, C. (2014). *The cultivation of taste: Chefs and the organization of fine dining*. Oxford University Press.

Leong, M. W. A., Yeh, S.-S., Fan, Y.-L., & Huan, T.-C. (2020). The effect of cuisine creativity on customer emotions. *International Journal of Hospitality Management*, *85*(August), 102346. Advance online publication. doi:10.1016/j.ijhm.2019.102346

Litvin, S. W., Goldsmith, R. E., & Pan, B. (2008). Electronic word-of-mouth in hospitality and tourism management. *Tourism Management*, *29*(3), 458–468. doi:10.1016/j.tourman.2007.05.011

Liu, Y., & Jang, S.-C. (2009). Perceptions of Chinese restaurants in the U.S.: What affects customer satisfaction and behavioral intentions? *International Journal of Hospitality Management*, *28*(3), 338–348. doi:10.1016/j.ijhm.2008.10.008

Loureiro, S. M. C., & Kastenholz, E. (2011). Corporate reputation, satisfaction, delight, and loyalty towards rural lodging units in Portugal. *International Journal of Hospitality Management*, *30*(3), 575–583. doi:10.1016/j.ijhm.2010.10.007

Loureiro, S. M. C., Miranda, F. J., & Breazeale, M. (2014). Who needs delight? The greater impact of value, trust and satisfaction in utilitarian, frequent-use retail. *Journal of Service Management, 25*(1), 101–124. doi:10.1108/JOSM-06-2012-0106

Lu, W., & Stepchenkova, S. (2012). Ecotourism experiences reported online: Classification of satisfaction attributes. *Tourism Management, 33*(3), 702–712. doi:10.1016/j.tourman.2011.08.003

Markovic, S., Raspor, S., & Šegaric, K. (2010). Does restaurant performance meet customers' expectations? An assessment of restaurant service quality using a modified DINESERV approach. *Tourism and Hospitality Management, 16*(2), 181–195.

Miranda, F. J., Rubio, S., & Chamorro, A. (2015). The Web as a marketing tool in the Spanish foodservice industry: Evaluating the websites of Spain's top restaurants. *Journal of Foodservice Business Research, 18*(2), 146–162.

Naccarato, P., & Lebesco, K. (2012). *Culinary capital*. Berg. doi:10.5040/9781350042131

Namin, A. (2017). Revisiting customers' perception of service quality in fast food restaurants. *Journal of Retailing and Consumer Services, 34*, 70–81. doi:10.1016/j.jretconser.2016.09.008

Neuendorf, K. A. (2002). *The content analysis guidebook*. Sage.

Ottenbacher, M., & Harrington, R. J. (2007). The innovation development process of Michelin-starred chefs. *International Journal of Contemporary Hospitality Management, 19*(6), 444–460. doi:10.1108/09596110710775110

Palmer, C., Cooper, J., & Burns, P. (2010). Culture, identity, and belonging in the 'culinary underbelly'. *International Journal of Culture, Tourism and Hospitality Research, 4*(4), 311–326. doi:10.1108/17506181011081497

Pan, B., MacLaurin, T., & Crotts, J. C. (2007). Travel blogs and the implications for destination marketing. *Journal of Travel Research, 46*(1), 35–45. doi:10.1177/0047287507302378

Parasuraman, A., Zeithaml, V., & Berry, L. (1988). SERVQUAL: A Multiple-Item Scale for Measuring Consumer Perceptions of Service Quality. *Journal of Retailing, 64*(1), 12–40.

Peng, N., & Chen, A. H. (2015). Diners' loyalty toward luxury restaurants: The moderating role of product knowledge. *Marketing Intelligence & Planning, 33*(2), 179–196. doi:10.1108/MIP-03-2014-0049

Pizam, A. (2010). Creating memorable experiences. *International Journal of Hospitality Management, 29*(3), 343. doi:10.1016/j.ijhm.2010.04.003

Romano, N. C., Donovan, C., Chen, H., & Nunamaker, J. F. (2003). A methodology for analyzing web-based qualitative data. *Journal of Management Information Systems, 19*(4), 213–246. doi:10.1080/07421222.2003.11045741

Rousseau, S. (2012). *Food and social media*. Rowaan & Littlefield Publishers. doi:10.5040/9781350042193

Ryu, K., & Han, H. (2010). Influence of the Quality of Food, Service, and Physical Environment on Customer Satisfaction and Behavioral Intention in Quick-Casual Restaurants: Moderating Role of Perceived Price. *Journal of Hospitality & Tourism Research (Washington, D.C.)*, *34*(3), 310–329. doi:10.1177/1096348009350624

Stepchenkova, S., & Morrison, A. M. (2006). The destination image of Russia: From the online induced perspective. *Tourism Management*, *27*(5), 943–956. doi:10.1016/j.tourman.2005.10.021

Stevens, P., Knutson, B., & Patton, M. (1995). DINESERV: A tool for measuring service quality in restaurants. *The Cornell Hotel and Restaurant Administration Quarterly*, *36*(2), 56–60. doi:10.1177/001088049503600226

Stokes, D., & Lomax, W. (2002). Taking control of word-of-mouth marketing: The case of an entrepreneurial hotelier. *Journal of Small Business and Enterprise Development*, *9*(4), 349–357. doi:10.1108/14626000210450531

Surlemont, B., & Johnson, C. (2005). The role of guides in artistic industries – The special case of the 'star system' in the haute-cuisine sector. *Managing Service Quality*, *15*(6), 577–590. doi:10.1108/09604520510634032

Tommaso, S., Petruzzelli, A. M., & Vito, A. (2017). Teams and lead creators in cultural and creative industries: Evidence from the Italian haute cuisine. *Journal of Knowledge Management*, *21*(3), 607–622. doi:10.1108/JKM-09-2016-0381

Vasquez, C. (2011). Complaints online: The case of TripAdvisor. *Journal of Pragmatics*, *43*(6), 1707–1717. doi:10.1016/j.pragma.2010.11.007

Vásquez, C., & Chik, A. (2015). 'I am not a foodie . . .': Culinary capital in online reviews of Michelin restaurants. *Food & Foodways*, *23*(4), 231–250. doi:10.1080/07409710.2015.1102483

Wenger, A. (2008). Analysis of travel bloggers' characteristics and their communication about Austria as a tourism destination. *Journal of Vacation Marketing*, *14*(2), 169–176. doi:10.1177/1356766707087525

Westbrook, R. A. (1987). Product/consumption-based affective responses and postpurchase processes. *JMR, Journal of Marketing Research*, *24*(3), 258–270. doi:10.1177/002224378702400302

Zhang, J. J., & Mao, Z. (2012). Image of all hotel scales on travel blogs: Its impact on customer loyalty. *Journal of Hospitality Marketing & Management*, *21*(2), 113–131. doi:10.1080/19368623.2011.615017

Zhang, Y., & Cole, S. T. (2016). Dimensions of lodging guest satisfaction among guests with mobility challenges: A mixed-method analysis of web-based texts. *Tourism Management*, *53*, 13–27. doi:10.1016/j.tourman.2015.09.001

Zhang, Z., Ye, Q., Song, H., & Liu, T. (2015). The structure of customer satisfaction with cruise-line services: An empirical investigation based on online word of mouth. *Current Issues in Tourism*, *18*(5), 450–464. doi:10.1080/13683500.2013.776020

Chapter 7
Negative Customer Experience in Lifestyle Hotels:
A Netnography Perspective

Manoel Vitor Santos
University of Porto, Portugal

Amélia M. P. C. Brandão
https://orcid.org/0000-0003-2751-7272
University of Porto, Portugal

ABSTRACT

The primary purpose of the present research is to develop a methodology which can accurately analyse online public reviews on Google using Netnography studies combined with text mining analyses. By analysing the current techniques applied to a lifestyle hotel brand in nine properties in different countries and carefully studying how negative reviews are expressed online by costumers, this study aims to create a pattern of lifestyle customer complaints. This research seeks to demonstrate patterns of consumer behaviour that are not fully satisfied with the hotel service and how it can negatively affect the brand. This study identifies the areas that five stars lifestyle hoteliers and hotel managers need to pay attention to improve services, considering online reviews on online platforms, such as social networks and other tourism sites. Today, online reviews and customer experiences have a significant impact on the choice of a hotel.

INTRODUCTION

The tourism and hotel paradigm is changing. After years of standardisation, in which brands provided consumers with products that were consistent across the marketplace, there is growing attention to more differentiated products offering in the lodging sector (Kosar, 2014). Nowadays there is a concern on the part of the hoteliers in providing unique and unforgettable experiences to their customers. It is in this

DOI: 10.4018/978-1-7998-4369-6.ch007

Copyright © 2021, IGI Global. Copying or distributing in print or electronic forms without written permission of IGI Global is prohibited.

context that the boutique and lifestyles hotels emerge, being one of the trends with higher growth in the area of tourism.

The concept of lifestyle hotel is frequently used as a synonym for a boutique hotel, even though they refer to two distinct hotel typologies. Therefore, it is imperative to differentiate a boutique hotel from a lifestyle hotel. Studies have demonstrated that some of the main attributes of boutique hotels are related to their visitor's preferences, namely to their location, their personalised services, their quality and the uniqueness of the hotel itself (Aggett, 2007; McIntosh & Siggs, 2005). Furthermore, some other characteristics of this typology of hotels are related to the focus on the customer experience and the interior design, not being necessarily small and independent hotels, since they have several properties with different types of capacity (Kosar, 2014).

Nevertheless, the entrance of global hotel brands within the boutique hotel sector ended up imposing the need to distinguish small, independent, classic, original – real boutique hotels. Therefore, brand hotel operators started to use the concept of lifestyle hotel to refer to new specific chains under their portfolio. According to the Boutique and Lifestyle Lodging Association (BLLA) (2011, cit. in Kosar, 2014), a lifestyle hotel is a subcategory of a boutique hotel, the term of lifestyle referring to a property that combines activities and living elements into functional design, allowing customers to explore the experiences that they truly desire. With a classification that is valid to date, Day et al. (cit. in Kosar, 2014) defined the concepts of boutique hotels and lifestyle hotels as follows:

1) Boutique hotels are frequently small hotels with high-quality services, providing authentic cultural or historical experiences, as well as exciting services, being considered as unique hotels;
2) Lifestyle hotels are often small to medium-sized hotels, providing innovative services and features. These hotels also tend to present some contemporary design features, providing highly personalised service to their customers, what truly differentiates them from larger hotel brands.

Still, lifestyle hotels imply more than just a small or medium-sized contemporary designed property, given the fact that they suggest the integration of parts for an entirely meaningful live-work-play environment. Overall, these hotels include design, dynamic, art, fashion and colourful environments, which are related to an entire demographic segment. They are frequently focused and specialised, aiming to provide a differentiated quality to their customers, making them feel very exclusive and essential. Moreover, lifestyle hotels tend to offer a very full-balanced stay, since they use experiential branding as a component of positioning strategies, providing their customers with a pleasurable experience and promoting the customer interaction with the hotel brand itself (Kosar, 2014).

In sum, lifestyle hotels include all types of hotels that are genuinely able to manage the experience of distinct market segments successfully, and at all levels of the products. Such ability is achieved through uniqueness, especially by monitoring consumer behaviour and lifestyle, since it recognises what constitutes their uniqueness. In other words, lifestyle hotels combine their uniqueness with the consumer's individuality, providing them with the best experience they can ever have when visiting such hotels. According to Kosar (2014, p. 48), "(…), the hotel will harmonise its services to the guests' lifestyles and thus acquire the attributes of 'lifestyle' hotels".

Even though lifestyle hotels are generally 5-stars and are based on the quality of service, what are the main issues that can lead this consumer to make a complaint on a public review platform? Is it possible to identify and catalogue such complaints in an organised and secure manner to improve services?

Nowadays, there are several platforms where customers can leave their opinion about their experiences, and these will largely influence the opinion of other potential customers. One way to analyse customer opinions is by using Netnography techniques. As the term itself suggests, Netnography is an adaptation of ethnographic research that considers the characteristics of digital environments and computer-mediated communication (Corrêa & Rozados, 2017). Netnography has as a basis the collection of consumers reviews containing detailed information about their experiences in published on the Internet (Thanh & Kirova, 2018). The Netnography permits telling a story, understanding complex social phenomena, and assists the researcher in developing themes from the consumer's points of view (Thanh & Kirova, 2018).

The primary purpose of the present research is to develop a methodology which can accurately analyse online public reviews on Google using Netnography studies combined with text mining analyses, to catalogue the chief complaints subsequently and thus improve the services offered by the hotel. By reviewing and understanding customers opinions of their hotel experiences, managers could gain knowledge concerning which element influence to form a positive brand image (Barreda & Bilgihan, 2013).

This work was divided into several chapters. The first chapter corresponds to the literature review, in order to frame the main theoretical aspects of the subject, using monographs, scientific articles and other relevant documents.

In the second chapter, the methodology is presented, describing the data collection and analysis techniques.

The third chapter analyses and discusses the results based on previous studies.

Finally, the fourth chapter corresponds to the conclusions of the study, limitations and future lines of research.

LITERATURE REVIEW

Social Networks

Online social networks, such as Facebook, Tinder, YouTube, Instagram, Twitter and virtual communities, are networks where individuals can construct their public profiles in order to share their experiences and knowledge, as well as to post information about themselves and contact with other individuals who share the same interests. These networks have changed the way people think about companies and marketing in general, and consumers are genuinely able to interact and maintain a relationship with one another in a straightforward way. Indeed, the current way of interaction between consumers and companies is a direct result of the introduction of online social networks, also changing the power from companies to consumers (Cheung & Lee, 2010).

Nowadays, consumers genuinely have a significant impact on brands and products, mainly due to the growth of their online participation. Overall, the changes in the consumer's behaviour and action result from social influences which comprehend, in turn, three distinct modes:

1) Compliance (subjective norms), which occurs when individuals recognise that a social actor wants to influence their behaviour;
2) Internalisation (group norm), which occurs when individuals want to adapt themselves to the goals that a specific group of people share, aiming to belong to such a group;

3) Identification (social identity), which occurs when individuals accept the group's influence, given the fact that they want to establish a relationship with such a group of individuals (Kelman, 1958).

The leading roles of online social networks are related to the distribution of information, opinions and influences, especially amongst their members. Furthermore, these networks have been recognised as an essential and useful tool and source of information, namely for services and products. Social networking sites are one of the most critical communication channels within these online social networks, providing the facilities to interact with other people and to join virtual communities that share the same opinions and interests (Heinrichs, Lim & Lim, 2011).

According to Evans, Jamal and Foxall (2009), online social networks are a more relevant and credible information source than direct information from companies, which is why consumers seek products or services on these networks. Moreover, and given the fact that consumers genuinely enjoy the communication and interaction with each other and like to receive advice, either positive or negative, about products or services, virtual communities end up having a significant impact on the consumers' purchasing decision and behaviour.

Lastly, the study conducted by Riegner (2007) supports all these assumptions, once it demonstrates that online users spent 27% of their time on several communication activities, more precisely in social networking sites, as well as 27% of the time on leisure and entertainment activities. Hence, it is obvious the significance and relevance of online social networks in the consumers' lives, since they use several social networking sites daily.

Online Review Platforms

Holleschovsky (2015) claims that the existing literature distinguishes different types of an online review or opinion platforms, especially from the consumer's point of view. Such classification of these platforms entails all those platforms that are consciously designed for reviews, such as video-sharing platforms and independent reviewing platforms. Indeed, retail websites, but also personal blogs, independent consumer review platforms and video-sharing platforms, are classified containing customer-generated content, more precisely in the form of consumer reviews (Fan & Gordon, 2014).

Retail platforms are websites of retail stores, focusing on selling their services/goods through the Internet. Thus, the main content of these platforms is created by marketers of retail shops, which is why their ownership is classified as private. Even though the primary goal of retail platforms is to sell products/services, reviews also support them by increasing the quality of the provided services and customer satisfaction. Simultaneously, future customers can inform themselves about the retail shop products/services by analysing other customers reviews (Fan & Gordon, 2014). It is essential to add that the content of the reviews on retail websites can be done in the form of open-ended customer-authored comments about the product in a written text and, of aggregated, numerical star ratings. Moreover, a product review function includes a scoring system, therefore allowing the customer to vote on the review helpfulness and the places that are the most voted. The customer can choose between a date range or a sorting option of helpfulness, analyse the reviews, in order to obtain feedback that is provided by past customers, elucidating them about their levels of satisfaction (Li, Hitt & Zhang, 2011).

In turn, independent consumer review platforms display reviews on their websites, being designated as independent, because they are not connected to retail stores, not offering services/products on the websites. The main goal of these websites is to display different services/products and its reviews, aiming to facilitate comparisons, being considered as public websites. The content of these reviews can also be structured as open-ended customer-authored comments about the product/service and, of aggregated, numerical star ratings. However, in these independent consumer review platforms, the consumer's profiles can be seen as a great source of information, since, despite presenting the number of reviews written, they also have some personal information about the user (Holleschovsky, 2015).

Personal blogs, or blogging sites, contain reviews that are written by bloggers, who write about their experiences with a specific product/service, which is why their own is considered as private. The goal of these platforms is to share purchasing experiences about specific products/services, as well as to give recommendations to other consumers. In sum, consumers often use the platforms to inform themselves before purchasing a product/service. The review content is frequently displayed through open-ended customer-authored texts, possibly including videos or photos (Huang, 2015).

Lastly, video-sharing platforms allow posting videos, which can include products advertisements, personal videos and political messages. However, consumers also use these video-sharing platforms to post product reviews in video format. Therefore, these platforms aim to allow consumers to upload and share any video with private content freely. The review content is shown in the form of a video, which includes a written heading that elucidates about the video's focus (product/service). Finally, video reviews in those specific platforms can be found by entering search terms, or keywords, in the platforms, where there are several options to categorise the results: by most popular, most discussed, most relevant, date of upload and top-rated (Holleschovsky, 2015).

A study carried out by Ye, Law & Gu (2009) revealed the importance that online reviews have in hotel bookings. The results obtained showed that positive reviews increase the number of hotel bookings, while a significant variance or polarity in opinions have a negative impact on the number of online sales. At the same time, hotels with more rating stars receive more online bookings, but room ratings have a negative impact on the number of online bookings. Therefore, hotel managers should consider online reviews, especially when they are posted on online reviews platforms.

The study conducted by Ruhanen (2019) also demonstrates the importance of online reviews for the purchase of ecotourism experiences. For most reviewers, service is the most crucial aspect in post-purchase reflections and evaluations of the ecotourism establishment.

Word of Mouth

Word of mouth (WOM) is the oral, person-to-person interaction, more precisely between a communicator and a receiver, consisting of informal marketing communication (Buttle, 1998). The receiver perceives the communicator to be a non-commercial, namely regarding a specific product, service or brand. Kimmel and Kitchen (2014) stated that WOM refers to the action of a consumer distributing and generating marketing-relevant information, more precisely to other consumers.

As it is pointed out by Alexandrov, Lilly and Babakus (2013), WOM results from the intention to engage in a social interaction, which is initiated in order to satisfy the self-needs of individuals. The authors also establish that positive WOM is motivated by the need for self-enhancement, while the need for self-affirmation motivates negative WOM. Kimmel and Kitchen (2014) add that both the self-enhancement and the opportunities motivate the spreading of WOM, explaining how and why such a phenomenon is widely spread.

Returning to Buttle (1998), the author has demonstrated that WOM truly influences several conditions, namely: expectations, attitudes, awareness, behavioural intentions, perceptions and behaviour.

Nevertheless, several studies have shown that there are many reasons for people to engage in WOM truly. Regarding such issue, Alexandrov et al. (2013) claimed that the foremost vital drivers of WOM, and considering the brand-related aspects, are related to 1) loyalty; 2) trust; 3) satisfaction; 4) commitment; 5) quality; and 6) perceived value.

As it was previously mentioned, decisions are influenced by WOM, either positively or negatively, even though the negative WOM seems to be more potent than the positive WOM. Still, Kimmel and Kitchen (2014) proved that when there are high levels of negative WOM, there are also high levels of positive WOM and that positive WOM is more memorable than the negative WOM. Moreover, it is noteworthy to mention that emotions also affect WOM, frequently expressing achievement, by a therapeutic feeling and confirmation seeking (Alexandrov et al., 2013).

Kimmel and Kitchen (2014) emphasise that negative WOM has a much stronger effect on the receivers when it comes from dissatisfied customers, especially when compared to the effect of positive WOM when satisfied customers deliver it. Hence, negative WOM ends up drawing more attention because it is not that frequent, turning negative WOM way more surprising to consumers.

Finally, it is crucial to establish that the WOM model contains two sets of variables: 1) the intrapersonal variables; and 2) the extrapersonal variables. The intrapersonal variables are processes or situations that are correlated either with precipitating output WOM or seeking input WOM. Overall, positive WOM is motivated by the delight and satisfaction of the customer, while negative WOM is an outcome of a disproportion between perceptions and expectations. In turn, the extrapersonal variables are contextual circumstances, affecting the production of output WOM or the seeking of input WOM (Buttle, 1998).

Brand Image and WOM

Shahrinaz et al. (2016) claim that brand image can be defined as any information that is related to the brand within the consumer's memory. That is, brand image is related to the beliefs and associations that consumers have towards a specific brand. Over the past few decades, companies have been creating and developing their brands, which demonstrates their continuous efforts to maintain an active and appealing brand by investing in it. In order to position their brands, as well as to create brand awareness amongst consumers, companies must carefully plan and execute several advertising campaigns, since these will help consumers to recognise it and to create brand loyalty.

Moreover, companies also created a specific method of communication in the form of a brand, aiming to enhance the target groups' ability to link a set of associations with the brand image. Jalilvand and Samiei (2012, cit. in Shahrinaz et al., 2016, p. 119) conceptualise brand equity as "a set of brand and liabilities linked to a brand, its name and symbol that add to or subtract from the value provided by a product or service to a firm and/or to the firm's consumers".

On the other hand, Lim (2009) has demonstrated that the destination preferences of consumers were influenced by the image of the consumer-based brand equity, which ends up extending to products that are directly associated to the destination itself. In Lim's (2009) study, it is possible to conclude that there is a positive relationship between the images of the destination and the preference for products that are associated with the destination's brand. Therefore, brand image truly influences the consumers' reference regarding a specific product.

According to Shahrinaz et al. (2016), some of the main tools that are used in order to create brand image are related to WOM, media, celebrities and advertising, since it has been established that consumers are more likely to feel that they are a part of the cultural environment, as well as of certain groups when the brand that they are associated with has a specific and significant meaning. Brands are unique, being distinguished from each other, as well as recognised by their consumers, who do not mind paying a premium price for branded items, which also encourages the spread of loyalty towards the brand.

In sum, the brand image consists of benefits and attributes that are offered by a brand in order to distinguish itself from other brands. The benefits of brand image are related to the personal value that consumers indeed attach to the brand attributes, being directly associated with what the brand can do for them. On the other hand, the brand's attributes are a characteristic feature of it, is perceived by consumers and influencing their purchase or consumption decision (Webster & Keller, 2004).

Finally, Tariq, Abbas, Abrar and Iqbal (2017) suggest that online social networks and the internet have more impact, especially when creating and establishing a brand image. However, the most substantial impact of the brand image is achieved through WOM since it creates a substantial impact on brand judgement. Overall, WOM is a very influential and useful tool, presenting a positive impact on consumer purchase intention and brand image, besides helping to create a right brand image for the company and its products/services, maintaining the customers' loyalty and preference, also influencing their purchase behaviour.

Consumer Negativity Towards Brands

Consumer negativity towards brands is related to harmful forms of consumer-brand relationships, which can be associated with anti-consumption, boycotts and brand avoidance. Anti-consumption means that consumers are against consumption, arising when they resist, reject of resenting consumption. According to Iyer and Muncy (2009), there are two types of anti-consumption: 1) the general resistance against consumption; and 2) the more specific resistance against consumption, where consumers reject specific products/brands. Table 1 presents the main types of anti-consumers, according to the authors perspective.

Table 1. Types of anti-consumers (Iyer & Muncy, 2009, p. 161)

		Purpose of anti-consumption	
		Societal concerns	**Personal concerns**
Object of anti-consumption	General (all consumption)	Global impact consumers	Simplifiers
	Specific (individual products/ brands)	Market Activists	Anti-Loyal Consumers

In more details, global impact consumers reject consumption due to their belief that the consumption level negatively impacts and affects the society and planet. Simplifiers reject consumption based on their perception that the current society is highly consumption-focused, being necessary to decrease consumption in order to achieve higher levels of well-being. On the other hand, Market Activists reject the consumption of specific products/brands due to their belief that they cause a specific societal problem, such as negative social behaviour or environmental damage. Lastly, Anti-Loyal Consumers reject the consumption of specific products/brands as a result of a negative experience, which influences their decision when buying specific products/brands (Iyer & Muncy, 2009).

Boycotting is a form of anti-consumption and consumer resistance, being defined as "(...) an attempt by one or more parties to achieve certain objectives by urging individual consumers to refrain from making selected purchases in the marketplace" (Friedman, 1985, p. 97). As a matter of fact, boycotting is a very effective tool for consumers to declare a discontent towards a company's business practices. Overall, there are two types of boycotts: 1) economic boycotts, which occurs when consumers refuse to purchase services/products due to the company's discriminatory marketing practices; and 2) social or ethical boycotts, which occur when a consumer rejects a business due to its unethical or socially irresponsible behaviour (Sen, Gürhan-Canli & Morwitz, 2001).

Finally, the brand avoidance concept is multifaceted, since the main reasons for engaging in it can differ amongst consumers. As it is pointed out by Lee, Conroy and Motion (2009), four distinct categories constitute the main reasons for brand avoidance, more precisely:

1) Experiential avoidance: when expectations are not met, occurring when consumers avoid specific brands as a result of previous negative experiences;
2) Identity avoidance: which arises from unappealing promises, such as a brand's inability to reflect a consumer's self-concept;
3) Moral avoidance: which arises due to detrimental promises, being associated with the consumers' perspectives of what is moral and immoral;
4) Deficit-value avoidance: which arises when a brand gives inadequate promises, leading to an unacceptable trade-off (Lee, Conroy & Motion, 2009).

Online Activism

Online activism is also designated as clicktivism, hashtag activism and slacktivism. This form of participation is prevalent because it is a low cost and low-risk activity. Indeed, online campaigns frequently seek to make participatory action easy, aiming to attract and encourage a higher level of engagement and support by consumers. Furthermore, some authors claim that online activism can genuinely help people that feel that they are voiceless and helpless, inspiring them to engage and join discussions. Such participation is possible due to the internet, which reduces the barriers to such online activism (Lee & Hsieh, 2013).

One of the most used tools in online activism is the hashtags, which were primarily a method of indexing information. Hashtags can be used to locate information within conversations, allowing for quick retrieval of specific information. Bonilla and Rosa (2015) argue that hashtags do not only provide a system for the indexing and retrieval of information, also functioning semiotically, namely by marking the real significance of a specific utterance. Even though some people use the number of posts containing a specific hashtag as a way to analyse how successful a hashtag campaign is, Bonilla and Rosa (2015) establish that there are some limitations to this specific method. Indeed, the authors claim that just because there is a large number of posts with the specific hashtag, it does not mean that the campaign is substantial. Hence, it is tough to know what the intentions behind a post are, since we do not know the true meaning that people apply to such hashtag when posting with it.

However, some opponents genuinely believe that online activism has little, or no value at all, to activist campaigns. For example, Breindl (2013) suggests that people are speedy to disqualify online activism since it is considered as a low-input action. Still, some of the opponents of online activism believe that this participation is slacktivism, endangering activism and activists themselves, since it promotes an oversimplification of issues, despite relying on the most traditional form of activism.

In sum, critics of online activism consider such type of participation as a lazy substitution that has emerged at the expense of more meaningful forms of engagement, such as donating money, time and participating in protests. Budish (2012) claims that organisations can lay claim to having several supporters, which range between thousands and millions, even though they solely contribute by clicking on a button or by forwarding emails.

Emotions and Consumer Behaviour

Emotions are aroused or provoked conditions of an organism, immediately followed by body changes and visible changes in one person's behaviour, therefore pointing to emotional processes or conditions. The emotional mind of an individual is quicker than the cognitive mind since it reacts without stopping. As an example, people do not need fast cars to get somewhere, even though they enjoy the feeling of energy and power which fast cars genuinely embody. Affect refers to a specific type of a mental phenomenon, including subjective feelings, moods, emotions and conscious experiences. Therefore, and based on people's emotions, consumer affective responses to companies' actions may either be positive or negative (Bagozzi, Gopinath & Nyer, 1999; Dunne, 2005; Fournier & Alvarez, 2013; Romani, Grappi & Dalli, 2012).

In 2013 Trandafilović, Pašić and Perunović (2013) argued that affective consumer behaviour, or impulsive shopping, is a response to a sudden stimulus, being characteristic of a situation in which the customers' emotions truly dominate other ways of knowledge regarding the product/service/brand. The main features of affective customer behaviour, differentiating it from cognitive behaviour, are the following ones:

1) Temporary loss of self-control;
2) Reduced logic and rational evaluations;
3) A sudden, spontaneous urge to buy the product/service/brand;
4) Spending regardless of the consequences;
5) Emotional conflicts and tensions.

Coca Cola is one of the world's most famous brands, recognising and using emotions and impulses that are underneath the consumers' conscious mind. Despite being a mass consumption and use product, this brand carries a message with positive energy, excitement, satisfaction, youth and positive mood, therefore affecting consumers to buy such product/brand. One of the essential paradigms and secrets of Coca Cola Company's success is related to the fact that the brand possesses human qualities and emotional values, which distinguishes it from other brands within the market (Trandafilović et al., 2013).

In sum, this example of Coca Cola brand truly demonstrates how emotions influence consumer's behaviours when buying some product/service/brand, since it is a brand that affects emotions of consumers, making them feel satisfied and positively excited, which makes them want to buy a specific product. Therefore, the marketing strategy is fundamental since it is what makes consumers feel different emotions, which will ultimately define their buying decisions (Trandafilović et al., 2013).

Brand Hate

Weingarten (2006) establishes that hate requires an object and subject, camouflaging different beliefs, attitudes and feelings. In turn, Rempel and Burris (2005) claim that hate is a motivation, being directly associated with diminishing or destroying the object's well-being.

Applying the concept of hate within the context of brand and/ product acquisition, Hogg (1998) argues that a consumer's decision to not purchase two aspects can cause a specific product: non-choice or anti-choice. Overall, the non-choice is related to three specific situations, namely: accessibility, affordability and availability. Thus, the consumer does not influence these situations, being affected by them. On the other hand, the anti-choice refers to aversion, abandonment and avoidance, being associated with situations where consumers can make a clear choice (Fournier & Alvarez, 2013; Veloutsou & Guzman, 2017).

In this specific context, it is pertinent to remember the study conducted by Lee et al. (2009), since it approaches the three motives for consumers to avoid a brand, being directly related to their feelings of hate or love: 1) experiential brand avoidance; 2) identity avoidance; and 3) moral avoidance, all represented and explained in Figure 1, which summarises the theoretical model of brand avoidance proposed by Lee et al. (2009).

Figure 1. Theoretical model of brand avoidance by Lee et al. (2009)

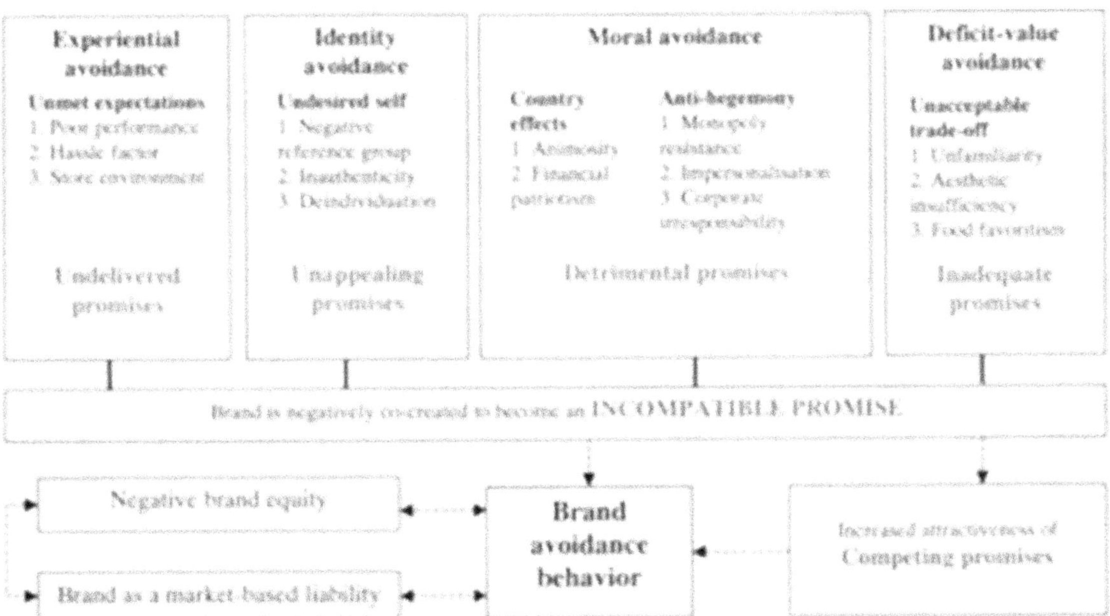

In turn, Funches, Markley and Davis (2009) establish that there are different behavioural categories for consumer retaliation:

1) Exit and rejection: it explains the reaction of consumers after a service/product failure. Exit means the end of the relationship, namely by stopping the purchase of products from a specific company,

while rejection, much stronger than brand exit, is related to a set of incidents that make consumers reject a brand;

2) Indirect revenge behaviours: which take place outside the company's border. One of these behaviours is related to negative WOM, where customers share their bad experiences with others, denigrating the company's services or products. Other behaviour is the online public complaining about negative publicity, which refers to the act of using an online feature to warn other consumers about the misbehaviour of a specific company;
3) Direct revenge behaviours: which point out to face-to-face responses between consumers and company. There is vindictive complaining, referring to customers that demonstrate their displeasure to frontline employees, and marketplace aggression, referring to actions that aim directly to harm a company or its employees.

However, for Grégoire, Tripp and Legoux (2009), consumers' hate can turn into revenge or avoidance. These authors have discovered that, over time, the revenge behaviour decreases, given the fact that it costs the consumer way more energy than avoidance behaviour. Revenge is defined as the harm that customer cause to a company after an unacceptable service/product, is a behaviour that can be divided into indirect behaviours (such as complaining) and direct behaviours (payback).

One way to fight brand hate is through brand authenticity. For example, the success of hotel brands increasingly depends on the customer's perceptions of authenticity. Authenticity can be defined by everything genuine, honest, unaltered concerning superficial characteristics as well as deeper characteristics (Manthiou *et al.*, 2018). In recent times, authenticity has been the main driving force in the area of tourism and hospitality, making consumers travel long distances to live authentic experiences (Cohen, 1988 *cit in* Manthiou et al., 2018). The authors conclude that "brand love should be understood as the outcome of the perceived authentic experience which is attributable to the circumstances in which several needs, wants, desires and aspirations of customers are satisfied by the brand" (Manthiou *et al.*, 2018, p.45).

METHODOLOGY

This following segment of the research portrays both the data collection and data analysis approaches considered in the study. The broad goal of the study is to determine how travellers communicate in the cyberspace concerning the negative experiences they had when staying or enjoying a lifestyle Hotel, which are the themes with the most significant number of complaints and what is the feeling of each consumer when writing the review.

A 5-star lifestyle brand was chosen that currently has nine hotels in operation, and the brand's primary market is placed in the USA, but there is also a large number of Hotels in Asia. At the moment of data collection, there were nine hotels in the brand, 15 pipeline properties, counting 2,312 open rooms and 3,357 pipeline rooms.

Netnography

The concept of Netnography refers to a virtual or internet ethnography, more precisely, from a consumer perspective. Netnography is defined as a qualitative, interpretative research methodology, is based on ethnography, which analyses and studies online cultures and communities that are constituted through computer-mediated communication (Beckmann & Langer, 2005; Kozinets, 2015).

This qualitative, interpretative research methodology has several advantages, which are mainly related to the fact that it is less obtrusive than the traditional survey methods, being unelicited and consequently more naturalistic. Furthermore, it also provides the researcher with ongoing, fresh material that illustrates daily experiences. In terms of its information, it is bottom-up generated material, therefore providing some background into the symbolism and consumption patterns of consumer groups (Hookway, 2008).

It is noteworthy to mention that most traditional forms of ethnography required the researcher to physically move into the field of search since this was the only way to analyse the target culture. However, virtual ethnography can provide unprecedented access to some unobservable behaviour of groups, namely by analysing the online interaction. In more detail, this methodology allows the researcher to have access to cultural rituals, realities and practices, which are essential to analyse and understand these digital groups. In sum, the researcher can access a broader spectrum of information from his/her desk since people put their own lives on display to others within social networks. Such display can be visual, textual or both, being instantly available to be viewed (Kozinets, 2015; Masten & Plowman, 2003).

According to Lugosi, Janta and Watson (2012), Netnography aims to understand, and not to measure, which is why it is an advantageous research method when the more traditional methods are not appropriated. The online communities are significant to their members, is constituted according to rules, norms, customs, a private language with several conversational conventions, shared value systems and linguistic and in-jokes shortcuts. Therefore, the researcher must interpret and understand such a complex context, which is why Netnography is very useful to do so.

Internet-Based methods can genuinely provide a desirable source of information, especially when studying consumer behaviour and experiences. Nowadays, there is a growing number of websites and social networks that allow consumers to share their reviews about their experiences, contributing to the discussion of several topics of their interest. These online communities are sometimes designated as neo-tribes since they are linked by a shared interest or passion, even though they are heterogeneous in terms of their economic, geographic and demographic characteristics. Hence, and truly unites these online communities is the shared experience of reality, being expressed through consumer interpretations of such experiences (Cova & Cova, 2001; Kozinets, 2015).

Kozinets define four major Netnography, represented in Figure 2. For this study by the information researcher and the type of result obtained was adopted the Symbolic. The Symbolic Netnography provide insights that are useful to managers, particularly managers in marketing. Symbolic Netnography, like commercial ethnography itself, attempt to help managers and another decode the everyday worlds of people or consumers (Kozinets, R.V. - 2015).

Although Netnography was initially developed as a tool for the business area to understand consumer behaviour, the importance of this method applies to various disciplines, such as tourism since it is essential for tourism stakeholders to understand how consumers behave and what experiences they value most (Tavakoli & Wijesinghe, 2019). Netnography in tourism can help the study of tourist experiences, suppliers and developers. However, the studies carried out using this technique focus mainly on the tourist experience, few focus on suppliers, and no study focuses on tourist developers (Tavakoli & Wijesinghe, 2019).

Figure 2. The four types of Netnography

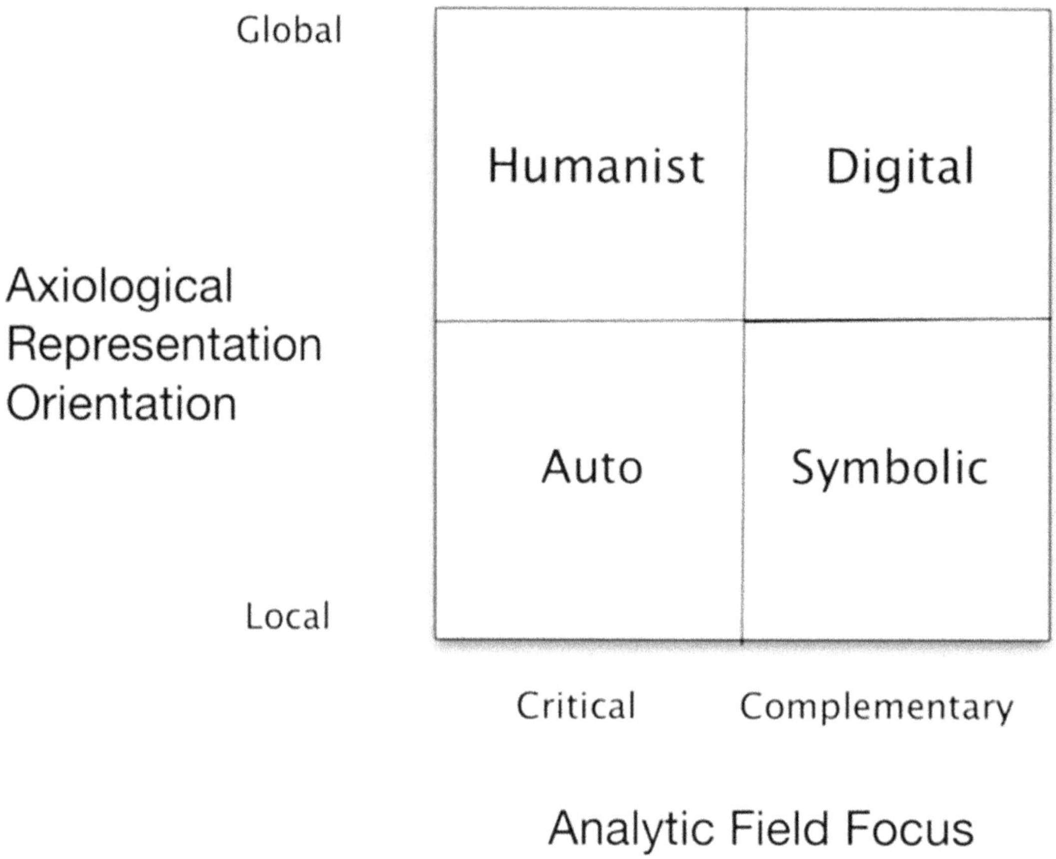

Data Collection

For this study, negative reviews posted online and shown at "Google My Business" of each hotel specific page were used. The selection was made based on the five stars evaluation system, which guides the user to rate the service/company from 1 to 5 stars, being five the maximum and one the minimum rate. Since the target is the negative experience, only reviews with 1-3 stars were selected, even though some 4 and 5 stars reviews could have complained too. Effectively, the reviews of unsatisfied customers appear in 1-3 stars rate reviews, and this is the primary motivation why they were selected to compose this study.

All data was copied from Google Reviews page and isolated so they would contain only the material produced by the client, not extra data that comes in the process of collecting. Understanding that we would have to isolate data, the decision of copy/paste the text individually was made. Each customer had its work document to each hotel folder, intending to understand cases in a micro world, not only as of the full analysis. In this first part, no specific program was used to collect data, the text analysis was made one by one, due to this study's nature, there was no intention of merely collecting material in a data basis, but the work developed aims the comprehension of the reviews and the customer himself.

Another crucial information is the indexation made by Google Review, at the moment of this work, not only reviews made at Google platforms were shown, but also the ones indexed from, for example, Booking, TripAdvisor and other review platforms. They were equally analysed since they appear and are part of the user's experience inside Google Reviews platform. Those were extracted but in the original platform to ensure that all data has been collected. Also, were collected reviews from clients and the responses from the hotels as well.

The data was collected from the reviews page of each of the Hotel. After collecting, the data was codified using and three more tools were used: NVivo, Iramuteq and Tableau, which will only be used to handle demographic data extracted from reviews in NVivo.

Data Analysis

Figure 3. Data collection model used in the research

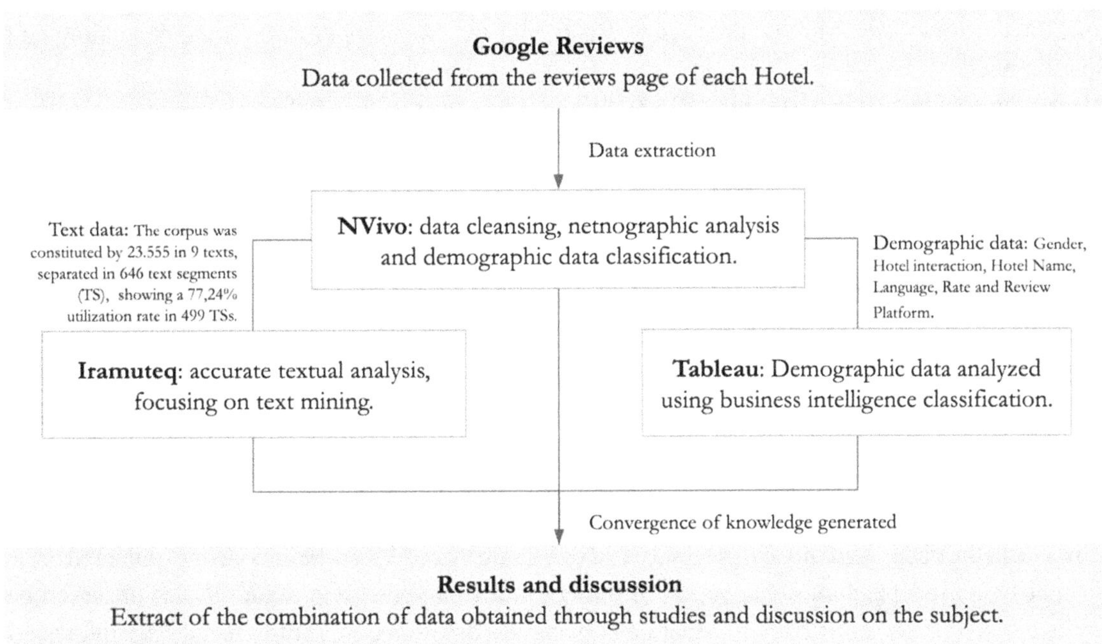

Considering the two different programs used for the data collection, each had an individual, but complementary role. NVivo was used to develop the individual analysis observing the reviews, the discourse and experiences, as well as perceiving and comprehending the guest's frustrations, in order to generate patterns and code them. Iramuteq was used for a more accurate textual analysis, focusing on text mining. Knowing that the final number of the material is 367 analysed reviews on nine hotels, generating 158 nodes divided into four principal themes group's and 11 subthemes, on NVivo. Finally, the content was collected in several different languages, not being valid for the analysis, due to that, the information was translated into English, in order to unify data and possibilities the study.

NVivo: qualitative data analysis (QDA)

NVivo 8 software served as the data analysis tool during the content analysis. NVivo is stated to be an instrument for discourse analysis, grounded theory method, conversation analysis, ethnography, phenomenology, mixed methods research and more (Schönfelder, 2011).

After the data has been collected online and separated by each review, they have been imported to NVivo. They were separated into different folders, one for each hotel, in order to also investigate the hotel variable in the analysis. One by one, they were transformed in cases; every client/customer was configuring a different case; namely, each review became an individual case. Since there was not any review from the same client, all of them originated a specific folder, with no duplicity. To the customers, was given a case classification with demographic data that was available: gender, hotel agenda, hotel interaction, hotel name, language, rate and review platform. For gender: masculine and feminine, when possible to determine by name or online profile, it was not possible "non-assigned". Hotel interaction: answered or unanswered, if the hotel has answered or not the review the complaint. The hotel name is the specific name of the hotel, to add information to further analysis. The language was described as the one the customer used to write the review. Rate: one star, two stars or three stars, depending on the evaluation made.

Moreover, review platform, because Google Reviews indexes other platforms was necessary to give this information. Each case was read and codified based on the complaints and issues every client has found. The codes were created in order to comprehend maximally the reason why the bad review was written, namely, the problem or issue portrayed by the client. Therefore, the codes are not for a particular department within the hotel, but it aims all of them. Among others, there are sections for front desk issues, neighbours, noises and physical issues, for example.

Coding

In this section, the coding process is explained, aiming comprehension of the process and the results. First, a code is defined as: "often a short word or phrase that symbolically assigns a summative, salient, essence-capturing, and evocative attribute for a portion of language-based or visual data." (Saldaña, 2012). For this work, the codes were nodes, precisely 158 ones, referenced 932 times inside the collected corpus.

Primarily, an independent organisation in themes and subthemes was made. It was observed need to create a more efficient structure to separate and analyse date since this study is not only interested in the general brand view, but also inner aspects of the customer-hotel relationship. For this, Lee's brand avoidance theoretical model was adopted, focusing on a more efficient method of textual separation and analysis. The begin of the coding was based on Netnography studies, considering the reviews not in a general view, for that, reading and understanding the customer's experiences, feelings and complaints were part of the methodology. After that, the automatic and statistical part of the research was the organization.

The codes were classified according to four main themes and respective subthemes, table 2. This chart follows Lee's model, divided into four categories, and 11 subcategories, it shows an overview of codes and references. Divided into four groups, it was able to perceive and comprehend the issues reported by the customers. Experiential avoidance has the most significant incidence of complaints, followed by identity avoidance, deficit-value avoidance and moral avoidance.

Specifically, the highest frequency of reviews regarding issues are in Poor Performance, Hassle Factor and Store Environment, 84% of the audience brings these aspects inside Experiential Avoidance group. Considering the client's focus on experience issues and their non-perception / discussion of other aspects, other topics, it is clear that this is the most substantial issue.

The second most referenced group is brand identification, about 10%, reviews provide information ranging from non-Marriott identification to partial identification. Moral Avoidance and Deficit-value Avoidance do not show a real expressive amount of issues, in comparison with the first two. Mention can be made about the nationality of the company, especially from North Americans, but the significance of this issue is less the 1%. Deficit-value is the second least expressive, but it shows 10% of the text and a little more than 4% in the analysis, the main issue is focused on food, aesthetic problems and no familiarity and understanding of the brand.

The coding model used has been chosen due to its ability to fulfil the objectives of this research, although this model is not entirely efficient for the study, the coding map, is available due to the understanding that this data is relevant and it shows a non-generic overview of the hotels.

Table 2. Codification Based on the Theoretical model of brand avoidance by Lee et al. (2009)

Name	Files	%	References	%
1-Experiential Avoidance	247	67.30%	787	84.44%
1.1-Poor Performance	189		408	
1.2-Hassle Factor	113		215	
1.3-Store Environment	99		164	
2-Identity Avoidance	76	20.71%	94	10.09%
2.1-Negative Reference Group	12		12	
2.2-Inauthenticity	39		42	
2.3-Deindividuation	36		40	
3-Moral avoidance	4	1.09%	8	0.86%
3.1.-Country effects	4		6	
3.2-Anti-hegemony	2		2	
4-Deficit-value Avoidance	40	10.90%	43	4.61%
4.1-Unfamiliarity	36		38	
4.2-Aesthetic Insufficiency	2		3	
4.3-Food Favoritism	2		2	

The Hierarchy Chart - Nodes, as can see below, is another construction of coding. It is a more visual way to understand and represent the analysed data in order to have different perspectives on the material. Also developed following Lee's model, the lexical choice is to maintain the semantical structured used by the customers. In this Chart is, once more, is clarified the issues related to Experience Avoidance, exemplified by the words: front desk, staff, food & beverage, housekeeping, financial, service, client feeling, client perception and physical problems. It is composing the majority of references computed by NVivo.

Figure 4. Hierarchy Chart from NVivo: Nodes compared by the number of coding references

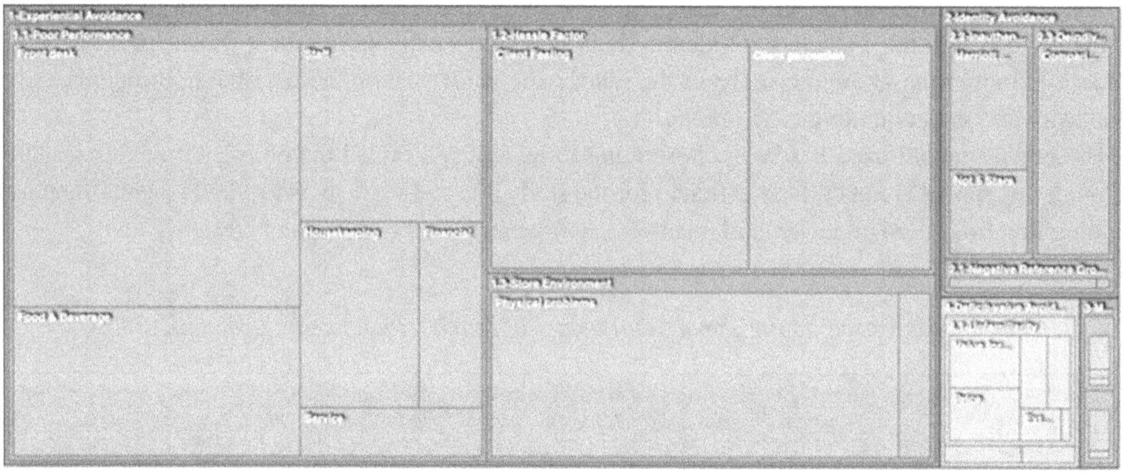

The coding process clarifies in a quantitative way the value of experience customers gives, especially when writing a review which is going to serve as the basis for other client's decision-making process. Few reviews are approaching the corporate experiences, usually made by fidelity members, Marriott or non-Marriott. The useful worry is the experience, and the hotel stays as an overview, not merely about the brand.

Word Cloud and Word Tree

The Word Cloud is a tool that is based on textual analysis, made by NVivo. When using this resource, it is possible to select a few configurations about the words inside the cloud, for example, the number of letters, the frequency they appear in the analysis, and also exclude vocabulary. For this work, we have selected only words with a minimum of 4 letters. The one-eighty more frequent, excluding "hotel" and all the individual hotel names, in order to have a more explicit cloud, not polluted. Finally, the words that do not have a specific meaning or relevance to the study, such as connectives, were as well not included. The main idea of the word cloud structure is to give the viewer a general portrait containing the principal issues found.

In the figure, the words appear in a proportion of their frequency in the data. The most prominent contrast can be found in the Words: services, check, staff, time and stay. Considering Services as the most constant mentioned word, our analysis shows this is a relevant issue in most hotels.

NVivo provides the ability to isolate a word and see its main correlations with reviews. A clipping of a World Tree, as an example, is shown below. Traditionally, many types of research begin by analysing the central frequencies of words in cloud or tree format, but as already explained, due to the nature of this research it was decided to read and encode each review indicatively.

Figure 5. Word Cloud from NVivo: The eighty more reelevates words cited in the texts

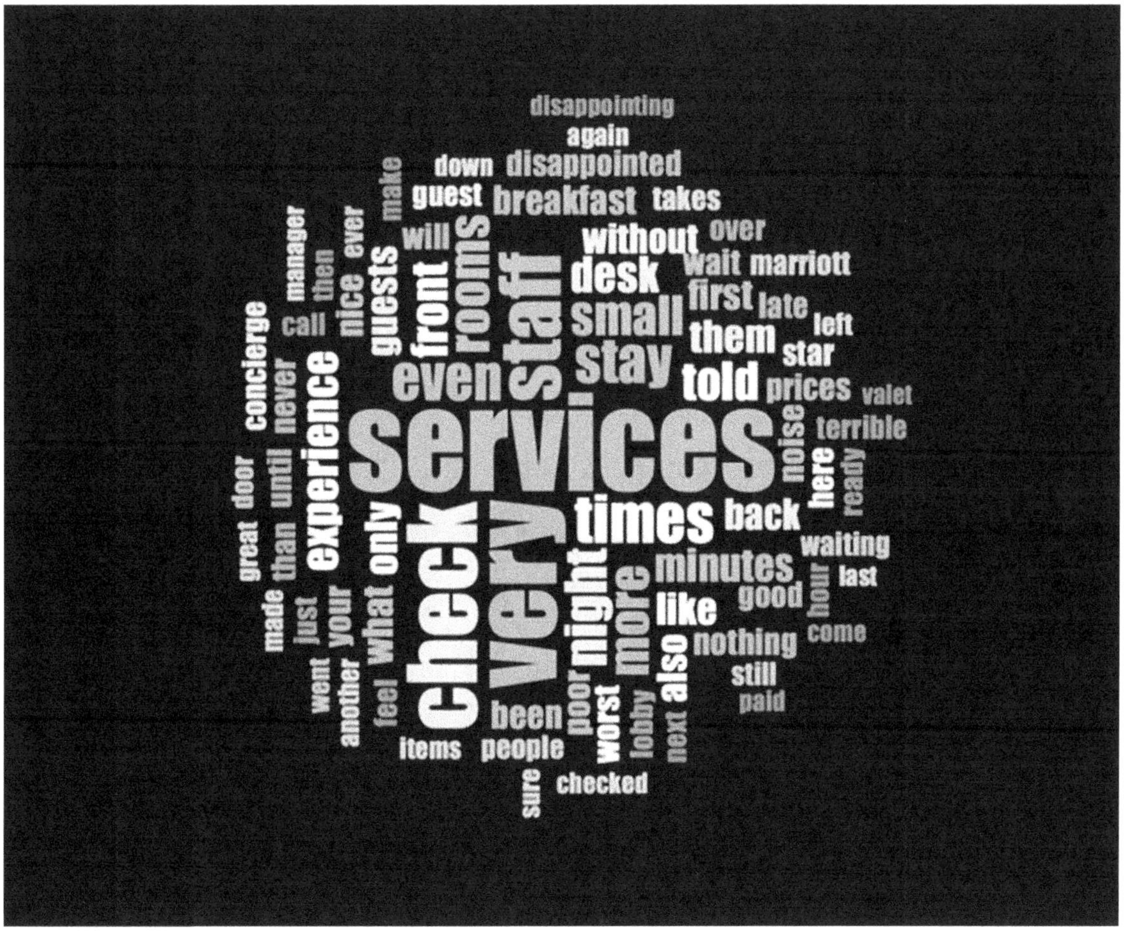

Using the word "Services" with the most prominent example of complaints, it is possible some extract many different negative reviews and visions about, the service.

...In addition to the management above the intermediate level, the quality of service and speed of ordinary staff except catering/room cleaning are horrendous.

(Vivian15, About the Hotel localised in Sanya).

Not a luxury hotel: Front desk services are good, but honestly the services at the pool and restaurants are quite underwhelming. I don't paying for money if that equates to value. This is by no means a category 8 hotel. More like a Category 3 or so. It's overpriced for service.

The pool service are quite underwhelming and staff is

slow/forgetful in the pool/beach/restaurant area.

Figure 6. Word Tree from NVivo: Connexion between a word and reference in the texts

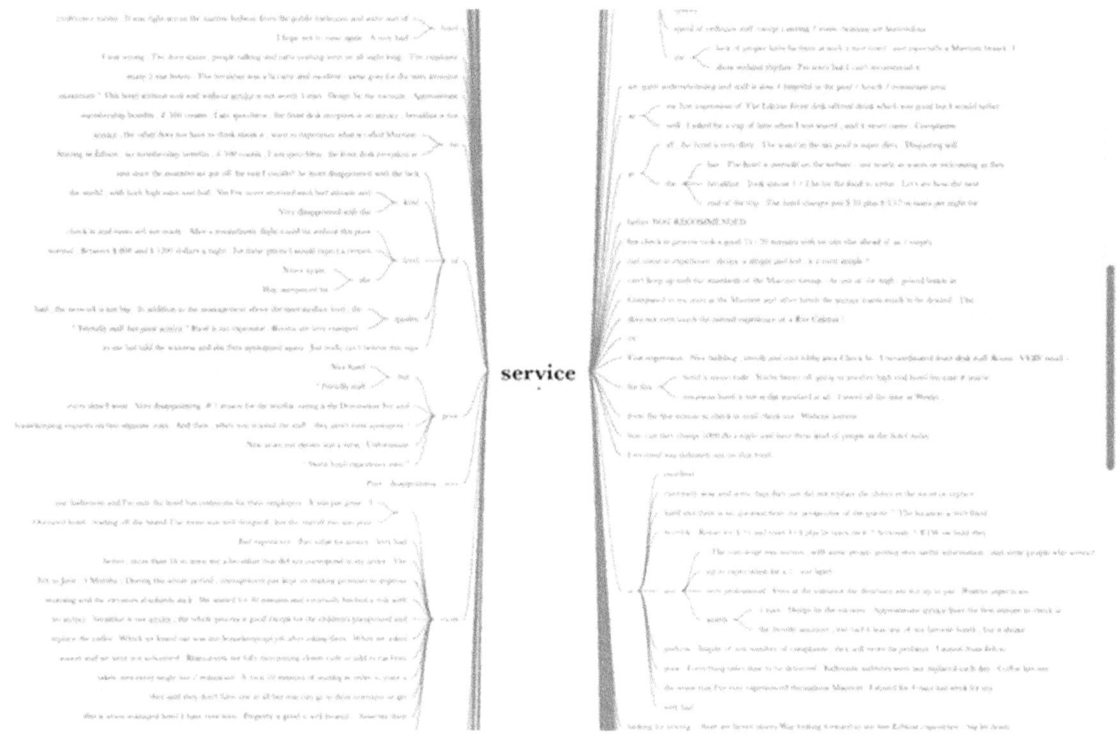

(RamitKumar about the hotel localised in Miami)

Lousy service: no loyalty to elite members, slow service, no customer service. (AVIICZKOVITS)

The first review - Vivian15 - mentioned problems about the quality of services and also the management, mixing our frustration in diversions parts of the hotel. The second declassified the Hotel and comparing the quantity of money paid with the services. Furthermore, the last example showed complains about the time of the service and the customer service as well. In the same review, it is possible to identify that customer is a member of the program of loyalty and does not feel prestigious as such.

Tableau: Demographic Data

Demographic data were collected and catalogued during coding: gender, hotel interaction, hotel name, language and review platform. Is important to highlight that all data was found in Google Reviews, and for that reason, not all individual profiles were complete. The essential aspects of this study are focused on minimally identifying customers, and their experience with the hotel, as well as the hotel's most frequent issues, reported. The gender analysis had three variables: female, male and not signed - when it was not possible to identify it. The results showed us that in New York, for example, most of the reviews were made by men, also in the other hotels, except Shanghai, the identifiable public is mainly masculine. The hotel interaction was measured by: answered or unanswered. For that aspect, the results are, one more time, only different in Shanghai, the other reviews had fewer answers than unanswered. The language variable brings the numbers for most reviews in English in seven of the nine hotels, other than Bodrum and Sanya, respectively Turkish and Chinese. Finally, the three platforms that were more used, in order of incidence are Google Reviews, Tripadvisor and Marriott.

The complete analysis is available, and it reveals an unsatisfied public composed by English speaker men, connected to 2 of the most significant review platforms - Google and TripAdvisor and a portion composed by Marriott regular clients. As the study is directed to reviews on Google, it is normal for the most substantial proportion to be from this platform, but 31% of the reviews come from TripAdvisor (a company that belongs to the Expedia group) indicating the need for cross-platform verification.

Iramuteq: R Interface for Multidimensional Analysis of Texts and Questionnaires

The analysis developed with Iramuteq started when all information was in English and grouped by the hotel. For this analysis objective, the clients' individuality was not necessary. Therefore, all data were exported in UFT-8 in order to attend the program's specifications. The corpus was constituted by nine texts, separated in 646 text segments (TS), showing a 77,24% utilisation rate in 499 TSs. From that, emerged 23.558 words, being 3.158 different words and 1.596 with a single appearance.

Afterwards, the analysis has begun. At its first option, Textual Statistics, the software brings the accurate number of texts and TS, incidence, average word frequency, as well as, the total frequency of each form and its grammar classification according to the short form dictionary. In the results interface, is possible visualised the Zipf diagram (Figure 7), which shows the behaviour of word frequencies in the corpus, using a graphic that illustrates the X rang frequency distribution — knowing that further analysis can be explained.

DHC (Descending Hierarchical Classification - Dendrogram)

The analysed content was categorised into 4 clusters or classes by Iramuteq: Cluster 1 with 131 TS's (26.25%), Cluster 2 with 118 TS's (23.65%), Cluster 3 with 145 TS's (29.06%) and Cluster 4 with 105 TS's (21.04) %) according to the dendrograms, in a descending classification. Cluster 1, in red, is linked to issues of Front Office of Hotels. Cluster 2 and Cluster 3, blue and green, respectively, are liked to groups experience-versus-value issues and experience and quality issues. The last one, Cluster 4, in purple, brings more structural and physical hotel issues.

Each classification represents a group that by word analysis, it is possible to divide into two different branches: A, which is directly linked to Cluster 1, and B which is directly related to customer experience. Branch A is composed only by Cluster 1, while branch B is composed by Cluster 2, 3 and 4, and further subdivided in B1 (Clusters 2 and 3) and B2 (Cluster 4) generating three different Clusters. This separation shows that even being separately less significative than Cluster 1, Clusters 2, 3 and 4 are connected, forming a group with over 70% of the complaints. Also, B1 is more expressive than B2. Knowing that it is possible to affirm that the customer's experience and the hotel structure are the aspects with most issues.

Factorial Correspondence Analysis

The factorial correspondences analysis uses a cartesian system to separate the data, showing the differences between each hotel place. The first relevant aspect is the proximity of hotels to the centre; six of the

Figure 7. Diagrama de Zipf from Iramuteq

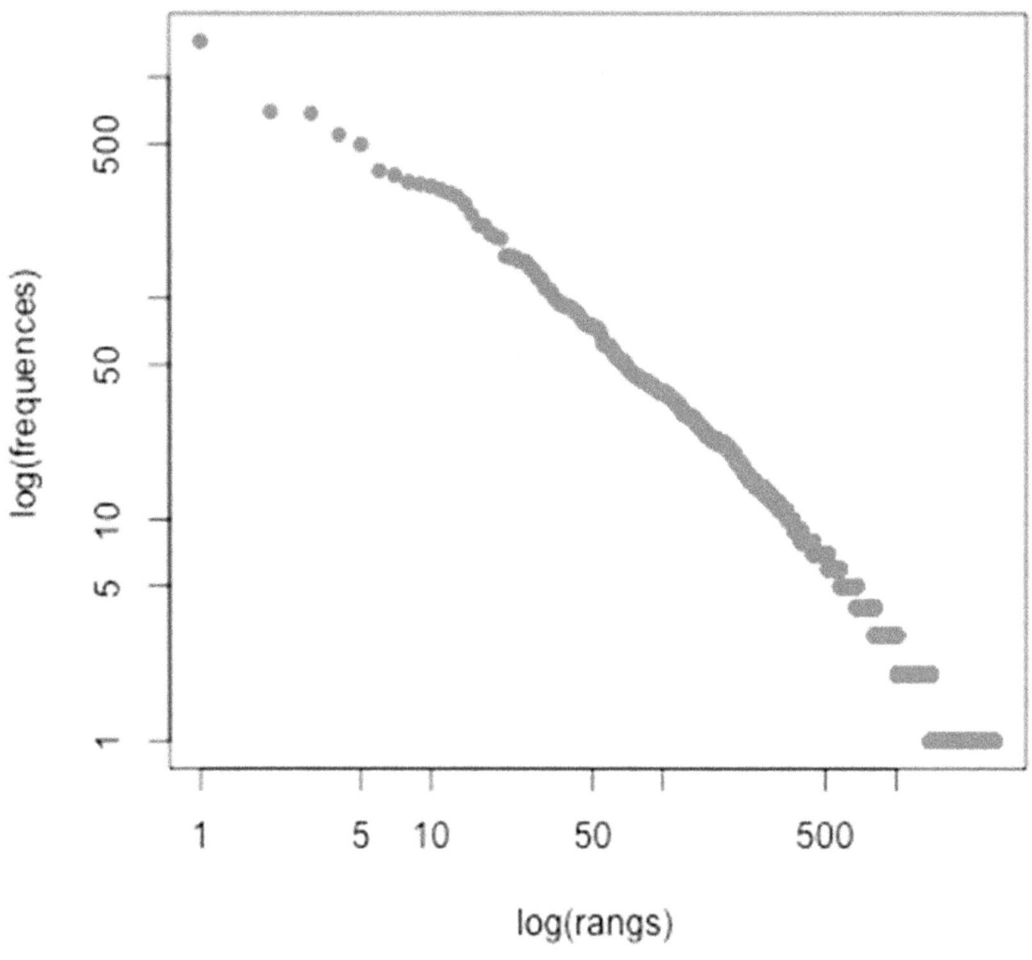

nine are between -1 and 1 in both axes. On the x-axis, representing 38.21% of the body of data, Cluster 2, 3 and 4 (negative x-axis) is clearly separate from class 1 (positive x-axis). On the y-axis, representing 34.96% of the body of data, Clusters 2 and 3 (positive y-axis) is clearly separate from Cluster 1 and 4 (negative y-axis), while class 3 is more centred.

The combination of these two axes offers a two-dimensional view of the text corpus and distinguishes three zones: Firstly, a zone of positive x and negative y, quadrant IV, showing Cluster 1, which is relational with Front Office of the hotels, more close to the variables London and Miami; A left bottom, quadrant III, a zone of negative y and x is close to Shanghai, bellower, Times Square and Sanya, on the left very close to the x and y=(0) and are related with physical issues; finally, a zone x negative and y positive, quadrant II, showing Cluster 2 (value for money) - more on top - and Cluster 3 (experience and quality) are, top to bottom: Bodrum, Abu Dhabi, Barcelona and New York. Quadrant I has no occurrences.

Figure 8. Factorial analysis combined - Text and Cluster

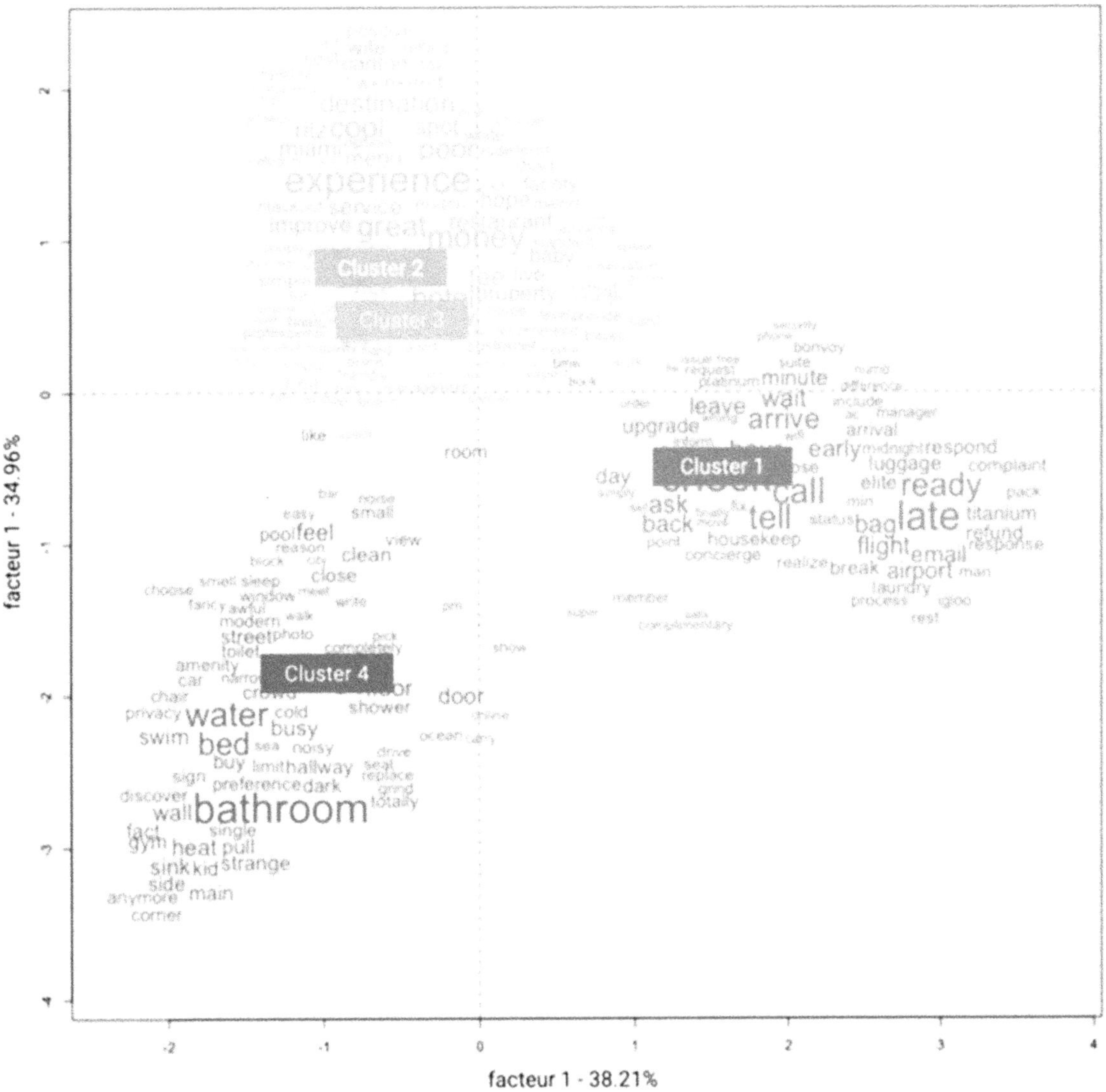

This analysis uses the Reinert method. Therefore, it is clear that as of the factorial analysis is possible to relate the associations of words and texts considering frequency and incidence of words in Clusters, represented in a cartesian plane. The Cluster 2 and the Cluster 4 are well delimited, but Clusters 1 and 3 are very close, with frontiers not so clear, reinforcing the dendrogram.

Similarities Analysis

Iramuteq, when working on similarities analysis, is focused on the connection between words in the text body. From that, is constructed a text with relevant themes, giving highlighting the most important words. For a cleaner result, the excess of meaningless words - in this specific analysis - was removed, in order to concentrate the relevant lexic.

Besides, the most influential word analysis was made in NVivo, as already seen. Even though a significant number of words match in both programs like Experience, Service, Small, Check and Noise.

Figure 9. Similarities analysis

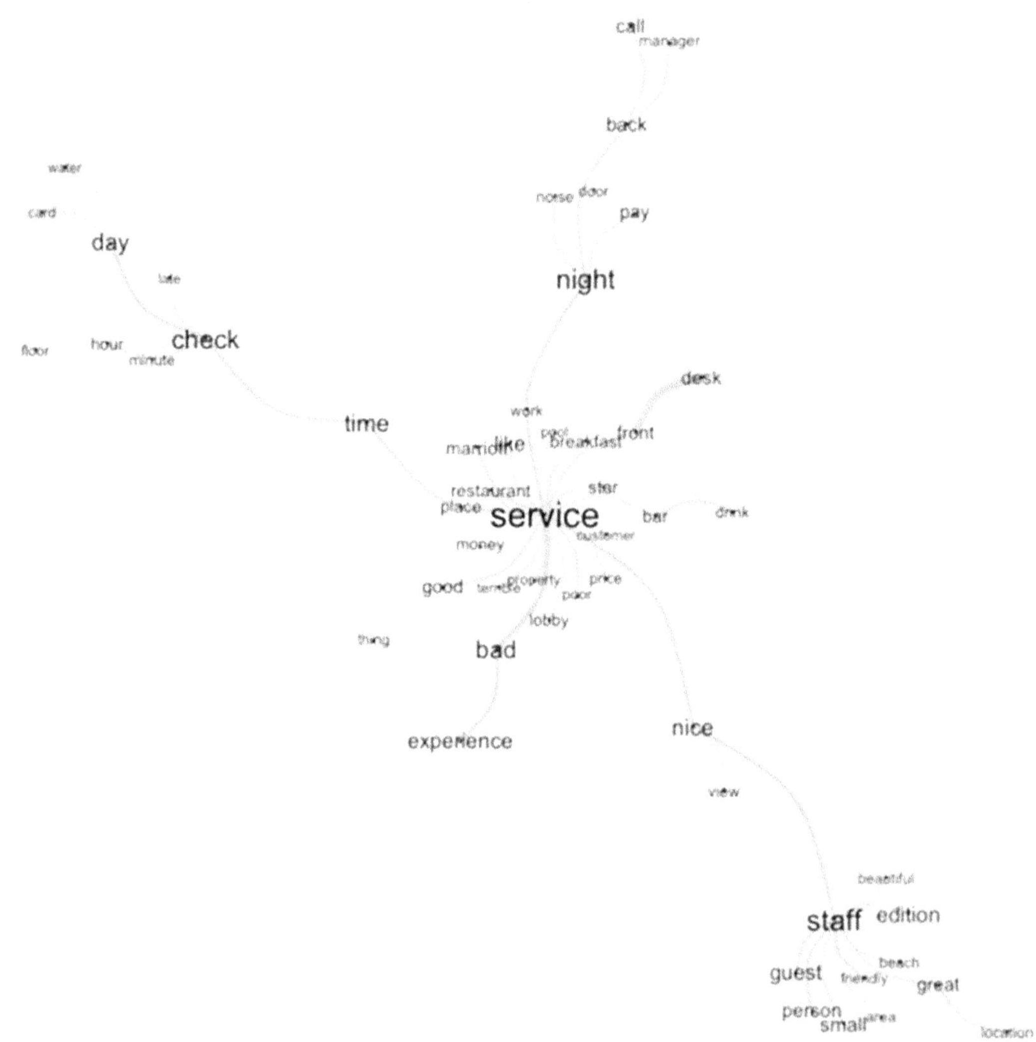

Once more, the similarities study brings a structure that converges to the other aspects of analysis made by Iramuteq.

DISCUSSION

In this part, we will discuss the results of the two methods applied to the same reviews, being the main character of this study using Netnography and in contrast, the text mining using Iramuteq. For the sake of clarity, the choice of a second technique did not have the character of confrontation of techniques, but of complement, understanding that the combination of the two improves the clarity of the data and can generate new perspectives.

After having the clarity of the data extracted from an extensive analysis on the prism of Netnography, the investigation proceeded in the process of grouping codes within the Theoretical model of brand avoidance as shown in Table - 2. The core of the study focused on Symbolic Netnography analysis of customer complaints 5-star hotels in lifestyle hotels and understanding their motivation to write their frustrations on a public review platform, in this case, Google, and seek to create a categorisation system for better understanding.

In the analysis of the coding themes 84.44% of the complaints are classified as Experiential Avoidance and as is possible to see in the Chats about 50% of the field is filled by Poor Performance which indicates a significant breach of the expectations of customers towards to the hotel. The front desk leads negative experiences with an emphasis on check-in, waiting time and check-out. A similar result is observed in Factorial Analyzes (Figure 8) where Cluster 1, in which London and Miami hotels are closest, refer to problems with Front Office.

It is possible to observe the same behaviour the Word Cloud (Figure 5) has among the main words Check, Staff, Desk and Service, all of them with strong relationships with Poor Performance in Front Desk. Still using the Similarities analysis (Figure 9) again, we see the same pattern associated with the word Service in the centre. Finally, looking at Word Tree we extracted some reviews, reported below, which show the negative experience.

Check-in:

The long check in time was unnecessary. We were so tired.

It was incredibly uncomfortable to wait.

(PainDoctor, About the Hotel localised in Abu Dhabi).

Waiting Time:

Wait time at check in was terrible and not efficient (multiple people checking in one party and a manager that stood there doing nothing but told his team he was "to busy to check in guests. (trvl2, About the Hotel localised in Barcelona).

Check-out:

... in addition to having already paid the agency from Italy we have

requested payment again at the time of check out. A fall of .

(Paola P, About the Hotel localised in London)

Following the analysis of the Chart now about Hassle Factor, which comprises 27.31% of the 84.44% of Experiential Avoidance, a large proportion was identified in Client feeling, especially in Disappointed, Sarcastic and Uncomfortable, showing the primary feelings of customers concerning the service provided. Below are some examples.

Disappointed:

...He does not answer me, and the last call told me that he would solve it already go 25 days And the hotel does not give me the disappointing face of Rita

Charneira's attention Guest service....

(Paola P, About the Hotel localised in London)

Sarcastic:

The genius valet even left my car to roast in the sun all day

in the scorching heat and damaged my car.

(PainDoctor, About the Hotel localised in Abu Dhabi)

Uncomfortable:

The staff at this hotel spoil my vacation. I have never been so uncomfortable in a 5 star hotel.

(Ogier, About the Hotel localised in Miami)

Finally, we discuss the third major experimental dropout point, especially the store environment that occupies 20.83% of the problems. The most relevant ones in this chart involve topics related to Small Places, which are related to room size, Noise related to both external noises, and lack of soundproofing of rooms and elevators which in this case is directly related to the New York Hotel.

Small Places:

...It is said that the Platinum Card has been upgraded, but the room is still the smallest room type, no landscape, and there is no Platinum Card Welcome..

(FYI, About the Hotel localised in Shanghai)

Noises:

Not bad, but the ventilation noise in the middle is incredibly uncomfortable,

they need to produce a professional solution..

(Emin Polat, About the Hotel localised in Bodrum)

Elevators:

I first had a 4 star rating for this hotel. But the lifts are such a problem that I take 3 stars back. Of the 4 lifts, only 1 works, we sometimes waited 10 minutes for the lift, unacceptable!...

(Heinz Nixdorf, About the Hotel localised in New York)

In addition to the analysis highlighted in the research, this study brings or confronts negative opinions with the brand precepts that, in this case, blend with the concept of lifestyle of the hotel. As explained in the introduction of this category, some crucial assumptions such as offering personalised service, differentiated quality and making customers very important. Within this line of reasoning, an analysis is required without major problems referenced by the data, but also those that can have the most significant impact on the concept of the hotel and negative WOM. These include some comments that consider essential points for maintaining a brand image and values.

Bad Customer Service:

... is 5 stars but the customer service I received was definitely not on that level.

(Daniel King, About the Hotel localised in Times Square)

Friend had a gift sent over and was never delivered to our room

as promised for our special anniversary wknd. Ruined the entire gift.

(Verified Traveler - Expedia-, About the Hotel localised in New York)

Bad Experience:

Do not stay at this property until they get it together and properly train their staff.

Horrible experience across the board except with the higher level management.

(Jillian Michaels, About the Hotel localised in Miami)

They all try to act like everybody here is super cool or whatever but I experienced receiving different treatment from the person who checked in in front of me, which I REALLY DID NOT APPRECIATE.

(Peter586, About the Hotel localised in New York)

Not 5 Stars:

You are not treated special, there is no soul or feeling of being treated as a guest, you just have a simple and small room with basic facilities and you can leave ASAP please! I won't even give this hotel 3 stars!!.

(Negar Ezmailzadeh, About the Hotel localised in Miami)

The price-service relationship has nothing to do, they charge much more than they should and should not be advertised as a 5-star hotel because they are not.

(Gustavoz56, About the Hotel localised in New York)

Marriott Member:

As a proud Marriott Ambassador, I stay over 100 nights in hotels... They obviously don't care. BEWARE, this is HORRIBLE customer service and a month later I'm still dealing with this. Once I showed them their error this should have been resolved and nothing.!!

(Jeff M, About the Hotel localised in London)

...As a Marriott platinum membership, I don't feel any special and feel unworthy to stay here.

(Li Wei, About the Hotel localised in Miami)

Comparisons with Others:

This is not a representation of the Ritz Carlton line, if you like a luxurious hotel

DO NOT STAY HERE!!! This was the worst hotel stay I have ever had.

(Stephanie, About the Hotel localised in Miami)

I would normally stay at Baccarat or Greenwhich Hotel - which are both superb but I wanted to be close to Madison Square Gardens for 3 events in 3 days I was attending. But after having a trickle of a shower (Greenwhich Hotel maybe he best shower in NYC) I kinda wish I had just caught an uber and stayed at a Genuine 5 star hotel.

(John Wall, About the Hotel localised in New York)

Understanding beyond numbers and words in repetition is the challenge and at the same time, the most significant advantage of Netnography. Over the last ten reviews presented above are translated by customer words, part of what is expected in the services of a 5-star hotel.

Finally, speculatively motivated by the experience of the researcher and the reviews reviewed, it can be said that in addition to common problems that a hotel operation may have, a lifestyle hotel can often suffer a misinterpretation of brand and positioning in the hotel.

Consumers head noting that online travel agencies (OTAs) offer several 5-star hotels, many customers may believe that a Lifestyle will offer the same services in the same way, which is not valid, as we can read in reviews about services or comparisons with other 5-star hotels. Thus, there is likely a traditional luxury consumer attraction that has very different standards, and there may be a confusion of expectation.

CONCLUSION

The Netnography is a specific approach to study social interaction experience from a human perspective (Kozinets, 2015). It is is a central part of this research totally oriented to understand and create one relationship between the consumer expectative, service delivered in the hotel and the negative review. It is extensive studies using numbers or even text mining to try understanding the motivations of client negative feelings, but with Netnography was possible in this study to see different sides, including essential perspectives to the lifestyle concept.

This work presents two crucial conceptual contributions. Firstly, this study offers an in-depth integrative analysis of a specific conceptual framework in order to explore the experiences related to lifestyles hotels, in particular, the negative ones. Secondly, the empirical results provide more information for this area of study, having identified the main patterns/areas of complaints reported in online reviews regarding the stay in lifestyle hotels.

It should also be noted that the present work has significant theoretical and empirical contributions to studies in the field of tourism, to the extent that which presents Netnography and, more specifically, Iramuteq software as powerful tool for the analysis of the behaviour of people (tourists) in virtual environments and can be used as a useful tool to lifestyle tourism and hotels management. As a destination management tool, the results provide useful information on the areas that need to be improved in order to offer better services with more quality, authenticity and a unique character to make the hotel brand associated with luxury worthwhile.

As for the use of Iramuteq, specifically, it is necessary to consider the character of the present study which, in a pioneering way, positions itself as one of the first references using such a textual data analysis tool for the conduct of research in the field of lifestyle hotels and tourism, particularly, in the negative experiences related to this niche. Therefore, it is useful to have new investigations that use the Iramuteq for the analysis of other aspects within the social phenomenon that is lifestyle tourism based on textual information from as many different sources as possible. It is crucial to emphasise that the present study, although it brings essential insights and inferences, did not claim to be conclusive and paradigmatic and new studies and new reflections should be conducted within this field of study.

REFERENCES

Aggett, M. (2007). What has influenced growth in the UK's boutique hotel sector? *International Journal of Contemporary Hospitality Management*, *19*(2), 169–177. doi:10.1108/09596110710729274

Alexandrov, A., Lilly, B., & Babakus, E. (2013). The effects of social- and self-motives on the intentions to share positive and negative word of mouth. *Journal of the Academy of Marketing Science*, *41*(5), 531–546. doi:10.100711747-012-0323-4

Bagozzi, R., Gopinath, M., & Nyer, P. (1999). The role of emotions in Marketing. *Journal of the Academy of Marketing Science*, *27*(2), 184–206. doi:10.1177/0092070399272005

Barreda, A., & Bilgihan, A. (2013). An analysis of user-generated content for hotel experiences. *Journal of Hospitality and Tourism Technology*, *4*(3), 263–280. doi:10.1108/JHTT-01-2013-0001

Beckmann, S. C., & Langer, R. (2005). Netnography: Rich insights from online research. *Insights*, *8*(2), 149–155.

Bonilla, Y., & Rosa, J. (2015). #Ferguson: Digital protest, hashtag ethnography, and the racial politics of social media in the United States. *American Ethnologist*, *42*(1), 4–17. doi:10.1111/amet.12112

Breindl, Y. (2013). Assessing success in internet campaigning. *Information Communication and Society*, *16*(9), 1419–1440. doi:10.1080/1369118X.2012.707673

Budish, R. H. (2012). Click to change: Optimism despite online activism's unmet expectations. *Emory International Law Review*, *26*(2), 745–772.

Buttle, F. A. (1998). Word of mouth: Understanding and managing referral marketing. *Journal of Strategic Marketing*, *6*(3), 241–254. doi:10.1080/096525498346658

Cheung, C. M. K., & Lee, M. K. O. (2010). A theoretical model of intentional social action in online social networks. *Decision Support Systems*, *49*(1), 24–30. doi:10.1016/j.dss.2009.12.006

Corrêa, M., & Rozados, H. (2017). A netnografia como método de pesquisa em Ciência da Informação. Encontros Bibli. *Revista Eletrônica de Biblioteconomia e Ciência da Informação*, *22*(49), 1–18. doi:10.5007/1518-2924.2017v22n49p1

Cova, B., & Cova, V. (2001). Tribal aspects of postmodern consumption research: The case of French in-line roller skaters. *Journal of Consumer Behaviour*, *1*(1), 67–76. doi:10.1002/cb.54

Dunne, D. (2005). *Consumers don't need a thing*. Marketing.

Evans, M., Jamal, A., & Foxall, G. (2009). *Consumer behaviour* (2nd ed.). John Wiley & Sons.

Fan, W., & Gordon, M. D. (2014). The power of social media analytics. *Communications of the ACM*, *57*(6), 74–81. doi:10.1145/2602574

Fournier, S., & Alvarez, C. (2013). Relating badly to brands. *Journal of Consumer Psychology*, *23*(2), 253–264. doi:10.1016/j.jcps.2013.01.004

Friedman, M. (1985). Consumer boycotts in the United States, 1970-1980: Contemporary events in historical perspective. *The Journal of Consumer Affairs*, *19*(1), 96–117. doi:10.1111/j.1745-6606.1985.tb00346.x

Funches, V., Markley, M., & Davis, L. (2009). Reprisal, retribution and requital: Investigating customer retaliation. *Journal of Business Research*, *62*(2), 231–238. doi:10.1016/j.jbusres.2008.01.030

Grégoire, Y., Tripp, T., & Legoux, R. (2009). When customer love turns into lasting hate: The effects of relationship strength and time on customer revenge and avoidance. *Journal of Marketing*, *73*(6), 18–32. doi:10.1509/jmkg.73.6.18

Heinrichs, J. H., Lim, J.-S., & Lim, K.-S. (2011). Influence of social networking site and user access method on social media evaluation. *Journal of Consumer Behaviour*, *10*(6), 347–355. doi:10.1002/cb.377

Hogg, M. K. (1998). Anti-constellations: Exploring the impact of negation on consumption. *Journal of Marketing Management*, *14*(1-3), 133–158. doi:10.1362/026725798784959354

Holleschovsky, N. I. (2015). *The social influence factor: Impact of online product review characteristics on consumer purchasing decisions.* 5th IBA Bachelor Thesis Conference, Enschede, The Netherlands.

Hookway, N. (2008). 'Entering the blogosphere': Some strategies for using blogs in social research. *Qualitative Research*, *8*(1), 91–113. doi:10.1177/1468794107085298

Huang, L.-S. (2015). Trust in product review blogs: The influence of self-disclosure and popularity. *Behaviour & Information Technology*, *34*(1), 33–44. doi:10.1080/0144929X.2014.978378

Iyer, R., & Muncy, J. A. (2009). Purpose and object of anti-consumption. *Journal of Business Research*, *62*(2), 160–168. doi:10.1016/j.jbusres.2008.01.023

Kelman, H. C. (1958). Compliance, identification, and internalization: Three processes of attitude change. *The Journal of Conflict Resolution*, *2*(1), 51–60. doi:10.1177/002200275800200106

Kimmel, A. J., & Kitchen, P. J. (2014). WOM and social media: Presaging future directions for research and practice. *Journal of Marketing Communications*, *20*(1), 5–20. doi:10.1080/13527266.2013.797730

Kosar, L. (2014). Lifestyle hotels – New paradigm of modern hotel industry. *Broj*, *14*(14), 39–50. doi:10.5937/TurPos1414039K

Kozinets, R. V. (2015). *Management Netnography: Axiological and Methodological Developments in Online Cultural Business Research.* Schulich School of Business, York University.

Kozinets, R. V. (2015). *Netnography: Redefined* (2nd ed.). SAGE Publications.

Lee, M. S. W., Conroy, D., & Motion, J. (2009). Brand avoidance: A negative promises perspective. *Advances in Consumer Research. Association for Consumer Research (U. S.), 36*, 421–429.

Lee, Y., & Hsieh, G. (2013). Does slacktivism hurt activism?: The effects of moral balancing and consistency in online activism. *Proceedings of the SIGCHI Conference on Human Factors in Computing Systems*. 10.1145/2470654.2470770

Li, X., Hitt, L. M., & Zhang, Z. (2011). Product reviews and competition in markets for repeat purchase products. *Journal of Management Information Systems, 27*(4), 9–31. doi:10.2753/MIS0742-1222270401

Lim, Y. M. (2009). *Customer-based brand equity: The effect of destination image on preference for products associated with a destination brand* (Master thesis). Virginia Polytechnic Institute and State University.

Lugosi, P., Janta, H., & Watson, P. (2012). Investigative management and consumer research on the internet. *International Journal of Contemporary Hospitality Management, 24*(6), 838–854. doi:10.1108/09596111211247191

Manthiou, A., Kang, J., Hyun, S., & Fu, X. (2018). The impact of brand authenticity on building brand love: An investigation of impression in memory and lifestyle-congruence. *International Journal of Hospitality Management, 75*, 38–47. doi:10.1016/j.ijhm.2018.03.005

Masten, D., & Plowman, T. (2003). Digital ethnography: The next wave in understanding the consumer experience. *Design Management Journal, 14*(2), 75–81. doi:10.1111/j.1948-7169.2003.tb00044.x

McIntosh, A., & Siggs, A. (2005). An exploration of the experiential nature of boutique accommodation. *Journal of Travel Research, 44*(1), 74–81. doi:10.1177/0047287505276593

Rempel, J. K., & Burris, C. T. (2005). Let me count the ways: An integrative theory of love and hate. *Personal Relationships, 12*(2), 297–313. doi:10.1111/j.1350-4126.2005.00116.x

Riegner, C. (2007). Word of mouth on the web: The impact of web 2.0 on consumer purchase decisions. *Journal of Advertising Research, 47*(4), 436–447. doi:10.2501/S0021849907070456

Romani, S., Grappi, S., & Dalli, D. (2012). Emotions that drive consumers away from brands: Measuring negative emotions towards brands and their behavioral effects. *International Journal of Research in Marketing, 29*(1), 55–67. doi:10.1016/j.ijresmar.2011.07.001

Ruhanen, L. (2019). The prominence of eco in ecotourism experiences: An analysis of post-purchase online reviews. *Journal of Hospitality and Tourism Management, 39*, 110–116. doi:10.1016/j.jhtm.2019.03.006

Saldaña, J. (2012). *The coding manual for qualitative research* (2nd ed.). SAGE.

Schönfelder, W. (2011). *CAQDAS and qualitative syllogism logic – NVivo 8 and MAXQDA 10 compared*. Paper presented at the Forum Qualitative Sozialforschung (Forum: Qualitative Social Research).

Sen, S., Gürhan-Canli, Z., & Morwitz, V. (2001). Withholding consumption: A social dilemma perspective on consumer boycotts. *The Journal of Consumer Research, 28*(3), 399–417. doi:10.1086/323729

Shahrinaz, I., Kasuma, J., Yacob, Y., Rahman, D. H. A. A., & Mahdi, A. F. (2016). Relationship and impact of e-WOM and brand image towards purchase intention of smartphone? *Journal of Scientific Research and Development*, *3*(5), 117–124.

Tariq, M., Abbas, T., Abrar, M., & Iqbal, A. (2017). EWOM and brand awareness impact on consumer purchase intention: Mediating role of brand image. *Pakistan Administrative Review*, *1*(1), 84–102.

Tavakoli, V., & Wijesinghe, S. N. R. (2019). The evolution of the web and netnography in tourism. *Systematic Reviews*.

Thanh, T., & Kirova, V. (2018). Wine tourism experience: A netnography study. *Journal of Business Research*, *83*, 30–37. doi:10.1016/j.jbusres.2017.10.008

Trandafilović, I., Pašić, V., & Perunović, S. (2013). The research of cognitive and affective behavior during shopping. *Economics and Organization*, *10*(2), 147–164.

Veloutsou, C., & Guzman, F. (2017). The evolution of brand management thinking over the last 25 years as recorded in the Journal of Product and Brand Management. *Journal of Product and Brand Management*, *26*(1), 2–12. doi:10.1108/JPBM-01-2017-1398

Webster, F. E. Jr, & Keller, K. L. (2004). A roadmap for branding in the industrial markets. *Brand Management*, *11*(5), 388–402. doi:10.1057/palgrave.bm.2540184

Weingarten, K. (2006). On hating to hate. *Family Process*, *45*(3), 277–288. doi:10.1111/j.1545-5300.2006.00170.x PMID:16984070

Ye, Q., Law, R., & Gu, B. (2009). The impact of online user reviews on hotel room sales. *International Journal of Hospitality Management*, *28*(1), 180–182. doi:10.1016/j.ijhm.2008.06.011

Chapter 8
Consumer-Brand Relationship and Use of the Website in Virtual Communication in the Luxury Furniture Industry

Vera Lúcia Lourenço
Urbanização Quinta de São José, Portugal

André Whiteman Catarino
https://orcid.org/0000-0003-2907-6845
Textile Engineering Department, University of Minho, Portugal

Manuel José Fonseca
https://orcid.org/0000-0002-3290-8449
Polytechinc Institute of Viana do Castelo (IPVC), Portugal

Bruno Barbosa Sousa
https://orcid.org/0000-0002-8588-2422
Polytechinc Institute of Cávado and Ave, Portugal

ABSTRACT

Luxury management can be considered the management of paradoxes between intangibility and functionality, rationality and emotion, modern technology with traditional craftsmanship, showing that luxury comes from creation, timelessness, emotion, excellence, heritage, and authenticity. This chapter results from two methods, a qualitative analysis, which presents an analysis grid with the most varied characteristics; these are divided into six groups: identification, content, product page, utility, entertainment and complementary relationship, speed and other presences visible on three websites of luxury furniture brands. The other method is the quantitative one, which was a questionnaire with the understanding the perceived quality of the website using the WebQual scale, as well as understanding the purchase intention and the importance of the internet in the purchase decision process.

DOI: 10.4018/978-1-7998-4369-6.ch008

Copyright © 2021, IGI Global. Copying or distributing in print or electronic forms without written permission of IGI Global is prohibited.

INTRODUCTION

The luxury market needs specific behaviors such as marketing strategies in order for these brands to differentiate themselves from mass consumer brands, and it is important to know which means have the most impact on all luxury values and which the positioning is not lost. "*Luxury*" is intrinsically inserted in society, and is usually defined as rarity and exclusivity, which is sought when a status or social position is desired. However, the term "*luxury*" in a systematized and integrated way is directly linked to exclusivity, desire, dream and exuberance, particularities that can become overly derogatory and ostentatious. Throughout the history of humanity, and based on the historical framework of luxury, its importance and its impact on society is understood from the earliest times to today's society, which is positioned in the social differentiation that it produces, such as the appearance of a quality of life, the beauty and the pleasure of the products by consumers. Thus, the symbolic grandeur and social dimension of the concept of luxury, as well as its value, is not easy to define because it is treated and represented by subjective meaning, and because over time it has also undergone several changes in its characteristics. Lipovetsky's Ephemeral Empire shows that the notion of luxury has changed, and nowadays this term has assumed a "more intimate than emotional character" (Lipovetsky, 2009) presenting itself to society as a way to satiate themselves, and not as an element of social differentiation, as was observed in past times. Thus, luxury is lived more emotionally than the essence of the product by consumers, where it is seen by the author of a "behavioral act that is based on the maxim of why I want and not why I can". A brand, can have much more value than their products, because its positioning in the market allows its target audience to create perceptions and identify with the brand identity and image, so that it can create its preferences, where "building a luxury brand is inseparable from the symbolic management of its roots, the work of building a myth" (Lipovetsky and Roux, 2005). The brand is a guarantee of luxury, that is, the consumer when looking for a certain brand, this unconsciously associates with luxury, adding an identity to the product. On the other hand, consumers can also associate luxury with a particular brand simply by the positioning it occupies in their mind, however, the greater the perceived value of a brand, linked to exclusivity, the greater the preference for that same brand. But at the same time, the luxury consumer, being aware of the high value that the brand can adopt, will also perceive a devaluation of its prestige, where the desire may diminish. The fact that the world owns and confronts consumers daily with new brands in the market shows that competition will have to increase their ability to have a good management of their attributes, as their main objective to differentiate themselves from others and achieve their desired success.

Brands are increasingly consumed according to what they represent, whether in lifestyles, a concept, or even emotions and not so much product related. For the postmodern brand enriches the shopping experience by offering a fantasy or aspiration that gives specific meaning to any consumed product, brand and service. Today, the vast majority of consumers learn to manage and make life decisions based on information taken from the Internet. Proving that the internet is increasingly the beginning for buying products and services, where the advantages are significant, such as convenience, diversity of supply and saving time and money. The Internet has the ability to transform the way consumers relate to brands where, this transformation is affecting the marketing economy while making many of the traditional features and strategies outdated. In this sense, brands are increasingly looking for marketing solutions that use the internet as the main tool for publicizing goods and services. This is because the internet is used by the general public to gather information, surpassing the users of radio, television and others. Internet usage has been increasing over the years, as has its benefit. The communication of luxury goods is associated with exclusivity, both in the choice of media and in the way it displays its messages, especially in an industry that does not only want to sell its products, but also wants to sell the concept associated with the brand (Lipovetsky, 2009). Thus, there is a need to understand how luxury brands communicate by creating the desire and dream to acquire not only their products, but also their concept, where the luxury universe needs agreement across communication, from messages to the use of various channels and segments starting with the format, colors, language and voices must always be in harmony and interconnected (Mazzon et al., 2012).

BACKGROUND

The Luxury

Lipovetsky (2005) presents luxury in the form of a social distinction between different social classes, proving through societies that, today, luxury is where individuals can differentiate and assert themselves before others in their social hierarchy. This proves that throughout history, luxury has been considered a privilege for high royal groups to be displayed and admired in public and visibly spawning the social hierarchy (Abbott, 2008). According to Lipovetsky and Roux (2005), the "notion of luxury has changed over time", where today it is considered a more intimate, emotional character, presenting itself in the form of the individual's desire to satisfy not only himself as well as being distinguished in society. Luxury is based on the emotions that it provides more than the product itself, showing that luxury is behavioral, proving that individuals buy for emotional reasons, but always justifying with logic, showing that luxury is an individual choice, but above all, is a way of expression. Luxury is no longer what it was. Expensive products, limited supply and high demand were once the luxury features where only a few people, those who had the money or access, could afford luxury goods that is bought by individuals who had a comfortable economic level life. Danziger (2004) argues that "old luxury was about two things" by showing that luxury is no longer defined solely by the wealth or income of consumers, nowadays almost any individual can be part of the luxury universe where they want luxury and they are willing to pay for it. To this new trend, Danziger (2004) presents two new concepts, the "democratization of luxury" or "new luxury". The meaning of luxury is entirely intertwined with the time period in which it was lived, where its interpretations may vary (Nwankwo, Hamelin form of goods and services considered as non-basic needs, and Khaled, 2014). Luxury is also defined under, associated with a high price and quality, where prestige and exclusivity then have a symbolic value (Tynan et al., 2010).

Thus, contrary to the past, luxury symbol depends not only on the quality and exclusivity attribute of a product and/or service, but also on the brand. Chandon et al. (2015) state that luxury is created by brands, and these are not only brands that sell luxury products, but sell dreams with a name and a symbolism. For many authors, the definition of luxury is considered an arduous task, as each author has his own definition, where this term fits perfectly with the high quality, high price and brand effect (Lipovetsky and Roux, 2005). It can almost be said that luxury can be related to the exclusive, rare and consequently high cost. Other authors argue that luxury is deeply linked to social stratification, a notion of utility as well as in the relation of wealth distribution. Luxury is linked to society in general, as Kapferer and Bastien (2009) state, that society itself defines the concept of luxury.

In the most concrete point of view, luxury can be associated with grandeur, fortune, extravagance, superfluous, frivolity, appearance and material power (Braga, 2004). But in contrast, for purists, luxury has a concrete value, expensive and scarce, almost seen as an investment, a heritage initiative (Castarède, 2005). Luxury has the ability to disassociate itself from behavior, a code, comfort, vanity, recognition, pleasure and satisfaction, conferring a different degree of elegance (Braga, 2004). Regarding the accessibility of luxury, some authors claim that it is based on a hierarchy, and currently there is not only one category of luxury, but different levels for different consumers. Thus, making the inaccessible accessible is still one of the biggest adversities that the luxury market has, without putting aside the prestige and magic of a given product (Galhanone, 2005). For a consumer to remain at the level of unreachable luxury is a tricky task, because on the one hand, all consumers of this level have increasing purchasing power, just as the number of affordable and intermediate luxury consumers increases, but it is not common to cross to the level of inaccessible luxury. Thus Allérès (2006) establishes a classification for luxury in three categories: affordable luxury, intermediate luxury, inaccessible luxury. Inaccessible luxury is the highest level of them all. This level is in many cases a brand-generating category so that in the future intermediate and affordable luxuries can be sold. These are unique products, authentic creations, with a thorough selection of their raw materials, design, finishes, service and customer customization (García, 2003). Thus it can be said that this higher category reflects fullness and its products have a high added value because the price of exclusivity and inaccessibility is paid by its consumers (Castarède, 2005). Intermediate luxury may be considered the lowest level of unreachable luxury or even the highest for the lowest level brands (García, 2003). This type of luxury is defined as a production made in limited quantities (Castarède, 2005 and Allèrés, 2006). In short, this kind of luxury is considered almost perfect, although it has a high price, the prices are lower and less rare than those of inaccessible luxury, where these products have a quality of excellence, but less perfect (Paixão, 2006). Finally, affordable luxury encompasses the full range of products that, even though they belong to the luxury sector, can still accommodate a different target audience and have never been allowed to access this universe. These products also have a high level of aspiration as they will allow a social distinction. At this level can be found products made in series with lower costs and lower quality (Paixão, 2006).

For centuries around the world, consumers have been satisfied with the purchase of products, but nowadays this phenomenon has intensified as consumers buy more luxury goods. However traditionally luxury products have been defined as the refinement of human needs, making them enjoyable and desired (Berry, 1994, in Kemp, 1998). It is still possible to observe the difficulty that the authors have in defining luxury. But after several controversies, some factors considered essential, mentioned by several authors in order to define luxury products and services, were identified: for the concept of luxury, quality is an important requirement; the upper classes are the target audiences of these products; only by visual attributes such as design and style can you identify them as luxury products; limited production; selectivity and limitation in distribution; rarity is its intrinsic quality; the differentiation they offer helps define social status; the price should be high in order to increase its added value; the symbology of the dream and seduction; appeal to the senses by creating a hedonic experience; hereditary history linked to traditions and immortality; value related more to superfluous particularity than to its utility.

According to Garcia (2003), the luxury market is divided into two types of products, the timeless or classic, where you can find prestigious brands and innovative or fashion products, which give the current position of the brand in the market. Trying to understand which of the products is more appealing, where the answer would be given according to the taste of each consumer, because it depends on social and cultural factors.

Luxury Brands

Figure 1. Luxury goods
Source: *Adaptation of Madeira (2009)*

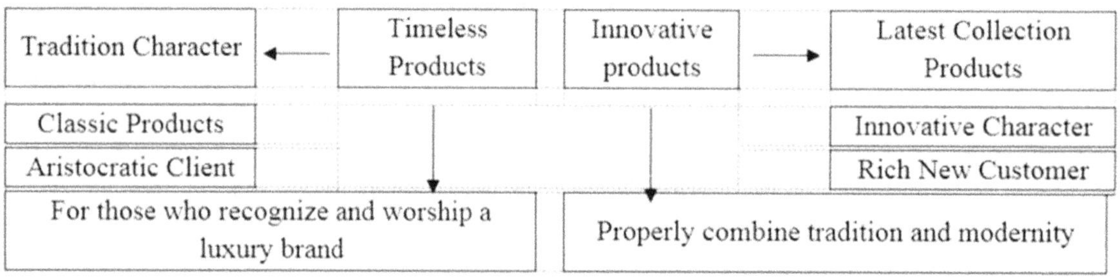

The importance of the role of luxury brands has grown, as the foundation of a brand is its intangible values that are associated with a product allowing its consumers to differentiate and make choices between similar products (Ueltschy and Laroche, 2004). That is, what differentiates products regardless of place of manufacture is the value added by the brand, also referred to as brand equity (Ueltschy and Laroche, 2004). From a more generalist perspective, a brand is not just a name, but it is much more than that (Farhana, 2012; Kotler and Armstrong, 2006), there are more elements that provide a great influence for a brand to succeed. Most of these elements are known, such as the symbol, logo, packaging and slogans (Kotler and Keller, 2006), as well as the feelings and perceptions that consumers have about the product or service and its performance (Kotler and Amstrong, 2006), as these have important elements in building a strong brand. Thus, "from the beginning of its birth, the brand name must express an interesting, inspiring and credible message of a promise that will attract consumers' attention in a competitive context" (Farhana, 2012). Luxury brands achieve something that "normal" brands fail, evoke feelings and emotions in the people who consume them. In addition to its limited production, it can generate a certain recognition towards others (Vigneron and Johnson, 2004). In the same opinion, Jackson and Haid (2002) show that luxury brands are desired because they can guarantee their consumer a perception of social status through acquired goods. Kapferer (2015) argues that it is the exclusivity of a brand that distinguishes it from others and that makes them a unique brand. Phau and Prendergast (2000) add that luxury brands evoke exclusivity, have their own identity and perceived quality by their consumers. In line with this definition, luxury brands are seen as unique and stand out for their unique elements as they cannot be found in non-luxury brands (Hudders et al, 2013). As noted earlier, Nueno and Quelch (1998) state that a luxury brand has certain characteristics: premium quality; heritage in the concept of crafts; style and design identifies the brand; limited quantities; premium price; international brand excellence; uniqueness of design in products; varied strategic capacity; the brand has the personality and values of its creator.

Vigneron and Johnson (2004) argue that while certain brands may be perceived as luxurious, they are not all alike, as how their consumers understand luxury brands and their respective "quantity" of luxury is dependent on the consumer's context. Parente (2007) stated that a brand would be the guarantee of luxury, that is, the consumer when looking for a brand unconsciously makes an association with luxury thus adding an identity to the product. However, the opposite also happens: luxury is associated with a brand by its positioning. Still, if a brand maintains its high levels of perceived value, it can maintain its prestige by implementing differentiated marketing strategies tailored to its markets.

Nevertheless, if a luxury consumer is aware of the high value that the brand has but has an undervalued perception of its prestige, the desire for this brand will decrease (Prendergast and Wong, 2003). Thus, building a consistent luxury brand requires effort and management, media segmentation, press relations, logistics, legal issues, a well-defined positioning, a specific target audience, among others (Nascimento, 2000). The luxury brand is something that needs to be achieved and the greater the inaccessibility and exclusivity, the greater the desire (Kapferer and Bastien, 2009). However, these brands are not only premium brands or a status symbol, they convey characteristics with their historical background (Nueno and Quelch, 1998). Lipovetsky (2005) states that luxury brands should justify their added value in their legitimacy and identity. Legitimacy, on the other hand, is based on quality, refinement, because the luxury brand is the excellence of know-how, the tradition of quality, creativity, but also the myth" (Castarède, 2005).

Luxury Marketing vs Traditional Marketing

Kapferer and Bastien (2009) argue that to build a luxury brand it is necessary to know the classic rules of marketing. In large consumer marketing, positioning is embedded within any brand strategy, and the difference that will lead to consumer preference is established. On the other hand, in luxury, being unique is the feature that matters most, and not being compared to competitors, where they are considered "irrelevant". As mentioned before, each brand has its own history, identity proving that each brand is an individual brand and never comparative, because when the goal is to win customers to the competition only demonstrates a true lack of visible identity even in premium brands but never in brands luxurious.

Table 1. Luxury marketing vs. traditional marketing

Traditional Marketing	Luxury Marketing
Brand Positioning	Brand identity
Comparative	Superlative
Pursuit of perfection (premium)	Failure equals charm and authenticity
Customer is the center	The center of the brand is its creator
Customer Approach	Customer Domain
Foster product accessibility	Obstacles to accessibility
Advertising Goal: Increased Sales	Advertising Goal: Recreating the Dream of Getting the Product
Advertising Effectiveness: Reaching the Audience	Advertising Effectiveness: Going Beyond Your Audience
Lowering Price Equals Increasing Demand	Price increase, demand increases

Source: Kapferer e Bastien (2009) K

In traditional marketing the customer is the center of the whole business, always being the basis of product creation, the opposite happens in luxury marketing, the products are born from the mind of its creator and is driven by a long term vision.

Desire increases when inaccessibility increases proving that the luxury segment is something that needs to be conquered with its consumers, because there is a need to create financial, cultural, logistical and time barriers (Peneda de Oliveira & Sousa, 2020). According to Kapferer and Bastien (2009), it is through communication that luxury brands reformulate the concept of social stratification, one of the most important functions of luxury, because this communication aims to create the dream and not increase sales. The communication is made before the sale is made and should reach as many people as possible, thus having to be direct, very vague and allusive, but very artistic. Kapferer and Bastien (2009) add that, in the luxury market, communication is important, but in a secondary way, that is, these brands usually advertise only in selected magazines, along with other luxury brands, but it is also necessary to press office and public relations. These marks are displayed in movies, celebrities who later appear in physical and / or online photographs. Yan and Qu (2014) believe that a brand should select well its media where they perform advertising, selecting magazines or other publications, however, television can never be the object of communication, as it may devalue the brand.

6 P's of Luxury Marketing

"Marketing-mix" is a concept that has been in use since the twentieth century, but it was in the 1960s that McCarthy popularized the term "4p's of marketing," namely price, product, place, and promotion. Allérès (2000) applied the previous strategy to the luxury segment, but later, Winsper (2009) presents a paper, "The 6P's of Luxury Marketing" that allows the assessment of luxury consumer behavior in today's times. In short, this study argues that marketers to analyze consumers in this market used only demographic criteria, profession studies, income, among others. However, according to Laurent et al (2001), today's luxury consumers are complex and diverse, thus defining the way they purchase goods. This approach allows Winsper (2007) to state that marketers should be able to better understand their target audience and build more lasting and profitable relationships. The 6P's of luxury marketing are:

- People - They have a very important role in building relationships because they can customize, create, develop and maintain strong relationships;
- Product - This should be intertwined with the characteristics of a brand's success, such as quality, heritage, integrity, price, rarity and ultimately superfluity;
- Passion - Aims at the passion of consumers or brand collectors, thus expressing the advantages of it, as well as passion can lead to irrational and impulsive behaviors;
- Pleasure - This is purchased when shopping, which should be an experience based on emotions and senses, as these are difficult to forget adding a different dimension to the purchase;
- Purpose / reason - This is entirely related to the utility of the luxury product, which is not important to all consumers. In other words, luxury goods are considered superfluous, but on the other hand it must be understood that there is an added utility built by luxury brands;
- Price - This should be set not only for your most extravagant target audience, but also for rational consumers.

THE CONSUMPTION OF LUXURY

Culture and behavior when inherent are an act of consumption, where many authors deal with symbols, feelings and values related to consumption (e.g. Sousa & Alves, 2019; Sousa & Magalhães, 2019). According to D'Angelo (2004), consumption "are rational and objective choices, always aiming for an 'ideal' purchase - one in which the maximum utility and the lowest monetary expenditure are combined". In agreeing with D'Angelo, Solomon (2006) argues that, for a long time, the act of consuming was explained in a technical way, but that behind it, there are the motivations, desires, culture and other elements relevant to the process of consumption purchase. Lipovetsky, on the other hand, asserts that consumption increases the pleasure of the consumer, but even so, the search for the satisfaction of his desires does not define the cessation of the idea of consumption by distinction (Lipovetsky and Roux, 2005).

According to Lipovetsky and Roux (2005), almost nobody has the objective of acquiring what is strictly necessary, thus, the overvaluation of consumption, leisure and welfare associated with the purchase of products that may be superfluous, being important the understanding that needs go through in cultural issues and their social position. Obviously, what is a necessity, so for some does not have the same value for others it is complex in response to a moral and universal definition of necessity, but some authors have developed its definition. For Allérès (2000), needs start from priorities ranging from instinctive (food, safety) to social (dreams, fantasy, beauty, leisure), as is the classification between true (physical) needs and false needs. (social), however, Allérès (2000) adds that the distinction makes no sense, since the fact that it is a false necessity is nevertheless a necessity. D'Angelo (2004) presented two meanings for the concept of luxury consumption: Pleasure - Luxury consumer experiences are labeled by both consumers and professionals as pleasurable and understand the pursuit of pleasure as a motivation for consumption and Impulsiveness / Understanding - The act of consuming luxury goods is wholly related to impulses where consumers cannot deny their buying desires.

Consumers in this market place a high value on both product exclusivity and brand tradition, as well as product customization and price. This has a great feature, which is their purchasing power, where their needs can be divided into functional and symbolic. Symbolic needs are considered intangible, mainly linked to dimensions with emotional and psychological benefits of the consumer in relation to the acquired good. On the other hand, functional needs are tangible and generate practical benefits. Thus, when it comes to a luxury consumer, the need he needs is a symbolic need and an intangible benefit that the product offers (Allérès, 2006). Theories on the consumption of luxury goods give two types of basic motivations for luxury goods: "luxury for others", based on extrinsic (interpersonal and social) motivations, and luxury "for oneself", only with a personal meaning (intrinsic motivation) (Kapferer and Bastien, 2009). Intrinsic and extrinsic motivations influence the acquisition of a luxury good individually or simultaneously. (Amatulli, Guido, and Nataraajan, 2015; Truong and McColl, 2011). A study by Truong et al. (2010) shows that consumers' intrinsic aspirations (personal, self-esteem, relational) have a negative effect on luxury brand preferences, where they have great relevance to their personal growth as well also in their values, distancing themselves from luxury goods because they confer a higher status and visibility.

The use of the Website in Virtual Communication and Luxury Brands

One of the defining characteristics of a luxury brand is "careful distribution control via a selective channel strategy" (Keller, 2009). Many luxury brands use their own retail network thus ensuring brand logistics align with their promise, however, the online platform encourages luxury brands to harness their potential (Keller, 2009).

From what has been observed, luxury brands have attributes such as rarity, exclusivity and, in addition to all its intrinsic characteristics, apparently the internet may be the opposite of what is intended to be communicated, i.e. the promotion or sale of a Luxury brand. Kapferer (2000) states that e-commerce represents both an opportunity and a threat to luxury brands. Porter (2001) noted that online differentiation is more difficult to achieve because there is a decrease in differentiation points, such as stores or personal service (Goh, Heng & Lin, 2013), however, the same author stated that the critical factor for Luxury goods professionals are not about the need for an online presence, but how the internet will be used to translate a brand's value into economic issues (Seringhaus, 2005).

However, Kapferer (2012) states a set of essential points in order to ensure a better penetration of the luxury brand to the e-commerce market without dissolving its value: 1) not to publish in order to generate sales; 2) communication is not intended for buyers; 3) the omnichannel should be controlled; 4) Inflate the price; 5) strengthen the direct relationship with customers using personalization and interactivity; 6) production of limited editions to promote rarity (virtual); 7) Capitalize on the use of brand ambassadors. Proper use of the Internet could contribute to greater cost efficiency by increasing the speed of raw materials and shipping products, where the reduction in sales, purchasing and operating processing costs is allowed.

E-commerce was born in 1995, when the Netscape.com website published its first online advertisements, thus popularizing the idea that the internet could be an advertising medium, helping to increase sales volume. Malheiro, Sousa and Ferreira (2019) states that e-commerce is considered to be a type of business transaction made especially through an electronic tool, however, it would be very simplistic to characterize a phenomenon that has been causing considerable and rapid changes in market structures. Turban et al. (2006) advocate a more complete definition of e-commerce, where this is a process of buying, selling, transmitting or exchanging goods, services and / or information through a network. "The online store, like physical stores, provides an atmosphere through its website that affects shoppers and their experience" (Eroglu et al., 2000), thus, luxury brand websites should recreate the characteristics and ambience of luxury stores (Seringhaus, 2005) while preserving brand-online congruence. "Luxemosphere" is a concept developed by Luxe Corp., defining it as "a strategy for reproducing a luxurious atmosphere in both offline and online environments. It can be applied online by integrating specific web elements that are directly linked to the five human senses" (Okonkwo, 2010, p. 347).

Consumer Attitude Towards the Internet

In the online environment consumers' attitude towards the internet can be fostered by the creativity of websites and as consumers are increasingly demanding and active, the ease of switching websites is high when it doesn't interest them (Ferreira & Sousa, 2020). A website portrays a utilitarian dimension ranging from providing consumer information to communicating new ideas and innovations (Carrera, 2009). But as regards experience some authors claim that it is defined as a personal event, usually with an emotional meaning and based on emotional stimuli (Hirschman and Holbrook, 1982). However, this online consumer shopping experience needs a thorough analysis as behavior focuses on purchasing and consumption being driven into the experience. Indeed, the buying and consuming process begins when the consumer develops intrinsic or extrinsic reasons for a particular good or service by establishing a longer-lasting connection with it (Hoffman and Novak, 1996). Therefore, the attitude that the consumer has about e-commerce becomes important at the moment the purchase decision occurs. Specifically, what consumers want from this experience is to use the internet for business purposes (Engel et al, 1995). In this thought, Lee and Turban (2001) portray the main benefits of e-commerce for consumers: 1) possibility of making price comparisons; 2) diversify in choices; 3) convenience of time; 4) customization of products; 5) possible interaction with other consumers.

Moreover, many consumers consider the in-store shopping experience a generation of pleasure and opportunity for social interaction. This can reduce the intent to shop online and the lack of instant access to goods, repulsing technology and the apathy to shop online (Sheth, Gardner and Garret, 1988). Purchase intention can be defined as the "possibility for consumers to buy again in the future" (Kim and Ko, 2010), thus having a direct relationship with consumer behavior and their perception of purchase. The reasons for the rapid development of internet shopping are many, much due to the benefits they offer. The internet has the ability to offer different conveniences to your consumer as they do not need to travel in order to get as much information as possible about a particular product or service, as the internet can help you get the information you need at varying levels and on various websites. The internet can increase the consumption of products, where the use is easier and more efficient compared to other channels. Through different search engines, consumers save their time by accessing information such as information with images, sound, detailed descriptions in order to choose the best product (Moon, 2004).

Consumer behavior can be seen as a set of processes involving the selection, acquisition, use and offer by consumers or group of products, services or experiences to meet their needs and wants. (Solomon, 1999), of which consumer behavior is influenced by many factors, whether social, cultural and psychological (Kotler, 2000). Lindon et al (2008) state that consumer behavior can be defined as an activity that seeks to obtain and consume goods and services. These authors also report that behavior and decision-making process are influenced by individual, sociological and psychosociological explanatory variables. It's important to note that explanatory variables can define the individual perceptions, motivations, needs your consumers have about a good or service.

It is necessary to mention that in the online shopping process when consumers have the need to buy something, they use the internet as a means of searching for information always related to what they want in order to satisfy that need (Liang and Lai, 2000). With the excess of information, sometimes consumers try to evaluate from existing alternatives, selecting the one that best suits their needs and, at a later stage, make a transaction that can be done with an after sales service (Lee and Turban, 2001). The motivation of online shopping can be described as an internal force of people that drives them to an action in order to satisfy a certain need (Schiffman and Kanuk, 2000). In this sense, motivational factors play a key role in the consumer's willingness to search for goods and purchase on the internet (Joines et al., 2003).

WebQual

The WebQual USA model belongs to the current measurement of website quality based on research and theories of systems and information technology, using the TRA - Theory of Reasoned Action (developed by Fishbein and Ajzen, 1975 apud Loiacono, 2000) and the TAM - Technology Acceptance Model (developed by Davis, 1989). Loiacono (2000) concluded that TAM can only identify ease of use and utility as a determinant of intended use. In order that the model could be applied to the virtual environment, the author proposes the inclusion of other important factors. Thus, it was able to identify which other categories should also be considered relevant in determining the intended use of a website. Moreover, this was the guideline used to develop the WebQual model, where it defines the website as an information system where users interact and generate beliefs about the user experience.

Figure 2. Expanded Technology Acceptance Template for web application

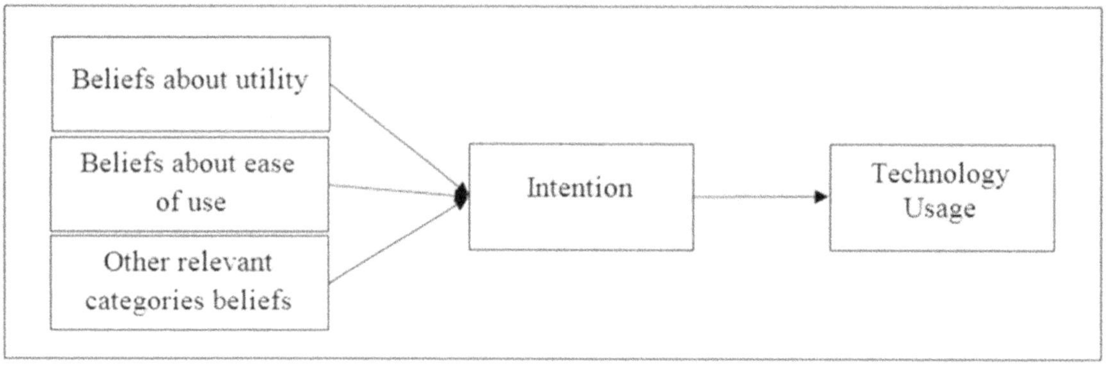

Thus, figure 3 shows the result of the expansion of TAM to add the dimension "other relevant belief categories" to determine the intended use of a website. From this, Loiacono (2000) researched in order to identify the component variables of WebQual.

METHODOLOGY

Digital communication channels are increasingly influencing the competitive environment (Alves, Sousa & Machado, 2020), where companies need to change their strategies to explore new ways to relate to their target audiences. Luxury brands are not exempt from constant technological changes and their significant influence on consumer behavior. In this context, the question for this sector is to understand how virtual communication influences the purchase decision in the luxury furniture sector. Thus, the present study intends to develop the approach to luxury brands and their buying behavior, so that the main factors that influence the purchase decision, as well as their motivations to consume luxury furniture are identified. Thus, in this work an empirical investigation was adopted using the case study, which aims to investigate a contemporary phenomenon introduced in a context of real action (Yin, 1994). The case study uses the methodology that seeks the perception and interpretation of certain facts and phenomena, and is used in studies that require exploration or description of events in certain contexts (Quivy and Campenhoudt, 2005). Cordova and Silveira (2009) show that exploratory research is used to gather various information about a central problem, in order to be clearer and enabling the generation of objectives around it.

Thus the methodology adopted will be quantitative and qualitative. In qualitative terms, an analysis will be made of the virtual communication developed in this sector of activity. In quantitative terms, questionnaires was administered through the Likert scale, from 1 to 5, which will study the attitude of consumers towards the communication of the luxury furniture industry in the virtual sphere and their influence on their decision to decide purchase. The surveys was applied to a database that uses websites related to luxury furniture companies, and this database is based on real consumers from three different brands, Boca do Lobo, BRABBU and DelightFULL.

Websites have a dynamic nature, where the content varies regularly. After an assessment has been made, the analyst may not have control over the record due to the constant changes on the websites, finding some variations throughout the study, making it necessary to repeat its entire assessment.

The content analysis used in the present work result from a selection of some of the analysis variables used in the research studies of Riley and Lacroix (2003), Seringhaus, 2008, Lin (2009), Rowley (2009), Geerts (2013), Motta, Filipe, and Barbosa (2013, 2014), and Goswami (2015), as well as the help of Google PageSpeed Insights showing how fast a website is For the websites of the three brands, BRABBU, Boca do Lobo and DelightFULL, an analysis grid was performed where the websites are subjected to an evaluation by the author of the study, to be compared with the respondents' responses at a later stage divided into 6 major group: the identification, the content, the products page, the utility, entertainment and complementary relationship, the speed and other visible presences on the website. Thus, each group had a number of characteristics that were flagged only with the own and no answers, as well as the speed group had answers in seconds and in percentage so that a better comparison in terms of speed was possible.

The questionnaire used in this study was designated as "Study of consumers attitude about communication in luxury furniture industry". This is divided into two distinct parts, the first part consists of 3 groups, all of which are measured under the Likert scale, ranging from: totally agree which is 5 to Strongly disagree equivalent to 1. This method was developed by Rensis Likert in 1932, more effectively assessing people's attitudes. The second part aims to survey potential buyers of luxury furniture brands, trying to find out their attitude towards a particular brand in their virtual environment. The first part of the questionnaire consists of an assessment of the websites of three luxury brands previously presented, using WebQual as a means of evaluating websites by the respondents and thus measuring 4 broad categories for website quality, ease of use, usefulness., entertainment and the complementary relationship. In the second part, we tried to know what is the attitude and the decision making process in a virtual environment, using a scale designed by Martins (2013) and Silva (2017), both master's theses. After completing the questionnaire, a pre-test email was sent to understand if respondents would understand the questions, as well as correct possible errors, in which case the pre-test respondents were members of the university, in which they gave feedback and with this it was possible to improve the questionnaire. Regarding database management, it was divided into three, with each set of contacts destined for a brand, never overlapping contacts, i.e., each respondent only responded to a specific brand. According to Aurélio (Version 3.0 - electronic), the construct is something elaborate or synthesized based on simple data. These were taken from the WebQual USA models, which aims at the correct evaluation of websites and their quality from the user's perspective, taking into account the different constructs of the WebQual model, such as ease of use, utility, entertainment and complementary relationship.

RESULTS

In terms of qualitative part, and according to the results of the analysis grids it is clear that they have many similarities, but also some differences, although not very expressive differences, but there is some degree of importance. In the first indicator it's visible that all brands are in equal circumstances, the information is available on all 3 websites in the same way i.e. all of them have proper identification in the

URL and browser title bar as well as the logo or the brand name at the top of the page. In the description or history of the brand can extract much information that the user considers important, is also visible the address, phone and mail, so they can contact the company should the need arise.

Its content already has some differences. The catalog for download can be found in all brands, but the news section is only visible on BRABBU, this is a website for sale, the importance of having this section is very, and Boca do Lobo and DelightFULL do not have it. But the opposite happens in the privacy policies that only BRABBU does not have, since the terms and conditions as well as the filling of online forms are presented in the three brands evaluated. Basic information about a particular product should be present on any website as well as images related to it, although zoom functionality is less important for many but very important for other users, only BRABBU does not have this extention tool on images. Both brands, Boca do Lobo and BRABBU have samples and materials available for their products, unlike DelightFULL which does not have this customization tool. Price is something that is not visible in any brand, it may be because companies want to be contacted to be able to provide more information to their customers or to keep the value of products anonymous.

The remaining topics, product sheet, project page, product category breakdown and press area are present on all websites. In the following indicator called utility, entertainment and complementary relationship, there are many similarities, starting with ease of understanding, interactive elements, attractive design, innovation and creativity and in cohesive design with products, all brands received a positive score according to your websites. Although all websites are considered an alternative to the phone, only DelightFULL has an online store. It is at the speed that we see the biggest differences in the entire analysis grid, starting with the first content fill, where Boca do Lobo takes only 4,2 seconds and BRABBU and DelightFULL have the same values with 4,4 seconds. The speed index presented by Google PageSpeed Insights shows that Boca do Lobo takes 3,3 seconds, BRABBU 4 seconds and a value twice higher, with 8,1 seconds is DelightFULL. In the time it takes the user to make an interaction, BRABBU has the shortest time, with only 2,1 seconds, unlike Boca do Lobo and DelightFULL, which take an average of 5,6 seconds. These indicators translate an overall speed of 87%, 94% and 69% for the brands Boca do Lobo, BRABBU and DelightFULL respectively.

With regard to data collection, and quantitative part, it is relevant to highlight that of the 26 responses obtained, 10 were not counted for the lack of response study, where they only answered the first and last question, where the respondents are website users are linked to the interior design and architecture sector, namely luxury furniture brands. The vast most of the sample works within the interior design sector (42,3%), the function of distributor and furniture stores has 15,4% each respondent, finally 11 (19,2%) respondents answered another Professional occupation.

The questionnaire applied to all brands was able to highlight very important and at the same time distinct answers in certain indicators. Thus, in the first indicator, the utility, where it refers to the degree of utility that the respondent attributes to the website, all brands have almost all their indicators above the average level (3), except for the speed issue. The website has a negative score, showing that users disagree with the fact that the Boca do Lobo and DelightFULL website take some time to load their pages, but at the same time the standard deviation of this issue is high proving that the disagreement of data exists. Evaluating the agreement of responses, only BRABBU has a more uniform data set, whose highest standard deviation is 0,6. Still speaking of consistency of results, the group's last question for all brands has a high disparity in responses. But overall, respondents show that when it comes to utility all brands have a positive average, where Boca do Lobo is 3,9, BRABBU is 3,7 and DelightFULL is, 6. Regarding the ease of use, in all brands, the consistency was excellent, and there were not many disparities in the answers, because in Boca do Lobo the average is 4,3 for all questions in the group. At BRABBU, only the first two questions regarding the ease of understanding of the website averaged 3,6, but these respondents consider this indicator to be indifferent in their assessments. DelightFULL ranks second on the average scale, thus averaging 4,1 out of all its questions.

In the following indicator, entertainment displays a total average of 3,8 and a standard deviation of 0,6, that is there is no high average standard deviation. However, there are questions where it is high as in Boca do Lobo in question number 4 and 6 regarding website innovation and creativity, although the average of these questions is 3,5, the standard deviation is 1, thus showing that there are respondents who have different answers from each other. The BRABBU website is cohesive because its average is 3,7 where the highest average was 3,8 and the lowest 3,2. Of the three brands addressed, DelightFULL has the highest average quality in all its responses (3,9), however its standard deviation is the highest with an average value of 0,7. Thus it can be proved that DelightFULL in terms of average rating is the one with the highest score, but at the same time with the highest standard deviation, i.e. respondents give an average of 3,9 for entertainment showing the stage of interest, but Boca do Lobo has the best cohesion in its responses with a standard deviation of 0,51. The complementary relationship, as already mentioned, aims at the relationship that the user has attributed as an alternative to other means. Also the level medium is negative (2,88), meaning that websites cannot respond to business processes in order to encourage buying. But at the same time the rest of the design questions are already showing positive signs, where Boca do Lobo respondents state on an average of 4 that the website has a design that is consistent with its pieces and brand identity. Also wants to visit the website more often. BRABBU has the same dynamics, ie the average of the following questions is 3,7, slightly lower than Boca do Lobo, but it is still at a positive level. Thus, it can be concluded that BRABBU has a higher average response than the other brands (3,4), followed by Boca do Lobo (3,3) and finally DelightFULL (3,3). Purchase intent evaluates consumers' intention to purchase a particular product while browsing their websites. Starting with the largest dispersion of data, DelightFULL has the highest mean standard deviation value (1,018), although the average response was positive (3,3), its respondents had many response disparities, with The question that had the highest average and the lowest standard deviation was related to the online store, which the brand actually owns. The other brands, BRABBU and Boca do Lobo, have very similar results, although they are not very different from DelightFULL. Finally, we try to assess with the respondents the influence of the internet in the purchase decision process. Thus, it is noticeable that the internet has a positive degree in its importance for all respondents with an average of answers of 4. Still, regarding the last two questions about the importance of the internet on the spot and after purchase, they have the deviation higher standard, showing that respondents have disparities in their responses. However, the average attributed to these questions was 3,8 for all brands.

CONCLUSIONS

The main findings allow us to state that most respondents think websites are very clear, can find the information according to their needs, as well as the security that websites convey, as some elements that evaluate speed. Websites have many elements that help their consumers find the most important information, but never fully satisfy their users. The ease-of-use indicator is one of the easiest to get true answers, because you just need to look at the website and see how it is presented, showing that websites have a very good degree of ease of use. In this way, brands should continue to focus their efforts on maintaining the ease of understanding of websites, thus leading to greater consumer retention and thus influencing their purchase intention, as it does not require too much knowledge of the website to navigate understand how he can convey his information. It was also possible to find out a lot of information relevant to the improvement of websites.

There are some disparities in answers, the associated questions of which are online transactions, whether your business can flow better through the website and the ease with which business is more easily conducted from the website than through other means. For business-related issues, these brands have some gaps, as their respondents say that they cannot easily do business, as a solution to the problem identified, it is suggested to create online stores for the brands Boca do Lobo and BRABBU. As already noted and in order to respond to the objective regarding the influence of website communication has on the purchase decision process, it was found that the difficulty in triggering business may have some implication in the purchase intention, as there are some factors that may be hindering business with respondents. They responded in the affirmative that they have already purchased products from these brands, thus creating a bigger picture as they compared, but their buying intention is relatively low, showing that the website may not even be the best option to make online purchases on these brands, having as soon as we resort to other means. There is a certain paradox in valuations between purchase intent and the purchase decision process. In this case, respondents show that websites have a high degree of importance in this indicator, even if they feel that the internet has a medium degree of importance during the buying process as well as in the post-purchase phase, however they consider that the internet is really important during the information seeking period. In general, it was possible to answer all the objectives where consumers' attitude towards virtual communication was verified and if it influences positively or negatively the purchase decision process as well as their purchase intention, as well as the degree of importance WebQual template for website quality. Thus evaluating each construct of the questionnaire according to the Likert scale, it can be stated that the utility is assessed as agree (3,7), ease of use is included in the agree (4) category, entertainment is also classified as I agree (3.8) on the part of its consumers and the complementary relationship is inserted in the degree of indifference with an average value of 3.3. Finally, the intention to buy is on the same level as the complementary relationship and with the same average value, ie 3.3 meaning yes some indifference, since the decision process has a value very close to the agreement of consumers (3, 9). In a final assessment, the average grade given to all the three brand constructs was 3.7, so that it is considered "in agreement" with its consumers, showing that there are some changes that websites will have to make in order to understand which the real ways to meet the needs and needs of such a narrow audience.

FUTURE DIRECTIONS

Primarily, it would be to carry out the same study with a substantially larger sample so that it was possible to represent the universe approached and perhaps achieve other more detailed and informative results. Another research that could be done only for this sector of activity would be to better assess its consumers against purchases made in the luxury sector virtual environment, in order to truly understand their needs vis-à-vis a buying website, and also understand by assessing which aspects they value in order to understand what their satisfactions can contribute to the increase of turnover from the virtual environment.

REFERENCES

Abbott, J. S. C. (2008). *Louis XIV, Makers of History Series* (D. Alexander & O. D. P. Team, Eds.). Gutenberg Project.

Allérès, D. (2006), Luxo... Estratégias, Marketing (2a Edição). Rio de Janeiro: Editora FGV.

Allérès, D., Gama, M., & Mouclier, J. (2000). *Luxo ...: Estratégias, marketing*. Ed. FGV.

Alves, G. M., Sousa, B. M., & Machado, A. (2020). The Role of Digital Marketing and Online Relationship Quality in Social Tourism: A Tourism for All Case Study. In J. Santos & Ó. Silva (Eds.), *Digital Marketing Strategies for Tourism, Hospitality, and Airline Industries* (pp. 49–70). IGI Global., doi:10.4018/978-1-5225-9783-4.ch003

Braga, J. (2004). *Sobre o Luxo*. Revista Costura Perfeita.

Carrera, F. (2009). *Marketing Digital na versão 2.0*. Edições Sílado.

Castarède, J. (2005). *O luxo: os segredos dos produtos mais desejados do mundo*. Ed. Barcarolla.

Chevalier, M., & Mazzalovo, G. (2008). Luxury Brand Management: A World of Privilege. *Mis Quartely*, *13*(3), 319–340.

D'Angelo, A. (2004). *Valores e significados do consumo de produtos de luxo*. Dissertação de mestrado, Escola de Administração, Universidade Federal do Rio Grande do Sul, Porto Alegre, Brasil.

Danziger, P. N. (2005). *Let them eat cake: Marketing luxury to the masses - as well as the classes*. Chicago: Dearborn trade.

Dubois, B., Laurent, G., & Czellar, S. (2001). Consumer rapport to luxury: analyzing complex and ambivalent attitudes, Consumer research working paper No. 736. *Les cahiers de Recherche Groupe HEC*, Jouy-en-Josas, France.

Engel, J., Blackwell, R., & Miniard, P. (1995). *Consumer Behavior* (8th ed.). The Dryden Press.

Farhana, M. (2012). Brand Elements Lead To Brand Equity: Differentiate or Die. *Information Management e Business Review*, *4*(4), 223–233. doi:10.22610/imbr.v4i4.983

Ferreira, L., & Sousa, B. B. (2020). Understanding the Role of Social Networks in Consumer Behavior in Tourism: A Business Approach. In C. Ramos, C. Almeida, & P. Fernandes (Eds.), *Handbook of Research on Social Media Applications for the Tourism and Hospitality Sector* (pp. 367–384). IGI Global. doi:10.4018/978-1-7998-1947-9.ch021

Galhanone, R. (2005). O mercado do luxo: aspetos de marketing. Academic Press.

García, S. (2003), El universo del lujo, Una visión global estratégica para profesionales y amantes del lujo. Instituto de Empresa, Mc Graw Hill.

Geerts, A. (2013). Cluster analysis of luxury brands on the internet. *International Journal of Management and Marketing Research*, *6*(2), 79–93.

Goh, K. Y., Heng, C. S., & Lin, Z. (2013). Social media brand community and consumer behavior: Quantifying the relative impact of user-and marketer-generated content. *Information Systems Research*, *24*(1), 88–107. doi:10.1287/isre.1120.0469

Goswami, S. (2015). *A Study on the Online Branding Strategies of Indian Fashion Retail Stores*. IUP Journal of Brand Management.

Hirschman, E. C., & Holbrook, M. B. (1982). Hedonic Consumption: Emerging Concepts, Methods and Propositions. *Journal of Marketing*, *46*(3), 92–101. Advance online publication. doi:10.1177/002224298204600314

Hoffman, D. L., & Novak, T. P. (1996). Marketing in Hypermedia Computer-Mediated Environments: Conceptual Foundations. *Journal of Marketing*, *60*(3), 50. doi:10.2307/1251841

Hudders, L., Pandelaere, M., & Vyncke, P. (2013). Consumer Meaning Making: The Meaning of Luxury Brands in a Democratised Luxury World. *International Journal of Market Research*, *55*(3), 391–412. doi:10.2501/IJMR-2013-036

Kapferer, J. (2012). *The new strategic brand management creating and sustaining brand equity long term* (5th ed.). Kogan Page.

Kapferer, J. (2015). *Kapferer on luxury: How luxury brands can grow yet remain rare*. Kogan Page Stylus.

Kapferer, J., & Bastien, V. (2009). The specificity of luxury management: Turning marketing upside down. *Journal of Brand Management*, *16*(5-6), 311–322. doi:10.1057/bm.2008.51

Kemp, S. (1998). Perceiving luxury and necessity. *Journal of Economic Psychology*, *19*(5), 591–606. doi:10.1016/S0167-4870(98)00026-9

Kim, A. J., & Ko, E. (2010). Impacts of Luxury Fashion Brand's Social Media Marketing on Customer Relationship and Purchase Intention. *Journal of Global Fashion Marketing*, *1*(3), 164–171. doi:10.1080/20932685.2010.10593068

Kotler, P. (2000). *Administração de Marketing: A Edição do Novo Milénio* (10th ed.). Prentice Hall.

Kotler, P., & Armstrong, G. (2006). *Principles of Marketing* (11th ed.). Pearson Education.

Lee, M. K., & Turban, E. (2001). A Trust Model for Consumer Internet Shopping. *International Journal of Electronic Commerce*, *6*(1), 75–91. doi:10.1080/10864415.2001.11044227

Liang, T., & Lai, H. (2000). Electronic store design and consumer choice: An empirical study. *Proceedings of the 33rd Annual Hawaii International Conference on System Sciences*. 10.1109/HICSS.2000.926863

Lindon, D., Lendrevie, J., Lévy, J., Dionísio, P., & Rodrigues, J. (2008). Mercator XXI. In Teoria e Prática do Marketing (11.a Ed.). Lisboa: Dom Quixote.

Lipovetsky, G., & Roux, E. (2005). *O luxo eterno: da idade do sagrado ao tempo das marca*. Cia. das Letras.

Loiacono, E. T. (2000). *WebQual: a web site quality instrumen*t. Dissertação de doutoramento, University of Georgia, Athens.

Malheiro, A., Sousa, B., & Ferreira, L. (2019). Compreender o papel das redes sociais no comportamento do consumidor: A perspetiva do setor hoteleiro na região norte. *Revista Ibérica de Sistemas e Tecnologias de Informação, E24*(11), 299–312.

Manganari, E. E., Siomkos, G. J., & Vrechopoulos, A. P. (2009). Store atmosphere in web retailing. *European Journal of Marketing, 43*(9/10), 1140–1153. doi:10.1108/03090560910976401

Mendes, M. S. (2012). *Programa de Marketing de Produtos e Serviços de Luxo*. Universidade Católica.

Moon, B. (2004). Consumer adoption of the internet as an information search and product purchase channel: Some research hypotheses. *International Journal of Internet Marketing and Advertising, 1*(1), 104. doi:10.1504/IJIMA.2004.003692

Motta, J., Filipe, S., & Barbosa, M. (2014). *Estratégia de Comunicação e Venda Online na Joalharia de Luxo Communications and Online Selling Strategy in Luxury Jewellery*. Academic Press.

Nascimento, M. (2000). *Marketing do varejo de luxo: desmistificando as verdades do varejo de luxo*. Universidade Salvador.

Nueno, J. L., & Quelch, J. A. (1998). The mass marketing of luxury. *Business Horizons, 41*(6), 61–68. doi:10.1016/S0007-6813(98)90023-4

Nwankwo, S., Hamelin, N., & Khaled, M. (2014). Consumer values, motivation and purchase intention for luxury goods. *Journal of Retailing and Consumer Services, 21*(5), 735–744. doi:10.1016/j.jretconser.2014.05.003

Ólafsdóttir, A. R. (2012). *Luxury Fashion Online*. Bifröst University.

Paixão, L. (2006). *Luxo – o Supérfluo Indispensável*. Jobson Brasil.

Parente, S. (2007), *Uma visão sobre o consumo de luxo – em busca da exclusividade*. Academic Press.

Peneda de Oliveira, C., & Sousa, B. M. (2020). Green Consumer Behavior and Its Implications on Brand Marketing Strategy. In V. Naidoo & R. Verma (Eds.), *Green Marketing as a Positive Driver Toward Business Sustainability* (pp. 69–95). IGI Global. doi:10.4018/978-1-5225-9558-8.ch004

Phau, I., & Prendergast, G. (2000). Consuming luxury brands: The relevance of the 'Rarity Principle'. *Journal of Brand Management, 8*(2), 122–138. doi:10.1057/palgrave.bm.2540013

Prendergast, G., & Wong, C. (2003). Parental influence on the purchase of luxury brands of infant apparel: An exploratory study in Hong Kong. *Journal of Consumer Marketing, 20*(2), 157–169. doi:10.1108/07363760310464613

Riley, F. D., & Lacroix, C. (2003). Luxury branding on the Internet: Lost opportunity or impossibility? *Marketing Intelligence & Planning, 21*(2), 96–104. doi:10.1108/02634500310465407

Rowley, J. (2010). Online branding strategies of UK fashion retailers. *Internet Research, 19*(3), 348–369. doi:10.1108/10662240910965397

Seringhaus, F. H. (2005). Selling Luxury Brands Online. *Journal of Internet Commerce, 4*(1), 1–25. doi:10.1300/J179v04n01_01

Sheth, J., Gardner, D., & Garret, D. (1988). *Marketing Theory - Evolution and Evaluation*. John Wiley e Sons.

Solomon, M. (1999). Consumer behavior – buying having and being (4.a Ed.). Upper Saddle River: Prentice Hall.

Solomon, M. R., Ribeiro, L. B., & Farias, S. A. (2006). *O comportamento do consumidor comprando, possuindo e sendo*. Bookman.

Sousa, B., & Alves, G. (2019). The role of relationship marketing in behavioural intentions of medical tourism services and guest experiences. *Journal of Hospitality and Tourism Insights*, *2*(3), 224–240. doi:10.1108/JHTI-05-2018-0032

Sousa, B. B., & Magalhães, F. C. (2019). An Approach on Attachment in Public Marketing and Higher Education Management Contexts. In C. Machado & J. Davim (Eds.), *Higher Education and the Evolution of Management, Applied Sciences, and Engineering Curricula* (pp. 151–171). IGI Global., doi:10.4018/978-1-5225-7259-6.ch006

Truong, Y., Mccoll, R., & Kitchen, P. J. (2010). Uncovering the relationships between aspirations and luxury brand preference. *Journal of Product and Brand Management*, *19*(5), 346–355. doi:10.1108/10610421011068586

Tynan, C., Mckechnie, S., & Chhuon, C. (2010). Co-creating value for luxury brands. *Journal of Business Research*, *63*(11), 1156–1163. doi:10.1016/j.jbusres.2009.10.012

Ueltschy, L. C., & Laroche, M. (2004). Co-Branding Internationally: Everyone Wins? *Journal of Applied Business Research*, *20*(3), 91–102.

Vigneron, F., & Johnson, L. W. (2004). Measuring perceptions of brand luxury. *Journal of Brand Management*, *11*(6), 484–506. doi:10.1057/palgrave.bm.2540194

Wiedmann, K., Hennigs, N., & Siebels, A. (2007). *Measuring Consumers" Luxury Value Perception: A Cross-Cultural Framework*. Institute of Marketing and Management, Leibniz University of Hanover.

Winsper, J. (2007). *The e P's of Luxury Marketing: The Advanced Model for Measuring Consumers.* Academic Press.

Yan, H., & Qu, X. (2014). Research on the marketing strategy of luxury goods. *Psychology and Marketing*, *26*(7), 625–651.

KEY TERMS AND DEFINITIONS

Consumer Behavior Online: The study of individuals, groups, or organizations and all the activities associated with the purchase, use and disposal of goods and services, including the consumer's emotional, mental and behavioral responses that precede or follow these activities in the online environment.

Digital Marketing: Is the marketing of products or services using digital technologies, mainly on the Internet, but also including mobile phones, display advertising, and any other digital medium.

Luxury Brands: In economics, a luxury good (or upmarket good) is a good for which demand increases more than proportionally as income rises, so that expenditures on the good become a greater proportion of overall spending.

Online Relationship: Is an integrative and multidimensional concept, such as relationship quality in an offline context.

Chapter 9
The Usage of Social Networks and Websites in International Luxury Brand Communication:
An Example of the Automotive Sector

Murat Arslandere
Karamanoglu Mehmetbey University, Turkey

ABSTRACT

Today, there are different digital communication opportunities that companies use to communicate with their customers. These are especially web sites and social networks. International brands are adapting to all changes in this communication environment while determining their communication strategies and then they communicate with their target audiences. Brands communicate with their target audiences and potential or unfamiliar audiences through communication opportunities without borders. This is also seen in the luxury brand market and consumers. In this study, luxury brand, luxury brand consumption, and finally website and social media applications used in international luxury brand communication are explained. In addition, comparative content analysis of corporate web sites and social media environments of Ferrari and Porsche companies, in which they are producing and marketing luxury products, were conducted and evaluations were made in the context of international luxury brand communication.

INTRODUCTION

Nowadays, generally all brands tend to leave from being only local brands and want to become a global brand. One of the main factors affecting this situation is communication technologies. Since the early 1990s, communication technologies have removed geographic distances and increased communication opportunities between companies and consumers, and also have given the opportunity to reach large masses in a short time. Together with these changes, due to increasing competition conditions, companies started to spread to different geographies faster and to offer their goods and services to different markets. This has led to the need for companies to develop international marketing strategies in these new markets

DOI: 10.4018/978-1-7998-4369-6.ch009

Copyright © 2021, IGI Global. Copying or distributing in print or electronic forms without written permission of IGI Global is prohibited.

that will enable them to be adopted by new consumers and to comply with competitive conditions. The companies have to answer many questions such as the ways of entering these new markets, the design of the marketing mix, the compose of effective strategies for success at the international level (Altuna, 2007). In this context, when considering luxury brands are generally international brands (Kapferer & Bastien, 2012b), and furthermore, according to Chevalier & Mazzalovo (2008) one of the three basic criteria for a brand to be a luxury brand is, operate in international level, brand communication activities of luxury brands on an international basis should be considered as an important element. In this context, nowadays, luxury brands have started to use Web 2.0 technologies in their brand communication activities. It has become necessary to change the established marketing approach of businesses with the emergence of Web 2.0 technologies (a set of tools that make it easier for individuals to create and publish content, share ideas, advise others, etc.). Consumers, who no longer enjoy the fact that advertising and other promotional activities are the only sources of information about the new product or service, adapt the social network, where they share their experiences with the brand or product and offer a more realistic view (Evans & McKee, 2010). Web 2.0 technologies have had three important effects on businesses. These are the transformation of the focus of activity into the web, the generation of value and power shift from the firm to the customer. Although Web 2.0 is a concept related to technology, its impact is sociological and it is a revolution for businesses in terms of its results. Active customers are the new value source of Web 2.0. Social media (Facebook, Twitter, Youtube, etc.) is the necessary tool for carrying the content that customers create to firms. Content in the form of words, text, photos, and videos has been developed by millions of consumers around the world and it is inspiring for firms to create value from a marketing perspective (Akyüz, 2013). Luxury brands use social media channels such as Facebook, Instagram, Twitter (Liu et al., 2019) and Youtube (Kim & Ko, 2012) as a means of communication. The reasons why luxury brand consumers use social media are different. For example, luxury brand consumers find Twitter useful for instant information and commenting on different events. They consider Facebook as a point of getting information about promotions. Additionally, luxury brand customers comment on the products they use and share their experiences about brands with the help of online communities, forums, and blogs (Liu et al., 2019).

Today, social media and websites are used by luxury brands both in national and international brand communication. Luxury consumption market is approximately 1 trillion euros per year worldwide and luxury cars constitute half of this market (Bain and Company Report, 2017). Despite this huge luxury spending int the world, there is a huge gap in the academic literature on luxury cars and brand communication that luxury car companies have established worldwide through websites and social networks. This chapter will make a great contribution to the literature at this point. From this point of view, in this chapter, international luxury brand communication is explained through social media and website, in addition, Ferrari and Porsche brands are examined in this context, and findings are shared.

BACKGROUND

Luxury Brand and Luxury Brand Consumption in the World

Dubois et al. (2001) proposed six basic variables to define luxury brands in consumer perception in their study which is conducted in Western Europe, America and Asia Pacific countries. These are unique product quality, very high price, rarity, aesthetics, having a long tradition and not necessary/useless.

According to Chevalier & Mazzalovo (2008), the luxury of a product depends on three criteria; having a strong artistic dimension, being produced as a result of hand workmanship and being international. Luxury brand consumers are more focused on the price than the benefit of the product they get. The function they gain is not important, the material value given to the product is important for them. Consumption has become a concept for them that they enjoy, satisfy, and enjoy life more. This situation can be called as hedonist consumption (Hopkinson & Pujari, 1999).

Capgemini and Merrill Lynch have named the best potential luxury customers as high net worth-individuals worldwide (HNWI-individuals worldwide that provide higher profits). HNWI consists of persons with assets over $1 million. According to 2006 data, this number is 9.5 million people worldwide. 3.3 million in North America, 2.9 million in Europe and 2.6 million people live in Asia (Kapferer & Bastien, 2009).

According to Bain and Company (2017), the global luxury market is approximately 1 trillion euros annually in total. Personal consumption luxury market is 262 billion euros, luxury cars expenditure is 489 billion euros, luxury hospitality expenditure is 191 billion euros, fine wines expenditure is 70 billion euros, fine food expenditure is 49 billion euros, fine art expenditure is 40 billion euros, designer furniture expenditure is 35 billion euros, private jets and yachts expenditure are 23 billion euros, and finally luxury cruises expenditure is 2 billion euros. These values are shown in Figure 1 below.

In the same wayaccording to the Bain and Companyreport (2017) within the scope of the evaluation of luxury products on a geographical basis globally, while Europe and the United States have both 33% share of the personal consumption market, Japan has 9%, China has 7%, remaining Asia has 14%, the rest of the world has 4% market share.

Figure 1. World Luxury Consumption Market (On Product Category Basis)
Source: (Bain and Company Report, 2017)

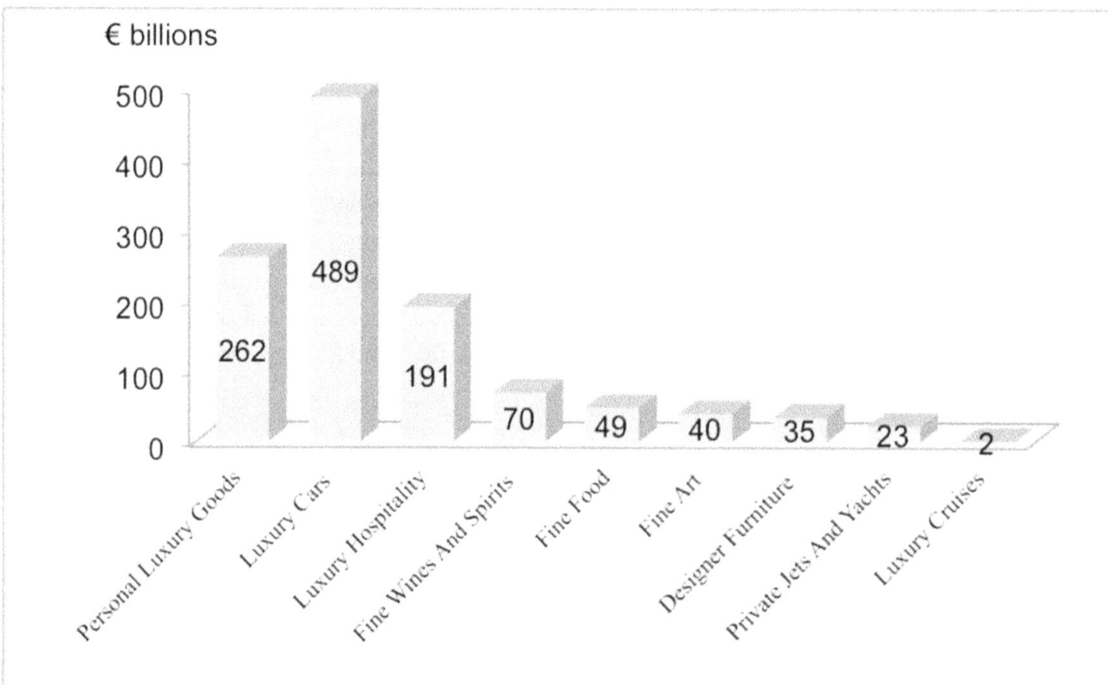

International Luxury Brand Communication

Brand communication is an integration of all communication activities that companies plan to achieve their objectives (Elmasoğlu, 2016). The aims of the brand communication are to reflect the brand ethics, to give real information about the brand, to make the brand remember, to emphasize the visual impact of the brand and to constitute feelings and attitudes towards the brand. All of these features are also valid for luxury brand communication (Kapferer &Bastien, 2012a).In today's luxury consumption market, rely solely on brands can no longer guarantee the company's performance and long-term progress and growth in the global competitive environment as customers' alternatives grow, and loyalty to a particular brand weakens. In this context, the long-term sustainability of brands and their existence depends on the strong relationships, they will establish with their customers (Kim &Ko, 2010). Especially considering the fact that in general luxury brands are global brands (Kapferer &Bastien, 2012b), it is inevitable that strong relations with customers should be carried out on an international basis. Nueno & Quelch (1998) stated that the cause of the global expansion of luxury brands on the macro scale, is largely related to the increasing wealth in Asia's emerging markets. Many European luxury brands, which are faced with stagnation in Europe and limited population growth, are expanding their operations rapidly and are trying to carry out their activities at the international level, to appealto rich Asian consumers who see Western luxury brands in a good position. At this point, luxury brands' establishing a strong level of international brand communication with customers gain importance.

Factors are seen in Figure 2 below, which are forming the luxury brand communication (Kapferer &Bastien, 2012a). The globalization of luxury brands is perceived as a rule (Kapferer &Bastien, 2012b), so in this context, it will be possible to examine luxury brand communication in the international context by adding standardization and/or adaptation to these factors.In many studies in the international marketing literature (Altuna, 2007; Theodosiou & Leonidou, 2003; Szymanski et al., 1993; Papavassiliou & Stathakopoulos, 1997), the adaptation of business strategies in the international arena is examined in the context of standardization and/or adaptation elements.

In luxury brands, communication strategies are used not only to increase sales, but also to aesthetically emphasize the brand's unique identity. In the world of luxury, communication is established to realize the customer's dream and increase brand value. However, since a dream cannot be realized without awareness, existingand potential consumers should be considered as the target audience. Therefore, luxury brands use communication to raise awareness and create positive attitudes and desires towards the brand. The most important reason for luxury brand communication is to create dreams with social and aesthetic dimensions and strong enough to distinguish luxury brands from others (Kale, 2016). For example, craftsmanship and attention to detail, contribute directly to the elements of rarity and preciousness, are steps to realize the customer dream (Kapferer & Bastien, 2012b). While the social dimension is an indicator of the social class and identifies the consumer with a certain identity and value, the aesthetic dimension offers an inner and emotional pleasure beyond being associated with a highly perceptive world and using functional products (Kale, 2016). Standardization and adaptation elements in international luxury brand communication are also issues that need to be emphasized. In this context, according to Kapferer & Bastien (2012b), international luxury brand communication strategies should be determined in central management and local managers should take the initiative and implement these decisions in the best way on the axis of these strategies on a local basis. At this point, it is important to preserve the core values of the brand.

Figure 2. Factors of International Luxury Brand Communication
Source: Adapted from Kapferer and Bastien (2012a)

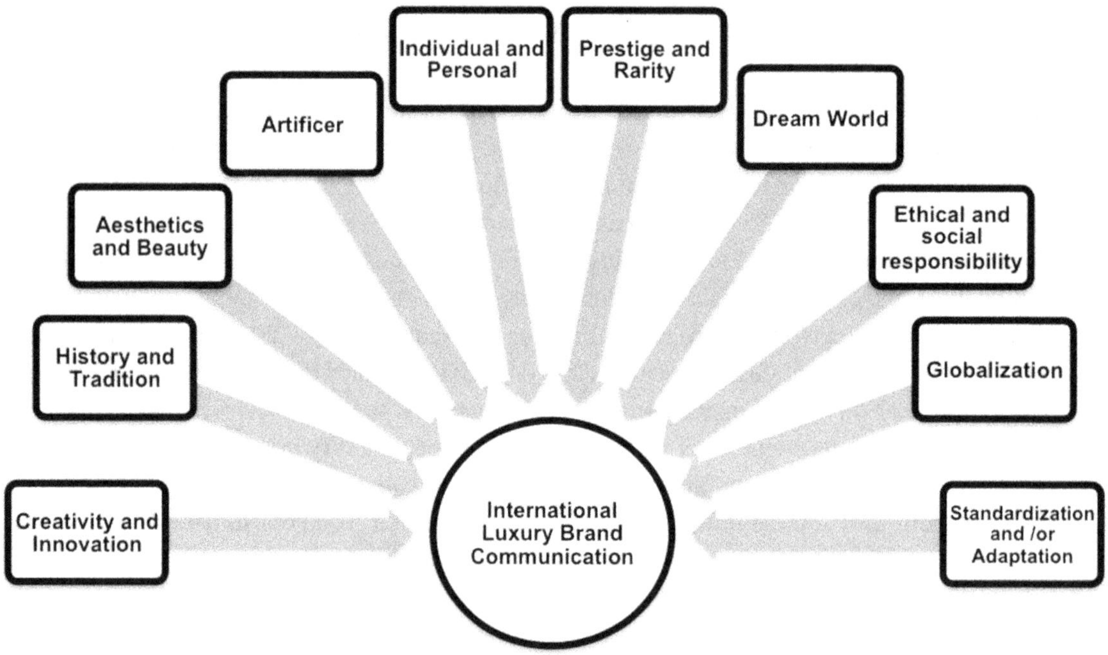

In addition to the factors of brand communication, brand communication channels are also the elements that companies should carefully consider. According to Bell (2008), it is possible to examine brand communication channels in two main categories as traditional and non-traditional communication channels. These can be listed as follows.

- **Classical communication channels**
    - Advertising (TV, radio, newspapers, magazines, billboards, cinema)
    - Sales promotion (price reduction, sampling, couponing, etc)
    - Public relation
    - Sponsoring (sport, culture, social)
    - Trade fairs and exhibitions
- **Non-Classical communication channels**
    - Events customer clubs
    - Product placement
    - Internet presence
    - Testimonials road-shows
    - Customer magazines
    - Telephone hotlines
    - Direct mailing
    - Mobile marketing
    - Ambient media (e.g.. postcards)

Brand communication channels are divided into two as classic and non-classic channels and they contain different activities. When the situation is evaluated in terms of luxury brands, there may be some differences in the use of these channels. Luxury brands, unlike other brands, prefer channels that can reach their target audiences more effectively. For instance, while the advertisement of a luxury car is rarely or never seen in daily newspapers, advertisements of other brands are seen more frequently in these channels. Instead of TV advertising, advertisements can be used in selected magazines or on the internet for luxury brands. The activities of luxury brands in the field of public relations also differ according to their target audiences (Değirmen et al., 2018). Also luxury brands use social media channels such as Facebook, Instagram, Twitter (Liu et al., 2019) and Youtube (Kim & Ko, 2012) as a means of communication.

It is also important to adapt the communication channels mentioned above to the international arena. In international markets, the most appropriate choice for the communication mix may be significantly different from the approach in the domestic market due to the role of different media regulations and channels. It is important to decide on the use of these communication channels in international markets (Bell, 2008).International marketers increasingly focusing on the importance of global brands' communication strategy and practices by considering the telecommunication and youth elements. In recent years, convergence has emerged in consumer tastes and values as a result of the developments in telecommunication with the internet. Intercultural interaction has increased with increased cross-border population mobility for entertainment or business, as well as increased intercultural communication mobility in the digital environment. The world is now being considered as a single marketwith this rising in interaction. Especially youths have quickly adapted to this change. It is important to consider these issues and elements in global brand communication (Quelch, 1999). Also, different strategies may be required in international markets due to the influence of different media rules, different channels (Bell, 2008), and diverse customer requests (Altuna, 2007). The simultaneous application of a company's international brand communication channels with a standard strategy really forces the companies. However, some communication rules are valid for all markets (Kotler & Keller, 2016).

How to establish a local or global distinction or balance in international luxury brand communication is among the important issues. The right strategy is that the headquarters defines all strategic communication, and adjust whole worldwide activities and communication channels in line with this strategy.These communication channels include social media, web sites, sponsorships etc. (Kapferer & Bastien, 2012b). Following this strategy design, local practitioners should implement them effectively (Ramchandani & Coste-Manière, 2012). Press relations, local public relations, relations with important customers and VIPs should be well managed within this context (Kapferer & Bastien, 2012b). Especially for luxury brands opening up to the world for the first time, operating internationally poses problems. One of the main reasons for this is that they are very centralized in terms of management and their identity is not open to the market in the first stage. In addition, the perception of the same brand in different cultures and countries may be diverse (Kapferer &Bastien, 2012b). Luxury brands need to carefully consider certain factors, such as geographic, demographic and psychographic / lifestyle models, as they spread their activities to various countries (Ramchandani & Coste-Manière, 2012). Consider the example of Louis Vuitton: in Asia, this brand is now perceived as the ultimate symbol of social ascensionand success. It is the symbol of an innovative genius with the influence of Mark Jacobs in the countries in which he was successful in Europe. If it is not very successful, it is associated with bling or considered as passé (Kapferer &Bastien, 2012b).

Website and Social Network Usage in International Luxury Brand Communication

The usage of websites and social networks in international luxury brand communication is examined under two separate headings below.

Social Network Usage in International Luxury Brand Communication

The way of communication with customers has changed as a consequence of the emergence of social media. The 21st century is a period of an explosion in internet-based messaging. These messages have been an important factor in influencing various aspects of customer behavior at raising awareness, acquiring knowledge, thoughts, attitudes, purchasing behavior and subsequent purchasing communication. Social media has emerged in a single dimension in marketing communication in the past, then this single dimension has turned into a multi-dimensional environment. Thus, the tools used in marketing communication have changed to a great extent with the emergence of social media. Because social media allows the consumer to communicate with the other consumer, the consumer with the firms and the firms with the consumer (Mangold & Faulds, 2009).

Companies use social networking sites to promote their brands and communicate with customers with the development of Web 2.0 technologies.The number of people on the Internet has exceeded 34% of the world's population. The activities of conducting brand communication using social media channels are on the agenda as a popular issue. For instance, brands are trying to connect with customers on the social networking site Facebook, which has 1.2 billion active users per month. Social media has completely changed traditional brand communication (Schivinski &Dabrowski, 2015).Internet users have begun to shape brand communication that marketers previously controlled and managed. Traditional one-way communication has now become multidimensional and bidirectional (Berthon et al., 2008). One of the most important issues in social media and brand communication activities is the issue of being interactive. Social media contributes directly to this element and supports the conduct of brand communication activities through two-way communication with customers (Adetunji et al., 2018). At this point, this situation is integrated with the concept of relational marketing, which puts customers completely at the center of focus. According to Keller (2009), the element of interaction is one of the most important differences in brand communication in digital and traditional marketing. Interaction is the ability to communicate and interact in two-way, with little or no obstructions such as long distances and time differences.

Brand communication activities conducted on social media can be evaluated in two main categories. These are the social media communication generatedby the company and generatedby the user. The social media communication generatedby the company is under the control of the company. Social media communication generated by users is independent of company control. Social media brand communication generatedby the company is shaped by word of mouth (WOM) and electronic word of mouth (eWOM) concept by academic researchers. The company-generatedWOM, which can be perceived as a fusion between the word consumer mouth and traditional advertising, is a term initiated by the firm but implemented by the consumer (Schivinski & Dabrowski, 2015). There is also a consensus in the current literature that this term can be defined as an online communication information dissemination source (Dellarocas et al., 2007). User-generated social media brand communication has been shaped in the literature with the concepts of vigilant marketing, user-generated branding (UGB) and user-generated content (UGC) (Schivinski & Dabrowski, 2015). At this point, customers' comments about the brand and their sharing of product experiences are the issues that need to be emphasized.

De Vries et al. (2012) examined the impact of 11 international brands' social media communication on their customers. As a result, in the aforementioned study it was found that international brands' usage of social media platforms in brand communication contributes to brand popularity.Also at this point, De Vries et al.(2012)emphasized that it is important to pay attention to the content generated by the customers,and to evaluate these contents, especially which are derived from social media. Social media contributes to businessescommunicating with customers, and developing this relationship in the international arena. It makes firms accessible to those interested in their product and makes it visible to those who do not know your productinternationally. It contributes to reflect the personality of the brand, creating loyal customers and increasing the recognition of the brand. Thanks to the diversity of social media platforms, it can be used in communication activities in the most appropriate way of enterprises' needs (Chary, 2014).It will not be true to apply social media activities to every country and region with a standard pattern on the international platform. Adaptations should be implemented taking into account the differences between countries on a national basis. An internationally operating company may find Levitt's (1983) global standardization approach attractive. The firm can implement this standardization strategy in terms of product, pricing, and distribution. However, implementing the adaptation strategy in brand communication through social media platforms in the international arena and making adjustments in brand communication according to regions will be beneficial and less risky for companies (Berthon et al., 2012).

In the first stage, luxury brands could not adaptto the usage of web and social media sufficiently. The main reason for this is the existence of an internet user group that they cannot control aside from their target audience, andtheaforementioned uncontrollable group being among their followers in the web environment. This situation leads to the fact that those who do not consume luxury products have a say about the brands, generate content and create a new target group that cannot be controlled from time to time.In this context, luxury brands are faced with the risk of losing their endurance, brand value and prestige (Dikmen, 2008).The brands in the luxury product market have stayed away from social media for many years because they think that social media and the internet will adversely affect brand image due to these and similar reasons.However, they had to take an active role in order to adapt to the era and not to be behind the day (Aksu & Ercan, 2014).But now in general luxury brands have turned their eyes to social media as a way of creating customer potential by communicating effectively with consumers. Today, social media has become an environment in which individuals communicate, show what they eat and wear, and comment on the products they buy. Activities such as sharing the restaurants visited and the luxury products consumed through social media have turned social media into a status races field (Sabuncuoğlu, 2015). Brands and customers communicate with each other without any restriction in time, space and environmentthrough social media, thus this situation transforming the old one-way communication interaction into two-way direct communication (Kim & Ko, 2012). Luxury brands use social media as a means of communication, such as Facebook, Instagram, Twitter (Liu et al., 2019) and Youtube (Kim &Ko, 2012). In addition, luxury brand consumers use social media just like luxury brand manufacturers. The reasons why luxury brand consumers use social media differentiates. For example, luxury brand consumers find Twitter useful for instant information and commenting on different events. They consider Facebook as a point of getting information about promotions. Additionally, luxury brand customers share comments about the products they use and their experiences about brands with the help of online communities, forums and blogs (Liu et al., 2019).

Social media channels offer both companies and customers new ways to connect. Companies hope to influence their perceptions about their products and brands by interacting with loyal consumers, then in the same way these firms hopes customers disseminate information about them and become a brand ambassador (Schivinski & Dabrowski, 2015). Social media luxury brand communication is a two-way communication that tries to empathize with young users and also forces the familiar feelings associated with existing luxury brands to a higher age group. Social media activities of brands provide an opportunity to increase brand value by reducing prejudice and misunderstanding against brands, and creating a platform that allows the exchanging of ideas among online people (Kim & Ko, 2012).Every luxury brand should pay particular attention to brand communities that consist of customers who use their products and especially who make purchasesfaithfully, in order for its product to be successful in the market. Current research indicates that luxury brand communities are critical and their multi-faceted experience can improve relationships with customers (Kim &Lee, 2019). At this point, it has become inevitable to give importance to social media brand communication, which enables interactive communication and enables an international level of development all over the world. It has been empirically shown that social media positively affects brand loyalty-building in luxury brand communication (Kim &Lee, 2019). Liu et al. (2019) showed that the applications of luxury brands to increase entertainment, interaction and trends in social media communication activities are beneficial in terms of developing customer relations. At this point, it is stated that investing in social media activities to increase activities based on interaction, entertainment and education, is important for luxury brands.

Traditional designers such as Louis Vuitton from luxury brands share live shows on their blogs. Ralph Lauren, Chanel, Donna Karan and Gucci have worked with Apple to create iPhone apps. Many luxury brands create their own Twitter accounts or share them on Facebook (Kim & Ko, 2012). As another example, Gucci, one of the luxury brands, has organized an innovative"Cut and Craft" campaign on its Facebook page, which offers fans the opportunity to design their own bags based on Stirrup, Jackie and New Bamboo. Activities in this scope were conducted in connection with Youtube and Twitter. Featured designs have found their place on the cover of Timeline on Gucci's Facebook page. Firms encouragethe user's interest and connect it to the iconic products of the brand by firm generated social media luxury brand communication activities (DeFanti et al., 2013). In addition, social media brand communication to generated by the user is also influenced automatically. Another example is Dolce & Gabbana use social media to conduct direct communication with its customers and conduct a brand communication effort by focusing on customer requests. In this context, Dolce & Gabbana invites fashion bloggers to the front seats of fashion shows and bloggers instantly send feedback from shows on Facebook and Twitter. Customers see their favorite models directly without fashion brand editors or sellers, and their purchase intentionsstarts to be affected by this situation. In this way, the company triggers social media brand communication content to be generated by the user. All these examples have been carried out internationally, open to the whole world. Likewise, Chanel, Louis Vuitton, Yves Saint Laurent and Stella McCartney now have Facebook, and Twitter accounts (Kim & Ko, 2012).

Website Usage in International Luxury Brand Communication

Websites are the main way in which businesses operating on the internet to promote their products or services and to attract consumers. The design of a successful website is all about consumer expectations. The website design should be started by defining consumer needs, expectations and problems. If the website does not look professional, the perception of the products and services will be negative even if the product is good (Bayram &Yaylı, 2009). A potential consumer can easily access and compare the websites of many businesses that offer products or services (Harridge, 2004). Therefore, in order to reach new consumers through the internet and to retain existing consumers, businesses should design their websites correctly and conveniently. Otherwise, potential consumers can easily opt for another business' website (Taylor & England, 2006). Also website design isa very important issue for companies operating at an international level. Companies that provide services at the global level have understood the importance of globalization in the design of websites (Rau &Liang, 2003). This is valid for both luxury brands and non-luxury brands. Unlike other brands, luxury brands should create areas where their target audience will feel privileged and different in their website designs. General features of websites; easy to be opened, accessible, correct management of e-mail or other feedback processes, clear and understandable information about the company and brand, easy and convenient navigation on the site and updated information (Değirmen et al., 2018).

Creating a website is not just about designing, technology (flash or html) and search engine optimization for luxury brands. In addition, it is not just efforts to create an e-boutique and ensure that sales are made as much as possible from here. Firms should givelife to a luxury brand in the virtual worldthrough the balanced integration of all the aforementioned features of the website, and at the same time ensure that these elements are fully reflected in everything the brand represents (Okonkwo, 2010).The website of a luxury brand should have sections such as corporate information (features such as history, mission, vision, philosophy), written and visual materials, detailed information about products, photo and video sharing, strategies providing bi-directional communication, questionnaire forms, option to respond to comments, and online aid (Değirmen et al., 2018). For all that, there should be much more to a luxury brand's website than to have beautiful multilingual text and photos. When creating a luxurious website, it should be taken into consideration that the customers who visit a luxurious website should be provided with a pleasant journey of discovery. The journey of creating a luxurious website is versatile. This includes a comprehensive understanding of the world of luxury, and in particular the universe of the brand with a balanced integration of design and innovation, technical competence, marketing and business expertise, and digital media expertise. The skills and expertise needed for a good website of a luxury brand can be assessed in five key areas.

1. Innovation and artistic talent (for aesthetics and design)
2. Technical skills in digital media and on the Web (for functionality)
3. Marketing and trade information (for e-retail, content and communication)
4. Interpretation skills and brand dynamics and (for the interpretation of the virtual brand)
5. Luxury industry experience (for online luxury brand positioning)

In fact, it is impossible for a luxury brand's website to be designed by one person by presenting all of the above elements as a whole. In order to create an effective website for a luxury brand, it is necessary; to form a team of members who display a high level of skills in a professional way, to combine the skills in a common area and to reflect these skills to the website in an integrated and efficient way (Okonkwo, 2010). According to the researchof Riley & Lacroix (2003), the participants, who visited the website of a luxury brand in the 18 months observed, reasons for visiting the luxury brand's website are; 22% seek information about the brand, 21% seek information about the product, 12% receive personalized advice. Only 5 percent had access to a luxury brand's website for purchase.

Customers have different levels of expectations from different dynamics of luxury brand websites, such as; 60% aesthetic, 47% communicate by e-mail, 44% information on products, 40% easy to navigate, 36% information on brands (PR events), 33% personalized advice (club, newsletters), 32% secure connection, 31% community (boards, chat), 28% clear postage and package charges, 27% real-time communication and world-wide availability, finally 26% purchase possibility (Riley&Lacroix, 2003).At this point, particularly the elements of interactive communication (communication via e-mail, personalized advice, community, real-time communication) are remarkable together with the aesthetics feature.

It is a general rule that luxury brands are international (Kapferer & Bastien, 2012b) and for international companies, the design and management of websites, not only in one country but in other countries, is an important issue. Country origin, as well as visitors' use and perception of the website, are effective on businesses' online communication strategies (Murphy &Scharl, 2007). It is important that international brands take into account country-based differences. There are many classifications in the literature regarding the globalization levels of websites. In a report published by the Global Sight Company, globalization in E-commerce is classified as centralized, decentralized, and distributed or hybrid. In the first level called a centralized model; web activities are centrally planned and executed with a small number of inputs from local offices. In the globalization of websites, at the second level, which is named as independent from the center; e-businesses are separate and developed and maintained by each local office. In the third level called distributed or a hybrid model; while determining a basic design on the website; it also has the flexibility to respond to local requirements (Singh &Boughton, 2005).Flexibility is important. A company needs to understand user preferences and how users interact with the web, in order to relate to online consumers (Geissler, 2001).For luxury brands, especially decentralized, and hybrid approaches can be used in international markets, within the framework of standardization or adaptation approaches and taking into account consumer preferences and requests.

MAIN FOCUS OF THE CHAPTER

Examples of Social Network and Website Implementation in International Luxury Brand Communication at Automotive Sector

In recent years, the luxury market has grown significantly, and luxury automotive manufacturers have traditionally been an essential part of this luxury brand market. Global competition has affected all businesses as well as luxury brand manufacturers. In order to stay competitive and increase customer demand, luxury automotive manufacturers also need to focus on customer requirements in their product development processes as early as possible (Wortmann et al., 1997). In this context, luxury brand communication activities on an international basis must be meticulously performed. Luxury automotive manufacturers always have a customer-centric product development approach and they carry out brand communication activities accordingly (Stylidis et al., 2016). In luxury brands, brand communication is a very important element. The most crucial component of this element is the customer. It is essential that luxury brands should contain different elements from the communication activities of non-luxury brands. For example, related to this situation, Stylidis et al. (2016) stated that the difference between how luxury car manufacturers obtain customer feedback unlike the premium segment can be considering. Traditionally, Italian luxury car manufacturers care about a close relationship with their customers individually.

These companies collect feedback from customers during the life of the vehicle. A dedicated team of engineers conducts face-to-face interviews, vehicle evaluations, and analyses in the post-sales period.

Luxury brand manufacturers should make full use of digital tools while conducting brand communication activities in the international arena. The most important of these are websites (Okonkwo, 2010) and social media tools (Liu et al., 2019). Keller (2009) stated that brand communication on social media platforms could have a great impact on brand perception, especially if brand managers can establish positive relationships with their customers and continue to maintain these positive relationships stably. Also, Okonkwo (2010) stated that the establishment of an effective website to be used in luxury brand communication would produce very significant and positive results. Adetunji et al. (2018) showed that the use of social media communication channels had an impact on the development of automotive brands. Dissemination of brand-related information of automotive brands provided with content generated by the users and by the company in social media channels, has good effects on brand development. At this point, automotive companies can influence consumer perception and consumer buying behaviors with similar actions (Adetunji et al., 2018).

The research sample includes corporate websites of Porsche and Ferrari companies and the social networks they use. Websites, as well as Facebook, Twitter, Instagram, Pinterest and Youtube contents were examined. In this study, the content analysis methodof Değirmen et al.(2018)was benefited for website and social networks in luxury brand communication. Değirmen et al. (2018) werebenefited from some studies while developing this content analysis method. These are, the content analysis method of Marangoz et al. (2012) used in e-commerce businesses for web and social networking sites, the content analysis method of Akbaş (2013) used to evaluate the applications of group shopping sites in social media, and finallywebsite analysis of Gibson et al. (2003) used for the comparative analysis of election campaigns in the US and the UK. Firstly, the content analysis data of the websitesare shown in Table 1.

In the comparative content analysis of Ferrari's and Porsche's corporate websites, it is observed that both sites have corporate information about the company.There is also content on company principles and social responsibility activities.The company's press releases option is availableon the website of both brands.There is a area on the Ferrari's website about the career section, while Porsche does not have this option.Company contact information, legal notice and specifications are available on both websites. In addition, there is no questionnaire for visitors/followers on both firms' websites. Both websites have a choice of help tools, a sitemap and a product search option. This is an important element for quick and easy use. Digital formats of electronic bulletins and corporate journals are also available.On both sites, customers have the opportunity to design and save their vehicles.Personalized applications can be thought to increase brand loyalty.Customers'comments on products have not been found on any of the two firms'websites.New products are featured on both websites. The multi-language option and applications are available on both sites. In both brandsthere are some changes on website by country, these are some ads and some content changes. However, the design, content and applications remain largely constant. In addition, there are no different currency options, cross-promotions, shopping call centers and live support applications. As mentioned above, Ferrari's website has its own application to design your own vehicles. Following the completion of the vehicle to be designed, your records are kept in the name of the meeting with the authorized person of the company, and the company can return to you if desired. A similar situation can be found on Porsche's website. The site design specific to mobile devices is included in the website of both brands. Both sites have links to social networks. Social Networks (Facebook, Twitter, Instagram, Youtube) are similar and used on both sites. The Pinterest application is available on Porsche's website and not on Ferrari's website. Porsche has mobile applications that include

Table 1. Website Analysis of Ferrari and Porsche

Website Analysis	Ferrari	Porsche
· Company information	+	+
· Company's media reflections	+	+
· Company's social responsibility activities	+	+
· Company principles	+	+
· Career section	+	-
· Company contact information	+	+
· Legal notices and specifications	+	+
· Survey form	-	-
· Help tools	+	+
· Electronic newsletter registration	+	+
· Magazine and so on. applications	+	+
· Sitemap	+	+
· Free services and facilities	-	-
· Loyalty program practitioners	-	-
· Customer comments	-	-
· Product search	+	+
· Highlighting new products	+	+
· Multi-language use	+	+
· Different currency options	-	-
· Cross promotion	-	-
· Product comparison	-	-
· Shopping call center	-	-
· Live support	-	-
· Special site design for mobile devices	+	+
· Mobile applications	-	-
· Access via Facebook	+	+
· Access via Twitter	+	+
· Access via Instagram	+	+
· Access via Youtube	+	+
· Access via Google+	-	-
· Access via Pinterest	-	+
· Events and presentations	+	+

elements such asthe introduction of its cars, rear-seat digital entertainment applications, smartwatches and race performance indicators. But no information is provided on the websiteassociated with these applications. Similarly, while Ferrari has an online magazine application within the scope of mobile applications, there is no information sharing about this issue on website.

Table 2. Facebook Analysis of Ferrari and Porsche

Facebook Analysis	FERRARI	PORSCHE
· Total likes	16.379.583	11.700.653
· Page response rate	-	-
· Company information	+	+
· Address of company	+	+
· Phone company	+	+
· Company establishment date	+	+
· Linking to other social networks and websites	+	+
· Support for users	-	-
· Facebook special contest and so on. applications	-	+
· Ad sharing	+	+
· Video ad sharing	+	+
· Congratulatory messages and greeting sharing	-	-
· Campaign information	-	-
· Product and image sharing	+	+
· Corporate magazine sharing	+	-
· Product & image sharing	+	+
· Customer comments	+	+
· Product comparisons	+	+

When Facebook, which is one of the social media environments of the two sites included in the research, is analysed it shows that the Ferrari brand has more likes compare to Porscheas can be seen in Table 2 above. Porsche has more than 11 million likes, while Ferrari has more than 16 million likes. It can be said that the response rate to the followers of the page is not specified in both brands.It is observed that both sites have company information in their accounts. Links are given to their own websites and other social networks they use.There is no element about the feature of support for users in both brands. Porsche organizes special competitions and applications for Facebook. Ad sharing, video ad sharing are available in both brand accounts. Congratulatory messages and greeting sharing are not available in both brands. It is seen that neither brand have a special campaign for Facebook. In addition, it is seen that both brands do not include information about product campaigns, but use products and images on their pages. Finally, while corporate magazine sharing exists in Ferrari, it is not available in Porshe.

When the Twitter accounts of the brands included in the research are examinedas can be seen in Table 3 above; it is seen that the number of followers is very different and Porsche is clearly ahead in this regard. Porsche brand has 1.8 million followers while the Ferrari brand has 566 thousand followers. Although Ferrari is far behind in the number of followers than Porsche, it is in front of Porsche in the number of tweets interestingly. Ferrari has over 6,000 tweets, while the Porsche brand has over 4,000 tweets. In both accounts, it is seen that special campaigns are organized for Twitter and advertising and video sharing aremade. Ferrari is far ahead of Porsche in this area. In total, the number of video advertisements is 4,000 and Porsche is around 1,400.Both sites have celebration messages and congratulations on their Twitter

Table 3. Twitter Analysis of Ferrari and Porsche

Twitter Analysis	FERRARI	PORSCHE
· Twitter followers	566.000	1.800.000
· Tweets	6.086	4.233
· Following count	9	1.400
· Twitter special campaigns	+	+
· Video ad sharing	4.015	1.454
· Congratulatory messages and greeting sharing	+	+
· Company information	+	+
· Company news	+	+
· Linking to other social networks and websites	+	+

accounts for special occasions. In both accounts, information is shared about the company, and links are givenfor the news about the company and its own website and other social media environments they used.

When the Instagram accounts of the sites included in the research are examinedas can be seen in Table 4 above; it is seen that Ferrari has more posts than Porsche.When looking following count, the Porsche is 338 Ferrari is only 4.Neither site has launched an Instagram-specific campaign. In addition, both sites share products and images and are not include any congratulatory messages. Ad sharing is made in Porsche while Ferrari is not available. Video ad sharing is available in both brands. It is seen that both sites share their corporate photos. Both brands also provide links to their own website and social media platforms.

Table 4. Instagram Analysis of Ferrari and Porsche

Instagram Analysis	FERRARI	PORSCHE
· Number of posts	21.186	1.768
· Number of followers	16.300.000	18.100.000
· Following count	4	338
· Instagram special offers	-	-
· Ad sharing	-	+
· Product and image sharing	+	+
· Video ad sharing	+	+
· Congratulatory messages and greeting sharing	-	-
· Corporate photo sharing	+	+
· Linking to other social networks and websites	+	+

When Pinterest accounts of Porsche and Ferrari brands is examinedas can be seen in Table 5 above, it is seen that the Ferrari brand hasn't a Pinterest account, Porsche has a Pinterest account and has 42 boards, 804 thousand pins and 41 thousand followers. In addition, it is found that 3.2 million people

Table 5. Pinterest Analysis of Ferrari and Porsche

Pinterest Analysis	FERRARI	PORSCHE
· Number of panels	-	42
· Number of pins	-	804.000
· Number of likes	-	-
· Number of followers	-	41.000
· Following count	-	878
· Corporate information / About section	-	+
· Product image / ad sharing	-	+
· Linking to other social networks and websites	-	+
· Viewers monthly	-	3.200.000

view monthly. In addition, giving the institutional information of their firm, and sharing information in the section about, linking to other social networks and their own websites, finally product and video sharing is made in Porsche's Instagram account.

Table 6. Youtube Analysis of Ferrari and Porsche

Yotube Analysis	Ferrari	Porsche
· Number of subscribers	687.000	816.000
· Total views	70.758.90	232.033.721
· Video ad sharing	+	+
· Linking to other social networks and websites	+	+
· Costumer comments	+	+

As can be seen in Table 6 abovethe Ferrari brand has 687 thousand subscribers and the Porsche brand has 816 thousand subscribers when Youtube channels of Ferrari and Porsche brands are analyzed. In the total number of views of videos, it can be said that Porsche is at the top. Porsche has more than 230 million views and Ferrari has more than 70 million views. Both brands use advertising sharing, linking to other social networks and providing customer comments.

When evaluated generally, it can be seen that there are some elements in both brands'websites, such as a logo that reflecting company brand image, a company information and principles, anda video advertising applications. When evaluated in the context of product differentiation, firms enable customers to make product differentiation within certain standards. Customers have the opportunity to design cars, and to make changes to their hardware on the website. When the subject is evaluated at the point of communication from websites, although there is a slight differentiation in language and advertising practices for some countries, it can be said that standardization strategy is applied generally. In social media applications, both companies commonlyshare advertisements and contents and allow customer comments. Ferrari and Porsche have additionally differentiated their Twitter accounts from some countries and regions, with the exception of their main accounts. For example, the Ferrari brand has separate

Twitter accounts for Japan, America, Northern Europe and the Far East.The same situation is seen in the Porsche brand. Apart from its main account, Porsche also has separate Twitter accounts for Japan, France, Mexico, Saudi Arabia, Netherlands, Canada and India. The same is valid for Instagram. Apart from Ferrari's own main account, for example, there is a separate account for Japan and the United States, also Porsche has separate Instagram accounts for France. The content and shares differ in these accounts.

CONCLUSION AND SUGGESTIONS

According to Kim & Ko (2010), trusting a brand can no longer guarantee the company's performance as competition in the luxury environment becomes difficult. Loyalty to a particular brand is weakened as a variety of alternatives are offered to customers in a competitive environment. Brands now need to build strong relationships with their existing customers to keep them as long as possible. Research has shown that consumers see social media as more reliable sources of information than traditional communication tools used by companies. Therefore, marketing and brand managers can assume that brand communication will increase through user-generated social media communication especially (Schivinski & Dabrowski, 2015). Also, in order to strengthen this communication, having a corporate website and designing it well is an inevitable factor for luxury brands (Okonkwo, 2010).

In today's globalizing world, businesses are trying to exist and continue to develop under the influence of intense competition. This is also valid for luxury brands. Luxury brands operate in both the national and international arena and try to cope with the competition. In this context, communication with customers is a very important element. The utilization of today's digital technologies in the conduct of brand communication activities has emerged as an inevitable element for luxury brands. This can apply to all categories of luxury products, including luxury cars. In this framework, luxury brands' usage of an effective website and social media applications in brand communication activities, is located as an indisputable reality both the national and international arena in today's world.

In this study, it was seen that Porsche and Ferrari brands used the website and social media applications, such as Facebook, Youtube, Twitter, Instagram, and Youtube within the scope of international brand communication activities. Porsche also uses the Pinterest application. Social media communication generated by the company and user-generated content (UGC) (Schivinski & Dabrowski, 2015), is seen on both Ferrari and Porsche's social media platforms. Furthermore it can be said that both brands implement the standardization approach (Theodosiou & Leonidou, 2003) worldwide within the scope of brand communication at the international level, which is conducted through Facebook, Youtube, and Pinterest accounts. But both Ferrari and Porsche brands differentiate in some countries and regions with separate accounts within the scope of brand communication established with their customers in the international arena via Twitter and Instagram. Thus it can be said that they have adopted the adaptation strategy (Theodosiou & Leonidou, 2003) in international brand communication via Twitter and Instagram with these countries and regions. Additionally it is possible to say that they adopt an approach between hybrid models and centralized models (Singh & Boughton, 2005) on their websites because they apply slight differences in advertising and content specific to certain countries. While maintaining the general personality of the brand with the standardization practices they make, they will also be able to appeal to different customer requests with their differentiation with the adaptation approach. When evaluated in general, in this study it was observed that Ferrari and Porsche companies actively use both their corporate websites and social media arguments in the international arena in their communication with their customers. This will enable companies to communicate more intimately, faster, less costly and more flexibly with their customers.

REFERENCES

Adetunji, R. R., Rashid, S. M., & Ishak, M. S. (2018). Social media marketing communication and consumer-based brand equity: An account of automotive brands in Malaysia. *Jurnal Komunikasi: Malaysian Journal of Communication*, *34*(1), 1–19.

Akbaş, H. (2013). *Grup Alışveriş Sitelerinin Sosyal Medyadaki Uygulamalarının Değerlendirilmesi* (UMI No. 345279) [Master thesis, University of Pamukkale]. Türk Ulusal Tez Merkezi Dissertations and Theses database.

Aksu, S., & Ercan, M. (2014). *Lüks marka iletişiminde sosyal medyaya uyum sağlamak: Gucci ve Vakko'nun Facebook ve Twitter kullanımları üzerine bir inceleme* [Paper presentation]. Internet Konferansı, Türkiye.

Akyüz, A. (2013). Sosyal medyada müşteri etkileşimi ve firmalar açısından önemi. *Kastamonu Üniversitesi İktisadi ve İdari Bilimler Fakültesi Dergisi*, *2*(2), 5–22.

Altuna, O. K. (2007). Uluslararası marka strateji formülasyonu: Standardizasyon ve uyarlama yaklaşımları. *İstanbul Üniversitesi Siyasal Bilgiler Fakültesi Dergisi*, (37), 159-171.

Bain and Company. (2017). *World Luxury Consumption Market*. Report Avaliable at: https://www.bain.com/insights/luxury-goods-worldwide-market-study-fall-winter-2017/

Bayram, M., & Yaylı, A. (2009). Otel web sitelerinin içerik analizi yöntemiyle değerlendirilmesi. *Elektronik Sosyal Bilimler Dergisi*, *8*(27), 347–379.

Bell, S. (2008). *International brand management of Chinese companies: Case studies on the Chinese household appliances and consumer electronics industry entering US and western European markets*. Physica-Verlag HD. doi:10.1007/978-3-7908-2030-0

Berthon, P. R., Pitt, L., & Campbell, C. (2008). Ad lib: When customers create the ad. *California Management Review*, *50*(4), 6–31. doi:10.2307/41166454

Berthon, P. R., Pitt, L. F., Plangger, K., & Shapiro, D. (2012). Marketing meets Web 2.0, social media, and creative consumers: Implications for international marketing strategy. *Business Horizons*, *55*(3), 261–271. doi:10.1016/j.bushor.2012.01.007

Chary, S. R. K. (2014). Social media marketing: The paradigm shift in international marketing. *IOSR Journal of Business and Management*, *16*(9), 11–13. doi:10.9790/487X-16921113

Chevalier, M., & Mazzalovo, G. (2008). *Luxury brand management: A world ofprivilege*. Wiley and Sons.

De Vries, L., Gensler, S., & Leeflang, P. S. H. (2012). Popularity of brand posts on brand fan pages: An investigation of the effects of social media marketing. *Journal of Interactive Marketing*, *26*(2), 83–91. doi:10.1016/j.intmar.2012.01.003

DeFanti, M., Bird, D., & Caldwell, H. (2013). *Forever now: Gucci's use of a partially borrowed heritage to establish a global luxury brand* [Paper presentation].The Biennial Conference on Historical Analysis and Research in Marketing (CHARM), Copenhagen, Denmark.

Değirmen, G. C., Vural, Z. B. A., & Ulaş, S. (2018). Lüks marka iletişiminde web sitesi ve sosyal ağ kullanımı: Karşılaştırmalı içerik analizi. *The Journal of International Social Research, 11*(57), 519–534. doi:10.17719/jisr.2018.2468

Dellarocas, C., Zhang, X., & Awad, N. F. (2007). Exploring the value of online product reviews in forecasting sales: The case of motion pictures. *Journal of Interactive Marketing, 21*(4), 23–45. doi:10.1002/dir.20087

Dikmen, G.Ö. (2008). Lüks marka pazarlaması, Vertu örneği. *İstanbul Üniversitesi İletişim Fakültesi Dergisi, 31*, 51-64.

Dubois, B., Laurent, G., & Czellar, S. (2001). *Consumer rapport to luxury: Analyzing complex and ambivalent attitudes*. Consumer Research Working Paper, No. 736, HEC, Patis.

Elmasoğlu, K. (2016). Marka kimlik öğesi olarak logoların marka iletişimi açısından incelenmesi: "Google Doodles" Örneği. *Erciyes İletişim Dergisi, 4*(4), 82–102.

Evans, D., & Mckee, J. (2010). *Social media marketing: The next generation of business engagement*. Wiley Publishing.

Geissler, G. L. (2001). Building customer relationships online: The website designers' perspective. *Journal of Consumer Marketing, 18*(6), 488–502. doi:10.1108/EUM0000000006154

Gibson, R. K., Margolis, M., Resnick, D., & Ward, S. J. (2003). Election campaigning on the www in the USA and UK: A comparative analysis. *Party Politics, 9*(1), 47–75. doi:10.1177/135406880391004

Harridge, M. S. (2004). Electronic marketing, the new kid on the block. *Marketing Intelligence & Planning, 22*(3), 297–309. doi:10.1108/02634500410536885

Hopkinson, G. C., & Pujari, D. (1999). A factor analytic study of the sources of meaning in hedonic consumption. *European Journal of Marketing, 33*(3/4), 273–290. doi:10.1108/03090569910253053

Kale, G. Ö. (2016). Lüks marka reklamlarında ünlü kullanımının önemi: Louis Vuitton örneği. *Istanbul Ticaret Üniversitesi Sosyal Bilimler Dergisi, 29*, 325.

Kapferer, J. N., & Bastien, V. (2009). *The luxury strategy: Break the rules ofmarketing to build luxury brands*. Kogan Page.

Kapferer, J. N., & Bastien, V. (2012a). *The luxury strategy*. Kogan Page.

Kapferer, J. N., & Bastien, V. (2012b). *The luxury strategy: Break the rules of marketing to build luxury brands*. Kogan Page.

Keller, K. L. (2009). Building strong brands in a modern marketing communications environment. *Journal of Marketing Communications, 15*(2-3), 139–155. doi:10.1080/13527260902757530

Kim, A. J., & Ko, E. (2010). Impacts of luxury fashion brand's social media marketing on customer relationship and purchase intention. *Journal of Global Fashion Marketing*, *1*(3), 164–171. doi:10.1080/20932685.2010.10593068

Kim, A. J., & Ko, E. (2012). Do social media marketing activities enhance customer equity? An empirical study of luxury fashion brand. *Journal of Business Research*, *65*(10), 1480–1486. doi:10.1016/j.jbusres.2011.10.014

Kim, J., & Lee, K. H. (2019). Influence of integration on interactivity in social media luxury brand communities. *Journal of Business Research*, *99*, 422–429. doi:10.1016/j.jbusres.2017.10.001

Kotler, P., & Keller, K. L. (2016). *Marketing Management*. Pearson Education Limited.

Levitt, T. (1983). The globalization of markets. *Harvard Business Review*, *61*(3), 2–11.

Liu, X., Shin, H., & Burns, A. C. (2019). Examining the impact of luxury brand's social media marketing on customer engagement: Using big data analytics and natural language processing. *Journal of Business Research*. Advance online publication. doi:10.1016/j.jbusres.2019.04.042

Mangold, W. G., & Faulds, D. J. (2009). Social media: The new hybrid element of the promotion mix. *Business Horizons*, *52*(4), 357–365. doi:10.1016/j.bushor.2009.03.002

Marangoz, M., Yeşildağ, B., & Saltık, I. A. (2012). E-Ticaret işletmelerinin web ve sosyal ağ sitelerinin içerik analizi yöntemiyle incelenmesi. *Internet Uygulamaları Dergisi*, *3*, 53–78.

Murphy, J., & Scharl, A. (2007). An investigation of global versus local online branding. *International Marketing Review*, *24*(3), 297–312. doi:10.1108/02651330710755302

Nueno, J. L., & Quelch, J. A. (1998). The mass marketing of luxury. *Business Horizons*, *41*(6), 61–68. doi:10.1016/S0007-6813(98)90023-4

Okonkwo, U. (2010). *Luxury online: Styles, systems, strategies*. Palgrave MacMillan. doi:10.1057/9780230248335

Papavassiliou, N., & Stathakopoulos, V. (1997). Standardization versus adaptation of international advertising strategies: Towards a framework. *European Journal of Marketing*, *31*(7), 504–527. doi:10.1108/03090569710176646

Quelch, J. (1999). Global brands: Taking stock. *Business Strategy Review*, *10*(1), 1–14. doi:10.1111/1467-8616.00085

Ramchandani, M., & Coste-Manière, I. (2012). Asymmetry in multi-cultural luxury communication: A comparative analysis on luxury brand communication in India and China. *Journal of Global Fashion Marketing*, *3*(2), 89–97. doi:10.1080/20932685.2012.10593111

Rau, P. P., & Liang, S. M. (2003). Internationalization and localization: Evaluating and testing a website for Asian users. *Ergonomics*, *46*(1), 255–270. doi:10.1080/00140130303527 PMID:12554410

Riley, F. D., & Lacroix, C. (2003). Luxury branding on the internet: Lost opportunity or impossibility? *Marketing Intelligence & Planning*, *21*(2), 96–104. doi:10.1108/02634500310465407

Sabuncuoğlu, A. (2015). Sosyal medyanın bir gösteriş tüketimi mecrası olarak kullanımı. In Z. Özgür & A. İşman (Eds.), *İletişim çalışmaları* (pp. 369–380). Sakarya Üni. Yayınları.

Schivinski, B., & Dabrowski, D. (2015). The impact of brand communication on brand equity through Facebook. *Journal of Research in Interactive Marketing*, *9*(1), 31–53. doi:10.1108/JRIM-02-2014-0007

Singh, N., & Boughton, P. D. (2005). Measuring website globalization: A cross- sectional country and level analysis. *Journal of Website Promotion*, *1*(3), 3–19. doi:10.1300/J238v01n03_02

Stylidis, K., Rossi, M., Wickman, C., & Söderberg, R. (2016). The communication strategies and customer's requirements definition at the early design stages: An empirical study on Italian luxury automotive brands. In *26th CIRP Design Conference*. Elsevier. 10.1016/j.procir.2016.04.062

Szymanski, D. M., Bharadwaj, S. G., & Varadarajan, P. R. (1993). Standardization versus adaptation of international marketing strategy: An empirical investigation. *Journal of Marketing*, *57*(4), 1–17. doi:10.1177/002224299305700401

Taylor, M. J., & England, D. (2006). Internet marketing: Web site navigation design issues. *Marketing Intelligence & Planning*, *24*(1), 77–85. doi:10.1108/02634500610641570

Theodosiou, M., & Leonidou, L. C. (2003). Standardization versus adaptation of international marketing strategy: An integrative assessment of the empirical research. *International Business Review*, *12*(2), 141–171. doi:10.1016/S0969-5931(02)00094-X

Wortmann, J.C., Muntslag, D. R., & Timmermans, P.J.M.(1997). *Customer-driven manufacturing*. Chapman & Hall.

KEY TERMS AND DEFINITIONS

Adaptation Strategy: Strategy that is made by enterprises to differentiating theiractivities on an international basis.

Company-Generated Content: Content that is made by firms and publicly available over the internet.

International Luxury Brand Communication: It is an integration of all the communication activities of luxury brands that they have planned to realize their aims at the international level.

Luxury Brands: Luxury brands are top brands in terms of quality and aesthetics, which are more difficult to reach due to their very high price and selectivity in the distribution network.

Social Networks: These are online applications, platform and media that facilitate interaction, collaboration and content sharing, like Facebook, Twitter, YouTube, etc.

Standardization Strategy: Strategy that is made by enterprises to standardize their activities on an international basis.

User-Generated Content: Content that is made by consumers and publicly available over the internet.

Chapter 10
The Rise of Islamic Luxury:
Current Trends

Muhammed Bilgehan Aytaç
Aksaray University, Turkey

ABSTRACT

As one of the essential elements of culture, the role of religiosity in consumer behavior has long been established and number of consumer research on Muslim individuals has been increasing rapidly in recent years. With the rapid increase of the Muslim population and the developing welfare level of the Islamic countries, it is observed that Islamic luxury consumption has also become widespread too. In this chapter, it is aimed to determine the conceptual framework of Islamic luxury consumption together with current trends. Three halal concepts which are considered as include more explicit examples of Islamic luxury are chosen and analyzed: halal fashion, halal cosmetics, and halal tourism. Throughout the text and in the conclusion part, it is aimed to create insights for marketers who interested in Islamic luxury.

INTRODUCTION

In the last decades, the world has witnessed significant shifts in social and cultural arenas, and socio-technological developments as well as intense and complex immigration have opened the way for transformation of diversity to super-diversity (Blommaert & Varis, 2015). In parallel with this trend, Islamic societies also have transformed and, especially with acculturation (Hirschman & Touzani, 2011), have become super-diversified. On the beaches of Dubai one can find a lady wearing a burqa and having a good time with family, alongside a single British lady wearing a bikini lying on the sand and enjoying her sunbath. Market transition of Islamic countries—especially the Gulf countries, Turkey, Malaysia and Indonesia—has been the main driving force of significant changes, with the adoption of a western lifestyle in which consumption of western-oriented consumer goods plays a central role. In consequence, the Islamic world created certain consumption patterns as well as a luxury consumption concept in which a western consumption lifestyle is blended with Islamic motives. Before delving into Islamic consumption and Islamic luxury, the role of religiosity in the consumer behavior literature should be analyzed.

DOI: 10.4018/978-1-7998-4369-6.ch010

Copyright © 2021, IGI Global. Copying or distributing in print or electronic forms without written permission of IGI Global is prohibited.

Religiosity is the level of the individual`s compliance with specific religious values and beliefs along with the related rituals. As one of the elements of culture, religiosity is accepted as a significant determinant of the decision-making process of consumers (Delener, 1990, 1994). According to Mittelstaedt (2002), religion affects (1) what consumers trade, (2) how they trade, and (3) when and where trade takes place. Religiosity is often used as an explanatory variable in consumer studies globally; and in general, religiosity and consumer behavior studies can be divided into two categories: (1) those that deal with individual level of religiosity and consumer behavior, and (2) those that compare consumer behavior of individuals in different cultures or subcultures (Moschis & Ong, 2011).

Although the effect of religiosity on consumer behavior has long since been established (Bailey and Sood, 1993; Wilkes et al., 1986) and Muslims have existed for centuries and have been involved in trade from their very beginnings, their relationship with marketing and consumer behavior have not been sufficiently investigated (Aslanbay et al., 2011; Prokopec & Kurdy, 2011).

Although not specific to Islam, Hirschman (1983) put forward three possible explanations for why religion and consumption have not been adequately analyzed[1] in tandem: (1) researchers are not aware of possible links between religion and consumption; (2) there is perceived prejudice against religion, and it is seen as a sensitive subject; and (3) because religion is everywhere, it may be overlooked by researchers. According to Mokhlis (2009), these explanations were valid for the year 2009; however, by the year 2020, it can be said that the paradigm is changing. It is observed that the ever-increasing population of Islam and the immigration of Muslims to non-Muslim countries, especially in the last decade, along with the economic growth of Islamic countries, have multiplied the number of studies on the Muslim market. As an example, since 2010 the *Journal of Islamic Marketing* has published three or four issues yearly and attracts scholars not just from the Islamic countries but all over the world. In addition, there are many academic and business events related to Islamic marketing being organized around the globe, including the Global Islamic Marketing Conference which has been organized yearly since 2011.

Nevertheless, some subjects are still ignored by Islamic marketing literature. One of these untouched subjects is luxury consumption. It is observed that, especially in rapidly growing economies like Turkey, Qatar, and the United Arab Emirates, a new high-class society has emerged, referred to in Turkish as "Süslüman"[2] (Meşe, 2015). This new social class is inclined to engage in luxury consumption within the halal context, such as halal tourism, halal cosmetics, or halal restaurants. Halal refers to anything that is permitted by the Shariah (Islamic Law), and means "lawful" or "permitted" (Battour et al., 2010).

This chapter aims to analyze the conceptual framework of Islamic luxury and current trends of luxury consumption in the Islamic world. Following this introduction, previous literature about Islamic religiosity and consumer behavior will first be briefly reviewed. Second, the term luxury will be analyzed. Third, the position of the concept of luxury in Islamic teaching will be examined according to the different perspectives of various scholars. Following this, three halal concepts—fashion, cosmetics, and tourism—will be analyzed within the luxury consumption context together with current trends among Muslims. In the concluding section, an overview of luxury trends in the Islamic world will be discussed together with implications for researchers and practitioners.

Islamic Religiosity and Consumer Behavior

It is known that religion-based values shape lifestyle and consumption patterns. Moreover, religiosity plays a crucial role in shaping consumer behavior by forbidding the consumption of some products or by encouraging the use of some products. Even it can be a predictor of consumers' switching behavior (Choi et al., 2013) or acceptance of novel products (Mansori et al., 2015; Rehman and Shabbir, 2010).

It is estimated that there are approximately 1.9 billion Muslims in the world, which makes Islam the second-largest religion in the world, following Christianity. It is also projected that the Muslim population will grow more than twice as fast as the total population of the all world between 2010 and 2050 and exceed the population of Christianity (Lipka and Hackett, 2017). This rapid rise increases the importance of analyzing the role of Islamic religiosity in consumer behavior. It is possible to say that in addition to the growing population and improved economic well-being of Muslims, their comparatively higher reliance on their religion (Bailey & Sood, 1993) makes paramount the subject of Islamic consumption.

Hashim and Mizerski (2010) found that consumers' motivation to follow Islamic teachings has a significant effect on some of their consumption patterns. Two primary resources of Islamic teaching are hadith and the Quran. Hadith are texts that consist of sayings of the Prophet Muhammad. When these resources are deficient in answering a specific question related to an issue, fatwa (legal opinion) comes into play. Fatwa means the adaptation of Qur'anic verses and hadith to contemporary issues, as declared by the ulama (singular alim), meaning "knowledgeable people" (Muhamad, 2011; Wiechman et al., 1996). Many controversial topics can be the subject of fatwa, such as smoking (Radwan et al., 2003; Yong et al., 2009), yoga exercise regime in Malaysia (Muhamad, 2011), and listening to popular music (Hashim & Mizerski, 2010).

Taking a glance at the consumer behavior literature reveals some attempts to identify Muslim consumers' distinct behaviors. Alam et al. (2011) empirically put forward that Muslims take Islam as a reference in their buying behavior. They also indicated that highly religious individuals tend to be less impulsive in buying. According to Gayatri et al. (2005), Islamic religiosity influences individuals' evaluation and use of services such as restaurants, hotels, and airlines. Correspondingly, Heiens et al. (2016) suggested using religiosity as a segmentation variable in Islamic markets.

In terms of reference groups, Vohra et al. (2009) have shown that family is the most significant factor in Muslim individuals' buying decisions. Vel and Rodrigues (2011) confirmed the influence of family in purchase decisions for Muslims who live in the United Arab Emirates.

How religiosity affects attitude towards the advertising of controversial products (gender/sex-related products, social/political groups, health and care products, and addictive products) is also examined in several studies (Fam et al., 2004; Farah and Samad, 2014; Wang et al., 2018). It was found that religious individuals are more likely to find advertisements of such products offensive, and that Muslims are the most offended among Christians, non-believers, and Buddhists (Fam et al., 2004). In addition, researchers found relatively weak government regulation of controversial advertising (Wang et al., 2018). Findings related to the relationship between religiosity and attitude towards offensive advertising were replicated by De Run et al. (2010) for Malaysian Muslims.

Luxury

The definition of luxury is context-dependent; the same product can be seen by one person as a luxury item, and by another as an everyday commodity (Nwankwo et al., 2014). Consequently, the definition of luxury remains highly subjective (Joy et al., 2017). As Ko et al. (2019) exemplified, the American Marketing Association's dictionary of terms does not suggest a definition for luxury. Some used the term luxury to describe, top-class prestigious brands (Vigneron & Johnson, 1999). Two of the definitions published by Cambridge Dictionary ("Luxury," n.d.) are parallel with the perspective of Berry (1994), who sees luxury as objects of desire that provide pleasure:

Something expensive that is pleasant to have but is not necessary.

Something that gives you a lot of pleasure but cannot be done often.

Thorstein Veblen (1899) contended that rich people consume conspicuous (luxury) goods for the sake of maintaining their higher position in society. Based on his interpretations, luxury can be accepted as a tool for signifying wealth and status. As income is directly related to one's wealth and status, consumption of luxury goods has long been considered as unique to rich people, and income has been found as a significant contributor for luxury consumption (Dubois & Duquesne, 1993). However especially together with spread of flexible payment methods, like credit cards (Vickers & Renand, 2003), consumers from all walks of life engage in luxury consumption today. Traditionally luxury has been associated with exclusivity, status, and quality (Atwal & Williams, 2017), but current trends in consumer behavior have created the term *neo-luxury* term which means "products and services that possess higher levels of quality, taste and aspiration than other goods in the category but are not so expensive as to be out of reach" (Silverstein et al., 2005, p. 1). Thus, this new concept describes the democratization of luxury.

According to Vickers and Renand (2003), luxury goods can be differentiated from non-luxury goods by analyzing three essential dimensions: functionalism, experientialism, and symbolic interactionism. Functionalism represents needs that motivate consumers to look for goods or services that help to solve a current problem, prevent potential problems, or resolve a conflict. Symbolic interactionism denotes desire for products that satisfy needs like self-enhancement or group membership. Experientialism denotes desire for products that provide sensory pleasure, variety, and/or cognitive stimulation. For Tynan et al. (2010, p. 1158), key identifiers of luxury brands are "high quality, expensive and non-essential products and services that appear to be rare, exclusive, prestigious and authentic, and offer high levels of symbolic and emotional/ hedonic values through customer experiences."

Islamic Luxury

Consumption of luxury goods has been hotly debated throughout history. While some claim that this is an unavoidable result of the movement from an agricultural society to a manufacturing society, others mention negative moral and political consequences (Ramos, 2011). It has also been a popular discussion topic among Islamic scholars because Islam has always suggested modesty to its followers (Sandikci & Ger, 2005). Several examples can be given from the Quran and from hadith that recommend not to waste by extravagance:

O children of Adam, take your adornment at every masjid, and eat and drink, but be not excessive. Indeed, He likes not those who commit excess. (Quran, 7-31)

Don't squander even if you are performing ablution from a running river. (Prophet Mohammed)

In addition, luxury consumption generally evokes materialistic attitudes and materialism related with low well-being and low life satisfaction (Hudders & Pandelaere, 2012). At this point, the term Islamic luxury creates a contradiction considering that one of the purposes of a religion is to provide its followers a happy life and high level of well-being. Also, as Arli et al. (2016) mention, most religious teachings suggest that money and materialism are at the root of all evil. However, by citing several hadith or verses from the Quran some scholars put forward that Islamic teaching does not stand against consumption of luxury goods (Alserhan et al., 2014):

Allah loves to see the sign of His Bounties on his servants. (Prophet Mohammad)

Say, "Who has forbidden the adornment of Allah which He has produced for His servants and the good [lawful] things of provision?" Say, "They are for those who believe during the worldly life [but] exclusively for them on the Day of Resurrection." Thus do We detail the verses for a people who know. (Quran 7-32)

According to Nwankwo et al. (2014), Islamic values do not solely drive consumer purchase orientation for luxury goods. Instead, the role of religion decreases as consumer affordability of luxury consumption increases. Ashraf et al. (2017) have found that religiosity does not moderate the relationship between attitude, belief, subjective norms, and perceived behavioral control (Theory of Planned Behavior components) and intention to buy luxury products for Pakistani consumers. In one study, Iranian consumers stated a neutral or even incentive role of religious beliefs on the decision to purchasing a luxury car (Forghani et al., 2019). Another study found that Muslims' intention to purchase luxury goods in Nigeria is not influenced by religious beliefs (Aksoy & Abdultatai, 2019). Dekhil et al. (2017) also found that Islamic religiosity does not inhibit luxury consumption in Tunisia. Alserhan et al. (2014) revealed that religiosity did not affect luxury brand consumption among Arab women in the United Arab Emirates. Further, Arli et al. (2016) found that intrinsic religiosity is positively related to affective attitudes towards luxury brands, whereas extrinsic religiousness is positively related to self-presentation attitudes.[3] Although some studies have shown the negative relationship between religiosity and attitude toward luxury brands (Abalkhail, 2020) or brand consciousness (Islam & Chandrasekaran, 2019), overall literature suggests that Islamic religiosity is not negatively related with luxury consumption and in some studies it even plays an incentive role.

Several Islamic scholars classify products in a hierarchical way, as illustrated in Figure 1. In this perspective, it is claimed that luxury consumption is accepted as halal (allowed) in Islam but it is discouraged to acquire those goods extravagantly (Alserhan et al., 2014).

According to Rice (1999), Islam's interpretation of needs can be evaluated together with Keynes's classification. According to Keynes the needs of humans fall into two classes: in the first class are the basic needs of all individuals regardless of the position of other people in their environment; whereas the second class comprises needs that make someone feel superior to others if satisfied. For Rice (1999), necessities (*daruriyyat*), conveniences (*hayiyyat*), and refinements (*tahsiniyyat*) overlap with Keynes's first class of needs, whereas luxuries that are acquired for vanity and do not affect one's well-being fall into the second class.

Whether it is allowed or not, it is evident that luxury consumption in Islam is rising especially for visible luxury goods. Muslims, and particularly those who live in Asian countries, live in a collectivist culture whereby they are interdependently self-focused rather than independently as in western individualistic cultures[4]. Consequently, visible luxury possessions are drawing substantial attention (Wong & Ahuvia, 1998).

Figure 1. Product hierarchy in Islam (Alserhan et al., 2014)

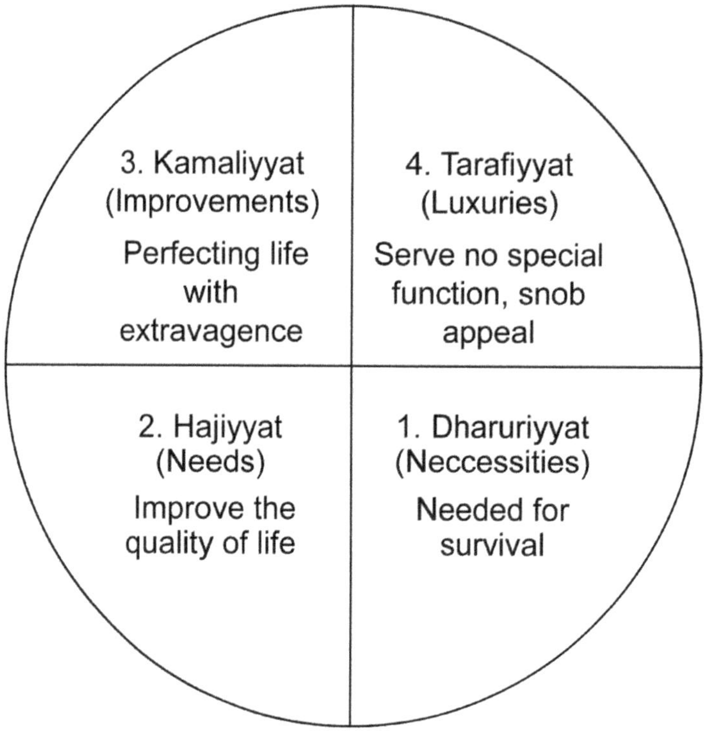

Figure 2, adapted from Okonkwo-Pézard (2017), illustrates how several luxury industries have evolved in an Islamic way. In this study, three industries will be analyzed within Islamic luxury: fashion, tourism, and cosmetics. These three industries are chosen because they exemplify the most visible and striking examples of Islamic luxury. Today, these are called as halal fashion, halal tourism, and halal cosmetics due to widespread applications for halal certification among businesses. Businesses use halal certification and logo in labeling for sharing the message that their products are halal and Shariah-compliant in order to encourage target customers (Hashim & Musa, 2014). Also, it is found that Muslim women are more inclined than men to buy luxury goods impulsively (Nwankwo et al., 2014; Hamelin & Thaichon, 2016), which increases the importance of halal cosmetics and halal fashion industry considering the more female-oriented structure of these industries.

Halal Fashion

As Sandikci and Ger (2005) illustrated, achieving a beautiful appearance is a difficult task considering that the main point about clothing emphasized repeatedly by Islamic scholars is modesty, which is positioned against indecency, vanity, and obscenity—while at the same time it is believed that Islam suggests to people to be clean, well-groomed, and pleasant looking. This difficult task opens the way for halal fashion. Halal fashion, also called modest fashion, has gained considerable attention even among giant players in the clothing sector, such as Nike which launched the Pro Hijab (see Figure 3). It has been estimated that Muslim consumers were spending $283 billion on clothing by 2019 (DinarStandard, 2019).

Figure 2. Islamic luxury industries

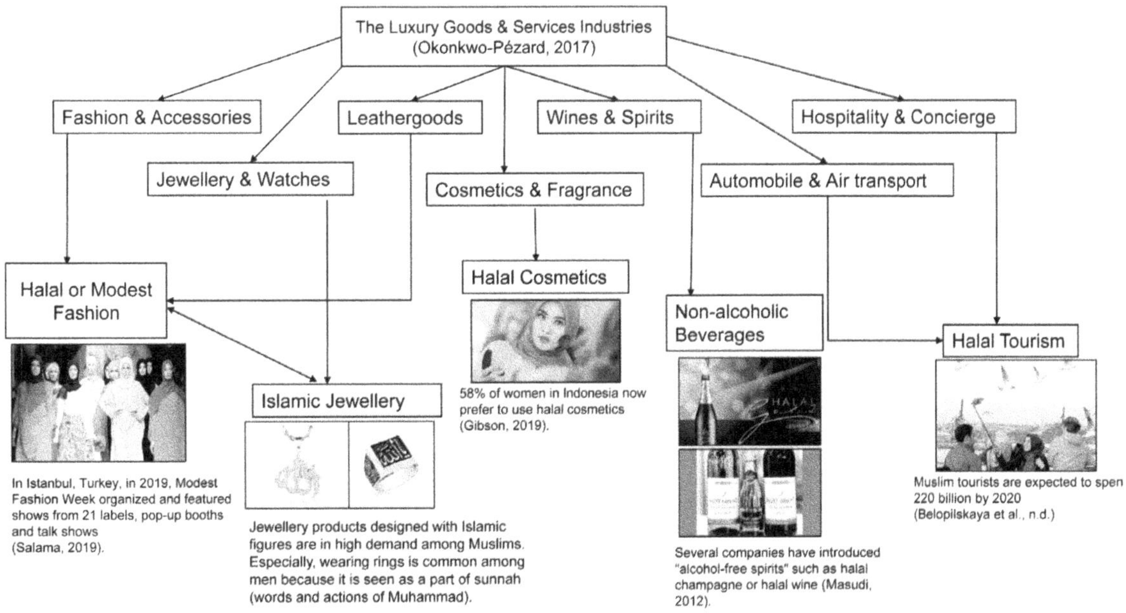

Although this is a controversial issue that has been discussed for decades, the majority of Muslims believe that the Quran orders Muslim women to cover themselves with the hijab, referring to the head covering or headscarf worn by women. Hence, the hijab is generally the first thing that comes to mind when talking about halal fashion. One of the trendiest terms is "hijabista," which refers to Muslim women who dress fashionably and/or design fashionable clothes in a halal way (Blommaert & Varis, 2015, p. 161). The term hijabista is lexicalized from "hijab" and "fashionista." A further term "hijabster" is lexicalized from "hijab" and "hipster," and represents more independent women whose fashion taste seen as more creative and independent (Williams & Kamaludeen, 2017).

Al-Mutawa (2013) revealed that Muslim female consumers of luxury fashion brands are involved because of the brand's symbolism, which gives them freedom of female sexuality. They are achieving a "modestly sexy" image by consuming these western brands. They are trying to balance modesty and sexuality to realize the "nice girl" ideal.

Halal or modest fashion has gained momentum since 9/11 as women who wear the hijab want to present themselves to society as "modern" or in other words as "normal". While this is the case in the western world, there is a reverse situation in some Muslim countries like Turkey, where political Islam is rising and gaining power. Islamic things and consumer products in this context have a function of differentiating individuals from so-called secular communities (Ger, 2013). As explained previously, halal food is not always eaten as a way to meet religious obligations. It can also be "a way of expressing an apparently chosen identity" (Varul, 2008, p. 250), and it can be a more significant contributor to the identity construction process in a non-Muslim environment. This determination can be valid for halal fashion also, which is even more evident due to its higher visibility in social life.

Halal fashion can be considered as an example of the super-diversity mentioned earlier because it is mainly considered as the interaction of faith, feminism, and identity (Durcanin, 2019). However, a common misconception in halal fashion is focusing on the female-oriented structure of the fashion

Figure 3. Nike Pro Hijab (Stanglin, 2017)

industry, thereby ignoring Muslim men who are eager to reflect their religious identity and lifestyle in their wearing style. Especially in countries like Turkey, politically motivated men are inclined to engage in historical consumption (Sandikci & Ger, 2007) by preferring products designed in an Ottoman style: for instance, wearing a shirt or necklace decorated with a *tughra* (Ottoman sultan's signature), carrying prayer beads in one hand while smoking his vintage-designed hookah in a luxury cafe. This kind of historical consumption is intertwined with religious consumption, considering that for many politically motivated consumers the Ottoman Empire signifies the "good old days" when a religious administrative mentality ruled in the state instead of the modern secular republic.

With brands like Dolce & Gabbana, Uniqlo, and Burberry entering the market of modest fashion for men, there are already some successful examples such as the German brand smartKhuffZ which released a sneaker for men with removable inners to fit prayer socks (Modest Man, 2019). While the Islamic dress code for men is not as clear as for women, it is suggested that clothing should be loose and tight trousers and shirts are not recommended (Buller, 2018).

One of the emerging trends in halal fashion is e-retailing. The Turkish halal fashion e-retailer modanisa.com, which was also the biggest sponsor of the Modest Fashion Week organized in Istanbul in 2019 (Sofia, 2019), has experienced rapid growth and obtained investment from the European Bank for Reconstruction and Development (United Kingdom), Goldman Sachs, and Wamda Capital (Wamda, 2019). Another contender is Dubai-based e-retailer The Modist, which attracted investment from British e-commerce fashion site Farfetch and Annabel Investment Holding (van Elven, 2019).

Another issue that is often neglected by marketers is that halal fashion trends are relevant only in Islamic countries. "Modest clothing" receives 8,000 Google searches monthly in the United States alone. It can be inferred that not only Muslims but also non-Muslim individuals are looking for modest fashion. One of the reasons is that today more women are questioning the rationale that being fashionable equates with being sexy instead of comfortable, and are thus seeking longer skirts or looser trousers (van Elven, 2019).

Halal Cosmetics

Although not as much discussed as food or finance within the halal economy, halal cosmetics is among the rapidly rising halal industries. The food, cosmetics, and pharmaceutical industries are particularly subject to concerns over whether manufacturers are using ingredients produced with pork or alcohol. These concerns have triggered the rise of halal cosmetics. Today halal cosmetics is not just about ingredients, it has become a consumption style. The Turkish YouTuber rimel askina ("for the love of mascara"), who focuses on different kinds of makeup for women with hijab, now has 430,000 followers (see Figure 4). The State of the Global Islamic Economy Report illustrated that global Muslim spending on cosmetics increased by 4.9% in 2018 from $61 billion to $64 billion (DinarStandard, 2019).

According to one report, in Iran in 2011 there were 14 million women aged between 15 and 45 living in big cities and spending an average of $7 per month on cosmetics (Teimourpour & Hanzaee, 2011). Another report revealed that Iran spends two times as much as Italy and three times the amount spent in England and Germany on cosmetics (Financial Tribune, 2017).

Figure 4. Screenshot of a makeup video recorded by Youtuber rimel askina

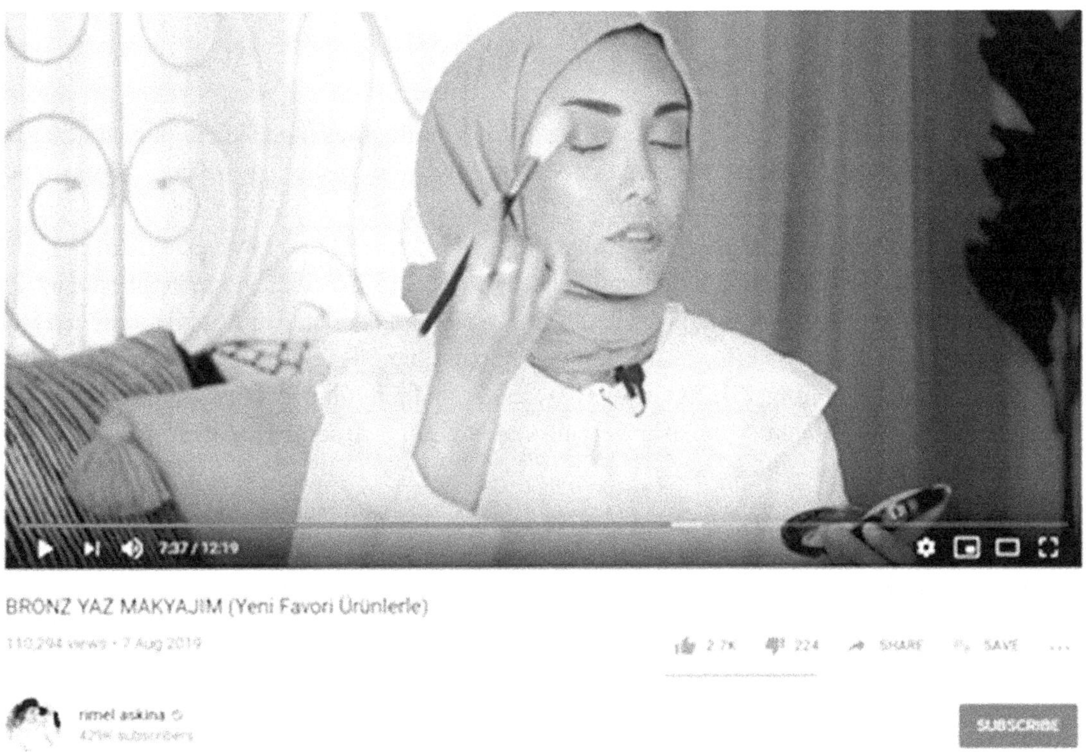

As discussed above, what is halal (permissible) or haram (prohibited) in Islam is decided according to the Quran and hadith, and when there is a contemporary issue that is not mentioned in these sources, fatwa declarations are issued by Islamic scholars. Concerning cosmetics, there some prominent fatwas online which put forward that wearing makeup is not allowed for Muslim women when they are with na-mahrams.[5] Al-Haj (2006) presents a clear fatwa example that actually summarizes the general understanding of makeup among Muslims:

With regards to kohl and similarly light makeup, there is some controversy, while some consider it from the ornament of the woman that may be shown (azzeenah azzahirah), others considered it not of it. It may be acceptable for a woman, particularly a single one seeking a partner to wear eye liner. It is however necessary for the woman to avoid tempting men, and if she felt she would be tempting, then she must avoid this act.

I advise the Muslim woman who is keen to please Allah to stay clear from the controversy and avoid the use of all forms of makeup unless in front of women, her husband and/or mahrams. The single woman who is seeking a husband may however be entitled to some leniency here based on the hadeeth of Subay`ah, in which it is indicated that she wore kohl and went out of her home, which was taken as a sign that she was readying herself for accepting proposals from willing suitors.

If the skin is abnormal as you hinted in the question, then I hope that some use of light powder to cover it up may be permissible.

Allah knows best.

In analyzing the suggestions of Islamic teaching about wearing makeup, Karabulut et al. (2020) ask the question, "Even though Islamic teaching is not supportive about wearing makeup, why is makeup consumption increasing among Muslim women?" Before answering the question, the authors prove the negative relationship between intrinsic religiosity and makeup intention. However, this negative relationship shifted with extrinsic makeup motivation but not with intrinsic makeup motivation, and social positioning (Karabulut et al., in press). Intrinsic satisfaction is mainly related to attractiveness and feeling good about one's own self. Extrinsic satisfaction on the other hand is related to social motivations and relationships. Social positioning reflects social roles, status, and feminine identity. All these motivations explain the perspective of Muslim women in wearing makeup and give considerable insights to marketers not only about marketing halal cosmetics.

Halal Tourism

Halal tourism is defined as "any tourism object or action which is permissible according to Islamic teachings to use or engage by Muslims in the tourism industry" (Battour & Ismail, 2016, p. 51). According to Battour and Ismail (2016), the definition has certain implications: first, Islamic law is the basis for market offerings in tourism that are directed to Muslims. Second, the location of the touristic activity is not limited to Muslim areas. In other words, touristic activities in non-Muslim countries designed for Muslim tourists by taking into consideration Islamic teaching can be accepted as halal tourism. Lastly, the main goal of the touristic activity may not be religious.

Report published by COMCEC (2017) creates a clear picture of the points that should be taken into consideration when designing a Muslim-friendly tourism (MFT) service (see Figure 5).

The main issue in halal tourism is privacy. As a highly successful example, some travel agencies offer exclusive villas for rent to their religiously sensitive consumers in Turkey. Many of these rentals are separate from their environment, protecting guests' privacy, and include a private swimming pool or even sometimes a small beach (see villasepeti.com). In addition, some agencies such as bookhalalhomes.com, a UK-based startup that could be called "halal Airbnb," have done a great job in targeting Muslim tourists in the past (Belopilskaya et al., n.d.). On the other hand, some simple design features in the setting of service may create significant impacts, for instance Muslim-friendly washrooms in hotels or restaurants, given that it is a big deal for Muslims who travel extensively to find an appropriate washroom not only for relieving but also performing ablutions.

Figure 5. Ratings, using a 5-point scale, on the importance of Muslim-friendly services being regulated by a Muslim-friendly accommodation standard (in percentage) (COMCEC, 2017)

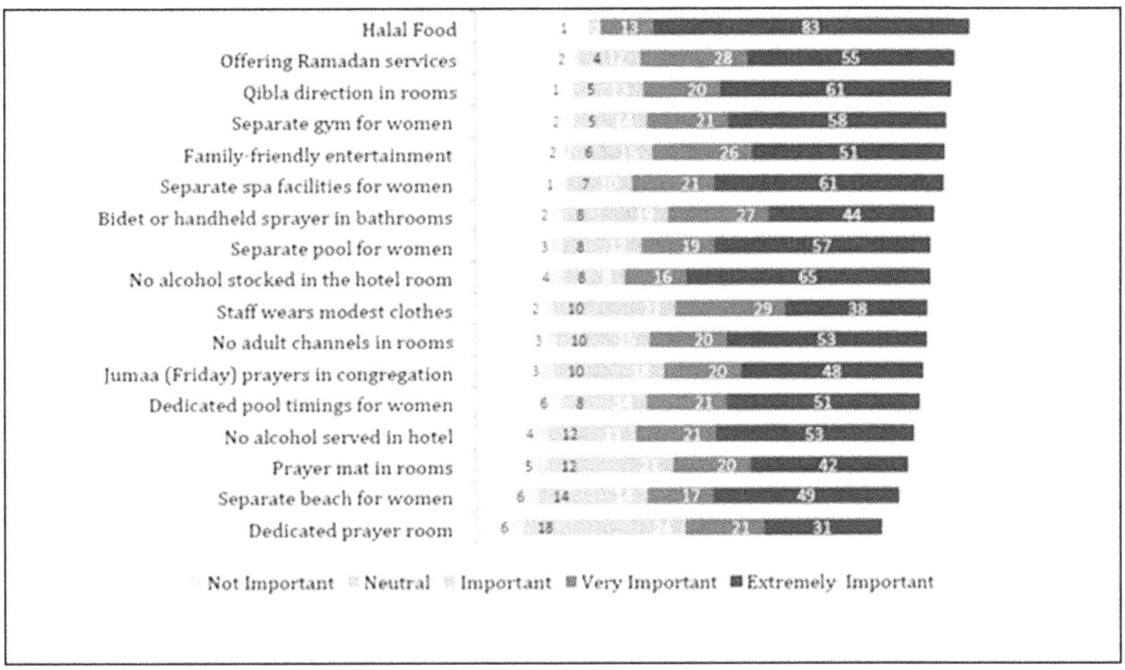

When talking about halal tourism, almost everyone pictures a family with two or more children, mom wearing hijab and the father most probably with a long beard, taking pictures in Islamic destinations like Mecca, Istanbul's Blue Mosque, or Jerusalem. This visualization may be correct to some extent but does not reflect the big picture. Findings of recent research conducted by MasterCard and CrescentRating illustrated that 28% of all female Muslims embarked on solo journeys, out of a total of 63 million trips that generated over USD80 billion in trip revenue in 2018 (The Jakarta Post, 2019).

Another rising trend in halal tourism is the halal honeymoon. It is well known that marriage and the marriage ceremony are vital in Islamic cultures. One of the reasons for this is that sexual intercourse is not halal[6] for Muslim couples if they are not married, which increases the significance of the honeymoon for these couples. In the World Halal Tourism Award held in 2016, Abu Dhabi, United Arab Emirates and Sembalun Village Region in Indonesia were chosen as the World's Best Halal Honeymoon Destination (Greenwood, 2016).

Figure 6. Sembalun Valley Region-Indonesia (Sembalunrinjanilombok, 2016)

CONCLUSION

This study has aimed to discuss the term Islamic luxury and illustrate how it is on the rise, especially in the last decade. Based on these arguments, some managerial implications and directions for marketers and researchers who are interested in the Muslim market segment can be offered.

Managerial Implications

First of all, demographics of Muslim population should be analyzed in detail. For example, the Muslim population is strikingly younger in many non-Muslim countries. As an example, the Muslim population of the United States is younger than the U.S. population. While millennials constitute 32% of the adult population of the U.S., Muslim millennials constitute 52% of all American Muslim adults (Diamant & Gecewwicz, 2017). It has been shown that millennials have an intense passion for luxury brands and especially for neo-luxury (Rodrigues & Rodrigues, 2019), which makes Islamic luxury more critical. As an example, it has been found that young Moroccan consumers are more inclined to buy luxury products than the elderly (Hamelin & Thaichon, 2016). On the other hand, as millennial consumers are more experience-focused and the importance of the experiential approach in luxury consumption is already known (Atwal & Williams, 2017), sufficient attention should be paid to the experiential approach in the design of halal luxury market offerings. Farrag's (2017) study confirmed this by finding that experiential needs are the most crucial factor that affects Qatari youth consumers' attitudes toward luxury brands. Also, millennials' high social media involvement (Smith, 2012) indicates the necessity of engagement in social media platforms for luxury brands (Brandão et al., 2019). Online relationships and the role of digital marketing should not be overlooked in halal tourism as well as in all sectors more generally, not only for halal luxury tourism but also for Muslims who seek affordable tourism options (Alves, Sousa, & Machado, 2020).

Muslims in Europe and the United States of America are more inclined to create their own consumption routines and also their tastes in social aspects of life like music, humor, or literature. In one prominent example, the Islamic hip-hop genre has risen significantly in the last decades, and is believed to promote a positive image of Islam. The UK female hip-hop band Poetic Pilgrimage tours throughout Europe and has been giving concerts since 2002 (Gazzah, 2014). These kinds of involvement should be followed closely by marketers because they affect luxury trends among consumers through creating reference groups.

Luxury brands that are active in or target the Muslim market segment should follow closely with fatwa rulings, considering that any luxury product can be the case for fatwa. One example is an online fatwa given by a famous Turkish Islamic scholar concerning whether or not buying a luxury car is permissible in Islam. In that discussion, Yildiz (2012) claims that one can buy a luxury product as long as one does not enter into debt in a way that causes trouble for oneself or one's family economically. Many online platforms can be used as a resource for following current developments in fatwa rulings, such as sorularlaislamiyet.com (Islam with questions, the most popular fatwa website in Turkish) and amjaonline.org (website of the Assembly of Muslim Jurists of America, with fatwa database).

It should be noted that Islamic consumer culture is not homogenous (Gorak-Sosnowska, 2012) and neither are preferences for luxury consumption harmonized across cultures (Kassim & Zain, 2016). For instance, Teimourpour and Hanzaee (2011) reviewed the dimensions of luxury values together with the cultural and religious values of Iranian consumers. They discussed how, for consumers, luxury values could depend on the country's culture; for Iranian Muslim consumers, some values like price, quality, or materialist values may outweigh others like hedonic or self-identity values.

One study found that Pakistani consumers show signs of less ethical behavior compared to UK consumers (Hussain et al., 2017). The majority of the participants were involved in buying counterfeit luxury products and described this behavior as ethical. As Hennings et al., (2012) suggest, people from around the world have different reasons to buy luxury products as well as globally available low-cost counterfeits of these products. Managers can unveil and focus on the specific value dimension regarded as the most important motivator for consumers of a luxury brand. In this case, the status associated with counterfeit luxury products was important for Pakistani consumers.

It should be also noted that Islamic societies are deeply community focused, such that each community imposes its own values on its members and thereby plays an important role in shaping consumption patterns and brand relationships (Karatas & Sandikci, 2013). Marketers should pay close attention to communities, given that some of them have millions of followers and can play a central role in shaping individuals' attitudes toward a luxury product.

Even though this chapter has shared some successful examples of launching halal products (e.g., Nike Pro Hijab), marketers may still face Islamophobia in western countries. For example, the French sportswear firm Decathlon planned the launch of hijab for women runners but had to cancel the project due to loud protests. Some believed that this product contradicted secular values (Chrisafis, 2019). The main takeaway from this case is that political institutions still play an important role in designing halal luxury. As an opposite example, in Turkey—which is also a secular country—the 1990s witnessed the rise of Islamic consumption culture together with resurgence of political Islam (Sandikci & Ger, 2005).

As offered before, advertising Halal products in a way that shows people with a high level of religiosity using those products cannot be valid for the luxury context. As a clear example, non-Muslim consumers also buy halal food products because they consider them to be safer (Bashir, 2019), or halal fashion is demanded by non-Muslim women because it avoids a sexy appeal (van Elven, 2019). Instead, and as Arli et al. (2016) proposed, focusing on quality and functionalism of the market offering by suppressing the materialistic aspect would be an effective marketing communication strategy for luxury goods, since focusing on the luxury side of a market offering may cause a conflict between Muslim's religious values in which modesty is a cornerstone and their desire towards luxury.

FUTURE STUDIES

Forghani et al. (2019) suggest that researchers should use various research methods to acquire in-depth insights, because religious beliefs are highly diversified. Ethnographic analyses would reveal many managerial implications for marketers who deal with the Muslim consumer segment, since culture has a dominant effect on interpretation of religion. For example, luxury goods are seen as appropriate for gift giving (Belk, 1996) and in Islamic cultures there are many traditions in which gift giving is considered essential. One of the most popular gift-giving practices, for example, in Turkey among Muslims, is giving gold, and to some extent it is given for religious purposes (Ertimur & Sandikci, 2014).

Although it is not analyzed in this study, when talking about halal economy food is among the first issues that come to mind. It is stated that instead of halal, millennial Muslims are now looking for *tayyab*, which means "ethical and wholesome," in which sustainability plays a central role together with other ethical issues like workers not being exploited. Also, the demand for organic halal food is rising (Sherwood, 2016). Future studies can analyze these trends, considering that organic food is still seen as a luxury.

Even though it is not analyzed deeply in the current study, some luxury markets are proliferating in Muslim countries. For Iran, the example of the luxury car market can be given (Forghani et al., 2019; Temourpour & Hanzaee, 2014). Market-specific research on items such as luxury cars can be conducted in future to reveal trends and potential cross-cultural differences among Muslim cultures.

Islamic technological consumption can also be a notable category of Islamic luxury and should not be overlooked. In 2004 a Dubai-based tech company launched an Islamic mobile phone that sends messages at prayer times and can point to the location of Mecca (Fischer, 2014). Today there are such many applications for mobile devices developed for religious people, varying from a halal food finder to a prayer timer. One example is Muzmatch, a dating app designed for single Muslims to meet and date, that now has more than 1.5 million users across 210 countries (Lomas, 2019). There are fruitful research opportunities for researchers in halal technological products or services.

Forghani et al. (2019) have found that certain peculiar beliefs among Muslims, like the evil-eye effect, are intertwined with religious beliefs and can affect their attitudes and behaviors toward luxury products. Future studies can look at the interaction of these peculiar belief with Islamic religious beliefs and effects on attitudes and behaviors toward luxury products and services.

ACKNOWLEDGMENT

The author thanks Feyzan Karabulut of the University of Alberta who shared her ideas and suggestions related to Islamic religiosity and consumer behavior.

REFERENCES

Abalkhail, T. (2020). The impact of religiosity on luxury brand consumption: The case of Saudi consumers. *Journal of Islamic Marketing*. Advance online publication. doi:10.1108/JIMA-11-2016-0091

Aksoy, H., & Abdulfatai, O. (2019). Exploring the impact of religiousness and culture on luxury fashion goods purchasing intention: A behavioural study on Nigerian Muslim consumers. *Journal of Islamic Marketing*, *10*(3), 768–789. doi:10.1108/JIMA-01-2018-0022

al-Haj, H. (2006, September 15). *What does Islam say about makeup?* Retrieved from https://www.amjaonline.org/fatwa/en/1987/what-does-islam-say-about-makeup

Al-Mutawa, F. S. (2013). Consumer-generated representations: Muslim women recreating western luxury fashion brand meaning through consumption. *Psychology and Marketing*, *30*(3), 236–246. doi:10.1002/mar.20601

Alam, S. S., Mohd, R., & Hisham, B. (2011). Is religiosity an important determinant on Muslim consumer behaviour in Malaysia? *Journal of Islamic Marketing*, *2*(1), 83–96. doi:10.1108/17590831111115268

Allport, G. W., & Ross, J. M. (1967). Personal religious orientation and prejudice. *Journal of Personality and Social Psychology*, *5*(4), 432–443. doi:10.1037/h0021212 PMID:6051769

Alserhan, B. A., Bataineh, M. K., Halkias, D., & Komodromos, M. (2014). Measuring luxury brand consumption and female consumers' religiosity in the UAE. *Journal of Developmental Entrepreneurship*, *19*(2), 1–16. doi:10.1142/S1084946714500095

Alves, G. M., Sousa, B. M., & Machado, A. (2020). The role of digital marketing and online relationship quality in social tourism: A tourism for all case study. In J. Santos & Ó. Silva (Eds.), Digital marketing strategies for tourism, hospitality, and airline industries (pp. 49–70). IGI Global. doi:10.4018/978-1-5225-9783-4.ch003

Arli, D., Cherrier, H., & Tjiptono, F. (2016). God blesses those who wear Prada: Exploring the impact of religiousness on attitudes toward luxury among the youth of Indonesia. *Marketing Intelligence & Planning*, *34*(1), 61–79. doi:10.1108/MIP-12-2014-0232

Ashraf, S., Hafeez, M. H., Yaseen, A., & Naqvi, A. (2017). Do they care what they believe? Exploring the impact of religiosity on intention to purchase luxury products. *Pakistan Journal of Commerce and Social Sciences*, *11*(2), 428–447.

Aslanbay, Y., Sanaktekin, Ö. H., & Ağırdır, B. (2011). Lifestyles of Islamic consumers in Turkey. In O. Sandikci & G. Rice (Eds.), *Handbook of Islamic Marketing* (pp. 129–146). Edward Elgar Publishing. doi:10.4337/9780857936028.00016

Atwal, G., & Williams, A. (2017). Luxury brand marketing–the experience is everything! In J. Kapferer, J. Kernstock, T. O. Brexendorf, & S. M. Powell (Eds.), *Advances in luxury brand management* (pp. 43–57). Palgrave Macmillan. doi:10.1007/978-3-319-51127-6_3

Aytaç, M. B. (2019). *Narsistik tüketim (Narcissistic consumption)*. Gazi Kitabevi.

Bailey, J. M., & Sood, J. (1993). The effects of religious affiliation on consumer behavior: A preliminary investigation. *Journal of Managerial Issues*, *5*(3), 328–352.

Bashir, A. (2019, August 14). Awareness of purchasing halal food among non-Muslim consumers: An explorative study with reference to Cape Town of South Africa. *Journal of Islamic Marketing*. Advance online publication. doi:10.1108/JIMA-04-2018-0077

Battour, M., & Ismail, M. N. (2016). Halal tourism: Concepts, practises, challenges and future. *Tourism Management Perspectives, 19*(B), 150–154.

Battour, M. M., Ismail, M. N., & Battor, M. (2010). Toward a halal tourism market. *Tourism Analysis*, *15*(4), 461–470. doi:10.3727/108354210X12864727453304

Belk, R. W. (1996). The perfect gift. In C. Otnes & R. F. Beltramini (Eds.), *Giftgiving: An interdisciplinary anthology* (pp. 59–85). Bowling Green University Popular Press.

Belopilskaya, Y., Visutthithada, C., & Wieser, T. (n.d.). *How halal tourism is reshaping the global tourism industry*. Retrieved from https://hospitalityinsights.ehl.edu/halal-tourism-global-industry

Berry, C. J. (1994). *The idea of luxury: A conceptual and historical investigation*. Cambridge University Press. doi:10.1017/CBO9780511558368

Blommaert, J., & Varis, P. (2015). Culture as accent: The cultural logic of hijabistas. *Semiotica*, *203*(203), 153–177. doi:10.1515em-2014-0067

Brandão, A., Pinho, E., & Rodrigues, P. (2019). Antecedents and consequences of luxury brand engagement in social media. *Spanish Journal of Marketing-ESIC*, *23*(2), 163–183. doi:10.1108/SJME-11-2018-0052

Buller, A. (2018, November 11). *Men's 'modest wear' set for global boom – experts*. Retrieved from https://www.arabianbusiness.com/style/407754-mens-modest-wear-set-for-global-boom-experts

Choi, Y., Paulraj, A., & Shin, J. (2013). Religion or religiosity: Which is the culprit for consumer switching behavior? *Journal of International Consumer Marketing*, *25*(4), 262–280.

Chrisafis, A. (2019, February 26). *Decathlon drops French sports hijab after politicians threaten boycott*. Retrieved from https://www.theguardian.com/world/2019/feb/26/decathlon-drops-french-sports-hijab-after-politicians-threaten-boycott

COMCEC. Standing Committee for Economic and Commercial Cooperation of the Organization of Islamic Cooperation. (2017). *Muslim friendly tourism: Regulating accommodation establishments in the OIC member countries*. Retrieved from http://www.sbb.gov.tr/wp-content/uploads/2018/11/Muslim_Friendly_Tourism_MFT_Regulating_Accommodation_Establishments_in_the_OIC_Member_Countries%E2%80%8B.pdf

Cutler, B. D. (1992). Religion and marketing: Important research area or a footnote in the literature? *Journal of Professional Services Marketing*, *8*(1), 153–164. doi:10.1300/J090v08n01_12

De Run, E. C., Butt, M. M., Fam, K.-S., & Jong, H. Y. (2010). Attitudes towards offensive advertising: Malaysian Muslims' views. *Journal of Islamic Marketing*, *1*(1), 25–36. doi:10.1108/17590831011026204

Dekhil, F., Boulebech, H., & Bouslama, N. (2017). Effect of religiosity on luxury consumer behavior: The case of the Tunisian Muslim. *Journal of Islamic Marketing*, *8*(1), 74–94. doi:10.1108/JIMA-09-2012-0051

Delener, N. (1990). The effects of religious factors on perceived risk in durable goods purchase decisions. *Journal of Consumer Marketing*, *7*(3), 27–38. doi:10.1108/EUM0000000002580

Delener, N. (1994). Religious contrasts in consumer decision behaviour patterns: Their –dimensions and marketing implications. *European Journal of Marketing*, *28*(5), 36–53. doi:10.1108/03090569410062023

Diamant, J., & Gecewicz, C. (2017, October 26). *5 facts about Muslim millennials in the U.S.* Retrieved from https://www.pewresearch.org/fact-tank/2017/10/26/5-facts-about-muslim-millennials-us/

DinarStandard. (2019). *State of the global Islamic economy report*. Retrieved from https://ceif.iba.edu.pk/pdf/state-of-global-islamic-economy-report-2019-20.pdf

Dubois, B., & Duquesne, P. (1993). The market for luxury goods: Income versus culture. *European Journal of Marketing*, *27*(1), 35–44. doi:10.1108/03090569310024530

Durcanin, C. (2019). *Conversation piece: San Francisco's de Young Museum celebrates 'Contemporary Muslim Fashions'*. Retrieved from https://www.artnews.com/art-news/news/conversation-piece-de-young-san-francisco-celebrates-contemporary-muslim-fashions-11630/

Ertimur, B., & Sandıkcı, Ö. (2014). Alienable gifts: Uses and meanings of gold in Turkey. *Journal of Consumer Behaviour, 13*(3), 204–211. doi:10.1002/cb.1479

Ertit, V. (2018). God is dying in Turkey as well: Application of secularization theory to a non-Christian society. *Open Theology, 4*(1), 192–211. doi:10.1515/opth-2018-0014

Essoo, N., & Dibb, S. (2004). Religious influences on shopping behaviour: An exploratory study. *Journal of Marketing Management, 20*(7–8), 683–712. doi:10.1362/0267257041838728

Fam, K. S., Waller, D. S., & Erdogan, B. Z. (2004). The influence of religion on attitudes towards the advertising of controversial products. *European Journal of Marketing, 38*(5/6), 537–555. doi:10.1108/03090560410529204

Farah, M. F., & El Samad, L. (2014). The effects of religion and religiosity on advertisement assessment among Lebanese consumers. *Journal of International Consumer Marketing, 26*(4), 344–369. doi:10.1080/08961530.2014.919126

Farrag, D. A. (2017). The young luxury consumer in Qatar. *Young Consumers, 18*(4), 393–407. doi:10.1108/YC-06-2017-00702

Financial Tribune. (2017, September 24). *Iran's cosmetics market on growth trajectory*. Retrieved from https://financialtribune.com/articles/economy/73022/iran-s-cosmetics-market-on-growth-trajectory

Fischer, J. (2014). Muslim material culture in the Western world. In R. Tottoli (Ed.), *Routledge handbook of Islam in the West* (pp. 348–362). Routledge.

Forghani, M. H., Kazemi, A., & Ranjbarian, B. (2019). Religion, peculiar beliefs and luxury cars' consumer behavior in Iran. *Journal of Islamic Marketing, 10*(2), 673–688. doi:10.1108/JIMA-06-2018-0101

Gayatri, G., Chan, C., Mort, G. S., & Hume, M. (2005). Understanding service quality from the Islamic customer perspective. In S. Purchase (Ed.), *Proceedings of the Australian and New Zealand Marketing Academy Conference*. University of Western Australia.

Gazzah, M. (2014). European Muslim youth and popular culture: At the crossroads of fun and faith. In R. Tottoli (Ed.), *Routledge handbook of Islam in the West* (pp. 334–347). Routledge.

Ger, G. (2013). Islamic marketing at the nexus of global markets–religions–politics and implications for research. *Marketing Theory, 13*(4), 497–503. doi:10.1177/1470593113499702

Gibson, S. (2019, September 11). *Brand-new Halal Cosmetics Zone to launch at in-cosmetics Asia 2019*. Retrieved from https://news.in-cosmetics.com/2019/09/11/brand-new-halal-cosmetics-zone-to-launch-at-in-cosmetics-asia-2019/#_ftnref2

Greenwood, G. (2016, December 9). *World Halal Tourism Awards 2016 winners announced*. Retrieved from https://www.traveldailymedia.com/world-halal-tourism-awards-2016-winners-announced/

Hamelin, N., & Thaichon, P. (2016). Consumer motives and impact of western media on the Moroccan luxury buyer. *Journal of Retailing and Consumer Services, 32*, 164–170. doi:10.1016/j.jretconser.2016.06.010

Hashim, A., & Musa, R. (2014). Factors influencing attitude towards halal cosmetics among young adult urban Muslim women: A focus group analysis. *Procedia: Social and Behavioral Sciences*, *130*, 129–134. doi:10.1016/j.sbspro.2014.04.016

Hashim, N. M., & Mizerski, D. (2010). Exploring Muslim consumers' information sources for fatwa rulings on products and behaviors. *Journal of Islamic Marketing*, *1*(1), 37–50. doi:10.1108/17590831011026213

Heiens, R. A., Pleshko, L. P., & Aldousari, A. A. (2016). Using direct observation to examine the relationship between religiosity, demographics, and consumption in a Middle Eastern retail services setting. *Journal of International Consumer Marketing*, *28*(4), 274–282. doi:10.1080/08961530.2016.1171741

Hennigs, N., Wiedmann, K. P., Klarmann, C., Strehlau, S., Godey, B., Pederzoli, D., ... Taro, K. (2012). What is the value of luxury? A cross-cultural consumer perspective. *Psychology and Marketing*, *29*(12), 1018–1034. doi:10.1002/mar.20583

Hirschman, E. C., & Touzani, M. (2011). Consumer acculturation in situ: The continuing legacy of French colonization in North Africa. In O. Sandikci & G. Rice (Eds.), Handbook of Islamic marketing (pp. 114–128). Cheltenham: Edward Elgar Publishing.

Hirschman, E. C. (1983). Religious affiliation and consumption processes: An initial paradigm. In J. N. Sheth (Ed.), *Research in marketing* (pp. 131–170). JAI Press.

Hudders, L., & Pandelaere, M. (2012). The silver lining of materialism: The impact of luxury consumption on subjective well-being. *Journal of Happiness Studies*, *13*(3), 411–437. doi:10.100710902-011-9271-9

Hussain, A., Kofinas, A., & Win, S. (2017). Intention to purchase counterfeit luxury products: A comparative study between Pakistani and the UK consumers. *Journal of International Consumer Marketing*, *29*(5), 331–346. doi:10.1080/08961530.2017.1361881

Islam, T., & Chandrasekaran, U. (2019). Religiosity, values and consumer behaviour: A study of young Indian Muslim consumers. *Journal of Consumer Marketing*, *36*(7), 948–961. doi:10.1108/JCM-10-2017-2415

Joy, A., Belk, R., & Bhardwaj, R. (2017). Luxury consumption and luxury brands: Past, present, and future. In M. Keller, B. Halkier, T. Wilska, & M. Truninger (Eds.), *Routledge handbook on consumption* (pp. 442–452). Routledge. doi:10.4324/9781315675015-44

Karabulut, F., Aytac, M. B., & Akin, E. (2020). Makeup Consumption and Islamic Religiosity. *Human Arenas*, *3*, 534–551. doi:10.100742087-020-00106-w

Karataş, M., & Sandıkcı, Ö. (2013). Religious communities and the marketplace: Learning and performing consumption in an Islamic network. *Marketing Theory*, *13*(4), 465–484. doi:10.1177/1470593113499697

Kassim, N. M., & Zain, M. M. (2016). Quality of lifestyle and luxury purchase inclinations from the perspectives of affluent Muslim consumers. *Journal of Islamic Marketing*, *7*(1), 95–119. doi:10.1108/JIMA-08-2014-0052

Ko, E., Costello, J. P., & Taylor, C. R. (2019). What is a luxury brand? A new definition and review of the literature. *Journal of Business Research*, *99*, 405–413. doi:10.1016/j.jbusres.2017.08.023

Lipka, M., & Hackett, C. (2017, April 6). *Why Muslims are the world's fastest-growing religious group*. Retrieved from https://www.pewresearch.org/fact-tank/2017/04/06/why-muslims-are-the-worlds-fastest-growing-religious-group/

Lomas, N. (2019, July 26). *Muzmatch adds $7M to swipe right on Muslim-majority markets*. Retrieved from https://techcrunch.com/2019/07/26/muzmatch-adds-7m-to-swipe-right-on-muslim-majority-markets/

Luxury. (n.d.). In *Cambridge dictionary* online. Retrieved from https://dictionary.cambridge.org/dictionary/english/luxury

Mansori, S., Sambasivan, M., & Md-Sidin, S. (2015). Acceptance of novel products: The role of religiosity, ethnicity and values. *Marketing Intelligence & Planning*, *33*(1), 39–66. doi:10.1108/MIP-03-2013-0050

Masudi. (2012, February 23). *Halal wine anyone?* Retrieved from https://gulfnews.com/uae/health/halal-wine-anyone-1.985002

Meşe, İ. (2015). İslami bir moda dergisi örneğinde moda ve tesettür: Ne türden bir birliktelik? *Fe Dergisi: Feminist Eleştiri*, *7*(1), 146–158.

Mittelstaedt, J. D. (2002). A framework for understanding the relationships between religions and markets. *Journal of Macromarketing*, *22*(1), 6–18. doi:10.1177/027467022001002

Modest Man. (2019, July 8). *The Islamic sneakers biz keeps exploding!* Retrieved from https://www.ifdcouncil.org/the-islamic-sneakers-biz-keeps-exploding/

Mokhlis, S. (2009). Relevancy and measurement of religiosity in consumer behavior research. *International Business Research*, *2*(3), 75–84. doi:10.5539/ibr.v2n3p75

Moschis, G. P., & Ong, F. S. (2011). Religiosity and consumer behavior of older adults: A study of subcultural influences in Malaysia. *Journal of Consumer Behaviour*, *10*(1), 8–17. doi:10.1002/cb.342

Muhamad, N. (2011). Fatwa rulings in Islam: A Malaysian perspective on their role in Muslim consumer behavior. In O. Sandikci & G. Rice (Eds.), *Handbook of Islamic marketing* (pp. 35–55). Edward Elgar Publishing. doi:10.4337/9780857936028.00010

Nwankwo, S., Hamelin, N., & Khaled, M. (2014). Consumer values, motivation and purchase intention for luxury goods. *Journal of Retailing and Consumer Services*, *21*(5), 735–744. doi:10.1016/j.jretconser.2014.05.003

Okonkwo-Pézard, U. (2017). The luxury brand strategy challenge. In J. Kapferer, J. Kernstock, T. O. Brexendorf, & S. M. Powell (Eds.), *Advances in luxury brand management* (pp. 59–64). Palgrave Macmillan. doi:10.1007/978-3-319-51127-6_4

Prokopec, S., & Kurdy, M. (2011). An international marketing strategy perspective on Islamic marketing. In O. Sandikci & G. Rice (Eds.), *Handbook of Islamic marketing* (pp. 208–225). Edward Elgar Publishing. doi:10.4337/9780857936028.00021

Radwan, G. N., Israel, E., El-Setouhy, M., Abdel-Aziz, F., Mikhail, N., & Mohamed, M. K. (2003). Impact of religious rulings (Fatwa) on smoking. *Journal of the Egyptian Society of Parasitology*, *330*(Suppl. 3), 1087–1101. PMID:15119472

Ramos, A. (2011). Luxury, crisis and consumption: Sir James Steuart and the eighteenth-century luxury debate. *History of Economics Review*, *53*(1), 55–72. doi:10.1080/18386318.2011.11682176

Rehman, A., & Shabbir, M. S. (2010). The relationship between religiosity and new product adoption. *Journal of Islamic Marketing*, *1*(1), 63–69. doi:10.1108/17590831011026231

Rice, G. (1999). Islamic ethics and the implications for business. *Journal of Business Ethics*, *18*(4), 345–358. doi:10.1023/A:1005711414306

Rodrigues, C., & Rodrigues, P. (2019). Brand love matters to Millennials: The relevance of mystery, sensuality and intimacy to neo-luxury brands. *Journal of Product and Brand Management*, *28*(7), 830–848. doi:10.1108/JPBM-04-2018-1842

Salama. (2019, April 23). *Turkey: Modanisa Istanbul modest fashion week*. Retrieved from https://halalfocus.net/turkey-modanisa-istanbul-modest-fashion-week/

Sandikci, O., & Ger, G. (2005). Aesthetics, ethics, and politics of the Turkish headscarf. In S. Kuechler & D. Miller (Eds.), *Clothing as material culture* (pp. 61–83). Berg. doi:10.2752/9780857854056/CLMATCULT0007

Sandikci, O., & Ger, G. (2007). Contemporary Turkish consumptionscape: Polarity and plurality. In J. Prasnikar & A. Cirman (Eds.), *New emerging economies and their culture* (pp. 139–153). Nova Science Pub Inc.

Sembalunrinjanilombok. (2016, December 12). *Sembalun-world's best halal honeymoon destination*. Retrieved from https://sembalunrinjanilombok.wordpress.com/2016/12/12/sembalun-worlds-best-halal-honeymoon-destination/

Sherwood, H. (2016). *Meet Generation M: The young, affluent Muslims changing the world*. Retrieved from https://www.theguardian.com/world/2016/sep/03/meet-generation-m-the-young-affluent-muslims-changing-the-world

Silverstein, M. J., Fiske, N., & Butman, J. (2005). *Trading up: Why consumers want new luxury goods – and how companies create them*. Portfolio.

Smith, K. T. (2012). Longitudinal study of digital marketing strategies targeting Millennials. *Journal of Consumer Marketing*, *29*(2), 86–92. doi:10.1108/07363761211206339

Sofia, N. (2019, February 18). *Modest fashion week: The "halal" showcase for trendy Muslim fashion*. Retrieved from https://www.halalzilla.com/modest-fashion-week-trendy-muslim-fashion/86638

Stanglin, D. (2017, December 20). *Nike begins selling sports hijab for Muslim female athletes*. Retrieved from https://www.usatoday.com/story/news/world/2017/12/20/nike-begins-selling-sports-hijab-muslim-female-athletes/970226001/

Teimourpour, B., & Hanzaee, K. (2011). The impact of culture on luxury consumption behaviour among Iranian consumers. *Journal of Islamic Research*, *2*(3), 309–328. doi:10.1108/17590831111164822

Teimourpour, B., & Hanzaee, K. H. (2014). An analysis of Muslims' luxury market in Iran: Challenges and opportunities. *Journal of Islamic Marketing*, *5*(2), 198–209. doi:10.1108/JIMA-01-2013-0002

The Jakarta Post. (2019, October 20). *More female Muslim travelers choose to travel solo: Report*. Retrieved from https://www.thejakartapost.com/travel/2019/10/19/more-female-muslim-travelers-choose-to-travel-solo-report.html

Tynan, C., McKechnie, S., & Chhuon, C. (2010). Co-creating value for luxury brands. *Journal of Business Research*, *63*(11), 1156–1163. doi:10.1016/j.jbusres.2009.10.012

van Elven, M. (2019, March 26). *Why The Modist has secured investments from Farfetch, Nicola Bulgari and Vaultier7*. Retrieved from https://fashionunited.uk/news/business/why-the-modist-has-secured-investments-from-farfetch-nicola-bulgari-and-vaultier7/2019032642385

Varul, M. Z. (2008). After heroism: Religion versus consumerism. Preliminaries for an investigation of Protestantism and Islam under consumer culture. *Islam & Christian-Muslim Relations*, *19*(2), 237–255. doi:10.1080/09596410801924046

Veblen, T. (1899). *The theory of the leisure class*. Reprint from Penguin.

Vel, K., Captain, A., Al-Abbas, R., & Al-Hashemi, B. (2011). Luxury buying in the United Arab Emirates. *Journal of Business and Behavioural Sciences*, *23*(3), 145–160.

Vickers, J. S., & Renand, F. (2003). The marketing of luxury goods: An exploratory study—Three conceptual dimensions. *The Marketing Review*, *3*(4), 459–478. doi:10.1362/146934703771910071

Vigneron, F., & Johnson, L. W. (1999). A review and a conceptual framework of prestige-seeking consumer behavior. *Academy of Marketing Science Review*, *1*, 1–15.

Vohra, M., Bhalla, G., & Chowdhury, A. (2009). Understanding the Islamic consumer. *Research World,* (February), 40–43.

Wamda. (2019, January 14). *Turkey's Modanisa sells minority stake to Goldman Sachs*. Retrieved from https://www.wamda.com/2019/01/turkeys-modanisa-sells-minority-stake-goldman-sachs

Wang, Z., Deshpande, S., Waller, D. S., & Erdogan, B. Z. (2018). Religion and perceptions of the regulation of controversial advertising. *Journal of International Consumer Marketing*, *30*(1), 29–44. doi:10.1080/08961530.2017.1358681

Wiechman, D. J., Kendall, J. D., & Azarian, M. K. (1996). Islamic law: Myths and realities. *Crime & Justice International Online, 12*(3). Retrieved from http://nur-al-islaam.tripod.com/id250.html

Wilkes, R. E., Burnett, J. J., & Howell, R. D. (1986). On the meaning and measurement of religiosity in consumer research. *Journal of the Academy of Marketing Science*, *14*(1), 47–56. doi:10.1007/BF02722112

Williams, J. P., & Kamaludeen, M. N. (2017). Muslim girl culture and social control in Southeast Asia: Exploring the hijabista and hijabster phenomena. *Crime, Media, Culture*, *13*(2), 199–216. doi:10.1177/1741659016687346

Wong, N. Y., & Ahuvia, A. C. (1998). Personal taste and family face: Luxury consumption in Confucian and Western societies. *Psychology and Marketing*, *15*(5), 423–441. doi:10.1002/(SICI)1520-6793(199808)15:5<423::AID-MAR2>3.0.CO;2-9

Yildiz, N. (2012, April 23). *Lüks araba caiz mi?* Retrieved from https://www.fetvameclisi.com/fetva-luks-araba-caiz-mi-14278.html

Yong, H. H., Hamann, S. L., Borland, R., Fong, G. T., & Omar, M. (2009). Adult smokers' perception of the role of religion and religious leadership on smoking and association with quitting: A comparison between Thai Buddhists and Malaysian Muslims. *Social Science & Medicine*, *69*(7), 1025–1031. doi:10.1016/j.socscimed.2009.07.042 PMID:19695758

Zainuddin, A. A., & Mahdy, Z. A. (2017). The Islamic perspectives of gender-related issues in the management of patients with disorders of sex development. *Archives of Sexual Behavior*, *46*(2), 353–360. doi:10.100710508-016-0754-y PMID:27102604

KEY TERMS AND DEFINITIONS

Fatwa: The adaptation of Qur'anic verses and hadiths to contemporary issues.

Halal: Anything that is permitted by the Shariah (Islamic Law).

Halal Cosmetics: Beauty products that have been manufactured, produced, and composed of ingredients that are halal.

Halal Fashion: Popular and modest style of clothing.

Halal Tourism: Any tourism object or action which is halal.

Haram: Opposite of Halal; anything that is not permitted by the Shariah (Islamic Law).

Islamic Luxury: Luxury products or services produced for Muslims.

Luxury: Something expensive that is pleasant to have but is not necessary.

ENDNOTES

1 Cutler (1992) noted 35 relevant articles out of 7,000 those published between 1959 and 1989.

2 In Turkish "Müslüman" describes an individual who is Muslim and "Süslü" means adorned. This term has gained attraction in media and academia in recent years because of rise of the luxury consumption among religious people in Turkey.

3 The intrinsic/extrinsic religiosity approach is widely used by Islamic scholars. In this approach, intrinsically religious people are assumed to be more sincere while extrinsically religious people are expected to be more goal-oriented (Allport & Ross, 1967). Essoo and Dibb (2004) found that extrinsically religious consumers are trendier, and care more about brand names. In contrast, intrinsically religious consumers were found to be more conservative, less innovative and trendy.

4 This point should be reviewed in light of current social upheavals. As an example, Turkey's culture has long been called collectivist but some researchers discuss the individualistic evolution of such cultures together with the spread of secularization (Ertit, 2018). Further, some explicit examples illustrate that these cultures can be classified as narcissistic (Aytaç, 2019).

5 Na-mahram means men that a woman would be allowed to marry. By contrast, mahram means a member of one's family with whom marriage would be considered haram, or not allowed (Zainuddin & Mahdy, 2017).

6 "And do not approach unlawful sexual intercourse. Indeed, it is ever an immorality and is evil as a way" (Quran, 17-32).

Chapter 11
The Role of Relational Marketing in Specific Contexts of Tourism:
A Luxury Hotel Management Perspective

Bruno Barbosa Sousa
https://orcid.org/0000-0002-8588-2422
Polytechnic Institute of Cávado and Ave, Portugal

Filipa Costa Magalhães
Polytechnic Institute of Cávado and Ave, Portugal

Daniela Braga Soares
University of Minho, Portugal

ABSTRACT

SMM (social media marketing) aims to produce content that users share in their various social media applications in order to increase brand exposure and broaden customer reach. There are numerous marketing techniques to apply in social media in order to involve the customer, some of which have costs and others do not. Digitization was a real challenge for any hotel company, requiring cautious and well-planned action to be successful. In this sense, the nature of social networks demands the adoption of a constructivist perspective, that is, a perspective that involves affirmations of knowledge based on individual and collective experiences. Presently, being present in social networks presents itself as a high value advantage, allowing to expose the brand, product, or idea, at a low cost, to a high audience. This chapter aims to systematize some relational marketing best practices that are identified in the luxury hotel segment in Europe (i.e., communication). Specifically, some examples of relational marketing (hotel/consumer) in terms of communication will be identified and analysed.

DOI: 10.4018/978-1-7998-4369-6.ch011

Copyright © 2021, IGI Global. Copying or distributing in print or electronic forms without written permission of IGI Global is prohibited.

INTRODUCTION

Brand attachment studies have a vital importance for marketing and tourism. There are few empirical studies that explicitly focus on the relation of brand attachment to other concepts, such as brand confidence, brand satisfaction, commitment and brand loyalty (Belaid & Temessek Behi, 2011; Sousa & Magalhães, 2019). For hospitality, such an approach can be very useful when operating within a global environment that sees companies often venture beyond their traditional geographical base into providing services to enhance tourist experience. Tourism, assuming itself as a multifaceted and geographically complex activity, increasingly originates new (and different) market segments with different individual interests (Ferreira & Sousa, 2019). These segments are characterized by the motivations that make them travel and, in turn, by the differentiation of the existing offer (Sousa, Malheiro & Veloso, 2019). Tourism is assumed as one of the major engines with more significant impact on the global development and growth of many economies. Year after year there has been an increase in competition in this sector, although this competition is established between tourism destinations (Becken & Simmons, 2002). Studies in tourism are increasing, although with different points of view and perspectives (Echtner & Jamal, 1997), for example on luxury hotel management perspective (Kimpakorn & Dimmitt, 2007; Mohsin & Lockyer, 2010; Li, Sanders & Frenkel, 2012) and on niche tourism perspective. According to Robinson and Novelli (2005) niche tourism has emerged in recent decades and is strongly associated with niche marketing theory. On the other hand, Dalgic and Leeuw (1994) state that niche marketing has been around for some time, what is new is the increasing diversity of markets, and the advanced technologies that allow new approaches to marketing and the deterioration of large companies and their traditional approaches. Focused marketing and micromarketing are other terms used interchangeably with niche marketing. Although they have similar characteristics, they differ to some extent (Dalgic & Leeuw, 1994). In the specific context of tourism, a review of the relevant literature (Atwal & Williams, 2017) suggests that luxury value involves experiential, symbolic and functional meanings, all connected with the brand. As stated by Veloutsou and Guzmán (2017), reasearch has been given growing attention to the fact that *"brands have moved from being transactional tools to human-like engagement entities, that consumers experience, interact with and cocreate via multiple channels"*. Thus, the main goal of this study is to explore and understand luxury hotels' value and its impact on tourists' attitude and attachment (i.e. relational marketing) specifically through the use of Social Media Marketing approaches. According to Koch (2011), the changing face of luxury holds the power to turn classic luxury brands into losers. A fear of dramatic loss of importance seems to be looming over these brands. Academics and practitioners alike have developed frameworks to help formulate strategies for developing experiential and relational branding strategies.

SMM (Social Media Marketing) goal is to produce content that users share in their various Social Media applications in order to increase brand exposure and broaden customer reach. There are numerous marketing techniques to apply in Social Media in order to involve the customer, some of which have costs and others do not. Digitization was a real challenge for any hotel company, requiring cautious and well-planned action to be successful. In this sense, the nature of social networks demands the adoption of a constructivist perspective, that is, a perspective that involves affirmations of knowledge based on individual and collective experiences. Being active on social networks presents itself as a high value advantage for companies, allowing to expose the brand, product or idea, at a low cost, to a high audience. Thus, this chapter pretends to identify some relational marketing best practices that are identified in the luxury hotel segment in Portugal (i.e. communication). Specifically, some examples of relational marketing (hotel/consumer) in terms of communication on Social Media will be further identified and analysed.

TOURISM SEGMENTATION AND LUXURY TOURISM MANAGEMENT

The study of consumer behavior has gathered particular interest in recent years in multiple contexts, notably with the development of the digital age (e.g. Pinto da Silva et al., 2019). Tourism, as said before, assumes itself as a multifaceted and geographically complex activity that increasingly generates new (and different) market segments with different individual interests. The term niche, in a marketing perspective, refers to two key interrelated ideas: that there is a place in the market for the product, and that there is an audience for that same product. This refers to a specific product capable of keeping up with the needs of a specific market segment (Sousa, Santos & Azevedo, 2020). Therefore, one should not look at the market in a simplistic and homogeneous way, since it represents a group of individuals with specific characteristics and needs (Figure 1).

Figure 1. Mass Tourism and Niche Tourism
Source: Robinson and Novelli (2005, p.9)

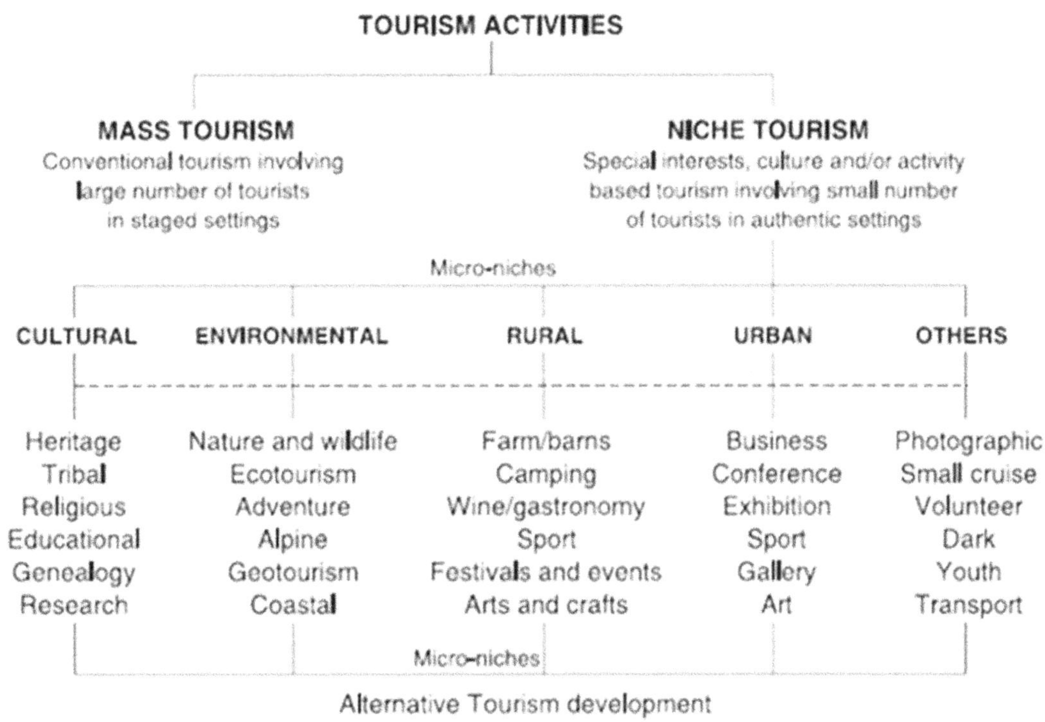

In this way, niche markets emerge as a response to the growing demand for sophisticated and specialized tourism, such as luxury tourism. Current trends show that luxury goes beyond the offer of simple products and services. The new luxury can now also include experiences and authenticity, in addition to tangible material products (Park et al., 2010). Luxury experiences may also be related with aspects of physical and mental wellness. The luxury of feeling and looking well is becoming the ultimate luxury of today's society (Bakker, 2005). According to Park et al. (2010), many luxury hotels and resorts are responding to this trend by offering wellness treatments and healthy meal options. Luxury products, services and experiences are offered today by the travel and tourism, entertainment, health, wellness and recreation, and beauty industries.

A review of the relevant literature in this field (Berthon et al., 2009; Han et al., 2010; Hung et al., 2011; Vigneron and Johnson, 2004) suggests that luxury value involves experiential, symbolic and functional values. Globally, the luxury goods market was estimated at over $220 billion in 2007 (Fortune, 2007). The annual growth rate in sales for the luxury goods market is approximately 7%. These numbers, however, differ depending on the markets alone. Some studies show that consumers perceive luxury products and services in terms of their beauty (79% of respondents), excellence (75%), magic (47%), uniqueness (46%), creativity (36%), sensuality (34%) and exclusiveness (30%) (Kapferer, 1998). Also, luxury products and services have to demonstrate superior quality and perceived prestige to enhance the social status of the buyer (Park et al., 2010). Following a review of literature, the first relationship to be examined in several studies about luxury hotels' functional value and its impact on lodgers' attitude toward luxury hotel. According to Wiedmann et al. (2009), functional value refers to a product' score benefits and quality (Chen & Peng, 2014). According to Narteh, Agbemabiese, Kodua & Braimah (2013), a study by Osman, Hemmington, and Bowie (2009) seem to suggest that transactional marketing based on differentiated products or services which offer value for money for customers could also be successful in building brand loyalty in luxury hotels. Thus, the need for further research on relationship marketing in the first-class and luxury hotel segment, especially in different geographical contexts in our view is very important and timely (Narteh et al., 2013). According to Bakker (2005), over the last 30 years, the concept of the luxury travel and tourism product has moved away from the traditional luxury product, such as five-star resorts and hotels, to a wide variety of exclusive and unique experiences. In this context, Park et al (2010) argues that the most frequently sought luxury expe-riences are unique dining (85% of respond-ents), being pampered in six-star spa resorts (63%) and being able to participate in exclusive and custom-designed experiential tours (50%). One of the most impor-tant and highly sought experiences is the feeling of privacy. Today, tourists want remote hotel suites, secluded tables at restaurants, private villas with a private beach or pool, per-sonal tour guides, trainers and cooking chefs. Many affluent travellers are concerned about privacy and are willing to pay for its high premium Price (Park et al., 2010).

BRAND ATTACHMENT AND LUXURY RELATIONAL MARKETING

According to Sousa & Magalhães (2019), brand attachment studies have a vital importance for marketing and tourism. There are few empirical studies that explicitly focus on the relation of brand attachment to other concepts, such as brand confidence, brand satisfaction, commitment and brand loyalty (Belaid & Temessek Behi, 2011). For hotels, such an approach can be very useful when operating within a global environment that sees organizations often venture beyond their traditional geographical base, but also into providing services to enhance tourist experience. According to Sousa and Magalhães (2019) brand attachment is the strength of the bond connecting the brand with the self. The studies developed are not conclusive regarding the role of affectivity in specific contexts of marketing and tourism management (e.g. luxury hotels). In this chapter, is intended to study the role of consumer's brand relations and to show the links between developments such as trust, satisfaction and loyalty of tourists in specific contexts of luxury tourism (i.e. best practices) through the content analysis. In this way, it was obtained evidence of the importance of the attachment for tourism marketing and hospitality management (in luxury contexts). Emotional behaviors of consumers earn increasingly interest in marketing studies because they provide important results for marketers including, among others, brand loyalty, consumer willingness to pay more expensive product or service and the positive word-of-mouth (Sousa & Magalhães, 2019). One of the most important experts in relationship marketing, Grönroos, a representative of the Nordic school, defines relationship marketing as, establishing, maintaining, enhancing relationships with customers and other partners, at a profit, so that the objectives of the parties involved are met (Sousa & Alves, 2019). Therefore, relationship marketing in luxury tourism can be defined as creating, maintaining and improving the mutually beneficial relations or possible termination of unfavorable relationships of luxury management with stakeholders. This is undertaken to satisfy the stakeholder's need and to seek consensus between guest and luxury management and tourism interests in development of tourism experiences.

In this context, trust has been studied for 30 years in several disciplines and continues to attract the interest of researchers in business-to-business (B2B) marketing (Akrout et al., 2016, p. 269). In relationship marketing, trust has been recognized as an important concept. According to some authors, trust is generally considered a fundamental to develop and maintain a long-term relationship (Sousa & Alves, 2019). This is an important concept in variety of relationships, whether interpersonal or interinstitutional, and consists of a factor to determine relationship quality. Trust is regarded as an essential key to maintaining continuity in the customer–provider relationship and trust likely leads to loyalty, irrespective of the magnitude of the level of the relationship between the company and its customers in specific tourism contexts (Yu et al., 2014). On the other hand, and according to Sousa and Alves (2019), satisfaction is a dimension of relationship quality that represents the emotional relationship (Palmatier et al., 2006) and cannot in the absence of several dimensions (trust, cooperation and commitment). The conceptualization of this term has been much discussed by the various research studies (Hennig-Thurau et al., 2002), but it, generally, describes the post-purchase process and allows consumers to evaluate the performance of a luxury product or service purchased. The literature highlights that satisfaction tends to favour the development of behavioural loyalty. These results are particularly evident in tourism contexts, as the example of the importance of satisfaction in revisiting or recommendation family or friends (Bigné et al., 2005; Prayag, 2008; Alves et al., 2020). Also, something that has been defended over the years is the urgent need to look at the challenges that brands, from every sector, face on the online environment due to its everchanging characteristics (Rowley, 2004). In fact, about this subject, Veloutsou and Guzmán (2017) add that *"the development and the speed of change of technology, in particular in social media, is one of the key current difficulties and challenges confronting brands"*.

Communication and Social Networks

The area of communication has become increasingly important over the years in our lives, in society, in companies and organizations, although it has not always been so. Lendrevie et al. (2015) recognize that today's role of communication is totally different given the pressure and strong competition that organizations face, and it plays a unique role in the success of an organization, a brand, a service or product. Prior to the dissemination of intended messages, communication has the function of designing, producing and disseminating them to achieve the intended targets. The choice of communication channels is also a fundamental task for the success of message transmission (Lendrevie et al., 2015). Kotler, Roberto and Lee (2002) consider that in order to develop strategic communication, it is essential to consider two main steps: the creation of messages and the selection of communication channels that best suit the specific case.

The marketer unfolds the message into two components: the message strategy (what one wants to communicate) and the message execution strategy (as it will be communicated) (Kotler & Armstrong, 2001). In the message strategy creation phase, you define what you want to communicate and why it will be communicated. Establishing message objectives, selecting effective delivery, and communicating strategies requires creating a document that will guide message development and media choice (Kotler, Roberto & Lee, 2002). Once the message strategy has been established, efforts now focus on executing it. The goal is to develop communications that capture the attention of the target audience and persuade them to adopt the desired behavior. The task is to consider and choose from a variety of potential communication elements, styles, tones, words and formats (Kotler & Armstrong, 2001). The marketing expert to inform and persuade must shape the message so that it attracts attention and is convincing (Kotler & Roberto, 1992). Thus, in the message execution strategy, it is essential to consider the four communication elements that act as calls for the adoption of the desired behavior: rationale, emotional, morals and nonverbal.

Andreasen (1995) explains that selecting the channels through which the message will be delivered is a difficult decision to make, as channels vary greatly in their ability to be effective and efficient in achieving the goals of the communication program. When selecting channels for promotional strategies, decisions are made by choosing the types of communication channels, selecting specific media vehicles, and determining campaign timing (Kotler, Roberto & Lee, 2002).

The Internet, as a new medium of communication, has brought with it new tools, and the advent of "Web 2.0" has enabled the emergence of other ways of communicating in digital communication, public relations, and relational marketing (Lendrevie et al., 2015). Digital communication encompasses all forms of communication over the Internet, including: website, blogs, portals, social networks, e-mails, e-newsletters. The Internet has gradually shifted its origins as a writing and reading tool, and is entering an increasingly social and participatory phase (Andersen, 2007).

According to Veloutsou and Guzmán (2017) virtual environments provide many opportunities and various contexts for individual and group brand-centric relationships to evolve. Due to brands almost ubiquitous online presence, consumers clearly form relationships with online brands (Veloutsou & Mafe, 2019). Online brand-enabled relationships can flourish in many platforms, including social media, primarily Facebook (where most online brand–enabled relationship research is conducted), but also on Twitter, Pinterest, and Google+, travel sites as TripAdvisor, trading platforms, such as eBay, general company web pages, dedicated brand-community websites and online forums.

Social media gives users the opportunity to interact with site content and other creators, enabling them to engage more with people (Weinreich (2011)). According to Kotler, Kartajaya and Setiawan (2017), social networks are considered "a powerful tool for consumer engagement" and have facilitated interaction between individuals, especially when it requires greater emotional involvement.

In a scenario of technological development, and change in the way people relate to brands, it is essential to adjust the communication strategies of companies that are required to be present in the most varied communication formats to reach the intended targets (Lendrevie et al., 2015).Social networks have already been perceived by companies as a great mechanism to help them reach their marketing goals and goals, especially in aspects such as customer engagement, customer relationship management and communication (Saxena & Khanna, 2013). In different contexts, companies look for ways to introduce social networks into the most diverse aspects of communicating with their customers, whether through interactivity, promotion, facilitating access to information, and even improving customer buying behavior (Zeng & Gerritsen, 2014). In this study we will focus on four extremely successful social networks, such as Facebook, Instagram, Youtube and Twitter. The choice of these stands for its huge popularity worldwide as well as its ability to expand a business (Ferreira & Sousa, 2020). In this context, and according to Ferreira and Sousa (2020), facebook is the most widely used social networking site in the world, allowing businesses to reach many more people and more occurrences than companies using other means such as calls, emails or through meetings / meetings. The Facebook is considered an attractive social network for digital marketing specialists and for online ads. These ads use social networks to connect customers to businesses, thereby creating new opportunities for customers to get to know their brands and products. To attract the attention of customers, digital marketers have commissioned social media platforms to customize their ads in order to have a greater impact on customers, resulting in a new online ad phase after IBM (International Business Machines) to Facebook on May 6, 2015, in an effort to create better ads on the world's largest social network, incorporating Facebook's targeting technology into IBM's services for marketers (Finley, 2015).

METHODOLOGY

The choice of a research approach, whether by qualitative, quantitative or mixed methods, is not only a question of ontological and epistemological orientation, it is also a question of specific research objectives as well as research questions. This research does not seek to test a specific theory, but to find causal explanations, thus not following a deductive path, which usually requires the adoption of a quantitative approach. This study seeks to explore a phenomenon more broadly, so as to be able to provide a broader understanding by describing participants' experiences (Creswell and Creswell, 2017). In this sense, the nature of social networks demands the adoption of a constructivist perspective, that is, a perspective that involves affirmations of knowledge based on individual and collective experiences. The focus of the research needs to shift the researcher's point of view to the participants' point of view, from the numbers to the words, from a form of structured data collection to a less structured one, from specific data to more generalized data (Ferreira & Sousa, 2020). Qualitative research presents four main methods of data collection, according to Marshall and Rossman (2014): individual interviews; focus groups; observation; and review of documents. For this chapter the selected method was the review of documents and social media analysis (content analysis). The flexibility of this approach allows the discovery or elaboration of information that is important to the participants but may not have been considered relevant by the researcher. Based on a qualitative approach, it also aims at analysing the good digital marketing and communication practices in social networks. In this chapter we will describe four luxury hotels with different characteristics, in order to take a more general approach and not focus too much on one type of (luxury) hotel.

CONTENT ANALYSIS (SOCIAL MEDIA ANALYSIS)

Luxury hospitality is one of the facets of tourism where competitiveness depends on the effective management of a set of key elements that customers perceive as superior, unique and prestigious. It is often relational marketing - based on the science of emotions and attachment - that makes it possible for luxury hospitality management to communicate these aspects to their clients and differentiate themselves from the competition. Next, it is applied the content analysis to present some examples of good relational marketing practices in hotels in Portugal, selected from its Social Media platforms.

Example 1 – Torre de Gomariz

Torre de Gomariz Wine and SPA Hotel is located in Portugal, in the Minho region. Considered one of the most luxurious countryside hotels in the world, Torre de Gomariz won the Condé Nast Johansens Award for Excellence 2020 in the category "Best Countryside or Lodge Hotel", for Europe and the Mediterranean. Torre de Gomariz is set in a verdant landscape, defined by the vinneyards and a leafy secular forest. The hotel consists of an emblematic historic building – Torre e Casa de Gomariz – and other newer buildings. The hotel combines history, nature and design in a romantic, sophisticated and elegante setting. In the most classic building, the hotel is made up of the Torre Medieval, which houses the Tower suites, the Solar de Gomariz, the Tower Bar, the Gomariz Restaurant and a vast duster. In the modern wing we find the Camellia Suites (consisting of 10 suites), the SPA, the pool and the Wine Bar.

Figure 2. Torre de Gomariz Wine & Spa Hotel Social Media

The hotel also has a multipurpose room and an audotorium for events. Torre de Gomariz Wine and SPA Hotel is the ideal place to drink wine, dine and relax, while enjoying the surrounding Minho landscapes.

The hotel to make known the services and products that the hotel offers, prices, conditions of access, as well as disseminate photos and videos of the experiences of that guests can enjoy, built a website and make a presence on social networks Facebook and Instagram. This makes it easier to create a close relationship with customers and/or potential customers. Posts made on social networks are characterized by colorful images and/or videos with simple customer-driven messages. The communication on Facebook is marked by the publication of images that promote the best of the hotel (such as the food) (figure 1), the dissemination of photographs taken by the guests themselves and the dissemination of specific campaigns are held to promote the hotel's leisure and wellness programs (figure 2).

Social networks are also used to make the customer aware of special corners, drawing their attention to details that can make all the difference. Through the Facebook comment box, the hotel responds directly to customer comments, creating a closer relationship (figure 3).

Figure 3. Torre de Gomariz Wine & Spa Hotel Customer Comments

Example 2 – Six Senses Douro Valley

Six Senses Douro Valley, a five-star resort located in Portugal, was named by the hotel magazine Gallivanter's Guide «the best resort hotel in Europe». This 19th century manor house is set high on a hill overlooking the vine-covered countryside of the Douro Valley and the river below. The surrounding landscape is considered a World Heritage Site. At the hotel you can enjoy the dreamily-designed and furnished rooms and suites, the expansive spa, fine and wholesome wining and dining and an outdoor pool. Six Senses Douro Valley is present on the social networks Facebook and Instagram where it shares various photos and videos of the products, services, activities and workshops that the hotel offers, and also to make known its history and all the surroundings in which it is inserted. In publications, the hotel interacts with guests by throwing questions and challenges about their experience (figure 4) and responds closely to customer comments.

Figure 4. Six Senses Douro Valley Social Media

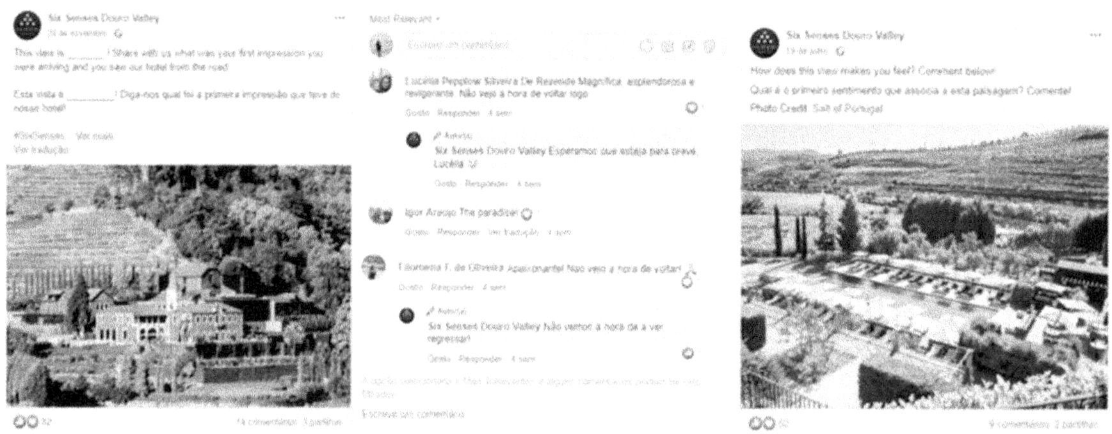

The posts published by the hotel share the moments experienced by guests in the organized workshops, disseminate the photos taken by the clients themselves (#sixsensesdourovalley) and require guest participation through the creation of polls (figure 5).

Example 3 (Ritz Four Seasons Hotel Lisbon*****):

The *Ritz Four Seasons* brand is highly recognized in the luxury hospitality market. In Lisbon, the hotel calls itself the "*most iconic address*" of the city, a reflection of the "*soul of the portuguese culture*". Its style is the result of a mix between modern and vintage with an artistic inspiration. In terms of accommodation, the *Ritz Four Seasons Hotel Lisbon* offers several guest rooms (superior, deluxe and *premier*) and suites (junior suite, central suite, grand suite, imperial suite, foundation suite, residency suite, royal suite and presidential suite) to ensure that it matches the interests and specificities of their target audience.

The hotel is very active when it comes to relational and experiential marketing strategies, specifically through their Social Media. It must be highlighted that on its website, the hotel gives clients the possibility to create an account, where they can login at any time and personalize their preferences while editing their profiles. In fact, when visiting the website, it often shows a pop-up where the hotel invites the client or potential client to sign in to access an exclusive offer. The promise is simple and clear: *"complimentary perks, best rate guaranteed and personalized service when you create your account"*.

The hotel also gives its clients a set of limited offers that might be useful and attractive according to their goals while staying at the hotel, e.g. "*stay longer – third or fourth night for free*"; "*Lisbon with children*"; and other special discounts. These are some examples of loyalty programs which are very common within relational marketing. In terms of Social Media, the hotel tries to keep its SMM strategies

Figure 5. Six Senses Douro Valley Consumer Survey

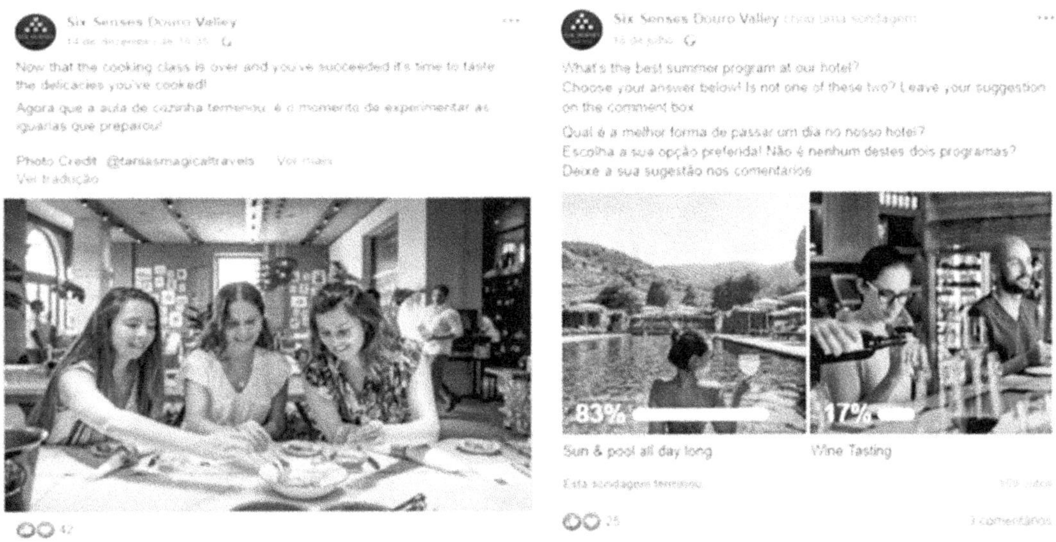

aligned in four different channels – Facebook, Instagram, Twitter and YouTube –, working on delivering creative content, through text, static and/or animated images and video.

On Facebook, the hotel counts with almost 20.000 likes and regular posts focused on a style of proximity and *call-to-action* messages, using very colourful photos (figure 6 and figure 7) and appealing short videos (figure 8) on a clear attempt to draw customers' attention to the details and to the best the hotel has to offer, specially writing about food and desserts. As shown in figure 9, the hotel also uses videos as a form of direct communication with followers, giving them tips and sharing experiences, something that clearly indicates the efforts the hotel puts on maintaining a close relationship with their customers, cherishing them and showing them they're important.

In the reviews and ratings section, Ritz Four Seasons Hotel Lisbon has a classification of 4,7 on 5 with reviewers emphasizing the quality of the customer service, the luxury experience and the sympathy of the staff.

Instagram has a preponderant role in the hotel's communication strategy. In fact, Ritz Four Seasons Hotel Lisbon's Instagram profile counts with more than 28.000 followers and people tend to be very active when it comes to commenting and give likes at the different publications the hotel posts daily. As said before, it's all aligned with the other digital communication channels, but Instagram has the particularity of being a more immediate and closer to reality kind of social network, often motivating unfiltered publications (that's the case with Instagram Stories).

Figure 10 shows an interesting post where the hotel was promoting interaction and engagement with its followers through a giveaway during Christmas season. The publication's scope exceeded expectations. Followers had to put a like on the post and to tag someone to share the prize with. The publication exceeded expectations and the hotel extended the offer to three people (plus three). The winners were randomly drawn. Other Instagram posts can be highlighted such as the ones where the hotel tries to give a call to the portuguese culture and history, referencing its heritage and significant traditions (Figure

Figure 6. Facebook post from October 18h, 2019, highlighting the room view to one of the most iconic places in Lisbon and the excellence of the hotel's breakfast/room service

11). For the portuguese tourists (as a target), it works as a way of enabling certain emotions, like the sense of belonging and even nostalgia. For the international tourists, it promotes curiosity and a desire to get to know new places.

Example 4 (VILA VITA Parc Algarve*****)

VILA VITA Parc Algarve is a 5-star luxury hotel and beach resort located in Porches, on the portuguese Algarve coast. The stylish hotel, which opened to the public in 1990, is a member of 'Leading Hotels of the World' and was named runner-up in the category 'Best Beach Resort in Europe' by the renowned travel magazine 'Geo Saison'. Additionally, it conquered notable prizes such as 'Top #3 Destination Spa Resort in The World', in 2019, by the Condé Nast Traveler as well as 'World's Leading Luxury Green Resort' and 'Europe's Leading Hotel Villas', in 2016, by the World Travel Awards. Other customer excellence and traveller awards were delivered to VILA VITA through the years.

Figure 7. Facebook post from January 6th, 2020, with a call-to-action message inviting guests to identify someone else in the comments section of the publication and focusing on colours and attractiveness

In terms of accommodation, the hotel guarantee that there are rooms available *"in various shapes and sizes, from chic, sea-inspired rooms and suites with ocean-view terraces to spacious whitewashed villas with private pools"* in order to attend the needs and preferences of every customer.

Relational marketing is a visible part of the hotel's management policies. As a matter of fact, Social Media plays an important role for the maintenance of a close and durable customer relationship, so the hotel has a consistent presence in Facebook, Twitter, Instagram, Pinterest and YouTube.

With more than 22.000 likes, its Facebook page is filled with captivating images of everything a customer can find at the hotel, from the food to the surrounding views and even to the most romantic moments and experiences (Figure 12). Keeping a language of proximity and a clear affective connection with its clients, the hotel promotes every aspect of its products, services and events receiving numerous compliments (Figure 13). As shown in Figure 14, VILA VITA Parc also takes to its social networks to announce different interactive, people-oriented, events organized by the hotel itself, such as the Christmas Food Market.

Figure 8. Facebook post from December 9th, 2019, consisting on a short video with sounds and effects about one of the hotel's Christmas trees

Besides its SMM strategy, VILA VITA Parc Algarve also develops other relational marketing techniques, such as a free newsletter sent to its subscribers in order to keep clients up to date on the hotel's latest news, articles, events and special offers. In fact, VILA VITA Parc Algarve tries to develop its experiences as personalized as possible.

CONCLUSIONS, LIMITATIONS AND NEXT STEPS

The present chapter focused on understanding the importance of relational marketing, specifically reflecting on constructs such as brand attachment, in the influence of tourists (as consumers), taking the luxury hospitality management as a context. Thus, it aimed to create a summary of good relational marketing practices in terms of social networks communication strategies observed in the luxury hotel segment in Portugal, in order to contribute to the scientific area under analysis. In general, considering that it was conducted a review of documents and a social media analysis by describing participants' experiences, results showed that social networks can, in fact, represent an important role on intensifying the connection and attachment between the hotels and its customer or potential customers, since it is easier to communicate directly and closely to followers on those platforms.

Figure 9. Facebook post from December 27th, 2019, where one of the hotel's chefs teaches how to do hot chocolate, step by step, through video

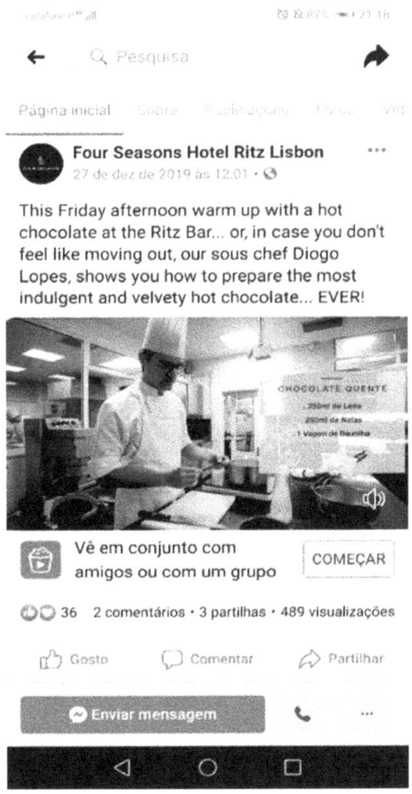

Figure 10. Giveaway promoted by the hotel, in December 2019, that consisted on winning the chance to enjoy an Evening Tea for two people at the hotel

Figure 11. Instagram post from July 26th, 2019, about three portuguese identity elements - 'Pastéis de Nata', 'Belém' Tower and the famous tile -, with a call-to-action message

Figure 12. Facebook posts from October 2019 that keep a focus on drawing attention to the potential of the hotel in terms of the set of experiences guests can enjoy during their stays

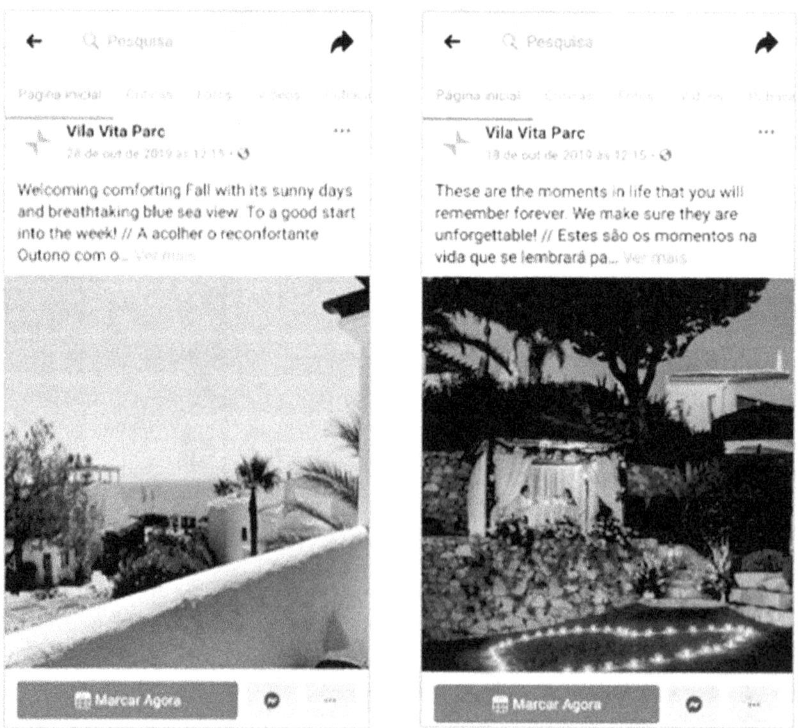

Figure 13. Comments posted on different publications by the followers of the hotel's Facebook page, most of them being real clients

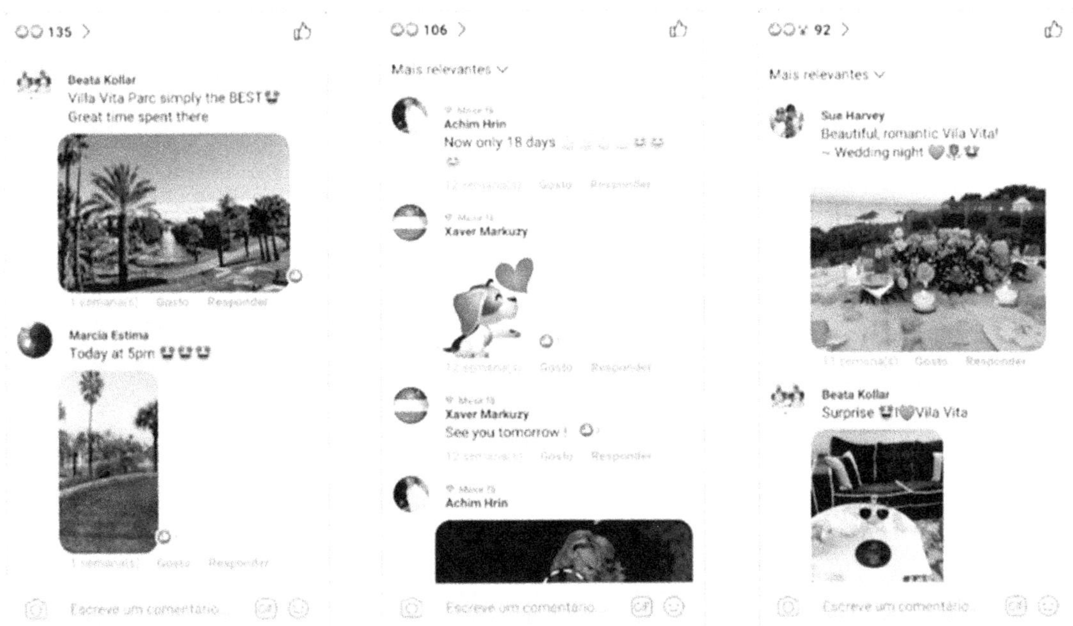

In conclusion, through this study, it was possible to observe that a good and consistent SMM strategy, based on improving brand attachment, satisfaction, commitment and, ultimately, loyalty, have an influence on tourists' behaviour and the extent of its relationship with the luxury hotels. Thus, social networks potential as a relational marketing tool for tourism must continue to be explored. In terms of limitations, while developing this study, it was possible to identify a main limitation regarding the fact that the methodology design selected for the study, considering its characteristics, does not made it possible to generalize the results obtained.

This study stands on a preliminary and exploratory research having a qualitative approach method on which conclusions derive from the researchers' perspective. For future research, it would be interesting to work with the insights of this study and to direct some attention to the limitation identified above trying to overcome it. Therefore, it is suggested a broader application of this study to the reality of luxury hospitality management in Portugal. In fact, it would be appropriate to consider conducting a research that would have into consideration more examples of good relational marketing practices in hotels in order to complement the findings and conclusions of this investigation. To get different perspectives of the subject, there is also, for example, the possibility of conducting this study through other qualitative and detailed methodologies like the development of focus groups or in-depth interviews.

On the other hand, it would be particularly interesting to deepen the investigation by applying a questionnaire and trying to test correlations between variables (quantitative methodology), such as brand attachment and satisfaction, or to develop a structural equations by adopting a SEM (Structural Equation Model) methodology and giving a clear focus to the studies (the hotel's perspective or the tourists/guests perspective), measuring the impact of those relational constructs on consumers'.

Figure 14. Announcement of the Christmas Food Market organized by VILA VITA Parc Algarve in December 2019 (an experience open to the public

REFERENCES

Akrout, H. (2014). Relationship quality in cross-border exchanges: A temporal perspective. *Journal of Business-To-Business Marketing*, *21*(3), 145–169. doi:10.1080/1051712X.2014.952179

Akrout, H., Diallo, M. F., Akrout, W., & Chandon, J.-L. (2016). Affective trust in buyer-seller relationships: A two-dimensional scale. *Journal of Business and Industrial Marketing*, *31*(2), 260–273. doi:10.1108/JBIM-11-2014-0223

Alves, G. M., Sousa, B. M., & Machado, A. (2020). The Role of Digital Marketing and Online Relationship Quality in Social Tourism: A Tourism for All Case Study. In J. Santos & Ó. Silva (Eds.), *Digital Marketing Strategies for Tourism, Hospitality, and Airline Industries* (pp. 49–70). IGI Global. doi:10.4018/978-1-5225-9783-4.ch003

Andersen, P. (2007). *What is Web 2.0?: ideas, technologies and implications for education*. JISC.

Andreasen, A. R. (1995). *Marketing social change: Changing behavior to promote health, social development, and the environment*. Jossey-Bass.

Atwal, G., & Williams, A. (2017). Luxury brand marketing–the experience is everything! In *Advances in luxury brand management* (pp. 43–57). Palgrave Macmillan. doi:10.1007/978-3-319-51127-6_3

Becken, S., Simmons, D. G., & Frampton, C. (2003). Energy use associated with different travel choices. *Tourism Management*, *24*(3), 267–277. doi:10.1016/S0261-5177(02)00066-3

Belaid, S., & Temessek Behi, A. (2011). The role of attachment in building consumer-brand relationships: An empirical investigation in the utilitarian consumption context. *Journal of Product and Brand Management*, *20*(1), 37–47. doi:10.1108/10610421111108003

Berthon, P., Pitt, L., Parent, M., & Berthon, J. P. (2009). Aesthetics and ephemerality: Observing and preserving the luxury brand. *California Management Review*, *52*(1), 45–66. doi:10.1525/cmr.2009.52.1.45

Bigné, J., Andreu, L., & Gnoth, J. (2005). The theme park experience: An analysis of pleasure, arousal and satisfaction. *Tourism Management*, *26*(6), 833–844. doi:10.1016/j.tourman.2004.05.006

Brenner, L., & Aguilar, A. G. (2002). Luxury tourism and regional economic development in Mexico. *The Professional Geographer*, *54*(4), 500–520. doi:10.1111/0033-0124.00346

Chen, A., & Peng, N. (2014). Examining Chinese consumers' luxury hotel staying behavior. *International Journal of Hospitality Management*, *39*, 53–56. doi:10.1016/j.ijhm.2014.01.002

Creswell, J. W., & Creswell, J. D. (2017). *Research design: Qualitative, quantitative, and mixed methods approaches*. Sage publications.

Dalgic, T., & Leeuw, M. (1994). Niche marketing revisited: Concept, applications and some European cases. *European Journal of Marketing*, *28*(4), 39–55. doi:10.1108/03090569410061178

Echtner, C. M., & Jamal, T. B. (1997). The disciplinary dilemma of tourism studies. *Annals of Tourism Research*, *24*(4), 868–883. doi:10.1016/S0160-7383(97)00060-1

Ferreira, J., & Sousa, B. (2020) Experiential Marketing as Leverage for Growth of Creative Tourism: A Co-creative Process. In Advances in Tourism, Technology and Smart Systems. Smart Innovation, Systems and Technologies, (vol 171, pp. 567-577). Springer. doi:10.1007/978-981-15-2024-2_49

Fortune. (2007). Luxury goes mass market. *Fortune Magazine*.

Han, Y. J., Nunes, J. C., & Drèze, X. (2010). Signaling status with luxury goods: The role of brand prominence. *Journal of Marketing*, *74*(4), 15–30. doi:10.1509/jmkg.74.4.015

Hennig-Thurau, T., Gwinner, K. P., & Gremler, D. D. (2002). Understanding relationship marketing outcomes: An integration of relational benefits and relationship quality. *Journal of Service Research*, *4*(3), 230–247. doi:10.1177/1094670502004003006

Hung, K. P., Huiling Chen, A., Peng, N., Hackley, C., Amy Tiwsakul, R., & Chou, C. L. (2011). Antecedents of luxury brand purchase intention. *Journal of Product and Brand Management*, *20*(6), 457–467. doi:10.1108/10610421111166603

Kimpakorn, N., & Dimmitt, N. (2007). Employer branding: The perspective of hotel management in the Thai luxury hotel industry. *Australasian Marketing Journal*, *15*(3), 49.

Koch, K. D. (2011). Luxury Tourism–Does This Market Segment Still Work? In *Trends and issues in global tourism 2011* (pp. 179–185). Springer. doi:10.1007/978-3-642-17767-5_19

Kotler, P., & Armstrong, G. (2001). *Principles of Marketing* (9th ed.). Prentice-Hall.

Kotler, P., Kartajaya, H., & Setiawan, I. (2017). *Marketing 4.0: Mudança do tradicional para o digital*. Conjuntura Actual Editora.

Kotler, P., & Roberto, E. L. (1992). *Marketing Social: Estratégias para alterar o comportamento público*. Campus.

Kotler, P., Roberto, N., & Lee, N. (2002). *Social Marketing: Improving the quality of life*. SAGE Publications.

Lendrevie, J., Lévy, J., Dionísio, P., & Rodrigues, J. V. (2015). *Mercator da Língua Portuguesa: Teoria e Prática do Marketing* (16th ed.). Publicações D. Quixote.

Li, X., Sanders, K., & Frenkel, S. (2012). How leader–member exchange, work engagement and HRM consistency explain Chinese luxury hotel employees' job performance. *International Journal of Hospitality Management*, *31*(4), 1059–1066. doi:10.1016/j.ijhm.2012.01.002

Marshall, C., & Rossman, G. B. (2014). *Designing qualitative research*. Sage publications.

Mohsin, A., & Lockyer, T. (2010). Customer perceptions of service quality in luxury hotels in New Delhi, India: An exploratory study. *International Journal of Contemporary Hospitality Management*, *22*(2), 160–173. doi:10.1108/09596111011018160

Narteh, B., Agbemabiese, G. C., Kodua, P., & Braimah, M. (2013). Relationship marketing and customer loyalty: Evidence from the Ghanaian luxury hotel industry. *Journal of Hospitality Marketing & Management*, *22*(4), 407–436. doi:10.1080/19368623.2012.660564

Palmatier, R. W., Dant, R. P., Grewal, D., & Evans, K. R. (2006). Factors influencing the effectiveness of relationship marketing: A meta-analysis. *Journal of Marketing*, *74*(4), 136–153. doi:10.1509/jmkg.70.4.136

Park, K. S., Reisinger, Y., & Noh, E. H. (2010). Luxury shopping in tourism. *International Journal of Tourism Research*, *12*(2), 164–178. doi:10.1002/jtr.744

Pinto da Silva, F., Brandão, F., & Sousa, B. (2019). Towards socially sustainable Tourism in cities: local community perceptions and development guidelins. *Enlightening Tourism. A Pathmaking Journal*, *9*(2), 168-198.

Prayag, G. (2008). Image, Satisfaction and Loyalty: The Case of Cape Town. Anatolia. *An International Journal of Tourism and Hospitality Research*, *19*(2), 205–224. doi:10.1080/13032917.2008.9687069

Rowley, J. (2004). Online branding. *Online Information Review*, *28*(2), 131–138. doi:10.1108/14684520410531637

Saxena, A., & Khanna, U. (2013). Advertising on social network sites: A structural equation modelling approach. *Vision (Basel)*, *17*(1), 17–25. doi:10.1177/0972262912469560

Sousa, B., & Alves, G. (2019). The role of relationship marketing in behavioural intentions of medical tourism services and guest experiences. *Journal of Hospitality and Tourism Insights*, *2*(3), 224–240. doi:10.1108/JHTI-05-2018-0032

Sousa, B.; Malheiro, A. & Veloso, C. M. (2019). O Marketing Territorial como Contributo para a Segmentação Turística: Modelo conceptual no turismo de shopping. *International Journal of Marketing, Communication and New Media*, 93-116.

Sousa, B. B., & Magalhães, F. C. (2019). An Approach on Attachment in Public Marketing and Higher Education Management Contexts. In C. Machado & J. Davim (Eds.), *Higher Education and the Evolution of Management, Applied Sciences, and Engineering Curricula* (pp. 151–171). IGI Global. doi:10.4018/978-1-5225-7259-6.ch006

Veloutsou, C., & Guzmán, F. (2017). The evolution of brand management thinking over the last 25 years as recorded in the Journal of Product & Brand Management. *Journal of Product and Brand Management*, *26*(1), 2–12. doi:10.1108/JPBM-01-2017-1398

Veloutsou, C., & Mafe, C. R. (2019). *Brands as relationship builders in the virtual world: A bibliometric analysis. Eletronic Commerce Research and Applications, 39*. doi:10.1016/j.elerap.2019.100901

Vigneron, F., & Johnson, L. W. (2004). Measuring perceptions of brand luxury. *Journal of Brand Management*, *11*(6), 484–506. doi:10.1057/palgrave.bm.2540194

Weinreich, N. K. (2011). *Hands-on social marketing: a step-by-step guide to designing change for good* (2nd ed.). SAGE Publications.

Yu, J. Y. (2009). A cross-cultural study on participation intention to medical tourism among Korean, Chinese and Japanese visitors in Korea. *The Korean Academic Society of Tourism*, *33*(3), 187–204.

Zeng, B., & Gerritsen, R. (2014). What do we know about social media in tourism? A review. *Tourism Management Perspectives*, *10*, 27–36. doi:10.1016/j.tmp.2014.01.001

Chapter 12
Luxury Counterfeiting:
Understanding Supply, Demand, and Anti-Counterfeiting Strategies

Nelson Borges Amaral
Ontario Tech University, Canada

ABSTRACT

Luxury counterfeits are appealing to certain shoppers because they provide the signaling value of luxury brands at a lower price. Because of the myriad challenges facing policymakers and law enforcement, the stigma of using counterfeits has been diminishing and counterfeit sales have been on the rise. Research has been conducted on the characteristics of those more likely to purchase counterfeits, and investigations into the social and emotional motives that underlie counterfeit use have also been undertaken. Despite all of this attention, it is still unclear which levers can be utilized by law enforcement to enact demand-side limitations that will reduce the on-going proliferation of counterfeits. The chapter reviews the literature, particularly in marketing, in order to provide some insight to brand managers, policymakers, and law enforcement agencies who are attempting to curb counterfeit consumption.

INTRODUCTION

The dramatic increase in the availability of counterfeit luxury goods has been motivated by returns on investment that are often greater than drug trafficking (IACC, 2015; Blakeney, 2009) with significantly lower levels of risk for the parties involved. This increase has negatively impacted brand owners, consumers, federal, state and local governments, and society as a whole. Despite the myriad negative effects of this industry, it has been noted that little is known about counterfeiting in general and even less is known about counterfeit luxury fashion goods in particular (Wall & Large, 2010). Moreover, the attention that counterfeiting has received is disparate in nature which makes it difficult for policy makers and practitioners to make informed decisions about the best ways to address the various drivers of luxury counterfeiting. The present chapter attempts to address this problem by first providing a thorough review of marketing research which has investigated the topic of luxury counterfeiting. This chapter then

DOI: 10.4018/978-1-7998-4369-6.ch012

Copyright © 2021, IGI Global. Copying or distributing in print or electronic forms without written permission of IGI Global is prohibited.

attempts to spur additional research from marketing practitioners and academics while also providing a base of knowledge that might inform professionals who are interested in the regulation of intellectual property and the formation of legal and policy changes that might curtail the spread of counterfeits.

The chapter begins with a working definition of luxury counterfeits and a summary of the reasons why the key stakeholders (i.e. brand managers, governments, consumers and society more generally) should be motivated to reduce the distribution and demand of counterfeit luxury goods. Next a review of the existing marketing literature on the topic of luxury counterfeits is provided. The chapter ends with proposed areas for future research aimed at addressing four key challenges facing key stakeholders in their attempts to reduce the proliferation of counterfeits and their negative downstream effects.

BACKGROUND

Luxury Branding

In order to understand the effects of luxury counterfeits it is necessary first to understand the unique status of luxury goods. Luxury goods display a different set of dynamics that often result in marketing actions that are directly opposed to standard marketing practices (Kapferer & Bastien, 2009). As a result, luxury branding is "much less understood and less well serviced by the literature" (Wall & Large, 2010, p. 6). It should come as no surprise then that there is no universally agreed upon definition of luxury brands (Wall & Large, 2010).

While there is little agreement on a single, succinct definition of "luxury" (see Wall & Large, 2010 and Wiedmann, Hennigs & Klarmann, 2012), experts appear to agree on some critical characteristics. For example, luxury goods are very high in quality and craftsmanship, they are associated with rarity and exclusivity (real and artifactual) and they are typically related to a history, heritage and tradition that usually goes back to an individual (e.g. Coco Chanel, Thierry Hermès, Ralph Lauren). The innately hedonic nature of luxury brands is strengthened and conveyed through high levels of service and, while quality and craftsmanship ensure functional satisfaction, luxury products provide more important psychological and social needs than other products (see e.g. Lu, 2013 and Amaral & Loken, 2016). The desire to fulfill these social and psychological needs has driven the luxury goods market to over $1 trillion in 2016. These characteristics also create brands that consumers form personal connections with, which further strengthens the usefulness of these products as signals about the social groups with whom the users wish to be affiliated.

The high signaling value, and low accessibility, of luxury products draws consumers to their counterfeits. As a result of lower prices, and more accessible distribution channels, counterfeiting has become a significant problem for luxury producers. Estimates of the annual costs of counterfeiting are as high as $600 billion (International Chamber of Commerce, 2013). This figure includes losses in diverted revenue for luxury goods manufacturers, losses in the labor market, and losses in tax revenues to various levels of government (Cunningham, 2011; Thomas, 2009). While counterfeiting is also a problem for many other sectors (e.g. pharmaceuticals and sporting goods; see Kollmannova, 2012), luxury brands are among the most commonly seized counterfeit items by the U.S. Customs and Border Protection Agency (Cunningham, 2011). At this point it would be informative to provide the definition of luxury counterfeits that will be the focus of this chapter.

Luxury Counterfeits

Broadly defined, counterfeits are unauthorized replicas of products. Policy makers have identified three categories of counterfeits: safety-critical goods, copyright piracy and counterfeiting of luxury goods (Wall & Large, 2010). Counterfeit luxury goods can be described as either deceptive (those that consumers purchase unwittingly), or non-deceptive (products that consumers recognize as replicas). This classification has particularly important implications for policy makers because a key argument against demand-side penalties (i.e. fining or imprisoning consumers) is that there is an intrinsic unfairness in penalizing individuals who are not able to identify a product as a counterfeit (Martinez, 2014). The evidence suggests, however, that consumers can identify luxury products as counterfeits by a number of important features such as their distribution channels, features and lower prices (Frerichs, 2008; Lai & Zaichkowsky, 1999).

Finally, a distinction could also be made between fashion design counterfeiting (design piracy, e.g. copying the pattern and look of a garment) and fashion brand counterfeiting (brand mark piracy, e.g. copying the brand or logo). Trademark laws are particularly important in understanding the value of these two classifications in the United States because trademark laws protect the designer's logo but do not extend protection to the fashion design itself (van Keymeulen & Nash, 2012) which encourages luxury designers to feature their brands prominently on their designs an example of which is provided by figure 1. Unfortunately, because luxury products are considered "useful articles" (Felice, 2011), even the U.S. Copyright Act, which protects creative works such as music, motion pictures and literary works, provides little protection for apparel and other luxury items because they are not considered creative productions (17 U.S.C. §§ 101; 102a [2010]).

LUXURY COUNTERFEITING: A REVIEW OF STAKEHOLDER HARMS

One of the key challenges for policymakers and brand managers is that there is not a clear pattern of victimization, in part because four distinct victim groups exist, each with unique concerns that would often require different action at various levels (i.e. local, national, international). The first two are the focus of the present chapter, consumers and luxury brand managers. The second pair of stakeholders are government agencies and the broader society. A summary of the concerns of these latter groups are beyond the scope of marketing academics, however a brief outline of their concerns is also provided in order to provide a broader context for practitioners and policy makers interested in this topic.

Consequences for Brand Managers and Luxury Brand Equity

Brand managers are greatly affected by the distribution of luxury counterfeits and, as a result, these effects have received the most attention. A key economic argument made to policymakers is that counterfeits cause brand owners financial losses through a direct loss of sales and reputational damage through complaints from dissatisfied customers. A review of the literature provides mixed support for these arguments. For example, research which has examined concurrent users of both genuine and counterfeit products (Triandewi & Tjiptono, 2013; Yoo & Lee, 2012) has shown that past experiences with genuine products reduced intentions to buy counterfeits, whereas previous experiences with counterfeits were not related to intentions to buy genuine products. A more important consequence to managers of luxury brands however, comes from the loss of intellectual property (i.e. designs and brand marks) as an asset (see Spence, 2007). A substantial set of results on this topic provides mixed results in support of this contention. For example, Zaichkowsky and Simpson (1996) found that a positive experience with a counterfeit product reduced evaluations of the genuine product. Also, Wilcox, Kim and Sen (2009) found that viewing counterfeit luxury products reduced consumers' perceptions of the genuine brand. Moreover, Commuri (2009) asked owners of genuine luxury products in India and Thailand how they might react to the proliferation of counterfeit versions of their products. The interviews revealed that consumers would react in one of three ways: flight (abandoning the brand), reclamation (emphasizing the distinctive heritage of the luxury brand), or abrading (preferring products that disguise the brand). The latter strategy is similar to the behavior of so-called Patricians (Han, Nunes & Drèze, 2010) (i.e. wealthy consumers who have a low need for signaling status. Most of these self-reported changes in perceptions showed a negative effect on preferences.

Other research, however, showed potential benefits from counterfeit use. For example, a series of studies with Mexican consumers who own both counterfeit and genuine products of the same brand revealed that they were more attached to the original brands than the counterfeits (Castaño & Perez, 2014). Stronger support for a potentially positive effect of counterfeiting on luxury brands comes from Romani, Gistri and Pace (2012), who demonstrated that the presence of counterfeits in a market increased consumer willingness to pay for the original brand. Additionally, Gabrielli, Grappi and Baghi (2012) found that when consumers were aware of counterfeit versions of a specific product, evaluations on numerous dimensions of the original product were enhanced. Research that relied on sales data (e.g. Qian, 2011) also suggested that counterfeits may have a favorable impact on sales of luxury goods.

Together, the available findings fail to show a consistent effect, or at least suggest a much more complex set of effects of counterfeits on the genuine luxury brands. A recent set of results from Amaral and Loken (2016) demonstrate this complexity. By drawing on previous research on the effects of social identity and social hierarchies they revealed that after viewing counterfeit use, high class consumers rated the genuine luxury brands more negatively if the counterfeit user came from a relatively lower social class. When the observer of the counterfeit was from a lower social class, however, and the counterfeit user was relatively higher in social class, perceptions of the original luxury brand were actually enhanced. It should also be noted that there is a substantial body of evidence in support of null effects of counterfeits on perceptions of the genuine luxury brand (e.g. Gabrielli et al., 2012; Hieke, 2010; Nia & Zaichkowsky, 2000).

Together these findings suggest that luxury counterfeits should be treated as a unique category by counterfeit researchers and policy makers. For example, the simultaneously positive and negative effects of counterfeit use on the original luxury brands run contrary to the standard zero-sum equation that is typically applied to the study of intellectual property which views the gains made by counterfeiters as losses to consumers and/or managers of the original brands.

Consequences for Consumers, Government and Society

Luxury counterfeits can also impact consumers in a number of negative ways. For example, luxury counterfeiting can have negative health consequences, such as the UV protection that consumers expect from the genuine luxury product. Consumers may also experience disappointment, and anger, at being deceived after the purchase of a counterfeit product. Finally, consumers who feel a connection to the brand can also be negatively impacted by the dissemination of counterfeit products if it weakens the symbolic value of their beloved brand.

Governments incur significant costs as a result of the time and effort expended on legislative tactics, however the main cost of counterfeiting to governments comes through the deprivation of sales and employment tax revenue. For example, Thomas (2009) reported that, in the United States alone, illegal counterfeits have resulted in $200 billion lost in sales and the loss of 750,000 domestic jobs. Data provided by the Anti-Counterfeiting Group (2010) estimates that Europe is deprived of over €7,000,000 in tax revenue each year.

A more insidious cost to governments comes from evidence that the revenue generated by counterfeit luxury goods are often tied to organized crime and the funding of terrorist organizations (e.g. Giambarrese, 2010; U.S. Chamber of Commerce, 2017). Despite these relationships, some U.S. laws allow counterfeit producers to circumvent trademark laws by engaging in the practice of finishing (Thomas, 2009) - distributors bring nearly completed counterfeit products into the United States (e.g. without any logos) and complete the product in the country to avoid seizures at the border.

Demand-side policies are also weak; U.S. Customs allows each traveler entering the country to bring one counterfeit product per category without penalty (USCBC, 2002). In addition to the ties to organized crime and terrorist organizations, counterfeits place additional burdens on society. For example, by profiting through the replication of innovative and creative works, the incentive to produce additional innovative and creative products is reduced. The counterfeit industry also causes potential damage to the environment as a result of the hidden production of these products and, relatedly, there are unwanted consequences from the unregulated manufacturing which might encourage worker exploitation, child labor and dangerous work environments.

To better address the myriad concerns of these stakeholders an understanding of the consumer motivations and downstream consequences of counterfeit use is helpful. In the next section a brief review of the factors that influence attitudes about counterfeits, such as individual differences and motivational factors (i.e. emotional, social, product-related), as well as product attributes that drive counterfeit demand are presented. The section concludes with a review of the research on ethical attitudes towards counterfeit use.

FACTORS ASSOCIATED WITH THE SUPPLY AND DEMAND OF COUNTERFEITING

Individual Differences

Perhaps the most important category of individual differences, because of the important role that social identity plays in the motivation to display luxury brands, is related to the social psychological motivations to purchase and display luxury counterfeit goods. For example, a number of findings have provided converging support for a significant role in materialism a motivating factor (e.g. Alsaid & Saleh, 2019; Wiedmann, Hennigs & Klarmann, 2012). Taormino and Chong (2010) also identified self-monitoring as an important individual difference and one that is related to the role of brand symbolism. They revealed that high self-monitors are more likely to purchase counterfeit luxury goods, and that these consumers were also more likely to purchase genuine versions of the products. The same series of studies also identified perfectionism as being related with lower purchase intentions of counterfeits. Finally, Penz and Stottinger (2005) demonstrated that counterfeit options were less attractive to consumers if they were in a product category in which those consumers reported high levels of personal involvement because it diminished the notion that purchasing counterfeits made them appear more savvy. Their findings also suggested that high involvement was associated with a higher fear of social embarrassment - a fear that their social group might identify their product as a counterfeit. These are useful findings for brand managers because they suggests that consumers who are loyal to, or even fans of a particular brand, are likely to view counterfeiting negatively.

A second category of individual differences, factors related to socioeconomic status, has also received a great deal of attention as an important consideration in understanding luxury counterfeit consumption (e.g. Coleman, 1983; Mandel, Petrova & Cialdini, 2006; Amaral et al., 2016). For the most part, however, relationships between these socioeconomic factors and counterfeit purchases have not provided clear relationships. For example, while some evidence suggests that lower income consumers, presumably those who can least afford genuine luxury products, are more likely to purchase counterfeit goods (e.g. Ang et al., 2001; Sharma & Chan, 2011), other results failed to find a consistent relationship (Vida, 2007) and many revealed that income had no influence at all (e.g. Bian & Moutinho, 2011; Cheung & Pendergast, 2006). The effect of education on counterfeit consumption is also inconclusive, with most of the evidence suggesting that there is no relationship between education and counterfeit consumption (e.g. Bian & Moutinho, 2009; 2011; Yoo & Lee, 2012) while other findings provided discrepant results. For example, two separate sets of results revealed that higher education resulted in less counterfeit consumption (Sharma & Chan, 2011; Wee, Tan & Cheok, 1995), but another set of results (Phau, Prendergast & Cheun, 2001) provided evidence to the contrary.

A third factor that has received a great deal of attention are demographic characteristics. While research seems to provide converging support for the notion that younger consumers are more likely to purchase counterfeits (e.g. Phau, Prendergast & Cheun, 2001; Tom et al., 1998; Wee, Tan & Cheok, 1995), the evidence for the role of gender is mixed. Most of the evidence fails to support any gender differences at all (e.g. Bian & Moutinho, 2009, 2011; Tom et al., 1998). Cheung and Prendergast (2006), however, found that males were less likely to purchase counterfeits than females. In contrast, others have found that counterfeit perceptions (Carpenter & Lear, 2011) and purchase intentions (e.g. Ang et al., 2001; Bian & Veloutsou, 2007; Sharma & Chan, 2011) are higher among men than women.

Affective Motivational Factors

A commonly used tactic by government agencies and luxury brand managers is to induce shame or embarrassment in order to deter counterfeit consumption, as illustrated by appendix A. These emotional drivers were alluded to in the previous section. Penz and Stöttinger (2012), however, investigated these directly through the use of focus groups. They found a distinction should be made between the emotions that drive the consumption of counterfeits, and those that drive the pursuit of counterfeits. While a great deal of research has investigated the emotions associated with the counterfeit shopping experience (e.g. Eisend & Schuchert-Güler, 2006; Gentry, Putrevu & Shultz, 2006), Penz and Stöttinger (2012) point out that these emotions are far more transient and less enduring than those of ownership.

The effect of ownership, because they are motivated by ego focused emotions, are more enduring (e.g. consumers' motivation to impress important others). Previous research clearly demonstrates that the strongest of these emotions are negative. For example, the fear of being detected as a counterfeit user can invoke a great deal of shame (e.g. Wee, Tan & Cheok, 1995; Bian & Moutinho, 2009). Koklik (2011) provides interesting corroboration for the role of these perceived social risks through a survey of 10,000 Slovenian consumers; the author demonstrated that levels of perceived social and legal risks were the strongest determinants of intentions to buy.

Together, this work suggests that reminding consumers of the potential negative emotions they may experience might deter them from purchasing counterfeits. Importantly, however, previous research provides an important caveat to this recommendation. Specifically, Stottinger and Penz (2015) found that only one of three types of consumers were influenced by these negative emotions, they called this group "guardians of authenticity." These consumers purchased counterfeits because they saw themselves as thrill seekers and described the purchase of counterfeits as fun and exciting. They reported feeling guilt and shame about their counterfeit ownership and recognized the inferior quality and ethical problems associated with counterfeiting. The other two groups, however, were driven by very different motives. The "nonchalant hedonist" thought counterfeits were fun to buy and wear and justified ownership by the belief that "everybody is doing it." As a result, these individuals felt very little shame or embarrassment. The third group, the "cautious cherry picker" was driven by utilitarian motives (e.g. lower prices) and also felt little shame as a result of fulfilling the goal of being a savvy shopper.

Social Motivational Factors

The importance of social shame and sanctions, demonstrated above, highlights the importance of the social meanings that luxury brands carry and how this motivates individuals to purchase counterfeits. The importance of these social motivations has been provided by a diverse set of results. For example, results have demonstrated that the desire to be viewed as part of the upper-class (Barnett, 2005), and more generally, the desire to be viewed positively by others (e.g. Phau & Teah, 2009; Penz & Stöttinger, 2005) are strong influencers. Related evidence has demonstrated that individuals who possess more stable self identities, and higher levels of self-esteem, are more likely to choose genuine luxury products over counterfeit versions (e.g. Wee, Soo-Jiuan & Cheok, 1995; Yoo & Lee, 2012). A particularly important example of the role of symbolic expression was demonstrated by Budiman and Wijaya (2014) who interviewed executive women in Yogyakarta-Indonesia, a location where counterfeit use was regarded as highly unethical. The results revealed that the intention to buy counterfeits was significantly lower when subjective norms were more important. The authors suggested that this result was a consequence of individuals feeling compelled to adhere to social rules and expectations.

Another indication of the importance of social pressure on counterfeit consumption was evident in a survey of Indian and Taiwanese counterfeit consumers that investigated the role of word-of-mouth (WOM) on counterfeit purchases (Lan et al., 2012). While WOM was instrumental in helping customers locate counterfeit dealers, what was more interesting was that the influence of WOM on purchase intentions was only evident when strong ties were involved (e.g. with family members and close friends).

Finally, the most intriguing research on the importance of social drivers of counterfeit consumption has been provided by Wilcox, Kim and Sen (2009). Their research demonstrated that attitudes toward luxury brands could be influenced by important elements of the marketing mix (e.g. product design, advertising). More to the point, the authors discovered that socially motivated, image-conscious consumers (i.e. those for whom luxury brands served a more social-adjustive, as opposed to a more value-expressive, role) were more motivated to purchase counterfeits with a prominent logo. In other words, among consumers for whom the counterfeit product played a predominantly social-adjustive role, there was a greater propensity to favor a luxury product with a more prominent brand.

Manufacturer and Product Factors

In addition to consumer-level factors, a number of product-level factors have been found to affect perceptions about, and intentions to buy, counterfeit luxury products. The role of price has received the most attention (e.g. Hansen & Moller, 2017; Penz & Stottinger, 2015; Harvey & Walls, 2003; Wee, Tan & Cheock, 1995). A key driver of counterfeit consumption is the ability to acquire the exclusive and prestigious symbolism associated with the luxury brand at a fraction of the price. Moreover, while it is generally acknowledged that counterfeits are lower in quality and durability (e.g. Bian & Veloutsou, 2007; Phau & Teah, 2009), perceived differences in quality between counterfeit and genuine luxury products have narrowed (Penz & Stöttinger, 2008b). As a result, consumers often justify the purchase of counterfeits by arguing that they are a good value (e.g. Ang et al., 2001; Wang et al., 2005). In one of the earliest studies on the role of price on counterfeit consumption, Bloch, Bush and Campbell (1993) found that the significantly lower price of luxury counterfeits could cause a large proportion of consumers to willingly purchase a counterfeit product over the genuine article. Interestingly, Han, Nunes and Drèze (2010) found that the price of various counterfeit luxury handbags mirrored those of the genuine goods: the counterfeit versions of more expensive items were priced higher. More importantly, consumers may be implicitly aware of the fact that a lower price product is not manufactured in the same conditions as a higher price product. This knowledge should be used by policymakers to remind consumers of the poor working conditions and environmental consequences that are likely to result from the production of these relatively lower quality products, as well as the potential health risks that may be incurred by the counterfeit consumer.

While price is the most investigated factor, other important product-level factors have been identified that affect consumer attitudes toward counterfeit products. For example, Wee, Ta and Cheok (1995) explored the role of eight non-price factors and revealed that only perceived quality and product appearance significantly influenced counterfeit perceptions; as expected, perceptions were more positive when quality was higher and appearance more appealing.

Two manufacturer characteristics have also been evaluated: corporate citizenship and country of origin. Research on corporate citizenship suggests that luxury brands can protect themselves from the negative effects of counterfeits by improving consumer perceptions about their role as responsible corporate citizens (Poddar et al., 2012). The results suggested that the strong motivating effects of lower prices to purchase counterfeit products can be counteracted when a luxury brand is associated with a higher degree of corporate citizenship. The importance of country of origin effects was revealed by data collected from American and Mexican consumers who were asked to describe their attitudes about counterfeits produced in one of three countries: China, Brazil, and the United States (Chapa, 2006). Their views were most positive about U.S.-made counterfeits, presumably as a result of higher perceived quality by U.S. manufacturers.

Finally, it should be noted that one related set of results also suggests that brand prominence may play a role in counterfeit consumption. Specifically, Han, Nunes, and Drèze (2010) found that the prominence of the brand name on luxury products was less important to consumers who were more established in high social positions. Relative newcomers to the higher social class, however, preferred products with more blatant brand signals. While this research focused on genuine luxury products, it supports the role of the brand mark as a key driver of counterfeit consumption. This helps to explain why counterfeiters make products that prominently display the luxury brand and why other research has found that these products are especially attractive to consumers for whom the counterfeit product plays a social role

(Stöttinger & Penz, 2015; Wilcox et al., 2009). As a consequence, the growing popularity of products with more subtle (or no) display of brand marks (Lutz, 2015) could help to make counterfeit goods less appealing by reducing the symbolic value of those products.

The Ethics of Counterfeit Consumption

The factor that has received the most attention in the counterfeit literature, by a sizable margin, is that of ethics. Unfortunately, consistent with the factors that have been included in the previous sections, there is still little clarity about the role of ethics in counterfeit consumption. Lai and Zaichkowsky (1999) found that consumers understand the unethical nature of counterfeit production, but that they do not perceive the purchase of those products as unethical. While other findings have suggested that consumers do believe that purchasing counterfeits is, in fact, unethical (Jiang et al., 2019; Lan et al., 2012). Gender differences have also been revealed. In contrast with previous research, which found that females had less favorable attitudes towards counterfeits (e.g. Ang et al., 2001; Cheung & Predergast, 2006), Carpenter and Lear (2011) found that females were less likely to see the sale of counterfeits as a crime. This may be the result of moral reasoning—females, for whom luxury fashion might play more important roles in fulfilling social goals (Wang & Griskevicius, 2014), might be motivated to downplay the unethical aspects of counterfeit use in order to feel more comfortable with the purchase and display of counterfeits (e.g. Mazar, Amir & Ariely, 2008). Additional evidence of this role of moral reasoning is provided by Wang, Stoner, and John (2019) and by Kim, Kim & Park (2012). In four experiments, the latter authors found that consumers were more likely to purchase counterfeits when cognitive resources were constrained, reducing their ability to think about the decision.

While ethical considerations typically have some effect on consumers' intention to purchase (e.g. Phau & Teah, 2009), this is not the case for all consumers. Norum and Cuno (2011) found that personal beliefs about the ethicality of counterfeiting failed to affect the purchase of counterfeit goods. Wilcox, Kim and Sen (2009) also found an important moderator which helped to explain the complex role of morality. In their research, the relationship between moral beliefs and brand preferences was only present when the consumers' brand attitudes served a value-expressive function (i.e. their product choice was associated with a need to communicate their core values and beliefs to others).

Finally, Gino, Norton and Ariely (2010) found that the perceived immorality of counterfeit use can also have important social consequences. Specifically, the researchers found that people who wear counterfeits, whether by choice (study 1) or by random assignment (study 2), behave less ethically, and view the behavior of others as less ethical. Importantly, the authors discovered that these effects were mediated by a reduction in feelings of authenticity, which were presumably a result of wearing the counterfeit (i.e. "fake") product.

TACTICS AND STRATEGIES AIMED AT ADDRESSING FOUR KEY CHALLENGES

Anti-counterfeiting agents (i.e. brand managers, policy makers, government and criminal agencies) face four categories of challenges when attempting to reduce the demand or supply of luxury counterfeit goods. This section summarizes a number of potential tactics and strategies that have been proposed to address each of the four categories of challenges.

Low Perceived Levels of Societal Harm

The first is the relative indifference that society exhibits towards luxury counterfeiting. There has been little political pressure to enact harsher penalties for the production and distribution of counterfeits. Ironically, the limited efforts to penalize producers and distributors, along with a failure to educate consumers about, for example, ties between counterfeiting and terrorist organizations, may facilitate the notion that counterfeiting is a victimless crime (Martinez 2014). There is ample evidence, for example, to support the role of public policy in influencing the perceived morality of consumption in several domains (Loureiro, et al., 2016). Moreover, as this chapter has demonstrated, ethical attitudes towards the production, distribution, and purchase of counterfeit goods vary greatly as a result of both cultural and individual personality factors (a recent framework by Sharma and Chan (2017), nicely summarizes these factors. This is due in part to the lower perceived harm inflicted by luxury goods when compared, for example, to pharmaceuticals or electrical components. A stronger case needs to be made about the costs inflicted on workers and the environment, and the evidence for ties between counterfeit luxury goods and criminal elements such as terrorist groups and organized crime. For example, the US House International Relations Committee (HIRC, 2003) claimed that the FBI had strong evidence to support a link between counterfeit textiles and the funds provided to the parties responsible for the 1993 attacks on the World Trade Centre (ICC, 2015: Kent, 2011).

Online Distribution of Counterfeit Luxury Goods

A second challenge is the growth of online counterfeit sales. In particular, the global and anonymous nature of the Internet, has made civil and criminal action even more difficult (e.g. Kopp & Suter, 2000). For example, imposing penalties on consumers becomes more difficult when these consumers are purchasing products without closely inspecting them. Moreover, new technologies like 3-D printers and new platforms like the dark Web are likely to make counterfeiting more accessible to more people. The important role of the Internet has recently attracted the attention of academics who found that lower prices (Radón, 2012) and factors like trust and competency (Key et al., 2013) increase online counterfeit purchases. Policy makers, however, are struggling with the challenge of eliminating traditional (i.e. on the ground) distribution activities and, as a result, have only recently started to address the problems that have arisen from Internet distribution. The lack of cooperation from platforms like EBay and Amazon have complicated the issue further, although a recent announcement by Amazon (Dastin 2020) provides some optimism. After implementing three new high tech tools to reduce counterfeit sales, Amazon disclosed that it would be sharing more data with law enforcement agencies in order to deter counterfeiters from using their platform.

Poor Coordination between Law Enforcement Agencies and Legislative Bodies

The third, and perhaps most significant challenge facing policymakers is that criminal provisions have developed in a very piecemeal fashion, a common characteristic of marketing regulations (Petty, 2005). As a result, policies vary greatly from one country to another (Mittelstaedt & Mittelstaedt, 1997). In most countries, anti-counterfeiting legislation is very weak and in many nations nonexistent. In the United States, for example, trademark counterfeiting is considered to be the most serious form of trademark infringement (Colman, 2015). The Lanham Act provides owners of a registered mark with the ability to recover monetary damages against producers and distributors of counterfeits. However, the Lanham Act does not extend to the individuals purchasing the counterfeits (Prager, 1996) and still places the burden of action on luxury brand managers.

However, even in countries where severe penalties exist, such as Italy, where the purchase of counterfeit luxury goods can result in fines of up to €2,000,000 and ten years in prison (repeat offenders could face up to a €5,000,000 fine and twenty years in prison), enforcement of those laws has been inconsistent (Chaudhry & Walsh, 1996). Moreover, while countries like France and Italy have enacted harsh penalties, the penalties vary greatly between nations, although attempts have been made to harmonize legislation across borders in the European Union (e.g. Wall & Large, 2010). Additionally, the piecemeal fashion that has been used to this point is particularly problematic in addressing the issue of counterfeiting because the industry has various components (i.e. manufacturing, transportation, sales) that are typically carried out by different parties, usually in different countries, making it very difficult for any individual law enforcement organization to effectively address the problem. Evidence for the potential effectiveness of a more coordinated effort exists in the newly formed Quality Brands Protection Committee (GACG 2019), an organization that began in China but now includes 23 countries and numerous luxury brands. In addition to the increase in cooperation between luxury producers, law enforcement activity has strategically focused their efforts at the point of sales and distribution, and some evidence suggests that this may be the most effective method because the strongest relationships between the counterfeiting industry and organized crime exist at the local level (ACG, 2010).

Stronger demand side penalties, such as those introduced in Italy and France, should be considered in the United States. Enacting laws that are targeted at stemming demand for counterfeits would not be unprecedented, and there is evidence to suggest that it could be effective. For example, U.S. law.142 made it illegal to download music through file sharing programs. A subsequent report revealed that the law increased consumer awareness of the risks of prosecution when engaging in piracy, which in turn increased perceptions that it was unethical and illegal (ICC WBO 5, 2009). Similar initiatives, coupled with an extensive education program, have been implemented by the motion pictures industry with similar results (Billboard, 2004). These two cases suggest that policies that target demand can be effective but, as the present review demonstrates, these laws need to be accompanied by a communication program that will change consumers' attitudes about counterfeits by informing them of the harms and financial costs of counterfeit activity. This is an important word of caution to lawmakers, like a New York Councilmember who proposed a bill that would impose a fine of up to $1000, and up to a year of imprisonment, to any consumer who purchased a product that he or she "knows, or should have known" was a counterfeit product (Int. No. 544 § 10-902, 2013).

Importantly, these policies and regulations often force brand managers to pursue mostly civil remedies. In a rare case in which significant penalties were assessed, Coach was awarded $257 million against online counterfeiters (Pearson, 2012). Unfortunately, the disparate and international nature of luxury counterfeiting makes such awards rare. As a result, these civil actions consume a great deal of resources, and often result in a net loss for the plaintiffs. Moreover, even when litigation leads to financial gains this strategy tends to result in only temporary losses to counterfeit producers while providing little in the way of permanent solutions.

Limitations on Evidence for the Effectiveness of Tactics and Strategies

Finally, the fourth challenge that is clear from the present review is the fact that despite the attention that counterfeits have received from academics and policy experts, our understanding of the effectiveness of various efforts at reducing counterfeit consumption is still lacking; table 1 summarizes the tactics and strategies that have been proposed. An important quality of the existing research that limits our current understanding of the problem is that most of the evidence provided is based on self-reports and main effects (Miyazaki, Rodriguez & Langenderfer, 2009). Therefore, a great deal more knowledge is needed about the various interactions between societal and psychological drivers of counterfeit consumption and the effectiveness of various tactics in reducing demand.

As an example of the need for more research on anti-counterfeit tactical effectiveness, France and Italy have been trying to address the demand for counterfeits by making such purchases illegal. For example, Article 474 of the Italian Criminal Code makes it illegal for consumers to bring counterfeit products into the country and in France, consumers must possess "documents evidencing the genuine origin" of luxury products being brought into the country (Douanes & Droits Indirects, 2009). Although a significant reduction in counterfeit consumption would be expected by such laws, it would be helpful to learn what other consequences such demand regulations might have. For example, would the consumption of these counterfeits become less acceptable?, do such laws increase the social stigma of counterfeit ownership?, and how would suppliers change their behavior in response to such laws? These are all important questions that remain unanswered. Moreover, most consumers are still not aware of the role that criminal organizations play in the production and distribution of counterfeit goods (UNODC, 2014). To raise awareness, the United Nations Office of Drugs and Crime recently launched a campaign to inform consumers of the connection between counterfeit products and organized crime; no data has been provided for the effectiveness of the campaign.

One group of consumers who may provide particularly useful insight on the effectiveness of these kinds of campaigns are those who concurrently own authentic and counterfeit versions of luxury products. This behavior provides evidence to suggest that, for some consumers, the "product" is the brand. For luxury products, the brand can symbolize more than other tangible product attributes, causing consumers to begin to view the brand as a product that can be purchased and consumed (e.g. Gentry et al., 2001). A greater understanding of this behavior and the role of the brand in counterfeit consumption would be helpful to policymakers and luxury manufacturers. For example, it is likely a lack of understanding of this role of brands that has caused legislators to permit the practice of finishing (Thomas, 2009) in the United States. On a related note, the most recent recession provided evidence to suggest that both the symbolic value of brands and the financial constraints associated with poor economic conditions motivate consumers to purchase counterfeits (Clifford, 2010) which raises new questions. For example, do consumers prefer louder brand signals from counterfeits when they feel more insecure about the economy, or about their personal financial situation? Work by Nunes, Drèze and Han (2011) found that products introduced during the 2008 recession displayed the brand far more prominently than products withdrawn from the market during that same time period. Future research should offer an explanation as to how consumers and luxury brand managers, respond to shifts in the economy, and the implications for counterfeit demand.

WHERE DO WE GO FROM HERE? POLICY IMPLICATIONS & FUTURE RESEARCH

Consumer-focused	
Make frequent changes to product design	v
Packaging with aspects that are hard to replicate	0
Emphasize warranties and after-sales service	0
Reduce prices on genuine goods	x
Emphasize benefits of genuine goods (e.g. quality)	0
Inform about the harmful effects of counterfeits	vx
Incorporate product features that are hard to replicate	0
Promote corporate citizenship efforts	0
Promote ties to organized crime and terrorism	0

Distribution-focused	
Educate channel members about counterfeits	v
Have distributors notify manufacturers or counterfeits	v
Provide financial incentives to reject counterfeits	v
Use tracking technology (e.g. RFID tags)	0
Monitor and investigate intermediaries	vx
Centralize distribution network	0

Counterfeiter-focused	
Create enforcement team	0
Use surveillance (e.g. private investigators)	v
Warn counterfeiters of legal action	0
Aggressively cut prices	v
Use covert actions	0
Reduce brand prominence on authentic luxury goods	0
Litigate counterfeit manufacturers, distributors, retailers	vx

Government-focused
Register trademarks and patents
Establish relationships with law enforcement
Establish relationships with customs officials
Injunctions against counterfeit goods
Lobby for legal protection (e.g. U.S. trade dress laws)
Seek assistance from tax authorities
Lobby for enforcement of laws

Cooperative Efforts
Monitor policy groups (e.g. WIPO)
Participate in IACC, CACN etc.
Use the TRIPS and WTO
Participate in multilateral groups
Lobby for stronger global IPR protections
Obtain support from local law enforcement
Coordinate with ISP providers (ID & shut down websites)

Internal (Corporate) focused
Educate employees about copycats
Acquire counterfeiters
Establish productions facilities in lower cost countries
Develop an anti-counterfeiting policy
Train employees to identify counterfeits

v denotes efficacy is supported; x efficacy not supported by literature 0 denotes success has not been tested empirically

As this chapter has demonstrated, marketing researchers have investigated the topic of counterfeiting from various cultural perspectives, but only rarely have different cultures been compared directly (see exceptions: Li, Ghaffari & Su, 2020; Bian & Veloutsou, 2007; Chan & Amaral, 2014). Moreover, what little research has been conducted has done little to provide consistent or actionable evidence. For example, research has suggested that Chinese consumers are more likely than Western (i.e. American) consumers to purchase counterfeits (Harvey & Walls, 2003), yet Bian and Veloutsou (2007) have found that Chinese consumers value counterfeits less than Westerners. Results from the latter survey also found that, compared to Chinese consumers, British consumers view counterfeit consumption as a riskier behavior. More importantly, the earlier call for cross-border, international cooperation by law enforcement is supported by this cross-cultural research, as well as historical international conflicts. For example, in 1996 the United States and China threatened sanctions against each other over a claim by the United States that China was not adequately policing counterfeits protected by U.S. copyright laws (Mittelstaedt & Mittelstaedt, 1997).

Relatedly, the greater acceptance and expertise in manufacturing counterfeit products in many East Asian countries has blurred the lines between authentic and “fake” luxury products through the production of very high-quality counterfeits. This is illustrated by the complex classification system of counterfeits in that part of the world. For example, in China and South Korea, counterfeit merchants often classify counterfeit products by quality levels: "A" (low), "AA" (high) and "SA" (superior), the latter group costing several hundred dollars. Despite this classification, researchers have treated counterfeits as a discrete category (i.e. fake or real). A more nuanced approach is needed to help understand, for example, cultural differences in counterfeit perceptions. Policy makers and brand managers must account for these differences because they have clear implications for the ways that stakeholders should communicate with different consumer groups about the value of genuine luxury products and the risks associated with counterfeit consumption.

The present chapter suggests that a more permanent solution can be achieved. For example, it seems clear that the negative emotions of ownership are more enduring than those of the experience and pursuit of counterfeits. The evidence also supports an important role for social pressures in counterfeit consumption and that young female consumers are more likely to purchase luxury counterfeit goods. This suggests that policymakers should target this group of consumers and increase the social stigma of counterfeit ownership. In the current geopolitical environment, making a direct link between counterfeit sales and the funding of recent terrorist activities could be very effective in accomplishing this goal. However, it is also clear that the current supply-side legislative environment (e.g. permitting counterfeit producers to "finish" products after crossing the border) and permissive demand-side regulations (e.g. allowing consumers to bring counterfeit goods into the United States) also needs to be addressed. Otherwise, the effectiveness of any public relations campaign will be limited by the signal that week legislation sends – the effectiveness of concurrent criminal and instructional initiatives has already been illustrated (e.g. the music and motion pictures industry).

CONCLUSION

While a great deal has been uncovered about the individual differences and motivational factors that are important in understanding counterfeit consumption, as table 1 demonstrates, we still know very little about the effectiveness of various tactics and strategies in combating counterfeit activity. More importantly, we have a limited understanding of the effects of counterfeit consumption on luxury brands. It is clear however, that our understanding of the effects of counterfeit consumption and the drivers of that consumption has greatly improved over the past decade. Moreover, recent findings about branding, information processing, and culture, particularly from social psychologists and marketing researchers, have provided theories and concepts that should aid managers, academics, and policy makers in developing a better understanding of counterfeit consumption, and the potential effectiveness of anti-counterfeiting initiatives. The hope is that this better understanding will help the various stakeholders mitigate the negative effects of counterfeiting and provide policymakers with more effective tools to reduce both the demand (e.g. appeal) and supply (i.e. production and distribution) of luxury counterfeits. The present chapter already provides one substantive recommendation: it is clear that any policy changes must be accompanied by programs aimed at increasing awareness of the personal and societal consequences of counterfeit consumption. Only when changes to both criminal penalties and consumer attitudes are made will a significant reduction in the supply and demand for counterfeits be realized.

REFERENCES

Alsaid, K. N., & Saleh, M. A. H. (2019). Perceived value and purchase intention of counterfeit luxury brands: Testing the moderation of materialism. *Amity Journal of Marketing*, *4*(1), 1–17.

Amaral, N. B., & Loken, B. (2016). Viewing usage of counterfeit luxury goods: Social identity and social hierarchy effects on dilution and enhancement of genuine luxury brands. *Journal of Consumer Psychology*, *26*(4), 483–495. doi:10.1016/j.jcps.2016.02.004

Ang, S. H., Cheng, P. S., Lim, E. A., & Tambyah, S. (2001). Spot the difference: Consumer responses towards counterfeits. *Journal of Consumer Marketing*, *18*(3), 219–235. doi:10.1108/07363760110392967

Anti-Counterfeiting Group (ACG). (2010). *Proceeds of Crime Act 2002: Examples of counterfeiting cases*. www.a-cg.org/guest/pdf/POCAcasesApril10.pdf

Bagwell, L. S., & Bernheim, B. D. (1996). Veblen effects in a theory of conspicuous consumption. *The American Economic Review*, *86*(3), 349–373.

Bain & Company. (2016). *Luxury good worldwide market study. FW 2016. As luxury resets to a new normal, strategy becomes paramount*. http://www.bain.com/Images/REPORT_Luxury_Goods_Worldwide_Market_Study_2016.pdf

Barnett, J. (2005). Shopping for Gucci on canal street: Reflections on status consumption, intellectual property and the incentive thesis. *Virginia Law Review, 91*, 1381-1423.

Berger, J., & Heath, C. (2008). Who drives divergence? Identity-signaling, outgroup dissimilarity, and the abandonment of cultural tastes. *Journal of Personality and Social Psychology*, *95*(3), 593–607. doi:10.1037/0022-3514.95.3.593 PMID:18729697

Bian, X., & Moutinho, L. (2009). An investigation of determinants of counterfeit purchase consideration. *Journal of Business Research*, *62*(3), 368–378. doi:10.1016/j.jbusres.2008.05.012

Bian, X., & Moutinho, L. (2011). The role of brand image, product involvement, and knowledge in explaining consumer purchase behaviour of counterfeits. *European Journal of Marketing*, *45*(1/2), 191–216. doi:10.1108/03090561111095658

Bian, X., & Veloutsou, P. (2007). Consumers' attitudes towards non-deceptive counterfeit brands in the UK and China. *Journal of Brand Management*, *14*(3), 211–222. doi:10.1057/palgrave.bm.2550046

Bird, R. C. (2007). Counterfeit drugs: A global consumer perspective. *Wake Forest Intellectual Property Law Journal*, *8*(3), 387–406.

Blakeney, M. (2009). *International proposals for the criminal enforcement of intellectual property rights: international concern with counterfeiting and piracy*. Queen Mary School of Law Legal Studies Research Paper, 29.

Bloch, P. H., Bush, R. F., & Campbell, L. (1993). Consumer accomplices in product counterfeiting: A demand side investigation. *Journal of Consumer Marketing*, *10*(4), 27–36. doi:10.1108/07363769310047374

Bloomberg. (Nov. 2, 2012). https://www.bloomberg.com/news/2012-11-02/coach-wins-257-million-court-ruling-against-counterfeiters-1-.html

Budiman, S., & Wijaya, T. (2014). Purchase intention of counterfeit products: The role of subjective norm. *International Journal of Marketing Studies*, *6*(2), 145–152. doi:10.5539/ijms.v6n2p145

Carpenter, J. M., & Lear, K. (2011). Consumer attitudes toward counterfeit fashion products: Does gender matter? *Journal of Textile and Apparel. Technology and Management*, *7*(1), 1–16.

Castaño, R., & Perez, M. E. (2014). A matter of love: Consumers' relationships with original brands and their counterfeits. *Journal of Consumer Marketing*, *31*(6/7), 475–482. doi:10.1108/JCM-05-2014-0970

Chan, S., & Amaral, N. B. (2014). Not all fakes are created equal. In B. Schmitt & L. Lee (Eds.), *The Psychology of the Asian Consumer* (Vol. 9, pp. 55–58). Routledge.

Chaudhry, P. E., & Walsh, M. G. (1996). An assessment of the impact of counterfeiting in international markets: The piracy paradox persists. *The Columbia Journal of World Business*, *31*(3), 34–48. doi:10.1016/S0022-5428(96)90039-3

Chaudry, P., Cordell, V., & Zimmerman, A. (2005). Modelling anti-counterfeiting strategies in response to protecting intellectual property rights in a global environment. *Marketing Review, 5*(1), 59-72. (97)

Cheung, W. L., & Prendergast, G. (2006). Buyers' perceptions of pirated products in china. *Marketing Intelligence & Planning*, *24*(5), 446–462. doi:10.1108/02634500610682854

Clifford, S. (2010). *Economic indicator: Even cheaper knockoffs.* https://www.nytimes.com/2010/08/01/business/economy/01knockoff.html

Coleman, R. P. (1983). The continuing significance of social class to marketing. *The Journal of Consumer Research*, *10*(3), 265–280. doi:10.1086/208966

Colman, C. E. (2015). The history and principles of American copyright protection for fashion design: On originality. *Harvard Journal of Sports & Entertainment Law*, *6*(2), 299–344.

Commuri, S. (2009). The impact of counterfeiting on genuine-item consumers' brand relationships. *Journal of Marketing*, *73*(3), 86–98.

Cunningham, L. L. (2011). *Trademark counterfeiting and individual purchaser liability*. https://www.iacc.org/aboutcounterfeiting/the-truth-about-counterfeiting.php

Dastin, J. (2020, January 13). *Amazon to ramp up counterfeit reporting to law enforcement.* https://www.reuters.com/article/us-amazon-com-counterfeit/amazon-to-ramp-up-counterfeit-reporting-to-law-enforcement-idUSKBN1ZC25U

Douanes & Droits Indirects. (n.d.). *La Douane Contre Le Fléau De La Contrefaçon: Chiffres 2009.* https://www.douane.gouv.fr/data/file/1249.pdf

Eisend, M., & Schuchert-Güler, P. (2006). Explaining counterfeit purchases: A review and preview. *Academy of Marketing Science Review*, *12*, 1–25.

Felice, K. B. (2011). Fashioning a solution for design piracy: Considering intellectual property law in the global context of fast fashion. *Syracuse J. Int'l L. & Com.*, *39*, 219–236.

Frerichs, A. (2008). Attitudes toward counterfeit fashion products: A South Dakota State University case study. *The Journal of Undergraduate Research*, *6*(6), 19–35.

Gabrielli, V., Grappi, S., & Baghi, I. (2012). Does counterfeiting affect luxury customer-based brand equity? *Journal of Brand Management*, *19*(7), 567–580. doi:10.1057/bm.2012.6

Gentry, J. W., Putrevu, S., & Shultz, C. J. (2006). The effects of counterfeiting on consumer search. *Journal of Consumer Behaviour*, *5*(3), 245–256. doi:10.1002/cb.176

Gentry, J. W., Putrevu, S., Shultz, C. J., & Commuri, S. (2001). How new Ralph Lauren? The separation of brand and product in a counterfeit culture. In M. C. Gilly & J. Meyers-Levy (Eds.), *Advances in Consumer Research* (Vol. 28, pp. 258–265). Association for Consumer Research.

Giambarrese, N. (2010). The look for less: A survey of intellectual property protections in the fashion industry. *Touro Law Review*, *26*(1), 243–286.

Gino, F., Norton, M. I., & Ariely, D. (2010). The counterfeit self: The deceptive costs of faking it. *Psychological Science*, *21*(5), 712–720. doi:10.1177/0956797610366545 PMID:20483851

Global Anti-Counterfeiting Network. (2019). http://www.gacg.org/Home

Han, Y. J., Nunes, J. C., & Drèze, X. (2010). Signaling status with luxury goods: The role of brand prominence. *Journal of Marketing*, *74*(4), 15–30. doi:10.1509/jmkg.74.4.015

Hansen, G. H., & Møller, H. K. (2017). Louis Vuitton in the bazaar: Negotiating the value of counterfeit goods in Shanghai's Xiangyang market. *International Journal of Entrepreneurship and Small Business*, *30*(2), 170–190. doi:10.1504/IJESB.2017.081437

Harvey, P. J., & Walls, W. D. (2003). Laboratory markets in counterfeit goods: Hong Kong versus Las Vegas. *Applied Economics Letters*, *10*(14), 883–887. doi:10.1080/1350485032000155431

Hieke, S. (2010). Effects of counterfeits on the image of luxury brands: An empirical study from the customer perspective. *Journal of Brand Management*, *18*(2), 159–173. doi:10.1057/bm.2010.28

HIRC. (2003). Are proceeds from counterfeited goods funding terrorism? *House International Relations Committee, Hearing on Intellectual Property Crimes,* www.foreignaffairs.house.gov/archives/108/88392.pdf

Int. No. 544 § 10-902 (2013). https://legistar.council.nyc.gov/LegislationDetail.aspx?ID=885894&GUID=926F900B-7A1E-48E8-991D-6A3CFE24EA90

International Chamber of Commerce report. (2009). http://www.iccwbo.org/Data/Documents/Bascap/Consumer-Perceptions/Consumer-Research-Report/

International Chamber of Commerce report. (2013). http://www.iccwbo.org/products-and-services/fighting-commercial-crime/counterfeiting-intelligence-bureau/

Jiang, Y., Miao, M., Jalees, T., & Zaman, S. I. (2019). Analysis of the moral mechanism to purchase counterfeit luxury goods: Evidence from China. *Asia Pacific Journal of Marketing and Logistics*, *31*(3), 647–669. doi:10.1108/APJML-05-2018-0190

Kapferer, J. N., & Bastien, V. (2009). The specificity of luxury management: Turning marketing upside down. *Journal of Brand Management*, *16*(5-6), 311–322. doi:10.1057/bm.2008.51

Kapferer, J. N., & Bastien, V. (2012). *The luxury strategy: Break the rules of marketing to build luxury brands*. Kogan Page Publishers.

Kent, M. H. (2011). *Counterfeits and infringements: Problems and solutions.* VENABLE L.L.P. https://www.venable.com/files/Publication/4166ad52-47e7-4ac6-9b52-2beaeafbaed1/Presentation/PublicationAttachment/64d85c1f-a0a8-40e6-82c3-32ee32363b3a/Counterfeits_and_Infringements.pdf

Key, T. M., Boostrom, R. E. Jr, Adjei, M. T., & Campbell, D. A. (2013). Watch out: Themes in timepiece communities of counterfeit consumption. *Journal of Consumer Behaviour*, *12*(4), 307–317. doi:10.1002/cb.1431

Kim, J., Kim, J. E., & Park, J. (2012). Effects of cognitive resource availability on consumer decisions involving counterfeit products: The role of perceived justification. *Marketing Letters*, *23*(3), 869–881. doi:10.100711002-012-9194-1

Koklic, M. K., & Vida, I. (2012). Counterfeiting purchase behavior: The role of perceived consequences and rationalization in forming attitudes and purchase intentions. *37th Macromarketing Conference*, 51-56.

Kollmannova, D. K. (2012). Fake product? Why not! Attitudes toward the consumption of counterfeit goods in CEE as shown on the example of Slovakia. *Central European Business Review*, *1*(2), 23–28. doi:10.18267/j.cebr.14

Kopp, S. W., & Suter, T. A. (2000). Trademark strategies online: Implications for intellectual property protection. *Journal of Public Policy & Marketing*, *19*(1), 119–131. doi:10.1509/jppm.19.1.119.16935

Lai, K. K. Y., & Zaichkowsky, J. L. (1999). Brand imitation: Do the Chinese have different views? *Asia Pacific Journal of Management*, *16*(2), 179–192. doi:10.1023/A:1015482707900

Lambkin, M., & Tyndall, Y. (2009). Brand counterfeiting: A marketing problem that won't go away. *Irish Marketing Review*, *20*(1), 35–46.

Lan, M. Y., Liu, F., Fang, C. H., & Lin, T. M. Y. (2012). Understanding word-of-mouth in counterfeiting. *Psychology (Irvine, Calif.)*, *3*(3), 289–295. doi:10.4236/psych.2012.33041

Li, J., Ghaffari, M., & Su, L. (2020). Luxury counterfeit consumption strategies in a collectivistic culture: The case of China. *Journal of Brand Management*, *27*(5), 546–560. doi:10.105741262-020-00197-4

Loureiro, Y. K., Bayuk, J., Tignor, S. M., Nenkov, G. Y., Baskentli, S., & Webb, D. (2016). The case for moral consumption: Examining and expanding the domain of moral behavior to promote individual and collective well-being. *Journal of Public Policy & Marketing*, *35*(2), 305–322. doi:10.1509/jppm.15.148

Lu, M. (2013). *An investigation of consumer motives to purchase counterfeit luxury-branded products.* [Unpublished Master's Thesis]. School of Management and Marketing, University of Wollongong.

Ludovica, C., Pastore, A., & Williams, P. (2017). Counterfeiting luxury goods. In P. E. Chaudhry (Ed.), *Handbook of research on counterfeiting and illicit trade* (pp. 193–222).

Lutz, A. (2015). *Millennial's Are rejecting a strategy Coach, Abercrombie & Fitch, and Michael Coors have relied on for years.* Business Insider. https://www.businessinsider.com/millennials-turn-away-from-logos-2015-12

LVMH. (2001). How does LVMH tackle counterfeiting of luxury products? http://www.LVMH.com/group/search.htm

Mandel, N., Petrova, P. K., & Cialdini, R. B. (2006). Images of success and the preference for luxury brands. *Journal of Consumer Psychology, 16*(1), 57–69. doi:10.120715327663jcp1601_8

Martinez, D. M. (2014). Fashionably late: Why the United States should copy France and Italy to reduce counterfeiting. *Boston University International Law Journal, 32*, 101–130.

Mazar, N., On, A., & Ariely, D. (2008). The dishonesty of honest people: A theory of self-concept maintenance. *JMR, Journal of Marketing Research, 45*(6), 633–644. doi:10.1509/jmkr.45.6.633

Mittelstaedt, J. D., & Mittelstaedt, R. A. (1997). The protection of intellectual property: Issues of origination and ownership. *Journal of Public Policy & Marketing, 16*(1), 14–25. doi:10.1177/074391569701600103

Miyazaki, A. D., Rodriguez, A. A., & Langenderfer, J. (2009). Price, scarcity, and consumer willingness to purchase pirated media products. *Journal of Public Policy & Marketing, 28*(1), 71–84. doi:10.1509/jppm.28.1.71

MPAA Expands Anti-Piracy Campaign. (June 21, 2004). Billboard. https://www.billboard.com/biz/articles/news/1431307/mpaa-expands-anti-piracy-campaign

Nia, A., & Zaichkowsky, J. L. (2000). Do counterfeits devalue the ownership of luxury brands? *Journal of Product and Brand Management, 9*(7), 485–497. doi:10.1108/10610420010351402

Norum, P. S., & Cuno, A. (2011). Analysis of the demand for counterfeit goods. *Journal of Fashion Marketing and Management, 15*(1), 27–40. doi:10.1108/13612021111112322

Nunes, J. C., Drèze, X., & Han, Y. J. (2011). Conspicuous consumption in a recession: Toning it down or turning it up? *Journal of Consumer Psychology, 21*(2), 199–205. doi:10.1016/j.jcps.2010.11.002

Paradise, P. R. (1999). *Trademark counterfeiting, product piracy, and the billion dollar threat to the US economy.* Greenwood Publishing Group.

Pearson, S. (2012). *Coach wins $257 million court ruling against counterfeiters.* Academic Press.

Penz, E., & Stöttinger, B. (2005). Forget the real thing - take the copy! An explanatory model for the volitional purchase of counterfeit products. *Advances in Consumer Research. Association for Consumer Research (U. S.), 32*(1), 568–575.

Penz, E., & Stöttinger, B. (2008b). Original brands and counterfeit brands - do they have anything in common? *Journal of Consumer Behaviour, 7*(2), 146–163. doi:10.1002/cb.243

Penz, E., & Stöttinger, B. (2012). A comparison of the emotional and motivational aspects in the purchase of luxury products. *Journal of Brand Management*, *19*(7), 581–594. doi:10.1057/bm.2012.7

Petty, R. D. (2005). Societal regulation of the marketing function: Does the patchwork create a quilt? *Journal of Public Policy & Marketing*, *24*(1), 63–74. doi:10.1509/jppm.24.1.63.63884

Phau, I., Prendergast, G., & Chuen, L. H. (2001). Profiling brand-piracy-prone consumers: An exploratory study in Hong Kong's clothing industry. *Journal of Fashion Marketing and Management*, *5*(1), 45–55. doi:10.1108/EUM0000000007278

Phau, I., & Teah, M. (2009). Devil wears (counterfeit) Prada: A study of antecedents and outcomes of attitudes towards counterfeits of luxury brands. *Journal of Consumer Marketing*, *26*(1), 15–27. doi:10.1108/07363760910927019

Poddar, A., Foreman, J., Banerjee, S. S., & Ellen, P. S. (2012). Exploring the Robin Hood effect: Moral profiteering motives for purchasing counterfeit products. *Journal of Business Research*, *65*(10), 1500–1506. doi:10.1016/j.jbusres.2011.10.017

Prager, E. A. (1996). The federal trademark dilution act of 1995: Substantial likelihood of confusion. *Fordham Intellectual Property. Media & Entertainment Law Journal*, *7*(1), 121–136.

Qian, Y. (2011). *Counterfeiters: foes or friends? How do counterfeits affect different product quality tiers? (No. w16785).* National Bureau of Economic Research. doi:10.3386/w16785

Radón, A. (2012). Counterfeit luxury goods online: An investigation of consumer perceptions. *International Journal of Marketing Studies*, *4*(2), 74–79.

Romani, S., Gistri, G., & Pace, S. (2012). When counterfeits raise the appeal of luxury brands. *Marketing Letters*, *23*(3), 807–824. doi:10.100711002-012-9190-5

Sharma, P., & Chan, R. Y. K. (2011). Counterfeit proneness: Conceptualisation and scale development. *Journal of Marketing Management*, *27*(5-6), 602–626. doi:10.1080/0267257X.2010.489829

2017 Special 301 Report from the Office of the U.S. Trade Representative. (2017). https://ustr.gov/sites/default/files/301/2017%20Special%20301%20Report%20FINAL.PDF

Spence, M. (2007). *Intellectual Property*. Clarendon Law Series. Oxford University Press. doi:10.1093/acprof:oso/9780198765011.001.0001

Stöttinger, B., & Penz, E. (2015). Concurrent ownership of brands and counterfeits: Conceptualization and temporal transformation from a consumer perspective. *Psychology and Marketing*, *32*(4), 373–391. doi:10.1002/mar.20786

Tajfel, H. (2010). *Social identity and intergroup relations*. Cambridge University Press.

Taormina, R. J., & Chong, K. Y. (2010). Purchasing counterfeit and legitimate products in China: Social and psychological correlates and predictors. *Journal of East-West Business*, *16*(2), 118–145. doi:10.1080/10669868.2010.486103

Thomas, D. (2009). The fight against fakes. *Harper's Bazaar*, *143*, 1–3.

Tom, G., Garibaldi, B., Zeng, Y., & Pilcher, J. (1998). Consumer demand for counterfeit goods. *Psychology and Marketing*, *15*(5), 405–421. doi:10.1002/(SICI)1520-6793(199808)15:5<405::AID-MAR1>3.0.CO;2-B

Triandewi, E., & Tjiptono, F. (2013). Consumer intention to buy original brands versus counterfeits. *International Journal of Marketing Studies*, *5*(2), 23–32. doi:10.5539/ijms.v5n2p23

United Nations Office on Drugs and Crime (UNODC). (2014). *Counterfeit: Don't buy into prganized crime' - UNODC launches new outreach campaign on $250 billion a year counterfeit business.* http://www.unodc.org/counterfeit/

U.S. Customs and Border Protection Directive 2310-011A, Personal use exemption: unauthorized trademarks (Cust. 2000). https://www.cbp.gov/sites/default/files/documents/2310-11a_3.pdf

van Keymeulen, E., & Nash, L. (2011). Fashionably Late. *Intellectual Property Magazine,* 54. Accessed Feb. 14, 2017: https://www.cov.com/~/media/files/corporate/publications/2011/12/fashionably-late.pdf

Vida, I. (2007). Determinants of Consumer willingness to purchase non-deceptive counterfeit products. *Marketing Global Transitions*, *5*(3), 253–270.

Wall, D. S., & Large, J. (2010). Jailhouse frocks locating the public interest in policing counterfeit luxury fashion goods. *British Journal of Criminology*, *50*(6), 1094–1116. doi:10.1093/bjc/azq048

Wang, F., Zhang, H., Zang, H., & Ouyang, M. (2005). Purchasing pirated software: An initial examination of Chinese consumers. *Journal of Consumer Marketing*, *22*(6), 340–351. doi:10.1108/07363760510623939

Wang, Y., & Griskevicius, V. (2014). Conspicuous consumption, relationships, and rivals: Women's luxury products as signals to other women. *The Journal of Consumer Research*, *40*(5), 834–854. doi:10.1086/673256

Wang, Y., Stoner, J. L., & John, D. R. (2019). Counterfeit luxury consumption in a social context: The effects on females' moral disengagement and behavior. *Journal of Consumer Psychology*, *29*(2), 207–225. doi:10.1002/jcpy.1071

Wee, C. H., Ta, S. J., & Cheok, K. H. (1995). Non-price determinants of intention to purchase counterfeit goods. *International Marketing Review*, *12*(6), 19–46. doi:10.1108/02651339510102949

Wiedmann, K. P., Hennigs, N., & Klarmann, C. (2012). Luxury consumption in the trade-off between genuine and counterfeit goods: What are the consumers' underlying motives and value-based drivers? *Journal of Brand Management*, *19*(7), 544–566. doi:10.1057/bm.2012.10

Wilcox, K., Kim, H. M., & Sen, S. (2009). Why do consumers buy counterfeit luxury brands? *JMR, Journal of Marketing Research*, *46*(2), 247–259. doi:10.1509/jmkr.46.2.247

Yoo, B., & Lee, S. H. (2012). Asymmetrical effects of past experiences with genuine fashion luxury brands and their counterfeits on purchase intention of each. *Journal of Business Research*, *65*(10), 1507–1515. doi:10.1016/j.jbusres.2011.10.018

Zaichkowsky, J. L., & Simpson, R. N. (1996). The effect of experience with a brand imitator on the original brand. *Marketing Letters*, *7*(1), 31–39. doi:10.1007/BF00557309

KEY TERMS AND DEFINITIONS

Counterfeit Luxury Goods: Unauthorized replicas of luxury goods. They differ from most other counterfeit products because they can be deceptive or non-deceptive. In the latter case consumers knowingly purchase the replica product.

Counterfeits: Unauthorized replicas of products, intended to deceive or defraud a consumer or business.

Fashion Design Counterfeiting: Products that are made and/or distributed by another company but is a replica of the overall look or design of a luxury product. Any product that displays the brand mark or logo of a luxury brand but is not produced and/or distributed by the luxury company is a fashion design counterfeit.

Intellectual Property: Refers to literary, musical, and otherwise artistic innovations as well symbols, names and even colors and scents that are unique to one producer or organization. It includes for categories of protections, trade secrets, trademarks, copyrights and patents.

Luxury Goods: Products, typically related to a heritage and/or traditional associated with a founding figure. They are high in quality and price and unique in the extent to which they convey important social signals to the user and serve as symbols of social status to others.

Trademark Counterfeiting: A broad term that describes replicas of the brand, logo (fashion brand) or overall appearance (fashion design) of a product. The definition differs in important ways between nations. For example, in the United States fashion design protections are typically not included in trademark laws, whereas in much of Europe they are.

Compilation of References

2017 Special 301 Report from the Office of the U.S. Trade Representative. (2017). https://ustr.gov/sites/default/files/301/2017%20Special%20301%20Report%20FINAL.PDF

Abalkhail, T. S. (2020). The impact of religiosity on luxury brand consumption: the case of Saudi consumers. *Journal of Islamic Marketing*. Ahead-of-print. doi:10.1108/JIMA-11-2016-0091

Abbott, J. S. C. (2008). *Louis XIV, Makers of History Series* (D. Alexander & O. D. P. Team, Eds.). Gutenberg Project.

Adapa, S., Fazal-e-Hasan, S. M., Makam, S. B., Azeem, M. M., & Mortimer, G. (2020). Examining the antecedents and consequences of perceived shopping value through smart retail technology. *Journal of Retailing and Consumer Services, 52*, 101901. doi:10.1016/j.jretconser.2019.101901

Adetunji, R. R., Rashid, S. M., & Ishak, M. S. (2018). Social media marketing communication and consumer-based brand equity: An account of automotive brands in Malaysia. *Jurnal Komunikasi: Malaysian Journal of Communication, 34*(1), 1–19.

Aggett, M. (2007). What has influenced growth in the UK's boutique hotel sector? *International Journal of Contemporary Hospitality Management, 19*(2), 169–177. doi:10.1108/09596110710729274

Agrawal, A. K., Gupta, A. A., & Vora, M. K. (2020). Pricing and lot-sizing policies for products with demand under Veblen effect. *Operations Management Research,* 1-9.

Akbaş, H. (2013). *Grup Alışveriş Sitelerinin Sosyal Medyadaki Uygulamalarının Değerlendirilmesi* (UMI No. 345279) [Master thesis, University of Pamukkale]. Türk Ulusal Tez Merkezi Dissertations and Theses database.

Akrout, H. (2014). Relationship quality in cross-border exchanges: A temporal perspective. *Journal of Business-To-Business Marketing, 21*(3), 145–169. doi:10.1080/1051712X.2014.952179

Akrout, H., Diallo, M. F., Akrout, W., & Chandon, J.-L. (2016). Affective trust in buyer-seller relationships: A two-dimensional scale. *Journal of Business and Industrial Marketing, 31*(2), 260–273. doi:10.1108/JBIM-11-2014-0223

Aksoy, H., & Abdulfatai, O. (2019). Exploring the impact of religiousness and culture on luxury fashion goods purchasing intention: A behavioural study on Nigerian Muslim consumers. *Journal of Islamic Marketing, 10*(3), 768–789. doi:10.1108/JIMA-01-2018-0022

Aksu, S., & Ercan, M. (2014). *Lüks marka iletişiminde sosyal medyaya uyum sağlamak: Gucci ve Vakko'nun Facebook ve Twitter kullanımları üzerine bir inceleme* [Paper presentation]. Internet Konferansı, Türkiye.

Akyüz, A. (2013). Sosyal medyada müşteri etkileşimi ve firmalar açısından önemi. *Kastamonu Üniversitesi İktisadi ve İdari Bilimler Fakültesi Dergisi, 2*(2), 5–22.

Alam, S. S., Mohd, R., & Hisham, B. (2011). Is religiosity an important determinant on Muslim consumer behaviour in Malaysia? *Journal of Islamic Marketing*, *2*(1), 83–96. doi:10.1108/17590831111115268

Alexandrov, A., Lilly, B., & Babakus, E. (2013). The effects of social- and self-motives on the intentions to share positive and negative word of mouth. *Journal of the Academy of Marketing Science*, *41*(5), 531–546. doi:10.100711747-012-0323-4

al-Haj, H. (2006, September 15). *What does Islam say about makeup?* Retrieved from https://www.amjaonline.org/fatwa/en/1987/what-does-islam-say-about-makeup

Allérès, D. (2006), Luxo... Estratégias, Marketing (2a Edição). Rio de Janeiro: Editora FGV.

Alleres, D. (1990). *Luxe—Strategies Marketing*. Economica.

Alleres, D. (1991). Spécificités et stratégies marketing des différents univers du luxe. *Revue Française du Marketing*, *132*(33), 71–95.

Allérès, D., Gama, M., & Mouclier, J. (2000). *Luxo ...: Estratégias, marketing*. Ed. FGV.

Allport, G. W., & Ross, J. M. (1967). Personal religious orientation and prejudice. *Journal of Personality and Social Psychology*, *5*(4), 432–443. doi:10.1037/h0021212 PMID:6051769

Al-Mutawa, F. S. (2013). Consumer-generated representations: Muslim women recreating western luxury fashion brand meaning through consumption. *Psychology and Marketing*, *30*(3), 236–246. doi:10.1002/mar.20601

Alsaid, K. N., & Saleh, M. A. H. (2019). Perceived value and purchase intention of counterfeit luxury brands: Testing the moderation of materialism. *Amity Journal of Marketing*, *4*(1), 1–17.

Alserhan, B. A., Bataineh, M. K., Halkias, D., & Komodromos, M. (2014). Measuring luxury brand consumption and female consumers' religiosity in the UAE. *Journal of Developmental Entrepreneurship*, *19*(2), 1–16. doi:10.1142/S1084946714500095

Altuna, O. K. (2007). Uluslararası marka strateji formülasyonu: Standardizasyon ve uyarlama yaklaşımları. *İstanbul Üniversitesi Siyasal Bilgiler Fakültesi Dergisi*, (37), 159-171.

Alves, G. M., Sousa, B. M., & Machado, A. (2020). The Role of Digital Marketing and Online Relationship Quality in Social Tourism: A Tourism for All Case Study. In J. Santos & Ó. Silva (Eds.), *Digital Marketing Strategies for Tourism, Hospitality, and Airline Industries* (pp. 49–70). IGI Global., doi:10.4018/978-1-5225-9783-4.ch003

Amaldoss, W., & Jain, S. (2005). Conspicuous Consumption and Sophisticated Thinking. *Management Science*, *51*(10), 1449–1466. doi:10.1287/mnsc.1050.0399

Amaldoss, W., & Jain, S. (2008). Trading up: A strategic analysis of reference group effects. *Marketing Science*, *27*(5), 932–942. doi:10.1287/mksc.1070.0350

Amaral, N. B., & Loken, B. (2016). Viewing usage of counterfeit luxury goods: Social identity and social hierarchy effects on dilution and enhancement of genuine luxury brands. *Journal of Consumer Psychology*, *26*(4), 483–495. doi:10.1016/j.jcps.2016.02.004

Amatulli, C., & Guido, G. (2011). Determinants of purchasing intentions of fashion luxury goods in the Italian market: A laddering approach. *Journal of Fashion Marketing and Management*, *15*(1), 123–136. doi:10.1108/13612021111112386

Amatulli, C., & Guido, G. (2012). Externalised vs. internalised consumption of luxury goods: Propositions and implications for luxury retail marketing. *International Review of Retail, Distribution and Consumer Research*, *22*(2), 189–207. doi:10.1080/09593969.2011.652647

Andersen, P. (2007). *What is Web 2.0?: ideas, technologies and implications for education*. JISC.

Andreasen, A. R. (1995). *Marketing social change: Changing behavior to promote health, social development, and the environment*. Jossey-Bass.

Andreini, D., Pedeliento, G., Zarantonello, L., & Solerio, C. (2018). A renaissance of brand experience: Advancing the concept through a multi-perspective analysis. *Journal of Business Research*, *91*, 123–133. doi:10.1016/j.jbusres.2018.05.046

Ang, S. H., Cheng, P. S., Lim, E. A., & Tambyah, S. K. (2001). Spot the difference: Consumer responses towards counterfeits. *Journal of Consumer Marketing*, *18*(3), 219–235. doi:10.1108/07363760110392967

Anti-Counterfeiting Group (ACG). (2010). *Proceeds of Crime Act 2002: Examples of counterfeiting cases*. www.a-cg.org/guest/pdf/POCAcasesApril10.pdf

Arli, D., Cherrier, H., & Tjiptono, F. (2016). God blesses those who wear Prada: Exploring the impact of religiousness on attitudes toward luxury among the youth of Indonesia. *Marketing Intelligence & Planning*, *34*(1), 61–79. doi:10.1108/MIP-12-2014-0232

Arnould, E. J., & Thompson, C. J. (2005). Consumer culture theory (CCT): Twenty years of research. *The Journal of Consumer Research*, *31*(4), 868–882. doi:10.1086/426626

Aron, A., & Aron, E. N. (1986). *Love and the expansion of self: Understanding attraction and satisfaction*. Hemisphere Publishing Corp/Harper & Row Publishers.

Arya, V., Sethi, D., & Paul, J. (2019). Does digital footprint act as a digital asset? Enhancing brand experience through remarketing. *International Journal of Information Management*, *49*, 142–156. doi:10.1016/j.ijinfomgt.2019.03.013

Ashraf, S., Hafeez, M. H., Yaseen, A., & Naqvi, A. (2017). Do they care what they believe? Exploring the impact of religiosity on intention to purchase luxury products. *Pakistan Journal of Commerce and Social Sciences*, *11*(2), 428–447.

Aslanbay, Y., Sanaktekin, Ö. H., & Ağırdır, B. (2011). Lifestyles of Islamic consumers in Turkey. In O. Sandikci & G. Rice (Eds.), *Handbook of Islamic Marketing* (pp. 129–146). Edward Elgar Publishing. doi:10.4337/9780857936028.00016

Atwal, G., & Williams, A. (2009). Luxury brand marketing – The experience is everything! *Journal of Brand Management*, *16*(5-6), 338–346. doi:10.1057/bm.2008.48

Atwal, G., & Williams, A. (2017). Luxury brand marketing–the experience is everything! In J. Kapferer, J. Kernstock, T. O. Brexendorf, & S. M. Powell (Eds.), *Advances in luxury brand management* (pp. 43–57). Palgrave Macmillan. doi:10.1007/978-3-319-51127-6_3

Au, N., Buhalis, D., & Law, R. (2014). Online complaining behavior in mainland China hotels: The perception of Chinese and non-Chinese customers. *International Journal of Hospitality & Tourism Administration*, *15*(3), 248–274. doi:10.1080/15256480.2014.925722

Aytaç, M. B. (2019). *Narsistik tüketim (Narcissistic consumption)*. Gazi Kitabevi.

Bagozzi, R., Gopinath, M., & Nyer, P. (1999). The role of emotions in Marketing. *Journal of the Academy of Marketing Science*, *27*(2), 184–206. doi:10.1177/0092070399272005

Bagwell, L. S., & Bernheim, B. D. (1996). Veblen effects in a theory of conspicuous consumption. *The American Economic Review*, *86*(3), 349–373.

Bahri-Ammari, N., Coulibaly, D., & Mimoun, M. S. B. (2020). The bandwagon luxury consumption in Tunisian case: The roles of independent and interdependent self concept. *Journal of Retailing and Consumer Services*, *52*, 101903. doi:10.1016/j.jretconser.2019.101903

Bailey, J. M., & Sood, J. (1993). The effects of religious affiliation on consumer behavior: A preliminary investigation. *Journal of Managerial Issues*, *5*(3), 328–352.

Bain & Company. (2016). *Luxury good worldwide market study. FW 2016. As luxury resets to a new normal, strategy becomes paramount.* http://www.bain.com/Images/REPORT_Luxury_Goods_Worldwide_Market_Study_2016.pdf

Bain & Company. (2019). *Luxury goods worldwide market study - – Spring 2019 Update Report.* Retrieved from https://www.bain.com/insights/luxury-report/

Bain and Company. (2017). *World Luxury Consumption Market.* Report Avaliable at: https://www.bain.com/insights/luxury-goods-worldwide-market-study-fall-winter-2017/

Bajwa, S., & Singh, S. (2019). Demographic characteristics and consumer purchase behaviour towards counterfeit cosmetic brands. *PIMT Journal of Research*, *12*(1), 83–93.

Baker, J., Ashill, N., Amer, N., & Diab, E. (2018). The internet dilemma: An exploratory study of luxury firms' usage of internet-based technologies. *Journal of Retailing and Consumer Services*, *41*, 37–47. doi:10.1016/j.jretconser.2017.11.007

Baloglu, S., & Mangaloglu, M. (2001). Tourism destination images of Turkey, Egypt, Greece, and Italy as perceived by US-based tour operators and travel agents. *Tourism Management*, *22*(1), 1–9. doi:10.1016/S0261-5177(00)00030-3

Banyai, M. (2012). Travel blogs: A reflection of positioning strategies? *Journal of Hospitality Marketing & Management*, *21*(4), 421–439. doi:10.1080/19368623.2012.624297

Banyai, M., & Glover, T. D. (2012). Evaluating research methods on travel blogs. *Journal of Travel Research*, *51*(3), 267–277. doi:10.1177/0047287511410323

Banyai, M., & Havitz, M. E. (2013). Analyzing travel blogs using a realist evaluation approach. *Journal of Hospitality Marketing & Management*, *22*(2), 229–241. doi:10.1080/19368623.2012.680239

Bapat, D. (2017). Impact of brand familiarity on brands experience dimensions for financial services brands. *International Journal of Bank Marketing*, *35*(4), 637–648. doi:10.1108/IJBM-05-2016-0066

Barber, N., Goodman, R. J., & Goh, B. K. (2011). Restaurant consumers repeat patronage: A service quality concern. *International Journal of Hospitality Management*, *30*(2), 329–336. doi:10.1016/j.ijhm.2010.08.008

Bardhi, F., & Eckhardt, G. M. (2017). Liquid consumption. *The Journal of Consumer Research*, *44*(3), 582–597. doi:10.1093/jcr/ucx050

Barnett, J. (2005). Shopping for Gucci on canal street: Reflections on status consumption, intellectual property and the incentive thesis. *Virginia Law Review*, *91*, 1381-1423.

Barreda, A., & Bilgihan, A. (2013). An analysis of user-generated content for hotel experiences. *Journal of Hospitality and Tourism Technology*, *4*(3), 263–280. doi:10.1108/JHTT-01-2013-0001

Bashir, A. (2019, August 14). Awareness of purchasing halal food among non-Muslim consumers: An explorative study with reference to Cape Town of South Africa. *Journal of Islamic Marketing*. Advance online publication. doi:10.1108/JIMA-04-2018-0077

Bastien, V., & Kapferer, J. N. (2012). *Luxe oblige*. Editions Eyrolles.

Battour, M., & Ismail, M. N. (2016). Halal tourism: Concepts, practises, challenges and future. *Tourism Management Perspectives*, *19*(B), 150–154.

Battour, M. M., Ismail, M. N., & Battor, M. (2010). Toward a halal tourism market. *Tourism Analysis*, *15*(4), 461–470. doi:10.3727/108354210X12864727453304

Baumeister, R. F., & Hutton, D. G. (1987). Self-presentation theory: Self-construction and audience pleasing. In B. Mullen & G. R. Goethals (Eds.), *Theories of Group Behavior* (pp. 71–87). Springer. doi:10.1007/978-1-4612-4634-3_4

Bayram, M., & Yaylı, A. (2009). Otel web sitelerinin içerik analizi yöntemiyle değerlendirilmesi. *Elektronik Sosyal Bilimler Dergisi*, *8*(27), 347–379.

Bearden, W. O., & Etzel, M. J. (1982). Reference group influence on product and brand purchase decisions. *The Journal of Consumer Research*, *9*(2), 183–194. doi:10.1086/208911

Becken, S., Simmons, D. G., & Frampton, C. (2003). Energy use associated with different travel choices. *Tourism Management*, *24*(3), 267–277. doi:10.1016/S0261-5177(02)00066-3

Beckmann, S. C., & Langer, R. (2005). Netnography: Rich insights from online research. *Insights*, *8*(2), 149–155.

Belaid, S., & Temessek Behi, A. (2011). The role of attachment in building consumer-brand relationships: An empirical investigation in the utilitarian consumption context. *Journal of Product and Brand Management*, *20*(1), 37–47. doi:10.1108/10610421111108003

Belk, R. W. (1988). Possessions and the extended self. *The Journal of Consumer Research*, *15*(2), 139–168. doi:10.1086/209154

Belk, R. W. (1996). The perfect gift. In C. Otnes & R. F. Beltramini (Eds.), *Giftgiving: An interdisciplinary anthology* (pp. 59–85). Bowling Green University Popular Press.

Belk, R. W. (2001). Materialism and you. *Journal of Research for Consumers*, *1*(1), 291–297.

Bell, S. (2008). *International brand management of Chinese companies: Case studies on the Chinese household appliances and consumer electronics industry entering US and western European markets*. Physica-Verlag HD. doi:10.1007/978-3-7908-2030-0

Belopilskaya, Y., Visutthithada, C., & Wieser, T. (n.d.). *How halal tourism is reshaping the global tourism industry*. Retrieved from https://hospitalityinsights.ehl.edu/halal-tourism-global-industry

Berger, J., & Heath, C. (2008). Who drives divergence? Identity signaling, outgroup dissimilarity, and the abandonment of cultural tastes. *Journal of Personality and Social Psychology*, *95*(3), 593–607. doi:10.1037/0022-3514.95.3.593

Berger, J., & Ward, M. (2010). Subtle signals of inconspicuous consumption. *The Journal of Consumer Research*, *37*(4), 555–569. doi:10.1086/655445

Berry, C. J. (1994). *The idea of luxury: A conceptual and historical investigation*. Cambridge University Press. doi:10.1017/CBO9780511558368

Berthon, P. R., Pitt, L. F., Plangger, K., & Shapiro, D. (2012). Marketing meets Web 2.0, social media, and creative consumers: Implications for international marketing strategy. *Business Horizons*, *55*(3), 261–271. doi:10.1016/j.bushor.2012.01.007

Berthon, P. R., Pitt, L., & Campbell, C. (2008). Ad lib: When customers create the ad. *California Management Review*, *50*(4), 6–31. doi:10.2307/41166454

Berthon, P., Pitt, L., Parent, M., & Berthon, J. P. (2009). Aesthetics and ephemerality: Observing and preserving the luxury brand. *California Management Review*, *52*(1), 45–66. doi:10.1525/cmr.2009.52.1.45

Beverland, M. (2004). Uncovering "theories-in-use": Building luxury wine brands. *European Journal of Marketing*, *38*(3/4), 446–466. doi:10.1108/03090560410518648

Beverland, M. (2006). The 'real thing': Branding authenticity in the luxury wine trade. *Journal of Business Research*, *59*(2), 251–258. doi:10.1016/j.jbusres.2005.04.007

Bhattarai, A. (2019, April 16). Consumers around the world are spending less on almost everything. Even booze. *The Washington Post*. Retrieved from https://www.washingtonpost.com/business/2019/04/16/consumers-around-world-are-spending-less-almost-everything-even-booze/

Bian, Q., & Forsythe, S. (2012). Purchase intention for luxury brands: A cross cultural comparison. *Journal of Business Research*, *65*(10), 1443–1451. doi:10.1016/j.jbusres.2011.10.010

Bian, X., & Moutinho, L. (2009). An investigation of determinants of counterfeit purchase consideration. *Journal of Business Research*, *62*(3), 368–378. doi:10.1016/j.jbusres.2008.05.012

Bian, X., & Moutinho, L. (2011). The role of brand image, product involvement, and knowledge in explaining consumer purchase behaviour of counterfeits. *European Journal of Marketing*, *45*(1/2), 191–216. doi:10.1108/03090561111095658

Bian, X., & Veloutsou, C. (2007). Consumers' attitudes regarding non-deceptive counterfeit brands in the UK and China. *Journal of Brand Management*, *12*(3), 211–222. doi:10.1057/palgrave.bm.2550046

Bian, X., Wang, K. Y., Smith, A., & Yannopoulou, N. (2016). New insights into unethical counterfeit consumption. *Journal of Business Research*, *69*(10), 4249–4258. doi:10.1016/j.jbusres.2016.02.038

Bigné, J., Andreu, L., & Gnoth, J. (2005). The theme park experience: An analysis of pleasure, arousal and satisfaction. *Tourism Management*, *26*(6), 833–844. doi:10.1016/j.tourman.2004.05.006

Bird, R. C. (2007). Counterfeit drugs: A global consumer perspective. *Wake Forest Intellectual Property Law Journal*, *8*(3), 387–406.

Bitner, M. J. (1990). Evaluating service encounters: The effects of physical surroundings and employee responses. *Journal of Marketing*, *54*(2), 69–82. doi:10.1177/002224299005400206

Blakeney, M. (2009). *International proposals for the criminal enforcement of intellectual property rights: international concern with counterfeiting and piracy*. Queen Mary School of Law Legal Studies Research Paper, 29.

Blevis, E., Makice, K., Odom, W., Roedl, D., Beck, C., & Blevis, S. A. (2007). Luxury; New Luxury, Quality; Equality. Sustainable Interaction Design Research Group, School of Informatics, Indiana University at Bloomington. doi:10.1145/1314161.1314188

Bloch, P. H., Bush, R. F., & Campbell, L. (1993). Consumer accomplices in product counterfeiting: A demand side investigation. *Journal of Consumer Marketing*, *10*(4), 27–36. doi:10.1108/07363769310047374

Blommaert, J., & Varis, P. (2015). Culture as accent: The cultural logic of hijabistas. *Semiotica*, *203*(203), 153–177. doi:10.1515em-2014-0067

Bloomberg. (Nov. 2, 2012). https://www.bloomberg.com/news/2012-11-02/coach-wins-257-million-court-ruling-against-counterfeiters-1-.html

Bóka, Z., & Kovács, I. S. (2015). Hungarian cuisine with respect to restaurant awards and consumers' opinions. *Journal of International Food & Agribusiness Marketing*, *27*(1), 33–49. doi:10.1080/08974438.2013.807417

Bonilla, Y., & Rosa, J. (2015). #Ferguson: Digital protest, hashtag ethnography, and the racial politics of social media in the United States. *American Ethnologist*, *42*(1), 4–17. doi:10.1111/amet.12112

Braga, J. (2004). *Sobre o Luxo*. Revista Costura Perfeita.

Brakus, J. J., Schmitt, B. H., & Zarantonello, L. (2009). Brand experience: What is it? How is it measured? Does it affect loyalty? *Journal of Marketing*, *73*(3), 52–68. doi:10.1509/jmkg.73.3.052

Brandão, A., Pinho, E., & Rodrigues, P. (2019). Antecedents and consequences of luxury brand engagement in social media. *Spanish Journal of Marketing-ESIC*, *23*(2), 163–183. doi:10.1108/SJME-11-2018-0052

Breindl, Y. (2013). Assessing success in internet campaigning. *Information Communication and Society*, *16*(9), 1419–1440. doi:10.1080/1369118X.2012.707673

Brenner, L., & Aguilar, A. G. (2002). Luxury tourism and regional economic development in Mexico. *The Professional Geographer*, *54*(4), 500–520. doi:10.1111/0033-0124.00346

Brochado, A., & Brochado, F. (2019). What makes a glamping experience great? *Journal of Hospitality and Tourism Technology*, *10*(1), 15–27. doi:10.1108/JHTT-06-2017-0039

Brochado, A., Oliveira, C., Rita, P., & Oliveira-Brochado, F. (2018). Shopping centres beyond purchasing of luxury goods: A tourism perspective. *Annals of Leisure Research*, *22*(4), 484–505. doi:10.1080/11745398.2018.1522594

Brochado, A., Troilo, M., Rodrigues, H., & Oliveira-Brochado, F. (2019). Dimensions of wine hotel experiences shared online. *International Journal of Wine Business Research*, *32*(1), 59–77. doi:10.1108/IJWBR-12-2018-0072

Brun, A., & Castelli, C. (2013). The nature of luxury: A consumer perspective. *International Journal of Retail & Distribution Management*, *41*(11/12), 823–847. doi:10.1108/IJRDM-01-2013-0006

Budiman, S., & Wijaya, T. (2014). Purchase intention of counterfeit products: The role of subjective norm. *International Journal of Marketing Studies*, *6*(2), 145–152. doi:10.5539/ijms.v6n2p145

Budish, R. H. (2012). Click to change: Optimism despite online activism's unmet expectations. *Emory International Law Review*, *26*(2), 745–772.

Bujisic, M., Hutchinson, J., & Parsa, H. G. (2014). The Effects of Restaurant Quality Attributes on Customer Behavioral Intentions. *International Journal of Contemporary Hospitality Management*, *26*(8), 1270–1291. doi:10.1108/IJCHM-04-2013-0162

Buller, A. (2018, November 11). *Men's 'modest wear' set for global boom – experts*. Retrieved from https://www.arabianbusiness.com/style/407754-mens-modest-wear-set-for-global-boom-experts

Bupalan, K., Rahim, S. A., Ahmi, A., & Rahman, N. A. A. (2019). Consumers' repurchase intention towards counterfeit products. *Int. J Sup. Chain. Mgt*, *8*(3), 973–981.

Buttle, F. A. (1998). Word of mouth: Understanding and managing referral marketing. *Journal of Strategic Marketing*, *6*(3), 241–254. doi:10.1080/096525498346658

Carbajal, J. C., Hall, J., & Li, H. (2015). Inconspicuous conspicuous consumption. Peruvian Economic Association, (38), 1-20.

Carpenter, J. M., & Lear, K. (2011). Consumer attitudes toward counterfeit fashion products: Does gender matter? *Journal of Textile and Apparel. Technology and Management*, *7*(1), 1–16.

Carrera, F. (2009). *Marketing Digital na versão 2.0*. Edições Sílado.

Carson, D. (2008). The 'blogosphere' as a market research tool for tourism destinations: A case study of Australia's Northern Territory. *Journal of Vacation Marketing*, *14*(2), 111–119. doi:10.1177/1356766707087518

Castano, R., & Perez, M. E. (2014). A matter of love: Consumers' relationships with original brands and their counterfeits. *Journal of Consumer Marketing*, *31*(6/7), 475–482. doi:10.1108/JCM-05-2014-0970

Castarède, J. (2005). *O luxo: os segredos dos produtos mais desejados do mundo*. Ed. Barcarolla.

Chandon, J. L., Laurent, G., & Valette-Florence, P. (2016). Pursuing the concept of luxury: Introduction to the JBR Special Issue on "Luxury Marketing from Tradition to Innovation". *Journal of Business Research*, *69*(1), 299–303. doi:10.1016/j.jbusres.2015.08.001

Chandon, J. L., Laurent, G., & Valette-Florence, P. (2017). In search of new planets in the luxury galaxy. *Journal of Business Research*, *77*(August), 140–146. doi:10.1016/j.jbusres.2017.04.006

Chan, S., & Amaral, N. B. (2014). Not all fakes are created equal. In B. Schmitt & L. Lee (Eds.), *The Psychology of the Asian Consumer* (Vol. 9, pp. 55–58). Routledge.

Charles, K., Hurst, E., & Roussanov, N. (2007). *Conspicuous consumption and race*. Working Paper 13392, National Bureau of Economic Research, Cambridge, MA.

Chary, S. R. K. (2014). Social media marketing: The paradigm shift in international marketing. *IOSR Journal of Business and Management*, *16*(9), 11–13. doi:10.9790/487X-16921113

Chatikavanij, K. (2019, February 12). The luxury brands taking personalisation to a new level. *The Style*. Retrieved from https://www.lifestyleasia.com/bk/style/fashion/the-luxury-brands-taking-personalisation-to-a-new-level/

Chattalas, M., & Paurav, S. (2015). Impact of value perceptions on luxury purchase intentions: A developed market comparison. *Luxury Research Journal*, *1*(1), 40–57. doi:10.1504/LRJ.2015.069806

Chaudhry, P. E., & Walsh, M. G. (1996). An assessment of the impact of counterfeiting in international markets: The piracy paradox persists. *The Columbia Journal of World Business*, *31*(3), 34–48. doi:10.1016/S0022-5428(96)90039-3

Chaudhuri, A. (2006). *Emotion and reason in consumer behavior*. Routledge. doi:10.4324/9780080461762

Chaudhuri, H. R., Mazumdar, S., & Ghoshal, A. (2011). Conspicuous consumption orientation: Conceptualisation, scale development and validation. *Journal of Consumer Behaviour. An International Research Review*, *10*(4), 216–224.

Chaudry, P., Cordell, V., & Zimmerman, A. (2005). Modelling anti-counterfeiting strategies in response to protecting intellectual property rights in a global environment. *Marketing Review, 5*(1), 59-72. (97)

Chen, A., & Peng, N. (2014). Examining Chinese consumers' luxury hotel staying behavior. *International Journal of Hospitality Management*, *39*, 53–56. doi:10.1016/j.ijhm.2014.01.002

Chen, Y. S., Raab, C., & Chen, C.-C. (2017). The influence of celebrity chefs on restaurant customers' behavior. *Journal of Hospitality Marketing & Management*, *26*(5), 489–510. doi:10.1080/19368623.2017.1269305

Cheung, C. M. K., & Lee, M. K. O. (2010). A theoretical model of intentional social action in online social networks. *Decision Support Systems*, *49*(1), 24–30. doi:10.1016/j.dss.2009.12.006

Cheung, W. L., & Prendergast, G. (2006). Buyers' perceptions of pirated products in china. *Marketing Intelligence & Planning*, *24*(5), 446–462. doi:10.1108/02634500610682854

Chevalier, M., & Mazzalovo, G. (2008). Luxury Brand Management: A World of Privilege. *Mis Quartely*, *13*(3), 319–340.

Chevalier, M., & Mazzalovo, G. (2008). *Luxury brand management: A world of privilege*. Wiley and Sons.

Chevalier, M., & Mazzalovo, G. (2013). *Luxury Brand Management: A World of Privilege*. Wiley.

Childers, T. L., & Rao, A. R. (1992). The influence of familial and peer-based reference groups on consumer decisions. *The Journal of Consumer Research*, *19*(2), 198–211. doi:10.1086/209296

Choi, W., Chan, A., & Wu, J. (1999). A qualitative and quantitative assessment of Hong Kong's image as a tourist destination. *Tourism Management*, *20*(3), 361–365. doi:10.1016/S0261-5177(98)00116-2

Choi, Y. K., Seo, Y., Wagner, U., & Yoon, S. (2018). (in press). Matching luxury brand appeals with attitude functions on social media across cultures. *Journal of Business Research*. Advance online publication. doi:10.1016/j.jbusres.2018.10.003

Choi, Y., Paulraj, A., & Shin, J. (2013). Religion or religiosity: Which is the culprit for consumer switching behavior? *Journal of International Consumer Marketing*, *25*(4), 262–280.

Chrisafis, A. (2019, February 26). *Decathlon drops French sports hijab after politicians threaten boycott*. Retrieved from https://www.theguardian.com/world/2019/feb/26/decathlon-drops-french-sports-hijab-after-politicians-threaten-boycott

Christodoulides, G., Michaelidou, N., & Li, C. H. (2009). Measuring perceived brand luxury: An evaluation of the BLI scale. *Journal of Brand Management*, *16*(5/6), 395–405. doi:10.1057/bm.2008.49

Chung, M., Ko, E., Joung, H., & Kim, S. J. (2018). (in press). Chatbot e-service and customer satisfaction regarding luxury brands. *Journal of Business Research*.

Clifford, S. (2010). *Economic indicator: Even cheaper knockoffs*. https://www.nytimes.com/2010/08/01/business/economy/01knockoff.html

Coelho, F. J., Bairrada, C. M., & de Matos Coelho, A. F. (2020). Functional brand qualities and perceived value: The mediating role of brand experience and brand personality. *Psychology and Marketing*, *37*(1), 41–55. doi:10.1002/mar.21279

Coleman, R. P. (1983). The continuing significance of social class to marketing. *The Journal of Consumer Research*, *10*(3), 265–280. doi:10.1086/208966

Colman, C. E. (2015). The history and principles of American copyright protection for fashion design: On originality. *Harvard Journal of Sports & Entertainment Law*, *6*(2), 299–344.

COMCEC. Standing Committee for Economic and Commercial Cooperation of the Organization of Islamic Cooperation. (2017). *Muslim friendly tourism: Regulating accommodation establishments in the OIC member countries*. Retrieved from http://www.sbb.gov.tr/wp-content/uploads/2018/11/Muslim_Friendly_Tourism_MFT_Regulating_Accommodation_Establishments_in_the_OIC_Member_Countries%E2%80%8B.pdf

Commuri, S. (2009). The impact of counterfeiting on genuine-item consumers' brand relationships. *Journal of Marketing*, *73*(3), 86–98.

Corbellini, E., & Saviolo, S. (2009). *Managing fashion and luxury companies*. Etas.

Cornell, A. (2002). Cult of luxury: The new opiate of the masses. *Australian Financial Review*, 47.

Cornell, A. (2002). Cult of luxury: The new opiate of the masses. *Australian Financial Review*, *27*(April), 47.

Corrêa, M., & Rozados, H. (2017). A netnografia como método de pesquisa em Ciência da Informação. Encontros Bibli. *Revista Eletrônica de Biblioteconomia e Ciência da Informação*, *22*(49), 1–18. doi:10.5007/1518-2924.2017v22n49p1

Cova, B., & Cova, V. (2001). Tribal aspects of postmodern consumption research: The case of French in-line roller skaters. *Journal of Consumer Behaviour*, *1*(1), 67–76. doi:10.1002/cb.54

Creswell, J. W., & Creswell, J. D. (2017). *Research design: Qualitative, quantitative, and mixed methods approaches*. Sage publications.

Cristini, H., Kauppinen-Räisänen, H., Barthod-Prothade, M., & Woodside, A. (2017). Toward a general theory of luxury: Advancing from workbench definitions and theoretical transformations. *Journal of Business Research*, *70*, 101–107. doi:10.1016/j.jbusres.2016.07.001

Cunningham, L. L. (2011). *Trademark counterfeiting and individual purchaser liability*. https://www.iacc.org/about-counterfeiting/the-truth-about-counterfeiting.php

Cutler, B. D. (1992). Religion and marketing: Important research area or a footnote in the literature? *Journal of Professional Services Marketing*, *8*(1), 153–164. doi:10.1300/J090v08n01_12

D'Angelo, A. (2004). *Valores e significados do consumo de produtos de luxo*. Dissertação de mestrado, Escola de Administração, Universidade Federal do Rio Grande do Sul, Porto Alegre, Brasil.

Dacko, S. G. (2017). Enabling smart retail settings via mobile augmented reality shopping apps. *Technological Forecasting and Social Change*, *124*, 243–256. doi:10.1016/j.techfore.2016.09.032

Dalgic, T., & Leeuw, M. (1994). Niche marketing revisited: Concept, applications and some European cases. *European Journal of Marketing*, *28*(4), 39–55. doi:10.1108/03090569410061178

Danziger, P. N. (2005). *Let them eat cake: Marketing luxury to the masses - as well as the classes*. Chicago: Dearborn trade.

Das, G., Agarwal, J., Malhotra, N. K., & Varshneya, G. (2019). Does brand experience translate into brand commitment?: A mediated-moderation model of brand passion and perceived brand ethicality. *Journal of Business Research*, *95*, 479–490. doi:10.1016/j.jbusres.2018.05.026

Dastin, J. (2020, January 13). *Amazon to ramp up counterfeit reporting to law enforcement*. https://www.reuters.com/article/us-amazon-com-counterfeit/amazon-to-ramp-up-counterfeit-reporting-to-law-enforcement-idUSKBN1ZC25U

De Barnier, V., Falcy, S., & Valette-Florence, P. (2012). Do consumers perceive three levels of luxury; A comparison of accessible, intermediate and inaccessible luxury brands. *Journal of Brand Management*, *19*(7), 623–636. doi:10.1057/bm.2012.11

de Kerviler, G., & Rodriguez, C. M. (2019). Luxury brand experiences and relationship quality for Millennials: The role of self-expansion. *Journal of Business Research*, *102*, 250–262. doi:10.1016/j.jbusres.2019.01.046

de Oliveira Santini, F., Ladeira, W. J., Sampaio, C. H., & Pinto, D. C. (2018). The brand experience extended model: A meta-analysis. *Journal of Brand Management*, *25*(6), 519–535. doi:10.105741262-018-0104-6

De Run, E. C., Butt, M. M., Fam, K.-S., & Jong, H. Y. (2010). Attitudes towards offensive advertising: Malaysian Muslims' views. *Journal of Islamic Marketing*, *1*(1), 25–36. doi:10.1108/17590831011026204

De Vries, L., Gensler, S., & Leeflang, P. S. H. (2012). Popularity of brand posts on brand fan pages: An investigation of the effects of social media marketing. *Journal of Interactive Marketing*, *26*(2), 83–91. doi:10.1016/j.intmar.2012.01.003

DeFanti, M., Bird, D., & Caldwell, H. (2013). *Forever now: Gucci's use of a partially borrowed heritage to establish a global luxury brand* [Paper presentation].The Biennial Conference on Historical Analysis and Research in Marketing (CHARM), Copenhagen, Denmark.

Değirmen, G. C., Vural, Z. B. A., & Ulaş, S. (2018). Lüks marka iletişiminde web sitesi ve sosyal ağ kullanımı: Karşılaştırmalı içerik analizi. *The Journal of International Social Research*, *11*(57), 519–534. doi:10.17719/jisr.2018.2468

Dekhil, F., Boulebech, H., & Bouslama, N. (2017). Effect of religiosity on luxury consumer behavior: The case of the Tunisian Muslim. *Journal of Islamic Marketing*, *8*(1), 74–94. doi:10.1108/JIMA-09-2012-0051

Delener, N. (1990). The effects of religious factors on perceived risk in durable goods purchase decisions. *Journal of Consumer Marketing*, *7*(3), 27–38. doi:10.1108/EUM0000000002580

Delener, N. (1994). Religious contrasts in consumer decision behaviour patterns: Their –dimensions and marketing implications. *European Journal of Marketing*, *28*(5), 36–53. doi:10.1108/03090569410062023

Delgado-Ballester, E., & Munuera-Alemán, J. L. (2001). Brand trust in the context of consumer loyalty. *European Journal of Marketing*, *35*(11/12), 1238–1258. doi:10.1108/EUM0000000006475

Dellarocas, C., Zhang, X., & Awad, N. F. (2007). Exploring the value of online product reviews in forecasting sales: The case of motion pictures. *Journal of Interactive Marketing*, *21*(4), 23–45. doi:10.1002/dir.20087

Deloitte. (2017). *Global powers of luxury goods 2017: The new luxury consumer*. Retrieved July 30, 2019, from https://www2.deloitte.com/content/dam/ Deloitte/global/Documents/consumer-industrial-products/gx-cip-globalpowers-luxury-2017.pdf

Dennis, C., Brakus, J. J., Gupta, S., & Alamanos, E. (2014). The effect of digital signage on shoppers' behavior: The role of the evoked experience. *Journal of Business Research*, *67*(11), 2250–2257. doi:10.1016/j.jbusres.2014.06.013

Desmichel, P., Ordabayeva, N., & Kocher, B. (2020). What if diamonds did not last forever? Signaling status achievement through ephemeral versus iconic luxury goods. *Organizational Behavior and Human Decision Processes*, *158*, 49–65. doi:10.1016/j.obhdp.2020.01.002

Dhillon, S., Rapindar, Y., & Roberts, J. (2020). *An exploration of children's understanding of luxury: A visual approach. Luxury: History, Culture*. Consumption.

Diamant, J., & Gecewicz, C. (2017, October 26). *5 facts about Muslim millennials in the U.S.* Retrieved from https://www.pewresearch.org/fact-tank/2017/10/26/5-facts-about-muslim-millennials-us/

Dikmen, G.Ö. (2008). Lüks marka pazarlaması, Vertu örneği. *İstanbul Üniversitesi İletişim Fakültesi Dergisi*, *31*, 51-64.

DinarStandard. (2019). *State of the global Islamic economy report*. Retrieved from https://ceif.iba.edu.pk/pdf/state-of-global-islamic-economy-report-2019-20.pdf

Ding, C. G., & Tseng, T. H. (2015). On the relationships among brand experience, hedonic emotions, and brand equity. *European Journal of Marketing*, *49*(7/8), 994–1015. doi:10.1108/EJM-04-2013-0200

Dion, D., & Arnould, E. J. (2011). Retail Luxury Strategy: Assembling Charisma through Art and Magic. *Journal of Retailing*, *87*(4), 502–520. doi:10.1016/j.jretai.2011.09.001

Dion, D., & Borraz, S. (2017). Managing Status: How luxury brands shape class subjectivities in the service encounter. *Journal of Marketing*, *81*(5), 67–85. doi:10.1509/jm.15.0291

Dittmar, H. (1992). Perceived material wealth and first impressions. *British Journal of Social Psychology*, *31*(4), 379–391. doi:10.1111/j.2044-8309.1992.tb00980.x

Dittmar, H. (1994). Material possessions as stereotypes: Material images of different socio-economic groups. *Journal of Economic Psychology*, *15*(4), 561–585. doi:10.1016/0167-4870(94)90011-6

Dolbec, P. Y., & Chebat, J. C. (2013). The impact of a flagship vs. a brand store on brand attitude, brand attachment and brand equity. *Journal of Retailing*, *89*(4), 460–466. doi:10.1016/j.jretai.2013.06.003

Dong, H. B., & Koo, J. (2018). Conspicuous and inconspicuous luxury consumption: a content analysis of BMW advertisements. reinvention. *An International Journal of Undergraduate Research*, *11*(2).

Douanes & Droits Indirects. (n.d.). *La Douane Contre Le Fléau De La Contrefaçon: Chiffres 2009*. https://www.douane.gouv.fr/data/file/1249.pdf

Drennan, J., Bianchi, C., Cacho-Elizondo, S., Loureiro, S., Guibert, N., & Proud, B. (2015). Examining the role of wine brand love on brand loyalty: A multi-country comparison. *International Journal of Hospitality Management*, *49*, 47–55. doi:10.1016/j.ijhm.2015.04.012

Dubois, B., Laurent, G., & Czellar, S. (2001). Consumer rapport to luxury: analyzing complex and ambivalent attitudes, Consumer research working paper No. 736. *Les cahiers de Recherche Groupe HEC*, Jouy-en-Josas, France.

Dubois, B., Laurent, G., & Czellar, S. (2001). *Consumer rapport to luxury: Analyzing complex and ambivalent attitudes*. Consumer Research Working Paper, No. 736, HEC, Patis.

Dubois, B., Laurent, G., & Czellar, S. (2001). *Consumer rapport to luxury: Analyzing complex and ambivalent attitudes*. Working Paper 736, HEC School of Management, Jouy-en-Josas.

Dubois, B., Czellar, S., & Laurent, G. (2005). Consumer Segments Based on Attitudes Toward Luxury: Empirical Evidence from Twenty Countries. *Marketing Letters*, *16*(2), 115–128. doi:10.100711002-005-2172-0

Dubois, B., & Duquesne, P. (1993). The market for luxury goods: Income versus culture. *European Journal of Marketing*, *27*(1), 35–45. doi:10.1108/03090569310024530

Dubois, B., & Laurent, G. (1995). Luxury Possessions and Practices, an Empirical Scale. In F. Hansen (Ed.), *European Advances in Consumer Research* (Vol. 2, pp. 69–77). Association for Consumer Research.

Dubois, B., & Laurent, G. (1996). Le luxe par-delà les frontières: Une etude exploratoire dans douze pays. *Décisions Marketing*, *9*, 35–43. doi:10.7193/DM.009.35.42

Duesenberry, J. S. (1949). *Income, Saving and The Theory of Consumer Behavior*. Harvard University Press.

Dunne, D. (2005). *Consumers don't need a thing*. Marketing.

Durcanin, C. (2019). *Conversation piece: San Francisco's de Young Museum celebrates 'Contemporary Muslim Fashions'*. Retrieved from https://www.artnews.com/art-news/news/conversation-piece-de-young-san-francisco-celebrates-contemporary-muslim-fashions-11630/

Dwivedi, A., Nayeem, T., & Murshed, F. (2018). Brand experience and consumers' willingness-to-pay (WTP) a price premium: Mediating role of brand credibility and perceived uniqueness. *Journal of Retailing and Consumer Services*, *44*, 100–107. doi:10.1016/j.jretconser.2018.06.009

Eagly, A. H., & Chaiken, S. (1993). *The psychology of attitudes*. Harcourt Brace Jovanovich College Publishers.

Eastman, J. K., Goldsmith, R. E., & Flynn, L. R. (1999). Status consumption in consumer behavior: Scale development and validation. *Journal of Marketing Theory and Practice*, *7*(3), 41–51. doi:10.1080/10696679.1999.11501839

Eastman, J. K., Shin, H., & Ruhland, K. (2020). The picture of luxury: A comprehensive examination of college student consumers' relationship with luxury brands. *Psychology and Marketing*, *37*(1), 56–73. doi:10.1002/mar.21280

Echtner, C. M., & Jamal, T. B. (1997). The disciplinary dilemma of tourism studies. *Annals of Tourism Research*, *24*(4), 868–883. doi:10.1016/S0160-7383(97)00060-1

Eckhardt, G. M., & Bardhi, F. (2019). New dynamics of social status and distinction. *Marketing Theory*, *20*(1), 85–102. doi:10.1177/1470593119856650

Eckhardt, G. M., Belk, R. W., & Wilson, J. A. (2015). The rise of inconspicuous consumption. *Journal of Marketing Management, 31*(7-8), 807–826. doi:10.1080/0267257X.2014.989890

Eisend, M., & Schuchert-Güler, P. (2006). Explaining counterfeit purchases: A review and preview. *Academy of Marketing Science Review, 12*, 1–25.

Ekiz, E., Khoo-Lattimore, C., & Memarzadeh, F. (2012). Air the anger: Investigating online complaints on luxury hotels. *Journal of Hospitality and Tourism Technology, 3*(2), 96–106. doi:10.1108/17579881211248817

Elliott, R., & Wattanasuwan, K. (1998). Brand as symbolic resources for the construction of identity. *International Journal of Advertising, 17*(2), 131–144. doi:10.1080/02650487.1998.11104712

Elmasoğlu, K. (2016). Marka kimlik öğesi olarak logoların marka iletişimi açısından incelenmesi: "Google Doodles" Örneği. *Erciyes İletişim Dergisi, 4*(4), 82–102.

Eng, T., & Bogaert, J. (2010). Psychological and cultural insights into consumption of luxury Western brands in India. *Journal of Customer Behaviour, 9*(1), 55–75. doi:10.1362/147539210X497620

Erickson, G. M., & Johansson, J. K. (1985). The role of price in multi-attribute product evaluations. *The Journal of Consumer Research, 12*(2), 195–199. doi:10.1086/208508

Ertimur, B., & Sandıkcı, Ö. (2014). Alienable gifts: Uses and meanings of gold in Turkey. *Journal of Consumer Behaviour, 13*(3), 204–211. doi:10.1002/cb.1479

Ertit, V. (2018). God is dying in Turkey as well: Application of secularization theory to a non-Christian society. *Open Theology, 4*(1), 192–211. doi:10.1515/opth-2018-0014

Escalas, J. E., & Bettman, J. R. (2003). You are what they eat: The influence of reference groups on consumers' connections to brands. *Journal of Consumer Psychology, 13*(3), 339–348. doi:10.1207/S15327663JCP1303_14

Essoo, N., & Dibb, S. (2004). Religious influences on shopping behaviour: An exploratory study. *Journal of Marketing Management, 20*(7–8), 683–712. doi:10.1362/0267257041838728

Evans, D., & Mckee, J. (2010). *Social media marketing: The next generation of business engagement*. Wiley Publishing.

Evans, M., Jamal, A., & Foxall, G. (2009). *Consumer behaviour* (2nd ed.). John Wiley & Sons.

Fam, K. S., Waller, D. S., & Erdogan, B. Z. (2004). The influence of religion on attitudes towards the advertising of controversial products. *European Journal of Marketing, 38*(5/6), 537–555. doi:10.1108/03090560410529204

Fan, W., & Gordon, M. D. (2014). The power of social media analytics. *Communications of the ACM, 57*(6), 74–81. doi:10.1145/2602574

Farah, M. F., & El Samad, L. (2014). The effects of religion and religiosity on advertisement assessment among Lebanese consumers. *Journal of International Consumer Marketing, 26*(4), 344–369. doi:10.1080/08961530.2014.919126

Farhana, M. (2012). Brand Elements Lead To Brand Equity: Differentiate or Die. *Information Management e Business Review, 4*(4), 223–233. doi:10.22610/imbr.v4i4.983

Farrag, D. A. (2017). The young luxury consumer in Qatar. *Young Consumers, 18*(4), 393–407. doi:10.1108/YC-06-2017-00702

Fazeli, Z., Shukla, P., & Perks, K. (2020). Digital buying behavior: The role of regulatory fit and self-construal in online luxury goods purchase intentions. *Psychology and Marketing, 37*(1), 15–26. doi:10.1002/mar.21276

Felice, K. B. (2011). Fashioning a solution for design piracy: Considering intellectual property law in the global context of fast fashion. *Syracuse J. Int'l L. & Com., 39*, 219–236.

Feltovich, N., Harbaugh, R., & To, T. (2002). Too cool for school? Signalling and Countersignalling. *The RAND Journal of Economics, 33*(4), 630–349. doi:10.2307/3087478

Fernandes, S. F., & Panda, R. (2018). Social reference group influence on women buying behaviour: A review. *Journal of Commerce and Management Thought, 9*(2), 273–291. doi:10.5958/0976-478X.2018.00019.8

Fernandes, S., & Panda, R. (2019). Influence of social reference groups on consumer buying behavior: A review. *Journal of Management Research, 19*(2), 131–142.

Ferraro, R., Kirmani, A., & Matherly, T. (2013). Look at me! Look at me! Conspicuous brand usage, self-brand connection, and dilution. *JMR, Journal of Marketing Research, 50*(4), 477–488. doi:10.1509/jmr.11.0342

Ferreira, J., & Sousa, B. (2020) Experiential Marketing as Leverage for Growth of Creative Tourism: A Co-creative Process. In Advances in Tourism, Technology and Smart Systems. Smart Innovation, Systems and Technologies, (vol 171, pp. 567-577). Springer. doi:10.1007/978-981-15-2024-2_49

Ferreira, L., & Sousa, B. B. (2020). Understanding the Role of Social Networks in Consumer Behavior in Tourism: A Business Approach. In C. Ramos, C. Almeida, & P. Fernandes (Eds.), *Handbook of Research on Social Media Applications for the Tourism and Hospitality Sector* (pp. 367–384). IGI Global. doi:10.4018/978-1-7998-1947-9.ch021

Ferreira, P., Rodrigues, P., & Rodrigues, P. (2019). Brand love as mediator of the brand experience-satisfaction-loyalty relationship in a retail fashion brand. *Management & Marketing. Challenges for the Knowledge Society, 14*(3), 278–291. doi:10.2478/mmcks-2019-0020

Festinger, L. (1954). A theory of social comparison processes. *Human Relations, 7*(2), 117–140. doi:10.1177/001872675400700202

Financial Tribune. (2017, September 24). *Iran's cosmetics market on growth trajectory*. Retrieved from https://financialtribune.com/articles/economy/73022/iran-s-cosmetics-market-on-growth-trajectory

Fionda, A. M., & Moore, C. M. (2009). The anatomy of the luxury fashion brand. *Journal of Brand Management, 16*(5), 347–363. doi:10.1057/bm.2008.45

Firat, A. F., & Venkatesh, A. (1995). Liberatory postmodernism and the reenchantment of consumption. *The Journal of Consumer Research, 22*(3), 239–267. doi:10.1086/209448

Fischer, J. (2014). Muslim material culture in the Western world. In R. Tottoli (Ed.), *Routledge handbook of Islam in the West* (pp. 348–362). Routledge.

Forghani, M. H., Kazemi, A., & Ranjbarian, B. (2019). Religion, peculiar beliefs and luxury cars' consumer behavior in Iran. *Journal of Islamic Marketing, 10*(2), 673–688. doi:10.1108/JIMA-06-2018-0101

Fortune. (2007). Luxury goes mass market. *Fortune Magazine*.

Fournier, S. (1998). Consumers and their brands: Developing relationship theory in consumer research. *The Journal of Consumer Research, 24*(4), 343–353. doi:10.1086/209515

Fournier, S., & Alvarez, C. (2013). Relating badly to brands. *Journal of Consumer Psychology, 23*(2), 253–264. doi:10.1016/j.jcps.2013.01.004

Francisco-Maffezzolli, E. C., Semprebon, E., & Prado, P. H. M. (2014). Construing loyalty through brand experience: The mediating role of brand relationship quality. *Journal of Brand Management, 21*(5), 446–458. doi:10.1057/bm.2014.16

Frerichs, A. (2008). Attitudes toward counterfeit fashion products: A South Dakota State University case study. *The Journal of Undergraduate Research*, *6*(6), 19–35.

Friedman, M. (1985). Consumer boycotts in the United States, 1970-1980: Contemporary events in historical perspective. *The Journal of Consumer Affairs*, *19*(1), 96–117. doi:10.1111/j.1745-6606.1985.tb00346.x

Fullerton, G. (2005). How commitment both enables and undermines marketing relationships. *European Journal of Marketing*, *39*(11/12), 1372–1388. doi:10.1108/03090560510623307

Funches, V., Markley, M., & Davis, L. (2009). Reprisal, retribution and requital: Investigating customer retaliation. *Journal of Business Research*, *62*(2), 231–238. doi:10.1016/j.jbusres.2008.01.030

Gabrielli, V., Grappi, S., & Baghi, I. (2012). Does counterfeiting affect luxury customer-based brand equity? *Journal of Brand Management*, *19*(7), 567–580. doi:10.1057/bm.2012.6

Galhanone, R. (2005). O mercado do luxo: aspetos de marketing. Academic Press.

García, S. (2003), El universo del lujo, Una visión global estratégica para profesionales y amantes del lujo. Instituto de Empresa, Mc Graw Hill.

Gardyn, R. (2002). Oh, the good life. *Advertising Age*, *24*(10), 31–35.

Gayatri, G., Chan, C., Mort, G. S., & Hume, M. (2005). Understanding service quality from the Islamic customer perspective. In S. Purchase (Ed.), *Proceedings of the Australian and New Zealand Marketing Academy Conference*. University of Western Australia.

Gazzah, M. (2014). European Muslim youth and popular culture: At the crossroads of fun and faith. In R. Tottoli (Ed.), *Routledge handbook of Islam in the West* (pp. 334–347). Routledge.

Gee, J. P. (2005). Social semiotic spaces and affinity spaces. In D. Barton & K. Tusting (Eds.), *Beyond communities of practice* (pp. 214–232). Cambridge University Press. doi:10.1017/CBO9780511610554.012

Geerts, A. (2013). Cluster analysis of luxury brands on the internet. *International Journal of Management and Marketing Research*, *6*(2), 79–93.

Gehrels, S. A., & Kristanto, S. (2007). Marketing of Dutch culinary restaurants: An exploration from the entrepreneur's perspective. *Journal of Culinary Science & Technology*, *5*(2/3), 23–37.

Geissler, G. L. (2001). Building customer relationships online: The website designers' perspective. *Journal of Consumer Marketing*, *18*(6), 488–502. doi:10.1108/EUM0000000006154

Gentile, C., Spiller, N., & Noci, G. (2007). How to sustain the customer experience: An overview of experience components that co-create value with the customer. *European Management Journal*, *25*(5), 395–410. doi:10.1016/j.emj.2007.08.005

Gentry, J. W., Putrevu, S., II, & Commuri, S. (2001). How now Ralph Lauren? The separation of brand and product in a counterfeit culture. *ACR North American Advances*, *28*, 258-265.

Gentry, J. W., Putrevu, S., & Shultz, C. J. (2006). The effects of counterfeiting on consumer search. *Journal of Consumer Behaviour*, *5*(3), 245–256. doi:10.1002/cb.176

Gentry, J. W., Putrevu, S., Shultz, C. J., & Commuri, S. (2001). How new Ralph Lauren? The separation of brand and product in a counterfeit culture. In M. C. Gilly & J. Meyers-Levy (Eds.), *Advances in Consumer Research* (Vol. 28, pp. 258–265). Association for Consumer Research.

Ger, G. (2013). Islamic marketing at the nexus of global markets–religions–politics and implications for research. *Marketing Theory, 13*(4), 497–503. doi:10.1177/1470593113499702

Giambarrese, N. (2010). The look for less: A survey of intellectual property protections in the fashion industry. *Touro Law Review, 26*(1), 243–286.

Gibson, S. (2019, September 11). *Brand-new Halal Cosmetics Zone to launch at in-cosmetics Asia 2019.* Retrieved from https://news.in-cosmetics.com/2019/09/11/brand-new-halal-cosmetics-zone-to-launch-at-in-cosmetics-asia-2019/#_ftnref2

Gibson, R. K., Margolis, M., Resnick, D., & Ward, S. J. (2003). Election campaigning on the www in the USA and UK: A comparative analysis. *Party Politics, 9*(1), 47–75. doi:10.1177/135406880391004

Gil, L. A., Kwon, K. N., Good, L. K., & Johnson, L. W. (2012). Impact of self on attitudes toward luxury brands among teens. *Journal of Business Research, 65*(10), 1425–1433. doi:10.1016/j.jbusres.2011.10.008

Gino, F., Norton, M. I., & Ariely, D. (2010). The counterfeit self: The deceptive costs of faking it. *Psychological Science, 21*(5), 712–720. doi:10.1177/0956797610366545 PMID:20483851

Giovannini, S., Xu, Y., & Thomas, J. (2015). Luxury fashion consumption and Generation Y consumers: Self, brand consciousness, and consumption motivations. *Journal of Fashion Marketing and Management, 19*(1), 22–40. doi:10.1108/JFMM-08-2013-0096

Global Anti-Counterfeiting Network. (2019). http://www.gacg.org/Home

Godey, B., Manthiou, A., Pederzoli, D., Rokka, J., Aiello, G., Donvito, R., & Singh, R. (2016). Social media marketing efforts of luxury brands: Influence on brand equity and consumer behavior. *Journal of Business Research, 69*(12), 5833–5841. doi:10.1016/j.jbusres.2016.04.181

Godey, B., Pederzoli, D., Aiell, G., Donvito, R., Wiedmann, K. P., & Hennigs, N. (2013). A cross-cultural exploratory content analysis of the perception of luxury from six countries. *Journal of Product and Brand Management, 22*(3), 229–237. doi:10.1108/JPBM-02-2013-0254

Godey, B., Pederzoli, D., Aiello, G., Donvito, R., Chan, P., Oh, H., Singh, R., Skorobogatykh, I. I., Tsuchiya, J., & Weitz, B. (2012). Brand and country-of-origin effect on consumers' decision to purchase luxury products. *Journal of Business Research, 65*(10), 1461–1470. doi:10.1016/j.jbusres.2011.10.012

Goffman, E. (1959). *The presentation of self in everyday life.* Doubleday Anchor.

Goh, K. Y., Heng, C. S., & Lin, Z. (2013). Social media brand community and consumer behavior: Quantifying the relative impact of user-and marketer-generated content. *Information Systems Research, 24*(1), 88–107. doi:10.1287/isre.1120.0469

Goldenberg, J., Libai, B., & Muller, E. (2001). Talk of the network: A complex systems look at the underlying process of word-of-mouth. *Marketing Letters, 12*(3), 211–223. doi:10.1023/A:1011122126881

Gong, Y. (2001). *Anomaly of consumption: Asian's extravagance in luxury goods.* Academic Press.

Goor, D., Odabayeva, N., Keinan, A. & Crener, S. (2020). The impostor syndrome from luxury consumption. *Journal of Consumer Research, 46*(6), 031–1051.

Goswami, S. (2015). *A Study on the Online Branding Strategies of Indian Fashion Retail Stores.* IUP Journal of Brand Management.

Granot, E., & Brashear, T. (2008). *From luxury to populence: Inconspicuous consumption as described by female consumers.* Paper presented at the Advances in Consumer Research Volume 35, Duluth, MN.

Granot, E., Russell, L. M., & Brashear-Alejandro, T. G. (2013). Populence: Exploring luxury for the masses. *Journal of Marketing Theory and Practice*, *21*(1), 31–44. doi:10.2753/MTP1069-6679210102

Greenberg, D., Ehrensperger, E., Schulte-Mecklenbeck, M., Hoyer, W. D., Zhang, Z. J., & Krohmer, H. (2020). The role of brand prominence and extravagance of product design in luxury brand building: What drives consumers' preferences for loud versus quiet luxury? *Journal of Brand Management*, *27*(2), 195–210. doi:10.105741262-019-00175-5

Green, M. C., & Brock, T. C. (2000). The role of transportation in the persuasiveness of public narratives. *Journal of Personality and Social Psychology*, *79*(5), 701–721. doi:10.1037/0022-3514.79.5.701

Greenwood, G. (2016, December 9). *World Halal Tourism Awards 2016 winners announced*. Retrieved from https://www.traveldailymedia.com/world-halal-tourism-awards-2016-winners-announced/

Grégoire, Y., Tripp, T., & Legoux, R. (2009). When customer love turns into lasting hate: The effects of relationship strength and time on customer revenge and avoidance. *Journal of Marketing*, *73*(6), 18–32. doi:10.1509/jmkg.73.6.18

Grewal, D., Baker, J., Levy, M., & Voss, G. B. (2003). The effects of wait expectations and store atmosphere evaluations on patronage intentions in service-intensive retail stores. *Journal of Retailing*, *79*(4), 259–268. doi:10.1016/j.jretai.2003.09.006

Grossman, G. M., & Shapiro, C. (1988). Foreign counterfeiting of status goods. *The Quarterly Journal of Economics*, *103*(1), 79–100. doi:10.2307/1882643

Grubb, E. L., & Grathwohl, H. L. (1967). Consumer self-concept, symbolism and market behavior: A theoretical approach. *Journal of Marketing*, *31*(4), 22–27. doi:10.1177/002224296703100405

Guido, G., Amatulli, C., Peluso, A. M., De Matteis, C., Piper, L., & Pino, G. (2020). Measuring internalized versus externalized luxury consumption motivations and consumers' segmentation. *Italian. Journal of Marketing*, 1–23.

Gurzki, H., & Woisetschläger, D. M. (2017). Mapping the luxury research landscape: A bibliometric citation analysis. *Journal of Business Research*, *77*, 147–166. doi:10.1016/j.jbusres.2016.11.009

Hagtveded, H., & Patrick, V. (2009). The broad embrace of luxury: Hedonic potential as a driver of brand extendibility. *Journal of Consumer Psychology*, *19*(4), 608–619. doi:10.1016/j.jcps.2009.05.007

Hagtvedt, H., & Patrick, V. M. (2008). Art infusion: The influence of visual art on the perception and evaluation of consumer products. *JMR, Journal of Marketing Research*, *45*(3), 379–389. doi:10.1509/jmkr.45.3.379

Hamelin, N., & Thaichon, P. (2016). Consumer motives and impact of western media on the Moroccan luxury buyer. *Journal of Retailing and Consumer Services*, *32*, 164–170. doi:10.1016/j.jretconser.2016.06.010

Han, H., & Hyun, S. S. (2017). Impact of hotel-restaurant image and quality of physical-environment, service, and food on satisfaction and intention. *International Journal of Hospitality Management*, *63*, 82–92. doi:10.1016/j.ijhm.2017.03.006

Hanks, L., Linea, N., & Kim, W. G. (2017). The impact of the social servicescape, density, and restaurant type on perceptions of interpersonal service quality. *International Journal of Hospitality Management*, *61*, 35–44. doi:10.1016/j.ijhm.2016.10.009

Hansen, G. H., & Møller, H. K. (2017). Louis Vuitton in the bazaar: Negotiating the value of counterfeit goods in Shanghai's Xiangyang market. *International Journal of Entrepreneurship and Small Business*, *30*(2), 170–190. doi:10.1504/IJESB.2017.081437

Hansen, K. V. (2014). Development of SERVQUAL and DINESERV for measuring meal experiences in eating establishments. *Scandinavian Journal of Hospitality and Tourism*, *14*(2), 116–134. doi:10.1080/15022250.2014.886094

Han, Y. J., Nunes, J. C., & Dreze, X. (2010). Signaling Status with Luxury Goods: The Role of Brand Prominence. *Journal of Marketing*, *74*(July), 15–30. doi:10.1509/jmkg.74.4.015

Harridge, M. S. (2004). Electronic marketing, the new kid on the block. *Marketing Intelligence & Planning*, *22*(3), 297–309. doi:10.1108/02634500410536885

Harun, A., Mahmud, M., Othman, B., Ali, R., & Ismael, D. (2020). Understanding experienced consumers towards repeat purchase of counterfeit products: The mediating effect of attitude. *Management Science Letters*, *10*(1), 13–28. doi:10.5267/j.msl.2019.8.019

Harvey, P. J., & Walls, W. D. (2003). Laboratory markets in counterfeit goods: Hong Kong versus Las Vegas. *Applied Economics Letters*, *10*(14), 883–887. doi:10.1080/1350485032000155431

Hashim, A., & Musa, R. (2014). Factors influencing attitude towards halal cosmetics among young adult urban Muslim women: A focus group analysis. *Procedia: Social and Behavioral Sciences*, *130*, 129–134. doi:10.1016/j.sbspro.2014.04.016

Hashim, N. M., & Mizerski, D. (2010). Exploring Muslim consumers' information sources for fatwa rulings on products and behaviors. *Journal of Islamic Marketing*, *1*(1), 37–50. doi:10.1108/17590831011026213

Heiens, R. A., Pleshko, L. P., & Aldousari, A. A. (2016). Using direct observation to examine the relationship between religiosity, demographics, and consumption in a Middle Eastern retail services setting. *Journal of International Consumer Marketing*, *28*(4), 274–282. doi:10.1080/08961530.2016.1171741

Heine, K. (2012). The concept of luxury brands. *Luxury Brand Management*, *1*.

Heine, K. (2012). *The Concept of Luxury*. Retrieved from https://upmarkit.com/sites/default/files/content/20130403_Heine_The_Concept_of_Luxury_Brands.pdf

Heine, K., & Berghaus, B. (2014). Luxury goes digital: How to tackle the digital luxury brand-consumer touchpoints. *Journal of Global Fashion Marketing*, *5*(3), 223–234. doi:10.1080/20932685.2014.907606

Heine, K., & Phan, M. (2011). Trading-up mass-market goods to luxury products. *Australasian Marketing Journal*, *19*(2), 108–114. doi:10.1016/j.ausmj.2011.03.001

Heinrichs, J. H., Lim, J.-S., & Lim, K.-S. (2011). Influence of social networking site and user access method on social media evaluation. *Journal of Consumer Behaviour*, *10*(6), 347–355. doi:10.1002/cb.377

Henke, L. L., & Fontenot, G. (2011). Why advertising does not cause smoking initiation. *Journal of Business & Economics Research*, *3*(5), 65–70. doi:10.19030/jber.v3i5.2778

Hennigs, N., Wiedmann, K. P., Behrens, S., & Klarmann, C. (2013). Unleashing the power of luxury: Antecedents of luxury brand perceptions and effect on luxury brand strength. *Journal of Brand Management*, *20*(8), 705–715. doi:10.1057/bm.2013.11

Hennigs, N., Wiedmann, K. P., Klarmann, C., Strehlau, S., Godey, B., Pederzoli, D., ... Taro, K. (2012). What is the value of luxury? A cross-cultural consumer perspective. *Psychology and Marketing*, *29*(12), 1018–1034. doi:10.1002/mar.20583

Hennigs, N., Wiedmann, K.-P., & Klarmann, C. (2012). Luxury brands in the digital age: Exclusivity versus ubiquity. *Marketing Review St. Gallen*, *29*(1), 30–35. doi:10.100711621-012-0108-7

Hennig-Thurau, T., Gwinner, K. P., & Gremler, D. D. (2002). Understanding relationship marketing outcomes: An integration of relational benefits and relationship quality. *Journal of Service Research*, *4*(3), 230–247. doi:10.1177/1094670502004003006

Hepola, J., Karjaluoto, H., & Hintikka, A. (2017). The effect of sensory brand experience and involvement on brand equity directly and indirectly through consumer brand engagement. *Journal of Product and Brand Management, 26*(3), 282–293. doi:10.1108/JPBM-10-2016-1348

Hieke, S. (2010). Effects of counterfeits on the image of luxury brands: An empirical study from the customer perspective. *Journal of Brand Management, 18*(2), 159–173. doi:10.1057/bm.2010.28

HIRC. (2003). Are proceeds from counterfeited goods funding terrorism? *House International Relations Committee, Hearing on Intellectual Property Crimes,* www.foreignaffairs.house.gov/archives/108/88392.pdf

Hirschman, E. C., & Touzani, M. (2011). Consumer acculturation in situ: The continuing legacy of French colonization in North Africa. In O. Sandikci & G. Rice (Eds.), Handbook of Islamic marketing (pp. 114–128). Cheltenham: Edward Elgar Publishing.

Hirschman, E. C. (1983). Religious affiliation and consumption processes: An initial paradigm. In J. N. Sheth (Ed.), *Research in marketing* (pp. 131–170). JAI Press.

Hirschman, E. C., & Holbrook, M. B. (1982). Hedonic Consumption: Emerging Concepts, Methods and Propositions. *Journal of Marketing, 46*(3), 92–101. Advance online publication. doi:10.1177/002224298204600314

Hlee, S., Lee, J., Yang, S.-B., & Koo, C. (2019). The moderating effect of restaurant type on hedonic versus utilitarian review evaluations. *International Journal of Hospitality Management, 77*, 195–206. doi:10.1016/j.ijhm.2018.06.030

Hoe, L., Hogg, G., & Hart, S. (2003). Faking it: Counterfeiting and consumer contradictions. *European Advances in Consumer Behaviour, 6*, 60–67.

Hoffman, D. L., & Novak, T. P. (1996). Marketing in Hypermedia Computer-Mediated Environments: Conceptual Foundations. *Journal of Marketing, 60*(3), 50. doi:10.2307/1251841

Hogg, M. K. (1998). Anti-constellations: Exploring the impact of negation on consumption. *Journal of Marketing Management, 14*(1-3), 133–158. doi:10.1362/026725798784959354

Holbrook, M. B., & Hirschman, E. C. (1982). The Experiential aspects of consumption: Consumer fantasies, feelings and fun. *The Journal of Consumer Research, 9*(2), 132–140. doi:10.1086/208906

Holleschovsky, N. I. (2015). *The social influence factor: Impact of online product review characteristics on consumer purchasing decisions.* 5th IBA Bachelor Thesis Conference, Enschede, The Netherlands.

Holmqvist, J., Ruiz, C. D., & Penaloza, L. (2019). Moments of luxury: Hedonic escapism as a luxury experience. *Journal of Business Research, 116*, 503–513. doi:10.1016/j.jbusres.2019.10.015

Hookway, N. (2008). "Entering the Blogosphere" Some Strategies for Using Blogs in Social Research. *Qualitative Research, 8*(1), 91–113. doi:10.1177/1468794107085298

Hopkinson, G. C., & Pujari, D. (1999). A factor analytic study of the sources of meaning in hedonic consumption. *European Journal of Marketing, 33*(3/4), 273–290. doi:10.1108/03090569910253053

Huang, C. C. (2017). The impacts of brand experiences on brand loyalty: Mediators of brand love and trust. *Management Decision, 55*(5), 915–934. doi:10.1108/MD-10-2015-0465

Huang, L.-S. (2015). Trust in product review blogs: The influence of self-disclosure and popularity. *Behaviour & Information Technology, 34*(1), 33–44. doi:10.1080/0144929X.2014.978378

Huang, R., Lee, S. H., Kim, H., & Evans, L. (2015). The impact of brand experiences on brand resonance in multichannel fashion retailing. *Journal of Research in Interactive Marketing, 9*(2), 129–147. doi:10.1108/JRIM-06-2014-0042

Hudders, L., & Pandelaere, M. (2012). The silver lining of materialism: The impact of luxury consumption on subjective well-being. *Journal of Happiness Studies*, *13*(3), 411–437. doi:10.100710902-011-9271-9

Hudders, L., Pandelaere, M., & Vyncke, P. (2013). Consumer meaning making: The meaning of luxury brands in a democratised luxury world. *International Journal of Market Research*, *55*(3), 391–412. doi:10.2501/IJMR-2013-036

Hughes, M. U., Bendoni, W. K., & Pehlivan, E. (2016). Storygiving as a co-creation tool for luxury brands in the age of the internet: A love story by Tiffany and thousands of lovers. *Journal of Product and Brand Management*, *25*(4), 357–364. doi:10.1108/JPBM-09-2015-0970

Hultén, B. (2011). Sensory marketing: The multi-sensory brand-experience concept. *European Business Review*, *23*(3), 256–273. doi:10.1108/09555341111130245

Hume, M., & Mills, M. (2013). Uncovering Victoria's Secret: Exploring women's luxury perceptions of intimate apparel and purchasing behaviour. *Journal of Fashion Marketing and Management*, *17*(4), 460–485. doi:10.1108/JFMM-03-2013-0020

Hung, K. P., Chen, A. H., Peng, N., Hackely, C., Tiwsakul, R. A., & Chou, C. I. (2011). Antecedents of luxury brand purchase intentions. *Journal of Product and Brand Management*, *20*(6), 457–467. doi:10.1108/10610421111166603

Hussain, A., Kofinas, A., & Win, S. (2017). Intention to purchase counterfeit luxury products: A comparative study between Pakistani and the UK consumers. *Journal of International Consumer Marketing*, *29*(5), 331–346. doi:10.1080/08961530.2017.1361881

Iglesias, O., Markovic, S., & Rialp, J. (2019). How does sensory brand experience influence brand equity? Considering the roles of customer satisfaction, customer affective commitment, and employee empathy. *Journal of Business Research*, *96*, 343–354. doi:10.1016/j.jbusres.2018.05.043

Iglesias, O., Singh, J. J., & Batista-Foguet, J. M. (2011). The role of brand experience and affective commitment in determining brand loyalty. *Journal of Brand Management*, *18*(8), 570–582. doi:10.1057/bm.2010.58

Int. No. 544 § 10-902 (2013). https://legistar.council.nyc.gov/LegislationDetail.aspx?ID=885894&GUID=926F900B-7A1E-48E8-991D-6A3CFE24EA90

Interbrand. (2013). *2013 ranking of the top 100 brands*. https://www.interbrand.com/en/best-global-brands/2013/Best-Global-Brands-2013-Brand-View.aspx

International Chamber of Commerce report. (2009). http://www.iccwbo.org/Data/Documents/Bascap/Consumer-Perceptions/Consumer-Research-Report/

International Chamber of Commerce report. (2013). http://www.iccwbo.org/products-and-services/fighting-commercial-crime/counterfeiting-intelligence-bureau/

Islam, J. U., Hollebeek, L. D., Rahman, Z., Khan, I., & Rasool, A. (2019). Customer engagement in the service context: An empirical investigation of the construct, its antecedents and consequences. *Journal of Retailing and Consumer Services*, *50*, 277–285. doi:10.1016/j.jretconser.2019.05.018

Islam, T., & Chandrasekaran, U. (2019). Religiosity, values and consumer behaviour: A study of young Indian Muslim consumers. *Journal of Consumer Marketing*, *36*(7), 948–961. doi:10.1108/JCM-10-2017-2415

Iyer, R., & Muncy, J. A. (2009). Purpose and object of anti-consumption. *Journal of Business Research*, *62*(2), 160–168. doi:10.1016/j.jbusres.2008.01.023

Jackson, T., & Shaw, D. (2009). *Mastering Fashion Marketing*. Palgrave Macmillan. doi:10.1007/978-1-137-09271-7

Jain, V. (2018). Luxury: Not for consumption but developing extended digital self. *Journal of Human Values*, *24*(1), 25–38. doi:10.1177/0971685817733570

Jain, V., Roy, S., & Ranchhod, A. (2015). Conceptualizing luxury buying behavior: The Indian perspective. *Journal of Product and Brand Management*, *24*(3), 211–228. doi:10.1108/JPBM-07-2014-0655

Jain, V., & Schultz, D. E. (2019). How digital platforms influence luxury purchase behavior in India? *Journal of Marketing Communications*, *25*(1), 41–64. doi:10.1080/13527266.2016.1197295

Japutra, A., & Molinillo, S. (2019). Responsible and active brand personality: On the relationships with brand experience and key relationship constructs. *Journal of Business Research*, *99*, 464–471. doi:10.1016/j.jbusres.2017.08.027

Jeong, M., & Jeon, M. M. (2008). Customer reviews of hotel experiences through consumer-generated media (CGM). *Journal of Hospitality & Leisure Marketing*, *17*(1/2), 121–138. doi:10.1080/10507050801978265

Jiang, Y., Miao, M., Jalees, T., & Zaman, S. I. (2019). Analysis of the moral mechanism to purchase counterfeit luxury goods: Evidence from China. *Asia Pacific Journal of Marketing and Logistics*, *31*(3), 647–669. doi:10.1108/APJML-05-2018-0190

Jin, N., Goh, B., Huffman, L., & Yuan, J. J. (2015). Predictors and outcomes of perceived image of restaurant innovativeness in fine-dining restaurants. *Journal of Hospitality Marketing & Management*, *24*(5), 457–485. doi:10.1080/19368623.2014.915781

Jin, N., Line, N. D., & Merkebu, J. (2016). Examining the Impact of Consumer Innovativeness and and Innovative Restaurant Image in Upscale Restaurants. *Cornell Hospitality Quarterly*, *57*(3), 268–281. doi:10.1177/1938965515619229

Johns, N., & Pine, R. (2002). Customer behavior in the food service industry: A review. *International Journal of Hospitality Management*, *21*(2), 119–134. doi:10.1016/S0278-4319(02)00008-7

Johnson, C., Surlemont, B., Nicod, P., & Revaz, F. (2005). Behind the stars – A concise typology of Michelin restaurants in Europe. *The Cornell Hotel and Restaurant Administration Quarterly*, *46*(2), 170–187. doi:10.1177/0010880405275115

Jordan Keane, M., & McMillan, Z. (2004). Above and beyond (brand papers). *Brand Strategy*, *187*, 30.

Joy, A., Belk, R., & Bhardwaj, R. (2017). Luxury consumption and luxury brands: Past, present, and future. In M. Keller, B. Halkier, T. Wilska, & M. Truninger (Eds.), *Routledge handbook on consumption* (pp. 442–452). Routledge. doi:10.4324/9781315675015-44

Joy, A., Wang, J. J., Chan, T. S., Sherry, J. F. Jr, & Cui, G. (2014). M (Art) worlds: Consumer perceptions of how luxury brand stores become art institutions. *Journal of Retailing*, *90*(3), 347–364. doi:10.1016/j.jretai.2014.01.002

Jung, J., Yu, J., Seo, Y., & Ko, E. (2019). (in press). Consumer experiences of virtual reality: Insights from VR luxury brand fashion shows. *Journal of Business Research*. Advance online publication. doi:10.1016/j.jbusres.2019.10.038

Kale, G. Ö. (2016). Lüks marka reklamlarında ünlü kullanımının önemi: Louis Vuitton örneği. *Istanbul Ticaret Üniversitesi Sosyal Bilimler Dergisi*, *29*, 325.

Kaminakis, K., Karantinou, K., Koritos, C., & Gounaris, S. (2019). Hospitality servicescape effects on customer-employee interactions: A multilevel study. *Tourism Management*, *72*, 130–144. doi:10.1016/j.tourman.2018.11.013

Kang, J., Manthiou, A., Sumarjan, N., & Tang, L. (2017). An investigation of brand experience on brand attachment, knowledge, and trust in the lodging industry. *Journal of Hospitality Marketing & Management*, *26*(1), 1–22. doi:10.1080/19368623.2016.1172534

Kapferer, J. (2015). *Kapferer on luxury: How luxury brands can grow yet remain rare*. Kogan Page Stylus.

Kapferer, J. (2012). *The new strategic brand management creating and sustaining brand equity long term* (5th ed.). Kogan Page.

Kapferer, J. N. (1997). Managing luxury brands. *Journal of Brand Management, 4*(4), 251–259. doi:10.1057/bm.1997.4

Kapferer, J. N. (1998). Why are we seduced by luxury brands? *Journal of Brand Management, 6*(1), 44–49. doi:10.1057/bm.1998.43

Kapferer, J. N. (2010). Luxury after the crisis: Pro logo or no logo. *European Business Review*, (September-October), 42–46.

Kapferer, J. N. (2017). Managing luxury brands. In J. N. Kapferer, J. Kernstock, T. Brexendorf, & S. Powell (Eds.), *Advances in Luxury Brand Management*. Palgrave Macmillan. doi:10.1007/978-3-319-51127-6_11

Kapferer, J. N., & Bastien, V. (2009). *The luxury strategy: Break the rules ofmarketing to build luxury brands*. Kogan Page.

Kapferer, J. N., & Bastien, V. (2009). The specificity of luxury management: Turning marketing upside down. *Journal of Brand Management, 16*(5-6), 311–322. doi:10.1057/bm.2008.51

Kapferer, J. N., & Bastien, V. (2012a). *The luxury strategy*. Kogan Page.

Kapferer, J. N., & Bastien, V. (2012b). *The luxury strategy: Break the rules of marketing to build luxury brands*. Kogan Page.

Kapferer, J. N., & Laurent, G. (2014). Where do consumers think luxury begins? A study of perceived minimum price for 21 luxury goods in 7 countries. *Journal of Business Research, 69*(1), 332–340. doi:10.1016/j.jbusres.2015.08.005

Kapferer, J. N., & Valette-Florence, P. (2018). The impact of brand penetration and awareness on luxury brand desirability: A cross country analysis of the relevance of the rarity principle. *Journal of Business Research, 83*, 38–50. doi:10.1016/j.jbusres.2017.09.025

Kapferer, J.-N. (2010). All that glitters is not green: The challenge of sustainable luxury'. *European Business Review*, (November–December), 40–45.

Kapferer, J.-N. (2012). Abundant rarity: The key to luxury growth. *Business Horizons, 55*(5), 453–462. doi:10.1016/j.bushor.2012.04.002

Kapferer, J.-N., & Bastien, V. (2012). *The Luxury Strategy: Break the Rules of Marketing to Build Luxury Brands*. Kogan Page.

Kapferer, J.-N., & Michaut, A. (2015). Luxury and sustainability: A common future? The match depends on how consumers define luxury. *Luxury Research Journal, 1*(1), 3–17. doi:10.1504/LRJ.2015.069828

Kapferer, J.-N., & Michaut, A. (2016). Pursuing the Concept of Luxury A cross-country comparison and segmentation of luxury buyers' perception of luxury. *Journal of International Marketing Strategy, 4*(1), 6–23.

Kapferer, J.-N., & Michaut-Denizeau, A. (2020). Are millennials really more sensitive to sustainable luxury? A cross-generational international comparison of sustainability consciousness when buying luxury. *Journal of Brand Management, 27*(1), 35–47. doi:10.105741262-019-00165-7

Kapferer, J.-N., & Valette-Florance, P. (2019). How self-success drives luxury demand: An integrated model of luxury growth and country comparisons. *Journal of Business Research, 102*(September), 273–288. doi:10.1016/j.jbusres.2019.02.002

Karabulut, F., Aytac, M. B., & Akin, E. (2020). Makeup Consumption and Islamic Religiosity. *Human Arenas, 3*, 534–551. doi:10.100742087-020-00106-w

Karahan, M. O., & Şahin, F. (2020). Tüketicilerin taklit ürün satın alma tutumlarını ve niyetlerini etkileyen faktörlerin belirlenmesi: Nicel bir araştırma. *Gümüşhane Üniversitesi Sosyal Bilimler Enstitüsü Elektronik Dergisi, 11*(1), 154–170.

Karataş, M., & Sandıkcı, Ö. (2013). Religious communities and the marketplace: Learning and performing consumption in an Islamic network. *Marketing Theory, 13*(4), 465–484. doi:10.1177/1470593113499697

Kassim, N. M., & Zain, M. M. (2016). Quality of lifestyle and luxury purchase inclinations from the perspectives of affluent Muslim consumers. *Journal of Islamic Marketing, 7*(1), 95–119. doi:10.1108/JIMA-08-2014-0052

Kastanakis, M. N., & Balabanis, G. (2012). Between the mass and the class: Antecedents of the "bandwagon" luxury consumption behavior. *Journal of Business Research, 65*(10), 1399–1407. doi:10.1016/j.jbusres.2011.10.005

Kastanakis, M. N., & Balabanis, G. (2014). Explaining variation in conspicuous luxury consumption: An individual differences' perspective. *Journal of Business Research, 67*(10), 2147–2154. doi:10.1016/j.jbusres.2014.04.024

Katz, D. (1960). The functional approach to the study of attitudes. *Public Opinion Quarterly, 24*(2), 163–204. doi:10.1086/266945

Kauppinen-Räisänen, H., Gummerus, J., von Koskull, C., Finne, A., Helkkula, A., Kowalkowski, C., & Rindell, A. (2014). Am I worth it? Gifting myself with luxury. *Journal of Fashion Marketing and Management, 18*(2), 112–132. doi:10.1108/JFMM-04-2013-0062

Kefi, H., & Maar, D. (2018). (in press). The power of lurking: Assessing the online experience of luxury brand fan page followers. *Journal of Business Research*. Advance online publication. doi:10.1016/j.jbusres.2018.08.012

Keller, K. L. (2009). Building strong brands in a modern marketing communications environment. *Journal of Marketing Communications, 15*(2-3), 139–155. doi:10.1080/13527260902757530

Kelman, H. C. (1958). Compliance, identification, and internalization: Three processes of attitude change. *The Journal of Conflict Resolution, 2*(1), 51–60. doi:10.1177/002200275800200106

Kemp, S. (1998). Perceiving luxury and necessity. *Journal of Economic Psychology, 19*(5), 591–606. doi:10.1016/S0167-4870(98)00026-9

Kent, M. H. (2011). *Counterfeits and infringements: Problems and solutions.* VENABLE L.L.P. https://www.venable.com/files/Publication/4166ad52-47e7-4ac6-9b52-2beaeafbaed1/Presentation/PublicationAttachment/64d85c1f-a0a8-40e6-82c3-32ee32363b3a/Counterfeits_and_Infringements.pdf

Key, T. M., Boostrom, R. E. Jr, Adjei, M. T., & Campbell, D. A. (2013). Watch out: Themes in timepiece communities of counterfeit consumption. *Journal of Consumer Behaviour, 12*(4), 307–317. doi:10.1002/cb.1431

Khalifa, D., & Shukla, P. (2017). Me, my brand and I: Consumer responses to luxury brand rejection. *Journal of Business Research, 81*, 156–162. doi:10.1016/j.jbusres.2017.05.032

Khamitov, M., Wang, X. S., & Thomson, M. (2019). How well do consumer-brand relationships drive customer brand loyalty? Generalizations from a meta-analysis of brand relationship elasticities. *The Journal of Consumer Research, 46*(3), 435–459. doi:10.1093/jcr/ucz006

Khan, I., & Fatma, M. (2017). Antecedents and outcomes of brand experience: An empirical study. *Journal of Brand Management, 24*(5), 439–452. doi:10.105741262-017-0040-x

Khan, I., & Rahman, Z. (2015). Brand experience anatomy in retailing: An interpretive structural modeling approach. *Journal of Retailing and Consumer Services, 24*, 60–69. doi:10.1016/j.jretconser.2015.02.003

Kiatkawsin, K., & Han, H. (2019). What drives customers' willingness to pay price premiums for luxury gastronomic experiences at Michelin-starred restaurants? *International Journal of Hospitality Management*, *82*, 209–219. doi:10.1016/j.ijhm.2019.04.024

Kim, A. J., & Ko, E. (2010). Impacts of Luxury Fashion Brand's Social Media Marketing on Customer Relationship and Purchase Intention. *Journal of Global Fashion Marketing*, *1*(3), 164–171. doi:10.1080/20932685.2010.10593068

Kim, A. J., & Ko, E. (2012). Do social media marketing activities enhance customer equity? An empirical study of luxury fashion brand. *Journal of Business Research*, *65*(10), 1480–1486. doi:10.1016/j.jbusres.2011.10.014

Kim, H., Choi, Y. J., & Lee, Y. (2015). Web atmospheric qualities in luxury fashion brand web sites. *Journal of Fashion Marketing and Management*, *19*(4), 384–401. doi:10.1108/JFMM-09-2013-0103

Kim, J. (2019). Luxury fashion goods ownership and collecting behavior in an omni-channel retail environment. *Research Journal of Textile and Apparel*, *23*(3), 212–231. doi:10.1108/RJTA-01-2019-0001

Kim, J. E., Lloyd, S., & Cervellon, M. C. (2016). Narrative-transportation storylines in luxury brand advertising: Motivating consumer engagement. *Journal of Business Research*, *69*(1), 304–313. doi:10.1016/j.jbusres.2015.08.002

Kim, J. H. (2019). Imperative challenge for luxury brands: Generation Y consumers' perceptions of luxury fashion brands' e-commerce sites. *International Journal of Retail & Distribution Management*, *47*(2), 220–244. doi:10.1108/IJRDM-06-2017-0128

Kim, J. H., & Kim, M. (2018). Conceptualization and assessment of e-service quality for luxury brands. *Service Industries Journal*, •••, 1–35. doi:10.1080/02642069.2018.1461842

Kim, J., Kim, J. E., & Park, J. (2012). Effects of cognitive resource availability on consumer decisions involving counterfeit products: The role of perceived justification. *Marketing Letters*, *23*(3), 869–881. doi:10.100711002-012-9194-1

Kim, J., & Lee, K. H. (2019). Influence of integration on interactivity in social media luxury brand communities. *Journal of Business Research*, *99*, 422–429. doi:10.1016/j.jbusres.2017.10.001

Kimmel, A. J., & Kitchen, P. J. (2014). WOM and social media: Presaging future directions for research and practice. *Journal of Marketing Communications*, *20*(1), 5–20. doi:10.1080/13527266.2013.797730

Kimpakorn, N., & Dimmitt, N. (2007). Employer branding: The perspective of hotel management in the Thai luxury hotel industry. *Australasian Marketing Journal*, *15*(3), 49.

Kim, W. G., Ng, C. Y. N., & Kim, Y.-S. (2009). Influence of institutional DINESERV on consumer satisfaction, return intentions, and word-of-mouth. *International Journal of Hospitality Management*, *28*(1), 10–17. doi:10.1016/j.ijhm.2008.03.005

Kirmani, A., Sood, S., & Bridges, S. (1999). The Ownership Effect in Consumer Responses to Brand Line Stretches. *Journal of Marketing*, *63*(January), 88–101. doi:10.1177/002224299906300107

Klein, J. F., Falk, T., Esch, F. R., & Gloukhovtsev, A. (2016). Linking pop-up brand stores to brand experience and word of mouth: The case of luxury retail. *Journal of Business Research*, *69*(12), 5761–5767. doi:10.1016/j.jbusres.2016.04.172

Knight, D. K., & Kim, E. Y. (2007). Japanese consumers' need for uniqueness: Effects on brand perceptions and purchase intention. *Journal of Fashion Marketing and Management*, *11*(2), 270–280. doi:10.1108/13612020710751428

Koch, K. D. (2011). Luxury Tourism–Does This Market Segment Still Work? In *Trends and issues in global tourism 2011* (pp. 179–185). Springer. doi:10.1007/978-3-642-17767-5_19

Ko, E., Costello, J. P., & Taylor, C. R. (2019). What is a luxury brand? A new definition and review of the literature. *Journal of Business Research, 99*, 405–413. doi:10.1016/j.jbusres.2017.08.023

Koklic, M. K., & Vida, I. (2012). Counterfeiting purchase behavior: The role of perceived consequences and rationalization in forming attitudes and purchase intentions. *37th Macromarketing Conference*, 51-56.

Kollmannova, D. K. (2012). Fake product? Why not! Attitudes toward the consumption of counterfeit goods in CEE as shown on the example of Slovakia. *Central European Business Review, 1*(2), 23–28. doi:10.18267/j.cebr.14

Kopp, S. W., & Suter, T. A. (2000). Trademark strategies online: Implications for intellectual property protection. *Journal of Public Policy & Marketing, 19*(1), 119–131. doi:10.1509/jppm.19.1.119.16935

Koronaki, E., Kyrousi, A. G., & Panigyrakis, G. G. (2018). The emotional value of arts-based initiatives: Strengthening the luxury brand-consumer relationship. *Journal of Business Research, 85*, 406–413. doi:10.1016/j.jbusres.2017.10.018

Kosar, L. (2014). Lifestyle hotels – New paradigm of modern hotel industry. *Broj, 14*(14), 39–50. doi:10.5937/TurPos1414039K

Kostritsa, M., Liebl, H., Beinhauer, R., & Turčínková, J. (2020). Consumer Brand Love for Luxury Brands in India. *Acta Universitatis Agriculturae et Silviculturae Mendelianae Brunensis, 68*(1), 189–197. doi:10.11118/actaun202068010189

Kotler, P. (2000). *Administração de Marketing: A Edição do Novo Milénio* (10th ed.). Prentice Hall.

Kotler, P., & Armstrong, G. (2006). *Principles of Marketing* (11th ed.). Pearson Education.

Kotler, P., Kartajaya, H., & Setiawan, I. (2017). *Marketing 4.0: Mudança do tradicional para o digital.* Conjuntura Actual Editora.

Kotler, P., & Keller, K. L. (2016). *Marketing Management.* Pearson Education Limited.

Kotler, P., & Roberto, E. L. (1992). *Marketing Social: Estratégias para alterar o comportamento público.* Campus.

Kotler, P., Roberto, N., & Lee, N. (2002). *Social Marketing: Improving the quality of life.* SAGE Publications.

Kozinets, R. V. (2015). *Management Netnography: Axiological and Methodological Developments in Online Cultural Business Research.* Schulich School of Business, York University.

Kozinets, R. V. (2015). *Netnography: Redefined* (2nd ed.). SAGE Publications.

Kressman, F., Sirgy, M. J., Herrman, A., Huber, F., Huber, S., & Lee, D.-J. (2006). Direct and indirect effects of self-image congruence on brand loyalty. *Journal of Business Research, 59*(6), 955–964. doi:10.1016/j.jbusres.2006.06.001

Krippendorff, K. (2004). *Content analysis: An introduction to its methodology.* Sage.

Kuo, T., Chen, C. T., & Cheng, W. J. (2018). Service quality evaluation: Moderating influences of first-time and revisiting customers. *Total Quality Management & Business Excellence, 29*(4), 429–440. doi:10.1080/14783363.2016.1209405

Kwon, J., Seo, Y., & Ko, D. (2016). Effective luxury-brand advertising: The es–if matching (entity–symbolic versus incremental–functional) model. *Journal of Advertising, 45*(4), 459–471. doi:10.1080/00913367.2016.1226995

Lai, K. K. Y., & Zaichkowsky, J. L. (1999). Brand imitation: Do the Chinese have different views? *Asia Pacific Journal of Management, 16*(2), 179–192. doi:10.1023/A:1015482707900

Lambkin, M., & Tyndall, Y. (2009). Brand counterfeiting: A marketing problem that won't go away. *Irish Marketing Review, 20*(1), 35–46.

Lane, C. (2014). *The cultivation of taste: Chefs and the organization of fine dining*. Oxford University Press.

Lan, M. Y., Liu, F., Fang, C. H., & Lin, T. M. Y. (2012). Understanding word-of-mouth in counterfeiting. *Psychology (Irvine, Calif.)*, *3*(3), 289–295. doi:10.4236/psych.2012.33041

Lannes, B., & Han, W. (2010). Selling luxury to the Chinese masses. *The Wall Street Journal Asia*.

Larraufie, A.-F. M., & Kourdoughli, A. (2014). The e-semiotics of luxury. *Journal of Global Fashion Marketing*, *5*(3), 197–208. doi:10.1080/20932685.2014.906120

Lascu, D. N., & Zinkhan, G. (1999). Consumer conformity: Review and applications for marketing theory and practice. *Journal of Marketing Theory and Practice*, *7*(3), 1–12. doi:10.1080/10696679.1999.11501836

Leary, M. R., & Kowalski, R. M. (1990). Impression management: A literature review and two-component model. *Psychological Bulletin*, *107*(1), 34–47. doi:10.1037/0033-2909.107.1.34

Leban, M., Seo, Y., & Voyer, B. G. (2019). Transformational effects of social media lurking practices on luxury consumption. *Journal of Business Research*, *116*, 514–521. doi:10.1016/j.jbusres.2019.09.010

Lee, H. C., Chen, W. W., & Wang, C. W. (2015). The role of visual art in enhancing perceived prestige of luxury brands. *Marketing Letters*, *26*(4), 593–606. doi:10.100711002-014-9292-3

Lee, M. K., & Turban, E. (2001). A Trust Model for Consumer Internet Shopping. *International Journal of Electronic Commerce*, *6*(1), 75–91. doi:10.1080/10864415.2001.11044227

Lee, M. S. W., Conroy, D., & Motion, J. (2009). Brand avoidance: A negative promises perspective. *Advances in Consumer Research. Association for Consumer Research (U. S.)*, *36*, 421–429.

Lee, Y., & Hsieh, G. (2013). Does slacktivism hurt activism?: The effects of moral balancing and consistency in online activism. *Proceedings of the SIGCHI Conference on Human Factors in Computing Systems*. 10.1145/2470654.2470770

Leibenstein, H. (1950). Bandwagon, snob, and Veblen effects in the theory of consumers' demand. *The Quarterly Journal of Economics*, *64*(2), 183–207. doi:10.2307/1882692

Lendrevie, J., Lévy, J., Dionísio, P., & Rodrigues, J. V. (2015). *Mercator da Língua Portuguesa: Teoria e Prática do Marketing* (16th ed.). Publicações D. Quixote.

Leong, M. W. A., Yeh, S.-S., Fan, Y.-L., & Huan, T.-C. (2020). The effect of cuisine creativity on customer emotions. *International Journal of Hospitality Management*, *85*(August), 102346. Advance online publication. doi:10.1016/j.ijhm.2019.102346

Levitt, T. (1983). The globalization of markets. *Harvard Business Review*, *61*(3), 2–11.

Liang, T., & Lai, H. (2000). Electronic store design and consumer choice: An empirical study. *Proceedings of the 33rd Annual Hawaii International Conference on System Sciences*. 10.1109/HICSS.2000.926863

Lichtenstein, D. R., Bloch, P. H., & Black, W. C. (1988). Correlates of price acceptability. *The Journal of Consumer Research*, *15*(2), 243–252. doi:10.1086/209161

Li, J., Ghaffari, M., & Su, L. (2020). Luxury counterfeit consumption strategies in a collectivistic culture: The case of China. *Journal of Brand Management*, *27*(5), 546–560. doi:10.105741262-020-00197-4

Lim, Y. M. (2009). *Customer-based brand equity: The effect of destination image on preference for products associated with a destination brand* (Master thesis). Virginia Polytechnic Institute and State University.

Lindon, D., Lendrevie, J., Lévy, J., Dionísio, P., & Rodrigues, J. (2008). Mercator XXI. In Teoria e Prática do Marketing (11.a Ed.). Lisboa: Dom Quixote.

Lipka, M., & Hackett, C. (2017, April 6). *Why Muslims are the world's fastest-growing religious group.* Retrieved from https://www.pewresearch.org/fact-tank/2017/04/06/why-muslims-are-the-worlds-fastest-growing-religious-group/

Lipovetsky, G. (2003). *De l'Age du sacré au temps des marques* [From the age of the sacred to the age of the brands]. Gallimard.

Lipovetsky, G., & Roux, E. (2005). *O luxo eterno: da idade do sagrado ao tempo das marca.* Cia. das Letras.

Litvin, S. W., Goldsmith, R. E., & Pan, B. (2008). Electronic word-of-mouth in hospitality and tourism management. *Tourism Management, 29*(3), 458–468. doi:10.1016/j.tourman.2007.05.011

Liu, F., Li, J., Mizerski, D., & Soh, H. (2012). Self-congruity, brand attitude, and brand loyalty: A study on luxury brands. *European Journal of Marketing, 46*(7/8), 922–937. doi:10.1108/03090561211230098

Liu, X., Shin, H., & Burns, A. C. (2019). (in press). Examining the impact of luxury brand's social media marketing on customer engagement: Using big data analytics and natural language processing. *Journal of Business Research.* Advance online publication. doi:10.1016/j.jbusres.2019.04.042

Liu, Y., & Jang, S.-C. (2009). Perceptions of Chinese restaurants in the U.S.: What affects customer satisfaction and behavioral intentions? *International Journal of Hospitality Management, 28*(3), 338–348. doi:10.1016/j.ijhm.2008.10.008

Li, X., Hitt, L. M., & Zhang, Z. (2011). Product reviews and competition in markets for repeat purchase products. *Journal of Management Information Systems, 27*(4), 9–31. doi:10.2753/MIS0742-1222270401

Li, X., Sanders, K., & Frenkel, S. (2012). How leader–member exchange, work engagement and HRM consistency explain Chinese luxury hotel employees' job performance. *International Journal of Hospitality Management, 31*(4), 1059–1066. doi:10.1016/j.ijhm.2012.01.002

Loiacono, E. T. (2000). *WebQual: a web site quality instrumen*t. Dissertação de doutoramento, University of Georgia, Athens.

Lomas, N. (2019, July 26). *Muzmatch adds $7M to swipe right on Muslim-majority markets.* Retrieved from https://techcrunch.com/2019/07/26/muzmatch-adds-7m-to-swipe-right-on-muslim-majority-markets/

Loureiro, S. M. C., de Plaza, M. A. P., & Taghian, M. (2020). The effect of benign and malicious envies on desire to buy luxury fashion items. *Journal of Retailing and Consumer Services, 52*, 101688. doi:10.1016/j.jretconser.2018.10.005

Loureiro, S. M. C., & Kastenholz, E. (2011). Corporate reputation, satisfaction, delight, and loyalty towards rural lodging units in Portugal. *International Journal of Hospitality Management, 30*(3), 575–583. doi:10.1016/j.ijhm.2010.10.007

Loureiro, S. M. C., Miranda, F. J., & Breazeale, M. (2014). Who needs delight? The greater impact of value, trust and satisfaction in utilitarian, frequent-use retail. *Journal of Service Management, 25*(1), 101–124. doi:10.1108/JOSM-06-2012-0106

Loureiro, Y. K., Bayuk, J., Tignor, S. M., Nenkov, G. Y., Baskentli, S., & Webb, D. (2016). The case for moral consumption: Examining and expanding the domain of moral behavior to promote individual and collective well-being. *Journal of Public Policy & Marketing, 35*(2), 305–322. doi:10.1509/jppm.15.148

Lu, M. (2013). *An investigation of consumer motives to purchase counterfeit luxury-branded products.* [Unpublished Master's Thesis]. School of Management and Marketing, University of Wollongong.

Ludovica, C., Pastore, A., & Williams, P. (2017). Counterfeiting luxury goods. In P. E. Chaudhry (Ed.), *Handbook of research on counterfeiting and illicit trade* (pp. 193–222).

Lugosi, P., Janta, H., & Watson, P. (2012). Investigative management and consumer research on the internet. *International Journal of Contemporary Hospitality Management, 24*(6), 838–854. doi:10.1108/09596111211247191

Lunardo, R., & Mouangue, E. (2019). Getting over discomfort in luxury brand stores: How pop-up stores affect perceptions of luxury, embarrassment, and store evaluations. *Journal of Retailing and Consumer Services, 49*, 77–85. doi:10.1016/j.jretconser.2019.03.005

Lundqvist, A., Liljander, V., Gummerus, J., & van Riel, A. (2013). The impact of storytelling on the consumer brand experience: The case of a firm-originated story. *Journal of Brand Management, 20*(4), 283–297. doi:10.1057/bm.2012.15

Lutz, A. (2015). *Millennial's Are rejecting a strategy Coach, Abercrombie & Fitch, and Michael Coors have relied on for years.* Business Insider. https://www.businessinsider.com/millennials-turn-away-from-logos-2015-12

Lu, W., & Stepchenkova, S. (2012). Ecotourism experiences reported online: Classification of satisfaction attributes. *Tourism Management, 33*(3), 702–712. doi:10.1016/j.tourman.2011.08.003

Luxury. (n.d.). In *Cambridge dictionary* online. Retrieved from https://dictionary.cambridge.org/dictionary/english/luxury

LVMH. (2001). How does LVMH tackle counterfeiting of luxury products? http://www.LVMH.com/group/search.htm

Lynn, M. (1991). Scarcity effects on value: A quantitative review of the commodity theory literature. *Psychology and Marketing, 8*(1), 45–57. doi:10.1002/mar.4220080105

MacInnis, D. J. (2011). A framework for conceptual contributions in marketing. *Journal of Marketing, 75*(4), 136–154. doi:10.1509/jmkg.75.4.136

Mainolfi, G. (2019). Exploring materialistic bandwagon behaviour in online fashion consumption: A survey of Chinese luxury consumers. *Journal of Business Research.* doi:10.1016/j.jbusres.2019.11.038

Makkar, M., & Yap, S. F. (2018a). Emotional experiences behind the pursuit of inconspicuous luxury. *Journal of Retailing and Consumer Services, 44*, 222–234. doi:10.1016/j.jretconser.2018.07.001

Makkar, M., & Yap, S. F. (2018b). The anatomy of the inconspicuous luxury fashion experience. *Journal of Fashion Marketing and Management, 22*(1), 129–156. doi:10.1108/JFMM-08-2017-0083

Malheiro, A., Sousa, B., & Ferreira, L. (2019). Compreender o papel das redes sociais no comportamento do consumidor: A perspetiva do setor hoteleiro na região norte. *Revista Ibérica de Sistemas e Tecnologias de Informação, E24*(11), 299–312.

Mandel, N., Petrova, P., & Cialdini, R. (2006). Images of success and the preference of luxury brands. *Journal of Consumer Psychology, 16*(1), 57–69. doi:10.120715327663jcp1601_8

Mandler, T., Johnen, M., & Grave, J. F. (2019). (in press). Can't help falling in love? How brand luxury generates positive consumer affect in social media. *Journal of Business Research.* Advance online publication. doi:10.1016/j.jbusres.2019.10.010

Mandrik, C., Fern, E., & Bao, Y. (2005). Intergenerational influence: Roles of conformity to peers and communication effectiveness. *Psychology and Marketing, 22*(10), 813–832. doi:10.1002/mar.20087

Manganari, E. E., Siomkos, G. J., & Vrechopoulos, A. P. (2009). Store atmosphere in web retailing. *European Journal of Marketing, 43*(9/10), 1140–1153. doi:10.1108/03090560910976401

Mangold, W. G., & Faulds, D. J. (2009). Social media: The new hybrid element of the promotion mix. *Business Horizons*, *52*(4), 357–365. doi:10.1016/j.bushor.2009.03.002

Mansori, S., Sambasivan, M., & Md-Sidin, S. (2015). Acceptance of novel products: The role of religiosity, ethnicity and values. *Marketing Intelligence & Planning*, *33*(1), 39–66. doi:10.1108/MIP-03-2013-0050

Manthiou, A., Kang, J., Hyun, S., & Fu, X. (2018). The impact of brand authenticity on building brand love: An investigation of impression in memory and lifestyle-congruence. *International Journal of Hospitality Management*, *75*, 38–47. doi:10.1016/j.ijhm.2018.03.005

Marangoz, M., Yeşildağ, B., & Saltık, I. A. (2012). E-Ticaret işletmelerinin web ve sosyal ağ sitelerinin íçerik analizi yöntemiyle íncelenmesi. *Internet Uygulamaları Dergisi*, *3*, 53–78.

Markovic, S., Raspor, S., & Šegaric, K. (2010). Does restaurant performance meet customers' expectations? An assessment of restaurant service quality using a modified DINESERV approach. *Tourism and Hospitality Management*, *16*(2), 181–195.

Marshall, C., & Rossman, G. B. (2014). *Designing qualitative research*. Sage publications.

Martinez, D. M. (2014). Fashionably late: Why the United States should copy France and Italy to reduce counterfeiting. *Boston University International Law Journal*, *32*, 101–130.

Mason, R. (1981). *Conspicuous consumption: A study of exceptional consumer behaviour*. Gower Publishing Company.

Mason, R. (1996). Measuring the demand for status goods: An evaluation of means-end chains and laddering. In F. Hansen (Ed.), *European Advances for Consumer Research* (pp. 78–82).

Masten, D., & Plowman, T. (2003). Digital ethnography: The next wave in understanding the consumer experience. *Design Management Journal*, *14*(2), 75–81. doi:10.1111/j.1948-7169.2003.tb00044.x

Masudi. (2012, February 23). *Halal wine anyone?* Retrieved from https://gulfnews.com/uae/health/halal-wine-anyone-1.985002

Matsuyama, K. (2002). The rise of mass consumption societies. *Journal of Political Economy*, *110*(5), 1035–1070. doi:10.1086/341873

Matthiesen, I., & Phau, I. (2005). The 'HUGO BOSS' connection: Achieving global brand consistency across countries. *Journal of Brand Management*, *12*(5), 325–338. doi:10.1057/palgrave.bm.2540229

Mazar, N., On, A., & Ariely, D. (2008). The dishonesty of honest people: A theory of self-concept maintenance. *JMR, Journal of Marketing Research*, *45*(6), 633–644. doi:10.1509/jmkr.45.6.633

McIntosh, A., & Siggs, A. (2005). An exploration of the experiential nature of boutique accommodation. *Journal of Travel Research*, *44*(1), 74–81. doi:10.1177/0047287505276593

McKendrick, N. (1984). *The birth of a consumer society: Commercialization of eighteenth century England*. Harper Collins Publishers Ltd.

Megehee, C. M., & Spake, D. F. (2012). Consumer enactments of archetypes using luxury brands. *Journal of Business Research*, *65*(10), 1434–1442. doi:10.1016/j.jbusres.2011.10.009

Mendes, M. S. (2012). *Programa de Marketing de Produtos e Serviços de Luxo*. Universidade Católica.

Meşe, İ. (2015). İslami bir moda dergisi örneğinde moda ve tesettür: Ne türden bir birliktelik? *Fe Dergisi: Feminist Eleştiri*, *7*(1), 146–158.

Meyers-Levy, J. (1989). Gender differences in information processing: A selectivity interpretation. In Cognitive and Affective Responses to Advertising. Lexington Press.

Meyers-Levy, J., & Loken, B. (2015). Revisiting gender differences: What we know and what lies ahead. *Journal of Consumer Psychology*, *25*(1), 129–149. doi:10.1016/j.jcps.2014.06.003

Michaud, Y. (2003). *Essai sur le triomphe de l'esthétique* [Essay on the triumph of the aesthetic]. Stock.

Miller, K. W., & Mills, M. K. (2012). Contributing clarity by examining brand luxury in the fashion market. *Journal of Business Research*, *65*(10), 1471–1479. doi:10.1016/j.jbusres.2011.10.013

Miranda, F. J., Rubio, S., & Chamorro, A. (2015). The Web as a marketing tool in the Spanish foodservice industry: Evaluating the websites of Spain's top restaurants. *Journal of Foodservice Business Research*, *18*(2), 146–162.

Mittelstaedt, J. D. (2002). A framework for understanding the relationships between religions and markets. *Journal of Macromarketing*, *22*(1), 6–18. doi:10.1177/027467022001002

Mittelstaedt, J. D., & Mittelstaedt, R. A. (1997). The protection of intellectual property: Issues of origination and ownership. *Journal of Public Policy & Marketing*, *16*(1), 14–25. doi:10.1177/074391569701600103

Miyazaki, A. D., Rodriguez, A. A., & Langenderfer, J. (2009). Price, scarcity, and consumer willingness to purchase pirated media products. *Journal of Public Policy & Marketing*, *28*(1), 71–84. doi:10.1509/jppm.28.1.71

Modest Man. (2019, July 8). *The Islamic sneakers biz keeps exploding!* Retrieved from https://www.ifdcouncil.org/the-islamic-sneakers-biz-keeps-exploding/

Mohsin, A., & Lockyer, T. (2010). Customer perceptions of service quality in luxury hotels in New Delhi, India: An exploratory study. *International Journal of Contemporary Hospitality Management*, *22*(2), 160–173. doi:10.1108/09596111011018160

Mokhlis, S. (2009). Relevancy and measurement of religiosity in consumer behavior research. *International Business Research*, *2*(3), 75–84. doi:10.5539/ibr.v2n3p75

Moon, B. (2004). Consumer adoption of the internet as an information search and product purchase channel: Some research hypotheses. *International Journal of Internet Marketing and Advertising*, *1*(1), 104. doi:10.1504/IJIMA.2004.003692

Moore, E., & Lutz, R. (1988). Intergenerational influences in the formation of consumer attitudes and beliefs about the marketplace: Mothers and daughters. *Advances in Consumer Research. Association for Consumer Research (U. S.)*, *15*, 461–467.

Mortelmans, D. (2005). Sign values in processes of distinction: The concept of luxury. *Semiotica*, *2005*(157), 497–520. doi:10.1515emi.2005.2005.157.1-4.497

Moschis, G. (1987). *Consumer socialization: A life cycle perspective*. Lexington Press.

Moschis, G. P., & Ong, F. S. (2011). Religiosity and consumer behavior of older adults: A study of subcultural influences in Malaysia. *Journal of Consumer Behaviour*, *10*(1), 8–17. doi:10.1002/cb.342

Mostafa, M. M., & Arnaout, J. P. (2020). What drives Kuwaiti consumers to purchase luxury brands? *International Review of Retail, Distribution and Consumer Research*, *30*(1), 86–102. doi:10.1080/09593969.2019.1626259

Motta, J., Filipe, S., & Barbosa, M. (2014). *Estratégia de Comunicação e Venda Online na Joalharia de Luxo Communications and Online Selling Strategy in Luxury Jewellery*. Academic Press.

MPAA Expands Anti-Piracy Campaign. (June 21, 2004). Billboard. https://www.billboard.com/biz/articles/news/1431307/mpaa-expands-anti-piracy-campaign

Muhamad, N. (2011). Fatwa rulings in Islam: A Malaysian perspective on their role in Muslim consumer behavior. In O. Sandikci & G. Rice (Eds.), *Handbook of Islamic marketing* (pp. 35–55). Edward Elgar Publishing. doi:10.4337/9780857936028.00010

Murphy, J., & Scharl, A. (2007). An investigation of global versus local online branding. *International Marketing Review, 24*(3), 297–312. doi:10.1108/02651330710755302

Mwihaki, B. W. (2020). Effects of personality factors on consumer attitude toward the acquisitions of counterfeit products. *African Multidisciplinary Journal of Research, 4*(2), 1–23.

Mylan, J. (2019). Sustainable innovation, consumption and everyday life. In F. Boons & A. McMeekin (Eds.), *Handbook of Sustainable Innovation* (pp. 252–266). Edward Elgar Publishing. doi:10.4337/9781788112574.00023

Naccarato, P., & Lebesco, K. (2012). *Culinary capital*. Berg. doi:10.5040/9781350042131

Namin, A. (2017). Revisiting customers' perception of service quality in fast food restaurants. *Journal of Retailing and Consumer Services, 34*, 70–81. doi:10.1016/j.jretconser.2016.09.008

Narteh, B., Agbemabiese, G. C., Kodua, P., & Braimah, M. (2013). Relationship marketing and customer loyalty: Evidence from the Ghanaian luxury hotel industry. *Journal of Hospitality Marketing & Management, 22*(4), 407–436. doi:10.1080/19368623.2012.660564

Nascimento, M. (2000). *Marketing do varejo de luxo: desmistificando as verdades do varejo de luxo*. Universidade Salvador.

Neuendorf, K. A. (2002). *The content analysis guidebook*. Sage.

Ngo, L. V., Northey, G., Tran, Q., & Septianto, F. (2020). The Devil might wear Prada, but Narcissus wears counterfeit Gucci! How social adjustive functions influence counterfeit luxury purchases. *Journal of Retailing and Consumer Services, 52*, 52. doi:10.1016/j.jretconser.2018.09.003

Ng, Y.-K. (1987). Diamonds are a government's best friend: Burden free taxes on goods valued for their values. *The American Economic Review, 77*, 186–191.

Nia, A., & Zaichkowsky, J. L. (2000). Do counterfeits devalue the ownership of luxury brands? *Journal of Product and Brand Management, 9*(7), 485–497. doi:10.1108/10610420010351402

Nierobisch, T., Toporowski, W., Dannewald, T., & Jahn, S. (2017). Flagship stores for FMCG national brands: Do they improve brand cognitions and create favorable consumer reactions? *Journal of Retailing and Consumer Services, 34*, 117–137. doi:10.1016/j.jretconser.2016.09.014

Nobre, H., & Simões, C. (2019). NewLux Brand Relationship Scale: Capturing the scope of mass-consumed luxury brand relationships. *Journal of Business Research, 102*, 328–338. doi:10.1016/j.jbusres.2019.01.047

Norum, P. S., & Cuno, A. (2011). Analysis of the demand for counterfeit goods. *Journal of Fashion Marketing and Management, 15*(1), 27–40. doi:10.1108/13612021111112322

Nueno, J. L., & Quelch, J. A. (1998). The mass marketing of luxury. *Business Horizons, 41*(6), 61–68. doi:10.1016/S0007-6813(98)90023-4

Nunes, J. C., Drèze, X., & Han, Y. J. (2011). Conspicuous consumption in a recession: Toning it down or turning it up? *Journal of Consumer Psychology, 21*(2), 199–205. doi:10.1016/j.jcps.2010.11.002

Nwankwo, S., Hamelin, N., & Khaled, M. (2014). Consumer values, motivation and purchase intention for luxury goods. *Journal of Retailing and Consumer Services, 21*(5), 735–744. doi:10.1016/j.jretconser.2014.05.003

Nysveen, H., Pedersen, P. E., & Skard, S. (2013). Brand experiences in service organizations: Exploring the individual effects of brand experience dimensions. *Journal of Brand Management*, *20*(5), 404–423. doi:10.1057/bm.2012.31

O'Cass, A., & Frost, H. (2002). Status brands: Examining the effects of non-product related brand associations on status and conspicuous consumption. *Journal of Product and Brand Management*, *11*(2), 67–88. doi:10.1108/10610420210423455

O'Guinn, T. C., & Shrum, L. J. (1997). The role of television in the construction of consumer reality. *The Journal of Consumer Research*, *23*(4), 278–294. doi:10.1086/209483

OECD/EUIPO. (2019, March 18). *Trends in Trade in Counterfeit and Pirated Goods.* . doi:10.1787/g2g9f533-en

Okonkwo-Pézard, U. (2017). The luxury brand strategy challenge. In J. Kapferer, J. Kernstock, T. O. Brexendorf, & S. M. Powell (Eds.), *Advances in luxury brand management* (pp. 59–64). Palgrave Macmillan. doi:10.1007/978-3-319-51127-6_4

Okonkwo, U. (2009). The luxury brand strategy challenge. *Journal of Brand Management*, *16*(5), 287–289. doi:10.1057/bm.2008.53

Okonkwo, U. (2010). *Luxury online: Styles, systems, strategies*. Palgrave MacMillan. doi:10.1057/9780230248335

Ólafsdóttir, A. R. (2012). *Luxury Fashion Online*. Bifröst University.

Olson, E. (1999). Bottled Water: Pure Drink or Pure Hype? Natural Resources Defense Council (NRDC).

Ong, C. H., Lee, H. W., & Ramayah, T. (2018). Impact of brand experience on loyalty. *Journal of Hospitality Marketing & Management*, *27*(7), 755–774. doi:10.1080/19368623.2018.1445055

Ordabayeva, N., & Chandon, P. (2011). Getting Ahead of the Joneses: When Equality Increases Conspicuous Consumption Among Bottom-Tier Consumers. *The Journal of Consumer Research*, *38*(1), 27–41. doi:10.1086/658165

Ottenbacher, M., & Harrington, R. J. (2007). The innovation development process of Michelin-starred chefs. *International Journal of Contemporary Hospitality Management*, *19*(6), 444–460. doi:10.1108/09596110710775110

Oyedele, A., & Simpson, P. (2018). Emerging adulthood, sharing utilities and intention to use sharing services. *Journal of Services Marketing*, *32*(2), 161–174. doi:10.1108/JSM-09-2016-0344

Paixão, L. (2006). *Luxo – o Supérfluo Indispensável.* Jobson Brasil.

Palmatier, R. W., Dant, R. P., Grewal, D., & Evans, K. R. (2006). Factors influencing the effectiveness of relationship marketing: A meta-analysis. *Journal of Marketing*, *74*(4), 136–153. doi:10.1509/jmkg.70.4.136

Palmer, C., Cooper, J., & Burns, P. (2010). Culture, identity, and belonging in the 'culinary underbelly'. *International Journal of Culture, Tourism and Hospitality Research*, *4*(4), 311–326. doi:10.1108/17506181011081497

Pan, B., MacLaurin, T., & Crotts, J. C. (2007). Travel blogs and the implications for destination marketing. *Journal of Travel Research*, *46*(1), 35–45. doi:10.1177/0047287507302378

Pantano, E., Passavanti, R., Priporas, C. V., & Verteramo, S. (2018). To what extent luxury retailing can be smart? *Journal of Retailing and Consumer Services*, *43*, 94–100. doi:10.1016/j.jretconser.2018.03.012

Pantzalis, I. (1995). *Exclusivity Strategies in Pricing and Brand Extension* (Unpublished Doctoral Dissertation). University of Arizona.

Papagiannidis, S., Pantano, E., See-To, E. W., Dennis, C., & Bourlakis, M. (2017). To immerse or not? Experimenting with two virtual retail environments. *Information Technology & People*, *30*(1), 163–188. doi:10.1108/ITP-03-2015-0069

Papavassiliou, N., & Stathakopoulos, V. (1997). Standardization versus adaptation of international advertising strategies: Towards a framework. *European Journal of Marketing, 31*(7), 504–527. doi:10.1108/03090569710176646

Paradise, P. R. (1999). *Trademark counterfeiting, product piracy, and the billion dollar threat to the US economy.* Greenwood Publishing Group.

Parasuraman, A., Zeithaml, V., & Berry, L. (1988). SERVQUAL: A Multiple-Item Scale for Measuring Consumer Perceptions of Service Quality. *Journal of Retailing, 64*(1), 12–40.

Parente, S. (2007), *Uma visão sobre o consumo de luxo – em busca da exclusividade.* Academic Press.

Park, H. J., Rabolt, N. J., & Jeon, K. S. (2008). Purchasing global luxury brands among young Korean consumers. *Journal of Fashion Marketing and Management, 12*(2), 244–259. doi:10.1108/13612020810874917

Park, K. S., Reisinger, Y., & Noh, E. H. (2010). Luxury shopping in tourism. *International Journal of Tourism Research, 12*(2), 164–178. doi:10.1002/jtr.744

Park, M., Im, H., & Kim, H. Y. (2018). (in press). "You are too friendly!" The negative effects of social media marketing on value perceptions of luxury fashion brands. *Journal of Business Research.*

Patsiaouras, G., & Fitchett, J. A. (2012). The evolution of conspicuous consumption. *Journal of Historical Research in Marketing, 4*(1), 154–176. doi:10.1108/17557501211195109

Pearson, S. (2012). *Coach wins $257 million court ruling against counterfeiters.* Academic Press.

Peneda de Oliveira, C., & Sousa, B. M. (2020). Green Consumer Behavior and Its Implications on Brand Marketing Strategy. In V. Naidoo & R. Verma (Eds.), *Green Marketing as a Positive Driver Toward Business Sustainability* (pp. 69–95). IGI Global. doi:10.4018/978-1-5225-9558-8.ch004

Peng, N., & Chen, A. (2019). Examining consumers' luxury hotel stay repurchase intentions-incorporating a luxury hotel brand attachment variable into a luxury consumption value model. *International Journal of Contemporary Hospitality Management, 31*(3), 1348–1366. doi:10.1108/IJCHM-04-2018-0332

Peng, N., & Chen, A. H. (2015). Diners' loyalty toward luxury restaurants: The moderating role of product knowledge. *Marketing Intelligence & Planning, 33*(2), 179–196. doi:10.1108/MIP-03-2014-0049

Penz, E., & Stöttinger, B. (2005). Forget the real thing - take the copy! An explanatory model for the volitional purchase of counterfeit products. *Advances in Consumer Research. Association for Consumer Research (U. S.), 32*(1), 568–575.

Penz, E., & Stöttinger, B. (2008). Original brands and counterfeit brands—Do they have anything in common? *Journal of Consumer Behaviour: An International Research Review, 7*(2), 146–163. doi:10.1002/cb.243

Penz, E., & Stöttinger, B. (2012). A comparison of the emotional and motivational aspects in the purchase of luxury products. *Journal of Brand Management, 19*(7), 581–594. doi:10.1057/bm.2012.7

Pepall, L., & Reiff, J. (2016). The "Veblen" effect, targeted advertising and consumer welfare. *Economics Letters, 145*, 218–220. doi:10.1016/j.econlet.2016.06.024

Petty, R. D. (2005). Societal regulation of the marketing function: Does the patchwork create a quilt? *Journal of Public Policy & Marketing, 24*(1), 63–74. doi:10.1509/jppm.24.1.63.63884

Pham, M., Valette-Florence, P., & Vigneron, F. (2018). Luxury brand desirability and fashion equity: The joint moderating effect on consumers' commitment toward luxury brands. *Psychology and Marketing, 35*(12), 902–912. doi:10.1002/mar.21143

Phau, I., & Prendergast, G. (2000). Consuming luxury brands: The relevance of the 'rarity principle'. *Journal of Brand Management*, *8*(2), 122–138. doi:10.1057/palgrave.bm.2540013

Phau, I., Prendergast, G., & Chuen, L. H. (2001). Profiling brand-piracy-prone consumers: An exploratory study in Hong Kong's clothing industry. *Journal of Fashion Marketing and Management*, *5*(1), 45–55. doi:10.1108/EUM0000000007278

Phau, I., & Teah, M. (2009). Devil wears (counterfeit) Prada: A study of antecedents and outcomes of attitudes towards counterfeits of luxury brands. *Journal of Consumer Marketing*, *26*(1), 15–27. doi:10.1108/07363760910927019

Pinto da Silva, F., Brandão, F., & Sousa, B. (2019). Towards socially sustainable Tourism in cities: local community perceptions and development guidelins. *Enlightening Tourism. A Pathmaking Journal*, *9*(2), 168-198.

Pizam, A. (2010). Creating memorable experiences. *International Journal of Hospitality Management*, *29*(3), 343. doi:10.1016/j.ijhm.2010.04.003

Poddar, A., Foreman, J., Banerjee, S. S., & Ellen, P. S. (2012). Exploring the Robin Hood effect: Moral profiteering motives for purchasing counterfeit products. *Journal of Business Research*, *65*(10), 1500–1506. doi:10.1016/j.jbusres.2011.10.017

Postrel, V. (2006, July/August). Inconspicuous consumption: A new theory of the leisure class. *The Atlantic*. Retrieved from https://www.theatlantic.com/magazine/archive/2008/07/inconspicuous-consumption/306845/

Prager, E. A. (1996). The federal trademark dilution act of 1995: Substantial likelihood of confusion. *Fordham Intellectual Property. Media & Entertainment Law Journal*, *7*(1), 121–136.

Pratt, S., & Zeng, C. Y. (2020). The economic value and determinants of tourists' counterfeit purchases: The case of Hong Kong. *Tourism Economics*, *26*(1), 155–178. doi:10.1177/1354816619834482

Prayag, G. (2008). Image, Satisfaction and Loyalty: The Case of Cape Town. Anatolia. *An International Journal of Tourism and Hospitality Research*, *19*(2), 205–224. doi:10.1080/13032917.2008.9687069

Prendergast, G., Hing Chuen, L., & Phau, I. (2002). Understanding consumer demand for non-deceptive pirated brands. *Marketing Intelligence & Planning*, *20*(7), 405–416. doi:10.1108/02634500210450846

Prendergast, G., & Wong, C. (2003). Parental influence on the purchase of luxury brands of infant apparel: An exploratory study in Hong Kong. *Journal of Consumer Marketing*, *20*(2), 157–169. doi:10.1108/07363760310464613

Prentice, C., Wang, X., & Loureiro, S. M. C. (2019). The influence of brand experience and service quality on customer engagement. *Journal of Retailing and Consumer Services*, *50*, 50–59. doi:10.1016/j.jretconser.2019.04.020

Priporas, C. V., Chen, Y., Zhao, S., & Tan, H. (2020). An exploratory study of the upper middle-class consumer attitudes towards counterfeiting in China. *Journal of Retailing and Consumer Services*, *53*, 101959. doi:10.1016/j.jretconser.2019.101959

Prokopec, S., & Kurdy, M. (2011). An international marketing strategy perspective on Islamic marketing. In O. Sandikci & G. Rice (Eds.), *Handbook of Islamic marketing* (pp. 208–225). Edward Elgar Publishing. doi:10.4337/9780857936028.00021

Pulh, M., Mencarelli, R., & Chaney, D. (2019). The consequences of the heritage experience in brand museums on the consumer-brand relationship. *European Journal of Marketing*, *53*(10), 2193–2212. doi:10.1108/EJM-03-2017-0233

Qian, Y. (2011). *Counterfeiters: foes or friends? How do counterfeits affect different product quality tiers? (No. w16785)*. National Bureau of Economic Research. doi:10.3386/w16785

Quelch, J. (1999). Global brands: Taking stock. *Business Strategy Review*, *10*(1), 1–14. doi:10.1111/1467-8616.00085

Radón, A. (2012). Counterfeit luxury goods online: An investigation of consumer perceptions. *International Journal of Marketing Studies*, *4*(2), 74–79.

Radwan, G. N., Israel, E., El-Setouhy, M., Abdel-Aziz, F., Mikhail, N., & Mohamed, M. K. (2003). Impact of religious rulings (Fatwa) on smoking. *Journal of the Egyptian Society of Parasitology*, *330*(Suppl. 3), 1087–1101. PMID:15119472

Ramaseshan, B., & Stein, A. (2014). Connecting the dots between brand experience and brand loyalty: The mediating role of brand personality and brand relationships. *Journal of Brand Management*, *21*(7-8), 664–683. doi:10.1057/bm.2014.23

Ramchandani, M., & Coste-Manière, I. (2012). Asymmetry in multi-cultural luxury communication: A comparative analysis on luxury brand communication in India and China. *Journal of Global Fashion Marketing*, *3*(2), 89–97. doi:10.1080/20932685.2012.10593111

Ramirez, R., & Merunka, D. (2019). Brand experience effects on brand attachment: The role of brand trust, age, and income. *European Business Review*, *31*(5), 610–645. doi:10.1108/EBR-02-2017-0039

Ramos, A. (2011). Luxury, crisis and consumption: Sir James Steuart and the eighteenth-century luxury debate. *History of Economics Review*, *53*(1), 55–72. doi:10.1080/18386318.2011.11682176

Rau, P. P., & Liang, S. M. (2003). Internationalization and localization: Evaluating and testing a website for Asian users. *Ergonomics*, *46*(1), 255–270. doi:10.1080/00140130303527 PMID:12554410

Rehman, A., & Shabbir, M. S. (2010). The relationship between religiosity and new product adoption. *Journal of Islamic Marketing*, *1*(1), 63–69. doi:10.1108/17590831011026231

Reimann, M., & Aron, A. (2009). Self-expansion motivation and inclusion of brands in self. In D. J. MacInnis, C. Whan Park, & J. W. Priester (Eds.), *Handbook of brand relationships* (pp. 87–103). Routledge.

Rempel, J. K., & Burris, C. T. (2005). Let me count the ways: An integrative theory of love and hate. *Personal Relationships*, *12*(2), 297–313. doi:10.1111/j.1350-4126.2005.00116.x

Rice, G. (1999). Islamic ethics and the implications for business. *Journal of Business Ethics*, *18*(4), 345–358. doi:10.1023/A:1005711414306

Richins, M. L. (1995). Social comparison, advertising, and consumer discontent. *The American Behavioral Scientist*, *3*(4), 593–607. doi:10.1177/0002764295038004009

Riegner, C. (2007). Word of mouth on the web: The impact of web 2.0 on consumer purchase decisions. *Journal of Advertising Research*, *47*(4), 436–447. doi:10.2501/S0021849907070456

Riley, F. D., & Lacroix, C. (2003). Luxury branding on the Internet: Lost opportunity or impossibility? *Marketing Intelligence & Planning*, *21*(2), 96–104. doi:10.1108/02634500310465407

Rodrigues, C., & Rodrigues, P. (2019). Brand Love Matters to Millenials: The relevance of mystery, sensuality and intimacy to neo-luxury brands. *Journal of Product and Brand Management*, *28*(7), 830–848. doi:10.1108/JPBM-04-2018-1842

Rodrigues, P., Brandao, A., & Rodrigues, C. (2018). The importance of self in brand love in consumer luxury brand relationships. *Journal of Customer Behaviour*, *18*(3), 189–210. doi:10.1362/147539218X15434304746036

Rojanasingsawad, M., Ryding, D., & Barnes, L. (2020). Consumer decision-making styles for grey luxury goods: a study on Thailand. *International Journal of Sales, Retailing & Marketing, 9*(1).

Romani, S., Gistri, G., & Pace, S. (2012). When counterfeits raise the appeal of luxury brands. *Marketing Letters*, *23*(3), 807–824. doi:10.100711002-012-9190-5

Romani, S., Grappi, S., & Dalli, D. (2012). Emotions that drive consumers away from brands: Measuring negative emotions towards brands and their behavioral effects. *International Journal of Research in Marketing*, *29*(1), 55–67. doi:10.1016/j.ijresmar.2011.07.001

Romano, N. C., Donovan, C., Chen, H., & Nunamaker, J. F. (2003). A methodology for analyzing web-based qualitative data. *Journal of Management Information Systems*, *19*(4), 213–246. doi:10.1080/07421222.2003.11045741

Roper, S., Caruana, R., Medway, D., & Murphy, P. (2013). Constructing luxury brands: Exploring the role of consumer discourse. *European Journal of Marketing*, *47*(3/4), 375–400. doi:10.1108/03090561311297382

Rousseau, S. (2012). *Food and social media*. Rowaan & Littlefield Publishers. doi:10.5040/9781350042193

Roux, E., Tafani, E., & Vigneron, F. (2017). Values associated with luxury brand consumption and the role of gender. *Journal of Business Research*, *71*, 102–113. doi:10.1016/j.jbusres.2016.10.012

Rowley, J. (2004). Online branding. *Online Information Review*, *28*(2), 131–138. doi:10.1108/14684520410531637

Rowley, J. (2010). Online branding strategies of UK fashion retailers. *Internet Research*, *19*(3), 348–369. doi:10.1108/10662240910965397

Roy, R., & Rabbanee, F. K. (2015). Antecedents and consequences of self-congruity. *European Journal of Marketing*, *49*(3/4), 444–466. doi:10.1108/EJM-12-2013-0739

Roy, S. K., Balaji, M. S., Quazi, A., & Quaddus, M. (2018). Predictors of customer acceptance of and resistance to smart technologies in the retail sector. *Journal of Retailing and Consumer Services*, *42*, 147–160. doi:10.1016/j.jretconser.2018.02.005

Rucker, D. D. (2020). Social rank: Implications for consumers as actors and observers. *Current Opinion in Psychology*, *33*, 57–61. doi:10.1016/j.copsyc.2019.07.024

Ruhanen, L. (2019). The prominence of eco in ecotourism experiences: An analysis of post-purchase online reviews. *Journal of Hospitality and Tourism Management*, *39*, 110–116. doi:10.1016/j.jhtm.2019.03.006

Ryu, K., & Han, H. (2010). Influence of the Quality of Food, Service, and Physical Environment on Customer Satisfaction and Behavioral Intention in Quick-Casual Restaurants: Moderating Role of Perceived Price. *Journal of Hospitality & Tourism Research (Washington, D.C.)*, *34*(3), 310–329. doi:10.1177/1096348009350624

Sabuncuoğlu, A. (2015). Sosyal medyanın bir gösteriş tüketimi mecrası olarak kullanımı. In Z. Özgür & A. İşman (Eds.), *İletişim çalışmaları* (pp. 369–380). Sakarya Üni. Yayınları.

Sahin, A., Kitapci, H., Altindag, E., & Gok, S. (2017). Investigating the impacts of brand experience and service quality. *International Journal of Market Research*, *59*(6), 707–724. doi:10.2501/IJMR-2017-051

Salama. (2019, April 23). *Turkey: Modanisa Istanbul modest fashion week*. Retrieved from https://halalfocus.net/turkey-modanisa-istanbul-modest-fashion-week/

Saldaña, J. (2012). *The coding manual for qualitative research* (2nd ed.). SAGE.

Sanderson, C. (2009). *Social psychology*. John Wiley & Sons, Ltd.

Sandikci, O., & Ger, G. (2005). Aesthetics, ethics, and politics of the Turkish headscarf. In S. Kuechler & D. Miller (Eds.), *Clothing as material culture* (pp. 61–83). Berg. doi:10.2752/9780857854056/CLMATCULT0007

Sandikci, O., & Ger, G. (2007). Contemporary Turkish consumptionscape: Polarity and plurality. In J. Prasnikar & A. Cirman (Eds.), *New emerging economies and their culture* (pp. 139–153). Nova Science Pub Inc.

Saxena, A., & Khanna, U. (2013). Advertising on social network sites: A structural equation modelling approach. *Vision (Basel), 17*(1), 17–25. doi:10.1177/0972262912469560

Schembri, S., & Latimer, L. (2016). Online brand communities: Constructing and co-constructing brand culture. *Journal of Marketing Management, 32*(7-8), 628–651. doi:10.1080/0267257X.2015.1117518

Schembri, S., Merrilees, B., & Kristiansen, S. (2010). Brand consumption and narrative of the self. *Psychology and Marketing, 27*(6), 623–637. doi:10.1002/mar.20348

Schivinski, B., & Dabrowski, D. (2015). The impact of brand communication on brand equity through Facebook. *Journal of Research in Interactive Marketing, 9*(1), 31–53. doi:10.1108/JRIM-02-2014-0007

Schlenker, B. R., Britt, T. W., & Pennington, J. (1996). Impression regulation and management: Highlights of a theory of self-identification. In R. M. Sorrentino & E. T. Higgins (Eds.), Handbook of motivation and cognition. Handbook of motivation and cognition, Vol. 3. The interpersonal context (pp. 118-147). New York, NY: The Guilford Press.

Schlenker, B. R. (2012). Self-presentation. In M. R. Leary & J. P. Tangney (Eds.), *Handbook of self and identity* (pp. 542–570). The Guilford Press.

Schmitt, B. (1999). Experiential marketing. *Journal of Marketing Management, 15*(1/3), 53–67. doi:10.1362/026725799784870496

Schönfelder, W. (2011). *CAQDAS and qualitative syllogism logic – NVivo 8 and MAXQDA 10 compared.* Paper presented at the Forum Qualitative Sozialforschung (Forum: Qualitative Social Research).

Selig Center for Economic Growth. (2014). *Multicultural Economy Report.* https://news.uga.edu/releases/article/multicultural-economy-report-2014/

Semaan, R. W., Lindsay, V., Williams, P., & Ashill, N. (2019). The influence of gender roles in the drivers of luxury consumption for women: Insights from the gulf region. *Journal of Retailing and Consumer Services, 51*(November), 165–175. doi:10.1016/j.jretconser.2019.06.006

Sembalunrinjanilombok. (2016, December 12). *Sembalun-world's best halal honeymoon destination.* Retrieved from https://sembalunrinjanilombok.wordpress.com/2016/12/12/sembalun-worlds-best-halal-honeymoon-destination/

Sen, S., Gürhan-Canli, Z., & Morwitz, V. (2001). Withholding consumption: A social dilemma perspective on consumer boycotts. *The Journal of Consumer Research, 28*(3), 399–417. doi:10.1086/323729

Seo, Y., & Buchanan-Oliver, M. (2019). Constructing a typology of luxury brand consumption practices. *Journal of Business Research, 99*, 414–421. doi:10.1016/j.jbusres.2017.09.019

Seringhaus, F. H. (2005). Selling Luxury Brands Online. *Journal of Internet Commerce, 4*(1), 1–25. doi:10.1300/J179v04n01_01

Shahrinaz, I., Kasuma, J., Yacob, Y., Rahman, D. H. A. A., & Mahdi, A. F. (2016). Relationship and impact of e-WOM and brand image towards purchase intention of smartphone? *Journal of Scientific Research and Development, 3*(5), 117–124.

Shaikh, S. (2019). The malleable self-concept-relationships between young adolescents' self-concept and bandwagon luxury consumption. *Journal of Marketing Development and Competitiveness, 13*(5), 33–44.

Shao, W., Grace, D., & Ross, M. (2019). Consumer motivation and luxury consumption: Testing moderating effects. *Journal of Retailing and Consumer Services, 46*, 33–44. doi:10.1016/j.jretconser.2018.10.003

Shao, W., Grace, D., & Ross, M. (2019a). Investigating brand visibility in luxury consumption. *Journal of Retailing and Consumer Services, 49*, 357–370. doi:10.1016/j.jretconser.2019.04.017

Sharma, P., & Chan, R. Y. (2017). Exploring the role of attitudinal functions in counterfeit purchase behavior via an extended conceptual framework. *Psychology and Marketing*, *34*(3), 294–308. doi:10.1002/mar.20989

Sharma, P., & Chan, R. Y. K. (2011). Counterfeit proneness: Conceptualisation and scale development. *Journal of Marketing Management*, *27*(5-6), 602–626. doi:10.1080/0267257X.2010.489829

Sharma, R. W., & Dasgupta, P. (2009). Marketing to children: A planning framework. *Young Consumers*, *10*(3), 180–187. doi:10.1108/17473610910985991

Shen, K. N., Vel, P., & Khalifa, M. (2016). Website design: Place for luxury brands in cyberspace? *Behaviour & Information Technology*, *35*(12), 1115–1129. doi:10.1080/0144929X.2016.1188987

Sherwood, H. (2016). *Meet Generation M: The young, affluent Muslims changing the world*. Retrieved from https://www.theguardian.com/world/2016/sep/03/meet-generation-m-the-young-affluent-muslims-changing-the-world

Sheth, J., Gardner, D., & Garret, D. (1988). *Marketing Theory - Evolution and Evaluation*. John Wiley e Sons.

Shimul, A. S., Phau, I., & Lwin, M. (2019). Conceptualising luxury brand attachment: Scale development and validation. *Journal of Brand Management*, *26*(6), 675–690. doi:10.105741262-019-00158-6

Shin, H., Eastman, J. K., & Mothersbaugh, D. (2017). The effect of a limited-edition offer following brand dilution on consumer attitudes toward a luxury brand. *Journal of Retailing and Consumer Services*, *38*, 59–70. doi:10.1016/j.jretconser.2017.05.009

Shobeiri, S., Mazaheri, E., & Laroche, M. (2018). Creating the right customer experience online: The influence of culture. *Journal of Marketing Communications*, *24*(3), 270–290. doi:10.1080/13527266.2015.1054859

Shove, E., & Warde, A. (2002). Inconspicuous consumption: the sociology of consumption, lifestyles and the environment. *Sociological Theory and the Environment: Classical Foundations. Contemporary Insights*, *230*, 51.

Shukla, P. (2012). The influence of value perceptions on luxury purchase intentions in developed and emerging markets. *International Marketing Review*, *29*(6), 574–596. doi:10.1108/02651331211277955

Shukla, P., Banerjee, M., & Singh, J. (2016). Customer commitment to luxury brands: Antecedents and consequences. *Journal of Business Research*, *69*(1), 323–331. doi:10.1016/j.jbusres.2015.08.004

Shukla, P., & Purani, K. (2012). Comparing the importance of luxury value perceptions in cross-national contexts. *Journal of Business Research*, *65*(10), 1417–1424. doi:10.1016/j.jbusres.2011.10.007

Silverstein, M. J., & Fiske, N. (2003). Luxury for themasses. *Harvard Business Review*, *81*, 48–57.

Silverstein, M. J., Fiske, N., & Butman, J. (2005). *Trading up: Why consumers want new luxury goods – and how companies create them*. Portfolio.

Silverstein, M., & Fiske, N. (2003). Luxury for the masses. *Harvard Business Review*, *81*(4), 48–57.

Silverstein, M., & Fiske, N. (2005). *Trading up: Why consumers want new luxury goods, and how companies create them* (rev. ed.). Portfolio.

Singh, N., & Boughton, P. D. (2005). Measuring website globalization: A cross- sectional country and level analysis. *Journal of Website Promotion*, *1*(3), 3–19. doi:10.1300/J238v01n03_02

Smith, A. (1776). *An Inquiry into the Nature and Causes of the Wealth of Nations*. Strahan & T. Cadell.

Smith, J. B., & Colgate, M. (2007). Customer value creation: A practical framework. *Journal of Marketing Theory and Practice*, *15*(1), 7–23. doi:10.2753/MTP1069-6679150101

Smith, K. T. (2012). Longitudinal study of digital marketing strategies targeting Millennials. *Journal of Consumer Marketing*, *29*(2), 86–92. doi:10.1108/07363761211206339

Smith, M. B., Bruner, J. S., & White, R. W. (1956). *Opinions and personality*. Wiley.

Snyder, C. R., & Fromkin, H. L. (1977). Abnormality as a positive characteristic: The development and validation of a scale measuring need for uniqueness. *Journal of Abnormal Psychology*, *86*(5), 518–527. doi:10.1037/0021-843X.86.5.518

Sofia, N. (2019, February 18). *Modest fashion week: The "halal" showcase for trendy Muslim fashion*. Retrieved from https://www.halalzilla.com/modest-fashion-week-trendy-muslim-fashion/86638

Solomon, M. (1999). Consumer behavior – buying having and being (4.a Ed.). Upper Saddle River: Prentice Hall.

Solomon, M. R. (1994). *Consumer Behavior* (2nd ed.). Allyn and Bacon.

Solomon, M. R., Ribeiro, L. B., & Farias, S. A. (2006). *O comportamento do consumidor comprando, possuindo e sendo*. Bookman.

Som, A., & Blanckaert, C. (2015). *The Road To Luxury, The Evoluation, Markets, and Strategies of Luxury Brand Management*. Wiley. doi:10.1002/9781118814321

Sousa, B.; Malheiro, A. & Veloso, C. M. (2019). O Marketing Territorial como Contributo para a Segmentação Turística: Modelo conceptual no turismo de shopping. *International Journal of Marketing, Communication and New Media*, 93-116.

Sousa, B. B., & Magalhães, F. C. (2019). An Approach on Attachment in Public Marketing and Higher Education Management Contexts. In C. Machado & J. Davim (Eds.), *Higher Education and the Evolution of Management, Applied Sciences, and Engineering Curricula* (pp. 151–171). IGI Global., doi:10.4018/978-1-5225-7259-6.ch006

Sousa, B., & Alves, G. (2019). The role of relationship marketing in behavioural intentions of medical tourism services and guest experiences. *Journal of Hospitality and Tourism Insights*, *2*(3), 224–240. doi:10.1108/JHTI-05-2018-0032

Spence, M. (2007). *Intellectual Property*. Clarendon Law Series. Oxford University Press. doi:10.1093/acprof:oso/9780198765011.001.0001

Srivastava, R. K., Bhanot, S., & Srinivasan, R. (2016). Segmenting markets along multiple dimensions of luxury values: The Case of India. *Journal of Promotion Management*, *22*(1), 175–193. doi:10.1080/10496491.2015.1088925

Stanglin, D. (2017, December 20). *Nike begins selling sports hijab for Muslim female athletes*. Retrieved from https://www.usatoday.com/story/news/world/2017/12/20/nike-begins-selling-sports-hijab-muslim-female-athletes/970226001/

Stathopoulou, A., & Balabanis, G. (2019). The effect of cultural value orientation on consumers' perceptions of luxury value and proclivity for luxury consumption. *Journal of Business Research*, *102*, 298–312. doi:10.1016/j.jbusres.2019.02.053

Steenkamp, J. B., Batra, R., & Alden, D. (2003). How perceived brand globalness creates brand value. *Journal of International Business Studies*, *34*(1), 53–65. doi:10.1057/palgrave.jibs.8400002

Stepchenkova, S., & Morrison, A. M. (2006). The destination image of Russia: From the online induced perspective. *Tourism Management*, *27*(5), 943–956. doi:10.1016/j.tourman.2005.10.021

Stępień, B. (2018). Snobbish bandwagoners: Ambiguity of luxury goods' perception. *Journal of Management and Business Administration. Central Europe*, *26*(1), 79–99.

Stevens, P., Knutson, B., & Patton, M. (1995). DINESERV: A tool for measuring service quality in restaurants. *The Cornell Hotel and Restaurant Administration Quarterly*, *36*(2), 56–60. doi:10.1177/001088049503600226

Stokburger-Sauer, N., & Teichmann, K. (2011). Influences of culture, gender, and age: why is luxury appealing? Exploring consumer's brand response with a special focus on gender. Chicago, IL: American Marketing Association.

Stokburger-Sauer, N. E., & Teichmann, K. (2013). Is luxury just a female thing? The role of gender in luxury brand consumption? *Journal of Business Research, 66*(7), 889–896. doi:10.1016/j.jbusres.2011.12.007

Stokburger-Sauer, N., Ratneshwar, S., & Sen, S. (2012). Drivers of consumer–brand identification. *International Journal of Research in Marketing, 29*(4), 406–418. doi:10.1016/j.ijresmar.2012.06.001

Stokes, D., & Lomax, W. (2002). Taking control of word-of-mouth marketing: The case of an entrepreneurial hotelier. *Journal of Small Business and Enterprise Development, 9*(4), 349–357. doi:10.1108/14626000210450531

Stöttinger, B., & Penz, E. (2015). Concurrent ownership of brands and counterfeits: Conceptualization and temporal transformation from a consumer perspective. *Psychology and Marketing, 32*(4), 373–391. doi:10.1002/mar.20786

Stylidis, K., Rossi, M., Wickman, C., & Söderberg, R. (2016). The communication strategies and customer's requirements definition at the early design stages: An empirical study on Italian luxury automotive brands. In *26th CIRP Design Conference*. Elsevier. 10.1016/j.procir.2016.04.062

Sun, G., D'Alessandro, S., & Johnson, L. W. (2016). Exploring luxury value perceptions in China direct and indirect effects. *International Journal of Market Research, 58*(5), 711–731. doi:10.2501/IJMR-2016-021

Sun, G., Wang, W., Cheng, Z., Li, J., & Chen, J. (2017). The intermediate linkage between materialism and luxury consumption: Evidence from the emerging market of China. *Social Indicators Research, 132*(1), 475–487. doi:10.100711205-016-1273-x

Sung, Y., Choi, S. M., Ahn, H., & Song, Y. A. (2015). Dimensions of luxury brand personality: Scale development and validation. *Psychology and Marketing, 32*(1), 121–132. doi:10.1002/mar.20767

Surlemont, B., & Johnson, C. (2005). The role of guides in artistic industries – The special case of the 'star system' in the haute-cuisine sector. *Managing Service Quality, 15*(6), 577–590. doi:10.1108/09604520510634032

Sweeney, J. C., & Soutar, G. N. (2001). Consumer perceived value: The development of a multiple item scale. *Journal of Retailing, 77*(2), 203–220. doi:10.1016/S0022-4359(01)00041-0

Szymanski, D. M., Bharadwaj, S. G., & Varadarajan, P. R. (1993). Standardization versus adaptation of international marketing strategy: An empirical investigation. *Journal of Marketing, 57*(4), 1–17. doi:10.1177/002224299305700401

Tajfel, H. (1981). *Human groups and social categories: Studies in social psychology*. Cambridge University Press.

Tajfel, H. (2010). *Social identity and intergroup relations*. Cambridge University Press.

Tajfel, H., & Turner, J. C. (1979). An integrative theory of intergroup conflict. *The Social Psychology of Intergroup Relations, 33*(47), 74.

Tanner, R. J., Ferraro, R., Chartrand, T. L., Bettman, J. R., & Van Baaren, R. (2008). Of chameleons and consumption: The impact of mimicry on choice and preferences. *The Journal of Consumer Research, 34*(6), 754–766. doi:10.1086/522322

Taormina, R. J., & Chong, K. Y. (2010). Purchasing counterfeit and legitimate products in China: Social and psychological correlates and predictors. *Journal of East-West Business, 16*(2), 118–145. doi:10.1080/10669868.2010.486103

Tariq, M., Abbas, T., Abrar, M., & Iqbal, A. (2017). EWOM and brand awareness impact on consumer purchase intention: Mediating role of brand image. *Pakistan Administrative Review, 1*(1), 84–102.

Taube, J., & Warnaby, G. (2017). How brand interaction in pop-up shops influences consumers' perceptions of luxury fashion retailers. *Journal of Fashion Marketing and Management*, *21*(3), 385–399. doi:10.1108/JFMM-08-2016-0074

Tavakoli, V., & Wijesinghe, S. N. R. (2019). The evolution of the web and netnography in tourism. *Systematic Reviews.*

Taylor, M. J., & England, D. (2006). Internet marketing: Web site navigation design issues. *Marketing Intelligence & Planning*, *24*(1), 77–85. doi:10.1108/02634500610641570

Teimourpour, B., & Hanzaee, K. (2011). The impact of culture on luxury consumption behaviour among Iranian consumers. *Journal of Islamic Research*, *2*(3), 309–328. doi:10.1108/17590831111164822

Teimourpour, B., & Hanzaee, K. H. (2014). An analysis of Muslims' luxury market in Iran: Challenges and opportunities. *Journal of Islamic Marketing*, *5*(2), 198–209. doi:10.1108/JIMA-01-2013-0002

Thanh, T., & Kirova, V. (2018). Wine tourism experience: A netnography study. *Journal of Business Research*, *83*, 30–37. doi:10.1016/j.jbusres.2017.10.008

The Jakarta Post. (2019, October 20). *More female Muslim travelers choose to travel solo: Report*. Retrieved from https://www.thejakartapost.com/travel/2019/10/19/more-female-muslim-travelers-choose-to-travel-solo-report.html

Theodosiou, M., & Leonidou, L. C. (2003). Standardization versus adaptation of international marketing strategy: An integrative assessment of the empirical research. *International Business Review*, *12*(2), 141–171. doi:10.1016/S0969-5931(02)00094-X

Thomas, D. (2007). *Deluxe: How Luxury Lost Its Luster*. The Penguin Press.

Thomas, D. (2009). The fight against fakes. *Harper's Bazaar*, *143*, 1–3.

Thomsen, T. U., Holmqvist, J., von Wallpach, S., Hemetsberger, A., & Belk, R. W. (2020). *Conceptualizing unconventional luxury. Journal of Business Research*. Ahead-of-print., doi:10.1016/j.jbusres.2020.01.058

Tian, K. T., Bearden, W. O., & Hunter, G. L. (2001). Consumers' need for uniqueness: Scale development and validation. *The Journal of Consumer Research*, *28*(1), 50–66. doi:10.1086/321947

Tice, D. M., Butler, J. L., Muraven, M. B., & Stillwell, A. M. (1995). When modesty prevails: Differential favorability of self-presentation to friends and strangers. *Journal of Personality and Social Psychology*, *69*(6), 1120–1138. doi:10.1037/0022-3514.69.6.1120

Ting, M. S., Goh, Y. N., & Isa, S. M. (2018). Inconspicuous consumption of luxury fashion goods among Malaysian adults: An investigation. *Global Business and Management Research*, *10*(1), 313–330.

Tom, G., Garibaldi, B., Zeng, Y., & Pilcher, J. (1998). Consumer demand for counterfeit goods. *Psychology and Marketing*, *15*(5), 405–421. doi:10.1002/(SICI)1520-6793(199808)15:5<405::AID-MAR1>3.0.CO;2-B

Tommaso, S., Petruzzelli, A. M., & Vito, A. (2017). Teams and lead creators in cultural and creative industries: Evidence from the Italian haute cuisine. *Journal of Knowledge Management*, *21*(3), 607–622. doi:10.1108/JKM-09-2016-0381

Trandafilović, I., Pašić, V., & Perunović, S. (2013). The research of cognitive and affective behavior during shopping. *Economics and Organization*, *10*(2), 147–164.

Triandewi, E., & Tjiptono, F. (2013). Consumer intention to buy original brands versus counterfeits. *International Journal of Marketing Studies*, *5*(2), 23–32. doi:10.5539/ijms.v5n2p23

Trigg, A. B. (2001). Veblen, Bourdieu, and conspicuous consumption. *Journal of Economic Issues*, *35*(1), 99–115. doi:10.1080/00213624.2001.11506342

Truong, Y., & McColl, R. (2011). Intrinsic motivations, self-esteem, and luxury goods consumption. *Journal of Retailing and Consumer Services*, *18*(6), 555–561. doi:10.1016/j.jretconser.2011.08.004

Truong, Y., McColl, R., & Kitchen, P. J. (2009). New luxury brand positioning and the emergence of masstige brands. *Journal of Brand Management*, *16*(5/6), 375–382. doi:10.1057/bm.2009.1

Truong, Y., McColl, R., & Kitchen, P. J. (2009). Uncovering the relationships between aspirations and luxury brand preference. *Journal of Product and Brand Management*, *19*(5), 346–355. doi:10.1108/10610421011068586

Truong, Y., Simmons, G., McColl, R., & Kitchen, P. J. (2008). Status and conspicuousness – are they related? Strategic marketing implications for luxury brands. *Journal of Strategic Marketing*, *16*(3), 189–203. doi:10.1080/09652540802117124

Tsai, S. P. (2005). Impact of personal orientation on luxury-brand purchase value: An international investigation. *International Journal of Market Research*, *47*(4), 429–454. doi:10.1177/147078530504700403

Tsai, W. S., Yang, Q., & Liu, Y. (2013). Young Chinese consumers' snob and bandwagon luxury consumption preferences. *Journal of International Consumer Marketing*, *25*(5), 290–304. doi:10.1080/08961530.2013.827081

Turunen, L. L. M., & Laaksonen, P. (2011). Diffusing the boundaries between luxury and counterfeits. *Journal of Product and Brand Management*, *20*(6), 468–474. doi:10.1108/10610421111166612

Tynan, C., McKechnie, S., & Chhuon, C. (2010). Co-creating value for luxury brands. *Journal of Business Research*, *63*(11), 1156–1163. doi:10.1016/j.jbusres.2009.10.012

U.S. Customs and Border Protection Directive 2310-011A, Personal use exemption: unauthorized trademarks (Cust. 2000). https://www.cbp.gov/sites/default/files/documents/2310-11a_3.pdf

Ueltschy, L. C., & Laroche, M. (2004). Co-Branding Internationally: Everyone Wins? *Journal of Applied Business Research*, *20*(3), 91–102.

United Nations Office on Drugs and Crime (UNODC). (2014). *Counterfeit: Don't buy into prganized crime' - UNODC launches new outreach campaign on $250 billion a year counterfeit business.* http://www.unodc.org/counterfeit/

van der Westhuizen, L. M. (2018). Brand loyalty: Exploring self-brand connection and brand experience. *Journal of Product and Brand Management*, *27*(2), 172–184. doi:10.1108/JPBM-07-2016-1281

van Elven, M. (2019, March 26). *Why The Modist has secured investments from Farfetch, Nicola Bulgari and Vaultier7.* Retrieved from https://fashionunited.uk/news/business/why-the-modist-has-secured-investments-from-farfetch-nicola-bulgari-and-vaultier7/2019032642385

van Keymeulen, E., & Nash, L. (2011). Fashionably Late. *Intellectual Property Magazine,* 54. Accessed Feb. 14, 2017: https://www.cov.com/~/media/files/corporate/publications/2011/12/fashionably-late.pdf

Varul, M. Z. (2008). After heroism: Religion versus consumerism. Preliminaries for an investigation of Protestantism and Islam under consumer culture. *Islam & Christian-Muslim Relations*, *19*(2), 237–255. doi:10.1080/09596410801924046

Vasquez, C. (2011). Complaints online: The case of TripAdvisor. *Journal of Pragmatics*, *43*(6), 1707–1717. doi:10.1016/j.pragma.2010.11.007

Vásquez, C., & Chik, A. (2015). 'I am not a foodie . . .': Culinary capital in online reviews of Michelin restaurants. *Food & Foodways*, *23*(4), 231–250. doi:10.1080/07409710.2015.1102483

Veblen, T. (1899). *The Theory of The Leisure Class.* Macmillan.

Veblen, T. (1899). *The Theory of the Leisure Class.* Penguin.

Veblen, T. (1899). *The theory of the leisure class.* Reprint from Penguin.

Veblen, T. (1994). *The collected works of Thorstein Veblen.* Routledge/Thoemms Press.

Vel, K. P., Captain, A., Al-Abbas, R., & Al Hashemi, B. (2011). Luxury buying in the United Arab Emirates. *Journal of Business and Behavioural Sciences*, *23*(3), 145–160.

Veloutsou, C., & Guzman, F. (2017). The evolution of brand management thinking over the last 25 years as recorded in the Journal of Product and Brand Management. *Journal of Product and Brand Management*, *26*(1), 2–12. doi:10.1108/JPBM-01-2017-1398

Veloutsou, C., & Mafe, C. R. (2019). *Brands as relationship builders in the virtual world: A bibliometric analysis. Eletronic Commerce Research and Applications, 39.* doi:10.1016/j.elerap.2019.100901

Verhallen, T. M. (1982). Scarcity and consumer choice behavior. *Journal of Economic Psychology*, *2*(2), 299–321. doi:10.1016/0167-4870(82)90034-4

Vickers, J. S., & Renand, F. (2003). The marketing of luxury brands: An exploratory study – three conceptual dimensions. *The Marketing Review*, *3*(4), 459–479. doi:10.1362/146934703771910071

Vida, I. (2007). Determinants of Consumer willingness to purchase non-deceptive counterfeit products. *Marketing Global Transitions*, *5*(3), 253–270.

Vigneron, F., & Johnson, L. W. (1999). A Review and a Conceptual Framework of Prestige Seeking Consumer Behavior. Academy of Marketing Science Review, (3/1), 2-8.

Vigneron, F., & Johnson, L. W. (1999). A review and a conceptual framework of prestige-seeking consumer behavior. *Academy of Marketing Science Review*, *1*(1), 1–15.

Vigneron, F., & Johnson, L. W. (2004). Measuring perceptions of brand luxury. *Brand Management*, *11*(6), 484–506. doi:10.1057/palgrave.bm.2540194

Vohra, M., Bhalla, G., & Chowdhury, A. (2009). Understanding the Islamic consumer. *Research World,* (February), 40–43.

Wall, D. S., & Large, J. (2010). Jailhouse frocks locating the public interest in policing counterfeit luxury fashion goods. *British Journal of Criminology*, *50*(6), 1094–1116. doi:10.1093/bjc/azq048

Wamda. (2019, January 14). *Turkey's Modanisa sells minority stake to Goldman Sachs.* Retrieved from https://www.wamda.com/2019/01/turkeys-modanisa-sells-minority-stake-goldman-sachs

Wang, F., Zhang, H., Zang, H., & Ouyang, M. (2005). Purchasing pirated software: An initial examination of Chinese consumers. *Journal of Consumer Marketing*, *22*(6), 340–351. doi:10.1108/07363760510623939

Wang, J., & Foosiri, P. (2018). Factors related to consumer behavior on luxury goods purchasing in China. *UTCC International Journal of Business & Economics*, *10*(1), 19–36.

Wang, O., & Somogyi, S. (2020). Motives for luxury seafood consumption in first-tier cities in China. *Food Quality and Preference*, *79*, 103780. doi:10.1016/j.foodqual.2019.103780

Wang, Y., & Griskevicius, V. (2014). Conspicuous consumption, relationships, and rivals: Women's luxury products as signals to other women. *The Journal of Consumer Research*, *40*(5), 834–854. doi:10.1086/673256

Wang, Y., Stoner, J. L., & John, D. R. (2019). Counterfeit luxury consumption in a social context: The effects on females' moral disengagement and behavior. *Journal of Consumer Psychology*, *29*(2), 207–225. doi:10.1002/jcpy.1071

Wang, Z., Deshpande, S., Waller, D. S., & Erdogan, B. Z. (2018). Religion and perceptions of the regulation of controversial advertising. *Journal of International Consumer Marketing*, *30*(1), 29–44. doi:10.1080/08961530.2017.1358681

Ward, S. (1974). Consumer socialization. *The Journal of Consumer Research*, *1*(2), 1–14. doi:10.1086/208584

Webster, F. E. Jr, & Keller, K. L. (2004). A roadmap for branding in the industrial markets. *Brand Management*, *11*(5), 388–402. doi:10.1057/palgrave.bm.2540184

Wee, C. H., Ta, S. J., & Cheok, K. H. (1995). Non-price determinants of intention to purchase counterfeit goods: An exploratory study. *International Marketing Review*, *12*(6), 19–46. doi:10.1108/02651339510102949

Weingarten, K. (2006). On hating to hate. *Family Process*, *45*(3), 277–288. doi:10.1111/j.1545-5300.2006.00170.x PMID:16984070

Weinreich, N. K. (2011). *Hands-on social marketing: a step-by-step guide to designing change for good* (2nd ed.). SAGE Publications.

Wenger, A. (2008). Analysis of travel bloggers' characteristics and their communication about Austria as a tourism destination. *Journal of Vacation Marketing*, *14*(2), 169–176. doi:10.1177/1356766707087525

Westbrook, R. A. (1987). Product/consumption-based affective responses and postpurchase processes. *JMR, Journal of Marketing Research*, *24*(3), 258–270. doi:10.1177/002224378702400302

Wiechman, D. J., Kendall, J. D., & Azarian, M. K. (1996). Islamic law: Myths and realities. *Crime & Justice International Online, 12*(3). Retrieved from http://nur-al-islaam.tripod.com/id250.html

Wiedmann, K. P., Hennigs, N., & Klarmann, C. (2012). Luxury consumption in the trade-off between genuine and counterfeit goods: What are the consumers' underlying motives and value-based drivers? *Journal of Brand Management*, *19*(7), 544–566. doi:10.1057/bm.2012.10

Wiedmann, K. P., Hennigs, N., & Siebels, A. (2007). Measuring consumers' luxury value perception: A cross-cultural framework. *Academy of Marketing Science Review*, *7*(7), 333–361.

Wiedmann, K. P., Hennings, N., & Siebels, A. (2009). Value based segmentation of luxury consumption behaviour. *Psychology and Marketing*, *26*(7), 625–651. doi:10.1002/mar.20292

Wiedmann, K. P., Labenz, F., Haase, J., & Hennigs, N. (2018). The power of experiential marketing: Exploring the causal relationships among multisensory marketing, brand experience, customer perceived value and brand strength. *Journal of Brand Management*, *25*(2), 101–118. doi:10.105741262-017-0061-5

Wiedmann, K., Hennigs, N., & Siebels, A. (2007). *Measuring Consumers" Luxury Value Perception: A Cross-Cultural Framework*. Institute of Marketing and Management, Leibniz University of Hanover.

Wijanarko, B., & Fachrodji, A. (2020). The analysis towards the ınfluence of motivation, brand ımage, price, and groups reference on purchasing decisions of original perfume products (Study Case of Meruya Campus Undergraduate Students, Mercu Buana University). *International Journal of Innovative Science and Research Technology*, *5*(1), 932–941.

Wilcox, K., Kim, H. M., & Sen, S. (2009). Why do consumers buy counterfeit luxury brands? *JMR, Journal of Marketing Research*, *46*(2), 247–259. doi:10.1509/jmkr.46.2.247

Wilke, R., & Zaichkowsky, J. L. (1999). Brand imitation and its effects on innovation, competition, and brand equity. *Business Horizons*, *42*(6), 9–9. doi:10.1016/S0007-6813(99)80033-0

Wilkes, R. E., Burnett, J. J., & Howell, R. D. (1986). On the meaning and measurement of religiosity in consumer research. *Journal of the Academy of Marketing Science*, *14*(1), 47–56. doi:10.1007/BF02722112

Williams, J. P., & Kamaludeen, M. N. (2017). Muslim girl culture and social control in Southeast Asia: Exploring the hijabista and hijabster phenomena. *Crime, Media, Culture, 13*(2), 199–216. doi:10.1177/1741659016687346

Winsper, J. (2007). *The e P's of Luxury Marketing: The Advanced Model for Measuring Consumers.* Academic Press.

Wong, N. Y., & Ahuvia, A. C. (1998). Personal taste and family face: Luxury consumption in Confucian and Western societies. *Psychology and Marketing, 15*(5), 423–432. doi:10.1002/(SICI)1520-6793(199808)15:5<423::AID-MAR2>3.0.CO;2-9

Wortmann, J.C., Muntslag, D. R., & Timmermans, P.J.M.(1997). *Customer-driven manufacturing.* Chapman & Hall.

Yadav, M. S. (2014). Enhancing theory development in marketing. *AMS Review, 4*(1-2), 1–4. doi:10.100713162-014-0059-z

Yang, W., & Mattila, A. (2016). Why do we buy luxury experiences? Measuring value perceptions of luxury hospitality services. *International Journal of Contemporary Hospitality Management, 28*(9), 1848–1867. doi:10.1108/IJCHM-11-2014-0579

Yang, W., & Mattila, A. S. (2004). Do affluent customers care when luxury brands go mass? The role of product type and status seeking on luxury brand attitude. *International Journal of Contemporary Hospitality Management, 26*(4), 526–543. doi:10.1108/IJCHM-03-2013-0124

Yan, H., & Qu, X. (2014). Research on the marketing strategy of luxury goods. *Psychology and Marketing, 26*(7), 625–651.

Yann, T. (2010). Personal aspirations and the consumption of luxury goods. *International Journal of Market Research, 52*(5), 653–671.

Yeoman, I. (2011). The changing behaviours of luxury consumption. *Journal of Revenue and Pricing Management, 10*(1), 47–50. doi:10.1057/rpm.2010.43

Yeoman, I., & McMahon-Beattie, U. (2005). Luxury Markets and Premium Pricing. *Journal of Revenue and Pricing Management, 4*(4), 319–328. doi:10.1057/palgrave.rpm.5170155

Ye, Q., Law, R., & Gu, B. (2009). The impact of online user reviews on hotel room sales. *International Journal of Hospitality Management, 28*(1), 180–182. doi:10.1016/j.ijhm.2008.06.011

Yildiz, N. (2012, April 23). *Lüks araba caiz mi?* Retrieved from https://www.fetvameclisi.com/fetva-luks-araba-caiz-mi-14278.html

Yong, H. H., Hamann, S. L., Borland, R., Fong, G. T., & Omar, M. (2009). Adult smokers' perception of the role of religion and religious leadership on smoking and association with quitting: A comparison between Thai Buddhists and Malaysian Muslims. *Social Science & Medicine, 69*(7), 1025–1031. doi:10.1016/j.socscimed.2009.07.042 PMID:19695758

Yoo, B., & Lee, S. H. (2012). Asymmetrical effects of past experiences with genuine fashion luxury brands and their counterfeits on purchase intention of each. *Journal of Business Research, 65*(10), 1507–1515. doi:10.1016/j.jbusres.2011.10.018

Young, W., Hwang, K., McDonald, S., & Oates, C. J. (2010). Sustainable consumption: Green consumer behavior when purchasing products. *Sustainable Development, 18*(1), 20–31.

Yu, J. Y. (2009). A cross-cultural study on participation intention to medical tourism among Korean, Chinese and Japanese visitors in Korea. *The Korean Academic Society of Tourism, 33*(3), 187–204.

Zaichkowsky, J. L., & Simpson, R. N. (1996). The effect of experience with a brand imitator on the original brand. *Marketing Letters, 7*(1), 31–39. doi:10.1007/BF00557309

Zainuddin, A. A., & Mahdy, Z. A. (2017). The Islamic perspectives of gender-related issues in the management of patients with disorders of sex development. *Archives of Sexual Behavior*, *46*(2), 353–360. doi:10.100710508-016-0754-y PMID:27102604

Zeng, B., & Gerritsen, R. (2014). What do we know about social media in tourism? A review. *Tourism Management Perspectives*, *10*, 27–36. doi:10.1016/j.tmp.2014.01.001

Zhang, J. J., & Mao, Z. (2012). Image of all hotel scales on travel blogs: Its impact on customer loyalty. *Journal of Hospitality Marketing & Management*, *21*(2), 113–131. doi:10.1080/19368623.2011.615017

Zhang, L., & Zhao, H. (2019). Personal value vs. luxury value: What are Chinese luxury consumers shopping for when buying luxury fashion goods? *Journal of Retailing and Consumer Services*, *51*, 62–71. doi:10.1016/j.jretconser.2019.05.027

Zhang, Q., Chen, J., & Zaccour, G. (2020). Market targeting and information sharing with social influences in a luxury supply chain. *Transportation Research Part E, Logistics and Transportation Review*, *133*, 133. doi:10.1016/j.tre.2019.101822

Zhang, W. (2019). Politicizing fashion: Inconspicuous consumption and anti-intellectualism during the Cultural Revolution in China. *Journal of Consumer Culture*. Advance online publication. doi:10.1177/1469540519889989

Zhang, Y., & Cole, S. T. (2016). Dimensions of lodging guest satisfaction among guests with mobility challenges: A mixed-method analysis of web-based texts. *Tourism Management*, *53*, 13–27. doi:10.1016/j.tourman.2015.09.001

Zhang, Z., Ye, Q., Song, H., & Liu, T. (2015). The structure of customer satisfaction with cruise-line services: An empirical investigation based on online word of mouth. *Current Issues in Tourism*, *18*(5), 450–464. doi:10.1080/13683500.2013.776020

About the Contributors

Paula Rodrigues holds a Ph.D. in Management, in Faculty of Economics at the University of Porto, Portugal. She is an Associate Professor in Brand Management at the School of Economics and Management, Lusíada University - North, Portugal. Since 1995, she teaches Brand Management, Consumer Behaviour, Econometrics, Statistic and Quantitative Methods at the Lusíada University - North. She has published several scientific papers, chapters, and books. Her on-going research projects concern consumer-brand relationships in the field of luxury, tourism and hospitality and consumer goods.

* * *

Nelson Amaral is a consumer psychologist (Ph.D. University of Minnesota) with an interest in understanding the interrelationship between consumers' social identities and products or brands. Dr. Amaral has investigated questions related to understanding cognitive processes that underlie unethical behaviour as well as the effects of counterfeits on luxury brands and cultural differences in the evaluation of counterfeit consumption. He has been invited to present his research on luxury counterfeits in Singapore, France, Monaco and Portugal. His research has been featured in Journal of Consumer Psychology, Journal of Experimental Social Psychology and Rutgers Business Review. He has been awarded research grants from The Marketing Science Institute and Asian Consumer Insights fund at Nanyang Technological University in Singapore.

Esra Arıkan is an assistant professor of marketing at Istanbul Bilgi University, Turkey. She received her Ph.D. in marketing from Bogazici University in 2010. Her research interests focus on consumer-brand relationships, brand extensions, social media marketing, service encounters and social marketing.

Murat Arslandere was born in 1982 in Karaman-Turkey. After graduating from Karaman Anatolian High School in 2000, Arslandere completed the Department of Econometrics at the Faculty of Economics and Administrative Sciences of Bursa Uludağ University in 2004. He completed his Master's Degree in Business Administration at Karamanoğlu Mehmetbey University in 2010 and received his Ph.D. degree in 2017 with completing his Ph.D. in Business Administration at Selçuk University in 2017. Arslandere has more than 10 years of experience in the private sector in supply chain management, business management, and foreign trade. Arslandere has been working as an Assistant Professor at Karamanoğlu Mehmetbey University since 2018. He works in the field of foreign trade. Arslandere is married and has two children.

Muhammed Bilgehan Aytaç received his bachelor's degree in Business Administration in 2007 and MS degree in Management Information Systems in 2013 from Gazi University-Ankara. He holds a Ph.D. degree from Aksaray University since 2019. His main area of interests are consumer behavior and consumer psychology. He is currently working on several fields like; Islamic consumption, narcissistic consumption, and ambush marketing.

Ana Pinto Borges holds a PhD in Economics at Faculty of Economics, University of Porto and the Economic Degree in Lusíada University - North. She is coordinating Professor at ISAG - European Business School (ISAG) since 2010, President of the Pedagogical Council since 2015 and has been the Executive Coordinator of the ISAG Research Center (NIDISAG) since 2014. She is one of the founding members of the Research Center in Business Sciences and Tourism (CICET). She is the author of more than 40 publications in scientific journals with peer review and indexed in the various international databases. The researcher has been participating in various national and international congresses and member of the Scientific Commissions and Organizing Committees in academic events. Editor and one of the founding members of the academic journal European Journal of Applied Business and Management (EJABM). She was consultant at Accenture in the financial area. Economist at the Portuguese Healthcare Regulation Authority since 2010.

Amélia Brandão is graduated in Enterprises Management from the Universidade Portucalense Infante D. Henrique, Porto, in 1995. She holds a Master degree in Finance from the Universidade Portucalense Infante D. Henrique, 2003. She has a Ph.D. graduation at the Faculdade de Economia do Porto (FEP) in the Brand Management valuation. Presently she is Services Management Master Director at FEP.UP and PostGraduate Programme Director at Porto Business School (PBS) She is lecturer of Marketing and Brand Management subjects at FEP, since 2004. Additionally she is teaching Managerial Communication, Strategy Communication and Marketing at Faculdade de Letras da Universidade do Porto, since 2008 until present. She is Scientific Committee member of the International Journal of Marketing, Communication and New Media. She is book author and reviewer of Master's theses at HSE, St. Petersburg (Rusia) and UFSM, Brazil. Her previous work experience was in brand communication consultancy at Associação Nacional de Jovens Empresários (ANJE), Associação Empresarial de Portugal (AEP), Markamos and XZ Consultores. She was coordinator and trainer for various projects and was senior consultant in micro enterprises (Formação e Ação em Micro Empresas -Fame project). She was Supervisor of Work Placements and Assistant Teacher at Universidade Portucalense Infante D. Henrique, 1995-2005, in undergraduate course, of Managerial Communication, Marketing Research, Brand Management and Marketing Management subjects. From 2000 to 2004 she was Visiting Assistant Teacher at Faculdad de Ciencias Economicas y Empresariales, Universidad de Sevilla, in Marketing Undergraduate course.

André Catarino received his graduation in electrical and computers engineering in 1992, at the University of Porto's Faculty of Engineering (FEUP). He started to work at Textile Engineering Department in the University of Minho (UM) in 1994 up to the present days where he is assistant professor. He received his MSc in 1998 and PhD in 2005 by the Scholl of Engineering (EEUM), both in the textile engineering and technology areas. He is a permanent researcher of the Center of Textile Science and Technology (2C2T). His specific interests lie on knitting technology and processes, interactive textiles, textile based sensors, especially applied on health and sports.

Senem Ergan is an assistant professor in Gökçeada School of Applied Sciences Tourism Management at Çanakkale Onsekiz Mart University. She received BA, MA and Ph.D degrees in Business from Trakya University, Turkey. Her research interests consumer behavior, place marketing, tourism marketing, marketing research, e-retailing, reverse logistics, contemporary issues in marketing.

Manuel José Fonseca, PhD in Information Sciences, Manuel José Serra da Fonseca was born in Lisbon in 1971. He played professional activities such as marketing communications technician and professor of higher education. He is currently Adjunct Professor at the Polytechnic Institute of Viana do Castelo (Portugal) and Coordinator of Marketing Master's degree at its Business School (ESCE-IPVC). He is a researcher at UNIAG (Applied Management Research Unit, since 2014). He participated in 3 national projects I&D and supervised about 40 undergraduate and masterworks in the areas of Communication Sciences and Business Sciences. He published several publications in peer-reviewed journals, book chapters and proceedings and has several communications at national and international scientific conferences. He collaborates as a reviewer with several journals. He acts in the Social Sciences field with an emphasis in Communication and Marketing Sciences. In his academic curriculum, the most frequent terms in the context of scientific production are: attitude towards advertising, attitude towards communication skills, road safety communication campaigns, consumer behavior, integrated marketing communications, social marketing, public service advertising, viral marketing and organizational communication.

Christine M. Kowalczyk holds a Ph.D. from the University of Memphis and is an associate professor of marketing at East Carolina University. Her research focuses on branding, celebrities and non-traditional advertising.

Asli Tolunay Kuscu completed her PhD in Marketing at Bogazici University, Turkey, Asli and is currently working as an Assistant Professor in Marketing teaching marketing courses at Yeditepe University, Istanbul Turkey. Her research interests and previous publications cover consumer-brand relationships and interactive marketing.

Vera Lourenço has a Master in Design of Communication of Fashion, by Faculty of Engineering of University of Minho, Portugal.

Filipa Magalhães has a Master's Degree in Marketing and Strategy, by School of Economics and Management (EEG), University of Minho, Braga (Portugal) and a Bachelor's Degree in Communication Sciences, by Institute of Social Sciences (ICS), from the same university. Currently, working as a Teaching Assistant at Polytechnic Institute of Cávado and Ave (IPCA), Barcelos (Portugal), lecturing marketing, strategic management and consumer behavior classes. At the same time, I work as a Marketing and Communication Manager at a non-profit organization, in Braga (Portugal). My main areas of research and interest are related to Emotional Marketing, Educational Marketing, Social Marketing and Consumer Behaviour.

Natalie A. Mitchell earned a Ph.D. at the University of Texas-Austin and is an instructor of marketing at University of North Florida. Her research interests include transformative consumer research, consumer culture, stigma identity, luxury branding, and marketing communications.

Manoel Vitor Santos is graduated in Bachelor in Social Communication from the FAESA - Faculdades Integradas Espírito-Santenses -, Vitória, in 2005. He holds an MBA in Marketing Management from the FGV - Fundação Getúlio Vargas - Rio de Janeiro, in 2015 and, a Master in Marketing from FEP - Faculdade de Economia do Porto -, Porto, in 2019. With more than 15 years of experience in the areas of communication, advertising and marketing, he has acquired a strong experience in several market segments in the management of marketing projects and is currently dedicated to the corporate market, external consultants and private courses.

Bruno Miguel Barbosa de Sousa Professor in Polytechnic Institute of Cavado and Ave (IPCA, Portugal) Head of Master Program - Tourism Management (ESHT - IPCA) - PhD Marketing and Strategy (Researcher in Tourism Marketing) at University of Minho - Market Analist at Sonae Distribuição – Modelo e Continente, S.A. (2006 to 2009) - Marketing Assistant - Jornal O Jogo at Controlinveste (2005) - Teaching Award of the School of Economics and Management of the University of Minho 2015/2016 - Best Thesis in Tourism Award - ICIEMC 2015 - Management Graduation, University of Minho Award - Best performance (2006) - Merit Scholarship for Students in Public Higher Education Awards of Merit Scholarship by University of Minho in 2001/02 - 2002/03 - 2003/04

Pınar Yürük-Kayapınar is working as Assistant Professor in the departman of Public Relations and Advertising, Uzunköprü School of Applied Sciences at Trakya University. Her research interests are consumer behavior at contemporary marketing approach, marketing research, event marketing.

Index

T

U

V

W

Purchase Print, E-Book, or Print + E-Book

IGI Global's reference books are available in three unique pricing formats:
Print Only, E-Book Only, or Print + E-Book.
Shipping fees may apply.
www.igi-global.com

Recommended Reference Books

ISBN: 978-1-5225-6201-6
© 2019; 341 pp.
List Price: $345

ISBN: 978-1-5225-7262-6
© 2019; 360 pp.
List Price: $215

ISBN: 978-1-5225-8003-4
© 2019; 216 pp.
List Price: $205

ISBN: 978-1-5225-5763-0
© 2019; 304 pp.
List Price: $205

ISBN: 978-1-5225-6980-0
© 2019; 325 pp.
List Price: $235

ISBN: 978-1-5225-7808-6
© 2019; 397 pp.
List Price: $215

Do you want to stay current on the latest research trends, product announcements, news and special offers?
Join IGI Global's mailing list today and start enjoying exclusive perks sent only to IGI Global members.
Add your name to the list at **www.igi-global.com/newsletters.**

Publisher of Peer-Reviewed, Timely, and Innovative Academic Research

IGI Global
DISSEMINATOR OF KNOWLEDGE

www.igi-global.com Sign up at www.igi-global.com/newsletters facebook.com/igiglobal twitter.com/igiglobal linkedin.com/igiglobal

Ensure Quality Research is Introduced to the Academic Community

Become an IGI Global Reviewer for Authored Book Projects

The overall success of an authored book project is dependent on quality and timely reviews.

In this competitive age of scholarly publishing, constructive and timely feedback significantly expedites the turnaround time of manuscripts from submission to acceptance, allowing the publication and discovery of forward-thinking research at a much more expeditious rate. Several IGI Global authored book projects are currently seeking highly-qualified experts in the field to fill vacancies on their respective editorial review boards:

Applications and Inquiries may be sent to:
development@igi-global.com

Applicants must have a doctorate (or an equivalent degree) as well as publishing and reviewing experience. Reviewers are asked to complete the open-ended evaluation questions with as much detail as possible in a timely, collegial, and constructive manner. All reviewers' tenures run for one-year terms on the editorial review boards and are expected to complete at least three reviews per term. Upon successful completion of this term, reviewers can be considered for an additional term.

If you have a colleague that may be interested in this opportunity, we encourage you to share this information with them.

IGI Global Proudly Partners With eContent Pro International

Receive a 25% Discount on all Editorial Services

Editorial Services

IGI Global expects all final manuscripts submitted for publication to be in their final form. This means they must be reviewed, revised, and professionally copy edited prior to their final submission. Not only does this support with accelerating the publication process, but it also ensures that the highest quality scholarly work can be disseminated.

English Language Copy Editing

Let eContent Pro International's expert copy editors perform edits on your manuscript to resolve spelling, punctuaion, grammar, syntax, flow, formatting issues and more.

Scientific and Scholarly Editing

Allow colleagues in your research area to examine the content of your manuscript and provide you with valuable feedback and suggestions before submission.

Figure, Table, Chart & Equation Conversions

Do you have poor quality figures? Do you need visual elements in your manuscript created or converted? A design expert can help!

Translation

Need your documjent translated into English? eContent Pro International's expert translators are fluent in English and more than 40 different languages.

Hear What Your Colleagues are Saying About Editorial Services Supported by IGI Global

"The service was very fast, very thorough, and very helpful in ensuring our chapter meets the criteria and requirements of the book's editors. I was quite impressed and happy with your service."

– Prof. Tom Brinthaupt,
Middle Tennessee State University, USA

"I found the work actually spectacular. The editing, formatting, and other checks were very thorough. The turnaround time was great as well. I will definitely use eContent Pro in the future."

– Nickanor Amwata, Lecturer,
University of Kurdistan Hawler, Iraq

"I was impressed that it was done timely, and wherever the content was not clear for the reader, the paper was improved with better readability for the audience."

– Prof. James Chilembwe,
Mzuzu University, Malawi

Email: customerservice@econtentpro.com

www.igi-global.com/editorial-service-partners

IGI Global
DISSEMINATOR OF KNOWLEDGE
www.igi-global.com

Celebrating Over 30 Years of Scholarly Knowledge Creation & Dissemination

InfoSci®-Books

A Database of Over 5,300+ Reference Books Containing Over 100,000+ Chapters Focusing on Emerging Research

InfoSci®-Books Database

The **InfoSci®-Books** database is a collection of over 5,300+ IGI Global single and multi-volume reference books, handbooks of research, and encyclopedias, encompassing groundbreaking research from prominent experts worldwide that span over 350+ topics in 11 core subject areas including business, computer science, education, science and engineering, social sciences and more.

Open Access Fee Waiver (Offset Model) Initiative

For any library that invests in IGI Global's InfoSci-Journals and/ or InfoSci-Books databases, IGI Global will match the library's investment with a fund of equal value to go toward **subsidizing the OA article processing charges (APCs) for their students, faculty, and staff** at that institution when their work is submitted and accepted under OA into an IGI Global journal.*

INFOSCI® PLATFORM FEATURES

- No DRM
- No Set-Up or Maintenance Fees
- A Guarantee of No More Than a 5% Annual Increase
- Full-Text HTML and PDF Viewing Options
- Downloadable MARC Records
- Unlimited Simultaneous Access
- COUNTER 5 Compliant Reports
- Formatted Citations With Ability to Export to RefWorks and EasyBib
- No Embargo of Content (Research is Available Months in Advance of the Print Release)

**The fund will be offered on an annual basis and expire at the end of the subscription period. The fund would renew as the subscription is renewed for each year thereafter. The open access fees will be waived after the student, faculty, or staff's paper has been vetted and accepted into an IGI Global journal and the fund can only be used toward publishing OA in an IGI Global journal. Libraries in developing countries will have the match on their investment doubled.*

To Learn More or To Purchase This Database:
www.igi-global.com/infosci-books

eresources@igi-global.com • Toll Free: 1-866-342-6657 ext. 100 • Phone: 717-533-8845 x100

IGI Global
DISSEMINATOR OF KNOWLEDGE
www.igi-global.com

IGI Global
DISSEMINATOR OF KNOWLEDGE
www.igi-global.com

Publisher of Peer-Reviewed, Timely, and Innovative Academic Research Since 1988

IGI Global's Transformative Open Access (OA) Model: How to Turn Your University Library's Database Acquisitions Into a Source of OA Funding

In response to the OA movement and well in advance of Plan S, IGI Global, early last year, unveiled their OA Fee Waiver (Read & Publish) Initiative.

Under this initiative, librarians who invest in IGI Global's InfoSci-Books (5,300+ reference books) and/or InfoSci-Journals (185+ scholarly journals) databases will be able to subsidize their patron's OA article processing charges (APC) when their work is submitted and accepted (after the peer review process) into an IGI Global journal. *See website for details.

How Does it Work?

1. When a library subscribes or perpetually purchases IGI Global's InfoSci-Databases and/or their discipline/subject-focused subsets, IGI Global will match the library's investment with a fund of equal value to go toward subsidizing the OA article processing charges (APCs) for their patrons.

   ***Researchers:* Be sure to recommend the InfoSci-Books and InfoSci-Journals to take advantage of this initiative.**
2. When a student, faculty, or staff member submits a paper and it is accepted (following the peer review) into one of IGI Global's 185+ scholarly journals, the author will have the option to have their paper published under a traditional publishing model or as OA.
3. When the author chooses to have their paper published under OA, IGI Global will notify them of the OA Fee Waiver (Read and Publish) Initiative. If the author decides they would like to take advantage of this initiative, IGI Global will deduct the US$ 2,000 APC from the created fund.
4. This fund will be offered on an annual basis and will renew as the subscription is renewed for each year thereafter. IGI Global will manage the fund and award the APC waivers unless the librarian has a preference as to how the funds should be managed.

Hear From the Experts on This Initiative:

"I'm very happy to have been able to make one of my recent research contributions, "Visualizing the Social Media Conversations of a National Information Technology Professional Association" featured in the *International Journal of Human Capital and Information Technology Professionals*, freely available along with having access to the valuable resources found within IGI Global's InfoSci-Journals database."

– **Prof. Stuart Palmer**,
Deakin University, Australia

For More Information, Visit: www.igi-global.com/publish/contributor-resources/open-access/read-publish-model or contact IGI Global's Database Team at eresources@igi-global.com.

Are You Ready to Publish Your Research?

IGI Global
DISSEMINATOR OF KNOWLEDGE

IGI Global offers book authorship and editorship opportunities across 11 subject areas, including business, computer science, education, science and engineering, social sciences, and more!

Benefits of Publishing with IGI Global:

- Free one-on-one editorial and promotional support.
- Expedited publishing timelines that can take your book from start to finish in less than one (1) year.
- Choose from a variety of formats including: Edited and Authored References, Handbooks of Research, Encyclopedias, and Research Insights.
- Utilize IGI Global's eEditorial Discovery® submission system in support of conducting the submission and blind review process.
- IGI Global maintains a strict adherence to ethical practices due in part to our full membership with the Committee on Publication Ethics (COPE).
- Indexing potential in prestigious indices such as Scopus®, Web of Science™, PsycINFO®, and ERIC – Education Resources Information Center.
- Ability to connect your ORCID iD to your IGI Global publications.
- Earn royalties on your publication as well as receive complimentary copies and exclusive discounts.

Get Started Today by Contacting the Acquisitions Department at:

acquisition@igi-global.com

www.igi-global.com/infosci-ondemand

InfoSci®-OnDemand

Continuously updated with new material on a weekly basis, InfoSci®-OnDemand offers the ability to search through thousands of quality full-text research papers. Users can narrow each search by identifying key topic areas of interest, then display a complete listing of relevant papers, and purchase materials specific to their research needs.

Comprehensive Service

- Over 125,000+ journal articles, book chapters, and case studies.
- All content is downloadable in PDF and HTML format and can be stored locally for future use.

No Subscription Fees

- One time fee of **$37.50** per PDF download.

Instant Access

- Receive a download link immediately after order completion!

"It really provides an excellent entry into the research literature of the field. It presents a manageable number of highly relevant sources on topics of interest to a wide range of researchers. The sources are scholarly, but also accessible to 'practitioners'."

- Lisa Stimatz, MLS, University of North Carolina at Chapel Hill, USA

"It is an excellent and well designed database which will facilitate research, publication, and teaching. It is a very useful tool to have."

- George Ditsa, PhD, University of Wollongong, Australia

"I have accessed the database and find it to be a valuable tool to the IT/IS community. I found valuable articles meeting my search criteria 95% of the time."

- Prof. Lynda Louis, Xavier University of Louisiana, USA

Recommended for use by researchers who wish to immediately download PDFs of individual chapters or articles.

www.igi-global.com/e-resources/infosci-ondemand

IGI Global
DISSEMINATOR OF KNOWLEDGE
www.igi-global.com

www.ingramcontent.com/pod-product-compliance
Lightning Source LLC
LaVergne TN
LVHW062140300926
849161LV00010B/2581